THE LIFE

OF

SAMUEL JOHNSON, LL.D.

INCLUDING

A JOURNAL OF A TOUR TO THE HEBRIDES

BY

JAMES BOSWELL

Vol. I.

GEORGE ROUTLEDGE AND SONS

New York: 9 Lafayette Place
London, Manchester, and Glasgow

"After my death I wish no other herald,
No other speaker of my living actions,
To keep mine honour from corruption,
But such an honest chronicler as Griffith."[1]

SHAKSPEARE, *Henry VIII.*

[1] See Dr. Johnson's letter to Mrs. Thrale, dated Ostick in Skie, September 30, 1773:
"Boswell writes a regular Journal of our travels, which I think contains as much of what I
say and do, as of all other occurrences together: *for such a faithful chronicler is Griffith*."—
BOSWELL.

BOSWELL'S
LIFE OF JOHNSON

ILLUSTRATED

L. 2

SAMUEL JOHNSON, LL.D.

VOL. I.

GEORGE ROUTLEDGE AND SONS

New York : 9 Lafayette Place

London, Glasgow, and Manchester

BJ63.

"Seven years, my lord, have now passed, since I waited in your outward rooms, or was repulsed from your door."—JOHNSON'S *Letter to Lord Chesterfield.*

CONTENTS OF VOLUME I.

CHAPTER I.—1709—1731.

Birth and Infancy of Johnson—Account of his Parents—Anecdotes of his Childhood—Taken to London to receive the Royal Touch for Scrofula—School Days at Lichfield—His Uncle Cornelius Ford, and Cousin the Rev. Dr. Ford Sent to School at Stourbridge—Translations and original Compositions while at this Place—Return Home—Arrival at Pembroke College, Oxford—His Tutor—Latin Translation of Pope's "Messiah"—Attack of Hypochondria—Religious Impressions—Course of Reading—Love of Literature—Apparent Recklessness—Real State of Mind—Struggles with Poverty—Leaves the University 29

CHAPTER II.—1731—1736.

Death of Johnson's Father—Intercourse with Society in Lichfield, Gilbert Walmesley, Dr. Swinfen, &c.—Tribute to Walmesley's Memory—Becomes Usher at Market Bosworth School—Removal to Birmingham; Mr. Hector, Mr. Porter, &c.—Translation of Lobo's Voyage to Abyssinia—Specimen of Early Style—Return to Lichfield — Birmingham again — First Letter to Cave, Proprietor of "Gentleman's Magazine"—Youthful Amatory Verses—Marriage with Mrs. Porter—Her Family, and Incidents of the Wedding—Opens a private Academy at Edial—Garrick becomes his Pupil—School unsuccessful—Great part of Tragedy of "Irene" written . . 46

CHAPTER III.—1737—1738.

Johnson arrives in London accompanied by Garrick—Letter relating to them from Walmesley to the Rev. Mr. Colson—First Residence and Mode of Life in the Metropolis—Retires to Greenwich—Progress of "Irene"—Projected translation of "Father Paul's History of Council of Trent"—Going back to Lichfield—Original MS. of "Irene"—Extracts—Return to London with Mrs. Johnson—First Contribution to "Gentleman's Magazine"—Reports Debates in Parliament—Publishes Poem of "London"—Pope admires it—Remarks and Extracts—Conditional Offer of Mastership of a Country School—Pope's Recommendation of Johnson to Lord Gower 56

CHAPTER XI.—1760—1763.

CHAPTER XII.—1763.

CHAPTER XIII.—1763.

CHAPTER XIV.—1763—1765.

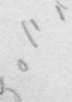

LIST OF ILLUSTRATIONS.

———◆———

DEDICATION.

TO

SIR JOSHUA REYNOLDS.

My DEAR Sir,

Every liberal motive that can actuate an Author in the dedication of his labours, concurs in directing me to you, as the person to whom the following Work should be inscribed.

If there be a pleasure in celebrating the distinguished merit of a contemporary, mixed with a certain degree of vanity not altogether inexcusable, in appearing fully sensible of it, where can I find one, in complimenting whom I can with more general approbation gratify those feelings? Your excellence, not only in the art over which you have long presided with unrivalled fame, but also in Philosophy and elegant Literature, is well known to the present, and will continue to be the admiration of future ages. Your equal and placid temper, your variety of conversation, your true politeness, by which you are so amiable in private society, and that enlarged hospitality which has long made your house a common centre of union for the great, the accom plished, the learned, and the ingenious ; all these qualities 1 can, in perfect confidence of not being accused of flattery, ascribe to you.

If a man may indulge an honest pride in having it known to the world that he has been thought worthy of particular attention by a person of the first eminence in the age in which he lived, whose company has been universally courted, I am justified in availing myself of the usual privilege of a Dedication, when I mention that there has been a long and uninterrupted friendship between us.

If gratitude should be acknowledged for favours received, I have this opportunity, my dear Sir, most sincerely to thank you for the many happy hours which I owe to your kindness,—for the cordiality with which you have at all times been pleased to welcome me,—for the number of valuable acquaintances to whom you have introduced me,—for the *noctes cœnæque Deûm*, which I have enjoyed under your roof.

If a work should be inscribed to one who is master of the subject of it, and whose approbation, therefore, must ensure it credit and success, the Life of Dr. Johnson is, with the greatest propriety, dedicated to Sir Joshua Reynolds, who was the intimate and beloved friend of that great man ; the friend whom he declared to be " the most invulnerable man he knew; whom, if he should quarrel with him, he should find the most difficulty how to abuse." You, my dear Sir, studied him, and knew him well : you venerated and admired him. Yet, luminous as he was upon the whole, you perceived all the shades w¹ ich mingled in the grand composition ; all the little peculiarities and slight blemishes which marked the literary Colossus. Your very warm commendation of the specimen which I gave, in my " Journal of a Tour to the Hebrides," of my being able to preserve his conversation in an authentic and lively manner, which opinion the Public has confirmed, was the best encouragement for me to persevere in my purpose of producing the whole of my stores.

In one respect, this work will, in some passages, be different from the former. In my " Tour," I was almost unboundedly open in my communications, and from my eagerness to display the wonderful fertility and readiness of Johnson's wit, freely showed to the world its dexterity, even when I was myself the object of it. I trusted that I should be liberally understood, as knowing very well what I was about, and by no means as simply unconscious of the pointed effects of the satire. I own, indeed, that I was arrogant enough to suppose that the tenour of the rest of the book would sufficiently guard me against such a strange imputation. But it seems I judged too well of the world; for, though I could scarcely believe it, I have been undoubtedly informed, that many persons, especially in distant quarters, not penetrating enough into Johnson's character, so as to understand his mode of treating his friends, have arraigned my judgment, instead of seeing that I was sensible of all that they could observe.

It is related of the great Dr. Clarke, that when, in one of his leisure hours, he was unbending himself with a few friends in the most playful and frolicsome manner, he observed Beau Nash approaching; upon which he suddenly stopped:—"My boys," said he, "let us be grave; here comes a fool." The world, my friend, I have found to be a great fool, as to that particular on which it has become necessary to speak very plainly. I have, therefore, in this work been more reserved; and though I tell nothing but the truth, I have still kept in my mind that the whole truth is not always to be exposed. This, however, I have managed so as to occasion no diminution of the pleasure which my book should afford; though malignity may sometimes be disappointed of its gratifications.

> I am, my dear Sir,
>> Your much obliged friend,
>>> And faithful humble servant,
>>>> JAMES BOSWELL

London, April 20, 1791.

JAMES BOSWELL.

ADVERTISEMENT TO THE FIRST EDITION.

I AT last deliver to the world a work which I have long promised, and of which, I am afraid, too high expectations have been raised. The delay of its publication must be imputed, in a considerable degree, to the extraordinary zeal which has been shown by distinguished persons in all quarters to supply me with additional information concerning its illustrious subject; resembling in this the grateful tribes of ancient nations, of which every individual was eager to throw a stone upon the grave of a departed Hero, and thus to share in the pious office of erecting an honourable monument to his memory.

The labour and anxious attention with which I have collected and arranged the materials of which these volumes are composed, will hardly be conceived by those who read them with careless facility. The stretch of mind and prompt assiduity by which so many conversations were preserved, I myself, at some distance of time, contemplate with wonder; and I must be allowed to suggest that the nature of the work in other respects, as it consists of innumerable detached particulars, all which, even the most minute, I have spared no pains to ascertain with a scrupulous authenticity, has occasioned a degree of trouble far beyond that of any other species of composition. Were I to detail the books which I have consulted, and the inquiries which I have found it necessary to make by various channels, I should probably be thought ridiculously ostentatious. Let me only observe, as a specimen of my trouble, that I have sometimes been obliged to run half over London, in order to fix a date correctly; which, when I had accomplished, I well knew would obtain me no praise, though a failure would have been to my discredit. And after all, perhaps, hard as it may be, I shall not be surprised if omissions or mistakes be pointed out with invidious severity. I have also been extremely careful as to the exactness of my quotations; holding that there is a respect due to the public, which should oblige every author to attend to this, and never to presume to introduce them with, "I think I have read," or, "If I remember right," when the originals may be examined.

I beg leave to express my warmest thanks to those who have been pleased to favour me with communications and advice in the conduct of my work. But I cannot sufficiently acknowledge my obligations to my friend Mr. Malone, who was so good as to allow me to read to him almost the whole of my manuscript, and make such remarks as were greatly for the advantage of the work ; though it is but fair to him to mention, that upon many occasions I differed from him, and followed my own judgment. I regret exceedingly that I was deprived of the benefit of his revision, when not more than one half of the book had passed through the press ; but after having completed his very laborious and admirable edition of Shakspeare, for which he generously would accept of no other reward but that fame which he had so deservedly obtained, he fulfilled his promise of a long-wished for visit to his relations in Ireland ; from whence his safe return *finibus Atticis* is desired by his friends here, with all the classical ardour of *Sic te Diva potens Cypri ;* for there is no man in whom more elegant and worthy qualities are united ; and whose society, therefore, is more valued by those who know him.

It is painful to me to think, that while I was carrying on this work, several of those to whom it would have been most interesting have died. Such melancholy disappointments we know to be incident to humanity ; but we do not feel them the less. Let me particularly lament the Reverend Thomas Warton, and the Reverend Dr. Adams. Mr. Warton, amidst his variety of genius and learning, was an excellent biographer. His contributions to my collection are highly estimable ; and as he had a true relish of my " Tour to the Hebrides," I trust I should now have been gratified with a larger share of his kind approbation. Dr. Adams, eminent as the head of a college, as a writer, and as a most amiable man, had known Johnson from his early years, and was his friend through life. What reason I had to hope for the countenance of that venerable gentleman to this work, will appear from what he wrote to me upon a former occasion from Oxford, November 17, 1785 :—" Dear Sir, I hazard this letter not knowing where it will find you, to thank you for your very agreeable 'Tour,' which I found here on my return from the country, and in which you have depicted our friend so perfectly to my fancy, in every attitude, every scene and situation, that I have thought myself in the company, and of the party almost throughout. It has given very general satisfaction ; and those who have found most fault with a passage here and there, have agreed that they could not help going through, and being entertained with the whole. I wish, indeed, some few gross expressions had been softened, and a few of our hero's foibles had been a little more shaded ; but it is useful to see the weaknesses incident to great minds ; and you have given us Dr. Johnson's authority that in history all ought to be told."

Such a sanction to my faculty of giving a just representation of Dr. Johnson I could not conceal. Nor will I suppress my satisfaction in the consciousness, that by recording so considerable a portion of the wisdom and wit of "the brightest ornament of the eighteenth century,"[1] I have largely provided for the instruction and entertainment of mankind.

London, April 20, 1791.

J. BOSWELL.

See Mr. Malone's Preface to his edition of Shakspeare.

ADVERTISEMENT TO THE SECOND EDITION.

THAT I was anxious for the success of a work which had employed mucn o. my time and labour, I do not wish to conceal ; but whatever doubts I at any time entertained, have been entirely removed by the very favourable reception with which it has been honoured. That reception has excited my best exertions to render my book more perfect ; and in this endeavour I have had the assistance not only of some of my particular friends, but of many other learned and ingenious men, by which I have been enabled to rectify some mistakes, and to enrich the work with many valuable additions. These I have ordered to be printed separately in quarto, for the accommodation of the purchasers of the first edition. May I be permitted to say that the typography of both editions does honour to the press of Mr. Henry Baldwin, now Master of the Worshipful Company of Stationers, whom I have long known a worthy man and an obliging friend.

In the strangely mixed scenes of human existence, our feelings are often at once pleasing and painful. Of this truth, the progress of the present work furnishes a striking instance. It was highly gratifying to me that my friend, Sir Joshua Reynolds, to whom it is inscribed, lived to peruse it, and to give the strongest testimony to its fidelity ; but before a second edition, which he contributed to improve, could be finished, the world has been deprived of that most valuable man ; a loss of which the regret will be deep, and lasting, and extensive, proportionate to the felicity which he diffused through a wide circle of admirers and friends.

In reflecting that the illustrious subject of this work, by being more extensively and intimately known, however elevated before, has risen in the veneration and love of mankind, I feel a satisfaction beyond what fame can afford. We cannot, indeed, too much or too often admire his wonderful powers of mind, when we consider that the principal store of wit and wisdom which this work contains was not a particular selection from his general conversation, but was merely his occasional talk at such times as I had the good fortune to be in his company ; and, without doubt, if his discourse at other periods had been collected with the same attention, the whole tenour of what he uttered would have been found equally excellent.

His strong, clear, and animated enforcement of religion, morality, loyalty and subordination, while it delights and improves the wise and the good, will, I trust, prove an effectual antidote to that detestable sophistry which has been lately imported from France, under the false name of Philosophy, and with a malignant industry has been employed against the peace, good order, and happiness of society, in our free and prosperous country ; but, thanks be to God, without producing the pernicious effects which were hoped for by its propagators.

It seems to me, in my moments of self-complacency, that this extensive biographical work, however inferior in its nature, may in one respect be assimilated to the "Odyssey." Amidst a thousand entertaining and instructive episodes the hero is never long out of sight ; for they are all in some degree connected with him ; and he, in the whole course of the history, is exhibited by the Author for the best advantage of his readers :

> —*Quid virtus et quid sapientia possit,*
> *Utile proposuit nobis exemplar Ulyssen.*

Should there be any cold-blooded and morose mortals who really dislike this book, I will give them a story to apply. When the great Duke of Marlborough, accompanied by Lord Cadogan, was one day reconnoitring the army in Flanders, a heavy rain came on, and they both called for their cloaks. Lord Cadogan's servant, a good-humoured alert lad, brought his lordship's in a minute. The Duke's servant, a lazy sulky dog, was so sluggish, that his Grace, being wet to the skin, reproved him, and had for answer with a grunt, "I came as fast as I could ; " upon which the Duke calmly said, " Cadogan, I would not for a thousand pounds have that fellow's temper."

There are some men, I believe, who have, or think they have, a very small share of vanity. Such may speak of their literary fame in a decorous style of diffidence. But I confess, that I am so formed by nature and by habit, that to restrain the effusion of delight, on having obtained such fame, to me would be truly painful. Why then should I suppress it? Why "out of the abundance of the heart" should I not speak? Let me then mention with a warm but no insolent exultation, that I have been regaled with spontaneous praise of my work, by many and various persons eminent for their rank, learning, talents, and accomplishments ; much of which praise I have under their hands to be reposited in my archives at Auchinleck. An honourable and reverend friend speaking of the favourable reception of my volumes, even in the circles of fashion and elegance, said to me, "You have made them all talk Johnson." Yes, I may add, I have Johnsonised the land ; and I trust they will not only talk, but think, Johnson.

To enumerate those to whom I have been thus indebted would be tediously ostentatious. I cannot, however, but name one whose praise is truly valuable, not only on account of his knowledge and abilities, but on account of the magnificent, yet dangerous embassy, in which he is now employed, which makes every thing that relates to him peculiarly interesting. Lord Macartney favoured me with his own copy of my book, with a number of notes, of which I have availed myself. On the first leaf I found, in his lordship's handwriting, an inscription of such high commendation, that even I, vain as I am, cannot prevail on myself to publish it.

July 1, 793.   ' BOSWELL.

EDMUND MALONE.

ADVERTISEMENT TO THE THIRD EDITION.

SEVERAL valuable letters, and other curious matter, having been communicated to the author too late to be arranged in that chronological order which he had endeavoured uniformly to observe in his work, he was obliged to introduce them in his second edition, by way of Addenda, as commodiously as he could. In the present edition they have been distributed in their proper places. In revising his volumes for a new edition he had pointed out where some of these materials should be inserted; but unfortunately, in the midst of his labours, he was seized with a fever, of which, to the great regret of all his friends, he died on the 19th of May, 1795. All the Notes that he had written in the margin of the copy which he had in part revised, are here faithfully preserved; and a few new Notes have been added, principally by some of those friends to whom the author in the former editions acknowledged his obligations. Those subscribed with the letter B. were communicated by Dr. Burney; those to which the letters J. B. are annexed, by the Rev. J. B. Blakeway, of Shrewsbury, to whom Mr. Boswell acknowledged himself indebted for some judicious remarks on the first edition of his work; and the letters J. B.—O. are annexed to some remarks furnished by the author's second son, a student of Brazen-Nose College, in Oxford. Some valuable observations were communicated by James Bindley, Esq., First Commissioner in the Stamp Office, which have been acknowledged in their proper places. For all those without any signature Mr. Malone is answerable.—Every new remark, not written by the author, for the sake of distinction, has been inclosed within crotchets; in one instance, however, the printer, by mistake, has affixed this mark to a note relative to the Rev. Thomas Fysche Palmer (see vol. iv. p. 92), which was written by Mr. Boswell, and therefore ought not to have been thus distinguished.

I have only to add, that the proof-sheets of the present edition not having passed through my hands, I am not answerable for any typographical errors that may be found in it. Having, however, been printed at the very accurate press of Mr. Baldwin, I make no doubt it will be found not less perfect than the former edition; the greatest care having been taken, by correctness and elegance, to do justice to one of the most instructive and entertaining works in the English language.

April 8, 1799.   EDM MALONE.

ADVERTISEMENT TO THE FOURTH EDITION.

IN this edition are inserted some new letters of which the greater part has been obligingly communicated by the Reverend Doctor Vyse, Rector of Lambeth. Those written by Dr. Johnson concerning his mother in her last illness, furnish a new proof of his great piety and tenderness of heart, and therefore cannot but be acceptable to the readers of this very popular work. Some new Notes also have been added, which, as well as the observations inserted in the third edition, and the letters now introduced, are carefully included within crotchets, that the author may not be answerable for anything which had not the sanction of his approbation. The remarks of his friends are distinguished as formerly, except those of Mr. Malone, to which the letter M. is now subjoined. Those to which the letter K. is affixed were communicated by my learned friend, the Reverend Doctor Kearney, formerly Senior Fellow of Trinity College, Dublin, and now beneficed in the diocese of Raphoe in Ireland, of which he is Archdeacon.

Of a work which has been before the public for thirteen years with increasing approbation, and of which near four thousand copies have been dispersed, it is not necessary to say more; yet I cannot refrain from adding, that, highly as it is now estimated, it will, I am confident, be still more valued by posterity a century hence, when all the actors in the scene shall be numbered with the dead; when the excellent and extraordinary man, whose wit and wisdom are here recorded, shall be viewed at a still greater distance; and the instruction and entertainment they afford will at once produce reverential gratitude, admiration, and delight.   E. M.

June 20, 1804.

ADVERTISEMENT TO THE FIFTH EDITION.

IN this fifth edition some errors of the press, which had crept into the text and notes, in consequence of repeated impressions, have been corrected. Two letters written by Dr. Johnson, and several new notes, have been added; by which, it is hoped, this valuable work is still further improved.   E. M.

January 1, 1807.

ADVERTISEMENT TO THE SIXTH EDITION.

GREAT pains have been taken to make this sixth edition accurate, in point of typography.   With this view the entire work has been read over by the author's second son, James Boswell, of the Inner Temple, Esq. ; by which means many errors of the press, occasioned by repeated impressions, have been discovered.   All these have been carefully amended.—Several new notes and some letters have been added ; and in the Index,—a very useful appendage to a book containing so much miscellaneous and unconnected matter,—many new articles have been inserted.

By these improvements, the present impression has been rendered the amplest, and it is hoped, will be found the most correct edition of this valuable work, which has yet appeared.   E. M.

May 2, 1811.

*** This edition (the 6th) is the last that was published under the superintendence of the accurate and judicious Malone.   He was in the author's confidence (as will be seen on reference to the first advertisement) in the original preparation of the work.   After Boswell's death, Malone brought out the third and subsequent editions, up to the sixth inclusive, receiving in the course of his labours that various and valuable assistance to which he adverts in the notices prefixed to his successive publications.

Malone's last edition is dated May, 1811 (about twenty years after the first appearance of the work); and he died in the same month of the following year.   This edition we have followed, as fairly settling the text of the work.

March, 1851.

This edition of "Boswell's Life of Johnson" has been divided into chapters for the reader's convenience, in the perusal of so great a body of matter.

The Chronological List of the works of Dr. Johnson, prepared by Boswell, will be found at the end of the Biography.

THE LIFE

OF

SAMUEL JOHNSON, LL.D.

INTRODUCTORY CHAPTER.

To write the Life of him who excelled all mankind in writing the lives of others, and who, whether we consider his extraordinary endowments, or his various works, has been equalled by few in any age, is an arduous, and may be reckoned in me a presumptuous task.

Had Dr. Johnson written his own Life, in conformity with the opinion which he has given,[1] that every man's life may be best written by himself; had he employed in the preservation of his own history, that clearness of narration and elegance of language in which he has embalmed so many eminent persons, the world would probably have had the most perfect example of biography that was ever exhibited. But although he at different times, in a desultory manner, committed to writing many particulars of the progress of his mind and fortunes, he never had persevering diligence enough to form them into a regular composition. Of these memorials a few have been preserved; but the greater part was consigned by him to the flames, a few days before his death.

As I had the honour and happiness of enjoying his friendship for upwards of twenty years; as I had the scheme of writing his life constantly in view; as he was well apprised of this circumstance, and from time to time obligingly satisfied my inquiries, by communicating to me the incidents of his early years; as I acquired a facility in recollecting, and was very assiduous in recording, his conversation, of which the extraordinary vigour and vivacity constituted one of the first features of his character; and as I have spared no pains in obtaining

[1] Idler, No. 84:—"Those relations are commonly of most value, in which the writer tells his own story."—BOSWELL.

materials concerning him, from every quarter where I could discover that they were to be found, and have been favoured with the most liberal communications by his friends ; I flatter myself that few biographers have entered upon such a work as this with more advantages, independent of literary abilities, in which I am not vain enough to compare myself with some great names who have gone before me in this kind of writing.

Since my work was announced, several Lives and Memoirs of Dr. Johnson have been published, the most voluminous of which is one compiled for the booksellers of London, by Sir John Hawkins, Knight,[1] a man whom, during my long intimacy with Dr. Johnson, I never saw in his company, I think, but once, and I am sure not above twice. Johnson might have esteemed him for his descent, religious demeanour, and his knowledge of books and literary history; but from the rigid formality of his manners, it is evident that they never could have lived together with companionable ease and familiarity ; nor had Sir John Hawkins that nice perception which was necessary to mark the finer and less obvious parts of Johnson's character. His being appointed one of his executors, gave him an opportunity of taking possession of such fragments of a diary and other papers as were left ; of which, before delivering them up to the residuary legatee, whose property they were, he endeavoured to extract the substance. In this he has not been very successful, as I have found upon a perusal of those papers, which have been since transferred to me. Sir John Hawkins's ponderous labours, I must acknowledge, exhibit a *farrago*, of which a considerable portion is not devoid of entertainment to the lovers of literary gossiping; but besides its being swelled out with long unnecessary extracts from various works (even one of several leaves from Osborne's Harleian Catalogue, and those not compiled by Johnson, but by Oldys), a very small part of it relates to the person who is the subject of the book ; and, in that, there is such an inaccuracy in the statement of facts, as in so solemn an author is hardly excusable, and certainly makes his narrative very unsatisfactory. But what is still worse, there is throughout the whole of it a dark uncharitable cast, by which the most unfavourable construction is put upon a   every circumstance in the character

---

[1] The greatest part of this book was written while Sir John Hawkins was alive ; and I avow, that one object of my strictures was to make him feel some compunction for his illiberal treatment of Dr. Johnson. Since his decease I have suppressed several of my remarks upon his work. But though I would not "war with the dead" *offensively*, I think it necessary to be strenuous in *defence* of my illustrious friend, which I cannot be without strong animadversions upon a writer who has greatly injured him. Let me add, that though I doubt I should not have been very prompt to gratify Sir John Hawkins with any compliment in his lifetime, I do now frankly acknowledge, that, in my opinion his volume, however inadequate and improper as a life of Dr. Johnson, and however discredited by unpardonable inaccuracies in other respects, contains a collection of curious anecdotes and observations, which few men but its author could have brought together. —BOSWELL.

and conduct of my illustrious friend ; who, I trust, will, by a true and fair delineation, be vindicated both from the injurious misrepresentations of this author, and from the slighter aspersions of a lady who once lived in great intimacy with him.

There is, in the British Museum, a letter from Bishop Warburton to Dr. Birch, on the subject of biography : which, though I am aware it may expose me to a charge of artfully raising the value of my own work, by contrasting it with that of which I have spoken, is so well conceived and expressed, that I cannot refrain from here inserting it :—

" I shall endeavour," says Dr. Warburton, " to give you what satisfaction I can in any thing you want to be satisfied in any subject of Milton, and am extremely glad you intend to write his life. Almost all the life-writers we have had before Toland and Desmaiseaux are indeed strange insipid creatures ; and yet I had rather read the worst of them, than be obliged to go through with this of Milton's, or the other's life of Boileau, where there is such a dull, heavy succession of long quotations of disinteresting passages, that it makes their method quite nauseous. But the verbose, tasteless Frenchman seems to lay it down as a principle that every life must be a book, and what's worse, it proves a book without a life ; for what do we know of Boileau, after all his tedious stuff? You are the only one (and I speak it without a compliment), that by the vigour of your style and sentiments, and the real importance of your materials, have the art (which one would imagine no one could have missed), of adding agreements to the most agreeable subject in the world, which is literary history." [1] [*Nov.* 24, 1737.]

Instead of melting down my materials into one mass, and constantly speaking in my own person, by which I might have appeared to have more merit in the execution of the work, I have resolved to adopt and enlarge upon the excellent plan of Mr. Mason, in his Memoirs of Gray. Wherever narrative is necessary to explain, connect, and supply, I furnish it to the best of my abilities ; but in the chronological series of Johnson's life, which I trace as distinctly as I can year by year, I produce, wherever it is in my power, his own minutes, letters, or conversation, being convinced that this mode is more lively, and will make my readers better acquainted with him, than even most of those were who actually knew him, but could know him only partially ; whereas there is here an accumulation of intelligence from various points, by which his character is more fully understood and illustrated.

Indeed, I cannot conceive a more perfect mode of writing any man's life, than not only relating all the most important events of it in their order, but interweaving what he privately wrote, and said, and thought ; by which mankind are enabled, as it were, to see him live, and to " live o'er each scene " with him, as he actually advanced through the several stages of his life. Had his other friends been as diligent and ardent as

[1] Brit. Mus. 4320, Ayscough's Catal. Sloane MSS.— Boswell.

I was, he might have been almost entirely preserved. As it is, I will venture to say, that he will be seen in this work more completely than any man who has ever yet lived.

And he will be seen as he really was; for I profess to write, not his panegyric, which must be all praise, but his Life; which, great and good as he was, must not be supposed to be entirely perfect. To be as he was, is indeed subject of panegyric enough to any man in this state of being; but in every picture there should be shade as well as light, and when I delineate him without reserve, I do what he himself recommended, both by his precept and his example.

"If the biographer writes from personal knowledge, and makes haste to gratify the public curiosity, there is danger lest his interest, his fear, his gratitude, or his tenderness, overpower his fidelity, and tempt him to conceal, if not to invent. There are many who think it an act of piety to hide the faults or failings of their friends, even when they can no longer suffer by their detection; we therefore see whole ranks of characters adorned with uniform panegyric, and not to be known from one another but by extrinsic and casual circumstances. 'Let me remember,' says Hale, 'when I find myself inclined to pity a criminal, that there is likewise a pity due to the country.' If we owe regard to the memory of the dead, there is yet more respect to be paid to knowledge, to virtue, and to truth." [Rambler, No. 60.]

What I consider as the peculiar value of the following work, is, the quantity it contains of Johnson's conversation, which is universally acknowledged to have been eminently instructive and entertaining; and of which the specimens that I have given upon a former occasion [1] have been received with so much approbation that I have good grounds for supposing that the world will not be indifferent to more ample communications of a similar nature.

That the conversation of a celebrated man, if his talents have been exerted in conversation, will best display his character, is, I trust, too well established in the judgment of mankind to be at all shaken by a sneering observation of Mr. Mason, in his "Memoirs of Mr. William Whitehead," in which there is literally no *Life*, but a mere dry narrative of facts. I do not think it was quite necessary to attempt a depreciation of what is universally esteemed, because it was not to be found in the immediate object of the ingenious writer's pen; for in truth, from a man so still and so tame, as to be contented to pass many years as the domestic companion of a superannuated lord and lady, conversation could no more be expected than from a Chinese mandarin on a chimney-piece, or the fantastic figures on a gilt leather screen.

If authority be required, let us appeal to Plutarch, the prince of ancient biographers. Οὔτε ταῖς ἐπιφανεστάταις πράξεσι πάντως ἔδεστι δήλωσις ἀρετῆς ἢ κακίας ἀλλὰ πρᾶγμα βραχὺ πολλάκις καὶ ῥῆμα, καὶ παίδιά τις ἔμφασιν

---

[1] Boswell alludes to the "Journal of a Tour to the Hebrides."—ED.

ἤθους ἐποίησεν μᾶλλον ἢ μάχαι μυριόνεκροι, παρατάξεις αἱ μέγισται, καὶ πολιορκία πόλεων. "Nor is it always in the most distinguished achievements that men's virtues or vices may be best discerned; but very often an action of small note, a short saying, or a jest, shall distinguish a person's real character more than the greatest sieges, or the most important battles."[1]

To this may be added the sentiments of the very man whose life I am about to exhibit.

"The business of the biographer is often to pass slightly over those performances and incidents which produce vulgar greatness to lead the thoughts into domestic privacies, and display the minute details of daily life, where exterior appendages are cast aside, and men excel each other only by prudence and by virtue. The account of Thuanus is with great propriety said by its author to have been written, that it might lay open to posterity the private and familiar character of that man, *cujus ingenium et candorem ex ipsius scriptis sunt olim semper miraturi*,—whose candour and genius will to the end of time be by his writings preserved in admiration.

"There are many invisible circumstances, which, whether we read as inquirers after natural or moral knowledge, whether we intend to enlarge our science or increase our virtue, are more important than public occurrences. Thus Sallust, the great master of nature, has not forgot in his account of Catiline to remark, that his walk was now quick, and again slow, as an indication of a mind revolving with violent commotion. Thus the story of Melancthon affords a striking lecture on the value of time, by informing us, that when he had made an appointment, he expected not only the hour but the minute to be fixed, that the day might not run out in the idleness of suspense; and all the plans and enterprises of De Witt are now of less importance to the world than that part of his personal character, which represents him as careful of his health, and negligent of his life.

"But biography has often been allotted to writers, who seem very little acquainted with the nature of their task, or very negligent about the performance. They rarely afford any other account than might be collected from public papers, but imagine themselves writing a life, when they exhibit a chronological series of actions or preferments; and have so little regard to the manners or behaviour of their heroes, that more knowledge may be gained of a man's real character, by a short conversation with one of his servants, than from a formal and studied narrative, begun with his pedigree, and ended with his funeral.

"There are, indeed, some natural reasons why these narratives are often written by such as were not likely to give much instruction or delight, and why most accounts of particular persons are barren and useless. If a life be delayed till interest and envy are at an end, we may hope for impartiality, but must expect little intelligence; for the incidents which give excellence to biography are of a volatile and evanescent kind, such as soon escape the memory, and are rarely transmitted by tradition. We know how few can portray a living acquaintance, except by his most prominent and observable particularities, and the grosser features of his mind ; and it may be easily imagined how much of this little knowledge may be lost in imparting it, and how soon a succession of copies will lose all resemblance of the original." [Rambler, No. 60.]

I am fully aware of the objections which may be made to the minuteness on some occasions of my detail of Johnson's conversation, and how happily it is adapted for the petty exercise of ridicule, by men of superficial understanding and ludicrous fancy : but I remain firm and confident in my opinion, that minute particulars are frequently characteristic, and always amusing, when they relate to a distinguished man. I am, therefore, exceedingly unwilling that any thing, however slight, which my illustrious friend thought it worth his while to express, with any degree of point, should perish. For this almost superstitious reverence I have found very old and venerable authority, quoted by our great modern prelate, Secker, in whose tenth sermon there is the following passage :—

"Rabbi David Kimchi,[1] a noted Jewish commentator, who lived about five hundred years ago, explains that passage in the first Psalm, 'His leaf also shall not wither,' from Rabbins yet older than himself, thus : That 'even the idle talk,' so he expresses it, 'of a good man ought to be regarded;' the most superfluous things he saith are always of some value. And other ancient authors have the same phrase, nearly in the same sense."

Of one thing I am certain, that considering how highly the small portion which we have of the table-talk and other anecdotes of our celebrated writers is valued, and how earnestly it is regretted that we have not more, I am justified in preserving rather too many of Johnson's sayings, than too few ; especially as from the diversity of dispositions it cannot be known with certainty beforehand, whether what may seem trifling to some, and, perhaps, to the collector himself, may not be most agreeable to many ; and the greater number that an author can please in any degree, the more pleasure does there arise to a benevolent mind.

To those who are weak enough to think this is a degrading task, and the time and labour which have been devoted to it misemployed, I shall content myself with opposing the authority of the greatest man of any age, JULIUS CÆSAR, of whom Bacon observes, that

"In his book of Apophthegms which he collected, we see that he esteemed it more honour to make himself but a pair of tables, to take the wise and pithy words of others, than to have every word of his own to be made an apophthegm or an oracle." [Advancement of Learning, Book I.]

Having said thus much by way of introduction, I commit the following pages to the candour of the public.

[1] A Spanish Rabbi, considered the best grammarian of his nation. He died in 1240.— ED

BIRTHPLACE OF DR. JOHNSON.

CHAPTER I.—1709—1731.

AMUEL JOHNSON was born at Lichfield in
Staffordshire, on the 18th of September, N. S.
1709; and his initiation into the Christian church
was not delayed; for his baptism is recorded, in
the register of St. Mary's parish in that city, to
have been performed on the day of his birth: his
father is there styled *Gentleman*, a circumstance of
which an ignorant panegyrist has praised him for
not being proud; when the truth is, that the
appellation of Gentleman, though now lost in the indiscriminate assump-
tion of *Esquire*, was commonly taken by those who could not boast of

gentility.   His father was Michael Johnson, a native of Derbyshire, of
obscure extraction, who settled in Lichfield as a bookseller and stationer.
His mother was Sarah Ford, descended of an ancient race of substantial
yeomanry in Warwickshire.   They were well advanced in years when
they married, and never had more than two children, both sons ;
Samuel their first born, who lived to be the illustrious character whose
various excellence I am to endeavour to record, and Nathanael, who
died in his twenty-fifth year.[1]

Mr. Michael Johnson was a man of a large and robust body, and of

MICHAEL JOHNSON.

a strong and active mind ; yet, as in
the most solid rocks veins of unsound
substance are often discovered, there
was in him a mixture of that disease,
the nature of which eludes the most
minute inquiry, though the effects
are well known to be a weariness of
life, an unconcern about those things
which agitate the greater part of
mankind, and a general sensation of
gloomy wretchedness.   From him
then his son inherited, with some
other qualities, " a vile melancholy,"
which in his too strong expression of
any disturbance of the mind, "made
him mad all his life, at least not

sober."[2]   Michael was, however, forced by the narrowness of his circumstances to be very diligent in business, not only in his shop, but by
occasionally resorting to several towns in the neighbourhood,[3] some of
which were at a considerable distance from Lichfield.   At that time
booksellers' shops, in the provincial towns of England were very rare :
so that there was not one even in Birmingham, in which town old Mr.
Johnson used to open a shop every market-day.   He was a pretty good
Latin scholar, and a citizen so creditable as to be made one of the
magistrates of Lichfield ; and being a man of good sense, and skill in
his trade, he acquired a reasonable share of wealth, of which, however,

---

[1] Nathanael was born in 1712, and died in 1737.   Their father, Michael Johnson, was born
at Cubley, in Derbyshire, in 1656, and died at Lichfield in 1731, at the age of seventy-six
Sarah Ford, his wife, was born at King's-Norton, in the county of Warwick, in 1669, and
died at Lichfield in January, 1759, in her ninetieth year.—MALONE.

[2] "Journal of a Tour to the Hebrides," 3rd edit., p. 213.—BOSWELL.

[3] Extract of a letter dated " Trentham, St. Peter's Day, 1716," written by the Rev. George
Plaxton, Chaplain at that time to Lord Gower, which may serve to show the high estimation
in which the father of our great moralist was held : " Johnson, the Lichfield librarian, is now
here ; he propagates learning all over this diocese, and advanceth knowledge to its just height·
all the clergy here are his pupils, and suck all they have from him.   Allen cannot make a
warrant without his precedent, nor our quondam John Evans draw a recognizance *sine direc-
tione Michaelis.*"—*Gentleman's Magazine*, October, 1791.—BOSWELL.

he afterwards lost the greatest part, by engaging unsuccessfully in a manufacture of parchment. He was a zealous high-churchman and royalist, and retained his attachment to the unfortunate house of Stuart, though he reconciled himself, by casuistical arguments of expediency and necessity, to take the oaths imposed by the prevailing power.

There is a circumstance in his life somewhat romantic, but so well authenticated, that I shall not omit it. A young woman of Leek, in Staffordshire, while ne served his apprenticeship there, conceived a violent passion for him; and though it met with no favourable return, followed him to Lichfield, where she took lodgings opposite to the house in which he lived, and indulged her hopeless flame. When he was informed that it so preyed upon her mind that her life was in danger, he with a generous humanity went to her and offered to marry her, but it was then too late: her vital power was exhausted; and she actually exhibited one of the very rare instances of dying for love. She was buried in the cathedral of Lichfield: and he, with a tender regard, placed a stone over her grave with this inscription:

Here lies the body of
Mrs. ELIZABETH BLANEY, a Stranger:
She departed this Life
20th of September, 1694.

Johnson's mother was a woman of distinguished understanding.[1] I asked his old schoolfellow, Mr. Hector, surgeon, of Birmingham, if she was not vain of her son. He said, "she had too much good sense to be vain, but she knew her son's value." Her piety was not inferior to her understanding; and to her must be ascribed those early impressions of religion upon the mind of her son, from which the world afterwards derived so much benefit. He told me, that he remembered distinctly having had the first notion of Heaven, "a place to which good people went," and Hell, "a place to which bad people went," communicated to him by her, when a little child in bed with her; and that it might be the better fixed in his memory, she sent him to repeat it to Thomas

[1] It was not, however, much cultivated, as we may collect from Dr. Johnson's own account of his early years, published by R. Phillips, 8vo, 1805. a work undoubtedly authentic. and which, though short, is curious, and well worthy of perusal. "My father and mother," says Johnson, "had not much happiness from each other. They seldom conversed; for my father could not bear to talk of his affairs; and my mother, *being unacquainted with books*, cared not to talk of anything else. Had my mother been more literate, they had been better companions. She might have sometimes introduced her unwelcome topic with more success, if she could have diversified her conversation. Of business she had no distinct conception; and therefore her discourse was composed only of complaint, fear, and suspicion. Neither of them ever tried to calculate the profits of trade or the expenses of living. My mother concluded that we were poor, because we lost by some of our trades; but the truth was, that my father having in the early part of his life contracted debts, never had trade sufficient to enable him to pay them, and to maintain his family; he got something, but not enough. It was not till about 1768, that I thought to calculate the returns of my father's trade, and, by that estimate, his probable profits. This I believe my parents never did."—MALONE.

Jackson, their man-servant; he not being in the way, this was not done; but there was no occasion for any artificial aid for its preservation.

In following so very eminent a man from his cradle to his grave, every minute particular, which can throw light on the progress of his mind, is interesting. That he was remarkable, even in his earliest years, may easily be supposed; for to use his own words in his " Life of Sydenham," " That the strength of his understanding, the accuracy of his discernment, and the ardour of his curiosity, might have been remarked from his infancy, by a diligent observer, there is no reason to doubt; for there is no instance of any man, whose history has been minutely related, that did not in every part of life discover the same proportion of intellectual vigour."

In all such investigations it is certainly unwise to pay too much attention to incidents which the credulous relate with eager satisfaction, and the more scrupulous or witty inquirer considers only as topics of ridicule : yet there is a traditional story of the infant Hercules of toryism, so curiously characteristic, that I shall not withhold it. It was communicated to me in a letter from Miss Mary Adye, of Lichfield.

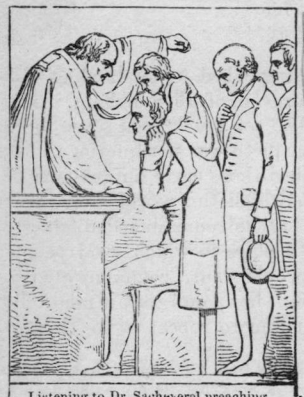
Listening to Dr. Sacheverel preaching.

" When Dr. Sacheverel was at Lichfield, Johnson was not quite three years old. My grandfather Hammond observed him at the cathedral perched upon his father's shoulders, listening and gaping at the much-celebrated preacher. Mr. Hammond asked Mr. Johnson how he could possibly think of bringing such an infant to church, and in the midst of so great a crowd. He answered, because it was impossible to keep him at home; for, young as he was, he believed he had caught the public spirit and zeal for Sacheverel, and would have stayed for ever in the church, satisfied with beholding him."[1]

Nor can I omit a little instance of that jealous independence of spirit, and impetuosity of temper, which never forsook him. The fact was acknowledged to me by himself, upon the authority of his mother. One day when the servant who used to be sent to school to conduct him home, had not come in time, he set out by himself, though he was then so near-sighted, that he was obliged to stoop down on his hands and knees to take a view of the kennel, before he ventured to step over it. His schoolmistress, afraid that he might miss his way, or fall into the kennel, or be run over by a cart, followed him at some distance. He happened to turn about and perceive her. Feeling her careful attention as an insult to his manliness, he ran back to her in a rage, and beat her, as well as his strength would permit.

PARLOUR IN THE HOUSE WHERE DR. JOHNSON WAS BORN.[1]

Of the power of his memory, for which he was all his life eminent to a degree almost incredible, the following early instance was told me in his presence at Lichfield, in 1776, by his step-daughter, Mrs. Lucy Porter, as related to her by his mother. When he was a child in petticoats, and had learned to read, Mrs. Johnson one morning put the Common Prayer Book into his hands, pointed to the collect for the day, and said, "Sam, you must get this by heart." She went up stairs, leaving him to study it; but by the time she had reached the second floor, she heard him following her. "What's the matter?" said she, "I can say it," he replied; and repeated it distinctly, though he could not have read it more than twice.

But there has been another story of his infant precocity generally circulated, and generally believed, the truth of which I am to refute upon his own authority. It is told,[2] that, when a child of three years old, he chanced to tread upon a duckling, the eleventh of a brood, and killed it; upon which, it is said, he dictated to his mother the following epitaph:—

> "Here lies good master duck,
>   Whom Samuel Johnson trod on;
> If it had lived, it had been *good luck*,
>   For then we'd had an *odd one*."

[1] This is the only room of the house which remains in the same state as when occupied by the Doctor's father.—Ed.   [2] Piozzi's Anecdotes and Sir John Hawkins's Life.—Boswell.

There is surely internal evidence, that this little composition combines in it what no child of three years old could produce, without an extension of its faculties by immediate inspiration; yet Mrs. Lucy Porter, Dr. Johnson's step-daughter, positively maintained to me, in his presence, that there could be no doubt of the truth of this anecdote, for she had heard it from his mother. So difficult is it to obtain an authentic relation of facts, and such authority may there be for error, for he assured me that his father made the verses, and wished to pass them for his child's. He added, " My father was a foolish old man; that is to say, foolish in talking of his children." [1]

Young Johnson had the misfortune to be much afflicted with the scrofula, or king's evil, which disfigured a countenance naturally well formed, and hurt his visual nerves so much, that he did not see at all with one of his eyes, though its appearance was little different from that of the other. There is amongst his prayers one inscribed " *When my* EYE *was restored to its use.*"[2] which ascertains a defect that many of his friends knew he had, though I never perceived it.[3] I supposed him to be only near-sighted: and, indeed, I must observe, that in no other respect could I discern any defect in his vision; on the contrary, the force of his attention and perceptive quickness made him see and distinguish all manner of objects, whether of nature or of art, with a nicety that is rarely to be found. When he and I were travelling in the Highlands of Scotland, and I pointed out to him a mountain which I observed resembled a cone, he corrected my inaccuracy, by showing me, that it was indeed pointed at the top, but that one side of it was larger than the other. And the ladies with whom he was acquainted agree, that no man was more nicely and minutely critical in the elegance of female dress. When I found that he saw the romantic beauties of Islam, in Derbyshire, much better than I did, I told him that he

[1] This anecdote of the duck, though disproved by internal and external evidence, has nevertheless, upon supposition of its truth, been made the foundation of the following ingenious and fanciful reflections of Miss Seward, amongst the communications concerning Dr. Johnson with which she has been pleased to favour me:—

" These infant numbers contain the seeds of those propensities which through his life so strongly marked his character; of that poetic talent which afterwards bore such rich and plentiful fruits; for, excepting his orthographic works, everything which Dr. Johnson wrote was poetry, whose essence consists, not in numbers, or in jingle, but in the strength and glow of a fancy to which all the stores of nature and of art stand in prompt administration; and in an eloquence which conveys their blended illustrations in a language ' more tuneable than needs or rhyme or verse to add more harmony.'

" The above little verses also show that superstitious bias which ' grew with his growth and strengthened with his strength,' and of late years particularly injured his happiness by presenting to him the gloomy side of religion, rather than that bright and cheering one which gilds the period of closing life with the light of pious hope."

This is so beautifully imagined, that I would not suppress it. But, like many other theories, it is deduced from a supposed fact, which is, indeed, a fiction.—BOSWELL.

[2] Johnson's " Prayers and Meditations," p. 27.—BOSWELL.

[3] Speaking himself of the imperfection of one of his eyes, he said, " The dog was never good for much."—BURNEY.

resembled an able performer upon a bad instrument. How false and ontemptible then are all the remarks which have been made to the prejudice either of his candour or of his philosophy, founded upon a supposition that he was almost blind. It has been said, that he contracted this grievous malady from his nurse.[1] His mother yielding to the superstitious notion, which it is wonderful to think, prevailed so long in this country, as to the virtue of the regal touch ; a notion which our king encouraged, and to which a man oi such inquiry and such judgment as Carte could give credit ; carried him to London, where he was actually touched by Queen Anne.[2] Mrs. Johnson, indeed, as Mr. Hector informed me, acted by the advice of the celebrated Sir John Floyer, then a physician in Lichfield. Johnson used to talk of this very frankly; and Mrs. Piozzi has preserved his very picturesque description of the scene as it remained upon his fancy. Being asked if he could remember Queen Anne,—" He had," he said, " a confused, but somehow a sort of solemn recollection of a lady in diamonds, and a long black hood." [3] This touch, however, was without any effect. I ventured to say to him, in allusion to the political principles in which he was educated, and of which he ever retained some odour, that " his mother had not carried him far enough ; she should have taken him to ROME." [4]

He was first taught to read English by Dame Oliver, a widow, who kept a school for young children in Lichfield. He told me she could read the black letter, and asked him to borrow for her, from his father, a Bible in that character. When he was going to Oxford, she came to take leave of him, brought him, in the simplicity of her kindness, a present of gingerbread, and said he was the best scholar she ever had. He delighted in mentioning this early compliment : adding, with a smile, that " this was as high a proof of his merit as he could conceive." His next instructor in English was a master, whom, when he spoke of him to me, he familiarly called Tom Brown, who, said he, " published a spelling-book, and dedicated it to the UNIVERSE ; but I fear no copy of it can now be had."

[1719. Age 10.] He began to learn Latin with Mr. Hawkins, usher, or under-master, of Lichfield school—" a man," said he, " very skilful

[1] Such was the opinion of Dr. Swinfen. Johnson's eyes were very soon discovered to be bad, and, to relieve them, an issue was cut in his left arm. At the end of ten weeks from his birth, he was taken home from his nurse, "a poor diseased infant, almost blind." See a work, already quoted, entitled " An Account of the Life of Dr. Samuel Johnson from his birth to his eleventh year; written by himself." 8vo, 1805.—MALONE.

[2] He was only thirty months old when he was taken to London to be touched for the evil. During this visit, he tells us, his mother purchased for him a small silver cup and spoon. " The cup," he affectingly adds, " was one of the last pieces of plate which dear Tetty sold in her distress. I have now the spoon. She bought at the same time two teaspoons, and till my manhood, she had no more."—MALONE.

[3] Mrs. Piozzi's Anecdotes, p. 1(BOSWELL.

[4] The Pretender.—ED.

in his little way." With him he continued two years, and then rose to be under the care of Mr. Hunter, the head master, who, according to his account, " was very severe, and wrongheadedly severe. He used,"

LICHFIELD SCHOOL.

said he, " to beat us unmercifully; and he did not distinguish between ignorance and negligence; for he would beat a boy equally for not knowing a thing, as for neglecting to know it. He would ask a boy a question, and if he did not answer it, he would beat him, without considering whether he had an opportunity of knowing how to answer it. For instance, he would call up a boy and ask him Latin for a candlestick, which the boy could not expect to be asked. Now, Sir, if a boy could answer every question, there would be no need of a master to teach him."

It is, however, but justice to the memory of Mr. Hunter to mention that though he might err in being too severe, the school of Lichfield was very respectable in his time. The late Dr. Taylor, Prebendary of Westminster, who was educated under him, told me, that " he was an excellent master, and that his ushers were most of them men of eminence; that Holbrook, one of the most ingenious men, best scholars, and best preachers of his age, was usher during the greatest part of the time that Johnson was at school. Then came Hague, of whom as much might be said, with the addition that he was an elegant poet. Hague was succeeded by Green, afterwards Bishop of Lincoln, whose character in the learned world is well known. In the same form with Johnson was Congreve, who afterwards became Chaplain to Archbishop Boulter, and by that connection obtained good preferment in Ireland.

He was a younger son of the ancient family of Congreve, in Staff
shire, of which the poet was a branch. His brother sold the estate.
There was also Lowe, afterwards Canon of Windsor."

Indeed, Johnson was very sensible how much he owed to Mr. Hunter.
Mr. Langton one day asked him how he had acquired so accurate a
knowledge of Latin, in which, I believe, he was exceeded by no man of
said, "My master whipt me very well. Without that,
have done nothing." He told Mr. Langton that while
was flogging his boys unmercifully, he used to say, "And this
o save you from the gallows." Johnson, upon all occasions,
10 ed his approbation of enforcing instruction by means of the
I would rather," said he, "have the rod to be the general terror
and, to make them learn, than tell a child, if you do thus, or thus,
you will be more esteemed than your brothers or sisters. The rod produces an effect which terminates in itself. A child is afraid of being
whipped, and gets his task, and there's an end on't: whereas, by ex-
citing emulation and comparisons of superiority, you lay the foundation
of lasting mischief; you make brothers and sisters hate each other."

When Johnson saw some young ladies in Lincolnshire who were
remarkably well behaved, owing to their mother's strict discipline and
severe correction, he exclaimed, in one of Shakspeare's lines a little
varied,[2]

> "*Rod*, I will honour thee for this thy duty."

That superiority over his fellows, which he maintained with so much
dignity in his march through life, was not assumed from vanity and
ostentation, but was the natural and constant effect of those extraordinary powers of mind, of which he could not but be conscious by comparison; the intellectual difference, which in other cases of comparison
of characters, is often a matter of undecided contest, being as clear in
his case as the superiority of stature in some men above others. Johnson did not strut or stand on tiptoe; he only did not stoop. From his
earliest years, his superiority was perceived and acknowledged. He
was from the beginning ἄναξ ἀνδρῶν, a king of men. His schoolfellow,
Mr. Hector, has obligingly furnished me with many particulars of his
boyish days; and assured me that he never knew him corrected at
school, but for talking and diverting other boys from their business.
He seemed to learn by intuition; for though indolence and procrasti
nation were inherent in his constitution, whenever he made an exertion
he did more than any one else. In short, he is a memorable instance
of what has been often observed, that the boy is the man in miniature;

---

[1] Johnson's observations to Dr. Burney, on this subject, may be found in a subsequent part
of this work. See vol. ii. near the end of the year 1775.—BURNEY.

More than a little. The line is in King Henry VI., Part ii. Act. iv. Scene last:—
" Sword I will hallow thee for this thy deed."—MALONE.

that the distinguishing characteristics of each individual are the same through the whole course of life. His favourites used to receive very liberal assistance from him ; and such was the submission and deference with which he was treated, such the desire to obtain his

Thus he was borne to School.

regard, that three of the boys, of whom Mr. Hector was sometimes one, used to come in the morning as his humble attendants, and carry him to school. One in the middle stooped while he sat upon his back, and one on each side supported him, and thus he was borne triumphant. Such a proof of the early predominance of intellectual vigour is very remarkable, and does honour to human nature. Talking to me once himself of his being much distinguished at school, he told me, "They never thought to raise me by comparing me to any one ; they never said Johnson is as good a scholar as such a one but such a one is as good a scholar as Johnson ; and this was said but of one, but of Lowe : and I do not think he was as good a scholar."

He discovered a great ambition to excel, which roused him to counteract his indolence. He was uncommonly inquisitive ; and his memory was so tenacious, that he never forgot anything that he either heard or read. Mr. Hector remembers having recited to him eighteen verses, which, after a little pause, he repeated *verbatim*, varying only one epithet, by which he improved the line.

He never joined with the other boys in their ordinary diversions : his only amusement was in winter, when he took a pleasure in being drawn upon the ice by a boy barefooted, who pulled him along by a garter fixed round him ; no very easy operation, as his size was remarkably large. His defective sight, indeed, prevented him from enjoying the common sports ; and he once pleasantly remarked to me, "how wonderfully well he had contrived to be idle without them." Lord Chesterfield, however, has justly observed in one of his letters, when earnestly cautioning a friend against the pernicious effects of idleness, that active sports are not to be reckoned idleness in young people ; and that the listless torpor of doing nothing, alone deserves that name. Of this dismal inertness of disposition, Johnson had all his life too great a share. Mr. Hector relates, that "he could not oblige him more than by sauntering away the hours of vacation in the fields, during which he was more engaged in talking to himself than to his companion."

Dr. Percy, the Bishop of Dromore, who was long intimately acquainted with him, and has preserved a few anecdotes concerning him, regretting that he was not a more diligent collector, informs me, that when a boy he was immoderately fond of reading romances of chivalry, and he retained his fondness for them through life; so that," adds his lordship, "spending part of a summer at my parsonage-house in the country, he chose for his regular reading the old Spanish romance of 'Felixmarte of Hircania,' in folio, which he read quite through. Yet I have heard him attribute to these extravagant fictions that unsettled turn of mind which prevented his ever fixing in any profession."

[1724. Aged 15.]—After having resided for some time at the house of his uncle, Cornelius Ford,[1] Johnson was, at the age of fifteen, removed to the school of Stourbridge, in Worcestershire, of which Mr. Wentworth was then master. This step was taken by the advice of his cousin, the Rev. Mr. Ford, a man in whom both talents and good dispositions were disgraced by licentiousness,[2] but who was a very able judge of what was right. At this school he did not receive so much benefit as was expected. It has been said, that he acted in the capacity of an assistant to Mr. Wentworth, in teaching the younger boys. "Mr. Wentworth," he told me, "was a very able man, but an idle man, and to me very severe; but I cannot blame him much. I was then a big boy; he saw I did not reverence him, and that he should get no honour by me. I had brought enough with me to carry me through; and all I should get at his school would be ascribed to my own labour, or to my former master. Yet he taught me a great deal."

PARSON FORD, FROM HOGARTH'S PICTURE.

He thus discriminated to Dr. Percy, Bishop of Dromore, his progress at his two grammar schools. "At one, I learned much in the school, but little from the master; in the other, I learned much from the master but little in the school."

The bishop also informs me, that Dr. Johnson's father, before he was received at Stourbridge, applied to have him admitted as a scholar and assistant to the Rev. Samuel Lee, M.A., head master of Newport school in Shropshire, (a very diligent good teacher, at that time in high reputation, under whom Mr. Hollis is said, in the Memoirs of his Life,

---

[1] Cornelius Ford, according to Sir John Hawkins, was his cousin german, being the son of Dr. Ford, an eminent physician, who was brother to Johnson's mother."—MALONE.

[2] He is said to be the original of the parson in Hogarth's Modern Midnight Conversation. —BOSWELL.

to have been also educated.)[1] This application to Mr. Lee was not successful; but Johnson had afterwards the gratification to hear that the old gentleman, who lived to a very advanced age, mentioned it as one of the most memorable events of his life, that "he was *very near* having that great man for his scholar."

He remained at Stourbridge little more than a year,[2] and then he returned home, where he may be said to have loitered, for two years, in a state very unworthy his uncommon abilities. He had already given several proofs of his poetical genius, both in his school exercises and in other occasional compositions. Of these I have obtained a considerable collection, by the favour of Mr. Wentworth, son of one of his masters, and of Mr. Hector,[3] his schoolfellow and friend; from which I select the following specimens:—

Translation of VIRGIL. Pastoral I.

MELIBŒUS.

Now, Tityrus, you, supine and careless laid,
Play on your pipe beneath this beechen shade;
While wretched we about the world must roam,
And leave our pleasing fields and native home,
Here at your ease you sing your amorous flame,
And the wood rings with Amarillis' name.

TITYRUS.

Those blessings, friend, a deity bestow'd,
For I shall never think him less than god:
Oft on his altar shall my firstlings lie,
Their blood the consecrated stones shall dye:
He gave my flocks to graze the flowery meads,
And me to tune at ease th' unequal reeds.

MELIBŒUS.

My admiration only I exprest
(No spark of envy harbours in my breast),
That, when confusion o'er the country reigns,
To you alone this happy state remains.
Here I, though faint myself, must drive my goats,
Far from their ancient fields and humble cots.
This scarce I lead, who left on yonder rock
Two tender kids, the hopes of all the flock.

---

[1] As was likewise the Bishop of Dromore many years afterwards.—BOSWELL.

[2] Yet here his genius was so distinguished, that although little better than a schoolboy, he was admitted into the best company of the place, and had no common attention paid to him; of which remarkable instances were long remembered there.—PERCY.

[3] Mr. Hector, to whom we are indebted for so many reminiscences of Johnson's early life was a native of Lichfield, and became an eminent surgeon in Birmingham, where he died September 2, 1794, aged 85. He resided for very many years at a house in the Old-square, where he was visited by Johnson in 1781, and again in 1784. This house, "much modernised," is now occupied by W. Scholefield, Esq., M.P. for Birmingham.—ED.

Had we not been perverse and careless grown,
This dire event by omens was foreshown ;
Our trees were blasted by the thunder stroke,
And left-hand crows, from an old hollow oak,
Foretold the coming evil by their dismal croak.

Translation of HORACE. Book I. Ode xxii.

THE man, my friend, whose conscious heart
   With virtue's sacred ardour glows,
Nor taints with death the envenom'd dart,
   Nor needs the guard of Moorish bows :

Though Scythia's icy cliffs he treads,
   Or horrid Afric's faithless sands ;
Or where the famed Hydaspes spreads
   His liquid wealth o'er barbarous lands.

For while by Chloe's image charm'd,
   Too far in Sabine woods I stray'd ;
Me singing, careless and unarm'd,
   A grizzly wolf surprised, and fled.

No savage more portentous stain'd
   Apulia's spacious wilds with gore ;
No fiercer Juba's thirsty land,
   Dire nurse of raging lions, bore.

Place me where no soft summer gale
   Among the quivering branches sighs ;
Where clouds condensed for ever veil
   With horrid gloom the frowning skies :

Place me beneath the burning line,
   A clime denied to human race ;
I 'll sing of Chloe's charms divine,
   Her heavenly voice, and beauteous face.

Translation of HORACE. Book II. Ode ix.

CLOUDS do not always veil the skies,
   Nor showers immerse the verdant plain ·
Nor do the billows always rise,
   Or storms afflict the ruffled main :

Nor, Valgius, on th' Armenian shores
   Do the chain'd waters always freeze :
Not always furious Boreas roars,
   Or bends with violent force the trees.

But you are ever drown'd in tears,
 For Mystes dead you ever mourn ;
No setting Sol can ease your cares,
 But finds you sad at his return.

The wise experienced Grecian sage
 Mourn'd not Antilochus so long ;
Nor did King Priam's hoary age
 So much lament his slaughter'd son.

Leave off, at length, these woman's sighs,
 Augustus' numerous trophies sing ;
Repeat that prince's victories,
 To whom all nations tribute bring.

Niphates rolls an humbler wave,
 At length the undaunted Scythian yields,
Content to live the Roman's slave,
 And scarce forsakes his native fields.

Translation of part of the Dialogue between HECTOR *and* ANDROMACHE ; *from the Sixth Book of* HOMER'S ILIAD.

SHE ceased ; then god-like Hector answer'd kind
(His various plumage sporting in the wind),
That post, and all the rest, shall be my care ;
But shall I, then, forsake the unfinish'd war ?
How would the Trojans brand great Hector's name !
And one base action sully all my fame,
Acquired by wounds and battles bravely fought !
O, how my soul abhors so mean a thought !
Long since I learn'd to slight this fleeting breath,
And view with cheerful eyes approaching death.
The inexorable sisters have decreed
That Priam's house, and Priam's self shall bleed :
The day will come, in which proud Troy shall yield,
And spread its smoking ruins o'er the field.
Yet Hecuba's, nor Priam's hoary age,
Whose blood shall quench some Grecian's thirsty rage,
Nor my brave brothers, that have bit the ground,
Their souls dismiss'd through many a ghastly wound,
Can in my bosom half that grief create,
As the sad thought of your impending fate :
When some proud Grecian dame shall tasks impose,
Mimic your tears, and ridicule your woes ;
Beneath Hyperia's waters shall you sweat,
And, fainting, scarce support the liquid weight :
Then shall some Argive loud insulting cry,
Behold the wife of Hector, guard of Troy !

Tears, at my name, shall drown those beauteous eyes,
And that fair bosom heave with rising sighs!
Before that day, by some brave hero's hand
May I lie slain, and spurn the bloody sand.

To a Young Lady on her Birthday.

This tributary verse receive, my fair,
Warm with an ardent lover's fondest prayer.
May this returning day for ever find
Thy form more lovely, more adorn'd thy mind;
All pains, all cares, may favouring Heaven remove,
All but the sweet solicitudes of love!
May powerful nature join with grateful art,
To point each glance, and force it to the heart!
O then, when conquer'd crowds confess thy sway,
When ev'n proud wealth and prouder wit obey
My fair, be mindful of the mighty trust:
Alas! 'tis hard for beauty to be just.
Those sovereign charms with strictest care employ;
Nor give the generous pain, the worthless joy:
With his own form acquaint the forward fool,
Shown in the faithful glass of ridicule;
Teach mimic consure her own faults to find,
No more let coquettes to themselves be blind,
So shall Belinda's charms improve mankind.

THE YOUNG AUTHOR.[2]

When first the peasant, long inclin'd to roam,
Forsakes his rural sports and peaceful home,
Pleas'd with the scene the smiling ocean yields,
He scorns the verdant meads and flow'ry fields;
Then dances jocund o'er the watery way,
While the breeze whispers, and the streamers play:
Unbounded prospects in his bosom roll,
And future millions lift his rising soul;
In blissful dreams he digs the golden mine,
And raptur'd sees the new-found ruby shine.
Joys insincere! thick clouds invade the skies,
Loud roar the billows, high the waves arise;
Sick'ning with fear, he longs to view the shore,
And vows to trust the faithless deep no more.

[1] Mr. Hector informs me, that this was made almost *impromptu*, in his presence.—BOSWELL.
[2] This he inserted, with many alterations, in the Gentleman's Magazine, 1743.—BOSWELL.
He however did not add his name.—MALONE.

So the young Author, panting after fame,
And the long honours of a lasting name,
Intrusts his happiness to human kind,
More false, more cruel, than the seas or wind.
" Toil on, dull crowd," in ecstacies he cries,
" For wealth or title, perishable prize;
" While I those transitory blessings scorn,
" Secure of praise from ages yet unborn."
This thought once form'd, all counsel comes too late.
He flies to press, and hurries on his fate;
Swiftly he sees the imagin'd laurels spread,
And feels the unfading wreath surround his head.
Warn'd by another's fate, vain youth, be wise;
Those dreams were Settle's once, and Ogilby's ·

The pamphlet spreads, incessant hisses rise,
To some retreat the baffled writer flies;
Where no sour critics snarl, no sneers molest,
Safe from the tart lampoon, and stinging jest
There begs of Heaven a less distinguish'd lot,
Glad to be hid, and proud to be forgot.

EPILOGUE, *intended to have been spoken by a* LADY *who was to personate
the Ghost of* HERMIONE.[1]

YE blooming train, who give despair or joy,
Bless with a smile, or with a frown destroy;
In whose fair cheeks destructive Cupids wait,
And with unerring shafts distribute fate;
Whose snowy breasts, whose animated eyes,
Each youth admires, though each admirer dies;
Whilst you deride their pangs in barb'rous play, ⎫
Unpitying see them weep, and hear them pray, ⎬
And unrelenting sport ten thousand lives away. ⎭
For you, ye fair, I quit the gloomy plains,
Where sable night in all her horror reigns;
No fragrant bowers, no delightful glades,
Receive the unhappy ghosts of scornful maids.
For kind, for tender nymphs, the myrtle blooms,
And weaves her bending boughs in pleasing glooms;
Perennial roses deck each purple vale,
And scents ambrosial breathe in every gale:
Far hence are banish'd vapours, spleen, and tears,
Tea, scandal, ivory teeth, and languid airs:
No pug, no favourite Cupid, there enjoys
The balmy kiss, for which poor Thyrsis dies;

[1] Some young ladies at Lichfield having proposed to act " The Distressed Mother"
Johnson wrote this, and gave it to Mr. Hector to convey it privately to them.—BOSWELL

Form'd to delight, they use no foreign arms,
Nor torturing whalebones pinch them into charms ;
No conscious blushes there their cheeks inflame,
For those who feel no guilt can know no **shame ;**
Unfaded still their former charms they show,
Around them pleasures wait, and joys for ever **new.**
But cruel virgins meet severer fates ;
Expell'd and exiled from the blissful seats,
To dismal realms, and regions void of peace,
Where furies ever howl, and serpents hiss.
O'er the sad plains perpetual tempests sigh,
And pois'nous vapours, black'ning all the sky,
With livid hue the fairest face o'ercast,
And every beauty withers at the blast :
Where'er they fly their lovers' ghosts pursue,
Inflicting all those ills which once they knew ;
Vexation, Fury, Jealousy, Despair,
Vex ev'ry eye, and every bosom tear ;
Their foul deformities by all descried,
No maid to flatter, and no paint to hide.
Then melt, ye fair, while crowds around you sigh.
Nor let disdain sit louring in your eye ;
With pity soften every awful grace,
And beauty smile auspicious in each face ;
To ease their pains exert your milder power,
So shall you guiltless reign, and all mankind adore.

[1728. Age 19.] The two years which he spent at home, after his return from Stourbridge, he passed in what he thought idleness, and was scolded by his father for his want of steady application. He had no settled plan of life, nor looked forward at all, but merely lived from day to day. Yet he read a great deal in a desultory manner, without any scheme of study ; as chance threw books in his way, and inclination directed him through them. He used to mention one curious instance of his casual reading when but a boy. Having imagined that his brother had hid some apples behind a large folio upon an upper shelf in his father's shop, he climbed up to search for them. There were no apples ; but the large folio proved to be Petrarch, whom he had seen mentioned in some preface, as one of the restorers of learning. His curiosity having been thus excited, he sat down with avidity, and read a great part of the book. What he read during these two years, he told me, was not works of mere amusement, "not voyages and travels, but all literature, Sir, all ancient writers, all manly : though but little Greek, only some of Anacreon and Hesiod ; but in this irregular manner," added he, "I had looked into a great many books, which were not commonly known at the Universities, where they seldom read any books but what are put into their hands by their tutors ; so that when I came to Oxford, Dr. Adams, now master of Pembroke College, told me I was the best qualified for the University that he had ever known come there."

In estimating the progress of his mind during these two years, as well as in future periods of his life, we must not regard his own hasty confession of idleness ; for we see, when he explains himself, that he was acquiring various stores ; and indeed he himself concluded the account, with saying, "I would not have you think I was doing nothing then." He might, perhaps, have studied more assiduously ; but it may be doubted whether such a mind as his was not more enriched by roaming at large in the fields of literature than if it had been confined to any single spot. The analogy between body and mind is very general, and the parallel will hold as to their food, as well as any other particular. The flesh of animals who feed excursively is allowed to have a higher flavour than that of those who are cooped up. May there not be the same difference between men who read as their taste prompts, and men who are confined in cells and colleges to stated tasks?

That a man in Mr. Michael Johnson's circumstances should think of sending his son to the expensive University of Oxford, at his own charge, seems very improbable. The subject was too delicate to question Johnson upon ; but I have been assured by Dr. Taylor, that the scheme never would have taken place, had not a gentleman of Shropshire, one of his schoolfellows, spontaneously undertaken to support him at Oxford, in the character of his companion ; though, in fact, he never received any assistance whatever from that gentleman.

He, however, went to Oxford, and was entered a commoner of Pembroke College, on the 31st of October, 1728, being then in his nineteenth year.

The Reverend Dr. Adams, who afterwards presided over Pembroke College with universal esteem, told me he was present, and gave me some account of what passed on the night of Johnson's arrival at Oxford. On that evening, his father, who had anxiously accompanied him, found means to have him introduced to Mr. Jorden, who was to be his tutor. His being put under any tutor, reminds us of what Wood says of Robert Burton, author of the "Anatomy of Melancholy," when elected student of Christ-church ; "for form's sake, *though he wanted not a tutor*, he was put under the tuition of Dr. John Bancroft, afterwards Bishop of Oxon."[1]

His father seemed very full of the merits of his son, and told the company he was a good scholar and a poet, and wrote Latin verses. His figure and manner appeared strange to them ; but he behaved modestly, and sat silent, till upon something which occurred in the course of conversation, he suddenly struck in and quoted Macrobius ;

---

[1] Athen. Oxon. edit. 1721, i. 627.—BOSWELL.

and thus he gave the first impression of that more extensive reading in which he had indulged himself.

His tutor, Mr. Jorden, fellow of Pembroke, was not, it seems, a man of such abilities as we should conceive requisite for the instructor of Samuel Johnson, who gave me the following account of him :—" He was a very worthy man, but a heavy man, and I did not profit much

CHRIST-CHURCH MEADOW.

by his instructions. Indeed, I did not attend him much. The first day after I came to college, I waited upon him, and then stayed away four. On the sixth, Mr. Jorden asked me why I had not attended. I answered, I had been sliding in Christ-church meadow : and this I said with as much *nonchalance* as I am now[1] talking to you. I had no notion that l was wrong or irreverent to my tutor." BOSWELL : " That, Sir, was great fortitude of mind." JOHNSON : " No, Sir ; stark insensibility."[2]

The fifth of November was at that time kept with great solemnity at Pembroke College, and exercises upon the subject of the day were required. Johnson neglected to perform his, which is much to be

[1] Oxford, 20th March, 1776.—BOSWELL.

[2] It ought to be remembered, that Dr. Johnson was apt, in his literary as well as moral exercises, to overcharge his defects. Dr. Adams informed me, that he attended his tutor s lectures, and also the lectures in the College Hall. very regularly.—BOSWELL.

regretted ; for his vivacity of imagination, and force of language, would probably have produced something sublime upon the gunpowder-plot. To apologise for his neglect, he gave in a short copy of verses, entitled *Somnium*, containing a common thought ; " that the Muse had come to him in his sleep, and whispered, that it did not become him to write on such subjects as politics; he should confine himself to humbler themes:" but the versification was truly Virgilian.

He had a love and respect for Jorden, not for his literature,[1] but for his worth. " Whenever," said he, " a young man becomes Jorden's pupil, he becomes his son."

Having given such a specimen of his poetical powers, he was asked by Mr. Jorden to translate Pope's " Messiah " into Latin verse, as a Christmas exercise. He performed it with uncommon rapidity, and in so masterly a manner, that he obtained great applause from it, which ever after kept him high in the estimation of his college, and, indeed, of all the University.

It is said, that Mr. Pope expressed himself concerning it in terms of strong approbation. Dr. Taylor told me, that it was first printed for old Mr. Johnson, without the knowledge of his son, who was very angry when he heard of it. A Miscellany of Poems, collected by a person of the name of Husbands, was published at Oxford in 1731. In that Miscellany Johnson's translation of the " Messiah " appeared, with this modest motto from Scaliger's Poetics : " *Ex alieno ingenio poeta, ex suo tantum versificator.*"

I am not ignorant that critical objections have been made to this and other specimens of Johnson's Latin poetry. I acknowledge myself not competent to decide on a question of such extreme nicety. But I am satisfied with the just and discriminative eulogy pronounced upon it by my friend Mr. Courtenay :—

> " And with like ease his vivid lines assume
> 　The garb and dignity of ancient Rome.—
> Let college *verse-men* trite conceits express,
> Trick'd out in splendid shreds of Virgil's dress
> From playful Ovid cull the tinsel phrase,
> And vapid notions hitch in pilfer'd lays ;
> Then with mosaic art the piece combine,
> And boast the glitter of each dulcet line :
> Johnson adventured boldly to transfuse
> His vigorous sense into the Latin muse ;
> Aspired to shine by unreflected light,
> And with a Roman's ardour *think* and write.
> He felt the tuneful Nine his breast inspire,
> And, like a master, waked the soothing lyre :

---

[1] Johnson used to say of Jorden, that " he scarcely knew a noun from an **adverb**."— NICHOLS.

> Horatian strains a grateful heart proclaim,
> While Sky's wild rocks resound his Thralia's name.—
> Hesperia's plant, in some less skilful hands,
> To bloom awhile factitious heat demands:
> Though glowing Maro a faint warmth supplies,
> The sickly blossom in the hot-house dies:
> By Johnson's genial culture, art, and toil,
> Its root strikes deep, and owns the fost'ring soil;
> Inbibes our sun through all its swelling veins,
> And grows a native of Britannia's plains."[1]

[1729. Age 20.] The "morbid melancholy," which was lurking in his constitution, and to which we may ascribe those particularities, and that aversion to regular life, which at a very early period marked his character, gathered such strength in his twentieth year, as to afflict him in a dreadful manner. While he was at Lichfield, in the college vacation of the year 1729, he felt himself overwhelmed with a horrible hypochondria, with perpetual irritation, fretfulness, and impatience; and with a dejection, gloom, and despair, which made existence misery. From this dismal malady he never afterwards was perfectly relieved; and all his labours, and all his enjoyments, were but temporary interruptions of its baleful influence. How wonderful, how unsearchable are the ways of God! Johnson, who was blest with all the powers of genius and understanding, in a degree far above the ordinary state of human nature, was at the same time visited with a disorder so afflictive, that they who know it by dire experience will not envy his exalted endowments. That it was, in some degree, occasioned by a defect in his nervous system, that inexplicable part of our frame, appears highly probable. He told Mr. Paradise that he was sometimes so languid and inefficient, that he could not distinguish the hour upon the town clock.

Johnson, upon the first violent attack of this disorder, strove to overcome it by forcible exertions. He frequently walked to Birmingham and back again, and tried many other expedients; but all in vain. His expression concerning it to me was, "I did not then know how to manage it." His distress became so intolerable, that he applied to Dr. Swinfen, physician in Lichfield, his godfather, and put into his hands a state of his case, written in Latin. Dr. Swinfen was so much struck with the extraordinary acuteness, research, and eloquence of this paper, that, in his zeal for his godson, he showed it to several people. His daughter, Mrs. Desmoulins, who was many years humanely supported in Dr. Johnson's house in London, told me, that upon his discovering that Dr. Swinfen had communicated his case, he was so much offended, that he was never afterwards fully reconciled to him. He indeed had good reason to be offended; for though Dr. Swinfen's motive was good, he

[1] "Poetical Review of the Literary and Moral Character of Dr. Johnson," by John Courtenay, Esq. M.P.—BOSWELL.

inconsiderately betrayed a matter deeply interesting and of great delicacy, which had been intrusted to him in confidence : and exposed a complaint of his young friend and patient, which, in the superficial opinion of the generality of mankind, is attended with contempt and disgrace.

But let not little men triumph upon knowing that Johnson was an HYPOCHONDRIAC, was subject to what the learned, philosophical, and pious Dr. Cheyne has so well treated under the title of " The English Malady." Though he suffered severely from it he was not therefore degraded. The powers of his great mind might be troubled, and their full exercise suspended at times ; but the mind itself was ever entire. As a proof of this, it is only necessary to consider that, when he was at the very worst, he composed that state of his own case, which showed an uncommon vigour, not only of fancy and taste, but of judgment. I am aware that he himself was too ready to call such a complaint by the name of *madness ;* in conformity with which notion, he has traced its gradations, with exquisite nicety, in one of the chapters of his " Rasselas." But there is surely a clear distinction between a disorder which affects only the imagination and spirits, while the judgment is sound, and a disorder by which the judgment itself is impaired. This distinction was made to me by the late Professor Gaubius, of Leyden, physician to the Prince of Orange, in a conversation which I had with him several years ago ; and he expounded it thus : " If," said he, " a man tells me that he is grievously disturbed, for that he *imagines* he sees a ruffian coming against him with a drawn sword, though at the same time he is *conscious* it is a delusion, I pronounce him to have a disordered imagination ; but if a man tells me that he *sees* this, and in consternation calls me to look at it, I pronounce him to be *mad.*"

It is a common effect of low spirits or melancholy, to make those who are afflicted with it imagine that they are actually suffering those evils which happen to be most strongly presented to their minds. Some have fancied themselves to be deprived of the use of their limbs, some to labour under acute diseases, others to be in extreme poverty ; when, in truth, there was not the least reality in any of the suppositions ; so that when the vapours were dispelled they were convinced of the delusion. To Johnson, whose supreme enjoyment was the exercise of his reason, the disturbance or obscuration of that faculty was the evil most to be dreaded. Insanity, therefore, was the object of his most dismal apprehension ; and he fancied himself seized by it, or approaching to it, at the very time when he was giving proofs of a more than ordinary soundness and vigour of judgment. That his own diseased imagination should have so far deceived him is strange ; but it is stranger still that some of his friends should have given credit to his groundless opinion, when they had such undoubted proofs that it was totally fallacious ; though it is by no means surprising that those who wish to depreciate him, should, since his death, have laid hold of this circumstance, and insisted upon it with very unfair aggravation.

Amidst the oppression, and distraction of a disease, which very few have felt in its full extent, but many have experienced in a slighter degree, Johnson, in his writings, and in his conversation, never failed to display all the varieties of intellectual excellence. In his march through this world to a better, his mind still appeared grand and brilliant, and impressed all around him with the truth of Virgil's noble sentiment—

"Igneus est ollis vigor et cœlestis origo."—Æn. vi. 730.

The history of his mind as to religion is an important article. I have mentioned the early impressions made upon his tender imagination by his mother, who continued her pious cares with assiduity, but, in his opinion not with judgment. "Sunday," said he, "was a heavy day to me when I was a boy. My mother confined me on that day, and made me read 'The Whole Duty of Man,' from a great part of which I could derive no instruction. When, for instance, I had read the chapter on theft, which, from my infancy I had been taught was wrong, I was no more convinced that theft was wrong than before ; so there was no accession of knowledge. A boy should be introduced to such books, by having his attention directed to the arrangement, to the style, and other excellencies of composition ; that the mind being thus engaged by an amusing variety of objects may not grow weary."

He communicated to me the following particulars upon the subject of his religious progress :—" I fell into an inattention to religion, or an indifference about it, in my ninth year. The church at Lichfield, in which we had a seat, wanted reparation, so I was to go and find a seat in other churches ; and having bad eyes, and being awkward about this, I used to go and read in the fields on Sunday. This habit continued till my fourteenth year ; and still I find a great reluctance to go to church. I then became a sort of lax *talker* against religion, for I did not much *think* against it ; and this lasted till I went to Oxford, where it would not be *suffered*. When at Oxford, I took up 'Law's Serious Call to a Holy Life,' expecting to find it a dull book (as such books generally are), and perhaps to laugh at it. But I found Law quite an overmatch for me ; and this was the first occasion of my thinking in earnest of religion, after I became capable of rational inquiry." [1]

[1] Mrs. Piozzi has given a strange fantastical account of the original of Dr. Johnson's belief in our most holy religion. "At the age of *ten* years his mind was disturbed by scruples of infidelity, which preyed upon his spirits, and made him very uneasy ; the more so, as he revealed his uneasiness to none, being naturally (as he said) of a sullen temper, and reserved disposition. He searched, however, diligently but fruitlessly, for evidences of the truth of revelation ; and, at length, *recollecting* a book he had *once* seen, [*I suppose at five years old,*] in his father's shop, entitled *De Veritate Religionis*, &c., he began to think himself *highly culpable* for neglecting such a means of information, and took himself severely to task for this *sin*, adding many acts of voluntary, and, to others, unknown *penance*. The first opportunity which offered

From this time forward religion was the predominant object of his thoughts; though, with the just sentiments of a conscientious Christian, he lamented that his practice of its duties fell far short of what it ought to be.

This instance of a mind such as that of Johnson being first disposed, by an unexpected incident, to think with anxiety of the momentous concerns of eternity, and of " what he should do to be saved," may for ever be produced in opposition to the superficial and sometimes profane contempt that has been thrown upon those occasional impressions, which it is certain many Christians have experienced; though it must be acknowledged that weak minds, from an erroneous supposition that no man is in a state of grace who has not felt a particular conversion, have, in some cases, brought a degree of ridicule upon them; a ridicule of which it is inconsiderate or unfair to make a general application.

How seriously Johnson was impressed with a sense of religion, even in the vigour of his youth, appears from the following passage in his minutes, kept by way of diary:—" Sept. 7, 1736. I have this day entered upon my 28th year. Mayest thou, O God, enable me, for Jesus Christ's sake, to spend this in such a manner, that I may receive comfort from it at the hour of death, and in the day of judgment! Amen."

The particular course of his reading while at Oxford, and during the time of vacation which he passed at home, cannot be traced. Enough has been said of his irregular mode of study. He told me, that from his earliest years he loved to read poetry, but hardly ever read any poem to an end; that he read Shakspeare at a period so early, that the speech of the Ghost in Hamlet terrified him when he was alone; that Horace's Odes were the compositions in which he took most delight, and it was long before he liked his Epistles and Satires. He told me what he read *solidly* at Oxford was Greek; not the Grecian historians, but Homer and Euripides, and now and then a little epigram; that the study of which he was the most fond was Metaphysics, but he had not read much, even in that way. I always thought that he did himself injustice in his account of what he had read, and that he must have been

of course, he seized the book with avidity; but, on examination, *not finding himself scholar enough to peruse its contents*, set his heart at rest; and not thinking to inquire whether there were any English books written on the subject, followed his usual amusements, and *considered his conscience as lightened of a crime.* He redoubled his diligence to learn the language that contained the information he most wished for; but from the pain which guilt [*namely, having omitted to read what he did not understand*] had given him, he now began to deduce the soul's immortality [*a sensation of pain in this world being an unquestionable proof of existence in another*], which was the point that belief first stopped at; *and from that moment resolving to be a Christian*, became one of the most zealous and pious ones our nation ever produced."—Anecdotes, p. 17.

This is one of the numerous misrepresentations of this lively lady, which it is worth while to correct; for if credit should be given to such a childish, irrational, and ridiculous statement of the foundation of Dr. Johnson's faith in Christianity, how little credit would be due to it. Mrs. Piozzi seems to wish that the world should think Dr. Johnson also under the influence of that easy logic, *Stet pro ratione voluntas.*—BOSWELL.

speaking with reference to the vast portion of study which is possible, and to which few scholars in the whole history of literature have attained ; for when I once asked him whether a person, whose name I have now forgotten, studied hard, he answered, "No, Sir ; I do not believe he studied hard. I never knew a man who studied hard. I conclude, indeed, from the effects, that some men have studied hard, as Bentley and Clarke." Trying him by that criterion upon which he formed his judgment of others, we may be absolutely certain, both from his writings and his conversation, that his reading was very extensive. Dr. Adam Smith, than whom few were better judges on this subject, once observed to me, that "Johnson knew more books than any man alive." He had a peculiar facility in seizing at once what was valuable in any book, without submitting to the labour of perusing it from beginning to end. He had, from the irritability of his constitution, at all times an impatience and hurry when he either read or wrote. A certain apprehension arising from novelty made him write his first exercise at College twice over ; but he never took that trouble with any other composition ; and we shall see that his most excellent works were struck off at a heat, with rapid exertion.[1]

Yet he appears, from his early notes or memorandums in my possession, to have at various times attempted, or at least planned, a methodical course of study, according to computation, of which he was all his life fond, as it fixed his attention steadily upon something without, and prevented his mind from preying upon itself. Thus I find in his handwriting the number of lines in each of two of Euripides's Tragedies, of the Georgics of Virgil, of the first six books of the Æneid, of Horace's Art of Poetry, of the three of the books of Ovid's Metamorphoses, of some parts of Theocritus, and of the tenth Satire of Juvenal ; and a table showing, at the rate of various numbers a day (I suppose verses to be read), what would be, in each case, the total amount in a week, month, and year.

No man had a more ardent love of literature, or a higher respect for it, than Johnson. His apartment in Pembroke College was that upon the second floor over the gateway.[2] The enthusiast of learning will ever contemplate it with veneration. One day, while he was sitting in it quite alone, Dr. Panting, then master of the college, whom he called "a fine Jacobite fellow," overheard him uttering this soliloquy in his strong emphatic voice : "Well, I have a mind to see what is done in other places of learning. I'll go and visit the universities abroad. I'll

[1] He told Dr. Burney that he never wrote any of his works that were printed, twice over. Dr. Burney's wonder at seeing several pages of his "Lives of the Poets," in manuscript, with scarce a blot or erasure, drew this observation from him.—MALONE.

[2] The illustration (p. 26) represents the gateway of Pembroke College as it appeared in Dr Johnson's time. Subsequently to that period, both the gateway and the interior of the apartment have undergone such extensive alterations as to preserve no resemblance to their original appearance.—ED.

go to France and Italy.   I'll go to Padua.—And I'll mind my business.
For an *Athenian* blockhead is the worst of all blockheads."[1]

PEMBROKE COLLEGE GATEWAY.[2]

Dr. Adams told me that Johnson, while he was at Pembroke College,
"was caressed and loved by all about him, was a gay and frolicsome
fellow, and passed there the happiest part of his life."   But this is a
striking proof of the fallacy of appearances, and how little any of us

[1] I had this anecdote from Dr. Adams, and Dr. Johnson confirmed it.   Bramston, in his
"Man of Taste," has the same thought:

"Sure, of all blockheads, scholars are the worst."—BOSWELL.

Johnson's meaning, however, is, that a scholar who is a blockhead must be the worst of all
blockheads, because he is without excuse.   But Bramston, in the assumed character of an
ignorant coxcomb, maintains that *all* scholars are blockheads on account of their scholarship.—
J. BOSWELL, Jun.

Johnson may also have alluded to the University of which he was a member, and whose
classical pre-eminence he so strenuously asserted.   His full meaning probably was, that if he
travelled, it behoved him, in justice to his renowned literary parent, not to betray ignorance
or incapacity, "for an Athenian (Oxford) blockhead is the worst of all blockheads."   Dryden
(who had studied at Cambridge) says, in one of his Prologues, complimenting the rival
University,—

"Oxford to him a dearer name shall be
Than his own mother University;
Thebes did his green unknowing youth engage,
He chooses *Athens* in his riper age."

It is possible that these lines may have impressed themselves on the mind of so zealous an
Oxonian as Johnson, and suggested the phrase in question."—ED.

know of the real internal state even of those whom we see most frequently; for the truth is, that he was then depressed by poverty, and irritated by disease When I mentioned to him this account as given me by Dr. Adams, he said, " Ah, Sir, I was mad and violent. It was bitterness which they mistook for frolic. I was miserably poor, and : thought to fight my way by my literature and my wit; so I disregarded all power and all authority."

The Bishop of Dromore observes in a letter to me, " The pleasure he took in vexing the tutors and fellows has been often mentioned. But I have heard him say, what ought to be recorded to the honour of the present venerable master of that college, the Reverend William Adams, D.D., who was then very young, and one of the junior fellows ; that the mild but judicious expostulations of this worthy man, whose virtue awed him, and whose learning he revered, made him really ashamed of himself, ' though I fear,' said he, ' I was too proud to own it.'

" I have heard from some of his contemporaries that he was generally seen lounging at the college gate, with a circle of young students round him, whom he was entertaining with wit, and keeping from their studies, if not spiriting them up to rebellion against the college discipline, which in his maturer years he so much extolled."

He very early began to attempt keeping notes or memorandums, by way of a diary of his life. I find, in a parcel of loose leaves, the following spirited resolution to contend against his natural indolence : " October, 1729. *Desidiæ valedixi ; syrenis istius, cantibus surdam posthac aurem obversurus.*—I bid farewell to sloth, being resolved henceforth not to listen to her syren strains." I have also in my possession a few leaves of another *Libellus,* or little book, entitled " Annales," in which some of the early particulars of his history are registered in Latin.

I do not find that he formed any close intimacies with his fellow-collegians. But Dr. Adams told me, that he contracted a love and regard for Pembroke College, which he retained to the last. A short time before his death he sent to that college a present of all his works, to be deposited in their library ; and he had thoughts of leaving to it his house at Lichfield ; but his friends who were about him very properly dissuaded him from it, and he bequeathed it to some poor relations. He took a pleasure of boasting of the many eminent men who had been educated at Pembroke. In this list are found the names of Mr. Hawkins, the Poetry Professor, Mr. Shenstone, Sir William Blackstone and others ;[1] not forgetting the celebrated popular preacher, Mr. George Whitefield, of whom, though Dr. Johnson did not think very highly, it must be acknowledged that his eloquence was powerful, his views pious and charitable, his assiduity almost incredible ; and that, since his

See Nash's History of Worcestershire, vol. i. p 529.—BOSWELL.

death, the integrity of his character has been fully vindicated. Being himself a poet, Johnson was peculiarly happy in mentioning how many of the sons of Pembroke were poets ; adding, with a smile of sportive triumph, " Sir, we are a nest of singing birds."

He was not, however, blind to what he thought the defects of his own college : and I have, from the information of Dr. Taylor, a very strong instance of that rigid honesty which he ever inflexibly preserved. Taylor had obtained his father's consent to be entered of Pembroke, that he might be with his schoolfellow Johnson, with whom, though some years older than himself, he was very intimate. This would have been a great comfort to Johnson. But he fairly told Taylor that he could not, in conscience, suffer him to enter where he knew he could not have an able tutor. He then made inquiry all round the University, and having found that Mr. Bateman, of Christ-church, was the tutor of highest reputation, Taylor was entered of that college. Mr. Bateman's lectures were so excellent, that Johnson used to come and get them at second-hand from Taylor, till his poverty being so extreme, that his shoes were worn out, and his feet appeared through them, he saw that this humiliating circumstance was perceived by the Christ-church men, and he came no more. He was too proud to accept of money, and somebody having set a pair of new shoes at his door, he threw them away with indignation. How must we feel when we read such an anecdote of Samuel Johnson !

His spirited refusal of an eleemosynary supply of shoes arose, no doubt, from a proper pride. But, considering his ascetic disposition at times, as acknowledged by himself in his " Meditations," and the exaggeration with which some have treated the peculiarities of his character, I should not wonder to hear it ascribed to a principle of superstitious mortification ; as we are told by Tursellinus, in his " Life of St. Ignatius Loyola," that this intrepid founder of the order of Jesuits, when he arrived at Goa, after having made a severe pilgrimage through the eastern deserts, persisted in wearing his miserable shattered shoes, and when new ones were offered him, rejected them as an unsuitable indulgence.

The *res angusta domi* prevented him from having the advantage of a complete academical education. The friend to whom he had trusted for support had deceived him. His debts in college, though not great, were increasing ; and his scanty remittances from Lichfield, which had all along been made with great difficulty, could be supplied no longer, his father having fallen into a state of insolvency. Compelled, therefore, by irresistible necessity, he left the college in autumn, 1731, without a degree, having been a member of it little more than three years.

Dr. Adams, the worthy and respectable master of Pembroke College, has generally had the reputation of being Johnson's tutor. The fact, however, is, that in 1731, Mr. Jorden quitted the college, and his pupils were transferred to Dr. Adams; so that, had Johnson returned, Dr. Adams *would have been his tutor*. It is to be wished that this connection had taken place. His equal temper, mild disposition, and politeness of manners, might have insensibly softened the harshness of Johnson, and infused into him those more delicate charities, those *petites morales*, in which, it must be confessed, our great moralist was more deficient than his best friends could fully justify. Dr. Adams paid Johnson this high compliment. He said to me at Oxford, in 1776, " I was his nominal tutor; but he was above my mark." When I repeated it to Johnson, his eyes flashed with grateful satisfaction, and he exclaimed " That was liberal and noble."

LICHFIELD.—1730.

CHAPTER II.—1731—1736.

AND now (I had almost said *poor*) Samuel Johnson returned to his native city, destitute, and not knowing how he should gain even a decent livelihood. His father's misfortunes in trade rendered him unable to support his son; and for some time there appeared no means by which he could maintain himself. In the December of this year his father died.

The state of poverty in which he died, appears from a note in one of Johnson's little diaries of the following year, which strongly displays his spirit and virtuous dignity of mind. " 1732, *Julii* 15. *Undecim aureos deposui, quo die quicquid ante matris funus (quod serum sit precor) de paternis bonis sperari licet, viginti scilicet libras, accepi. Usque adeo mihi fortuna fingenda est. Interea, ne paupertate vires animi languescant, nec in flagitia egestas abigat, cavendum.*—I layed by eleven guineas on this day, when I received twenty pounds, being all that I have reason to hope for out of my father's effects, previous to the death of my mother; an event which I pray God may be very remote. I now, therefore, see that I must make my own fortune. Meanwhile, let me take care that the powers of my mind be not debilitated by poverty, and that indigence do not force me into any criminal act."

Johnson was so far fortunate, that the respectable character of his parents, and his own merit, had, from his earliest years, secured him a kind reception in the best families at Lichfield. Among these I can mention Mr. Howard, Dr. Swinfen, Mr. Simpson, Mr. Levett, Captain Garrick, father of the great ornament of the British stage; but above all, Mr. Gilbert Walmesley,[1] Registrar of the Ecclesiastical Court of Lichfield, whose character, long after his decease, Dr. Johnson has in his life of Edmund Smith, thus drawn in the glowing colours of gratitude:—

"Of Gilbert Walmesley, thus presented to my mind, let me indulge myself in the remembrance. I knew him very early; he was one of the first friends that literature procured me, and I hope, that at least my gratitude made me worthy of his notice.

"He was of an advanced age, and I was only not a boy, yet he never received my notions with contempt. He was a whig, with all the virulence and malevolence of his party; yet difference of opinion did not keep us apart. I honoured him and he endured me.

"He had mingled with the gay world without exemption from its vices or its follies; but had never neglected the cultivation of his mind. His belief of revelation was unshaken; his learning preserved his principles; he grew first regular, and then pious.

"His studies had been so various, that I am not able to name a man of equal knowledge. His acquaintance with books was great, and what he did not immediately know, he could, at least, tell where to find. Such was his amplitude of learning, and such his copiousness of communication, that it may be doubted whether a day now passes, in which I have not some advantage from his friendship.

"At this man's table I enjoyed many cheerful and instructive hours, with companions such as are not often found—with one who has lengthened, and one who has gladdened life; with Dr. James, whose skill in physic will be long remembered; and with David Garrick, whom I hoped to have gratified with this character of our common friend. But what are the hopes of man? I am disappointed by that stroke of death, which has eclipsed the gaiety of nations and impoverished the public stock of harmless pleasure."

[1] Mr. Warton informs me, "that this early friend of Johnson was entered a Commoner of Trinity College, Oxford, aged 17, in 1698; and is the author of many Latin verse translations in the "Gentleman's Magazine." One of them is a translation of
"My time, O ye Muses, was happily spent," &c
He died August 3rd, 1751, and a monument to his memory has been erected in the cathedral of Lichfield, with an inscription written by Mr. Seward, one of the Prebendaries.—BOSWELL.
His translation of "My time, O ye Muses," &c., may be found in the "Gentleman's Magazine" for 1745, vol. xv. p. 102. It is there subscribed with his name.—MALONE.

In these families he passed much time in his early years. In most of them, he was in the company of ladies, particularly at Mr. Walmesley's, whose wife and sisters-in-law, of the name of Aston, and daughters of a baronet, were remarkable for good breeding; so that the notion which has been industriously circulated and believed, that he never was in good company till late in life, and consequently had been confirmed in coarse and ferocious manners by long habits, is wholly without foundation. Some of the ladies have assured me, they recollected him well when a young man, as distinguished for his complaisance.

And that his politeness was not merely occasional and temporary, or confined to the circles of Lichfield, is ascertained by the testimony of a lady, who, in a paper with which I have been favoured by a daughter of his intimate friend and physician, Dr. Lawrence, thus describes Dr. Johnson some years afterwards:

"As the particulars of the former part of Dr. Johnson's life do not seem to be very accurately known, a lady hopes that the following information may not be unacceptable.

"She remembers Dr. Johnson on a visit to Dr. Taylor, at Ashbourne, some time between the end of the year '37, and the middle of the year '40; she rather thinks it to have been after he and his wife were removed to London. During his stay at Ashbourne, he made frequent visits to Mr. Meynell, at Bradley, where his company was much desired by the ladies of the family, who were, perhaps, in point of elegance and accomplishments, inferior to few of those with whom he was afterwards acquainted. Mr. Meynell's eldest daughter was afterwards married to Mr. Fitzherbert, father to Mr. Alleyne Fitzherbert, lately minister to the court of Russia. Of her, Dr. Johnson said, in Dr. Lawrence's study, that she had the best understanding he ever met with in any human being. At Mr. Meynell's he also commenced that friendship with Mrs. Hill Boothby, sister to the present Sir Brook Boothby, which continued till her death. The *young woman whom he used to call Molly Aston,*[1] was sister to Sir Thomas Aston, and daughter to a baronet; she was also sister to the wife of his friend, Mr. Gilbert Walmesley.[2] Besides his intimacy with the above-mentioned persons, who were surely people of rank and education, while he was at Lichfield he used to be frequently at the house of Dr. Swinfen, a gentleman of very ancient family in Staffordshire, from which, after the death of his elder brother, he inherited a good estate. He was, besides, a physician of very extensive practice; but for want of due attention to the management of his domestic concerns, left a very large family in indigence. One of his daughters, Mrs. Desmoulins, afterwards found an asylum in the house of her old friend, whose doors were always open to the

---

[1] The words of Sir John Hawkins, p. 316—BOSWELL.

[2] Sir Thomas Aston, Bart., who died in January, 1724-5, left one son, named Thomas also and eight daughters. Of the daughters, Catherine married Johnson's friend, the Hon. Henry Hervey; Margaret, Gilbert Walmesley. Another of these ladies married the Rev. Mr. Gastrell. Mary, or *Molly* Aston, as she was usually called, became the wife of Captain Brodie, of the Navy. Another sister, who was unmarried, was living at Lichfield in 1776.—MALONE

unfortunate, and who well observed the precept of the Gospel, for he 'was kind to the unthankful and to the evil.'"

In the forlorn state of his circumstances, he accepted of an offer to be employed as usher in the school of Market-Bosworth, in Leices shire, to which it appears, from one of his little fragments of a diary that he went on foot, on the 16th of July.—" *Julii* 16. *Bosvortiam pedes petii*." But it is not true, as has been erroneously related, that

MARKET-BOSWORTH SCHOOL.

he was assistant to the famous Anthony Blackwall, whose merit has been honoured by the testimony of Bishop Hurd,[1] who was his scholar ; for Mr. Blackwall died on the 8th of April, 1730,[2] more than a year before Johnson left the University.

This employment was very irksome to him in every respect, and he complained grievously of it in his letters to his friend, Mr. Hector, who was now settled as a surgeon at Birmingham. The letters are lost ; but Mr. Hector recollects his writing " that the poet had described the dull sameness of his existence in these words, ' *Vitam continet una dies* ' (one day contains the whole of my life) ; that it was unvaried as the

---

[1] There is here (as Mr. James Boswell observes to me) a slight inaccuracy. Bishop Hurd, in the Epistle Dedicatory prefixed to his "Commentary on Horace's Art of Poetry," &c., does not praise Blackwall, but the Rev. Mr. Budworth, Head Master of the Grammar School at Brewood, in Staffordshire, who had himself been bred under Blackwall. See vol. iv., near the end, where, from the information of Mr. John Nichols, Johnson is said to have applied in 1736 to Mr. Budworth, to be received by him as an assistant in his school in Staffordshire. MALONE.

[2] See "Gentleman's Magazine," December, 1784, p. 957.—BOSWELL.

note of the cuckoo; and that he did not know whether it was more disagreeable for him to teach, or the boys to learn, the grammar rules." His general aversion to this painful drudgery was greatly enhanced by a disagreement between him and Sir Wolstan Dixie, the patron of the school, in whose house, I have been told, he officiated as a kind of domestic chaplain, so far, at least, as to say grace at table, but was treated with what he represented as intolerable harshness; and, after suffering for a few months such complicated misery,[1] he relinquished a situation which all his life afterwards he recollected with the strongest aversion, and even a degree of horror. But it is probable that at this period, whatever uneasiness he may have endured, he laid the foundation of much future eminence by application to his studies.

Being now again totally unoccupied, he was invited by Mr. Hector to pass some time with him at Birmingham, as his guest, at the house

BIRMINGHAM, 1730.

of Mr. Warren, with whom Mr. Hector lodged and boarded. Mr. Warren was the first established bookseller in Birmingham, and was very attentive to Johnson, who he soon found could be of much service to him in his trade, by his knowledge of literature; and he even obtained the assistance of his pen in furnishing some numbers of a periodical Essay printed in the newspaper of which Warren was proprietor.

---

1 It appears from a letter of Johnson's to a friend, which I have read, dated Lichfield, July 27, 1732, that he had left Sir Wolstan Dixie's house recently before that letter was written. He then had hopes of succeeding, either as master or usher, in the school of Ashbourne.—MALONE.

After very diligent inquiry, I have not been able to recover those early specimens of that particular mode of writing by which Johnson afterwards so greatly distinguished himself.

He continued to live as Mr. Hector's guest for about six months, and then hired lodgings in another part of the town,[1] finding himself as well situated at Birmingham as he supposed he could be any where, while he had no settled plan of life, and very scanty means of subsistence. He made some valuable acquaintances there, amongst whom were Mr. Porter, a mercer, whose widow he afterwards married, and Mr. Taylor, who by his ingenuity in mechanical inventions, and his success in trade, acquired an immense fortune. But the comfort of being near Mr. Hector, his old schoolfellow and intimate friend, was Johnson's chief inducement to continue here.

In what manner he employed his pen at this period, or whether he derived from it any pecuniary advantage, I have not been able to ascertain. He probably got a little money from Mr. Warren ; and we are certain that he executed here one piece of literary labour, of which Mr. Hector has favoured me with a minute account. Having mentioned that he had read at Pembroke College a "Voyage to Abyssinia," by Lobo, a Portuguese Jesuit, and that he thought an abridgment and translation of it from the French into English might be an useful and profitable publication, Mr. Warren and Mr. Hector joined in urging him to undertake it. He accordingly agreed ; and the book not being to be found in Birmingham, he borrowed it of Pembroke College. A part of the work being very soon done, one Osborn, who was Mr. Warren's printer, was set to work with what was ready, and Johnson engaged to supply the press with copy as it should be wanted, but his constitutional indolence soon prevailed, and the work was at a stand. Mr. Hector, who knew that a motive of humanity would be the most prevailing argument with his friend, went to Johnson, and represented to him, that the printer could have no other employment till this undertaking was finished, and that the poor man and his family were suffering. Johnson, upon this, exerted the powers of his mind, though his body was relaxed. He lay in bed with the book, which was a quarto, before him, and dictated while Hector wrote. Mr. Hector carried the sheets to the press, and corrected almost all the proof sheets, very few of which were ever seen by Johnson. In this manner, with the aid of Mr. Hector's active friendship, the book was completed, and was published in 1735, with London upon the title-page, though it was in reality printed at Birmingham, a device too common with provincial publishers. For this work, he had from Mr. Warren only the sum of five guineas.

[1] Sir John Hawkins states, from one of Johnson's diaries, that in June, 1733, he lodged in Birmingham at the house of a person named Jarvis, probably a relation of Mrs. Porter, whom he afterwards married.—MALONE.

This being the first prose work of Johnson, it is a curious object of inquiry how much may be traced in it of that style which marks his subsequent writings with such pecular excellence; with so happy an union of force, vivacity, and perspicuity. I have perused the book with this view, and have found that here, as I believe in every other translation, there is in the work itself no vestige of the translator's own style; for the language of translation being adapted to the thoughts of another person, insensibly follows their cast, and as it were runs into a mould that is ready prepared.

Thus, for instance, taking the first sentence that occurs at the opening of the book, p. 4:—

"I lived here above a year, and completed my studies in divinity; in which time some letters were received from the fathers of Ethiopia, with an account that Sultan Segned, Emperor of Abyssinia, was converted to the church of Rome; that many of his subjects had followed his example, and that there was a great want of misssionaries to improve these prosperous beginnings. Every body was very desirous of seconding the zeal of our fathers, and of sending them the assistance they requested; to which we were the more encouraged, because the Emperor's letter informed our Provincial that we might easily enter his dominions by the way of Dancala; but, unhappily, the secretary wrote Geila for Dancala, which cost two of our fathers their lives."

Every one acquainted with Johnson's manner will be sensible that there is nothing of it here; but that this sentence might have been composed by any other man.

But, in the Preface, the Johnsonian style begins to appear; and though use had not yet taught his wing a permanent and equable flight, there are parts of it which exhibit his best manner in full vigour. I had once the pleasure of examining it with Mr. Edmund Burke, who confirmed me in this opinion, by his superior critical sagacity, and was, I remember, much delighted with the following specimen:—

"The Portuguese traveller, contrary to the general vein of his countrymen, has amused his reader with no romantic absurdity, or incredible fictions; whatever he relates, whether true or not, is at least probable; and he who tells nothing exceeding the bounds of probability, has a right to demand that they should believe him who cannot contradict him.

"He appears by his modest and unaffected narration, to have described things as he saw them, to have copied nature from the life, and to have consulted his senses, not his imagination. He meets with no basilisks that destroy with their eyes, his crocodiles devour their prey without tears, and his cataracts fall from the rocks without deafening the neighbouring inhabitants.

"The reader will here find no regions cursed with irremediable barrenness, or blest with spontaneous fecundity; no perpetual gloom, or unceasing sunshine; nor are the nations here described, either devoid of all sense of humanity, or consummate in all private or social virtues. Here are no Hottentots without religious policy or articulate language; no Chinese perfectly polite, and completely skilled in all sciences; he will discover, what will always be discovered by a diligent and impartial inquirer, that wherever human nature is to be found, there is a mixture of vice and virtue, a contest of passion and reason; and that the Creator doth not appear partial in his distributions, but has balanced, in most countries, their particular inconveniences by particular favours."

Here we have an early example of that brilliant and energetic expression, which, upon innumerable occasions in his subsequent life, justly impressed the world with the highest admiration.

Nor can any one, conversant with the writings of Johnson, fail to discern his hand in this passage of the Dedication to John Warren, Esq., of Pembrokeshire, though it is ascribed to Warren the bookseller.

" A generous and elevated mind is distinguished by nothing more certainly than an eminent degree of curiosity;[1] nor is that curiosity ever more agreeably or usefully employed, than in examining the laws and customs of foreign nations. I hope, therefore, the present I now presume to make will not be thought improper, which, however, it is not my business as a dedicator to commend, nor as a bookseller to depreciate."

It is reasonable to suppose, that his having been thus accidentally led to a particular study of the history and manners of Abyssinia, was the remote occasion of his writing, many years afterwards, his admirable philosophical tale, the principal scene of which is laid in that country.[2]

Johnson returned to Lichfield early in 1734, and in August that year he made an attempt to procure some little subsistence by his pen; for he published proposals for printing by subscription the Latin Poems of " Politian;"[3] *Angeli Politiani Poemata Latina, quibus, Notas cum historiâ Latinæ poeseos à Petrarchæ ævo ad Politiani tempora deductâ, et vitâ Politiani fusius quam antehac enarratâ, addidit* SAM. JOHNSON.[4]

It appears that his brother Nathanael had taken up his father's trade; for it is mentioned that "subscriptions are taken in by the Editor, or N. Johnson, bookseller, of Lichfield." Notwithstanding the merit of Johnson, and the cheap price at which this book was offered, there were not subscribers enough to ensure a sufficient sale; so the work never appeared, and probably, never was executed.

We find him again this year at Birmingham, and there is preserved

[1] See " Rambler," No. 103, " Curiosity is the thirst of the soul," &c.—BOSWELL.

[2] " Rasselas."

[3] May we not trace a fanciful similarity between Politian and Johnson? Huetius, speaking of Paulus Pelissonius Fontanerius, says, " —— in quo Natura, ut olim in Angelo Politiano, deformitatem oris excellentis ingenii præstantiâ compensavit." Comment. de reb. ad eum pertin. Edit. Amstel., 1718, p. 200.—BOSWELL.

[4] The book was to contain more than thirty sheets, the price to be two shillings and sixpence at the time of subscribing, and two shillings and sixpence at the delivery of a perfect book in quires.—BOSWELL.

the following letter from him to Mr. Edward Cave,[1] the original compiler and editor of the " Gentleman's Magazine :"—

" TO MR. CAVE.

" Sir.   *Nov.* 25, 1734.

" As you appear no less sensible than your readers of the defects of your poetical article, you will not be displeased, if, in order to the improvement of it,

EDWARD CAVE.

I communicate to you the sentiments of a person, who will undertake on reasonable terms, sometimes to fill a column.

"His opinion is, that the public would not give you a bad reception, if, beside the current wit of the month, which a critical examination would generally reduce to a narrow compass, you admitted not only poems, inscriptions, &c., never printed before, which he will sometimes supply you with, but likewise short literary dissertations in Latin or English, critical remarks on authors, ancient or modern, forgotten poems, that deserve revival, or loose pieces, like Floyer's[2] worth preserving. By this method, your literary article, for so it might be called, will, he thinks, be better recommended to the public than by low jests, awkward buffoonery, or the dull scurrilities of either party.

" If such a correspondence will be agreeable to you, be pleased to inform me in two posts, what the conditions are on which you shall expect it. Your late offer[3] gives me no reason to distrust your generosity. If you engage in any literary projects besides this paper, I have other designs to impart, if I could be secure from having others reap the advantage of what I should hint.

" Your letter by being directed to *S. Smith,* to be left at the Castle, in Birmingham, Warwickshire, will reach

" Your humble servant."

Mr. Cave has put a note to this letter, " Answered, Dec. 2." But whether anything was done in consequence of it we are not informed.

Johnson had, from his early youth, been sensible to the influence of

---

[1] Miss Cave, the grand-niece of Mr. Edward Cave, has obligingly shown me the originals of this and the other letters of Dr. Johnson to him, which were first published in the " Gentleman's Magazine," with notes by Mr. John Nichols, the worthy and indefatigable editor of that valuable miscellany, signed N ; some of which I shall occasionally transcribe in the course of this work.—BOSWELL.

[2] Sir John Floyer's Treatise on Cold Baths. " Gentleman's Magazine," 1734, p. 197.——BOSWELL.

[3] A prize of fifty pounds for the best poem " on Life, Death, Judgment, Heaven, and Hell." See " Gentleman's Magazine," vol. iv. p. 560.—NICHOLS.

female charms.   When at Stourbridge school, he was much enamoured
of Olivia Lloyd, a young quaker, to whom he wrote a copy of verses,
which I have not been able to recover ;[1] but with what facility and
elegance he could warble the amorous lay, will appear from the following
lines which he wrote for his friend Mr. Edmund Hector :—

Verses to a Lady, on receiving from her a Sprig of Myrtle.

> " What hopes, what terrors does thy gift create,
>   Ambiguous emblem of uncertain fate !
>   The myrtle, ensign of supreme command,
>   Consign'd by Venus to Melissa's hand ;
>   Not less capricious than a reigning fair,
>   Now grants, and now rejects a lover's prayer.
>   In myrtle shades oft sings the happy swain,
>   In myrtle shades despairing ghosts complain ;
>   The myrtle crowns the happy lovers' heads,
>   The unhappy lover's grave the myrtle spreads ;
>   Oh then the meaning of thy gift impart,
>   And ease the throbbings of an anxious heart !
>   Soon must this bough, as you shall fix his doom,
>   Adorn Philander's head, or grace his tomb."[2]

[1] He also wrote some amatory verses, before he left Staffordshire, which our author appears
not to have seen. They were addressed "To Miss Hickman, playing on the Spinet." At the
back of this early poetical effusion, of which the original copy, in Johnson's handwriting, was
obligingly communicated to me by Mr. John Taylor, is the following attestation :—

> "Written by the late Dr. Samuel Johnson, on my mother, then Miss Hickman,
>   playing on the Spinet. J. Turton."

Dr. Turton, the physician, the writer of this certificate, who 'ied in April, 1806, in his
71st year, was born in 1735. The verses in question therefore, wl ch have been printed in
some late editions of Johnson's poems, must have been writter before that year.—Miss
Hickman, it is believed, was a lady of Staffordshire.

The concluding lines of this early copy of verses have much oi the vigour of Johnson's
poetry in his maturer years :—

> " When old Timotheus struck the vocal string,
>   Ambitious fury fir'd the Grecian king :
>   Unbounded projects lab'ring in his mind,
>   He pants for room, in one poor world confin'd.
>   Thus wak'd to rage by music's dreadful power,
>   He bids the sword destroy, the flame devour.
>   Had Stella's gentle touches mov'd the lyre,
>   Soon had the monarch felt a nobler fire;
>   No more delighted with disastrous war,
>   Ambitious only now to please the fair,
>   Resign'd his thirst of empire to her charms,
>   And found a thousand worlds in Stella's arms."
>   MALONE.

[2] Mrs. Piozzi gives the following account of this little composition from Dr. Johnson's own
relation to her, on her inquiring whether it was rightly attributed to him. "I think it is now,
just forty years ago, that a young fellow had a sprig of myrtle given him by a girl he courted,
and asked me to write him some verses that he might present her in return. I promised, but
forgot; and when he called for his lines at the time agreed on—' Sit still a moment,' says I,
' dear Mund, and I 'll fetch them thee'—so stepped aside for five minutes, and wrote the nonsense you now keep such a stir about."—Anecdotes. p. 34.

His juvenile attachments to the fair sex were, however, very transient ; and it is certain, that he formed no criminal connection whatsoever Mr. Hector, who lived with him in his younger days in the utmost intimacy and social freedom, has assured me, that even at that ardent season his conduct was strictly virtuous in that respect ; and that though he loved to exhilarate himself with wine, he never knew him intoxicated but once.

In a man whom religious education has secured from licentious indulgences, the passion of love, when once it has seized him, is exceedingly strong ; being unimpaired by dissipation and totally concentrated in one object. This was experienced by Johnson, when he became the fervent admirer of Mrs. Porter, after her first husband's death.[1] Miss Porter told me, that when he was first introduced to her mother, his appearance was very forbidding ; he was then lean and lank, so that his

---

In my first edition I was induced to doubt the authenticity of this account, by the following circumstantial statement in a letter to me from Miss Seward, of Lichfield :—" I *know* those verses were addressed to Lucy Porter, when he was enamoured of her in his boyish days, two or three years before he had seen her mother, his future wife. He wrote them at my grandfather's, and gave them to Lucy in the presence of my mother, to whom he showed them on the instant. She used to repeat them to me, when I asked her for *the Verses Dr. Johnson gave her* " *On a Sprig of Myrtle* " *which he had stolen or begged from her bosom.* We all know honest Lucy Porter to have been incapable of the mean vanity of applying to herself a compliment not *intended* for her." Such was this lady's statement, which I make no doubt she supposed to be correct ; but it shows how dangerous it is to trust too implicitly to traditional testimony and ingenious inference ; for Mr. Hector has lately assured me that Mrs. Piozzi's account is in this instance accurate, and that he was the person for whom Johnson wrote those verses, which have been erroneously ascribed to Mr. Hammond.

I am obliged in so many instances to notice Mrs. Piozzi's incorrectness of relation, that I gladly seize this opportunity of acknowledging, that however often, she is not always inaccurate.

The author having been drawn into a controversy with Miss Anna Seward, in consequence of the preceding statement (which may be found in the " Gentleman's Magazine," vols. lxiii. and lxiv.), received the following letter from Mr. Edmund Hector, on the subject :—

" DEAR SIR,

" I am sorry to see you are engaged in altercation with a lady who seems unwilling to be convinced of her errors. Surely it would be more ingenuous to acknowledge than to persevere.

" Lately, in looking over some papers I meant to burn, I found the original manuscript of ' The Myrtle,' with the date on it, 1731, which I have enclosed.

" The true history (which I could swear to) is as follows :—Mr. Morgan Graves, the elder brother of a worthy clergyman near Bath, with whom I was acquainted, waited upon a lady in this neighbourhood, who at parting presented him the branch. He showed it me, and wished much to return the compliment in verse. I applied to Johnson, who was with me, and in about half an hour dictated the verses which I sent to my friend.

" I most solemnly declare, at that time, Johnson was an entire stranger to the Porter family ; and it was almost two years after that I introduced him to the acquaintance of Porter, whom I bought my clothes of.

" If you intend to convince this obstinate woman, and to exhibit to the public the truth of your narrative, you are at liberty to make what use you please of this statement.

" I hope you will pardon me for taking up so much of your time. Wishing you *multos et felices annos,* I shall subscribe myself   Your obliged humble servant,

" E. HECTOR, Birmingham, Jan. 9, 1794."—BOSWELL.

[1] It appears, from Mr. Hector's letter, that Johnson became acquainted with her three years before he married her.—MALONE.

immense structure of bones was hideously striking to the eye, and the scars of the scrofula were deeply visible. He also wore his hair, which was straight and stiff, and separated behind; and he often had, seemingly, convulsive starts and odd gesticulations, which tended to excite at once surprise and ridicule. Mrs. Porter was so much engaged by his conversation that she overlooked all these external disadvantages, and said to her daughter, "this is the most sensible man that I ever saw in my life."

Though Mrs. Porter was double the age of Johnson,[1] and her person and manner, as described to me by the late Mr. Garrick, were by no means pleasing to others,[2] she must have had a superiority of understanding and talents,[3] as she certainly inspired him with a more

MRS. JOHNSON

[1] Mrs. Johnson's maiden name was Jervis.— Though there was a great disparity of years between her and Dr. Johnson, she was not quite so old as she is here represented, having only completed her forty-eighth year in the month of February preceding her marriage, as appears by the following extract from the parish register of Great Peatling, in Leicestershire, which was obligingly made, at my request, by the Hon. and Rev. Mr. Ryder, Rector of Lutterworth, in that county :—

"Anno Dom. 1688-9. Elizabeth, the daughter of William Jervis, Esq., and Mrs. Anne, his wife, born the fourth day of February and *mané*, baptised 16th day of the same month by Mr. Smith, Curate of Little Peatling. John Allen, Vicar."

The family of Jervis, Mr. Ryder informs me, once possessed nearly the whole lordship of Great Peatling (about 2000 acres), and there are many monuments of them in the church; but the estate is now much reduced. The present representative of this ancient family is Mr. Charles Jervis, of Hinckley, Attorney-at-Law.—MALONE.

[2] That in Johnson's eyes she was handsome, appears from the epitaph which he caused to be inscribed on her tombstone not long before his own death, and which may be found in a subsequent page, under the year 1752.—MALONE.

[3] The following account of Mrs. Johnson and her family, is copied from a paper (chiefly relating to Mrs. Anna Williams) written by Lady Knight, at Rome, and transmitted by her to the late John Hoole, Esq., the translator of "Metastasio," &c., by whom it was inserted in the "European Magazine" for October, 1799 :—

"Mrs. Williams's account of Mrs. Johnson was, that she had a good understanding, and great sensibility, but inclined to be satirical. Her first husband died insolvent; her sons were much disgusted with her for her second marriage, perhaps because they, being struggling to get advanced in life, were mortified to think she had allied herself to a man who had not any visible means of being useful to them; however, she always retained her affection for them. While they [Dr. and Mrs. Johnson] resided in Gough Square, her son, the officer, knocked at the door, and asked the maid if her mistress was at home. She answered, 'Yes, sir, but she is sick in bed.' 'Oh,' says he, 'if it's so, tell her that her son Jervis called to know how she did;' and was going away. The maid begged she might run up to tell her mistress, and, without attending his answer, left him. Mrs. Johnson, enraptured to hear her son was below, desired the maid to tell him she longed to embrace him. When the maid descended, the gentleman

than ordinary passion; and she having signified her willingness to accept of his hand, he went to Lichfield to ask his mother's consent to the marriage, which he could not but be conscious was a very imprudent scheme, both on account of their disparity of years, and her want of fortune. But Mrs. Johnson knew too well the ardour of her son's temper, and was too tender a parent to oppose his inclinations.

I know not for what reason the marriage ceremony was not performed at Birmingham; but a resolution was taken that it should be at Derby, for which place the bride and bridegroom set out on horseback, I suppose in very good humour. But though Mr. Topham Beauclerk used archly to mention Johnson's having told him with much gravity, " Sir, it was a love marriage on both sides," I have heard from my illustrious friend the following curious account of their journey to church upon the nuptial morn [9th July]:—" Sir, she had read the old romances, and had got into her head the fantastical notion that a woman of spirit should use her lover like a dog. So, Sir, at first she told me that I rode too fast, and she could not keep up with me : and, when I rode a little slower, she passed me, and complained that I lagged behind. I was not to be made the slave of caprice ; and I resolved to begin as I meant to end. I therefore pushed on briskly, till I was fairly out of her sight. The road lay between two hedges, so I was sure she could not miss it ; and I contrived that she should soon come up with me. When she did I observed her to be in tears."

This, it must be allowed, was a singular beginning of connubial felicity ; but there is no doubt that Johnson, though he thus showed a manly firmness, proved a most affectionate and indulgent husband to the last moments of Mrs. Johnson's life : and in his " Prayers and Meditations," we find very remarkable evidence that his regard and fondness for her never ceased, even after her death.

He now set up a private academy, for which purpose he hired a large

was gone, and poor Mrs. Johnson was much agitated by the adventure : it was the only time he ever made an effort to see her. Dr. Johnson did all he could to console his wife, but told Mrs. Williams, ' Her son is uniformly undutiful ; so I conclude, like many other sober men, he might, once in his life, be drunk, and in that fit nature got the better of his pride.' "

The following anecdotes of Dr. Johnson are recorded by the same lady :—

" One day that he came to my house to meet many others, we told him that we had arranged our party to go to Westminster Abbey : would not he go with us ? ' No,' he replied, ' not while I can keep out.'

" Upon our saying that the friends of a lady had been in great fear lest she should make a certain match, he said, ' We that are his friends have had great fears for him.'

" Dr. Johnson's political principles ran high, both in Church and State ; he wished power to the King and to the Heads of the Church, as the laws of England have established ; but I know he disliked absolute power; and I am very sure of his disapprobation of the doctrines of the Church of Rome ; because, about three weeks before we came abroad, he said to my Cornelia, ' You are going where the ostentatious pomp of Church ceremonies attracts the imagination ; but, if they want to persuade you to change, you must remember, that by increasing your faith, you may be persuaded to become Turk.' If these were not the words, I have kept up to the express meaning."—MALONE.

house, well situated near his native city. In the "Gentleman's Magazine" for 1736, there is the following advertisement :—

"At Edial, near Lichfield, in Staffordshire, young gentlemen are boarded and taught the Latin and Greek languages, by Samuel Johnson."

But the only pupils that were put under his care were the celebrated David Garrick and his brother George, and a Mr. Offely, a young gentleman of good fortune who died early. As yet his name had nothing of that celebrity which afterwards commanded the highest attention and respect of mankind. Had such an advertisement appeared after the publication of his "London," or his "Rambler," or his "Dictionary," how would it have burst upon the world! with what eagerness would the great and the wealthy have embraced an opportunity of putting their sons under the learned tuition of Samuel Johnson. The truth, however, is, that he was not so well qualified for being a teacher of elements, and a conductor in learning by regular gradations, as men of inferior powers of mind. His own acquisitions

EDIAL HOUSE

had been made by fits and starts, by violent irruptions into the regions of knowledge; and it could not be expected that his impatience would be subdued, and his impetuosity restrained, so as to fit him for a quiet guide to novices. The art of communicating instruction, of whatever kind, is much to be valued; and I have ever thought that those who devote themselves to this employment, and do their duty with diligence and success, are entitled to very high respect from the community, as Johnson himself often maintained. Yet I am of opinion, that the greatest abilities are not only not required for this office, but render a man less fit for it.

While we acknowledge the justness of Thomson's beautiful remark,

> "Delightful task! to rear the tender thought,
> And teach the young idea how to shoot!"

we must consider that this delight is perceptible only by "a mind at ease," a mind at once calm and clear: but that a mind gloomy and impetuous like that of Johnson, cannot be fixed for any length of time in minute attention, and must be so frequently irritated by unavoidable slowness and error in the advances of scholars, as to perform the duty, with little pleasure to the teacher, and no great advantage to the pupils. Good temper is a most essential requisite in a preceptor. Horace paints the character as *bland*:

> "———— Ut pueris olim dant crustula *blandi*
> Doctores, elementa velint ut discere prima."

Johnson was not more satisfied with his situation as the master of an academy, than with that of the usher of a school; we need not wonder, therefore, that he did not keep his academy above a year and a half. From Mr. Garrick's account he did not appear to have been profoundly reverenced by his pupils. His oddities of manner and uncouth gesticulations, could not but be the subject of merriment to them; and in particular, the young rogues used to listen at the door of his bedchamber, and peep through the key-hole, that they might turn into ridicule his tumultuous and awkward fondness for Mrs. Johnson, whom he used to name by the familiar appellation of *Tetty* or *Tetsey*, which, like *Betty* or *Betsey*, is provincially used as a contraction for *Elizabeth*, her Christian name, but which to us seems ludicrous, when applied to a woman of her age and appearance. Mr. Garrick described her to me as very fat, with a bosom of more than ordinary protuberance, with swelled cheeks, of a florid red, produced by thick painting, and increased by the liberal use of cordials; flaring and fantastic in her dress, and affected both in her speech and her general bahaviour. I have seen Garrick exhibit her, by his exquisite talent of mimicry, so as to excite the heartiest bursts of laughter; but he, probably, as is the case in all such representations, considerably aggravated the picture.

That Johnson well knew the most proper course to be pursued in the instruction of youth, is authentically ascertained by the following paper in his own handwriting, given about this period to a relation, and now in the possession of Mr. John Nichols :—

SCHEME FOR THE CLASSES OF A GRAMMAR SCHOOL.

" When the introduction, or formation of nouns and verbs, is perfectly mastered, let them learn

" Corderius by Mr. Clarke, beginning at the same time to translate out of the introduction, that by this means they may learn the syntax. Then let them proceed to

" Erasmus, with an English translation, by the same author.

" Class II. Learns Eutropius and Cornelius Nepos, or Justin, with the translation.

" N.B. The first class gets for their part every morning the rules which they have learned before, and in the afternoon learns the Latin rules of the nouns and verbs.

" They are examined in the rules which they have learned, every Thursday and Saturday.

" The second class does the same whilst they are in Eutropius ; afterwards their part is in the irregular nouns and verbs, and in the rules for making and scanning verses. They are examined as the first.

" Class III. Ovid's Metamorphoses in the morning, and Cæsar's Commentaries in the afternoon.

" Practice in the Latin rules till they are perfect in them ; afterwards in Mr. Leeds's Greek Grammar. Examined as before.

" Afterwards they proceed to Virgil, beginning at the same time to write themes and verses, and to learn Greek ; from thence passing on to Horace, &c., as shall seem most proper.

————————

" I know not well what books to direct you to, because you have not informed me what study you will apply yourself to. I believe it will be most for your advantage to apply yourself wholly to the languages, till you go to the university. The Greek authors I think it best for you to read are these :—

Cebes.	
Ælian.	
Lucian by Leeds.	} Attic.
Xenophon.	
Homer.	Ionic.
Theocritus.	Doric.
Euripides.	Attic and Doric.

" Thus you will be tolerably skilled in all the dialects, beginning with the Attic, to which the rest must be referred.

" In the study of Latin, it is proper not to read the latter authors, till you are well versed with those of the purest ages ; as Terence, Tully, Cæsar, Sallust, Nepos, Velleius Paterculus, Virgil, Horace, Phædrus.

" The greatest and most necessary task still remains, to attain a habit of expression, without which knowledge is of little use. This is necessary in

Latin, and more necessary in English; and can only be acquired by a daily imitation of the best and correctest authors.

"SAM. JOHNSON."

While Johnson kept his academy, there can be no doubt that he was insensibly furnishing his mind with various knowledge; but I have not discovered that he wrote any thing except a great part of his tragedy of "Irene." Mr. Peter Garrick, the elder brother of David, told me that he remembered Johnson's borrowing the Turkish History of him, in order to form his play from it. When he had finished some part of it, he read what he had done to Mr. Walmesley, who objected to his having already brought his heroine into great distress, and asked him, "How can you contrive to plunge her into deeper calamity?" Johnson, in sly allusion to the supposed oppressive proceedings of the court of which Mr. Walmesley was registrar, replied, "Sir, I can put her into the Spiritual Court!"

Mr. Walmesley, however, was well pleased with this proof of Johnson's abilities as a dramatic writer, and advised him to finish the tragedy and produce it on the stage.

ST JOHN'S GATEWAY.

CHAPTER III.—1737—1738.

JOHNSON now thought of trying his fortune in London, the great field of genius and exertion, where talents of every kind have the fullest scope, and the highest encouragement. It is a memorable circumstance that his pupil, David Garrick, went thither at the same time,[1] with intent to complete his education, and follow the profession

---

[1] Both of them used to talk pleasantly of this their first journey to London. Garrick, evidently meaning to embellish a little, said one day in my hearing, "We rode and tied." And the Bishop of Killaloe (Dr. Barnard) informed me, that at another time, when Johnson and Garrick were dining together in a pretty large company, Johnson humorously ascertaining

of the law, from which he was soon diverted by his decided preference for the stage.

This joint expedition of those two eminent men to the metropolis, was many years afterwards noticed in an allegorical poem on Shakspeare's Mulberry-tree, by Mr. Lovibond, the ingenious author of "The Tears of Old May-day."

They were recommended to Mr. Colson,[1] an eminent mathematician and master of an academy, by the following letter from Mr. Walmesley:—

REV. JOHN COLSON.

"TO THE REVEREND MR. COLSON.

"Dear Sir,   *Lichfield, March*, 2, 1737.

"I had the favour of yours, and am extremely obliged to you; but I cannot say I had a greater affection for you upon it than I had before, being long since so much endeared to you, as well by an early friendship, as by your many excellent and valuable qualifications; and, had I a son of my own, it would be my ambition, instead of sending him to the University, to dispose of him as this young gentleman is.

"He, and another neighbour of mine, one Mr. Samuel Johnson, set out this morning for London together. Davy Garrick is to be with you early the next week, and Mr. Johnson to try his fate with a Tragedy, and to see to get himself employed in some translation, either from the Latin or the French. Johnson is a very good scholar and poet, and I have great hopes will turn out a fine tragedy-writer. If it should in any way lie in your way, doubt not but you would be ready to recommend and assist your countryman.

"G. Walmesley."

How he employed himself upon his first coming to London is not

the chronology of something, expressed himself thus: "That was the year when I came to London with twopence halfpenny in my pocket." Garrick overhearing him, exclaimed, "Eh? what do you say; with twopence halfpenny in your pocket?"—Johnson: "Why, yes; when I came with twopence halfpenny in *my* pocket, and thou, Davy, with three halfpence in thine." Boswell.

[1] The Reverend John Colson was bred at Emanuel College, in Cambridge, and in 1728, when George the Second visited the University, was created Master of Arts. About that time he became First Master of the Free School at Rochester, founded by Sir Joseph Williamson. In 1739, he was appointed Lucasian Professor of Mathematics in the University of Cambridge, on the death of Professor Sanderson, and held that office till 1759, when he died. He published Lectures on Experimental Philosophy, translated from the French of l'Abbé Nodet, 8vo, 1732, and some other tracts. Our author, it is believed, was mistaken in stating him to have been Master of an Academy. Garrick, probably, during his short residence at Rochester, lived in his house as a private pupil."--Boswell.

The character of *Gelidus*, the philosopher, in the "Rambler" (No. 24), was meant to represent this gentleman. See Mrs. Piozzi's Anecdotes, &c., p. 49.—Malone.

particularly known.[1] I never heard that he found any protection or encouragement by the means of Mr. Colson, to whose academy David Garrick went. Mrs. Lucy Porter told me, that Mr. Walmesley gave him a letter of introduction to Lintot, his bookseller, and that Johnson wrote some things for him; but I imagine this to be a mistake, for I have discovered no trace of it, and I am pretty sure he told me that Mr. Cave was the first publisher by whom his pen was engaged in London.

He had a little money when he came to town, and he knew how he could live in the cheapest manner. His first lodgings were at the house of Mr. Norris, a staymaker, in Exeter-street, adjoining Catherine-street, in the Strand. "I dined," said he, "very well for eightpence, with very good company, at the Pine-Apple, in New-street, just by. Several of them had travelled. They expected to meet every day; but did not know one another's names. It used to cost the rest a shilling, for they drank wine; but I had a cut of meat for sixpence, and bread for a penny, and gave the waiter a penny; so that I was quite well served, nay, better than the rest, for they gave the waiter nothing."

He at this time, I believe, abstained entirely from fermented liquors: a practice to which he rigidly conformed for many years together, at different periods of his life.

His *Ofellus*,[2] in the "Art of Living in London," I have heard him relate, was an Irish painter, whom he knew at Birmingham, and who had practised his own precepts of economy for several years in the British capital. He assured Johnson, who, I suppose, was then meditating to try his fortune in London, but was apprehensive of the expense, "that thirty pounds a year was enough to enable a man to live there without being contemptible. He allowed ten pounds for clothes and linen. He said a man might live in a garret at eighteen-pence a week; few people would inquire where he lodged; and if they did, it was easy to say, 'Sir, I am to be found at such a place.' By spending threepence in a coffee-house, he might be for some hours every day in very good company; he might dine for sixpence, breakfast on bread and milk for a penny, and do without supper. On *clean-shirt-day* he went abroad, and paid visits." I have heard him more than once talk of his frugal friend, whom he recollected with esteem and kindness, and did not like to have one smile at the recital. "This man," said he, gravely, "was a very sensible man, who perfectly understood common affairs; a man of a great deal of knowledge of the world, fresh from life, not strained through books. He borrowed a

---

[1] One curious anecdote was communicated by himself to Mr. John Nichols. Mr. Wilcox the bookseller, on being informed by him that his intention was to get his livelihood as an author, eyed his robust frame attentively, and with a significant look, said, "You had better buy a porter's knot." He however added, "Wilcox was one of my best friends."—BOSWELL.

[2] *Ofellus* was a philosophic countryman, commemorated by Horace, Sat. ii. lib. 2.—BOSWELL.

horse and ten pounds at Birmingham. Finding himself master of so much money, he set off for West Chester, in order to get to Ireland. He returned the horse, and probably the ten pounds too, after he got home."

Considering Johnson's narrow circumstances in the early part of his life, and particularly at the interesting æra of his launching into the ocean of London, it is not to be wondered at, that an actual instance, proved by experience, of the possibility of enjoying the intellectual luxury of social life upon a very small income, should deeply engage his attention, and be ever recollected by him as a circumstance of much importance. He amused himself, I remember, by computing how much more expense was absolutely necessary to live upon the same scale with that which his friend described, when the value of money was diminished by the progress of commerce. It may be estimated that double the money might now with difficulty be sufficient.

Amidst this cold obscurity, there was one brilliant circumstance to cheer him; he was well acquainted with Mr. Henry Hervey,[1] one of the branches of the noble family of that name, who had been quartered at Lichfield as an officer of the army, and had at this time a house in London, where Johnson was frequently entertained, and had an opportunity of meeting genteel company. Not very long before his death, he mentioned this, among other particulars of his life, which he was kindly communicating to me; and he described this early friend, "Harry Hervey," thus: "He was a vicious man, but very kind to me. If you call a dog Hervey, I shall love him."

He told me he had now written only three acts of his "Irene," and that he retired for some time to lodgings at Greenwich, where he proceeded in it somewhat further, and used to compose, walking in the park; but did not stay long enough at that place to finish it.

At this period we find the following letter from him to Mr. Edward Cave, which, as a link in the chain of his literary history, it is proper to insert:—

"TO MR. CAVE.

"SIR,

"*Greenwich, next door to the Golden Heart, Church-street*
July 12, 1737.

"Having observed in your papers very uncommon offers of encouragement to men of letters, I have chosen, being a stranger in London, to communicate to you the following design, which, I hope, if you join in it, will be of advantage to both of us.

"The History of the Council of Trent having been lately translated into

[1] The Honourable Henry Hervey, third son of the first Earl of Bristol, quitted the army and took orders. He married a sister of Sir Thomas Ayston, by whom he got the Aston Estate, and assumed the name and arms of that family.—BOSWELL.
The Honourable Henry Hervey was nearly of the same age with Johnson, having been

French, and published with large Notes by Dr. Le Courayer, the reputation of that book is so much revived in England, that, it is presumed, a new translation of it from the Italian, together with Le Courayer's Notes from the French, could not fail of a favourable reception.

"If it be answered, that the history is already in English, it must be remembered, that there was the same objection against Le Courayer's undertaking, with this disadvantage, that the French had a version by one of their best translators, whereas you cannot read three pages of the English history without discovering that the style is capable of great improvements; but whether those improvements are to be expected from this attempt, you must judge from the specimen, which, if you approve the proposal, I shall submit to your examination.

"Suppose the merit of the versions equal, we may hope that the addition of the notes will turn the balance in our favour, considering the reputation of the annotator.

"Be pleased to favour me with a speedy answer, if you are not willing to engage in this scheme; and appoint me a day to wait upon you, if you are.

"I am, Sir,

"Your humble servant,

"SAMUEL JOHNSON."

It should seem from this letter, though subscribed with his own name, that he had not yet been introduced to Mr. Cave. We shall presently see what was done in consequence of the proposal which it contains.

In the course of the summer he returned to Lichfield, where he had left Mrs. Johnson, and there he at last finished his tragedy, which was executed with his rapidity of composition upon other occasions, but was slowly and painfully elaborated. A few days before his death, while burning a great mass of papers, he picked out from among them the original uniform sketch of this tragedy, in his own handwriting, and gave it to Mr. Langton, by whose favour a copy of it is now in my possession. It contains fragments of the intended plot, and speeches for the different persons of the drama, partly in the raw materials of prose, partly worked up into verse; as also a variety of hints for illustration, borrowed from the Greek, Roman, and modern writers. The handwriting is very difficult to be read, even by those who were best acquainted with Johnson's mode of penmanship, which at all times was very particular. The King having graciously accepted of this manuscript as a literary curiosity, Mr. Langton made a fair and distinct copy of it, which he ordered to be bound up with the original and the printed tragedy; and the volume is deposited in the King's

born about nine months before him, in the year 1709. He married Catherine, the sister of Sir Thomas Aston, in 1739; and as that lady had seven sisters, she probably succeeded to the Aston estate on the death of her brother under his will. Mr. Hervey took the degree of Master of Arts at Cambridge, at the late age of thirty-five, in 1774; about which time, it is believed, he entered into holy orders.—MALONE.

library.[1] His Majesty was pleased to permit Mr. Langton to take a copy of it for himself.

The whole of it is rich in thought and imagery, and happy expressions; and of the *disjecta membra* scattered throughout, and as yet unarranged, a good dramatic poet might avail himself with considerable advantage. I shall give my readers some specimens of different kinds, distinguishing them by the asterisk (*).

> * " Nor think to say here will I stop,
>   Here will I fix the limits of transgression,
>   Nor farther tempt the avenging rage of heaven.
>   When guilt like this once harbours in the breast,
>   Those holy beings, whose unseen direction
>   Guides through the maze of life the steps of man,
>   Fly the detested mansions of impiety,
>   And quit their charge to horror and to ruin."

A small part only of this interesting admonition is preserved in the play, and is varied, I think, not to advantage :—

> " The soul once tainted with so foul a crime,
>   No more shall glow with friendship's hallow'd ardour,
>   Those holy beings whose superior care
>   Guides erring mortals to the paths of virtue,
>   Affrighted at impiety like thine,
>   Resign their charge to baseness and to ruin."

> " I feel the soft infection
>   Flush in my cheek, and wander in my veins.
>   Teach me the Grecian arts of soft persuasion."

* " Sure this is love, which heretofore I conceived the dream of idle maids, and wanton poets."

* " Though no comets or prodigies foretold the ruin of Greece, signs which heaven must by another miracle enable us to understand, yet it might be foreshown, by tokens no less certain, by the vices which always bring it on."

This last passage is worked up in the tragedy itself, as follows :—

LEONTIUS.

> " ———————That power that kindly spreads
>   The clouds, a signal of impending showers,
>   To warn the wand'ring linnet to the shade
>   Beheld, without concern, expiring Greece,
>   And not one prodigy foretold our fate.

---

[1] The "King's library" (that of George III.) was given by his son and successor, George IV., to the British Museum.—MALONE.

It has recently transpired, if we are to believe such an authority as the "Quarterly Review," that the Government of the day bought the library of George IV., just as he was on the eve of concluding a sale of it to the Emperor of Russia. The statement of the "Quarterly" is denied by a writer—probably Mr. Croker—in "Notes and Queries," Vol. 4, No. 96.—ED.

DEMETRIUS.

A thousand horrid prodigies foretold it ;
A feeble government, eluded laws,
A factious populace, luxurious nobles,
And all the maladies of sinking States.
When public villany, too strong for Justice,
Shows his bold front, the harbinger of ruin,
Can brave Leontius call for airy wonders,
Which cheats interpret, and which fools regard ;
When some neglected fabric nods beneath
The weight of years, and totters to the tempest,
Must heaven despatch the messengers of light,
Or wake the dead, to warn us of its fall ?"

* MAHOMET (to IRENE). "I have tried thee, and joy to find that thou deservest to be loved by Mahomet,—with a mind great as his own. Sure, thou art an error of nature, and an exception to the rest of thy sex, and art immortal; for sentiments like thine were never to sink into nothing. I thought all the thoughts of the fair had been to select the graces of the day, dispose the colours of the flaunting (flowing) robe, tune the voice and roll the eye, place the gem, choose the dress, and add new roses to the fading cheek, but—sparkling."

Thus in the tragedy :—

"Illustrious maid, new wonders fix me thine ;
Thy soul completes the triumphs of thy face ;
I thought, forgive my fair, the noblest aim,
The strongest effort of a female soul
Was but to choose the graces of the day,
To tune the tongue, to teach the eyes to roll,
Dispose the colours of the flowing robe,
And add new roses to the faded cheek."

I shall select one other passage, on account of the doctrine which it illustrates, IRENE observes,

* "That the Supreme Being will accept of virtue, whatever outward circumstances it may be accompanied with, and may be delighted with varieties of worship :" but is answered, "That variety cannot affect that Being, who, infinitely happy in his own perfections, wants no external gratifications; nor can infinite truth be delighted with falsehood; that though he may guide or pity those he leaves in darkness, he abandons those who shut their eyes against the beams of day."

Johnson's residence at Lichfield, on his return to it at this time, was only for three months ; and as he had as yet seen but a small part of the wonders of the metropolis, he had little to tell his townsmen. He related to me the following minute anecdote of this period :—" In the last age, when my mother lived in London, there were two sets of people, those who gave the wall, and those who took it ; the peaceable and the quarrelsome. When I returned to Lichfield, after having been in London, my mother asked me, whether I was one of those who gave the wall, or those who took it. *Now* it is fixed that every man keeps to the right ; or, if one is taking the wall, another yields it ; and it is never a dispute." [1]

He now removed to London with Mrs. Johnson ; but her daughter, who had lived with them at Edial, was left with her relations in the country. His lodgings were for some time in Woodstock-street, near Hanover-square, and afterwards in Castle-street, near Cavendish-square. As something pleasingly interesting, to many, in tracing so great a man through all his different habitations, I shall, before this work is concluded, present my readers with an exact list of his lodgings and houses, in order of time, which, in placid condescension to my respectful curiosity, he one evening dictated to me, but without specifying how long he lived at each. In the progress of his life I shall have occasion to mention some of them as connected with particular incidents, or with the writing of particular parts of his works. To some, this minute attention may appear trifling ; but when we consider the punctilious exactness with which the different houses in which Milton resided have been traced by the writers of his life, a similar enthusiasm may be pardoned in the biographer of Johnson.

His tragedy being by this time, as he thought, completely finished and fit for the stage, he was very desirous that it should be brought forward. Mr. Peter Garrick told me, that Johnson and he went together to the Fountain tavern, and read it over, and that he afterwards solicited Mr. Fleetwood, the patentee of Drury Lane theatre, to have it acted at his house ; but Mr. Fleetwood would not accept it, probably because it was not patronised by some man of high rank ; and it was not acted till 1749, when his friend David Garrick was manager of that theatre.

" The Gentleman's Magazine," begun and carried on by Mr. Edward Cave, under the name of Sylvanus Urban, had attracted the notice and esteem of Johnson, in an eminent degree, before he came to London as an adventurer in literature. He told me that when he first saw St. John's Gate, the place where that deservedly popular miscellany was originally printed, he "beheld it with reverence." I suppose, indeed, that every young author has had the same kind of feeling for the magazine or periodical publication which has first entertained him, and in which he has first had an opportunity to see himself in print, without the risk of exposing his name. I myself recollect such impressions from "The Scots Magazine," which was begun at Edinburgh in the year 1739, and has been ever conducted with judgment

---

[1] " Journal of a Tour to the Hebrides." —BOSWELL.

accuracy, and propriety. I yet cannot help thinking of it with an affectionate regard. Johnson has dignified the "Gentleman's Magazine," by the importance with which he invests the life of Cave; but he has given it still greater lustre by the various admirable Essays which he wrote for it.

Though Johnson was often solicited by his friends to make a complete list of his writings, and talked of doing it, I believe with a serious intention that they should all be collected on his own account, he put it off from year to year, and at last died without having done it perfectly. I have one in his own handwriting, which contains a certain number; I, indeed, doubt if he could have remembered every one of them, as they were so numerous, so various, and scattered in such a multiplicity of unconnected publications; nay, several of them published under the names of other persons, to whom he liberally contributed from the abundance of his mind. We must, therefore, be content to discover them, partly from occasional information given by him to his friends, and partly from internal evidence.[2]

His first performance in the "Gentleman's Magazine," which for many years was his principal source for employment and support, was a copy of Latin verses, in March, 1738, addressed to the editor in so happy a style of compliment, that Cave must have been destitute both of taste and sensibility, had he not felt himself highly gratified.

Ad URBANUM.*

URBANE, nullis fesse laboribus,
URBANE, nullis victe calumniis,
 Cui fronte sertum in eruditâ
  Perpetuò viret et virebit;

Quid moliatur gens imitantium,
Quid et minetur, solicitus parùm,
 Vacare solis perge Musis,
  Juxta animo studiisque felix.

Linguæ procacis plumbea spicula,
Fidens, superbo frange silentio;
 Victrix per obstantes catervas
  Sedulitas animosa tendet.

Intende nervos, fortis, inanibus
Risurus olim nisibus æmuli;
 Intende jam nervos, habebis
  Participes operæ Camœnas.

 · While in the course of my narrative I enumerate his writings, I shall take care that my readers shall not be left to waver in doubt, between certainty and conjecture, with regard to their authenticity; and, for that purpose, shall mark with an *asterisk* (*) those which he acknowledged to his friends, and with a *dagger* (†) those which are ascertained to be his by internal evidence. When any other pieces are ascribed to him, I shall give my reasons.— BOSWELL

> Non ulla Musis pagina gratior,
> Quam quæ severis ludicra jungere
> Novit, fatigatamque nugis
>   Utilibus recreare mentem.
>
> ɪexente Nymphis serte Lycoride,
> Rosæ ruborem sic viola adjuvat
> Immista, sic Iris refulget
>   Æthereis variata fucis.[1]   S. J.

It appears that he was now enlisted by Mr. Cave as a regular coadjutor in his magazine, by which he probably obtained a tolerable livelihood.   At what time, or by what means, he had acquired a competent knowledge both of French and Italian, I do not know; but he was so well skilled in them, as to be sufficiently qualified for a translator.   That

---

[1] A translation of this Ode, by an unknown correspondent, appeared in the Magazine for the month of May following :—

> "Hail, URBAN! indefatigable man,
>   Unwearied yet by all thy useful toil!
> Whom num'rous slanderers assault in vain;
>   Whom no base calumny can put to foil.
> But still the laurel on thy learned brow
> Flourishes fair, and shall for ever grow.
>
> "What mean the servile, imitating crew,
>   What their vain blust'ring, and their empty noise.
> Ne'er seek; but still thy noble ends pursue,
>   Unconquer'd by the rabble's venal voice,
> Still to the Muse thy studious mind apply,
> Happy in temper as in industry.
>
> "The senseless sneerings of an haughty tongue,
>   Unworthy thy attention to engage,
> Unheeded pass; and tho' they mean thee wrong,
>   By manly silence disappoint their rage.
> Assiduous diligence confounds its foes,
> Resistless, tho' malicious crowds oppose.
>
> "Exert thy powers, nor slacken in thy course,
>   Thy spotless fame shall quash all false reports:
> Exert thy powers, nor fear a rival's force,
>   Then thou shalt smile at all his main efforts;
> Thy labours shall be crown'd with large success:
> The Muse's aid thy Magazine shall bless.
>
> "No page more grateful to th' harmonious nine
>   Than that wherein thy labours we survey;
> Where solemn themes in fuller splendour shine,
>   (Delightful mixture) blended with the gay,
> Where in improving, various joys we find,
> A welcome respite to the wearied mind.
>
> "Thus when the nymphs in some fair verdant mead
>   Of various flow'rs a beauteous wreath compose,
> The lovely violet's azure-painted head
>   Adds lustre to the crimson-blushing rose.
> Thus splendid Iris, with her varied dye,
> Shines in the æther, nd adorns the sky."
>   "BRITON."

part of his labour which consisted in emendation and improvement of the productions of other contributors, like that employed in levelling ground, can be perceived only by those who had an opportunity of comparing the original with the altered copy. What we certainly know to have been done by him in this way, was the Debates in both houses of Parliament, under the name of "The Senate of Lilliput," sometimes with feigned denominations of the several speakers, sometimes with denominations formed of the letters of their real names, in the manner of what is called anagram, so that they may easily be deciphered. Parliament then kept the press in a kind of mysterious awe, which made it necessary to have recourse to such devices. In our time it has acquired an unrestrained freedom, so that the people in all parts of the kingdom have a fair, open, and exact report of the actual proceedings of their representatives and legislators, which in our constitution is highly to be valued; though, unquestionably, there has of late been too much reason to complain of the petulance with which obscure scribblers have presumed to treat men of the most respectable character and situation.

This important article of the "Gentleman's Magazine" was, for several years, executed by Mr. William Guthrie, a man who deserves to be recorded in the literary annals of this country. He was descended of an ancient family in Scotland; but having a small patrimony, and being an adherent of the unfortunate house of Stuart, he could not accept of any office in the state; he, therefore, came to London, and employed his talents and learning as an "author by profession." His writings in history, criticism, and politics, had considerable merit.[1] He was the first English historian who had recourse to that authentic source of information, the Parliamentary Journals; and such was the power of his political pen, that, at an early period, Government thought it worth their while to keep it quiet by a pension, which he enjoyed till his death. Johnson esteemed him enough to wish that his life should be written. The debates in Parliament, which were brought home and digested by Guthrie, whose memory, though surpassed by others who have since followed him in the same department, was yet very quick and tenacious, were sent by Cave to Johnson for his revision; and, after some time, when Guthrie had attained to greater variety of employment, and the speeches were more and more enriched by the accession of Johnson's genius, it was resolved that he should do the whole himself, from the scanty notes furnished by persons employed to attend in both houses of Parliament. Sometimes, however, as he himself told me, he had nothing more communicated to him than the names of the several speakers, and the part which they had taken in the debate.

[1] How much poetry he wrote, I know not; but he informed me that he was the author of the beautiful little piece, "The Eagle and the Robin Redbreast," in the collection of poems entitled the "Union," though it is there said to be written by Archibald Scott, before the year 1600.—BOSWELL.

Thus was Johnson employed during some of the best years of his life, as a mere literary labourer, "for gain, not glory," solely to obtain an honest support. He, however, indulged himself in occasional little sallies, which the French so happily express by the term *jeux d'esprit*, and which will be noticed in their order, in the progress of this work.

But what first displayed his transcendent powers, and "gave the world assurance of the man," was his "London, a Poem, in Imitation of the third Satire of Juvenal;" which came out in May this year and burst forth with a splendour, the rays of which will for ever encircle his name. Boileau had imitated the same satire with great success, applying it to Paris; but an attentive comparison will satisfy every reader, that he is much excelled by the English Juvenal. Oldham had also imitated it, and applied it to London: all which performances concur to prove, that great cities, in every age, and in every country, will furnish similar topics of satire. Whether Johnson had previously read Oldham's imitation, I do not know; but it is not a little remarkable, that there is scarcely any coincidence found between the two performances, though upon the very same subject. The only instances are, in describing London as the *sink* of foreign worthlessness :—

> "———— the *common shore,*
>   Where France does all her filth and ordure pour;"
>
> OLDHAM.
>
> "The *common shore* of Paris and of Rome."
>
> JOHNSON.

And,

> "No calling or profession comes amiss,
>   A *needy monsieur* can be what he please."
>
> OLDHAM.
>
> "All sciences a *fasting monsieur* knows."
>
> JOHNSON.

The particulars which Oldham has collected, both as exhibiting the horrors of London, and of the times, contrasted with better days, are different from those of Johnson, and in general well chosen, and well expressed.[1]

There are, in Oldham's imitation, many prosaic verses and bad rhymes, and his poem sets out with a strange inadvertent blunder :—

> "Tho' much concern'd to *leave* my dear old friend,
>   I must, however, *his* design commend
>   Of fixing in the country."

I own it pleased me to find amongst them one trait of the manners of the age in London, in the last century, to shield from the sneer of English ridicule, what was some time ago too common a practice in my native city of Edinburgh!
> "If what I have said can't from the town affright,
>   Consider other *dangers of the night ;*
>   When brickbats are from upper stories thrown,
>   And *emptied chamberpots come pouring down*
>   *From garret windows.*"—BOSWELL.

It is plain he was not going to leave his *friend ;* his friend was going to leave *him.* A young lady at once corrected this with good critical sagacity, to

> " Tho' much concern'd to *lose* my old dear friend."

There is one passage in the original, better transfused by Oldham than by Johnson :—

> " *Nil habet infelix paupertas durius in se,*
> *Quàm quod ridiculos homines facit—*"

which is an exquisite remark on the galling meanness and contempt annexed to poverty; Johnson's imitation is,—

> " Of all the griefs that harass the distrest,
> Sure the most bitter is a scornful jest."

Oldham's, though less elegant, is more just ;—

> " Nothing in poverty so ill is borne,
> As its exposing men to grinning scorn."

Where, or in what manner this poem was composed, I am sorry that I neglected to ascertain with precision, from Johnson's own authority. He has marked upon his corrected copy of the first edition of it, " Written in 1738 ;" and, as it was published in the month of May in that year, it is evident that much time was not employed in preparing it for the press. The history of its publication I am enabled to give in a very satisfactory manner ; and judging from myself, and many of my friends, I trust that it will not be uninteresting to my readers.

We may be certain, though it is not expressly named in the following letter to Mr. Cave, in 1738, that they all relate to it :—

" TO MR. CAVE.

" *Castle-street, Wednesday Morning.*
" SIR,   [*March,* 1738.]

" When I took the liberty of writing to you a few days ago, I did not expect a repetition of the same pleasure so soon ; for a pleasure I shall always think it, to converse in a manner with an ingenious and candid man ; but having the enclosed poem in my hands to dispose of for the benefit of the author (of whose abilities I shall say nothing, since I send you his performance), I believe I could not procure more advantageous terms from any person than from you, who have so much distinguished yourself by your generous encouragement of poetry; and whose judgment of that art nothing but your commendation of my trifle[1] can give me any occasion to call in question. I do not doubt but you will look over this poem with another eye, and reward it in a different manner from a

His Ode " Ad Urbanum," probably.—NICHOLS.

mercenary bookseller, who counts the lines he is to purchase, and considers nothing but the bulk. I cannot help taking notice that besides what the author may hope for on account of his abilities, he likewise has another claim to your regard, as he lies at present under very disadvantageous circumstances of fortune. I beg, therefore, that you will favour me with a letter to-morrow, that I may know what you can afford to allow him, that he may either part with it to you, or find out (which I do not expect), some other way more to his satisfaction.

"I have only to add, that as I am sensible I have transcribed it very coarsely, which, after having altered it, I was obliged to do, I will, if you please to transmit the sheets from the press, correct it for you ; and take the trouble of altering any stroke of satire which you may dislike.

"By exerting on this occasion your usual generosity, you will not only encourage learning, and relieve distress, but (though it be, in comparison of the other motives, of very small account) oblige in a very sensible manner, Sir,

"Your very humble servant,

"SAMUEL JOHNSON."

"TO MR. CAVE.

"SIR,   "Monday, No. 6, Castle-street.

"I am to return you thanks for the present you were so kind as to send by me, and to entreat that you will be pleased to inform me by the penny-post, whether you resolve to print the poem. If you please to send it me by the post, with a note to Dodsley, I will go and read the lines to him, that we may have his consent to put his name in the title-page. As to the printing, if it can be set immediately about, I will be so much the author's friend, as not to content myself with mere solicitations in his favour. I propose, if my calculation be near the truth, to engage for the reimbursement of all that you shall lose by an impression of 500; provided, as you very generously propose, that the profit, if any, be set aside for the author's use, excepting the present you made, which, if he be a gainer, it is fit he should repay. I beg that you will let one of your servants write an exact account of the expense of such an impression, and send it with the poem, that I may know what I engage for. I am very sensible, from your generosity on this occasion, of your regard to learning, even in its unhappiest state; and cannot but think such a temper deserving the gratitude of those who suffer so often from a contrary disposition. I am, Sir,

"Your most humble servant,

"SAM. JOHNSON."

"TO MR. CAVE.

"SIR,   [No date.]

"I waited on you to take the copy of Dodsley's ; as I remember the number of lines which it contains, it will be no longer than 'Eugenio,'[1] with the quotations, which must be subjoined at the bottom of the page; part of the beauty of the performance (if any beauty be allowed it) consisting in adapting

A poem, published in 1737, of which see an account in vol. ii. under April 30, 1773.

Juvenal's sentiments to modern facts and persons. It will, with those additions, very conveniently make five sheets. And since the expense will be no more, I shall contentedly insure it, as I mentioned in my last. If it be not, therefore, gone to Dodsley's, I beg it may be sent me by the penny post, that I may have it in the evening. I have composed a Greek Epigram to Eliza,[1] and think she ought to be celebrated in as many different languages as Lewis le Grand. Pray send me word when you will begin upon the poem, for it is a long way to walk. I will leave my Epigram, but have not daylight to transcribe it. I am, Sir,

"Yours, &c.

"Sam. Johnson."

"TO MR. CAVE.

· Sir, [*No date.*]

"I am extremely obliged by your kind letter, and will not fail to attend you to-morrow with ' Irene,' who looks upon you as one of her best friends.

"I was to-day with Mr. Dodsley, who declares very warmly in favour of the paper you sent him, which he desires to have a share in, it being, as he says, *a creditable thing to be concerned in.* I knew not what answer to make till I had consulted you, nor what to demand on the author's part, but am very willing that, if you please, he should have a part in it, as he will undoubtedly be more diligent to disperse and promote it. If you can send me word to-morrow what I shall say to him, I will settle matters, and bring the poem with me for the press, which, as the town empties, we cannot be too quick with. I am, Sir,

"Yours, &c.

"Sam. Johnson."

To us who have long known the manly force, bold spirit, and masterly versification of this poem, it is a matter of curiosity to observe the diffidence with which its author brought it forward into public notice, while he is so cautious as not to avow it to be his own production ; and with what humility he offers to allow the printer to " alter any stroke of satire which he might dislike." That any such alteration was made, we do not know. If we did, we could not but feel an indignant regret ; but how painful is it to see that a writer of such vigorous powers of mind was actually in such distress, that the small profit which so short a poem, however excellent, could yield, was courted as a " relief."

It has been generally said, I know not with what truth, that Johnson offered his " London " to several booksellers, none of whom would purchase it. To this circumstance Mr. Derrick alludes in the following lines of his " Fortune, a Rhapsody :"

> " Will no kind patron Johnson own ?
> Shall Johnson friendless range the town ?
> And every publisher refuse
> The offspring of his happy Muse ?"

[1] The learned Mrs. Elizabeth Carter. This lady, of whom frequent mention will be found in these Memoirs, was daughter of Nicholas Carter, D.D. She died in Clarges-street, Feb. 19, 1806, in her eighty-ninth year.—Malone.

But we have seen that the worthy, modest, and ingenious Mr. Robert Dodsley, had taste enough to perceive its uncommon merit, and thought it creditable to have a share in it. The fact is, that, at a future confer-

ence, he bargained for the whole property of it, for which he gave Johnson ten guineas ; who told me, "I might perhaps have accepted of less ; but that Paul Whitehead had a little before got ten guineas for a poem ; and I would not take less than Paul Whitehead."

I may here observe, that Johnson appeared to me to undervalue Paul Whitehead upon every occasion when he was mentioned, and, in my opinion, did not do him justice ; but when it is considered that Paul Whitehead was a member of a riotous and profane club, we may account

ROBERT DODSLEY.

for Johnson having a prejudice against him. Paul Whitehead was, indeed, unfortunate in being not only slighted by Johnson, but violently attacked by Churchill, who utters the following imprecation :—

> "May I (can worse disgrace on manhood fall ?)
> Be born a Whitehead, and baptised a Paul !"

yet I shall never be persuaded to think meanly of the author of so brilliant and pointed a satire as "Manners."

Johnson's "London" was published in May, 1738 ;[1] and it is remarkable, that it came out on the same morning with Pope's satire, entitled "1738 ;" so that England had at once its Juvenal and Horace as poetical monitors. The Reverend Dr. Douglas, now Bishop of Salisbury, to whom I am indebted for some obliging communications, was then a student at Oxford, and remembers well the effect which "London" produced. Every body was delighted with it ; and there

---

[1] Sir John Hawkins, p. 86, tells us, "The event is *antedated*, in the poem of 'London;' but in every particular, except the difference of a year, what is there said of the departure of Thales, must be understood of Savage, and looked upon as *true history*." This conjecture is, I believe, entirely groundless. I have been assured that Johnson said he was not so much as acquainted with Savage, when he wrote his "London." If the departure mentioned in it was 'he departure of Savage, the event was not *antedated* but *foreseen ;* for "London" was published in May, 1738, and Savage did not set out for Wales till July, 1739. However well Johnson could defend the credibility of *second sight*, he did not pretend that he himself was possessed of that faculty.

The assertion that Johnson was not even acquainted with Savage, when he published his "London," may be doubtful. Johnson took leave of Savage when he went to Wales in 1739, and must have been acquainted with him before that period. See his "Life of Savage."— A. CHALMERS.

being no name to it, the first buzz of the literary circle was, "Here is an unknown poet, greater even than Pope." And it is recorded in the "Gentleman's Magazine" of that year, that it "got to the second edition in the course of a week."

One of the warmest patrons of this poem on its first appearance was General Oglethorpe, whose strong "benevolence of soul" was unabated during the course of a very long life; though it is painful to think, that he had but too much reason to become cold and callous, and discontented with the world, from the neglect which he experienced of his public and private worth by those in whose power it was to gratify so gallant a veteran with marks of distinction. This extraordinary person was as remarkable for his learning and taste, as for his other eminent qualities; and no man was more prompt, active, and generous, in encouraging merit. I have heard Johnson gratefully acknowledge, in his presence, the kind and effectual support which he gave to his "London," though unacquainted with its author.

Pope, who then filled the poetical throne without a rival, it may reasonably be presumed, must have been particularly struck by the sudden appearance of such a poet; and, to his credit, let it be remembered, that his feelings and conduct on the occasion were candid and liberal. He requested Mr. Richardson, son of the painter, to endeavour to find out who this new author was. Mr. Richardson, after some inquiry, having informed him that he had discovered only that his name was Johnson, and that he was some obscure man, Pope said, "He will soon be *déterré*."[1] We shall presently see, from a note written by Pope,[2] that he was himself afterwards more successful in his inquiries than his friend.

That in this justly celebrated poem may be found a few rhymes which the critical position of English prosody at this day would disallow, cannot be denied; but with this small imperfection, which in the general blaze of its excellence is not perceived, till the mind has subsided into cool attention, it is, undoubtedly, one of the noblest productions in our language, both for sentiment and expression. The nation was then in that ferment against the court and the ministry, which some years after ended in the downfall of Sir Robert Walpole; and it has been said, that Tories are Whigs when out of place, and Whigs Tories when in place; so, as a Whig Administration ruled with what force it could, a Tory Opposition had all the animation and all the eloquence of resistance to power, aided by the common topics of patriotism, liberty, and independence. Accordingly, we find in Johnson's "London" the most spirited invectives against tyranny and oppression, the warmest predilection for his own country, and the purest love of virtue; interspersed with traits of his own particular character and situation, not omitting his prejudices as a

By Joshua Reynolds, from the information of the younger Richardson.—BOSWELL.
See p. 73.—MALONE.

" true born Englishman "[1] not only against foreign countries, but against Ireland and Scotland. On some of these topics I shall quote a few passages : —

> " The cheated nation's happy fav'rites see ;
>   Mark whom the great caress, who frown on me."

> " Has heaven reserv'd, in pity to the poor,
>   No pathless waste, or undiscover'd shore ?
>   No secret island in the boundless main ?
>   No peaceful desert yet unclaim'd by Spain ?
>   Quick let us rise, the happy seats explore,
>   And bear Oppression's insolence no more."

> " How, when competitors like these contend,
>   Can *surly Virtue* hope to find a friend ? "

> " This mournful truth is every where confess'd,
>   SLOW RISES WORTH, BY POVERTY DEPRESS'D ! "

We may easily conceive with what feeling a great mind like his, cramped and galled by narrow circumstances, uttered this last line, which he marked by capitals. The whole of the poem is eminently excellent, and there are in it such proofs of a knowledge of the world, and of a mature acquaintance with life, as cannot be contemplated without wonder, when we consider that he was then only in his twenty-ninth year, and had yet been so little in the " busy haunts of men."

Yet, while we admire the poetical excellence of this poem, candour obliges us to allow, that the flame of patriotism and zeal for popular resistance with which it is fraught, had no just cause. There was, in truth, *no* " oppression ;" the " nation " was *not* " cheated." Sir Robert Walpole was a wise and benevolent minister, who thought that the happiness and prosperity of a commercial country like ours would be best promoted by peace, which he accordingly maintained with credit, during a very long period. Johnson himself afterwards [October 21, 1773,] honestly acknowledged the merit of Walpole, whom he called " a fixed star ;" while he characterised his opponent, Pitt, as " a meteor." But Johnson's juvenile poem was naturally impregnated with the fire of opposition, and upon every account was universally admired.

Though thus elevated into fame, and conscious of uncommon powers, he had not that bustling confidence, or, I may rather say, that animated ambition, which one might have supposed would have urged him to endeavour at rising in life. But such was his inflexible dignity of character, that he could not stoop to court the great ; without which, hardly any man has made his way to a high station. He could not expect to produce many such works as his " London," and he felt the

---

[1] It is, however, remarkable, that he uses the epithet, which undoubtedly, since the union between England and Scotland, ought to denominate the natives of both parts of our island;—
    " Was early taught a Briton's rights to prize."—BOSWELL.

hardships of writing for bread ; he was therefore willing to resume the office of a schoolmaster, so as to have a sure, though moderate income for his life ; and an offer being made to him of the mastership of a school,[1] provided he could obtain the degree of Master of Arts, Dr. Adams was applied to, by a common friend, to know whether that could be granted him as a favour from the University of Oxford. But though he had made such a figure in the literary world, it was then thought too great a favour to be asked.

Pope, without any knowledge of him but from his " London," recommended him to Earl Gower, who endeavoured to procure for him a degree from Dublin, by the following letter to a friend of Dean Swift ·

"Sir,   *Trentham, August* 1, 1739.

"Mr. Samuel Johnson (author of London, a satire, and some other poetical pieces) is a native of this country, and much respected by some worthy gentlemen in his neighbourhood, who are trustees of a charity-school now vacant ; the certain salary is sixty pounds a year, of which they are desirous

---

[1] In a billet written by Mr. Pope in the following year, this school is said to have been in *Shropshire;* but as it appears from a letter from Earl Gower, that the trustees of it were "some worthy gentlemen in Johnson's neighbourhood," I in my first edition suggested that Mr. Pope must have, by mistake, written Shropshire, instead of Staffordshire. But I have since been obliged to Mr. Spearing, attorney-at-law, for the following information:—" William Adams, formerly citizen and haberdasher of London, founded a school at Newport, in the county of Salop, by deed dated 27th November, 1656, by which he granted the ' yearly sum of *sixty pounds* to such able and learned schoolmaster, from time to time, being of godly life and conversation, who should have been educated at one of the Universities of Oxford or Cambridge, and had taken the degree of *Master of Arts,* and was well read in the Greek and Latin tongues, as should be nominated from time to time by the said William Adams, during his life, and after the decease of the said William Adams by the governors (namely, the Master and Wardens of the Haberdashers' Company of the City of London) and their successors. The manor and lands out of which the revenues for the maintenance of the school were to issue, are situate *at Knighton and Adbaston in the County of Stafford.*" From the foregoing account of this foundation, particularly the circumstances of the salary being sixty pounds, and the degree of Master of Arts being a requisite qualification in the teacher, it seemed probable that this was the school in contemplation ; and that Lord Gower erroneously supposed that the gentlemen who possessed the lands, out of which the revenues issued, were trustees of the charity.

Such was the probable conjecture. But in the "Gentleman's Magazine" for May, 1793, there is a letter from Mr. Henn, one of the masters of the school of Appleby, in Leicestershire, in which he writes as follows :—

"I compared time and circumstances together, in order to discover whether the school in question might not be this of Appleby. Some of the trustees at that period were ' worthy gentlemen of the neighbourhood of Lichfield.' Appleby itself is not far from the neighbourhood of Lichfield: the salary, the degree requisite, together with the *time of election,* all agreeing with the statutes of Appleby. The election, as said in the letter ' could not be delayed longer than the 11th of next month,' which was the 11th of September, just three months after the annual audit-day of Appleby school, which is always on the 11th of June ; and the statutes enjoin *ne ullius præceptorum electio diutius tribus mensibus moraretur, &c.*

"These I thought to be convincing proofs that my conjecture was not ill-founded, and that in a future edition of that book, the circumstance might be recorded as fact.

"But what banishes every shadow of doubt is the *Minute-book* of the school, which declares the head-mastership to be *at that time* VACANT."

I cannot omit returning thanks to this learned gentleman for the very handsome manner in which he has in that letter been so good as to speak of this work.—BOSWELL.

to make him master ; but, unfortunately, he is not capable of receiving their bounty, which 'would make him happy for life,' by not being 'a Master of Arts ;' which, by the statutes of this school, the master of it must be.

"Now these gentlemen do me the honour to think that I have interest enough in you, to prevail upon you to write to Dean Swift, to persuade the University of Dublin to send a diploma to me, constituting this poor man Master of Arts in their University. They highly extol the man's learning and probity; and will not be persuaded, that the University will make any difficulty of conferring such a favour upon a stranger, if he is recommended by the Dean. They say, he is not afraid of the strictest examination, though he is of so long a journey ; and will venture it, if the Dean thinks it necessary ; choosing rather to die upon the road, 'than be starved to death in translating for booksellers ;' which has been his only subsistence for some time past.

"I fear there is more difficulty in this affair, than those good-natured gentlemen apprehend; especially as their election cannot be delayed longer than the 11th of next month. If you see this matter in the same light that it appears to me, I hope you will burn this, and pardon me for giving you so much trouble about an impracticable thing ; but, if you think there is a probability of obtaining the favour asked, I am sure your humanity, and propensity to relieve merit in distress, will incline you to serve the poor man, without my adding any more to the trouble I have already given you, than assuring you that I am, with great truth, Sir,

"Your faithful servant,

"Gower."

It was, perhaps, no small disappointment to Johnson that this respectable application had not the desired effect ; yet how much reason has there been, both for himself and his country, to rejoice that it did not succeed, as he might probably have wasted in obscurity those hours in which he afterwards produced his incomparable works.

JOHNSON, RICHARDSON, AND HOGARTH.

CHAPTER IV.—1738—1743.

ABOUT this time he made one other effort to emancipate himself
from the drudgery of authorship. He applied to Dr. Adams, to
consult Dr. Smalbroke of the Commons, whether a person might be
permitted to practise as an advocate there, without a doctor's degree
in Civil Law. "I am," said he, "a total stranger to these studies;
but whatever is a profession, and maintains numbers, must be within
the reach of common abilities, and some degree of industry." Dr
Adams was much pleased with Johnson's design to employ his talents
in that manner, being confident he would have attained to great
eminence. And, indeed, I cannot conceive a man better qualified to
make a distinguished figure as a lawyer; for he would have brought
to his profession a rich store of various knowledge, an uncommon

acuteness, and a command of language, in which few could have equalled, and none have surpassed, him. He who could display eloquence and wit in defence of the decision of the House of Commons upon Mr. Wilkes's election for Middlesex, and of the unconstitutional taxation of our fellow subjects in America, must have been a powerful advocate in any cause. But here, also, the want of a degree was an insurmountable bar.

He was, therefore, under the necessity of persevering in that course to which he had been forced ; and we find that his proposal from Greenwich to Mr. Cave, for a translation of Father Paul Sarpi's History, was accepted.[1]

Some sheets of this translation were printed off, but the design was dropped ; for it happened, oddly enough, that another person of the name of Samuel Johnson, Librarian of St. Martin's-in-the-Fields, and curate of that parish, engaged in the same undertaking, and was patronised by the clergy, particularly by Dr. Pearce, afterwards Bishop of Rochester. Several light skirmishes passed between the rival translators, in the newspapers of the day ; and the consequence was that they destroyed each other, for neither of them went on with the work. It is much to be regretted that the able performance of that celebrated genius, Fra Paolo, lost the advantage of being incorporated into British literature by the masterly hand of Johnson.

I have in my possession, by the favour of Mr. John Nichols, a paper in Johnson's handwriting, entitled "Account between Mr. Edward Cave and Sam. Johnson, in relation to a version of Father Paul, &c., begun August the 2nd, 1738 ; " by which it appears, that from that day to the 21st of April, 1739, Johnson received for this work 49l. 7s. in sums of one, two, three, and sometimes four guineas at a time, most frequentl two. And it is curious to observe the minute and scrupulous accuracy with which Johnson had pasted upon it a slip of paper, which he has entitled " Small Account," and which contains one article, " Sept. 9th, Mr. Cave laid down 2s. 6d." There is subjoined to this account, a list of some subscribers to the work, partly in Johnson's handwriting, partly

---

[1] In the " Weekly Miscellany," October 21, 1738, there appeared the following advertisement :—" Just published, proposals for printing the History of the Council of Trent, translated from the Italian of Father Paul Sarpi ; with the Author's life, and Notes, Theological, Historical, and Critical, from the French edition of Dr. Le Courayer ; to which are added, Observations on the History, and Notes and Illustrations from various Authors, both printed and manuscript. By S. Johnson. 1. The work will consist of two hundred sheets, and be two volumes in quarto, printed on good paper and letter. 2. The price will be 18s. each volume, to be paid, half a guinea at the delivery of the first volume, and the rest at the delivery of the second volume in sheets. 3. Twopence to be abated for every sheet less than two hundred. It may be had on a large paper, in three volumes, at the price of three guineas one to be paid at the time of subscribing, another at the delivery of the first, and the rest at the delivery of the other volumes. The work is now in the press, and will be diligently prosecuted. Subscriptions are taken in by Mr. Dodsley, in Pall Mall, Mr. Rivington, in St. Paul's Churchyard, by E. Cave, at St. John's Gate, and the Translator, at No. 6, in Castle-street, by Cavendish-square."—BOSWELL.

in that of another person ; and there follows a leaf or two, on which are
written a number of characters which have the appearance of a short-
hand, which, perhaps, Johnson was then trying to learn.

" TO MR. CAVE.

" SIR,   *Wednesday.*

" I did not care to detain your servant while I wrote an answer to your
letter, in which you seem to insinuate that I had promised more than I am
ready to perform.   If I have raised your expectations by any thing that may
have escaped my memory, I am sorry ; and if you remind me of it, shall thank
you for the favour.   If I made fewer alterations than usual in the debates, it
was only because there appeared, and still appears to be, less need of
alteration.   The verses to Lady Firebrace[1] may be had when you please, for
you know that such a subject neither deserves much thought, nor requires it.

" The Chinese Stories[2] may be had folded down when you please to send, in
which I do not recollect that you desired any alterations to be made.

" An answer to another query I am very willing to write, and had consulted
with you about it last night, if there had been time ; for I think it the most
proper way of inviting such a correspondence as may be an advantage to the
paper, not a load upon it.

" As to the Prize Verses, a backwardness to determine their degrees of
merit is not peculiar to me.   You may, if you please, still have what I can
say ; but I shall engage with little spirit in an affair, which I shall *hardly* end
to my own satisfaction, and *certainly* not to the satisfaction of the parties
concerned.[3]

" As to Father Paul, I have not yet been just to my proposal, but have met
with impediments, which, I hope, are now at an end ; and if you find the
progress hereafter not such as you have a right to expect, you can easily
stimulate a negligent translator.

" If any or all of these have contributed to your discontent, I will endeavour
to remove it ; and desire you to propose the question to which you wish for an
answer.   I am, Sir, your humble servant,

                                                    " SAM. JOHNSON."

" TO MR. CAVE.

" SIR,   [*No date.*]

" I am pretty much of your opinion, that the Commentary cannot be
prosecuted with any appearance of success ; for, as the names of the authors
concerned are of more weight in the performance than its own intrinsic merit,
the public will be soon satisfied with it.   And I think the Examen should be
pushed forward with the utmost expedition.   Thus, ' This day, &c.   An

---

[1] They afterwards appeared in the " Gentleman's Magazine," with this title—" Verses to
Lady Firebrace, at Bury Assizes."—BOSWELL.

[2] Du Halde's " Description of China" was then publishing by Mr. Cave in weekly
numbers, whence Johnson was to select pieces for the embellishment of the Magazine.—
NICHOLS.

[3] The premium of forty pounds proposed for the best poem on the Divine Attributes is here
alluded to.—NICHOLS.

Examen of Mr. Pope's Essay, &c., containing a succinct Account of the Philosophy of Mr. Leibnitz on the System of the Fatalists, with a Confutation of their Opinions and an illustration of the Doctrine of Free-will;' (with what else you think proper.)

"It will, above all, be necessary to take notice, that it is a thing distinct from the Commentary.

"I was so far from imagining they stood still,[1] that I conceived them to have a good deal beforehand, and therefore was less anxious in providing them more. But if ever they stand still on my account, it must doubtless be charged to me; and whatever else shall be reasonable, I shall not oppose; but beg a suspense of judgment till morning, when I must entreat you to send me a dozen proposals, and you shall then have copy to spare.

> "I am, Sir, yours, *impransus,*
>
> > "SAM. JOHNSON."

"Pray muster up the proposals if you can, or let the boy recal them from the booksellers."

But although he corresponded with Mr. Cave concerning a translation of Crousaz's Examen of Pope's Essay on Man, and gave advice as one anxious for its success, I was long ago convinced by a perusal of the preface that this translation was erroneously ascribed to him; and I have found this point ascertained beyond all doubt by the following article in Dr. Birch's manuscripts in the British Museum :—

"ELISÆ CARTERÆ S. P. D. THOMAS BIRCH.

"*Versionem tuam Examinis Crousaziani jam perlegi. Summam styli et elegantiam, et in re difficillimâ proprietatem, admiratus.*

"*Dabam Novemb.* 27°, 1738."[2]

Indeed Mrs. Carter has lately acknowledged to Mr. Seward that she was the translator of the "Examen."

It is remarkable that Johnson's last quoted letter to Mr. Cave concludes with a fair confession that he had not a dinner; and it is no less remarkable, that, though in this state of want himself, his benevolent heart was not insensible to the necessities of an humble labourer in literature, as appears from the very next letter :—

"TO MR. CAVE.

"DEAR SIR,   [*No date.*]

"You may remember I have formerly talked with you about a Military Dictionary. The eldest Mr. Macbean, who was with Mr. Chambers, has very good materials for such a work, which I have seen, and will do it at a very low rate.[3] I think the terms of war and navigation might be comprised, with good

---

[1] The compositors in Mr. Cave's printing-office, who appear by this letter to have then waited for copy.—NICHOLS.

[2] Birch MSS., Brit. Mus. 4323.—BOSWELL.   [3] This book was published.—BOSWELL.

explanations, in one 8vo pica, which he is willing to do for twelve shillings a sheet, to be made up a guinea at the second impression. If you think on it I will wait on you with him.

> "I am, Sir, your humble servant,
>
> "Pray lend me Topsel on Animals."   "SAM. JOHNSON."

I must not omit to mention that this Mr. Macbean was a native of Scotland.

In the "Gentleman's Magazine" of this year Johnson gave a life of Father Paul ;* and he wrote the preface to the volume,† which, though prefixed to it when bound, is always published with the appendix, and is, therefore, the last composition belonging to it. The ability and nice adaptation with which he could draw up a prefatory address, was one of his peculiar excellencies.

It appears, too, that he paid a friendly attention to Mrs. Elizabeth Carter ; for, in a letter from Mr. Cave to Dr. Birch, November 28th, this year, I find " Mr. Johnson advises Miss C. to undertake a translation of *Boethius de Cons.*, because there is prose and verse, and to put her name to it when published." This advice was not followed ; probably from an apprehension that the work was not sufficiently popular for an extensive sale. How well Johnson himself could have executed a translation of this philosophical poet we may judge from the following specimen which he has given in the "Rambler" (*Motto to No.* 7) :—

> "O qui perpetuâ mundum ratione gubernas,
> Terrarum cœlique sator !————
> Disjice terrenæ nebulas et pondera molis,
> Atque tuo splendore mica! Tu namque serenum,
> Tu requies tranquilla piis. Te cernere finis,
> Principium, vector, dux, semita, terminus, idem."

> "O Thou whose power o'er moving worlds presides,
> Whose voice created, and whose wisdom guides,
> On darkling man in pure effulgence shine,
> And cheer the clouded mind with light divine.
> 'Tis thine alone to calm the pious breast,
> With silent confidence and holy rest ;
> From thee, great God! we spring, to thee we tend,
> Path, motive, guide, original, and end!"

In 1739, besides the assistance which he gave to the "Parliamentary Debates," his writings in the "Gentleman's Magazine " were, "The Life of Boerhaave,"* in which it is to be observed, that he discovers that love of chemistry which never forsook him ; "An appeal to the Public in behalf of the Editor ;"† "An Address to the Reader ;"† "An Epigram both in Greek and Latin to Eliza ;"* and also English verses to her ;* and "A Greek Epigram to Dr. Birch."* It has been erroneously supposed that an essay, published in that Magazine this year, entitled "The Apotheosis of Milton," was written by Johnson; and on that supposition it has been improperly inserted in the edition of his works by the booksellers after his decease. Were there no positive testimony as to this point, the style of the performance, and the name of Shakspeare not being mentioned in an essay professedly reviewing the principal English poets, would ascertain it not to be the production of Johnson. But there is here no occasion to resort to internal evidence; for my Lord Bishop of Salisbury (Dr. Douglas) has assured me that it was written by Guthrie. His separate publications were, "A Complete Vindication of the Licensers of the Stage, from the malicious and scandalous Aspersions of Mr. Brooke, author of 'Gustavus Vasa,'"* being an ironical attack upon them for their suppression of that tragedy; and "Marmor Norfolciense; or, an Essay on an Ancient Prophetical Inscription, in Monkish Rhyme, lately discovered near Lynne, in Norfolk, by Probus Britannicus." * In this performance he, in a feigned inscription, supposed to have been found in Norfolk, the county of Sir Robert Walpole, then the obnoxious prime minister of this country, inveighs against the Brunswick succession, and the measures of government consequent upon it.[1] To this supposed prophecy he added a Commentary, making each expression apply to the times, with warm anti-Hanoverian zeal.

This anonymous pamphlet, I believe, did not make so much noise as was expected, and, therefore, had not a very extensive circulation. Sir John Hawkins relates, that " warrants were issued and messengers employed to apprehend the author; who, though he had forborne to subscribe his name to the pamphlet, the vigilance of those in pursuit of him had discovered;" and we are informed that he lay concealed in Lambeth-marsh till the scent after him grew cold. This, however, is altogether without foundation; for Mr. Steele, one of the Secretaries of the Treasury, who, amidst a variety of important business, politely obliged me with his attention to my inquiry, informed me that "he directed every possible search to be made in the records of the Treasury and Secretary of State's Office, but could find no trace whatever of any warrant having been issued to apprehend the author of this pamphlet."

" Marmor Norfolciense" became exceedingly scarce, so that I, for many years, endeavoured in vain to procure a copy of it. At last I was indebted to the malice of one of Johnson's numerous petty adversaries, who in 1775, published a new edition of it, " with Notes and a Dedication to Samuel Johnson, L.L.D., by Tribunus;" in which some puny scribbler invidiously attempted to found upon it a charge of inconsistency against its author, because he had accepted of a pension from his present Majesty, and had written in support of the measures of government. As a mortification to such impotent malice, of which there are so many

---

[1] The Inscription and the Translation of it are preserved in the " London Magazine" for the year 1739, p. 244.—BOSWELL.

instances towards men of eminence, I am happy to relate that this *telum imbelle* did not reach its exalted object till about a year after it thus appeared, when I mentioned it to him, supposing that he knew of the republication. To my surprise he had not yet heard of it. He requested me to go directly and get it for him, which I did. He looked at it and laughed, and seemed to be much diverted with the feeble efforts of his unknown adversary, who, I hope, is alive to read this account. "Now," said he, "here is somebody who thinks he has vexed me sadly ; yet if it had not been for you, you rogue, I should probably never have seen it."

As Mr. Pope's note concerning Johnson, alluded to in a former page, refers both to his "London," and his "Marmor Norfolciense," I have deferred inserting it till now. I am indebted for it to Dr. Percy, the Bishop of Dromore, who permitted me to copy it from the original in his possession. It was presented to his Lordship by Sir Joshua Reynolds, to whom it was given by the son of Mr. Richardson the painter, the person to whom it is addressed. I have transcribed it with minute exactness, that the peculiar mode of writing, and imperfect spelling of that celebrated poet, may be exhibited to the curious in literature. It justifies Swift's epithet of "paper-sparing Pope," for it is written on a slip no larger than a common message-card, and was sent to Mr. Richardson, along with the imitation of Juvenal.

"This is imitated by one Johnson who put in for a Public-school in Shropshire,[1] but was disappointed. He has an infirmity of the convulsive kind, that attacks him sometimes so as to make Him a sad Spectacle. Mr. P. from the Merit of This Work which was all the knowledge he had of him, endeavour'd to serve him without his own application ; & wrote to my Ld. gore, but he did not succeed. Mr. Johnson published afterwds. another Poem in Latin with Notes the whole very humerous call'd the Norfolk Prophecy.

"P."

Johnson had been told of this note : and Sir Joshua Reynolds informed him of the compliment which it contained, but, from delicacy, avoided showing him the paper itself. When Sir Joshua observed to Johnson that he seemed very desirous to see Pope's note, he answered, "Who would not be proud to have such a man as Pope so solicitous in inquiring about him ?"

The infirmity to which Mr. Pope alludes, appeared to me also, as I have elsewhere[2] observed, to be of the convulsive kind, and of the nature of that distemper called St. Vitus's dance ; and in this opinion I am confirmed by the description which Sydenham gives of that disease : "This disorder is a kind of convulsion. It manifests itself by halting, or unsteadiness of one of the legs, which the patient draws after him

- See note, p. 65.—Boswell.
[2] "Journal of a Tour to the Hebrides," 3rd edit. p. 8.—Boswell.

like an idiot. If the hand of the same side be applied to the breast, or any other part of the body, he cannot keep it a moment in the same posture, but it will be drawn into a different one by a convulsion, notwithstanding all his efforts to the contrary." Sir Joshua Reynolds, however, was of a different opinion, and favoured me with the following paper :—

" Those notions or tricks of Dr. Johnson are improperly called convulsions. He could sit motionless when he was told so to do, as well as any other man. My opinion is, that it proceeded from a habit [1] which he had indulged himself in, of accompanying his thoughts with certain untoward actions, and those actions always appeared to me as if they were meant to reprobate some part of his past conduct. Whenever he was not engaged in conversation, such thoughts were sure to rush into his mind; and, for this reason, any company, any employment whatever, he preferred to being alone. The great business of his life, he said, was to escape from himself; this disposition he considered as the disease of his mind, which nothing cured but company.

" One instance of his absence of mind and particularity, as it is characteristic of the man, may be worth relating. When he and I took a journey together into the West, we visited the late Mr. Banks, of Dorsetshire; the conversation turning upon pictures, which Johnson could not well see, he retired to a corner of the room, stretching out his right leg as far as he could reach before him, then bringing up his left leg, and stretching his right still further on. The old gentleman observing him, went up to him and in a very courteous manner assured him, though it was not a new house, the flooring was perfectly safe. The Doctor started from his reverie, like a person waked out of his sleep, but spoke not a word."

While we are on this subject, my readers may not be displeased with another anecdote, communicated to me by the same friend, from the relation of Mr. Hogarth.

Johnson used to be a pretty frequent visitor at the house of Mr. Richardson, author of " Clarissa," and other novels of extensive reputation. Mr. Hogarth came one day to see Richardson, soon after the execution of Dr. Cameron, for having taken arms for the house of Stuart in 1745-6 ; and being a warm partisan of George the Second, he observed to Richardson, that certainly there must have been some very unfavourable circumstances lately discovered in this particular case, which had induced the King to approve of an execution for rebellion so long after the time when it was committed, as this had the appearance of putting a man to death in cold blood,[2] and was very unlike his Majesty's usual

---

[1] Sir Joshua Reynolds's notion on this subject is confirmed by what Johnson himself said to a young lady, the niece of his friend Christopher Smart. See a note by Mr. Boswell on some particulars communicated by Reynolds, under March 30th, 1783.—MALONE.

[2] Impartial posterity may, perhaps, be as little inclined as Dr. Johnson was, to justify the uncommon rigour exercised in the case of Dr. Archibald Cameron. He was an amiable and truly honest man ; and his offence was owing to a generous, though mistaken principle of duty. Being obliged, after 1746, to give up his profession as a physician, and to go into foreign parts,

clemency. While he was talking, he perceived a person standing at a window in the room, shaking his head, and rolling himself about in a strange ridiculous manner. He concluded that he was an idiot, whom his relations had put under the care of Mr. Richardson, as a very good man. To his great surprise, however, this figure stalked forwards, to where he and Mr. Richardson were sitting, and all at once took up the argument, and burst out into an invective against George the Second, as one, who, upon all occasions, was unrelenting and barbarous ; mentioning many instances ; particularly, that when an officer of high rank had been acquitted by a court-martial, George the Second had with his own hand struck his name off the list. In short, he displayed such a power of eloquence, that Hogarth looked at him with astonishment, and actually imagined that this idiot had been at the moment inspired. Neither Hogarth nor Johnson were made known to each other at this interview.

In 1740 he wrote for the Gentleman's Magazine the " Preface,"† the " Life of Admiral Blake,"* and the first parts of those of " Sir Francis Drake,"* and "Philip Barretier,"*[1] both which he finished the following year. He also wrote an " Essay on Epitaphs,"* and an " Epitaph on Phillips, a Musician,"* which was afterwards published with some other pieces of his, in Mrs. Williams's Miscellanies. This Epitaph is so exquisitely beautiful, that I remember even Lord Kaimes, strangely prejudiced as he was against Dr. Johnson, was compelled to allow it very high praise. It has been ascribed to Mr. Garrick, from its appearing at first with the signature G. ; but I have heard Mr. Garrick declare, that it was written by Dr. Johnson, and give the following account of the manner in which it was composed. Johnson and he were sitting together ; when, amongst other things, Garrick repeated an Epitaph upon this Phillips, by a Dr. Wilkes, in these words :

> " Exalted soul ! whose harmony could please
> The love-sick virgin, and the gouty ease ;
> Could jarring discord, like Amphion, move
> To beauteous order and harmonious love ;
> Rest here in peace, till angels bid thee rise,
> And meet thy blessed Saviour in the skies."

Johnson shook his head at these common-place funereal lines, and

he was honoured with the rank of Colonel, both in the French and Spanish service. He was a son of the ancient and respectable family of Cameron of Lochiel ; and his brother, who was the Chief of that brave clan, distinguished himself by moderation and humanity, while the Highland army marched victorious through Scotland. It is remarkable of this Chief, that though he had earnestly remonstrated against the attempt as hopeless, he was of too heroic a spirit not to venture his life and fortune in the cause, when personally asked by him whom he thought his Prince.—BOSWELL.

[1] To which in 1742 he made very large additions, which have never yet been incorporated in any edition of Barretier's life.—A. CHALMERS.

said to Garrick, " I think, Davy, I can make a better." Then, stirring about his tea for a little while, in a state of meditation, he almost extempore produced the following verses :—

> "Phillips, whose touch harmonious could remove
> The pangs of guilty power or hapless love ;
> Rest here, distress'd by poverty no more,
> Here find that calm thou gav'st so oft before :
> Sleep, undisturb'd, within this peaceful shrine,
> Till angels wake thee with a note like thine !"[1]

In 1741 he wrote for the Gentleman's Magazine the " Preface,"† " Conclusion of his Lives of Drake and Barretier,"* " A free Translation of the Jests of Hierocles, with an Introduction ;" and, I think, the following pieces :—" Debate on the Proposal of Parliament to Cromwell, to assume the Title of King, abridged, modified, and digested ;" † " Translation of Abbe Guyon's Dissertation on the Amazons ;" † " Translation of Fontenelle's Panegyric on Dr. Morin." † Two notes upon this appear to me undoubtedly his. He this year, and the two following, wrote the " Parliamentary Debates." He told me himself that he was the sole composer of them for those three years only. He was not, however, precisely exact in his statement, which he mentioned from hasty recollection ; for it is sufficiently evident, that his composition of them began November 19, 1740, and ended February 23, 1742-43.

It appears from some of Cave's letters to Dr. Birch, that Cave had better assistance for that branch of his Magazine, than has been generally supposed ; and that he was indefatigable in getting it made as perfect as he could.

[1] The epitaph of Phillips is in the porch of Wolverhampton Church. The prose part of it is curious : -

> " Near this place lies
> CHARLES CLAUDIUS PHILLIPS,
> Whose absolute contempt of riches
> and inimitable performances upon the violin
> made him the admiration of all that knew him.
> He was born in Wales,
> made the tour of Europe,
> And, after the experience of both kinds of fortune,
> Died in 1732."

Mr. Garrick appears not to have recited the verses correctly, the original being as follows One of the various readings is remarkable, as it is the germ of Johnson's concluding line :-

> " Exalted soul, *thy various sounds* could please
> The love-sick virgin, and the gouty ease ;
> Could jarring *crowds*, like *old* Amphion, move
> To beauteous order and harmonious love ;
> Rest here in peace, till angels bid thee rise,
> And meet thy SAVIOUR'S *consort* in the skies."

Dr. Wilkes, the author of these lines, was a Fellow of Trinity College in Oxford, and Rector of Pitchford, in Shropshire. He collected materials for a history of that county, and is spoken of by Brown Willis, in his " History of Mitred Abbies," vol. ii. p. 189. But he was a native of Staffordshire; and to the antiquities of that county was his attention chiefly confined. Mr. Shaw has had the use of his papers.—J. BLAKEWAY.

Thus, 21st July, 1735,

"I trouble you with the enclosed, because you said you could easily correct what is here given for Lord Chesterfield's speech. I beg you will do so as soon as you can for me, because the month is far advanced."

And 15th July, 1737,

"As you remember the debates so far as to perceive the speeches already printed are not exact, I beg the favour that you will peruse the enclosed, and, in the best manner your memory will serve, correct the mistaken passages, or any thing that is omitted. I should be very glad to have something of the Duke of Newcastle's speech, which would be particularly of service.

"A gentleman has Lord Bathurst's speech to add something to."

And July 3, 1744,

"You will see what stupid, low, abominable stuff is put[1] upon your noble and learned friend's[2] character, such as I should quite reject, and endeavour to do something better towards doing justice to the character. But as I cannot expect to attain my desire in that respect, it would be a great satisfaction, as well as an honour to our work, to have the favour of the genuine speech. It is a method that several have been pleased to take, as I could show, but I think myself under a restraint. I shall say so far, that I have had some by a third hand, which I understood well enough to come from the first; others by penny-post, and others by the speakers themselves, who have been pleased to visit St. John's Gate, and show particular marks of their being pleased."[3]

There is no reason, I believe, to doubt the veracity of Cave. It is, however, remarkable that none of these letters are in the years during which Johnson alone furnished the debates, and one of them is in the very year after he ceased from that labour. Johnson told me, that as soon as he found that the speeches were thought genuine, he determined that he would write no more of them ; "for he would not be accessory to the propagation of falsehood." And such was the tenderness of his conscience, that a short time before his death he expressed his regret for his having been the author of fictions which had passed for realities.

He nevertheless agreed with me in thinking, that the debates which he had framed were to be valued as orations upon questions of public importance. They have accordingly been collected in volumes, properly arranged, and recommended to the notice of parliamentary speakers by a preface written by no inferior hand.[4] I must, however, observe, that although there is in those debates a wonderful store of political information and very powerful eloquence, I cannot agree that they exhibit the manner of each particular speaker, as Sir John Hawkins seems to

---

[1] I suppose in another compilation of the same kind.—BOSWELL.

[2] Doubtless, Lord Hardwicke.—BOSWELL.

[3] Birch's MSS. in the British Museum, 4302.—BOSWELL.

[4] I am assured that the editor is Mr. George Chalmers, whose commercial works are well known and esteemed.—BOSWELL.

think. But, indeed, what opinion can we have of his judgment and taste in public speaking, who presumes to give as the characteristics of two celebrated orators, "the deep-mouthed rancour of Pulteney, and the yelping pertinacity of Pitt."[1]

This year I find that his tragedy of "Irene" had been for some time ready for the stage, and that his necessities made him desirous of getting as much as he could for it without delay ; for there is the following letter from Mr. Cave to Dr. Birch in the same volume of manuscripts in the British Museum, from which I copied those above quoted. They were most obligingly pointed out to me by Sir William Musgrave, one of the Curators of that noble repository.

"Sept. 9, 1741.

"I have put Mr. Johnson's play into Mr. Gray's[2] hands, in order to sell it to him, if he is inclined to buy it ; But I doubt whether he will or not. He would dispose of the copy, and whatever advantage may be made by acting it. Would your society,[3] or any gentleman, or body of men that you know, take such a bargain? He and I are very unfit to deal with theatrical persons. Fleetwood was to have acted in it last season, but Johnson's diffidence or   [4] prevented it."

I have already mentioned that "Irene," was not brought into public notice till Garrick was manager of Drury-lane Theatre.

In 1742[5] he wrote for the Gentleman's Magazine the "Preface,"† the "Parliamentary Debates,"* "Essay on the Account of the Conduct of the Duchess of Marlborough,"* then the popular topic of conversation. This essay is a short but masterly performance. We find him in No. 13 of his "Rambler," censuring a profligate sentiment in that "Account ;"[6] and again insisting upon it strenuously in conversation.[7] "An Account of the Life of Peter Burman,"* I believe chiefly taken from a foreign publication ; as, indeed, he could not himself know much about Burman ;

[1] Sir G. Hawkins's "Life of Johnson," pp. 94—132. 100.—BOSWELL.

[2] A London bookseller of the time.—BOSWELL.

[3] Not the Royal Society ; but the Society for the Encouragement of Learning, of which Dr. Birch was a leading member. Their object was to assist authors in printing expensive works. It existed from about 1735 to 1746, when, having incurred a considerable debt, it was dissolved.—BOSWELL.

[4] There is no erasure here, but a mere blank to fill up which may be an exercise for ingenious conjecture.—BOSWELL.

[5] From one of his letters to a friend, written in June, 1742, it should seem that he then proposed to write a play on the subject of Charles the Twelfth, of Sweden, and to have it ready for the ensuing winter. The passage alluded to, however, is somewhat ambiguous, and the work which he then had in contemplation may have been a history of that monarch.—MALONE.

[6] The passage alluded to runs as follows :—"A late female minister of s te has been shameless enough to inform the world that she used, when she wanted to extract anything from her sovereign, to remind her of Montaigne's reasoning—who has determined that to tell a secret to a friend is no breach of fidelity, because the number of persons is not multiplied; a man and his friend being virtually the same.—WRIGHT.

[7] "Journal of a Tour to the Hebrides," 3rd edit p 167.—BOSWELL.

"Additions to his Life of Barretier;"* "The Life of Sydenham,"* afterwards prefixed to Dr. Swan's edition of his works ; "Proposals for printing the Bibliotheca Harleiana, or a Catalogue of the Library of the Earl of Oxford."* His account of that celebrated collection of books, in which he displays the importance to literature, of what the French call a *catalogue raisonné*, when the subjects of it are extensive and various, and it is executed with ability, cannot fail to impress all his readers with admiration of his philological attainments. It was afterwards prefixed to the first volume of the Catalogue, in which the Latin accounts of books were written by him. He was employed in this business by Mr. Thomas Osborne the bookseller, who purchased the library for 13,000*l.* a sum which Mr. Oldys says, in one of his manuscripts, was not more than the binding of the books had cost ; yet, as Dr. Johnson assured me, the slowness of the sale was such, that there was not much gained by it. It has been confidently related, with many embellishments, that Johnson one day knocked Osborne down in his shop, with a folio, and put his foot upon his neck. The simple truth I had from Johnson himself. "Sir, he was impertinent to me and I beat him. But it was not in his shop ; it was in my own chamber."

A very diligent observer may trace him where we should not easily suppose him to be found. I have no doubt that he wrote the little abridgment entitled "Foreign History," in the Magazine for December. To prove it, I shall quote the introduction :—

"As this is that season of the year in which Nature may be said to command a suspension of hostilities, and which seems intended, by putting a short stop to violence and slaughter, to afford time for malice to relent, and animosity to subside, we can scarce expect any other account than of plans, negotiations, and treaties, of proposals for peace, and preparations for war."

As also this passage :—

"Let those who despise the capacity of the Swiss, tell us by what wonderful policy, or by what happy conciliation of interests, it is brought to pass, that in a body made up of different communities and different religions, there should be no civil commotions, though the people are so warlike, that to nominate and raise an army is the same."

I am obliged to Mr. Astle[1] for his ready permission to copy the two following letters, of which the originals are in his possession. Their contents show that they were written about this time, and that Johnson was now engaged in preparing an historical account of the British Parliament.

"TO MR. CAVE.

"SIR, [*No date.*]

"I believe I am going to write a long letter, and have therefore taken a whole sheet of paper. The first thing to be written about is our historical design.

"You mentioned the proposal of printing in numbers, as an alteration in the

[1] Mr. Astle was Keeper of the Records of the Tower, and otherwise well known in the literary world.

scheme, but I believe you mistook, some way or other, my meaning; I had no other view than that you might rather print too many of five sheets, than of five-and-thirty.

"With regard to what I shall say on the manner of proceeding, I would have it understood as wholly indifferent to me, and my opinion only, not my resolution. *Emptoris sit eligere.*

"I think the insertion of the exact dates of the most important events in the margin, or of so many events as may enable the reader to regulate the order of facts with sufficient exactness, the proper medium between a journal, which has regard only to time, and a history which ranges facts according to their dependance on each other, and postpones or anticipates according to the convenience of narration. I think the work ought to partake of the spirit of history, which is contrary to minute exactness, and of the regularity of a journal, which is inconsistent with spirit. For this reason I neither admit numbers or dates, nor reject them.

"I am of your opinion with regard to placing most of the resolutions, &c., in the margin, and think we shall give the most complete account of parliamentary proceedings that can be contrived. The naked papers, without an historical treatise interwoven, require some other book to make them understood. I will date the succeeding facts with some exactness, but I think in the margin. You told me on Saturday that I had received mony on this work, and found set down 13*l.* 2*s.* 6*d.*, reckoning the half guinea of last Saturday. As you hinted to me that you had many calls for money, I would not press you too hard, and therefore shall desire only, as I send it in, two guineas for a sheet of copy ; the rest you may pay me when it may be more convenient; and even by this sheet-payment I shall, for some time, be very expensive.

"The Life of Savage I am ready to go upon; and in great primer and pica notes, I reckon on sending in half a sheet a day ; but the money for that shall likewise lie by in your hands till it is done. With the debates, shall not I have business enough? if I had but good pens.

"Towards Mr. Savage's Life, what more have you got? I would willingly have his trial, &c., and know whether his defence be at Bristol, and would have his collection of poems, on account of the Preface ;—" The Plain Dealer," [1]— all the magazines that have any thing of his or relating to him.

"I thought my letter would be long, but now it is ended ; and,

"I am, Sir, yours, &c.,

"SAM. JOHNSON."

"The boy found me writing this almost in the dark, when I could not quite easily read yours.

"I have read the Italian :—nothing in it is well.

"I had no notion of having any thing for the inscription.[2] I hope you don't think I kept it to extort a price. I could think of nothing, till to-day. If you could spare me another guinea for the history, I should take it very kindly, to-night; but if you do not, I shall not think it an injury.

"I am almost well again."

· The "Plain Dealer" was published in 1724, and contained some account of Savage.— BOSWELL.

[2] Perhaps the Runic Inscription ; ' Gentleman's Magazine," vol. xii. p. 132.—MALONE.

"TO MR. CAVE.

" SIR,

" You did not tell me your determination about the *Soldier's Letter*,[1] which I am confident was never printed. I think it will not do by itself, or in any other place so well as the Mag. Extraordinary. If you will have it all, I believe you do not think I set it high, and I will be glad if what you give, you will give quickly.

" You need not be in care about something to print, for I have got the State Trials, and shall extract Layer, Atterbury, and Macclesfield from them, and shall bring them to you in a fortnight ; after which I will try to get the South Sea Report."   [*No date, nor signature.*]

I would also ascribe to him an " Essay on the Description of China, from the French of Du Halde."†

His writings in the " Gentleman's Magazine," in 1743, are, the " Preface," † the " Parliamentary Debates,"† " Considerations on the Dispute between Crousaz and Warburton, on Pope's Essay on Man ;"† in which, while he defends Crousaz, he shows an admirable metaphysical acuteness and temperance in controversy ; " Ad Lauram parituram Epigramma ;[2]* and, " A Latin Translation of Pope's Verses on his

---

[1] I have not discovered what this was.—BOSWELL.

[2] " Angliacas inter pulcherrima Laura puellas,
    Mox uteri pondus depositura grave,
    Adsit, Laura, tibi facilis Lucina dolenti,
    Neve tibi noceat præenituisse Deæ."

Mr. Hector was present when this Epigram was made *impromptu*. The first line was proposed by Dr. James, and Johnson was called upon by the company to finish it, which he instantly did.- BOSWELL.

The following elegant Latin Ode, which appeared in the " Gentleman's Magazine " for 1743 (vol. xiii. p. 548), was many years ago pointed out to James Bindley, Esq., as writter by Johnson, and may safely be attributed to him :—

AD ORNATISSIMAM PUELLAM.

Vanæ sit arti, sit studio modus,
Formosa virgo ! sit speculo quies,
  Curamque quærendi decoris
    Mitte, supervacuosque cultus.

Ut fortuitis verna coloribus
Depicta vulgo rura magis placent,
  Nec invident horto nitenti
    Divitias operosiores :

Lenique fons cum murmure pulcrior
Obliquat ultro præcipitem fugam
  Inter reluctantes lapillos, et
    Ducit aquas temere sequentes :

Utque inter undas, inter et arbores,
Jam vere primo dulce strepunt aves,
  Et arte nulla gratiores
    Ingeminant sine lege cantus:

Grotto ;" and, as he could employ his pen with equal success upon a small matter as a great, I suppose him to be the author of an advertisement for Osborne, concerning the great Harleian Catalogue.

But I should think myself much wanting, both to my illustrious friend and my readers, did I not introduce here, with more than ordinary respect, an exquisitely beautiful Ode, which has not been inserted in any of the collections of Johnson's poetry, written by him at a very early period, as Mr. Hector informs me, and inserted in "The Gentleman's Magazine" of this year.

FRIENDSHIP, AN ODE.*

Friendship, peculiar boon of heaven,
   The noble mind's delight and pride,
To men and angels only given,
   To all the lower world denied.

While love unknown among the blest,
   Parent of thousand wild desires,
The savage and the human breast
   Torments alike with raging fires :

With bright, but oft destructive, gleam,
   Alike o'er all his lightnings fly ;
Thy lambent glories only beam
   Around the fav'rites of the sky.

Thy gentle flows of guiltless joys
   On fools and villains ne'er descend :
In vain for thee the tyrant sighs,
   And hugs a flatterer for a friend.

Nativa sic te gratia, te nitor
Simplex decebit, te Veneres tuæ ;
   Nudus Cupido suspicatur
     Artifices nimis apparatus.

Ergo fluentum tu, male sedula,
Ne sæva inuras semper acu comam
   Nec sparsa odorato nitentes
     Pulvere dedecores capillos ;

Quales nec olim Ptolemæia
Jactabat uxor, sidereo in chore
   Utcunque devotæ refulger,
     Verticis exuviæ decori ;

Nec diva mater, cum similem tuæ
Mentita formam, et pulcrior adspici,
   Permisit incomtas protervis
     Fusa comas agitare ventis.

In vol. xiv. p. 46, of the same work, an elegant Epigram was inserted, in answer to the foregoing Ode, which was written by Dr. Inyon of Norfolk, a physician, and an excellent classical scholar :—

"*Ad Authorem Carminis* AD ORNATISSIMAM PUELLAM.

"O cui non potuit, quia culta, placere puella,
   Qui speras Musam posse placere tuam !"—MALONE.

Directress of the brave and just,
O guide us through life's darksome way !
And let the tortures of mistrust
On selfish bosoms only prey.

Nor shall thine ardour cease to glow,
When souls to blissful climes remove :
What rais'd our virtue here below,
Shall aid our happiness above.

Johnson had now an opportunity of obliging his schoolfellow Dr. James, of whom he once observed, "No man brings more mind to his profession." James published this year his "Medicinal Dictionary," in three volumes folio. Johnson, as I understood from him, had written, or assisted in writing, the proposals for this work ; and being very fond of the study of physic, in which James was his master, he furnished some of the articles. He, however, certainly wrote for it the Dedication to Dr. Mead, † which is conceived with great address, to conciliate the patronage of that very eminent man.[1]

DR. BIRCH.

It has been circulated, I know not with what authenticity, that Johnson considered Dr. Birch as a dull writer, and said of him, "Tom

"TO DR. MEAD.

"Sir,
"That the 'Medicinal Dictionary' is dedicated to you, is to be imputed only to your reputation for superior skill in those sciences which I have endeavoured to explain and facilitate; and you are, therefore, to consider this address, if it be agreeable to you, as one of the rewards of merit; and if otherwise, as one of the inconveniences of eminence.

"However you shall receive it, my design cannot be disappointed, because this public appeal to your judgment will show that I do not found my hopes of approbation upon the ignorance of my readers, and that I fear his censure least whose knowledge is most extensive.
I am, Sir, your most obedient humble servant,
"R. James"—Boswell.

Birch is as brisk as a bee in conversation. but no sooner does he take a pen in his hand, than it becomes a torpedo to him, and benumbs all his faculties." That the literature of this country is much indebted to Birch's activity and diligence must certainly be acknowledged. We have seen that Johnson honoured him with a Greek Epigram ; and his correspondence with him, during many years, proves that he had no mean opinion of him.

' TO DR. BIRCH.

"SIR, Thursday, Sept. 29, 1743.

" I hope you will excuse me for troubling you on an occasion on which I know not whom else I can apply to ; I am at a loss for the Lives and Characters of Earl Stanhope, the two Craggs, and the minister Sunderland ; and beg that you will inform [me] where I may find them, and send any pamphlets, &c. relating to them to Mr. Cave to be perused for a few days by, Sir,

" Your most humble servant,

" SAM. JOHNSON."

His circumstances were at this time embarrassed ; yet his affection for his mother was so warm, and so liberal, that he took upon himself a debt of hers, which, though small in itself, was then considerable to him. This appears from the following letter which he wrote to Mr. Levett, of Lichfield, the original of which lies now before me :—

" TO MR. LEVETT, IN LICHFIELD.

"SIR, December 1, 1743.

" I am extremely sorry that we have encroached so much upon your forbearance with respect to the interest, which a great perplexity of affairs hindered me from thinking of with that attention that I ought, and which I am not immediately able to remit to you, but will pay it (I think twelve pounds) in two months. I look upon this, and on the future interest of that mortgage, as my own debt ; and beg that you will be pleased to give me directions how to pay it, and not mention it to my dear mother. If it be necessary to pay this in less time, I believe I can do it ; but I take two months for certainty, and beg an answer whether you can allow me so much time. I think myself very much obliged to your forbearance, and shall esteem it a great happiness to be able to serve you. I have great opportunities of dispersing any thing that you may think it proper to make public. I will give a note for the money, payable at the time mentioned, to any one here that you shall appoint. I am, Sir,

" Your most obedient and most humble servant,

" SAM. JOHNSON.

" At Mr. Osborne's, bookseller, in Gray's Inn."

LORD CHESTERFIELD.

CHAPTER V.—1744—1748.

JOHNSON PUBLISHES THE LIFE OF SAVAGE—MERITS OF THIS BIOGRAPHY—DISCUSSION AS TO SAVAGE'S PARENTAGE—PREFACE TO HARLEIAN MISCELLANY—"MISCELLANEOUS OBSERVATIONS ON THE TRAGEDY OF MACBETH"—GARRICK MANAGER OF DRURY-LANE THEATRE—JOHNSON'S "PROLOGUE" ON ITS OPENING—"PLAN" OF THE DICTIONARY ADDRESSED TO LORD CHESTERFIELD—RESIDENCE IN GOUGH SQUARE—INSTITUTION OF THE CLUB IN IVY LANE—WRITES LIFE OF ROSCOMMON CONTRIBUTIONS TO DODSLEY'S "PRECEPTOR."

IT does not appear that Johnson wrote anything in 1744 for the "Gentleman's Magazine," but the Preface.† His "Life of Barretier" was now published in a pamphlet by itself. But he produced one work this year, fully sufficient to maintain the high reputation which he had acquired. This was "The Life of Richard Savage;"* a man, of whom it is difficult to speak impartially, without wondering that he was for some time the intimate companion of Johnson; for his character [1] was marked by profligacy, insolence, and ingratitude: yet, as he undoubtedly had a warm and vigorous, though unregulated mind, had seen life in all its varieties, and been much in the company of the states-

---

[1] As a specimen of his temper, I insert the following letter from him to a noble Lord Tyrconnel] to whom he was under great obligations, but who, on account of his bad conduct, was obliged to discard him. The original was in the hands of the late Francis Cockayne Cust, Esq., one of his Majesty's Counsel, learned in the law :—

"*Right Honourable* BRUTE *and* BOOBY,

"I find you want (as Mr. ——— is pleased to hint) to swear away my life, that is, the life of your creditor, because he asks you for a debt.—The public shall soon be acquainted with this, to judge whether you are not fitter to be an Irish evidence, than to be an Irish Peer.—I defy and despise you. I am

"Your determined adversary,

"R. S."—BOSWELL.

men and wits of his time, he could communicate to Johnson an abundant supply of such materials as his philosophical curiosity most eagerly desired ; and as Savage's misfortunes and misconduct had reduced him to the lowest state of wretchedness as a writer for his bread, his visit to St. John's Gate naturally brought Johnson and him together.[1]

It is melancholy to reflect, that Johnson and Savage were sometimes in such extreme indigence,[2] that they could not pay for a lodging ; so that they have wandered together whole nights in the streets.[3] Yet in these almost incredible scenes of distress, we may suppose that Savage mentioned many of the anecdotes with which Johnson afterwards enriched the life of his unhappy companion, and those of other poets.

He told Sir Joshua Reynolds, that one night in particular, when Savage and he walked round St. James's-square for want of a lodging, they were not at all depressed by their situation, but in high spirits, and

[1] Sir John Hawkins gives the world to understand, that Johnson, "being an admirer of genteel manners, was captivated by the address and dem anour of Savage, who, as to his exterior, was to a remarkable degree accomplished."—Hawkins's Life, p. 52. But Sir John's notions of gentility must appear somewhat ludicrous, from his stating the following circumstance as presumptive evidence that Savage was a good swordsman :—"That he understood the exercise of a gentleman's weapon, may be inferred from the use made of it in that rash encounter which is related in his life." The dexterity here alluded to was, that Savage, in a nocturnal fit of drunkenness, stabbed a man at a coffee-house, and killed him : for which he was tried at the Old Bailey, and found guilty of murder.

Johnson, indeed, describes him as having "a grave and manly deportment, a solemn dignity of mien ; but which, upon a nearer acquaintance, softened into an engaging easiness of manners." How highly Johnson admired him for that knowledge which he himself so much cultivated, and what kindness he entertained for him, appears from the following lines in the "Gentleman's Magazine" for April, 1738, which I am assured were written by Johnson :—

"*Ad* RICARDUM SAVAGE.

"*Humani studium generis cui pectore fervet
O colat humanum te foveatque genus.*"—BOSWELL.

[2] The following striking proof of Johnson's extreme indigence, when he published the Life of Savage, was communicated to Mr. Boswell, by Mr. Richard Stowe, of Aspley, in Bedfordshire, from the information of Mr. Walter Harte, author of the Life of Gustavus Adolphus :—

"Soon after Savage's Life was published, Mr. Harte dined with Edward Cave, and occasionally praised it. Soon after, meeting him, Cave said, ' You made a man very happy t'other day.'—' How could that be?' says Harte ; ' nobody was there but ourselves Cave answered, by reminding him that a plate of victuals was sent behind a screen, which was to Johnson, dressed so shabbily, that he did not choose to appear ; but on hearing the conversation, he was highly delighted with the encomiums on his book."—MALONE.

[3] As Johnson was married before he settled in London, and must have always had a habitation for his wife, some readers have wondered how he ever could have been driven to stroll about with Savage, all night, for want of a lodging. But it should be remembered, that Johnson, at different periods, had lodgings in the vicinity of London ; and his finances certainly would not admit of a double establishment. When, therefore, he spent a convivial day in London, and found it too late to return to any country residence he may occasionally have had, having no lodging in town, he was obliged to pass the night in the manner described above ; for, though at that period, it was not uncommon for two men to sleep together, Savage, it appears, could accommodate him with nothing but his company in the open air. The Epigram given above, which doubtless was written by Johnson, shows, that their acquaintance commenced before April, 1738.—MALONE.

brimful of patriotism, traversed the square for several hours, inveighed against the minister, and "resolved they would *stand by their country*."

I am afraid, however, that by associating with Savage, who was habituated to the dissipation and licentiousness of the town, Johnson, though his good principles remained steady, did not entirely preserve that conduct, for which, in days of greater simplicity, he was remarked by his friend Mr. Hector, but was imperceptibly led into some indulgences which occasioned much distress to his virtuous mind.

That Johnson was anxious that an authentic and favourable account of his extraordinary friend should first get possession of the public attention, is evident from a letter which he wrote in the "Gentleman's Magazine" for August of the year preceding its publication.

"MR. URBAN,

"As your collections show how often you have owed the ornaments of your poetical pages to the correspondence of the unfortunate and ingenious Mr. Savage, I doubt not but you have so much regard to his memory, as to encourage any design that may have a tendency to the preservation of it from insults or calumnies, and therefore with some degree of assurance, entreat you to inform the public, that his life will speedily be published by a person who was favoured with his confidence, and received from himself an account of most of the transactions which he proposes to mention, to the time of his retirement to Swansea, in Wales.

"From that period, to his death in the prison of Bristol, the account will be continued from materials still less liable to objection: his own letters, and those of his friends, some of which will be inserted in the work, and abstracts of others subjoined in the margin.

"It may be reasonably imagined, that others may have the same design; but as it is not credible that they can obtain the same materials, it must be expected they will supply from invention the want of intelligence; and that under the title of 'The Life of Savage,' they will publish only a novel, filled with romantic adventures, and imaginary amours. You may therefore, perhaps, gratify the lovers of truth and wit, by giving me leave to inform them in your Magazine, that my account will be published in 8vo. by Mr. Roberts, in Warwick-lane."

[*No signature.*]

In February, 1744, it accordingly came forth from the shop of Roberts, between whom and Johnson I have not traced any connection except the casual one of this publication. In Johnson's "Life of Savage," although it must be allowed that its moral is the reverse of "*Respicere exemplar vitæ morumque jubebo*," a very useful lesson is inculcated, to guard men of warm passions from a too free indulgence of them; and the various incidents are related in so clear and animated a manner, and illuminated throughout with so much philosophy, that it is one of the most interesting narratives in the English language. Sir Joshua Reynolds told me, that upon his return from Italy he met with it in Devonshire, knowing nothing of its author, and began to read it while he was standing with his arm leaning against a chimney-piece. It seized his attention so strongly, that, not being able to lay down the book till he had finished it, when he attempted to move, he found his arm totally benumbed. The rapidity with which this work was composed, is a wonderful circumstance. Johnson has been heard to say, "I wrote forty-eight of the printed octavo pages of the 'Life of Savage' at a sitting; but then I sat up all night."[1]

He exhibits the genius of Savage to the best advantage, in the specimens of his poetry which he has selected, some of which are of uncommon merit. We, indeed, occasionally find such vigour and such point, as might make us suppose that the generous aid of Johnson had been imparted to his friend. Mr. Thomas Warton made this remark to me; and, in support of it, quoted from the poem entitled "The Bastard," a line in which the fancied superiority of one "stamped in Nature's mint with ecstasy," is contrasted with a regular lawful descendant of some great and ancient family:

> "No tenth transmitter of a foolish face."

But the fact is, that this poem was published some years before Johnson and Savage were acquainted.

It is remarkable, that in this biographical disquisition there appears a very strong symptom of Johnson's prejudice against players; a prejudice which may be attributed to the following causes: first, the imperfection of his organs, which were so defective that he was not susceptible of the fine impressions which theatrical excellence produces upon the generality of mankind; secondly, the cold rejection of his tragedy; and, lastly, the brilliant success of Garrick, who had been his pupil, who had come to London at the same time with him, not in a much more prosperous state than himself, and whose talents he undoubtedly rated low, compared with his own. His being outstripped by his pupil in the race of immediate fame, as well as of fortune, probably made him feel some indignation, as thinking that whatever might be Garrick's merits in his art, the reward was too great when compared with what the most successful efforts of literary labour could attain. At all periods of his life, Johnson used to talk contemptuously of players; but in this work he speaks of them with peculiar acrimony; for which, perhaps, there was formerly too much reason from the licentious and dissolute manners of those engaged in that profession. It is but justice to add, that in our own time such a change has taken place, that there is no longer room for such an unfavourable distinction.

His schoolfellow and friend, Dr. Taylor, told me a pleasant anecdote of Johnson's triumphing over his pupil, David Garrick. When that great actor had played some little time at Goodman's-fields, Johnson and Taylor went to see him perform, and afterwards passed the evening at a tavern with him and old Giffard. Johnson, who was ever depreciating stage-players, after censuring some mistakes in emphasis, which Garrick had committed in the course of that night's acting, said, " The players, Sir, have got a kind of rant, with which they run on, without any regard either to accent or emphasis." Both Garrick and Giffard were offended at this sarcasm, and endeavoured to refute it ; upon which Johnson rejoined, " Well, now, I'll give you something to speak, with which you are little acquainted, and then we shall see how just my observation is. That shall be the criterion. Let me hear you repeat the ninth Commandment, ' Thou shalt not bear false witness against thy neighbour.' " Both tried at it, said Dr. Taylor, and both mistook the emphasis, which should be upon *not* and *false witness.*' Johnson put them right, and enjoyed his victory with great glee.

His " Life of Savage " was no sooner published, than the following liberal praise was given to it, in " The Champion," a periodical paper :—

"This pamphlet is, without flattery to its author, as just and well-written a piece of its kind as I ever saw ; so that at the same time that it highly deserves, it certainly stands very little in need of this recommendation. As to the history of the unfortunate person whose memoirs compose this work, it is certainly penned with equal accuracy and spirit, of which I am so much the better judge, as I know many of the facts mentioned to be strictly true, and very fairly related. Besides, it is not only the story of Mr. Savage, but innumerable incidents relating to other persons, and other affairs, which renders this a very amusing, and, withal, a very instructive and valuable performance. The author's observations are short, significant, and just, as his narrative is remarkably smooth, and well-disposed. His reflections open to all the recesses of the human heart ; and in a word, a more just or pleasant, a more engaging or a more improving treatise, on all the excellencies and defects of human nature, is scarce to be found in our own, or, perhaps, any other language."[2]

Johnson's partiality for Savage made him entertain no doubt of his story, however extraordinary and improbable. It never occurred to him to question his being the son of the Countess of Macclesfield, of whose unrelenting barbarity he so loudly complained, and the particulars of which are related in so strong and affecting a manner in Johnson's life of him. Johnson was certainly well warranted in publishing his narrative, however offensive it might be to the lady and her relations,

---

[1] I suspect Dr. Taylor was inaccurate in his statement. The emphasis should be equally upon *shalt* and *not*, as both concur to form the negative injunction ; and *false witness*, like the other acts prohibited in the Decalogue, should not be marked by any peculiar emphasis, but only be distinctly enunciated.—BOSWELL.

A moderate emphasis should be placed on *false*.—KEARNEY.

[2] This character of the " Life of Savage" was not written by Fielding, as has been supposed, but most probably by Ralph, who, as appears from the minutes of the partners of " The Champion " in the possession of Mr. Reed, of Staple-inn, succeeded Fielding in his share of the paper before the date of that eulogium.—BOSWELL.

because her alleged unnatural and cruel conduct to her son, and shameful avowal of guilt, were stated in a "Life of Savage" now lying before me, which came out so early as 1727, and no attempt had been made to confute it, or to punish the author or printer as a libeller : but for the honour of human nature, we should be glad to find the shocking tale not true ; and from a respectable gentleman [1] connected with the lady's family, I have received such information and remarks, as, joined to my own inquiries, will, I think, render it at least somewhat doubtful, especially when we consider that it must have originated from the person himself who went by the name of Richard Savage.

If the maxim, *falsum in uno, falsum in omnibus,* were to be received without qualification, the credit of Savage's narrative, as conveyed to us, would be annihilated ; for it contains some assertions which, beyond a question, are not true.

1. In order to induce a belief that the Earl Rivers—on account of a criminal connection with whom, Lady Macclesfield is said to have been divorced from her husband, by Act of Parliament [1697]—had a peculiar anxiety about the child which she bore to him, it is alleged, that his lordship gave him his own name, and had it duly recorded in the register of St. Andrew's, Holborn. I have carefully inspected that register, but no such entry is to be found.[2]

2. It is stated, that "Lady Macclesfield having lived for some time

---

[1] The late Francis Cockayne Cust, Esq., one of his Majesty's (George III.) Counsel.—BOSWELL.

[2] Mr. Cust's reasoning, with respect to the filiation of Richard Savage, always appeared to me extremely unsatisfactory, and is entirely overturned by the following decisive observations, for which the reader is indebted to the unwearied researches of Mr. Bindley. The story on which Mr. Cust so much relies, that Savage was a supposititious child, not the son of Lord Rivers and Lady Macclesfield, but the offspring of a shoemaker, introduced in consequence of her real son's death, was, without doubt, grounded on the circumstance of Lady Macclesfield's having, in 1696, previously to the birth of Savage, had a daughter by the Earl Rivers, who died in her infancy ; a fact which, as the same gentleman observes to me, was proved in the course of the proceedings on Lord Macclesfield's Bill of Divorce. Most fictions of this kind have some admixture of truth in them.—MALONE.

From "the Earl of Macclesfield's Case," which, in 1697-8, was presented to the Lords, in order to procure an act of divorce, it appears that "Anne, Countess of Macclesfield, under the name of Madam Smith, was delivered of a male child in Fox-court, near Brook-street, Holborn, by Mrs. Wright, a midwife, on Saturday, the 16th of January, 1696-7, at six o'clock in the morning, who was baptised on the Monday following, and registered by the name of Richard, the son of John Smith, by Mr. Burbridge, assistant to Dr. Manningham's curate for St. Andrew's, Holborn ; that the child was christened on Monday, the 18th of January, in Fox-court ; and, from the privacy, was supposed by Mr. Burbridge to be 'a by-blow, or bastard.'" It also appears, that during her delivery the lady wore a mask ; and that Mary Pegler, on the next day after the baptism (Tuesday) took a male child, whose mother was called Madam Smith, from the house of Mrs. Pheasant, in Fox-court (running from Brook-street into Gray's-inn-lane), who went by the name of Mrs. Lee.

Conformable to this statement is the entry in the register of St. Andrew's, Holborn, which is as follows, and which unquestionably records the baptism of Richard Savage, to whom Lord Rivers gave his own Christian name, prefixed to the assumed surname of his mother : Jan. 1696-7. "Richard, son of John Smith and Mary, in Fox-court, in Gray's-inn-lane, baptised the 18th."—BINDLEY.

upon very uneasy terms with her husband, thought a public confession of adultery the most obvious and expeditious method of obtaining her liberty ;" and Johnson, assuming this to be true, stigmatises her with indignation, as "the wretch who had, without scruple, proclaimed herself an adulteress."[1] But I have perused the Journals of both houses of Parliament at the period of her divorce, and there find it authentically ascertained, that, so far from voluntarily submitting to the ignominious charge of adultery, she made a strenuous defence by her counsel ; the bill having been first moved the 15th of January, 1697-8, in the House of Lords, and proceeded on (with various applications for time to bring up witnesses at a distance, &c.) at intervals, till the 3rd of March, when it passed. It was brought to the Commons, by a message from the Lords, the 5th of March, proceeded on the 7th, 10th, 11th, 14th, and 15th, on which day, after a full examination of witnesses on both sides, and hearing of counsel, it was reported without amendments, passed, and carried to the Lords. That Lady Macclesfield was convicted of the crime of which she was accused, cannot be denied ; but the question now is, whether the person calling himself Richard Savage was her son.

It has been said,[2] that when Earl Rivers was dying, and anxious to provide for all his natural children, he was informed by Lady Macclesfield that her son by him was dead. Whether, then, shall we believe that this was a malignant lie, invented by a mother to prevent her own child from receiving the bounty of his father, which was accordingly the consequence, if the person whose life Johnson wrote, was her son ; or shall we not rather believe that the person who then assumed the name of Richard Savage was an impostor, being in reality the son of the shoemaker, under whose wife's care[3] Lady Macclesfield's child was placed ; that after the death of the real Richard Savage he attempted to personate him ; and that the fraud being known to Lady Macclesfield, he was therefore repulsed by her with just resentment.

There is a strong circumstance in support of the last supposition ; though it has been mentioned as an aggravation of Lady Macclesfield's unnatural conduct, and that is, her having prevented him from obtaining the benefit of a legacy left to him by Mrs. Lloyd, his godmother. For if there was such a legacy left, his not being able to obtain payment of it, must be imputed to his consciousness that he was not the real person. The just inference should be, that by the death of Lady Macclesfield's child before its godmother, the legacy became lapsed, and therefore that Johnson's Richard Savage was an impostor.

[1] No divorce can be obtained in the Courts on confession of the party. There must be proofs.—KEARNEY.

[2] By Johnson, in his "Life of Savage."—MALONE.

[3] This, as an accurate friend remarks to me, is not correctly stated. The shoemaker under whose care Savage was placed, with a view to his becoming his apprentice, was not the husband of this nurse.—See Johnson's "Life of Savage." "Lives of the Poets." vol. iii. p. 131, edit 1782.—BOSWELL.

If he had a title to the legacy he could not have found any difficulty in recovering it; for had the executors resisted his claim, the whole costs, as well as the legacy, must have been paid by them, if he had been the child to whom it was given.

The talents of Savage, and the mingled fire, rudeness, pride, meanness, and ferocity of his character,[1] concur in making it credible that he was fit to plan and carry on an ambitious and daring scheme of imposture, similar instances of which have not been wanting in higher spheres in the history of different countries, and have had a considerable degree of success.

Yet, on the other hand, to the companion of Johnson (who, through whatever medium he was conveyed into this world,—be it ever so doubtful "to whom related, or by whom begot," was, unquestionably, a man of no common endowments), we must allow the weight of general repute as to his *status* or parentage, though illicit; and supposing him to be an impostor, it seems strange that Lord Tyrconnel, the nephew of Lady Macclesfield, should patronise him, and even admit him as a guest in his family.[2] Lastly, it must ever appear very suspicious, that three different accounts of the life of Richard Savage, one published in " The Plain Dealer," in 1724, another in 1727, and another by the powerful pen of Johnson, in 1744, and all of them while Lady Macclesfield was alive, should, notwithstanding the severe attacks upon her, have been suffered to pass without any public and effectual contradiction.

I have thus endeavoured to sum up the evidence upon the case as fairly as I can, and the result seems to be, that the world must vibrate in a state of uncertainty as to what was the truth.

This digression, I trust, will not be censured, as it relates to a matter

[1] Johnson's companion appears to have persuaded that lofty minded man that he resembled him in having a noble pride; for Johnson, after painting in strong colours the quarrel between Lord Tyrconnel and Savage, asserts that " the spirit of Mr. Savage, indeed, never suffered him to solicit a reconciliation; he returned reproach for reproach, and insult for insult." But the respectable gentleman to whom I have alluded, has in his possession a letter from Savage, after Lord Tyrconnel had discarded him, addressed to the Reverend Mr. Gilbert, his lordship's chaplain, in which he requests him, in the humblest manner, to represent his case to the Viscount.—BOSWELL.

[2] Trusting to Savage's information, Johnson represents this unhappy man's being received as a companion by Lord Tyrconnel, and pensioned by his lordship, as posterior to Savage's conviction and pardon. But I am assured that Savage had received the voluntary bounty of Lord Tyrconnel, and had been dismissed by him long before the murder was committed, and that his lordship was very instrumental in procuring Savage's pardon, by his intercession with the Queen, through Lady Hertford. If, therefore, he had been desirous of preventing the publication by Savage, he would have left him to his fate. Indeed, I must observe, that although Johnson mentions that Lord Tyrconnel's patronage of Savage was "upon his promise to lay aside his design of exposing the cruelty of his mother," the great biographer has forgotten that he himself has mentioned that Savage's story had been told several years before in "The Plain Dealer," from which he quotes this strong saying of the generous Sir Richard Steele, that the "inhumanity of his mother had given him a right to find every good man his father." At the same time it must be acknowledged that Lady Macclesfield and her relations might still wish that her story should not be brought into more conspicuous notice by the satirical pen of Savage.—BOSWELL

exceedingly curious, and very intimately connected with Johnson, both as a man and an author.[1]

He this year wrote the "Preface to the Harleian Miscellany."* The selection of the pamphlets of which it was composed was made by Mr. Oldys, a man of eager curiosity and indefatigable diligence, who first exerted that spirit of inquiry into the literature of the old English writers by which the works of our great dramatic poet have of late been so signally illustrated.

In 1745 he published a pamphlet entitled, "Miscellaneous Observations on the Tragedy of Macbeth, with Remarks on Sir. T. H.'s (Sir Thomas Hanmer's) Edition of Shakspeare."* To which he affixed proposals for a new edition of that poet.

As we do not trace anything else published by him during the course of this year, we may conjecture that he was occupied entirely with that work. But the little encouragement which was given by the public to his anonymous proposals for the execution of a task which Warburton was known to have undertaken, probably damped his ardour. His pamphlet, however, was highly esteemed, and was fortunate enough to obtain the approbation even of the supercilious Warburton himself, who, in the Preface to his Shakspeare, published two years afterwards, thus mentioned it : "As to all those things which have been published under the titles of *Essays, Remarks, Observations*, &c., on Shakspeare, if you except some Critical Notes on Macbeth, given as a specimen of a projected edition, and written, as appears, by a man of parts and genius, the rest are absolutely below a serious notice."

Of this flattering distinction shown to him by Warburton, a very grateful remembrance was ever entertained by Johnson, who said, "He praised me at a time when praise was of value to me."

In 1746 it is probable that he was still employed upon his Shakspeare, which perhaps he laid aside for a time, on account of the high expectations which were formed of Warburton's edition of that great poet. It is somewhat curious, that his literary career appears to have been almost totally suspended in the years 1745 and 1746, those years which were marked by a civil war in Great Britain, when a rash attempt was made to restore the House of Stuart to the throne. That he had a tenderness for that unfortunate House, is well known ; and some may

---

* Miss Mason, after having forfeited the title of Lady Macclesfield by divorce, was married to Colonel Brett, and it is said was well known in all the polite circles. Colley Cibber, I am informed, had so high an opinion of her taste and judgment as to genteel life and manners, that he submitted every scene of his "Careless Husband" to Mrs. Brett's revisal and correction. Colonel Brett was reported to be free in his gallantry with his lady's maid. Mrs. Brett came into a room one day in her own house, and found the Colonel and her maid both fast asleep in two chairs. She tied a white handkerchief round her husband's neck, which was a sufficient proof that she had discovered his intrigue; but she never at any time took notice of it to him. This incident, as I am told, gave occasion to the well-wrought scene of Sir Charles and Lady Easy, and Edging.—BOSWELL.

fancifully imagine, that a sympathetic anxiety impeded the exertion of his intellectual powers ; but I am inclined to think, that he was, during this time, sketching the outlines of his great philological work.

None of his letters during those years are extant, so far as I can discover. This is much to be regretted. It might afford some entertainment to see how he then expressed himself to his private friends concerning state affairs. Dr. Adams informs me, that "at this time a favourite object which he had in contemplation was 'The Life of Alfred ;' in which, from the warmth with which he spoke about it, he would, I believe, had he been master of his own will, have engaged himself, rather than on any other subject."

In 1747 it is supposed that the "Gentleman's Magazine" for May was enriched by him with five short poetical pieces, distinguished by three asterisks. The first is a translation, or rather a paraphrase, of a Latin Epitaph on Sir Thomas Hanmer. Whether the Latin was his, or not, I have never heard, though I should think it probably was, if it be certain that he wrote the English ; as to which my only cause of doubt is, that his slighting character of Hanmer as an editor, in his "Observations on Macbeth," is very different from that in the Epitaph. It may be said, that there is the same contrariety between the character in the Observations, and that in his own Preface to Shakspeare ; but a considerable time elapsed between the one publication and the other, whereas the Observations and the Epitaph came close together. The others are, "To Miss ——, on her giving the author a gold and silk network Purse of her own weaving ;" "Stella in Mourning ;" "The Winter's Walk ;" " An Ode ;" and, "To Lyce, an elderly Lady." I am not positive that all these were his productions ;[1] but as "The Winter's Walk" has never been controverted to be his, and all of them have the same mark, it is reasonable to conclude that they are all written by the same hand. Yet to the Ode, in which we find a passage very characteristic of him, being a learned description of the gout,

> " Unhappy, whom to beds of pain
> *Arthritic* tyranny consigns,"

there is the following note, "The author being ill of the gout ;" but Johnson was not attacked with that distemper till a very late period of his life. May not this, however, be a poetical fiction ? Why may not a poet suppose himself to have the gout, as well as suppose himself to be in love, of which we have innumerable instances, and which has

---

[1] In the "Universal Visiter," to which Johnson contributed, the mark which is affixed to some pieces unquestionably his, is also found subjoined to others, of which he certainly was not the author. The mark therefore will not ascertain the poems in question to have been written by him. Some of them were probably the productions of Hawkesworth, who, it is believed, was afflicted with the gout. The verses "On a Purse," were inserted afterwards in Mrs. Williams's " Miscellanies," and are, unquestionably, Johnson's.—MALONE.

been admirably ridiculed by Johnson in his "Life of Cowley?" I have also some difficulty to believe that he could produce such a group of *conceits* as appear in the verses of Lyce, in which he claims for this ancient personage as good a right to be assimilated to *heaven*, as nymphs whom other poets have flattered ; he therefore ironically ascribes to her the attributes of the *sky*, in such stanzas as this :

> "Her teeth the *night* with *darkness* dies,
> She's *starr'd* with pimples o'er ;
> Her tongue like nimble *lightning* plies,
> And can with *thunder* roar."

But as at a very advanced age he could condescend to trifle in *namby-pamby* rhymes to please Mrs. Thrale and her daughter, he may have in his earlier years, composed such a piece as this.

It is remarkable, that in this first edition of "The Winter's Walk," the concluding line is much more Johnsonian than it was afterwards printed ; for in subsequent editions, after praying Stella to "snatch him to her arms," he says,

> "And *shield* me from the *ills* of life."

Whereas, in the first edition it is

> "And *hide* me from the *sight* of life."

A horror at life in general is more consonant with Johnson's habitual gloomy cast of thought.

I have heard him repeat with great energy the following verses, which appeared in the "Gentleman's Magazine" for April this year ; but I have no authority to say they were his own. Indeed one of the best critics of our age suggests to me, that "the word *indifferently* being used in the sense of *without concern*, and being also very unpoetical, renders it improbable that they should have been his composition.'"

"ON LORD LOVAT'S EXECUTION.

> "Pitied by *gentle minds* KILMARNOCK died ;
> The *brave*, BALMERINO, were on thy side ;
> RADCLIFFE, unhappy in his crimes of youth,
> Steady in what he still mistook for truth,
> Beheld his death so decently unmoved
> The *soft* lamented, and the *brave* approved.
> But LOVAT's fate indifferently we view,
> True to no *King*, to no *religion* true :
> No *fair* forgets the *ruin* he has done ;
> No *child* laments the *tyrant* of his *son* ;

No *tory* pities, thinking what he was ;
No *whig* compassions, *for he left the cause ;*
The *brave* regret not, for he was not brave ?
The *honest* mourn not, knowing him a knave !"[1]

This year his old pupil and friend, David Garrick, having become joint patentee and manager of Drury-lane Theatre, Johnson honoured his opening of it with a Prologue,* which, for just and manly dramatic criticism on the whole range of the English stage, as well as for poetical excellence,[2] is unrivalled. Like the celebrated Epilogue to the " Distressed Mother," it was, during the season, often called for by the audience. The most striking and brilliant passages of it have been so often repeated, and are so well recollected by all the lovers of the drama and of poetry, that it would be superfluous to point them out. In the " Gentleman's Magazine" for December this year he inserted an " Ode on Winter," which is, I think, an admirable specimen of his genius for lyric poetry.

But the year 1747 is distinguished as the epoch when Johnson's arduous and important work, his " DICTIONARY OF THE ENGLISH LAN-GUAGE," was announced to the world, by the publication of its plan or prospectus.

How long this immense undertaking had been the object of his con-

LORD LOVAT.

templation I do not know. I once asked him by what means he had attained to that astonishing knowledge of our language, by which he was enabled to realise a design of such extent and accumulated difficulty. He told me, that "it was not the effect of particular study, but

[1] These verses are somewhat too severe on the extraordinary person who is the chief figure in them ; for he was undoubtedly brave. His pleasantry during his solemn trial (in which, by the way, I have heard Mr. David Hume observe, that we have one of the very few speeches of Mr. Murray, now Earl of Mansfield authentically given) was very remarkable. When asked if he had any questions to put to Sir Everard Fawkener, who was one of the strongest witnesses against him, he answered, " I only wish him joy of his young wife." And after sentence of death, in the horrible terms in such cases of treason, was pronounced upon him, and he was retiring from the bar, he said, " Fare you well, my lords, we shall not all meet again in one place." He behaved with perfect composure at his execution, and called out, " *Dulce et decorum est pro patriâ mori.* BOSWELL.

[2] My friend Mr. Courtnay, whose eulogy on Johnson's Latin Poetry has been inserted in this work, is no less happy in praising his English Poetry.

But hark, he sings! the strain even Pope admires ;
Indignant virtue her own bard inspires,
Sublime as Juvenal he pours his lays,
And with the Roman shares congenial praise ;—
In glowing numbers now he fires the age,
And Shakspeare's sun relumes the clouded stage.—BOSWELL.

that it had grown up in his mind insensibly." I have been informed by Mr. James Dodsley, that several years before this period, when Johnson was one day sitting in his brother Robert's shop, he heard his brother suggest to him that a dictionary of the English language would be a work that would be well received by the public ; that Johnson seemed at first to catch at the proposition, but, after a pause, said, in his abrupt decisive manner, " I believe I shall not undertake it." That he, however had bestowed much thought upon the subject before he published his " Plan," is evident from the enlarged, clear, and accurate views which it exhibits ; and we find him mentioning in that tract, that many of the writers whose testimonies were to be produced as authorities were selected by Pope; which proves that he had been furnished, probably by Mr. Robert Dodsley, with whatever hints that eminent poet had contributed towards a great literary project, that had been the subject of important consideration in a former reign.

The booksellers who contracted with Johnson, single and unaided, for the execution of a work, which in other countries has not been effected but by the co-operating exertions of many, were Mr. Robert Dodsley, Mr. Charles Hitch, Mr. Andrew Millar, the two Messieurs Longman, and the two Messieurs Knapton. The price stipulated was fifteen hundred and seventy-five pounds.

The " Plan" was addressed to Philip Dormer, Earl of Chesterfield, then one of his Majesty's Principal Secretaries of State ; a nobleman who was very ambitious of literary distinction, and who, upon being informed of the design, had expressed himself in terms very favourable to its success. There is, perhaps, in everything of any consequence, a secret history which it would be amusing to know, could we have it authentically communicated. Johnson told me,[1] " Sir, the way in which the plan of my Dictionary came to be inscribed to Lord Chesterfield was this : I had neglected to write it by the time appointed. Dodsley suggested a desire to have it addressed to Lord Chesterfield. I laid hold of this as a pretext for delay, that it might be better done, and let Dodsley have his desire. I said to my friend, Dr. Bathurst, ' Now if any good comes of my addressing to Lord Chesterfield, it will be ascribed to deep policy, when, in fact, it was only a casual excuse for laziness.' "

It is worthy of observation that the " Plan" has not only the substantial merit of comprehension, perspicuity, and precision, but that the language of it is unexceptionably excellent ; it being altogether free from that inflation of style, and those uncommon but apt and energetic words, which in some of his writings have been censured with more petulance than justice ; and never was there a more dignified strain of compliment than that in which he courts the attention of one who, he had been persuaded to believe, would be a respectable patron.

[1] September 22, 1777, going from Ashbourne in Derbyshire to see Ilam.—BOSWELL

"With regard to questions of purity or propriety," says he, "I was once in doubt whether I should not attribute to myself too much in attempting to decide them, and whether my province was to extend beyond the proposition of the question, and the display of the suffrages on each side; but I have been since determined, by your lordship's opinion, to interpose my own judgment, and shall therefore endeavour to support what appears to me most consonant to grammar and reason. Ausonius thought that modesty forbade him to plead inability for a task to which Cæsar had judged him equal:—

> ' *Cur me posse negem, posse quod ille putat ?*'

And I may hope, my lord, that since you, whose authority in our language is so generally acknowledged, have commissioned me to declare my own opinion, I shall be considered as exercising a kind of vicarious jurisdiction: and that the power which might have been denied to my own claim will be readily allowed me as the delegate of your lordship."

This passage proves that Johnson's addressing his "Plan" to Lord Chesterfield was not merely in consequence of the result of a report by means of Dodsley that the earl favoured the design, but that there had been a particular communication with his lordship concerning it. Dr. Taylor told me that Johnson sent his "Plan" to him in manuscript for his perusal; and that when it was lying upon his table, Mr. William Whitehead happened to pay him a visit, and being shown it, was highly pleased with such parts of it as he had time to read, and begged to take it home with him, which he was allowed to do; that from him it got into the hands of a noble lord, who carried it to Lord Chesterfield. When Taylor observed this might be an advantage, Johnson replied, "No, Sir, it would have come out with more bloom if it had not been seen before by any body."

The opinion conceived of it by another noble author appears from the following extract of a letter from the Earl of Orrery to Dr. Birch:—

> "*Caledon, Dec.* 30, 1747.

"I have just now seen the specimen of Mr. Johnson's Dictionary, addressed to Lord Chesterfield. I am much pleased with the plan, and I think the specimen is one of the best that I have ever read. Most specimens disgust rather than prejudice us in favour of the work to follow; but the language of Mr. Johnson's is good, and the arguments are properly and modestly expressed. However, some expressions may be cavilled at, but they are trifles. I'll mention one: the *barren* laurel. The laurel is not barren, in any sense whatever; it bears fruits and flowers. *Sed hæ sunt nugæ,* and I have great expectations from the performance." [Birch MSS. Brit. Mus. 4303.]

That he was fully aware of the arduous nature of the undertaking he acknowledges, and shows himself perfectly sensible of it in the conclusion of his "Plan;" but he had a noble consciousness of his own abilities, which enabled him to go on with undaunted spirit.

Dr. Adams found him one day busy at his Dictionary, when the following dialogue ensued:—ADAMS : " This is a great work, Sir. How are you to get all the etymologies ?" JOHNSON : " Why, Sir, here is a shelf with Junius, and Skinner, and others ; and there is a Welsh gentleman who has published a collection of Welsh proverbs, who will help me with the Welsh." ADAMS : " But, Sir, how can you do this in three years ?" JOHNSON : " Sir, I have no doubt that I can do it in three years." ADAMS : " But the French Academy, which consists of forty members, took forty years to compile their Dictionary." JOHNSON : " Sir, thus it is : this is the proportion. Let me see ; forty times forty is sixteen hundred. As three to sixteen hundred, so is the proportion of an Englishman to a Frenchman." With so much ease and pleasantry could he talk of that prodigious labour which he had undertaken to execute.

The public has had, from another pen,[1] a long detail of what had been done in this country by prior lexicographers ; and no doubt Johnson was wise to avail himself of them, so far as they went, but the learned yet judicious research of etymology, the various yet accurate display of definition, and the rich collection of authorities were reserved for the superior mind of our great philologist. For the mechanical part he employed, as he told me, six amanuenses; and let it be remembered by the natives of North Britain, to whom he is supposed to have been so hostile, that five of them were of that country. There were two Messieurs Macbean ; Mr. Shiels, who, we shall hereafter see, partly wrote the "Lives of the Poets," to which the name of Cibber is affixed ;[2] Mr. Stewart, son of Mr. George Stewart, bookseller at Edinburgh ; and a Mr. Maitland. The sixth of these humble assistants was Mr. Peyton, who, I believe, taught French, and published some elementary tracts.

To all these painful labourers Johnson showed a never-ceasing kindness, so far as they stood in need of it. The elder Mr. Macbean had afterwards the honour of being librarian to Archibald Duke of Argyle, for many years, but was left without a shilling. Johnson wrote for him a Preface to " A System of Ancient Geography ;" and, by the favour of Lord Thurlow, got him admitted a poor brother of the Charter-house. For Shiels, who died of a consumption, he had much tenderness ; and it has been thought that some choice sentences in the " Lives of the Poets" were supplied by him. Peyton, when reduced to penury, had frequent aid from the bounty of Johnson, who at last was at the expense of burying him and his wife.

While the Dictionary was going forward, Johnson lived part of the time in Holborn, part in Gough-square, Fleet-street ; and he had an

---

[1] See Sir John Hawkins's " Life of Johnson."—BOSWELL.

Sir John Hawkins's list of former English Dictionaries is, however, by no means complete.—MALONE.

[2] See vol. iii. under April 10, 1776.—BOSWELL.

upper room fitted up like a counting-house for the purpose, in which he gave to the copyists their several tasks. The words, partly taken from other dictionaries, and partly supplied by himself, having been first written down with spaces left between them, he delivered in writing

JOHNSON'S RESIDENCE IN GOUGH SQUARE.

their etymologies, definitions, and various significations. The authorities were copied from the books themselves, in which he had marked the passages with a black-lead pencil, the traces of which could easily be effaced. I have seen several of them, in which that trouble had not been taken, so that they were just as when used by the copyists. It is remarkable, that he was so attentive in the choice of the passages in which words were authorised, that one may read page after page of his Dictionary with improvement and pleasure; and it should not pass unobserved, that he has quoted no author whose writings had a tendency to hurt sound religion and morality.

The necessary expense of preparing a work of such magnitude for the press must have been a considerable deduction from the price stipu-

TUNBRIDGE WELLS.—1748.

1748, *Aug.*
1 **Dr. Johnson**.
2 **Bishop** of Salisbury (*Dr. Gilbert*).
3 Lord Harcourt.
4 Mr. Cibber (*Colley*)
5 Mr. Garrick.

6 Mrs. Frasi (*the Singer*).
7 Mr. Nash.
8 Miss Chudleigh (*Duchess of Kingston*).
9 Mr. Pitt (*Earl of Chatham*).
10 A. Onslow, Esq (*the Speaker*).
11 Lord Fowis.

12 Duchess of Norfolk.
13 Miss Peggy Banks.
14 Lady Lincoln.
15 Mr. Lyttleton (*afterwards Ld. Lyttleton*).
16 The Baron (*a German gamester*)
17 Anonym. (*Mr Richardson*).

18 Mrs. Onslow.
19 Miss Onslow.
20 Mrs. Johnson (*the Doctor's wife*).
21 Mr. Whiston.
22 Loggan the Artist.
23 The Woman of the Well.

lated to be paid for the copyright. I understand that nothing was
allowed by the booksellers on that account ; and I remember his telling
me that a large portion of it having, by mistake, been written upon both
sides of the paper, so as to be inconvenient for the compositor, it cost
him twenty pounds to have it transcribed upon one side only.

He is now to be considered as "tugging at his oar," as engaged in
a steady continued course of occupation, sufficient to employ all his
time for some years, and which was the best preventive of that constitutional melancholy which was ever lurking about him, ready to trouble
his quiet. But his enlarged and lively mind could not be satisfied
without more diversity of employment, and the pleasure of animated
relaxation.[1] He therefore not only exerted his talents in occasional
composition, very different from Lexicography, but formed a club in
Ivy-lane, Paternoster-row, with a view to enjoy literary discussion, and
amuse his evening hours. The members associated with him in this
little society were, his beloved friend Dr. Richard Bathurst, Mr. Hawkesworth, afterwards well known by his writings ; Mr. John Hawkins, an
attorney,[2] and a few others of different professions.

In the "Gentleman's Magazine" for May of this year he wrote a
"Life of Roscommon,"* with Notes, which he afterwards much im
proved (indenting the notes into text), and inserted amongst his "Lives
of the English Poets."

Mr. Dodsley this year brought out his "Preceptor," one of the
most valuable books for the improvement of young minds that has
appeared in any language ; and to this meritorious work Johnson furnished "The Preface," * containing a general sketch of the book, with
a short and perspicuous recommendation of each article ; as also, "The
Vision of Theodore, the Hermit, found in his Cell," * a most beautiful
allegory of human life, under the figure of ascending the mountain of
Existence. The Bishop of Dromore heard Dr. Johnson say that he
thought this was the best thing he ever wrote.

[1] For the sake of relaxation from his literary labours, and probably, also, for Mrs. Johnson's
health, he this summer visited Tunbridge Wells, then a place of much greater resort than it is
at present. Here he met Mr. Cibber, Mr. Garrick, Mr. Samuel Richardson, Mr. Whiston, Mr.
Onslow (the Speaker), Mr. Pitt, Mr. Lyttleton, and several other distinguished persons. In a
print, representing some of "the remarkable characters" who were at Tunbridge Wells in
1748, and copied from a drawing of the same size (see "Richardson's Correspondence"), Dr
Johnson stands the first figure.—MALONE.

[2] He was afterwards for several years Chairman of the Middlesex Justices; and, upon occasion of presenting an address to the King, accepted the usual offer of Knighthood. He is
author of "A History of Music," in five volumes in quarto. By assiduous attendance upon
Johnson in his last illness, he obtained the office of one of his executors; in consequence of
which the booksellers of London employed him to publish an edition of Dr. Johnson's Works,
and to write his Life.—BOSWELL.

DAVID GARRICK.

CHAPTER VI.—1749—1750.

PUBLICATION OF "THE VANITY OF HUMAN WISHES"—TRAGEDY OF "IRENE" PERFORMED AT DRURY-LANE THEATRE — COMMENCEMENT OF THE "RAMBLER" — REPUBLISHED IN EDINBURGH — GENERAL ESTIMATE OF THE MERITS OF THIS WORK — PROLOGUE TO "COMUS," WHEN PERFORMED FOR THE BENEFIT OF MILTON'S GRAND-DAUGHTER, AND LETTER IN FAVOUR OF THE UNDERTAKING.

IN January, 1749, he published "The Vanity of Human Wishes, being the Tenth Satire of Juvenal imitated." * He, I believe, composed it the preceding year.[1] Mrs. Johnson, for the sake of country air, had lodgings at Hampstead, to which he resorted occasionally, and there the greatest part, if not the whole, of this "Imitation" was written. The fervid rapidity with which it was produced is scarcely credible. I have heard him say that he composed seventy lines of it in one day, without putting one of them upon paper till they were finished. I remember when I once regretted to him that he had not given us more of "Juvenal's Satires," he said he probably should give more, for he had them all in his head : by which I understood that he had the originals

---

[1] Sir John Hawkins, with solemn inaccuracy, represents this poem as a consequence of the indifferent reception of his tragedy. But the fact is, that the poem was published on the 9th of January, and the tragedy was not acted till the 6th of the February following — BOSWELL

and correspondent allusions floating in his mind, which he could, when he pleased, embody and render permanent without much labour. Some of them, however, he observed, were too gross for imitation.

The profits of a single poem, however excellent, appear to have been very small in the last reign, compared with what a publication of the same size has since been known to yield. I have mentioned, upon Johnson's own authority, that for his " London" he had only ten guineas ; and now, after his fame was established, he got for his " Vanity of Human Wishes " but five guineas more, as is proved by an authentic document in my possession.[1]

It will be observed that he reserves to himself the right of printing one edition of this satire, which was his practice upon occasion of the sale of all his writings ; it being his fixed intention to publish at some period, for his own profit, a complete collection of his works.

His " Vanity of Human Wishes " has less of common life, but more of a philosophic dignity than his "London." More readers, therefore, will be delighted with the pointed spirit of " London," than with the profound reflection of " The Vanity of Human Wishes." Garrick, for instance, observed in his sprightly manner, with more vivacity than regard to just discrimination, as is usual with wits, " When Johnson lived much with the Herveys, and saw a good deal of what was passing in life, he wrote his ' London,' which is lively and easy ; when he became more retired, he gave us his ' Vanity of Human Wishes,' which is as hard as Greek. Had he gone on to imitate another satire, it would have been as hard as Hebrew." [2]

But " The Vanity of Human Wishes " is, in the opinion of the best judges, as high an effort of ethic poetry as any language can show. The instances of variety of disappointment are chosen so judiciously, and painted so strongly, that, the moment they are read, they bring conviction to every thinking mind. That of the scholar must have depressed the too sanguine expectations of many an ambitious student.[3]

---

[1] " Nov. 25, 1748, I received of Mr. Dodsley fifteen guineas, for which I assign to him the right of copy of an ' Imitation of the Tenth Satire of Juvenal,' written by me, reserving to myself the right of printing one edition.   SAM. JOHNSON."
" London, 29 June, 1786. A true copy, from the original in Dr. Johnson's handwriting.
JAS. DODSLEY."—BOSWELL

[2] From Mr. Langton.—BOSWELL.

[3] In this poem one of the instances mentioned of unfortunate men is *Lydiat*:

" Hear Lydiat's life, and Galileo's end."

The history of Lydiat being little known, the following account of him may be acceptable to many of my readers. It appeared as a note in the Supplement to the " Gentleman's Magazine" for 1748, in which some passages extracted from Johnson's poem were inserted, and it should have been added in the subsequent editions.—" A very learned divine and mathematician, Fellow of New College, Oxon, and Rector of Okerton, near Banbury. He wrote, among many others, a Latin treatise, ' *De Natura Cœli, &c.*' in which he attacked the sentiments of Scaliger and Aristotle, not bearing to hear it urged, *that some things are true in philosophy, and false in divinity*. He made above six hundred Sermons on the Harmony of the Evangelists. Being unsuccessful in publishing his works, he lay in the prison of Bocardo at Oxford, and in

That of the warrior, Charles of Sweden, is, I think, as highly finished a picture as can possibly be conceived.

Were all the other excellences of this poem annihilated, it must ever have our grateful reverence from its noble conclusion ; in which we are consoled with the assurance that happiness may be attained, if we "apply our hearts" to piety :—

> " Where, then, shall hope and fear their objects find?
> Shall dull suspense corrupt the stagnant mind?
> Must helpless man, in ignorance sedate,
> Roll darkling down the torrent of his fate?
> Shall no dislike alarm, no wishes rise,
> No cries attempt the mercy of the skies?
> Inquirer, cease ; petitions yet remain,
> Which Heaven may hear, nor deem Religion vain.
> Still raise for good the supplicating voice,
> But leave to Heaven the measure and the choice.
> Safe in His hand, whose eye discerns afar
> The secret ambush of a specious prayer ;
> Implore his aid, in his decisions rest,
> Secure, whate'er he gives, he gives the best :
> Yet when the sense of sacred presence fires,
> And strong devotion to the skies aspires,
> Pour forth thy fervours for a healthful mind,
> Obedient passions, and a will resign'd ;
> For love, which scarce collective man can fill ;
> For patience, sovereign o'er transmuted ill ;
> For faith, which panting for a happier seat,
> Counts death kind Nature's signal for retreat,
> These goods for man the laws of Heaven ordain,
> These goods he grants, who grants the power to gain ;
> With these celestial wisdom calms the mind,
> And makes the happiness she does not find."[1]

the King's Bench, till Bishop Usher, Dr. Laud, Sir William Boswell, and Dr. Pink, released him by paying his debts. He petitioned King Charles I. to be sent into Ethiopia, &c. to procure MSS. Having spoken in favour of monarchy and bishops, he was plundered by the Parliament forces, and twice carried away prisoner from his rectory; and afterwards had not a shirt to shift him in three months, without he borrowed it, and died very poor in 1646." —Boswell.

[1] In this poem, a line in which the danger attending on female beauty is mentioned, has very generally, I believe, been misunderstood :—

> " Yet Vane could tell what ills from beauty spring,
> And Sedley curs'd the form that pleas'd a king."

The lady mentioned in the first of these verses, was not the celebrated Lady Vane, whose memoirs were given to the public by Dr. Smollett, but Anne Vane, who was mistress to Frederick, Prince of Wales, and died in 1736, not long before Johnson settled in London. Some account of this lady was published, under the title of " The Secret History of Vanella," 8vo. 1732. See also "Vanella in the Straw," 4to. 1732. In Mr. Boswell's " Tour to the Hebrides" (v. 37 4th edit.), we find some observations respecting the lines in question :—

Garrick being now vested with theatrical power by being manager of
Drury-lane Theatre, he kindly and generously made use of it to bring out
Johnson's tragedy, which had been long kept back for want of encouragement.   But in this benevolent purpose he met with no small difficulty
from the temper of Johnson, which could not brook that a drama which
he had formed with much study, and had been obliged to keep more
than the nine years of Horace, should be revised and altered at the
pleasure of an actor. Yet Garrick knew well, that without some alterations it would not be fit for the stage. A violent dispute having ensued
between them, Garrick applied to the Reverend Dr. Taylor to interpose.
Johnson was at first very obstinate.   "Sir," said he, "the fellow wants
me to make 'Mahomet' run mad, that he may have an opportunity of
tossing his hands and kicking his heels."[1]   He was, however, at last,
with difficulty, prevailed on to comply with Garrick's wishes, so as to
allow of some changes ; but still there were not enough.

Dr. Adams was present the first night of the representation of "Irene,"
and gave me the following account :—" Before the curtain drew up, there
were catcalls whistling, which alarmed Johnson's friends.   The Prologue, which was written by himself in a manly strain, soothed the
audience,[2] and the play went off tolerably, till it came to the conclusion,
when Mrs. Pritchard, the heroine of the piece, was to be strangled upon

" In Dr. Johnson's ' Vanity of Human Wishes,' there is the following passage :—

> ' The teeming mother, anxious for her race,
> Begs for each birth the fortune of a face :
> Yet Vane,' &c.

" Lord Hailes told him [Johnson] he was mistaken in the instances he had given of unfortunate fair ones, for neither Vane nor Sedley had a title to that description."—His lordship
therefore thought that the lines should rather have run thus :—

> " Yet *Shore* could tell ——
> And *Valiere* curs'd " ——

"Our friend, (he added in a subsequent note, addressed to Mr. Boswell on this subject),
chose Vane, who was far from being well-look'd, and Sedley, who was so ugly that Charles II
said—his brother had her by way of penance."—MALONE.

[1] *Mahomet* was in fact played by Mr. Barry, and *Demetrius* by Mr. Garrick ; but probably at
this time the parts were not yet cast.—BOSWELL.

[2] The expression used by Dr. Adams was "soothed." I should rather think the audience
was *awed* by the extraordinary spirit and dignity of the following lines : —

> " Be this at least his praise, be this his pride,
> To force applause no modern arts are tried :
> Should partial catcalls all his hopes confound,
> He bids no trumpet quell the fatal sound ;
> Should welcome sleep relieve the weary wit,
> He rolls no thunders o'er the drowsy pit ;
> No snares to captivate the judgment spreads,
> Nor bribes your eyes, to prejudice your heads.
> Unmov'd, though witlings sneer and rivals rail,
> Studious to please, yet not ashamed to fail,
> He scorns the meek address, the suppliant strain,
> With merit needless, and without it vain ;
> In Reason, Nature, Truth, he dares to trust ;
> Ye fops be silent, and ye wits be just ! "—BOSWELL

the stage, and was to speak two lines with the bow-string round her neck. The audience cried out '*Murder! Murder!*'[1] She several times attempted to speak; but in vain. At last she was obliged to go off the stage alive." This passage was afterwards struck out, and she was carried off to be put to death behind the scenes, as the play now has it. The Epilogue, as Johnson informed me, was written by Sir William Yonge. I know not how his play came to be thus graced by the pen of a person so eminent in the political world.

Notwithstanding all the support of such performers as Garrick, Barry, Mrs. Cibber, Mrs. Pritchard, and every advantage o' dress and decoration, the tragedy of Irene did not please the public.[2] Mr Garrick's zeal carried it through for nine nights, so that the author had his three nights' profit; and from a receipt signed by him, now in the hands of Mr. James Dodsley, it appears that his friend, Mr. Robert Dodsley,

[1] This shows how ready modern audiences are to condemn in a new play what they have frequently endured very quietly in an old one. Rowe has made *Moneses* in "Tamerlane" die by the bow-string, without offence.—MALONE.

[2] I know not what Sir John Hawkins means by the *cold reception* of "Irene." I was at the first representation, and most of the subsequent. It was much applauded the first night, particularly the speech on *to-morrow*. It ran nine nights at least. It did not indeed become a stock-play, but there was not the least opposition during the representation, except the first night in the last act, where *Irene* was to be strangled on the stage, which *John* could not bear, though a dramatic poet may stab or slay by hundreds. The bow-string was not a Christian nor an ancient Greek or Roman death. But this offence was removed after the first night, and *Irene* went off the stage to be strangled. Many stories were circulated at the time, of the author's being observed at the representation to be dissatisfied with some of the speeches and conduct of the play, himself; and, like La Fontaine, expressing his disapprobation aloud.—BURNEY.

Mr. Murphy, in his "Life of Johnson," p. 53, says, "The amount of the three benefit nights for the tragedy of 'Irene,' it is to be feared, were not very considerable, as the profit, that stimulating motive, never invited the author to another dramatic attempt."

On the word "profit," the late Mr. Isaac Reed in his copy of that Life, which I purchased at the sale of his library, has added a manuscript note, containing the following receipts on Johnson's three benefit nights:—

"Third night's receipt	£177	1	6
Sixth	106	4	0
Ninth	101	11	6
	384	17	0
Charges of the House	189	0	0
Profit	195	17	0
He also received for the Copy	100	0	0
In all	£295	17	0 "

In a preceding page (52) Mr. Murphy says, "'Irene' was acted at Drury-lane on Monday. Feb. 6, and from that time, without interruption, to Monday, February the 20th, being in all thirteen nights."

On this Mr. Reed somewhat indignantly has written—"This is false; it was acted only nine nights, and never repeated afterwards. Mr. Murphy, in making the above calculation, includes both the Sundays and Lent-days.'

The blunder, however, is that of the Monthly Reviewer, from whom Murphy took, without acknowledgment, the greater part of his Essay. M. R. vol. lxxvii. p. 135.—A. CHALMERS.

gave him one hundred pounds for the copy, with his usual reservation of the right of one edition.

"Irene," considered as a poem, is entitled to the praise of superior excellence. Analysed into parts, it will furnish a rich store of noble sentiments, fine imagery, and beautiful language; but it is deficient in pathos, in that delicate power of touching the human feelings, which is the principal end of the drama.[1] Indeed Garrick has complained to me that Johnson not only had not the faculty of producing the impressions of tragedy, but that he had not the sensibility to perceive them. His great friend Mr. Walmesley's prediction, that he would "turn out a fine tragedy writer," was, therefore, ill-founded. Johnson was wise enough to be convinced that he had not the talents necessary to write successfully for the stage, and never made another attempt in that species of composition.

When asked how he felt upon the ill success of his tragedy, he replied, "Like the Monument;" meaning that he continued firm and unmoved as that column. And let it be remembered, as an admonition to the *genus irritabile* of dramatic writers, that this great man, instead of peevishly complaining of the bad taste of the town, submitted to its decision without a murmur. He had, indeed, upon all occasions, a great deference for the general opinion : "A man," said he, "who writes a book, thinks himself wiser or wittier than the rest of mankind; he supposes that he can instruct or amuse them, and the public to whom he appeals must, after all, be the judges of his pretensions."

On occasion of this play being brought upon the stage, Johnson had a fancy, that as a dramatic author, his dress should be more gay than what he ordinarily wore; he therefore appeared behind the scenes, and even in one of the side boxes, in a scarlet waistcoat, with rich gold lace, and a gold laced hat. He humorously observed to Mr. Langton, "that when in that dress he could not treat people with the same ease as when in his usual plain clothes." Dress indeed, we must allow, has more effect even upon strong minds than one should suppose without having had the experience of it. His necessary attendance while his play was in rehearsal, and during its performance, brought him acquainted with many of the performers of both sexes, which produced a more favourable opinion of their profession than he had harshly expressed in his " Life of Savage." With some of them he kept up an acquaintance as long as ne and they lived, and was ever ready to show them acts of kindness. He, for a considerable time, used to frequent the *Green Room*, and seemed to take delight in dissipating his gloom, by mixing in the sprightly chit-chat of the motley circle then to be found there. Mr. David Hume related to me from Mr. Garrick, that Johnson at last denied

---

[1] Aaron Hill (vol. ii. p. 355), in a letter to Mr. Mallet, gives the following account of "Irene," after having seen it :—" I was at the anomalous Mr. Johnson's benefit, and found the play his proper representative; strong sense ungraced by sweetness or decorum."—BOSWELL.

himself this amusement, from considerations of rigid virtue, saying, " I'll come no more behind your scenes, David ; for the silk stockings and white bosoms of your actresses excite my amorous propensities."

THE GREEN ROOM OF DRURY LANE THEATRE.

Mr. Beard.	Mr. Baddeley.	Mr. Woodward.	Gentleman Aickin.	Gentleman Smith.
Mrs. Garrick.	Unknown.	Mr. Macklin.	Mrs. Yates.	Mrs. Abingdon.	Mr. O'Brien.
		Mr. Hogarth.	David Garrick.	P. Garrick.

In 1750 he came forth in the character for which he was eminently qualified, a majestic teacher of moral and religious wisdom. The vehicle which he chose, was that of a periodical paper, which he knew had been, upon former occasions, employed with great success. The "Tatler," " Spectator," and "Guardian," were the last of the kind published in England, which had stood the test of a long trial ; and such an interval had now elapsed since their publication, as made him justly think that, to many of his readers, this form of instruction would, in some degree, have the advantage of novelty. A few days before the first of his Essays came out, there started another competitor for fame in the same form, under the title of "The Tatler Revived," which I believe was "born but to die." Johnson was, I think, not very happy in the choice of his title,—" The Rambler ;" which certainly is not suited to a series of grave and moral discourses, which the Italians have literally but ludicrously, translated by *Il Vagabondo*, and which has been lately assumed as the denomination of a vehicle of licentious tales, "The Rambler's Magazine." He gave Sir Joshua Reynolds the following account of its getting this name :—" What *must* be done, Sir, *will* be done. When I was to begin publishing that paper, I was at a loss how to name it. I sat down at night upon my bedside, and resolved that I would not go to sleep till I had fixed its title. The 'Rambler' seemed the best that occurred, and I took it."[1]

With what devout and conscientious sentiments this paper was undertaken, is evidenced by the following prayer, which he composed and offered up on the occasion :—

" Almighty God, the giver of all good things, without whose help all labour is ineffectual, and without whose grace all wisdm is folly; grant, I beseech Thee, that in this undertaking thy Holy Spirit may not be withheld from me, but that I may promote thy glory, and the salvation of myself and others: grant this, O Lord, for the sake of thy Son, Jesus Christ. Amen."—[Pr. & Med. p. 9.]

The first paper of the "Rambler" was published on Tuesday the 20th of March, 1749-50; and its author was enabled to continue it, without interruption, every Tuesday and Saturday, till Saturday the 17th of March,[2] 1752, on which day it closed. This is a strong confirmation of the truth of a remark of his, which I have had occasion to quote elsewhere,[3] that " a man may write at any time, if he will set himself doggedly to it ;" for, notwithstanding his constitutional indolence, his depression of spirits, and his labour in carrying on his Dictionary, he answered the stated calls of the press twice a week from the stores of his mind, during all that time ; having received no assistance, except four billets in No. 10, by Miss Mulso, now Mrs. Chapone ; No. 30, by Mrs. Catherine Talbot ; No. 97, by Mr. Samuel Richardson, whom he describes in an introductory note as " An author who has enlarged the knowledge of human nature, and taught the passions to. move at the command of virtue ;" and Numbers 44 and 100, by Mrs. Elizabeth Carter.

Posterity will be astonished when they are told, upon the authority of Johnson himself, that many of these discourses, which we should suppose had been laboured with all the slow attention of literary leisure, were written in haste as the moment pressed, without even being read

---

[1] I have heard Dr. Warton mention, that he was at Mr. Robert Dodsley's with the late Mr. Moore, and several of his friends, considering what should be the name of the periodical paper which Moore had undertaken. Garrick proposed the " Salad," which, by a curious coincidence, was afterwards applied to himself by Goldsmith :—

" Our Garrick's a salad, for in him we see
     Oil, vinegar, sugar, and saltness agree!"

At last, the company having separated, without anything of which they approved having been offered, Dodsley himself thought of " The World."—Boswell.

[2] This is a mistake, into which the author was very pardonably led by the inaccuracy of the original folio edition of the "Rambler," in which the concluding paper of that work is dated on "Saturday, March 17." But Saturday was in fact the *fourteenth* of March. This circumstance, though it may at first appear of very little importance, is yet worth notice ; for Mrs. Johnson died on the *seventeenth* of March.—Malone.

[3] Journal of a Tour to the Hebrides 3rd edit. p. 28.—Boswell

over by him before they were printed.   It can be accounted for only in this way : that by reading and meditation, and a very close inspection of life he had accumulated a great fund of miscellaneous knowledge, which, by a peculiar promptitude of mind, was ever ready at his call, and which he had constantly accustomed himself to clothe in the most apt and energetic expression.   Sir Joshua Reynolds once asked him by what means he had attained his extraordinary accuracy and flow of language.   He told him, that he had early laid it down as a fixed rule to do his best on every occasion, and in every company, to impart whatever he knew in the most forcible language he could put it in ; and that by constant practice, and never suffering any careless expressions to escape him, or attempting to deliver his thoughts without arranging them in the clearest manner, it became habitual to him.[1]

Yet he was not altogether unprepared as a periodical writer ; for I have in my possession a small duodecimo volume in which he has written in the form of Mr. Locke's " Common-Place Book," a variety of hints for essays on different subjects.   He has marked upon the first blank leaf of it, " To the 128th page, collections for the ' Rambler ; ' " and in another place, " In fifty-two there were seventeen provided ; in 97—21 ; in 190—25."   At a subsequent period, probably after the work was finished, he added, " In all, taken of provided materials, 30."

Sir John Hawkins, who is unlucky upon all occasions, tells us, that " this method of accumulating intelligence had been practised by Mr. Addison, and is humorously described in one of the Spectators [No. 46], wherein he feigns to have dropped his paper of *notanda*, consisting of a diverting medley of broken sentences and loose hints, which he tells us he had collected and meant to make use of.   Much of the same kind is Johnson's ' Adversaria.' " [2]   But the truth is, that there is no resemblance at all between them.   Addison's note was a fiction, in which unconnected fragments of his lucubrations were purposely jumbled together in as odd a manner as he could, in order to produce a laughable effect. Whereas Johnson's abbreviations are all distinct, and applicable to each subject of which the head is mentioned.

For instance, there is the following specimen :—

Youth's Entry, &c.

" Baxter's account of things in which he had changed his mind as he grew up.   Voluminous.—No wonder.—If every man was to tell, or mark, on how many subjects he has changed, it would make vols. but the changes not always observed by man's self.—From pleasure to bus. [*business*] to quiet ; from

---

The rule which Dr. Johnson observed is sanctioned by the authority of two great writers of antiquity : " Ne id quidem tacendum est, quod eidem Ciceroni placet, nullum nostrum usquam negligentem esse sermonem : *quicquid loquemur, ubicunque, sit pro sua scilicet portione perfectum.*"   Quinctil. x. 7.—MALONE.

[2] Hawkins's Life of Johnson, p. 268.—BOSWELL.

thoughtfulness to reflect. to piety ; from dissipation to domestic. by impercept. gradat. but the change is certain.   Dial *non progredi progress. esse conspicimus.* Look back, consider what was thought at some dist. period.

Hope predom. in youth.   Mind not willingly indulges unpleasing thoughts. The world lies enamelled before him, as a distant prospect sun-gilt;[1]—the qualities only found by coming to it.   *Love is to be all joy—children excellent—* Fame to be constant—caresses of the great—applauses of the learned—smiles of beauty.

"*Fear of disgrace—Bashfulness*—Finds things of less importance.   Miscarriages forgot like excellencies;—if remembered of no import.   Danger of sink ing into negligence of reputation;—lest the fear of disgrace destroy activity.

"*Confidence in himself.* Long tract of life before him.—No thought of sickness.—-Embarrassment of affairs.—Distraction of Family.   Public calamities.— No sense of the prevalence of bad habits.   Negligent of time—ready to undertake—careless to pursue—all changed by time.

"*Confident of others*—unsuspecting as unexperienced—imagining himself secure against neglect, never imagines they will venture to treat him ill.   Ready to trust ; expecting to be trusted.   Convinced by time of the selfishness, the meanness, the cowardice, the treachery of men.

"Youth ambitious, as thinking honours easy to be had.

"Different kinds of praise pursued at different periods.   Of the gay in youth. dang. hurt, &c. despised.

"Of the fancy in manhood.   Ambit.—stocks—bargains.—Of the wise and sober in old age—seriousness—formality—maxims, but general—only of the rich, otherwise age is happy—but at last every thing referred to riches—no having fame, honour, influence, without subjection to caprice.

"Horace.

"Hard it would be if men entered life with the same views with which they leave it, or left as they enter it.—No hope—no undertaking—no regard to benevolence—no fear of disgrace, &c.

"Youth to be taught the piety of age—age to retain the honour of youth."

This, it will be observed, is the sketch of No. 196 of the "Rambler." I shall gratify my readers with another specimen —

"Confederacies difficult ; why.

"Seldom in war a match for single persons—nor in peace; therefore kings ake themselves absolute.   Confederacies in learning—every great work the ork of one.   *Bruy.* Scholars' friendship like ladies.   Scribebamus, &c., Mart.[2] The apple of discord—the laurel of discord—the poverty of criticism.   Swift's opinion of the power of six geniuses united.   That union scarce possible.   His remarks just;—man, a social, not steady nature.   Drawn to man by words, repelled by passions.   Orb. drawn by attraction, rep. [*repelled*] by centrifugal.

"Common danger unites by crushing other passions—but they return.

---

[1] This most beautiful image of the enchanting delusion of youthful prospect has not been used in any of Johnson's essays.—BOSWELL.

[2] Lib. xii. 96.   "In Tuccam æmulum omnium suorum studiorum."—MALONE.

Equality hinders compliance. Superiority produces insolence and envy. Too much regard in each to private interest;—too little.

"The mischiefs of private and exclusive societies.—The fitness of social attraction diffused through the whole. The mischiefs of too partial love of our country. Contraction of moral duties.—Οἵ φιλοι, οὐ φιλος.

"Every man moves upon his own centre, and therefore repels others from too near a contact, though he may comply with some general laws.

"Of confederacy with superiors every one knows the inconvenience. With equals, no authority; every man his own opinion—his own interest.

"Man and wife hardly united;—scarce ever without children. Computation, if two to one against two, how many against five? If confederacies were easy—useless; many oppresses many.—If possible only to some, dangerous. *Principum amicitias.*"

Here we see the embryo of No. 45 of "The Adventurer;" and it is a confirmation of what I shall presently have occasion to mention, that the papers in that collection marked T were written by Johnson.

This scanty preparation of materials will not, however, much diminish our wonder at the extraordinary fertility of his mind; for the proportion which they bear to the number of essays which he wrote is very small; and it is remarkable, that those for which he had made no preparation, are as rich and as highly-finished as those for which the hints were lying by him. It is also to be observed, that the papers formed from his hints are worked up with such strength and elegance that we almost lose sight of the hints, which become like "drops in the bucket." Indeed, in several instances, he has made a very slender use of them, so that many of them remain still unapplied.[1]

As the "Rambler"[2] was entirely the work of one man, there was, on

[1] Sir John Hawkins has selected from this little collection of materials what he calls the "Rudiments of two of the papers of the 'Rambler.'" But he has not been able to read the manuscript distinctly. Thus he writes, p. 266, "Sailor's fate any mansion;" whereas the original is "Sailor's life my aversion." He has also transcribed the unappropriated hints on *Writers for bread*, in which he deciphers these notable passages, one in Latin, *fatui non famœ*, instead of *frmi non famœ;* Johnson having in his mind what Thuanus says of the learned German antiquary and linguist, Xylander, who, he tells us, lived in such poverty, that he was supposed *fami non famœ scribere;* and another in French, *Degenté de fate et affamé d'argent*, instead of *Dégouté de fame* (an old word for *renommé*) *et affamé d'argent*. The manuscript being written in an exceedingly small hand, is indeed very hard to read; but it would have been better to have left blanks than to write nonsense.—BOSWELL.

[2] The "Ramblers" certainly were little noticed at first. Smart, the poet, first mentioned them to me as excellent papers, before I had heard any one else speak of them. When I went into Norfolk, in the autumn of 1751, I found but one person (the Rev. Mr. Squires, a man of learning, and a general purchaser of new books), who knew anything of them. But he had been misinformed concerning the true author, for he had been told they were written by a Mr. Johnson of Canterbury, the son of a clergyman who had had a controversy with Bentley; and who had changed the readings of the old ballad entitled "Norton Falgate," in Bentley's bold style (*meo periculo*), till not a single word of the original song was left. Before I left Norfolk in the year 1760, the "Ramblers" were in high favour among persons of learning and good taste. Others there were, devoid of both, who said that the hard *words* in the "Ramblor" were used by the author to render his Dictionary indispensably necessary.—BURNEY.

It may not be improper to correct a slight error in the preceding note, though it does not at

course, such a uniformity in its texture, as very much to exclude the charm of variety ; and the grave and often solemn cast of thinking, which distinguished it from other periodical papers, made it for some time not generally liked. So slowly did this excellent work, of which twelve editions have now issued from the press, gain upon the world at large, that even in the closing number the author says, "I have never been much a favourite of the public."

Yet, very soon after its commencement, there were who felt and acknowledged its uncommon excellence. Verses in its praise appeared in the newspapers ; and the editor of the " Gentleman's Magazine " mentions, in October, his having received several letters to the same purpose from the learned. " The Student of Oxford and Cambridge Miscellany," in which Mr. Bonnel Thornton and Mr. Colman were the principal writers, describes it as " a work that exceeds anything of the kind ever published in this kingdom, some of the 'Spectators' excepted—if, indeed, they may be excepted." And afterwards, " May the public favours crown his merits, and may not the English, under the auspicious reign of George the Second, neglect a man, who, had he lived in the first century, would have been one of the greatest favourites of Augustus." This flattery of the monarch had no effect. It is too well known, that the second George never was an Augustus to learning or genius.

Johnson told me, with an amiable fondness, a little pleasing circumstance relative to this work. Mrs. Johnson, in whose judgment and taste he had great confidence, said to him, after a few numbers of the " Rambler " had come out, " I thought very well of you before ; but I did not imagine you could have written anything equal to this." Distant praise, from whatever quarter, is not so delightful as that of a wife whom a man loves and esteems. Her approbation may be said to " come home to his *bosom ;*" and being so near, its effect is most sensible and permanent.

Mr. James Elphinston, who has since published various works, and who was ever esteemed by Johnson as a worthy man, happened to be in Scotland while the "Rambler" was coming out in single papers at London. With a laudable zeal at once for the improvement of his countrymen and the reputation of his friend, he suggested and took the charge of an

all affect the principal object of Dr. Burney's remark. The clergyman above alluded to, was Mr. Richard Johnson, schoolmaster at Nottingham, who in 1717 published an octavo volume in Latin, against Bentley's edition of Horace, entitled " Aristarchus Anti-Bentleianus." In the middle of this Latin work (as Mr. Bindley observes to me) he has introduced four pages of English criticism, in which he ludicrously corrects, in Bentley's manner, one stanza, not of the ballad the hero of which lived in Norton Falgate, but of a ballad celebrating the achievements of Tom Bostock ; who in a sea-fight performed prodigies of valour. The stanza on which this ingenious writer has exercised his wit, is as follows :—

" Then old Tom Bostock he fell to the work,
He pray'd like a Christian, but fought like a Turk.
And cut 'em off all in a jerk,
Which nobody can deny." &c.—MALONE

edition of those essays at Edinburgh, which followed progressively the London publication.[1]

The following letter written at this time, though not dated, will show how much pleased Johnson was with this publication, and what kindness and regard he had for Mr. Elphinston.

"TO MR. JAMES ELPHINSTON.

"Dear Sir,　　　　　　　　　　　　　　　　　　　　　[No date.]

"I cannot but confess the failures of my correspondence, but hope the same regard which you express for me on every other occasion, will incline you to forgive me. I am often, very often, ill; and, when I am well, am obliged to work; and, indeed, have never much used myself to punctuality. You are, however, not to make unkind inferences, when I forbear to reply to your kindness; for be assured, I never receive a letter from you without great pleasure, and a very warm sense of your generosity and friendship, which I heartily blame myself for not cultivating with more care. In this, as in many other cases, I go wrong, in opposition to conviction; for I think scarce any temporal good equally to be desired with the regard and familiarity of worthy men. I hope we shall be some time nearer to each other, and have a more ready way of pouring out our hearts.

"I am glad that you still find encouragement to proceed in your publication, and shall beg the favour of six more volumes to add to my former six, when you can, with any convenience, send them me. Please to present a set, in my name, to Mr. Ruddiman,[2] of whom, I hear, that his learning is not his highest excellence. I have transcribed the mottos and returned them, I hope not too late, of which I think many very happily performed. Mr. Cave has put the last in the Magazine,[3] in which I think he did well. I beg of you to write soon, and to write often, and to write long letters, which I hope in time to repay you; but you must be a patient creditor. I have, however, this of gratitude, that I think of you with regard, when I do not, perhaps, give the proofs which I ought, of being, Sir,

"Your most obliged and most humble servant,

"Sam. Johnson."

[1] It was executed in the printing-office of Sands, Murray, and Cochran, with uncommon elegance, upon writing-paper, of a duodecimo size, and with the greatest correctness; and Mr. Elphinston enriched it with translations of the mottos. When completed it made eight handsome volumes. It is, unquestionably, the most accurate and beautiful edition of this work; and there being but a small impression, it is now become scarce, and sells at a very nigh price.—Boswell.

With respect to the correctness of this edition, the author probably derived his information from some other person, and appears to have been misinformed; for it was *not* accurately printed, as we learn from Mr. A. Chalmers.—J. Boswell.

[2] Mr. Thomas Ruddiman, the learned grammarian of Scotland, well known for his various excellent works, and for his accurate editions of several authors. He was also a man of a most worthy private character. His zeal for the royal house of Stuart did not render him less estimable in Dr. Johnson's eye.—Boswell.

[3] If the Magazine here referred to be that for October, 1752 (see "Gent. Mag." vol. xxii., p. 68), then this letter belongs to a later period. If it relates to the Magazine for Sept. 1750 (see "Gent. Mag." vol. xx., p. 406), then it may be ascribed to the month of October in that year, and should have followed the subsequent letter.—Malone.

This year he wrote to the same gentleman another letter upon a mournful occasion.

"TO MR. JAMES ELPHINSTON.

"DEAR SIR,   *September* 25, 1750.

"You have, as I find by every kind of evidence, lost an excellent mother; and I hope you will not think me incapable of partaking of your grief. I have a mother, now eighty-two years of age, whom, therefore, I must soon lose, unless it please God that she should rather mourn for me. I read the letters in which you relate your mother's death to Mrs. Strahan, and think I do myself honour, when I tell you that I read them with tears; but tears are neither to *you* nor to *me* of any further use, when once the tribute of nature has been paid. The business of life summons us away from useless grief, and calls us to the exercise of those virtues of which we are lamenting our deprivation. The greatest benefit which one friend can confer upon another, is to guard, and excite, and elevate, his virtues. This your mother will still perform, if you diligently preserve the memory of her life, and of her death: a life, so far as I can learn, useful, wise, and innocent; and a death resigned, peaceful and holy. I cannot forbear to mention, that neither reason nor revelation denies you to hope, that you may increase her happiness by obeying her precepts; and that she may, in her present state, look with pleasure upon every act of virtue to which her instructions or example have contributed. Whether this be more than a pleasing dream, or a just opinion of separate spirits, is, indeed, of no great importance to us, when we consider ourselves as acting under the eye of God: yet, surely, there is something pleasing in the belief, that our separation from those whom we love is merely corporeal; and it may be a great incitement to virtuous friendship, if it can be made probable, that that union that has received the divine approbation shall continue to eternity.

"There is one expedient by which you may, in some degree, continue her presence. If you write down minutely what you remember of her from your earliest years, you will read it with great pleasure, and receive from it many hints of soothing recollection, when time shall remove her yet farther from you, and your grief shall be matured to veneration. To this, however painful for the present, I cannot but advise you, as to a source of comfort and satisfaction in the time to come; for all comfort and all satisfaction is sincerely wished you by, dear Sir,   Your most obliged, most obedient,

"And most humble servant,

"SAM. JOHNSON."

The "Rambler" has increased in fame as in age. Soon after its first folio edition was concluded, it was published in six duodecimo volumes;[1]

1 This is not quite accurate. In the "Gentleman's Magazine" for November, 1751, while the work was yet proceeding, is an advertisement, announcing that *four* volumes of the "Rambler" would speedily be published; and it is believed that they were published in the next month. The fifth and sixth volumes, with tables of contents and translations of the mottos, were published in July, 1752, by Payne (the original publisher), three months after the close of the work.

When the "Rambler" was collected into volumes, Johnson revised and corrected it throughout. Mr. Boswell was not aware of this circumstance, which has lately been discovered

and its author lived to see ten numerous editions of it in London, beside those of Ireland and Scotland.

I profess myself to have ever entertained a profound veneration for the astonishing force and vivacity of mind, which the "Rambler" exhibits. That Johnson had penetration enough to see, and seeing would not disguise the general misery of man in this state of being, may have given rise to the superficial notion of his being too stern a philosopher. But men of reflection will be sensible that he has given a true representation of human existence, and that he has, at the same time, with a generous benevolence displayed every consolation which our state affords us ; not only those arising from the hopes of futurity, but such as may be attained in the immediate progress through life. He has not depressed the soul to despondency and indifference. He has every where inculcated study, labour, and exertion. Nay, he has shown, in a very odious light, a man whose practice is to go about darkening the views of others, by perpetual complaints of evil, and awakening those considerations of danger and distress, which are, for the most part, lulled into a quiet oblivion. This he has done very strongly in his character of *Suspirius* [No. 55], from which Goldsmith took that of *Croaker*, in his comedy of "The Good-natured Man," as Johnson told me he acknowledged to him, and which is, indeed, very obvious.

To point out the numerous subjects which the "Rambler" treats, with a dignity and perspicuity which are there united in a manner which we shall in vain look for any where else, would take up too large a portion of my book, and would, I trust, be superfluous, considering how universally those volumes are now disseminated. Even the most condensed and brilliant sentences which they contain, and which have very properly been selected under the name of "Beauties,"[1] are of considerable bulk. But I may shortly observe, that the "Rambler" furnishes such an assemblage of discourses on practical religion and moral duty, of critical investigations, and allegorical and oriental tales, that no mind can be thought very deficient that has, by constant study and meditation, assimilated to itself all that may be found there. No. 7, written in Passion-week on abstraction and self-examination, and No. 110, on penitence and the placability of the Divine Nature, cannot be too often read. No. 54, on the effect which the death of a friend should have upon us, though rather too dispiriting, may be occasionally very medicinal to the mind. Every one must suppose the writer to have

---

and accurately stated by Mr. Alexander Chalmers in a new edition of these and various other periodical essays, under the title of "The British Essayists!"—MALONE.

[1] Dr. Johnson was gratified by seeing this selection, and wrote to Mr Kearsley, bookseller in Fleet-street, the following note :—

"Mr. Johnson sends compliments to Mr. Kearsley, and begs the favour of seeing him as soon as he can. Mr. Kearsley is desired to bring with him the last edition of what he has honoured with the name of 'Beauties.' May 20, 1782.'—BOSWELL.

been deeply impressed by a real scene ; but he told me that was not the case ; which shows how well his fancy could conduct him to the " house of mourning." Some of these more solemn papers, I doubt not, particularly attracted the notice of Dr. Young, the author of the " Night Thoughts," of whom my estimation is such, as to reckon his applause an honour even to Johnson. I have seen volumes of Dr. Young's copy of the " Rambler," in which he has marked the passages which he thought particularly excellent, by folding down a cornei of the page ; and such as he rated in a supereminent degree are marked by double folds. I am sorry that some of the volumes are lost. Johnson was pleased when told of the minute attention with which Young had signified his approbation of his Essays.

I will venture to say, that in no writings whatever can be found more *bark and steel for the mind,* if I may use the expression ; more that can brace and invigorate every manly and noble sentiment. No. 32, on patience, even under extreme misery, is wonderfully lofty, and ɩ⸲ much above the rant of stoicism, as the Sun of Revelation is brighter than the twilight of Pagan philosophy. I never read the following sentence without feeling my frame thrill : " I think there is some reason for questioning whether the body and mind are not so proportioned, that the one can bear all which can be inflicted on the other ; whether virtue cannot stand its ground as long as life, and whether a soul well principled will not be sooner separated than subdued."

Though instruction be the predominant purpose of the " Rambler," yet it is enlivened with a considerable portion of amusement. Nothing can be more erroneous than the notion which some persons have entertained, that Johnson was then a retired author, ignorant of the world ; and, of consequence, that he wrote only from his imagination, when he described characters and manners. He said to me, that before he wrote that work, he had been " running about the world," as he expressed it, more than almost any body ; and I have heard him relate, with much satisfaction, that several of the characters in the " Rambler," were drawn so naturally, that when it first circulated in numbers, a club in one of the towns in Essex imagined themselves to be severely exhibited in it, and were much incensed against a person who, they suspected, had thus made them objects of public notice ; nor were they quieted till authentic assurance was given them, that the " Rambler " was written by a person who had never heard of any one of them. Some of the characters are believed to have been actually drawn from the life, particularly that of *Prospero* from Garrick,[1] who never entirely forgave its

---

[1] That of *Gelidus,* in No. 24, from Professor Colson (see p. 48 of this vol.), and that of *Euphues* in the same paper, which, with many others, was doubtless drawn from the life. Euphues, I once thought, might have been intended to represent either Lord Chesterfield oi Soame Jenyns : but Mr. Bindleʃ, with more probability, thinks, that George Bubb Doddington, who was remarkable for the homeliness of his person, and the finery of his dress, was the person meant under that character.—MALONE.

pointed satire. For instances of fertility of fancy, and accurate description of real life, I appeal to No. 19, a man who wanders from one profession to another, with most plausible reasons for every change : No. 34, female fastidiousness and timorous refinement : No. 82, a virtuoso who has collected curiosities : No. 88, petty modes of entertaining a company, and conciliating kindness : No. 182, fortune-hunting : No. 194, 195, a tutor's account of the follies of his pupil : No. 197, 198, legacy-hunting. He has given a specimen of his nice observation of the mere external appearances of life, in the following passage in No. 179, against affectation. that frequent and most disgusting quality :—" He that stands to contemplate the crowds that fill the streets of a populous city will see many passengers, whose air and motions it will be difficult to behold without contempt and laughter ; but if he examine what are the appearances that thus powerfully excite his risibility, he will find among them neither poverty nor disease, nor any involuntary or painful defect. The disposition to derision and insult, is awakened by the softness of foppery, the swell of insolence, the liveliness of levity, or the solemnity of grandeur ; by the sprightly trip, the stately stalk, the formal strut, and the lofty mien ; by gestures intended to catch the eye, and by looks elaborately formed as evidences of importance."

Every page of the " Rambler" shows a mind teeming with classical allusion and poetical imagery : illustrations from other writers are, upon all occasions, so ready, and mingle so easily in his periods, that the whole appears of one uniform vivid texture.

The style of this work has been censured by some shallow critics as involved and turgid, and abounding with antiquated and hard words. So ill-founded is the first part of this objection, that I will challenge all who may honour this book with a perusal, to point out any English writer whose language conveys his meaning with equal force and perspicuity. It must, indeed, be allowed, that the structure of his sentences is expanded, and often has somewhat of the inversion of Latin ; and that he delighted to express familiar thoughts in philosophical language ; being in this the reverse of Socrates, who, it is said, reduced philosophy to the simplicity of common life. But let us attend to what he himself says in his concluding paper :—" When common words were less pleasing to the ear, or less distinct in their signification, I have familiarised the terms of philosophy, by applying them to popular ideas."⁴ And as to the second part of this objection, upon a late careful revision of the work, I can with confidence say, that it is amazing how few of those words, for which it has been unjustly characterised, are actually to be found in it ; I am sure, not the proportion of one to each paper. This idle charge has been echoed from one babbler to another, who have confounded Johnson's Essays with Johnson's Dictionary ; and because

---

¹ Yet his style did not escape the harmless shafts of pleasant humour; for the ingenious Bonnel Thornton published a mock Rambler in the " Drury-lane Journal."—BOSWELL.

he thought it right in a lexicon of our language to collect many words
which had fallen into disuse, but were supported by great authorities, it
has been imagined that all of these have been interwoven into his own
compositions. That some of them have been adopted by him unneces-
sarily, may, perhaps, be allowed ; but, in general they are evidently an
advantage, for without them his stately ideas would be confined and
cramped. " He that thinks with more extent than another, will want
words of larger meaning."[1] He once told me, that he had formed his
style upon that of Sir William Temple, and upon Chambers's Proposal
for his Dictionary.[2] He certainly was mistaken ; or if he imagined at
first that he was imitating Temple, he was very unsuccessful ;[3] for
nothing can be more unlike than the simplicity of Temple and the
richness of Johnson. Their styles differ as plain cloth and brocade.
Temple, indeed, seems equally erroneous in supposing that he himself
had formed his style upon Sandys's " View of the State of Religion in
the Western parts of the World."

The style of Johnson was, undoubtedly, much formed upon that of
the great writers in the last century, Hooker, Bacon, Sanderson, Hake-
well and others ; those " Giants," as they were well characterised by A
GREAT PERSONAGE, whose authority, were I to name him, would stamp
a reverence on the opinion.

We may, with the utmost propriety, apply to his learned style that
passage of Horace, a part of which he has taken as the motto to his
Dictionary :

> " Cum tabulis animum censoris sumet honesti ;
> Audebit quæcumque parùm splendoris habebunt
> Et sine pondere erunt, et honore indigna ferentur,
> Verba movere loco, quamvis invita recedant,
> Et versentur adhuc intra penetralia Vestæ.
> Obscurata diu populo bonus eruet, atque
> Proferet in lucem speciosa vocabula rerum,
> Quæ priscis memorata Catonibus atque Cethegis,
> Nunc situs informis premit et deserta vetustas :
> Adsciscet nova, quæ genitor produxerit usus :
> Vehemens, et liquidus, puroque simillimus amni,
> Fundet opes Latiumque beabit divite linguâ."

[1] Idler, No. 70.—BOSWELL.

[2] The paper here alluded to was, I believe, Chambers's Proposal for a second and improved
edition of his Dictionary, which, I think, appeared in 1738. This Proposal was probably in
circulation in 1737, when Johnson first came to London.—MALONE.

[3] The author appears to me to have misunderstood Johnson in this instance. He did not,
I conceive, mean to say, that, when he first began to write, he made Sir William Temple his
model, with a view to form a style that should resemble his in all its parts; but that he
formed his style on that of Temple and others; by taking from each those characteristic
excellencies which were most worthy of imitation.—See the matter further explained in vol. iii.
under April 9, 1778; where, in a conversation at Sir Joshua Reynolds's, Johnson himself
mentions the particular improvements which Temple made in the English style. These,
doubtless, were the objects of his imitation, so far as that writer was his model.—MALONE.

To so great a master of thinking, to one of such vast and variou
knowledge as Johnson, might have been allowed a liberal indulgence o
that licence which Horace claims in another place :

> " ———— Si fortè necesse est
> Indiciis monstrare recentibus abdita rerum,
> Fingere cinctutis non exaudita Cethegis
> Continget; dabiturque licentia sumpta pudenter :
> Et nova fictaque nuper habebunt verba fidem, si
> Græco fonte cadant, parcè detorta.   Quid autem
> Cæcilio Plautoque dabit Romanus, ademptum
> Virgilio Varioque?   Ego cur, acquirere pauca
> Si possum, invideor ; cum lingua Catonis et Ennî
> Sermonem patrium ditaverit, et nova rerum
> Nomina protulerit ?   Licuit, semperque licebit
> Signatum præsente notâ producere nomen."

Yet Johnson assured me, that he had not taken upon him to add more than four or five words to the English language, of his own formation ; and he was very much offended at the general licence by no means "modestly taken " in his time, not only to coin new words, but to use many words in senses quite different from their established meaning, and those frequently very fantastical.

Sir Thomas Brown, whose Life Johnson wrote, was remarkably fond of Anglo-Latin diction ; and to his example we are to ascribe Johnson's sometimes indulging himself in this kind of phraseology.[1] Johnson's comprehension of mind was the mould for his language. Had his conceptions been narrower, his expression would have been easier. His sentences have a dignified march ; and, it is certain that his example has given a general elevation to the language of his country, for many of our best writers have approached very near to him ; and, from the influence which he has had upon our composition, scarcely anything is written now that is not better expressed than was usual before he appeared to lead the national taste.

This circumstance, the truth of which must strike every critical reader, has been so happily enforced by Mr. Courtenay, in his "Moral and Literary Character of Dr. Johnson," that I cannot prevail on myself to withhold it, notwithstanding his, perhaps, too great partiality for one of his friends :

> " By nature's gifts ordain'd mankind to rule,
> He, like a Titian, form'd his brilliant school ,

[1] The observation of his having imitated Sir Thomas Brown has been made by many people; and lately it has been insisted on, and illustrated by a variety of quotations from Brown, in one of the popular Essays written by the Reverend Mr. Knox, master of Tunbridge-school, whom I have set down in my list of those who have sometimes not unsuccessfully imitated Dr. Johnson's style.—BOSWELL.

And taught congenial spirits to excel,
While from his lips impressive wisdom fell.
Our boasted GOLDSMITH felt the sovereign sway ;
From him deriv'd the sweet, yet nervous lay.
To Fame's proud cliff he bade our Raffaelle rise ;
Hence REYNOLDS' pen with REYNOLDS' pencil vies.
With Johnson's flame melodious BURNEY glows,
While the grand strain in smoother cadence flows.
And you, MALONE, to critic learning dear,
Correct and elegant, refin'd though clear,
By studying him, acquir'd that classic taste,
Which high in Shakspeare's fane thy statue plac'd.
Near Johnson STEEVENS stands, on scenic ground.
Acute, laborious, fertile, and profound.
Ingenious HAWKESWORTH to this school we owe.
And scarce the pupil from the tutor know.
Here early parts accomplish'd JONES sublimes.
And science blends with Asia's lofty rhymes :
Harmonious JONES ! who in his splendid strains
Sings Camdeo's sports on Agra's flowery plains.
In Hindu fictions while we fondly trace
Love and the Muses, deck'd with Attic grace.
Amid these names can BOSWELL be forgot,
Scarce by North Britons now esteem'd a Scot ?[1]
Who to the sage devoted from his youth,
Imbib'd from him the sacred love of truth ;
The keen research, the exercise of mind,
And that best art, the art to know mankind.—
Nor was his energy confin'd alone
To friends around his philosophic throne ;
Its influence wide improv'd our letter'd isle,
And lucid vigour mark'd the general style :
As Nile's proud waves, swoln from their oozy bed,
First o'er the neighbouring meads majestic spread ;
Till gathering force, they more and more expand,
And with new virtue fertilise the land."

Johnson's language, however, must be allowed to be too masculine for the delicate gentleness of female writing. His ladies, therefore, seem strangely formal, even to ridicule ; and are well denominated by the

---

[1] The following observation in Mr. Boswell's "Journal of a Tour to the Hebrides," may sufficiently account for that gentleman's being "now scarcely esteemed a Scot" by many of his countrymen :—" If he [Dr. Johnson] was particularly prejudiced against the Scots, it was because they were more in his way; because he thought their success in England rather exceeded the due proportion of their real merit; and because he could not but see in them that nationality which, I believe, no liberal-minded Scotchman will deny." Mr. Boswell, indeed, is so free from national prejudices, that he might with equal propriety have been described as—

" Scarce by *South* Britons now esteem'd a Scot."—COURTENAY.

names which he has given them, as Misella, Zozima, Properantia, Rhodoclia.

It has of late been the fashion to compare the style of Addison and Johnson, and to depreciate, I think, very unjustly, the style of Addison as nerveless and feeble, because it has not the strength and energy of that of Johnson. Their prose may be balanced like the poetry of Dryden and Pope. Both are excellent though in different ways. Addison writes with the ease of a gentleman. His readers fancy that a wise and accomplished companion is talking to them ; so that he insinuates his sentiments and taste into their minds by an imperceptible influence. Johnson writes like a teacher. He dictates to his readers as if from an academical chair. They attend with awe and admiration ; and his precepts are impressed upon them by his commanding eloquence. Addison's style, like a light wine, pleases everybody, from the first. Johnson's, like a liquor of more body, seems too strong at first, but, by degrees, is highly relished ; and such is the melody of his periods, so much do they captivate the ear, and seize upon the attention, that there is scarcely any writer, however inconsiderable, who does not aim in some degree, at the same species of excellence. But let us not ungratefully undervalue that beautiful style, which has pleasingly conveyed to us much instruction and entertainment. Though comparatively weak, opposed to Johnson's Herculean vigour, let us not call it positively feeble. Let us remember the character of his style, as given by Johnson himself :— " What he attempted, he performed ; he is *never feeble*, and he did not wish to be energetic ; he is never rapid, and he never stagnates. His sentences have neither studied amplitude nor affected brevity ; his periods, though not diligently rounded, are voluble and easy.[1] Whoever wishes to attain an English style, familiar but not coarse, and elegant but not ostentatious, must give his days and nights to the volumes of Addison." [2]

Though the "Rambler" was not concluded till the year 1752, I shall, under this year, say all that I have to observe upon it. Some of the translations of the mottos, by himself, are admirably done. He

[1] When Johnson showed me a proof-sheet of the character of Addison, in which he so highly extols his style, I could not help observing, that it had not been his own model, as no two styles could differ more from each other.—" Sir, Addison had his style, and I have mine." —When I ventured to ask him, whether the difference did not consist in this, that Addison's style was full of idioms, colloquial phrases, and proverbs, and his own more strictly grammatical, and free from such phraseology and modes of speech as can never be literally translated or understood by foreigners, he allowed the discrimination to be just.—Let any one who doubts it, try to translate one of Addison's Spectators into Latin, French, or Italian ; and though so easy, familiar, and elegant, to an Englishman, as to give the intellect no trouble, yet he would find the transfusion into another language extremely difficult, if not impossible. But a " Rambler," " Adventurer," or " Idler," of Johnson, would fall into any classical or European language, as easily as if it had been originally conceived in it.—Burney.

[2] I shall probably, in another work, maintain the merit of Addison's poetry, which has been very unjustly depreciated.—Boswell.

acknowledges to have received "elegant translations" of many of them from Mr. James Elphinston ; and some are very happily translated by a Mr. F. Lewis, of whom I never heard more, except that Johnson thus described him to Mr. Malone : "Sir, he lived in London, and hung loose upon society."[1] The concluding paper of his "Rambler" is at once dignified and pathetic. I cannot, however, but wish, that he had not ended it with an unnecessary Greek verse, translated[2] also into an English couplet. It is too much like the conceit of those dramatic poets, who used to conclude each act with a rhyme ; and the expression in the first line of his couplet, "*Celestial powers*," though proper in Pagan poetry, is ill suited to Christianity, with "a conformity" to which he consoles himself. How much better would it have been, to have ended with the prose sentence, "I shall never envy the honours which wit and learning obtain in any other cause, if I can be numbered among the writers who have given ardour to virtue, and confidence to truth."

His friend, Dr. Birch, being now engaged in preparing an edition of Ralegh's smaller pieces, Dr. Johnson wrote the following letter to that gentleman :—

"TO DR. BIRCH.

"SIR,   *Gough-square, May* 12, 1750.

"Knowing that you are now preparing to favour the public with a new edition of Ralegh's miscellaneous pieces, I have taken the liberty to send you a Manuscript, which fell by chance within my notice. I perceive no proofs of forgery in my examination of it ; and the owner tells me, that as *he* has heard, the handwriting is Sir Walter's. If you should find reason to conclude it genuine, it will be a kindness to the owner, a blind person,[3] to recommend it to the booksellers. I am, Sir,

"Your most humble servant,
"SAM. JOHNSON."

His just abhorrence of Milton's political notions was ever strong. But this did not prevent his warm admiration of Milton's great poetical merit, to which he has done illustrious justice, beyond all who have written upon the subject. And this year he not only wrote a Prologue,

---

[1] In the "Gentleman's Magazine" for October, 1752, p. 468, he is styled "the Rev Francis Lewis, of Chiswick." The late Lord Macartney, while he resided at Chiswick at my request, made some inquiry concerning him at that place, but no intelligence was obtained.

The translations of the mottos supplied by Mr. Elphinston, appeared first in the Edinburgh edition of the "Rambler," and in some instances were revised and improved, probably by Johnson, before they were inserted in the London octavo edition. The translations of the mottos affixed to the first thirty numbers of the "Rambler," were published from the Edinburgh edition, in the "Gentleman's Magazine" for September, 1750, before the work was collected into volumes.—MALONE.

[2] Not in the original edition, in folio.--MALONE.

[3] Mrs. Williams is probably the person meant.--BOSWELL.

which was spoken by Mr. Garrick, before the acting of "Comus," at Drury-Lane Theatre, for the benefit of Milton's grand-daughter, but took a very zealous interest in the success of the charity. On the day preceding the performance, he published the following letter in the " General Advertiser," addressed to the printer of that paper :—

"SIR,

"That a certain degree of reputation is acquired merely by approving the works of genius, and testifying a regard for the memory of authors, is a truth too evident to be denied ; and therefore to ensure a participation of fame with a celebrated poet, many, who would, perhaps, have contributed to starve him when alive have heaped expensive pageants upon his grave.[1]

"It must, indeed, be confessed, that this method of becoming known to posterity with honour, is peculiar to the great, or at least to the wealthy ; but an opportunity now offers for almost every individual to secure the praise of paying a just regard to the illustrious dead, united with the pleasure of doing good to the living. To assist industrious indigence, struggling with distress and debilitated by age, is a display of virtue, and an acquisition of happiness and honour.

"Whoever, then, would be thought capable of pleasure in reading the works of our incomparable Milton, and not so destitute of gratitude as to refuse to lay out a trifle in rational and elegant entertainment, for the benefit of his living remains, for the exercise of their own virtue, the increase of their reputation, and the pleasing consciousness of doing good, should appear at Drury-lane Theatre to-morrow, April 5, when 'Comus' will be performed for the benefit of Mrs. Elizabeth Foster, grand-daughter to the author,[2] and the only surviving branch of his family.

"N.B.—There will be a new prologue on the occasion, written by the author of 'Irene,' and spoken by Mr. Garrick ; and, by particular desire, there will be added to the masque a dramatic satire, called 'Lethe,' in which Mr. Garrick will perform."

[1] Alluding probably to Mr. Auditor Benson. See the "Dunciad," b. iv.—MALONE.
[2] Mrs. Elizabeth Foster died May 9, 1754.—A. CHALMERS.

JOHNSON, BEAUCLERK, AND LANGTON.

CHAPTER VII.—1751—1754.

PROGRESS OF THE "DICTIONARY AND "RAMBLER"—LAUDER'S FORGERIES—ACCOUNT OF MISS WILLIAMS—CLOSE OF THE "RAMBLER"—COMMENCEMENT OF HAWKESWORTH'S "ADVENTURER"—DEATH OF MRS. JOHNSON—ACCOUNT OF ROBERT LEVETT—JOHNSON'S FRIENDSHIP WITH REYNOLDS—LANGTON—BEAUCLERK—WRITINGS IN THE "ADVENTURER" —EXTRACT FROM DIARY—MRS. LENOX'S "SHAKSPEARE ILLUSTRATED."

IN 1751 we are to consider him as carrying on both his "Dictionary" and "Rambler." But he also wrote "The Life of Cheynel,"* in the miscellany called "The Student ;" and the Rev. Dr. Douglas having, with uncommon acuteness, clearly detected a gross forgery and imposition upon the public by William Lauder, a Scotch schoolmaster, who had, with equal impudence and ingenuity, represented Milton as a plagiary from certain modern Latin poets, Johnson, who had been so far imposed upon as to furnish a Preface and Postscript to his work, now dictated a letter for Lauder, addressed to Dr. Douglas, acknowledging his fraud in terms of suitable contrition.[1]

[1] Lest there should be any person, at any future period, absurd enough to suspect that Johnson was a partaker in Lauder's fraud, or had any knowledge of it, when he assisted him with his masterly pen, it is proper here to quote the words of Dr. Douglas, now Bishop of

This extraordinary attempt of Lauder was no sudden effort. He had brooded over it for many years : and to this hour it is uncertain what his principal motive was, unless it were a vain notion of his superiority, in being able, by whatever means, to deceive mankind. To effect this, he produced certain passages from Grotius, Masenius, and others, which had a faint resemblance to some parts of the " Paradise Lost." In these he interpolated some fragments of Hog's Latin translation of that poem, alleging that the mass thus fabricated was the archetype from which Milton copied. These fabrications he published from time to time in the " Gentleman's Magazine," and, exulting in his fancied success, he, in 1750, ventured to collect them into a pamphlet, entitled " An Essay on Milton's Use and Imitation of the Moderns in his Paradise Lost." To this pamphlet Johnson wrote a Preface, in full persuasion of Lauder's honesty, and a Postscript, recommending, in the most persuasive terms, a subscription for the relief of a granddaughter of Milton, of whom he thus speaks :—

" It is yet in the power of a great people to reward the poet whose name they boast, and from their alliance to whose genius they claim some kind of superiority to every other nation of the earth ; that poet, whose works may possibly be read when every other monument of British greatness shall be obliterated ; to reward him, not with pictures or with medals, which, if he sees, he sees with contempt, but with tokens of gratitude, which he, perhaps, may even now consider as not unworthy the regard of an immortal spirit."

Surely this is inconsistent with " enmity towards Milton," which Sir John Hawkins imputes to Johnson upon this occasion, adding,

" I could all along observe that Johnson seemed to approve, not only of the design, but of the argument; and seemed to exult in a persuasion, that the reputation of Milton was likely to suffer by this discovery. That he was not privy to the imposture, I am well persuaded ; that he wished well to the argument, may be inferred from the Preface, which indubitably was written by Johnson."

Is it possible for any man of clear judgment to suppose that Johnson, who so nobly praised the poetical excellence of Milton in a Postscript to

Salisbury, at the time when he detected the imposition. " It is to be hoped, nay it is *expected* that the elegant and nervous writer, whose judicious sentiments and inimitable style point out the author of Lauder's Preface and Postscript, will no longer allow one to *plume himself with his feathers*, who appeareth so little to deserve assistance: an assistance which I am persuaded would never have been communicated, had there been the least suspicion of those facts which I have been the instrument of conveying to the world in these sheets." " Milton no Plagiary," 2nd edit. p. 78. And his Lordship has been pleased now to authorise me to say, in the strongest manner, that there is no ground whatever for any unfavourable reflection against Dr. Johnson, who expressed the strongest indignation against Lauder.—BOSWELL.

Lauder afterwards went to Barbadoes where he died very miserably about the year 1771.—MALONE.

this very " discovery," as he then supposed it, could, at the same time, exult in a persuasion that the great poet's reputation was likely to suffer by it ? This is an inconsistency of which Johnson was incapable ; nor can anything more be fairly inferred from the Preface, than that Johnson, who was alike distinguished for ardent curiosity and love of truth, was pleased with an investigation by which both were gratified. That he was actuated by these motives, and certainly by no unworthy desire to depreciate our great epic poet, is evident from his own words ; for, after mentioning the general zeal of men of genius and literature, " to advance the honour, and distinguish the beauties of ' Paradise Lost,' " he says,

" Among the inquiries to which this ardour of criticism has naturally given occasion, none is more obscure in itself, or more worthy of rational curiosity, than a retrospect of the progress of this mighty genius in the construction of his work ; a view of the fabric gradually rising, perhaps, from small beginnings, till its foundation rests in the centre, and its turrets sparkle in the skies ; to trace back the structure through all its varieties, to the simplicity of its first plan, to find what was first projected, whence the scheme was taken, how it was improved, by what assistance it was executed, and from what stores the materials were collected, whether its founder dug them from the quarries of Nature, or demolished other buildings to embellish his own."[1]

Is this the language of one who wished to blast the laurels of Milton ?

Though Johnson's circumstances were at this time far from being easy, his humane and charitable disposition was constantly exerting itself. Mrs. Anna Williams, daughter of a very ingenious Welsh physician, and a woman of more than ordinary talents in literature, having come to London in hopes of being cured of a cataract in both her eyes, which afterwards ended in total blindness, was kindly received as a constant visitor at his house while Mrs. Johnson lived ; and, after her death, having come under his roof in order to have an operation upon her eyes performed with more comfort to her than in lodgings, she had an apartment from him during the rest of her life, at all times when he had a house.

In 1752 he was almost entirely occupied with his Dictionary. The last paper of his " Rambler " was published March 2,[2] this year ; after

[1] " Proposals [written evidently by Johnson] for printing the ' Adamus Exul' of Grotius, with a Translation and Notes by Wm. Lauder, A.M."—" Gent. Mag." 1747, vol. xvii. p. 404.—MALONE.

[2] Here the author's memory failed him, for, according to the account given in a former page (see p. 110), we should here read March 17 ; but, in truth, as has been already observed, the " Rambler" closed on Saturday, the *fourteenth* of March, at which time Mrs. Johnson was near her end, for she died on the following Tuesday, March 17. Had the concluding paper of that work been written on the day of her death, it would have been still more extraordinary than it is, considering the extreme grief into which the author was plunged by that event.— The melancholy cast of that concluding essay is sufficiently accounted for by the situation

which, there was a cessation for some time of any exertion of his talents as an essayist. But in the same year, Dr. Hawkesworth, who was his warm admirer, and a studious imitator of his style, and then lived in great intimacy with him, began a periodical paper, entitled, "The Adventurer," in connection with other gentlemen, one of whom was Johnson's much-loved friend, Dr. Bathurst ; and, without doubt, they received many valuable hints from his conversation, most of his friends having been so assisted in the course of their works.

That there should be a suspension of his literary labours during a part of the year 1752, will not seem strange, when it is considered that soon after closing his "Rambler," he suffered a loss which, there can be no doubt, affected him with the deepest distress. For on the 17th of March, O.S., his wife died. Why Sir John Hawkins should unwarrantably take upon him even to *suppose* that Johnson's fondness for her was *dissembled* (meaning simulated or assumed), and to assert, that if it was not the case, "it was a lesson he had learned by rote," I cannot conceive, unless it proceeded from a want of similar feelings in his own breast. To argue from her being much older than Johnson, or any other circumstances, that he could not really love her, is absurd, for love is not a subject of reasoning, but of feeling, and therefore there are no common principles upon which one can persuade another concerning it. Every man feels for himself, and knows how he is affected by particular qualities in the person he admires, the impressions of which are too minute and delicate to be substantiated in language.

The following very solemn and affecting prayer was found after Dr. Johnson's decease, by his servant, Mr. Francis Barber, who delivered it to my worthy friend, the Rev. Mr. Strahan, Vicar of Islington, who, at my earnest request, has obligingly favoured me with a copy of it, which he and I compared with the original. I present it to the world as an undoubted proof of a circumstance in the character of my illustrious friend, which, though some, whose hard minds I never shall envy, may attack as superstitious, will, I am sure, endear him more to numbers of good men. I have an additional, and that a personal motive for presenting it, because it sanctions what I myself have always maintained, and am fond to indulge :—

"April 26th, 1752, being after 12 at Night of the 25th.

"O Lord ! Governor of heaven and earth, in whose hands are embodied and departed spirits, if thou hast ordained the souls of the dead to minister to the living, and appointed my departed wife to have care of me, grant that I may enjoy the good effects of her attention and ministration, whether exercised by appearance, impulses, dreams, or in any other manner agreeable to thy government. Forgive my presumption, enlighten my ignorance, and however meaner

of Mrs. Johnson at the time it was written : and her death three days afterwards put an end to the Paper.—MALONE.

agents are employed, grant me the blessed influences of thy Holy Spirit, through Jesus Christ our Lord.   Amen."

What actually followed upon this most interesting piece of devotion by Johnson, we are not informed ; but I, whom it has pleased God to afflict in a similar manner to that which occasioned it, have certain experience of benignant communication by dreams.

That his love for his wife was of the most ardent kind, and, during the long period of fifty years, was unimpaired by the lapse of time, is evident from various passages in the series of his "Prayers and Meditations," published by the Rev. Mr. Strahan, as well as from other memorials, two of which I select, as strongly marking the tenderness and sensibility of his mind.

"March 28, 1753.   I kept this day as the anniversary of my Tetty's death, with prayers and tears in the morning.   In the evening I prayed for her conditionally, if it were lawful."

"April 23, 1753.   I know not whether I do not too much indulge the vain longings of affection ; but I hope they intenerate my heart, and that when I die like my Tetty, this affection will be acknowledged in a happy interview, and that in the mean time I am incited by it to piety.   I will, however, not deviate too much from common and received methods of devotion."

Her wedding-ring, when she became his wife, was, after her death, preserved by him, as long as he lived, with an affectionate care, in a little round wooden box, in the inside of which he pasted a slip of paper, thus inscribed by him in fair characters, as follows :—

> "*Eheu !*
> *Eliz. Johnson,*
> *Nupta Jul.* 9° 1736.
> *Mortua, eheu !*
> *Mart.* 17° 1752."

After his death, Mr. Francis Barber, his faithful servant and residuary legatee, offered this memorial of tenderness to Mrs. Lucy Porter, Mrs. Johnson's daughter ; but she having declined to accept of it, he had it enamelled as a mourning ring for his old master, and presented it to his wife, Mrs. Barber, who now has it.

The state of mind in which a man must be upon the death of a woman whom he sincerely loves, had been in his contemplation many years before.   In his "Irene," we find the following fervent and tender speech of *Demetrius*, addressed to his *Aspasia :*—

> "From those bright regions of eternal day,
> Where now thou shin'st amongst thy fellow saints,
> Arrayed in purer light, look down on me !
> In pleasing visions and assuasive dreams,
> O ! soothe my soul, and teach me how to lose thee."

I have, indeed, been told by Mrs. Desmoulins, who, before her marriage, lived for some time with Mrs. Johnson at Hampstead, that she indulged herself in country air and nice living, at an unsuitable expense, while her husband was drudging in the smoke of London, and that she by no means treated him with that complacency which is the most engaging quality in a wife. But all this is perfectly compatible with his fondness for her, especially when it is remembered that he had a high opinion of her understanding, and that the impressions which her beauty, real or imaginary, had orignally made upon his fancy, being continued by habit, had not been effaced, though she herself was doubtless much altered for the worse. The dreadful shock of separation took place in the night, and he immediately despatched a letter to his friend, the Rev. Dr. Taylor, which, as Taylor told me, expressed grief in the strongest manner he had ever read ; so that it is much to be regretted it has not been preserved.[1] The letter was brought to Dr. Taylor, at his house in the Cloisters, Westminster, about three in the morning ; and as it signified an earnest desire to see him, he got up, and went to Johnson as soon as he was dressed, and found him in tears and in extreme agitation. After being a little while together, Johnson requested him to join with him in prayer. He then prayed extempore, as did Dr. Taylor ; and thus by means of that piety which was ever his primary object, his troubled mind was, in some degree soothed and composed.

The next day he wrote as follows :—

"TO THE REVEREND DR. TAYLOR.

"DEAR SIR,   "*March* 18, 1752.

"Let me have your company and instruction. Do not live away from me My distress is great.

"Pray desire Mrs. Taylor to inform me what mourning I should buy for my mother and Miss Porter, and bring a note in writing with you.

"Remember me in your prayers, for vain is the help of man.

"I am, dear Sir, &c.,

"SAM. JOHNSON."

That his sufferings upon the death of his wife were severe, beyond what are commonly endured, I have no doubt, from the information of many who were then about him, to none of whom I give more credit than to Mr. Francis Barber, his faithful negro servant,[2] who came into

---

[1] In "The Gentleman's Magazine" for February, 1794 (p. 100), was printed a letter pretending to be that written by Johnson on the death of his wife. But it is merely a transcript of the 41st number of "The Idler," on the death of a friend. A fictitious date, March 17, 1751, O. S. was added by some person, previously to this paper's being sent to the publisher of that miscellany, to give a colour to this deception.—MALONE.

[2] Francis Barber was born in Jamaica, and was brought to England in 1750 by Colonel Bathurst, father of Johnson's very intimate friend, Dr. Bathurst. He was sent for some

his family about a fortnight after the dismal event. These sufferings were aggravated by the melancholy inherent in his constitution ; and although he probably was not oftener in the wrong than she was, in the little disagreements which sometimes troubled his married state during which, he owned to me, that the gloomy irritability of his existence was more painful to him than ever, he might very naturally after her death, be tenderly disposed to charge himself with slight omissions and offences, the sense of which would give him much uneasiness.[1] Accordingly we find, about a year after her decease, that he thus addressed the Supreme Being :—

"O Lord, who givest the grace of repentance, and hearest the prayers of the penitent, grant that by true contrition I may obtain forgiveness of all the sins committed, and of all duties neglected, in my union with the wife whom thou hast taken from me ; for the neglect of joint devotion, patient exhortation, and mild instruction." [Pr. and Med. p. 19.]

The kindness of his heart, notwithstanding the impetuosity of his temper, is well known to his friends ; and I cannot trace the smallest foundation for the following dark and uncharitable assertion by Sir John Hawkins :—" The apparition of his departed wife was altogether of the terrific kind, and hardly afforded him a hope that she was in a state of happiness."[2]   That he, in conformity with the opinion of many of the most able, learned, and pious Christians in all ages, supposed that there was a middle state after death, previous to the time at which departed souls are finally received to eternal felicity, appears, I think, unquestionably from his devotions :[3]—" And, O Lord, so far as it may be lawful in me, I commend to thy fatherly goodness *the soul of my departed wife ;* beseeching thee to *grant* her whatever is best in her *present state,* and *finally to receive her to eternal happiness.*" [Pr. and Med. p. 20.] But this state has not been looked upon with horror, but only as less gracious.

He deposited the remains of Mrs. Johnson in the church of Bromley in Kent,[3] to which he was probably led by the residence of his friend Hawkesworth at that place.   The funeral sermon which he composed

time, to the Rev. Mr. Jackson's school, at Barton, in Yorkshire. The Colonel by his will left him his freedom, and Dr. Bathurst was willing that he should enter into Johnson's service, in which he continued from 1752 till Johnson's death, with the exception of two intervals ; in one of which, upon some difference with his master, he went and served an apothecary in Cheapside, but still visited Dr. Johnson occasionally : in another, he took a fancy to go to sea. Part of the time, indeed, he was, by the kindness of his master, at a school in North-amptonshire, that he might have the advantage of some learning. So early, and so lasting a connection was there between Dr. Johnson and this humble friend.—Bo~~~

[1] See his beautiful and affecting " Rambler," No. 54.—MALONE.

[2] Hawkins's Life of Johnson, p. 316.

[3] It does not appear that Johnson was fully persuaded that there was a middle state : his prayers being only *conditional, i. e.* if such a state existed.—MALONE.

[4] A few months before his death, Johnson honoured her memory by the following epitaph

for her, which was never preached, but having been given to Dr
Taylor, has been published since his death, is a performance of uncommon excellence, and full of rational and pious comfort to such as are
depressed by that severe affliction which Johnson felt when he wrote it
When it is considered that it was written in such an agitation of mind
and in the short interval between her death and burial, it cannot be
read without wonder.

From Mr. Francis Barber I have had the following authentic and
artless account of the situation in which he found him recently after his
wife's death :—

" He was in great affliction. Mrs. Williams was then living in his house,
which was in Gough square. He was busy with the Dictionary. Mr. Shiels,
and some others of the gentlemen who had formerly written for him, used to
come about him. He had then little for himself, but frequently sent money to
Mr. Shiels when in distress. The friends who visited him at that time, were
chiefly Dr. Bathurst,[1] and Mr. Diamond, an apothecary in Cork-street, Burlington-gardens, with whom he and Mrs. Williams generally dined every Sunday.
There was a talk of his going to Iceland with him, which would probably have
happened, had he lived. There were also Mr. Cave, Dr. Hawkesworth, Mr
Ryland, merchant on Tower-hill, Mrs. Masters, the poetess, who lived with
Mr. Cave, Mrs. Carter, and sometimes Mrs. Macaulay; also Mrs. Gardiner,
wife of a tallow-chandler on Snow-hill, not in the learned way, but a worthy
good woman ; Mr. (now Sir Joshua) Reynolds ; Mr. Miller, Mr. Dodsley, Mr.
Bouquet, Mr. Payne, of Paternoster-row, bookseller ; Mr. Strahan, the printer ;
the Earl of Orrery, Lord Southwell, Mr. Garrick."

Many are, no doubt, omitted in this catalogue of his friends, and in
particular his humble friend Mr. Robert Levett, an obscure practiser in
physic amongst the lower people, his fees being sometimes very small
sums, sometimes whatever provisions his patients could afford him ; but
of such extensive practice in that way, that Mrs. Williams has told me

which was inscribed on her tombstone, in the church of Bromley :—

" Hic conduntur reliquiæ
ELIZABETHÆ
Antiquâ Jarvisiorum gente,
Peatlingæ, apud Leicestrienses, ortæ ;
Formosæ, cultæ, ingeniosæ, piæ ;
Uxoris, primis nuptiis, HENRICI PORTER,
Secundis, SAMUELIS JOHNSON :
Qui multum amatam, diuque defletam
Hoc lapide contexit.
Obiit Londini, Mense Mart.
A.D. MDCCLII."

MALONE.

[1] Dr. Bathurst, though a physician of no inconsiderable merit, had not the good fortune to
get much practice in London. He was, therefore, willing to accept of employment abroad,
and, to the regret of all who knew him, fell a sacrifice to the destructive climate, in the
expedition against Havannah. Mr. Langton recollects the following passage in a letter from
Dr. Johnson to Mr. Beauclerk :—" The Havannah is taken—a conquest too dearly obtained ;
for, Bathust died before it.

" Vix Priamus tanti totaque Troja fuit."

BOSWELL.

his walk was from Hounsditch to Marylebone. It appears from John-son's diary, that their acquaintance commenced about the year 1746 ; and such was Johnson's predilection for him, and fanciful estimation of his moderate abilities, that I have heard him say he should not be satisfied, though attended by all the College of Physicians, unless he had Mr. Levett with him. Ever since I was acquainted with Dr. Johnson, and many years before, as I have been assured by those who knew him earlier, Mr. Levett had an apartment in his house or his chambers, and waited upon him every morning, through the whole course of his late and tedious breakfast. He was of a strange, grotesque appearance, stiff and formal in his manner, and seldom said a word while any company was present.[4]

The circle of his friends, indeed, at this time was extensive and various, far beyond what has been generally imagined. To trace his acquaintance with each particular person, if it could be done, would be a task, of which the labour would not be repaid by the advantage. But exceptions are to be made, one of which must be a friend so eminent as Sir Joshua Reynolds, who was truly his *dulce decus*, and with whom he maintained an uninterrupted intimacy to the last hour of his life. When Johnson lived in Castle-street, Cavendish-square, he used fre-quently to visit two ladies who lived opposite to him, Miss Cotterells, daughters of Admiral Cotterell. Reynolds used also to visit there, and thus they met. Mr. Reynolds, as I have observed above, had, from the first reading of his " Life of Savage," conceived a very high admiration of Johnson's powers of writing. His conversation no less delighted him ; and he cultivated his acquaintance with the laudable zeal of one who was ambitious of general improvement. Sir Joshua, indeed, was lucky enough, at their very first meeting, to make a remark, which was so much above the common-place style of conversation, that Johnson at once perceived that Reynolds had the habit of thinking for himself. The ladies were regretting the death of a friend, to whom they owed great obligations ; upon which Reynolds observed, " You have, however, the comfort of being relieved from a burthen of gratitude." They were shocked a little at this alleviating suggestion, as too selfish ; but John-son defended it in his clear and forcible manner, and was much pleased with the *mind*, the fair view of human nature,[2] which it exhibited, like some of the reflections of Rochefaucault. The consequence was, that he went home with Reynolds, and supped with him.

Sir Joshua told me a pleasant characteristical anecdote of Johnson, about the time of their first acquaintance. When they were one evening together at the Miss Cotterells,' the then Duchess of Argyle and another lady of high rank came in. Johnson thinking that the Miss Cotterells were too much engrossed by them, and that he and his friend were neglected, as low company of whom they were somewhat ashamed, grew angry; and resolving to shock their supposed pride, by making their great visitors imagine that his friend and he were low indeed, he addressed himself in a loud tone to Mr. Reynolds, saying, " How much do you think you and I could get in a week, if we were to *work as hard* as we could?"—as if they had been common mechanics.

His acquaintance with Bennet Langton, Esq., of Langton, in Lincolnshire, another much valued friend, commenced soon after the conclusion of his "Rambler;" which that gentleman, then a youth, had read with so much admiration, that he came to London chiefly with a view of endeavouring to be introduced to its author. By a fortunate chance, he happened to take lodgings in a house where Mr. Levett frequently visited; and having mentioned his wish to his landlady, she introduced him to Mr. Levett, who readily obtained Johnson's permission to bring Mr. Langton to him; as, indeed, Johnson, during the whole course of his life, had no shyness, real or affected, but was easy of access to all who were properly recommended, and even wished to see num-

BENNET LANGTON.

bers at his *levée*, as his morning circle of company might, with strict propriety, be called. Mr. Langton was exceedingly surprised when the sage first appeared. He had not received the smallest intimation of his figure, dress, or manner. From perusing his writings, he fancied he should see a decent, well-dressed, in short, a remarkably decorous philosopher. Instead of which, down from his bedchamber, about noon, came, as newly risen, a huge uncouth figure, with a little dark wig which scarcely covered his head, and his clothes hanging loose about him. But his conversation was so rich, so animated, and so forcible, and his religious and political notions so congenial with those in which Langton had been educated, that he conceived for him that veneration and attachment which he ever preserved. Johnson was not the less ready to love Mr. Langton, for his being of a very ancient family; for I have heard him say, with pleasure, "Langton, Sir, has a grant of free-warren from Henry the Second; and Cardinal Stephen Langton, in King John's reign, was of this family."

Mr. Langton afterwards went to pursue his studies at Trinity College, Oxford, where he formed an acquaintance with his fellow-

student, Mr. Topham Beauclerk ; who though their opinions and
modes of life were so different, that it seemed utterly improbable that
they should at all agree, had so ardent a love of literature, so acute an

understanding, such elegance of manners, and so well discerned the excellent qualities of Mr. Langton, a
gentleman eminent not only for worth
and learning, but for an inexhaustible
fund of entertaining conversation,
that they became intimate friends.

Johnson, soon after this acquaintance began, passed a considerable time
at Oxford. He at first thought it
strange that Langton should associate
so much with one who had the character of being loose, both in his
principles and practice ; but, by
degrees, he himself was fascinated.
Mr. Beauclerk's being of the St.
Alban's family, and having, in some

TOPHAM BEAUCLERK.

particulars, a resemblance to Charles II., contributed, in Johnson's
imagination, to throw a lustre upon his other qualities ; and in a short
time, the moral, pious Johnson, and the gay, dissipated Beauclerk, were
companions. "What a coalition!" said Garrick, when he heard of
this, "I shall have my old friend to bail out of the Round-house." But
I can bear testimony that it was a very agreeable association. Beauclerk
was too polite, and valued learning and wit too much, to offend Johnson
by sallies of infidelity or licentiousness ; and Johnson delighted in the
good qualities of Beauclerk, and hoped to correct the evil. Innumerable
were the scenes in which Johnson was amused by these young men.
Beauclerk could take more liberty with him, than any body with whom
I ever saw him ; but, on the other hand, Beauclerk was not spared by
his respectable companion, when reproof was proper. Beauclerk had
such a propensity to satire, that at one time Johnson said to him, "You
never open your mouth but with the intention to give pain ; and you have
often given me pain, not from the power of what you said, but from
seeing your intention." At another time applying to him, with a slight
alteration, a line of Pope, he said,

"Thy love of folly, and thy scorn of fools.

Every thing thou dost shows the one, and every thing thou say'st, the
other." At another time he said to him, "Thy body is all vice, and
thy mind all virtue." Beauclerk not seeming to relish the compliment
Johnson said, "Nay, Sir, Alexander the Great, marching in triumph
into Babylon, could not have desired to have had more said to him."

Johnson was some time with Beauclerk at his house at Windsor, where he was entertained with experiments in natural philosophy. One Sunday, when the weather was very fine, Beauclerk enticed him, insensibly, to saunter about all the morning. They went into a churchyard, in the time of divine service, and Johnson laid himself down at his ease upon one of the tombstones. "Now, Sir," said Beauclerk, "you are like Hogarth's Idle Apprentice." When Johnson got his pension, Beauclerk said to him, in the humorous phrase of Falstaff, "I hope you'll now purge, and live cleanly, like a gentleman."

One night when Beauclerk and Langton had supped at a tavern in London, and sat till about three in the morning, it came into their heads to go and knock up Johnson, and see if they could prevail on him to join them in a ramble. They rapped violently at the door of his chambers in the Temple, till at last he appeared in his shirt, with his little black wig on the top of his head, instead of a nightcap, and a poker in his hand, imagining, probably, that some ruffians were coming to attack him. When he discovered who they were, and was told their errand, he smiled, and with great good humour agreed to their proposal : "What, is it you, you dogs ! I'll have a frisk with you." [1] He was soon dressed and they sallied forth together into Covent-garden, where the greengrocers and fruiterers were beginning to arrange their hampers, just come in from the country. Johnson made some attempts to help them ; but the honest gardeners stared so at his figure and manner, and odd interference, that he soon saw his services were not relished. They then repaired to one of the neighbouring taverns, and made a bowl of that liquor called *bishop*, which Johnson had always liked ; while, in joyous contempt of sleep, from which he had been roused, he repeated the festive lines,

"Short, O short, then be thy reign,
And give us to the world again !"[2]

They did not stay long, but walked down to the Thames, took a boat, and rowed to Billingsgate. Beauclerk and Johnson were so well pleased with their amusement, that they resolved to persevere in dissipation for the rest of the day : but Langton deserted them, being engaged to breakfast with some young ladies. Johnson scolded him for "leaving his social friends, to go and sit with a set of wretched *un-idea'd* girls." Garrick being told of this ramble, said to him smartly, "I heard of your frolic t'other night. You'll be in the 'Chronicle.'" Upon

---

[1] Johnson, as Mr. Kemble observes to me, might here have had in his thoughts the words of Sir John Brute (a character which doubtless he had seen represented by Garrick), who uses nearly the same expression in "The Provoked Wife," Act iii., sc. i.—Malone.

[2] Mr. Langton recollected, or Dr. Johnson repeated, the passage wrong. The lines are in Lord Lansdowne's Drinking Song to Sleep, and run thus:—

"Short, very short, be then thy reign,
For I'm in haste to laugh and drink again."—Boswell.

which Johnson afterwards observed, "*He* durst not do such a thing His *wife* would not *let* him !"

He entered upon this year, 1753, with his usual piety, as appears from the following prayer, which I transcribed from that part of his diary which he burned a few days before his death :—

"Jan. 1, 1753, N.S., which I shall use for the future.

"Almighty God, who hast continued my life to this day, grant that, by the assistance of thy Holy Spirit, I may improve the time which thou sha!t grant me, to my eternal salvation. Make me to remember, to thy glory, thy judgments and thy mercies. Make me to consider the loss of my wife, whom thou hast taken from me, that it may dispose me, by thy grace, to lead the residue of my life in thy fear. Grant this, O Lord, for Jesus Christ's sake. Amen."

He now relieved the drudgery of his Dictionary, and the melancholy of his grief, by taking an active part in the composition of " The Adventurer," in which he began to write, April 10, marking his essays with the signature T., by which most of his papers in that collection are distinguished : those, however, which have that signature, and also that of *Mysargyrus*, were not written by him, but, as I suppose, by Dr. Bathurst. Indeed, Johnson's energy of thought and richness of language are still more decisive marks than any signature. As a proof of this, my readers, I imagine, will not doubt that No. 39, on Sleep, is his ; for it not only has the general texture and colour of his style, but the authors with whom he was peculiarly conversant are readily introduced in it in cursory allusion. The translation of a passage in Statius,[1] quoted in that paper, and marked C. B., has been erroneously ascribed to Dr. Bathurst, whose Christian name was Richard. How much this amiable man actually contributed to "The Adventurer," cannot be known. Let me add, that Hawkesworth's imitations of Johnson are sometimes so happy, that it is extremely difficult to distinguish them, with certainty, from the compositions of his great archetype. Hawkesworth was his closest imitator, a circumstance of which that writer would once have been proud to be told ; though when he had become elated by having risen into some degree of consequence, he, in a conversation with me, had the provoking effrontery to say he was not sensible of it.

Johnson was truly zealous for the success of "The Adventurer ;" and very soon after his engaging in it, he wrote the following letter :—

"TO THE REVEREND DR. JOSEPH WARTON.

"DEAR SIR,   *March*, 8, 1753.

"I ought to have written to you before now, but I ought to do many things which I do not ; nor can I, indeed, claim any merit from this letter ; for being

---

[1] This is a slight inaccuracy. The Latin Sapphics, translated by C. B. in that paper, were written by Cowley, and are in his fourth book on Plants.—MALONE.

desired by the authors and proprietor of "The Adventurer," to look out for another hand, my thoughts necessarily fixed upon you, whose fund of literature will enable you to assist them, with very little interruption of your studies.

"They desire you to engage to furnish one paper a month, at two guineas a paper, which you may very readily perform. We have considered that a paper should consist of pieces of imagination, pictures of life, and disquisitions of literature. The part which depends on the imagination is very well supplied, as you will find when you read the paper; for descriptions of life, there is now a treaty almost made with an author and an authoress;[1] and the province of criticism and literature they are very desirous to assign to the commentator on Virgil.

"I hope this proposal will not be rejected, and that the next post will bring us your compliance. I speak as one of the fraternity, though I have no part in the paper, beyond now and then a motto; but two of the writers are my particular friends, and hope the pleasure of seeing a third united to them, will not be denied to, dear Sir, your most obedient and most humble servant,

"SAM. JOHNSON."

The consequence of this letter was, Dr. Warton's enriching the collection with several admirable essays.

Johnson's saying, "I have no part in the paper, beyond now and then a motto," may seem inconsistent with his being the author of the papers marked T. But he had at this time written only one number;[2] and,

---

[1] It is not improbable, that the "author and authoress, with whom a treaty was almost made,—for descriptions of life," and who are mentioned in a manner that seems to indicate some connection between them, were Henry, and his sister Sally, Fielding, as she was then popularly called. Fielding had previously been a periodical essayist, and certainly was well acquainted with life in all its varieties, more especially within the precincts of London; and his sister was a lively and ingenious writer. To this notion it perhaps may be objected, that no papers in "The Adventurer" are known to be their productions. But it should be remembered, that of several of the essays in that work, the authors are unknown; and some of these may have been written by the persons here supposed to be alluded to. Nor would the objection be decisive, even if it were ascertained that neither of them contributed anything to "The Adventurer;" for the treaty above mentioned might afterwards have been broken off. The negotiator, doubtless, was Hawkesworth, and not Johnson. Fielding was at this time in the highest reputation; having, in 1751, produced his Amelia, of which the whole impression was sold off on the day of its publication.—MALONE.

[2] The author, I conceive, is here in an error. He had before stated, that Johnson began to write in "The Adventurer" on April 10th (when No. 45 was published), above a month after the date of his letter to Dr. Warton. The two papers published previously with the signature T., and subscribed MYSARGYRUS (Nos. 34 and 41), were written, I believe, by Bonnel Thornton, who contributed also all the papers signed A. This information I received several years ago; but do not precisely remember from whom I derived it. I believe, however, my informer was Dr. Warton.

With respect to No. 39, on Sleep, which our author has ascribed to Johnson (see p. 170), even if it were written by him, it would not be inconsistent with his statement to Dr. Warton for it appeared on March 20th, near a fortnight after the date of Johnson's letter to that gentleman. But on considering it attentively, though the style bears a strong resemblance to that of Johnson, I believe it was written by his friend Dr. Bathurst, and perhaps touched in a few places by Johnson. Mr. Boswell has observed that "this paper not only has the general texture and colour of his style, but the authors with whom he was peculiarly conversant are readily introduced in it in cursory allusion." Now the authors mentioned in

besides, even at any after period he might have used the same expression, considering it as a point of honour not to own them ; for Mrs. Williams told me that, " as he had *given* those essays to Dr. Bathurst, who sold them at two guineas each, he never would own them ; nay, he used to say he did not *write* them ; but the fact was, that he *dictated* them while Bathurst wrote." I read to him Mrs. Williams's account : he smiled, and said nothing.

I am not quite satisfied with the casuistry by which the productions of one person are thus passed upon the world for the productions of another. I allow that not only knowledge, but powers and qualities of mind may be communicated, but the actual effect of individual exertion never can be transferred, with truth, to any other than its own original cause. One person's child may be made the child of another person by adoption, as among the Romans, or by the ancient Jewish mode of a wife having children borne to her upon her knees, by her handmaid. But these were children in a different sense from that of nature. It was clearly understood that they were not of the blood of their nominal parents. So in literary children, an author may give the profits and fame of his composition to another man, but cannot make that other the real author. A Highland gentleman, a younger branch of a family, once consulted me if he could not validly purchase the Chieftainship of his family from the Chief, who was willing to sell it. I told him it was impossible for him to acquire, by purchase, a right to be a different person from what he really was ; for that the right of Chieftainship attached to the blood of primogeniture, and therefore was incapable of being transferred. I added, that though Esau sold his birthright, or the advantages belonging to it, he still remained the first-born of his parents ; and that whatever agreement a chief might make with any or the clan, the Heralds' Office could not admit of the metamorphosis, of with any decency attest that the younger was the elder : but I did not convince the worthy gentleman.

Johnson's papers in "The Adventurer" are very similar to those of " The Rambler ; " but being rather more varied in their subjects,[1] and

that paper are, Fontenelle, Milton, Ramazzini, Madlle. de Scuderi, Swift, Homer, Barratier Statius, Cowley, and Sir Thomas Browne. With many of these, doubtless, Johnson was particularly conversant; but I doubt whether he would have characterised the expression quoted from Swift as *elegant ;* and with the works of Ramazzini it is very improbable that he should have been acquainted. Ramazzini was a celebrated physician, who died at Padua, in 1714, at the age of 81; with whose writings Dr. Bathurst may be supposed to have been conversant. So also with respect to Cowley : Johnson, without doubt, had read his Latin poem on Plants, but Bathurst's profession probably led him to read it with more attention than his friend had given to it; and Cowley's eulogy on the Poppy would more readily occur to the naturalist and the physician than to a more general reader. I believe, however, that the last paragraph of the paper on Sleep, in which Sir Thomas Browne is quoted to show the propriety of prayer before we lie down to rest, was added by Johnson.—MALONE.

[1] Dr. Johnson lowered and somewhat disguised his style in writing " The Adventurers" in order that his papers might pass for those of Dr. Bathurst, to whom he consigned the profits. This was Hawkesworth's opinion.—BURNEY.

being mixed with essays by other writers, upon topics more generally attractive than even the most elegant ethical discourses, the sale of the work, at first, was more extensive. Without meaning, however, to depreciate "The Adventurer," I must observe, that, as the value of "The Rambler" came, in the progress of time, to be better known, it grew upon the public estimation, and that its sale far has exceeded that of any other periodical papers since the reign of Queen Anne.

In one of the books of his Diary I find the following entry :—

"Apr. 3, 1753. I began the second vol. of my Dictionary, room being left in the first for Preface, Grammar, and History, none of them yet begun.

"O God, who hast hitherto supported me, enable me to proceed in this labour, and in the whole task of my present state ; that when I shall render up at the last day an account of the talent committed to me, I may receive pardon, for the sake of Jesus Christ, Amen."

He this year favoured Mrs. Lenox [1] with a Dedication * to the Earl of Orrery, of her "Shakspeare Illustrated." [2]

---

[1] Mrs. Lenox was authoress of "The Female Quixote" and various other works that will be found mentioned in the common biographies. In her "Shakspeare Illustrated" she gives an account of the source whence the poet derived the plots of his plays.—Ed.

[2] Two of Johnson's letters addressed to Samuel Richardson, author of "Clarissa," &c., the former dated March 9, 1750-1, the other, September 26, 1753, are preserved in "Richardson's Correspondence," 8vo., 1804, vol. v., pp. 281—284. In the latter of these letters Johnson suggested to Richardson the propriety of making an index to his three works : "but while I am writing," he adds, "an objection arises ; such an Index to the three would look like the preclusion of a fourth, to which I will never contribute ; for if I cannot benefit mankind, I hope never to injure them." Richardson, however, adopted the hint ; for in 1755 he published in octavo, "A Collection of the Moral and Instructive Sentiments, Maxims, Cautions, and Reflections, contained in the Histories of ' Pamela,' ' Clarissa,' and ' Sir Charles Grandison,' digested under proper Heads."

It is remarkable, that both to this book, and to the first two volumes of "Clarissa," is prefixed a Preface, by a friend. The "friend," in this latter instance, was the celebrated Dr. Warburton.—Malone.

CHESTERFIELD HOUSE.

CHAPTER VIII.—1754—1755.

JOHNSON WRITES "THE LIFE OF CAVE"—LORD CHESTERFIELD'S PAPERS IN "THE WORLD," RECOMMENDING THE DICTIONARY—LETTER IN ANSWER TO HIS LORDSHIP—EXCURSION TO OXFORD—RECEIVES HIS DEGREE OF M.A.—PROJECTED "BIBLIOTHEQUE" —-LETTERS, REMARKS, &c., RELATING TO THE DICTIONARY—GARRICK'S PANEGYRIC—JOHNSON'S PAMPHLET ON THE LONGITUDE—SCHEME OF LIFE FOR SUNDAYS.

IN 1754 I can trace nothing published by him, except his numbers of "The Adventurer," and the "Life of Edward Cave," * in "The Gentleman's Magazine" for February. In biography there can be no question that he excelled, beyond all who have attempted that species of composition ; upon which, indeed, he set the highest value. To the minute selection of characteristical circumstances, for which the ancients were remarkable, he added a philosophical research, and the most perspicuous and energetic language. Cave was certainly a man of estimable qualities, and was eminently diligent and successful in his own business, which, doubtless, entitled him to respect. But he was peculiarly fortunate in being recorded by Johnson ; who, of the narrow life of a printer and publisher, without any digressions or adventitious circumstances, has made an interesting and agreeable narrative.

The Dictionary, we may believe, afforded Johnson full occupation this year. As it approached to its conclusion, he probably worked with redoubled vigour, as seamen increase their exertion and alacrity when they have a near prospect of their haven.

Lord Chesterfield, to whom Johnson had paid the high compliment of addressing to his Lordship the plan of his Dictionary, had behaved to him in such a manner as to excite his contempt and indignation. The world has been for many years amused with a story confidently told, and as confidently repeated with additional circumstances, that a sudden disgust was taken by Johnson upon occasion of his having been one day kept long in waiting in his lordship's antechamber, for which the reason assigned was, that he had company with him ; and that at last, when the door opened, out walked Colley Cibber ; and that Johnson was so violently provoked when he found for whom he had been so long excluded, that he went away in a passion, and never would return. I remember having mentioned this story to George Lord Lyttleton, who told me he was very intimate with Lord Chesterfield ; and holding it as a well-known truth, defended Lord Chesterfield by saying, that " Cibber, who had been introduced familiarly by the back-stairs, had probably not been there above ten minutes." It may seem strange even to entertain a doubt concerning a story so long and so widely current, and thus implicitly adopted, if not sanctioned, by the authority which I have mentioned ; but Johnson himself assured me, that there was not the least foundation for it. He told me, that there never was any particular incident which produced a quarrel between Lord Chesterfield and him ; but that his lordship's continued neglect was the reason why he resolved to have no connection with him.

When the Dictionary was upon the eve of publication, Lord Chesterfield, who, it is said, had flattered himself with expectations that Johnson would dedicate the work to him, attempted, in a courtly manner, to soothe and insinuate himself with the sage, conscious, as it should seem, of the cold indifference with which he had treated its learned author ; and further attempted to conciliate him, by writing two papers in " The World," in recommendation of the work ; and it must be confessed that they contain some studied compliments, so finely turned, that if there had been no previous offence, it is probable that Johnson would have been highly delighted. Praise, in general, was pleasing to him ; but by praise from a man of rank and elegant accomplishments, he was peculiarly gratified. His lordship says,—

"I think the public in general, and the republic of letters in particular, are greatly obliged to Mr. Johnson, for having undertaken and executed so great and desirable a work. Perfection is not to be expected from man ; but if we are to judge by the various works of Johnson already published, we have good reason to believe, that he will bring this as near to perfection as any man could do. The plan of it, which he published some years ago, seems to me to be a proof of it. Nothing can be more rationally imagined, or more accurately and elegantly

expressed. 1 therefore recommend the previous perusal of it to all those
who intend to buy the Dictionary, and who, I suppose, are all those who can
afford it. . . . . .

"It must be owned, that our language is, at present, in a state of anarchy,
and hitherto, perhaps, it may not have been the worse for it. During our free
and open trade, many words and expressions have been imported, adopted, and
naturalised from other languages, which have greatly enriched our own. Let
it still preserve what real strength and beauty it may have borrowed from
others; but let it not, like the Tarpeian maid, be overwhelmed and crushed by
unnecessary ornaments. The time for discrimination seems to be now come.
Toleration, adoption, and naturalization have run their length. Good order
and authority are now necessary. But where shall we find them, and at the
same time, the obedience due to them? We must have recourse to the old
Roman expedient in times of confusion, and choose a dictator. Upon this principle, I give my vote for Mr. Johnson, to fill that great and arduous post, and I
hereby declare, that I make a total surrender of all my rights and privileges in
the English language, as a free-born British subject, to the said Mr. Johnson,
during the term of his dictatorship. Nay, more—I will not only obey him like
an old Roman, as my dictator, but, like a modern Roman, I will implicitly
believe in him as my Pope, and hold him to be infallible while in the chair, but
no longer. More than this, he cannot well require; for, I presume, that obedience can never be expected, when there is neither terror to enforce, nor interest
to invite it. . . . . .

"But a Grammar, a Dictionary, and a History of our Language, through
its several stages, were still wanting at home, and importunately called for from
abroad. Mr. Johnson's labours will now, I dare say, very fully supply that
want, and greatly contribute to the farther spreading of our language in other
countries. Learners were discouraged, by finding no standard to resort to;
and, consequently, thought it incapable of any. They will now be undeceived
and encouraged."

This courtly device failed of its effect. Johnson, who thought that
"all was false and hollow," despised the honeyed words, and was even
indignant that Lord Chesterfield should, for a moment, imagine that he
could be the dupe of such an artifice. His expression to me concerning
Lord Chesterfield, upon this occasion, was, "Sir, after making great
professions, he had, for many years, taken no notice of me; but when
my Dictionary was coming out, he fell a scribbling in "The World"
about it. Upon which I wrote him a letter expressed in civil terms,
but such as might show him that I did not mind what he said or wrote,
and that I had done with him."

This is that celebrated letter of which so much has been said, and
about which curiosity has been so long excited, without being gratified.
I for many years solicited Johnson to favour me with a copy of it, that
so excellent a composition might not be lost to posterity. He delayed
from time to time to give it me;[1] till at last, in 1781, when we were on

[1] Dr. Johnson appeared to have had a remarkable delicacy with respect to the circulation

a visit at Mr. Dilly's, at Southill in Bedfordshire, he was pleased to dictate it to me from memory. He afterwards found among his papers a copy of it, which he had dictated to Mr. Baretti, with its title and corrections, in his own handwriting. This he gave to Mr. Langton ; adding, that if it were to come into print, he wished it to be from that copy. By Mr. Langton's kindness, I am enabled to enrich my work with a perfect transcript of what the world has so eagerly desired to see.

"TO THE RIGHT HONOURABLE THE EARL OF CHESTERFIELD.

" My Lord,   *February* 7, 1775.

" I have been lately informed, by the proprietor of " The World," that two papers, in which my Dictionary is recommended to the public, were written by your lordship. To be so distinguished is an honour, which, being very little accustomed to favours from the great, I know not well how to receive, or in what terms to acknowledge.

" When, upon some slight encouragement, I first visited your lordship, I was overpowered, like the rest of mankind, by the enchantment of your address, and could not forbear to wish that I might boast myself *Le vainqueur du vainqueur de la terre ;*—that I might obtain that regard for which I saw the world contending ; but I found my attendance so little encouraged, that neither pride nor modesty would suffer me to continue it.   When I had once addressed your lordship in public, I had exhausted all the art of pleasing which a retired and uncourtly scholar can possess.   I had done all that I could ; and no man is well pleased to have his all neglected, be it ever so little.

" Seven years, my lord, have now passed, since I waited in your outward rooms, or was repulsed from your door ; during which time I have been pushing on my work through difficulties, of which it is useless to complain, and have brought it, at last, to the verge of publication, without one act of assistance,[1] one word of encouragement, or one smile of favour.   Such treatment I did not expect, for I never had a patron before.

" The shepherd in ' Virgil ' grew at last acquainted with Love, and found him a native of the rocks.

" Is not a patron, my lord, one who looks with unconcern on a man struggling for life in the water, and, when he has reached ground, encumbers him with help ?   The notice which you have been pleased to take of my labours, had it been early, had been kind ; but it has been delayed till I am indifferent,

---

of this letter ; for Dr. Douglas, Bishop of Salisbury, informs me that, having many years ago pressed him to be allowed to read it to the second Lord Hardwicke, who was very desirous to hear it (promising at the same time, that no copy of it should be taken), Johnson seemed much pleased that it had attracted the attention of a nobleman of such a respectable character ; but after pausing some time, declined to comply with the request, saying, with a smile, " No, Sir ; I have hurt the dog too much already ; " or words to that purpose.—Boswell.

[1] The following note is subjoined by Mr. Langton :—" Dr. Johnson, when he gave me this copy of his letter, desired that I would annex to it his information to me, that whereas it is said in the letter that 'no assistance has been received,' he did once receive from Lord Chesterfield the sum of ten pounds ; but as that was so inconsiderable a sum, he thought the mention of it could not properly find a place in a letter of the kind that this was "—Boswell

and cannot enjoy it ; till I am solitary, and cannot impart it ;[1] till I am known, and do not want it.   I hope it is no very cynical asperity, not to confess obligations where no benefit has been received, or to be unwilling that the public should consider me as owing that to a patron, which Providence has enabled me to do for myself.

"Having carried on my work thus far with so little obligation to any favourer of learning, I shall not be disappointed though I shall conclude it, if less be possible, with less ; for I have been long wakened from that dream of hope, in which I once boasted myself with so much exultation,

" My Lord, your lordship's most humble,

" Most obedient servant,

" SAM. JOHNSON."[2]

" While this was the talk of the town," says Dr. Adams, in a letter to me, " I happened to visit Dr. Warburton, who, finding that I was acquainted with Johnson, desired me earnestly to carry his compliments to him, and to tell him that he honoured him for his manly behaviour in rejecting these condescensions of Lord Chesterfield, and for resenting the treatment he had received from him with a proper spirit.   Johnson was visibly pleased with this compliment, for he had always a high opinion of Warburton."[3]   Indeed, the force of mind which appeared in this letter was congenial with that which Warburton himself amply possessed.

There is a curious minute circumstance which struck me, in comparing the various editions of " Johnson's Imitations of Juvenal."   In the tenth Satire one of the couplets upon the vanity of wishes even for literary distinction, stood thus :—

" Yet think what ills the scholar's life assail,
Toil, envy, want, the *garret*, and the jail."

---

[1] In this passage Dr. Johnson evidently alludes to the loss of his wife.   We find the same tender recollection recurring to his mind upon innumerable occasions: and, perhaps, no man ever more forcibly felt the truth of the sentiment so elegantly expressed by my friend Mr. Malone, in his Prologue to Mr. Jephson's tragedy of " Julia :"—

" Vain—wealth, and fame, and fortune's fostering care,
If no fond breast the splendid blessings share :
And, each day's bustling pageantry once past,
There, only there, our bliss is found at last."—BOSWELL.

[2] Upon comparing this copy with that which Dr. Johnson dictated to me from recollection, the variations are found to be so slight, that this must be added to the many other proofs which he gave of the wonderful extent and accuracy of his memory.   To gratify the curious in composition, I have deposited both the copies in the British Museum.—BOSWELL.

[3] Soon after Edwards's " Canons of Criticism " came out, Johnson was dining at Tonson the Bookseller's, with Hayman the Painter and some more company.   Hayman related to Sir Joshua Reynolds, that the conversation having turned upon Edwards's book, the gentleman praised it much, and Johnson allowed its merit.   But when they went farther, and appeared to put that author upon a level with Warburton, " Nay," said Johnson, "he has given him some smart hits to be sure ; but there is no proportion between the two men ; they must not be named together.   A fly, Sir, may sting a stately horse, and make him wince ; but one is but an insect, and the other is a horse still "—BOSWELL.

But after experiencing the uneasiness which Lord Chesterfield's fallacious patronage made him feel, he dismissed the word *garret* from the sad group, and in all the subsequent editions the line stands,

" Toil, envy, want, the *patron,* and the jail.

That Lord Chesterfield must have been mortified by the lofty contempt, and polite, yet keen, satire with which Johnson exhibited him to himself in this letter, it is impossible to doubt. He, however, with that glossy duplicity which was his constant study, affected to be quite unconcerned. Dr. Adams mentioned to Mr. Robert Dodsley that he was sorry Johnson had written his letter to Lord Chesterfield. Dodsley, with the true feelings of trade, said, " he was very sorry too ; for that he had a property in the Dictionary, to which his Lordship's patronage might have been of consequence." He then told Dr. Adams, that Lord Chesterfield had shown him the letter. " I should have imagined," replied Dr. Adams, " that Lord Chesterfield would have concealed it." " Poh ! " said Dodsley, " do you think a letter from Johnson could hurt Lord Chesterfield ? Not at all, Sir. It lay upon his table, where any body might see it. He read it to me ; said, ' This man has great powers,' pointed out the severest passages, and observed how well they were expressed." This air of indifference, which imposed upon the worthy Dodsley, was certainly nothing but a specimen of that dissimulation which Lord Chesterfield inculcated as one of the most essential lessons for the conduct of life. His lordship endeavoured to justify himself to Dodsley from the charges brought against him by Johnson ; but we may judge of the flimsiness of his defence, from his having excused his neglect of Johnson, by saying, that " he had heard he had changed his lodgings, and did not know where he lived ; " as if there could have been the smallest difficulty to inform himself of that circumstance, by inquiring in the literary circle with which his lordship was well acquainted, and was, indeed, himself, one of its ornaments.

Dr. Adams expostulated with Johnson, and suggested, that his not being admitted when he called on him, was probably not to be imputed to Lord Chesterfield ; for his lordship had declared to Dodsley, that " he would have turned off the best servant he ever had, if he had known that he denied him to a man who would have been always more than welcome ; " and in confirmation of this, he insisted on Lord Chesterfield's general affability and easiness of access, especially to literary men. " Sir," said Johnson, " that is not Lord Chesterfield ; he is the proudest man this day existing." " No," said Dr. Adams, " there is one person, at least, as proud ; I think, by your own account, you are the prouder man of the two." " But mine," replied Johnson instantly, " was *defensive* pride." This, as Dr. Adams well observed, was one of those happy turns, for which he was so remarkably ready.

Johnson having now explicitly avowed his opinion of Lord Chester-

L 2

field, did not refrain from expressing himself concerning that nobleman with pointed freedom : " This man," said he, " I thought had been a lord among wits, but I find, he is only a wit among lords ! " [1] And when his Letters to his natural son were published, he observed, that " they teach the morals of a whore, and the manners of a dancing master." [2]

The character of a " respectable Hottentot," in Lord Chesterfield's Letters, has been generally understood to be meant for Johnson, and I have no doubt that it was. But I remember when the *Literary Property* of those letters was contested in the Court of Session in Scotland, and Mr. Henry Dundas,[3] one of the council for the proprietors, read this character as an exhibition of Johnson, Sir David Dalrymple, Lord Hailes, one of the judges, maintained with some warmth, that it was not intended as a portrait of Johnson, but of a late noble lord, distinguished for abstruse science. I have heard Johnson himself talk of the character, and say that it was meant for George Lord Lyttleton, in which I could by no means agree ; for his lordship had nothing of that violence which is a conspicuous feature in the composition. Finding that my illustrious friend could bear to have it supposed that it might be meant for him, I said, laughingly, that there was one trait which unquestionably did not belong to him ; " he throws his meat anywhere but down his throat." " Sir," said he, " Lord Chesterfield never saw me eat in his life."

On the 6th of March came out Lord Bolingbroke's works, published by Mr. David Mallet. The wild and pernicious ravings, under the name of " Philosophy," which were thus ushered into the world, gave great offence to all well-principled men. Johnson, hearing of their

[1] Johnson's character of Chesterfield seems to be imitated from—*inter doctos nobilissimus, inter nobiles doctissimus, inter utrosques optimus;* (ex Apuleio, v. Erasm.—Dedication of Adagies to Lord Mountjoy ;) and from ιδιωτης εν φιλοσοφοις, φιλοσοφος εν ιδιοταις. Proclus de Critia.— KEARNEY.

[2] That collection of letters cannot be vindicated from the serious charge, encouraging in some passages, one of the vices most destructive to the good order and comfort of society, which his lordship represents as mere fashionable gallantry ; and, in others, of inculcating the base practice of dissimulation, and recommending, with disproportionate anxiety, a perpetual attention to external elegance of manners But it must at the same time, be allowed, that they contain many good precepts of conduct, and much genuine information upon life and manners, very happily expressed, and that there was considerable merit in paying so much attention to the improvement of one who was dependent upon his lordship's protection : it has, probably, been exceeded in no instance by the most exemplary parent ; and though I can by no means approve of confounding the distinction between lawful and illicit offspring which is, in effect, insulting the civil establishment of our country, to look no higher ; I cannot help thinking it laudable to be kindly attentive to those, of whose existence we have, in any way been the cause. Mr. Stanhope's character has been unjustly represented as diametrically opposite to what Lord Chesterfield wished him to be. He has been called dull, gross, and awkward : but I knew him at Dresden, when he was Envoy to that court, and though he could not boast of the *graces*, he was, in truth, a sensible, civil, well-behaved man.—BOSWELL.

[3] Now [1792] one of his Majesty's principal Secretaries of State.— BOSWELL. Mr. Dundas was subsequently created Viscount Melville.

there, after quitting the University. The next morning after his arrival, he wished to see his old college, *Pembroke.* I went with him. He was highly pleased to find all the college-servants which he had left there still remaining, particularly a very old butler; and expressed great satisfaction at being recognised by them, and conversed with them familiarly. He waited on the master, Dr. Radcliffe, who received him very coldly. Johnson at least expected, that the master would order a copy of his Dictionary, now near publication; but the master did not choose to talk on the subject, never asked Johnson to dine, nor even to visit him, while he stayed at Oxford. After we had left the lodgings, Johnson said to me, ' *There* lives a man, who lives by the revenues of literature, and will not move a finger to support it. If I come to live at Oxford, I shall take up my abode at Trinity.' We then called on the Reverend Mr. Meeke, one of the fellows, and of Johnson's standing. Here was a most cordial greeting on both sides. On leaving him, Johnson said, ' I used to think Meeke had excellent parts, when we were boys together at the college; but, alas !

'Lost in a convent's solitary gloom !'

I remember, at the classical lecture in the Hall, I could not bear Meeke's superiority, and I tried to sit as far from him as I could, that I might not hear him construe.

RESIDENCE OF MR. WISE.

" As we were leaving the college, he said, ' Here I translated Pope's ' Messiah. Which do you think is the best line in it ?—My own favourite is,

' *Vallis aromaticas fundit Saronica nubes.*'

I told him, I thought it a very sonorous hexameter. I did not tell him, it was not in the Virgilian style. He much regretted that his *first* tutor was dead; for whom he seemed to retain the greatest regard. He said, 'I once had been - a whole morning sliding in Christ-church meadows, and missed his lecture in logic. After dinner he sent for me to his room. I expected a sharp rebuke for my idleness, and went with a beating heart. When we were seated, he told me he had sent for me to drink a glass of wine with him, and to tell me, he was *not* angry with me for missing his lecture. This was, in fact, a most severe reprimand. Some more of the boys were then sent for, and we spent a very pleasant afternoon.' Besides Mr. Meeke, there was only one other fellow of Pembroke now resident : from both of whom Johnson received the greatest civilities during this visit, and they pressed him very much to have a room in the college.

"In the course of this visit (1754), Johnson and I walked three or four times to Ellesfield, a village beautifully situated about three miles from Oxford, to see Mr. Wise, Radclivian librarian, with whom Johnson was much pleased. At this place, Mr. Wise had fitted up a house and gardens, in a singular manner, but with great taste. Here was an excellent library, particularly a valuable collection of books in Northern literature, with which Johnson was often very busy. One day Mr. Wise read to us a dissertation which he was preparing for the press, entitled, 'A History and Chronology of the Fabulous Ages.' Some old divinities of Thrace, related to the Titans, and called the Cabiri, made a very important part of the theory of this piece; and in conversation afterwards, Mr. Wise talked much of his Cabiri. As we returned to Oxford in the evening, I outwalked Johnson, and he cried out *Sufflamina*, a Latin word, which came from his mouth with peculiar grace, and was as much as to say, *Put on your drag chain*. Before we got home, I again walked too fast for him ; and he now cried out, 'Why, you walk as if you were pursued by all the Cabiri in a body.' In an evening we frequently took long walks from Oxford into the country, returning to supper. Once, in our way home, we viewed the ruins of the abbeys of Oseney and Rewley, near Oxford.

OSENEY ABBEY.

After at least half an hour's silence, Johnson said, 'I viewed them with indignation !' We had then a long conversation on Gothic buildings ; and in talking of the form of old halls, he said, 'In these halls, the fire-place was anciently always in the middle of the room, till the Whigs removed it on one side. About this time there had been an execution of two or three criminals at Oxford, on a Monday. Soon afterwards, one day at dinner, I was saying that Mr. Swinton, the chaplain of the gaol, and also a frequent preacher before the University, a learned man, but often thoughtless and absent, preached the condemnation sermon on repentance, before the convicts, on the preceding day,

Sunday; and that in the close he told his audience, that he should give them the remainder of what he had to say on the subject, the next Lord's day.　Upon

REWLEY ABBEY.

which, one of our company, a Doctor of Divinity, and a plain matter-of-fact man, by way of offering an apology for Mr. Swinton, gravely remarked, that he had probably preached the same sermon before the University : 'Yes, Sir,' says Johnson, 'but the University were not to be hanged the next morning.'

"I forgot to observe before, that when he left Mr. Meeke (as I have told above), he added, 'About the same time of life, Meeke was left behind at Oxford to feed on a Fellowship, and I went to London to get my living : now, Sir, see the difference of our literary characters!'"

The following letter was written by Dr. Johnson to Mr. Chambers, of Lincoln College, afterwards Sir Robert Chambers, one of the judges in India :—[1]

"TO MR. CHAMBERS, OF LINCOLN COLLEGE.

"Dear Sir,　　　　　　　　　　　　　　　　　　*Nov.* 21, 1754.

"The commission which I delayed to trouble you with at your departure, I am now obliged to send you; and beg that you will be so kind as to carry it to Mr. Warton, of Trinity, to whom I should have written immediately, but that I know not if he be yet come back to Oxford.

"In the Catalogue of MSS. of Gr. Brit. see vol. i. page 18, MSS. Bodl. Martyrium xv. *martyrum sub Juliano, auctore Theophylacto.*

"It is desired that Mr. Warton will inquire, and send word, what will be the cost of transcribing this manuscript.

"Vol. ii. p. 32. Num. 1022. 58. Coll. Nov.—*Commentaria in Acta Apostol.— Comment. in Septem Epistolas Catholicas.*

: Communicated by the Reverend Mr. Thomas Warton, who had the original.—Boswell.

" He is desired to tell what is the age of each of these manuscripts: and what it will cost to have a transcript of the two first pages of each.

" If Mr. Warton be not in Oxford, you may try if you can get it done by anybody else; or stay till he comes, according to your own convenience. It is for an Italian *literato*.

" The answer is to be directed to his Excellency Mr. Zon, Venetian Resident, Soho-square.

" I hope, dear Sir, that you do not regret the change of London for Oxford. Mr. Baretti is well, and Miss Williams;[1] and we shall be glad to hear from you, whenever you shall be so kind as to write to, Sir,

" Your most humble servant,

" SAM. JOHNSON."

The degree of Master of Arts, which, it has been observed, could not be obtained for him at an early period of his life, was now considered as an honour of considerable importance, in order to grace the title-page of his Dictionary; and his character in the literary world being by this time deservedly high, his friends thought that, if proper exertions were made, the University of Oxford would pay him the compliment.

" TO THE REVEREND MR. THOMAS WARTON.

" DEAR SIR,   *Nov.* 28, 1754.

" I am extremely obliged to you and to Mr. Wise, for the uncommon care which you have taken of my interest;[2] if you can accomplish your kind design, I shall certainly take me a little habitation among you.

" The books which I promised to Mr. Wise,[3] I have not been able to procure; but I shall send him a Finnick Dictionary, the only copy, perhaps, in England, which was presented me by a learned Swede; but I keep it back, that it may make a set of my own books of the new edition, with which I shall accompany it, more welcome. You will assure him of my gratitude.

I presume she was a relation of Mr. Zachariah Williams, who died in his eighty-third year, July 12, 1755. When Dr. Johnson was with me at Oxford, in 1755, he gave to the Bodleian Library a thin quarto of twenty-one pages, a work in Italian, with an English translation on the opposite page. The English title-page is this: " An Account of an Attempt to ascertain the Longitude at Sea, by an exact Variation of the Magnetical Needle, &c. By Zachariah Williams. London, printed for Dodsley, 1755." The English translation, from the strongest internal marks, is unquestionably the work of Johnson. In a blank leaf, Johnson has written the age, and time of death, of the author Z. Williams, as I have said above. On another blank leaf is pasted a paragraph from a newspaper, of the death and character of Williams, which is plainly written by Johnson. He was very anxious about placing this book in the Bodleian: and, for fear of any omission or mistake, he entered, in the great Catalogue, the title-page of it with his own hand.—WARTON.

In this statement there is a slight mistake. The English account, which was written by Johnson, was the *original;* the Italian was a *translation,* done by Baretti. See p. 170.— MALONE.

2 In procuring him the degree of Master of Arts by diploma at Oxford.—WARTON.

3 Lately Fellow of Trinity College, and at this time Radclivian librarian at Oxford. He was a man of very considerable learning, and eminently skilled in Roman and Anglo-Saxon antiquities. He died in 1767.—WARTON

"Poor dear Collins![1] Would a letter give him any pleasure? I have a mind to write.

"I am glad of your hindrance in your Spenserian design,[2] yet I would not have it delayed. Three hours a day stolen from sleep and amusement will produce it. Let a Servitor[3] transcribe the quotations, and interleave them with references, to save time. This will shorten the work, and lessen the fatigue.

"Can I do any thing to promoting the diploma ! I would not be wanting to co-operate with your kindness; of which, whatever be the effect, I shall be, dear Sir,   "Your most obliged, &c.

                                        "SAM. JOHNSON."

TO THE SAME.

"DEAR SIR,   Dec. 21, 1754.

"I am extremely sensible of the favour done me, both by Mr. Wise and yourself. The book [the Dictionary] cannot, I think, be printed in less than six weeks, nor probably so soon ; and I will keep back the title-page, for such an insertion as you seem to promise me. Be pleased to let me know what money I shall send you for bearing the expense of the affair ; and I will take care that you have it ready at your hand.

"I had lately the favour of a letter from your brother, with some account of poor Collins, for whom I am much concerned. I have a notion, that by very great temperance, or more properly abstinence, he may yet recover.

---

[1] Collins (the poet) was at this time at Oxford, on a visit to Mr. Warton; but labouring under the most deplorable languor of body, and dejection of mind.—WARTON.

In a letter to Dr. Joseph Warton, written some months before (March 8, 1754), Dr. Johnson thus speaks of Collins :—

"But how little can we venture to exult in any intellectual powers or literary attainments, when we consider the condition of poor Collins ! I knew him a few years ago full of hopes, and full of projects, versed in many languages, high in fancy, and strong in retention. This busy and forcible mind is now under the government of those, who lately could not have been able to comprehend the least and most narrow of his designs. What do you hear of him ? are there hopes of his recovery ? or is he to pass the remainder of his life in misery and degradation ? perhaps, with complete consciousness of his calamity."

In a subsequent letter to the same gentleman (Dec. 24, 1754), he thus feelingly alludes to their unfortunate friend :—

"Poor dear Collins ! Let me know whether you think it would give him pleasure if I should write to him. I have often been *near* his state, and therefore have it in great commiseration."

Again,—April 9, 1756 :—

"What becomes of poor dear Collins? I wrote him a letter which he never answered. I suppose writing is very troublesome to him. That man is no common loss. The moralists all talk of the uncertainty of fortune, and the transitoriness of beauty : but it is yet more dreadful to consider that the powers of the mind are equally liable to change, that understanding may make its appearance and depart, that it may blaze and expire."

See Biographical Memoirs of the Reverend Dr. Joseph Warton, by the Reverend John Wool, A.M. 4to. 1806.

Mr. Collins who was the son of a hatter at Chichester, was born December 25, 1720, and was released from the dismal state here so pathetically described, in 1756.—MALONE.

[2] Of publishing a volume of observations on the best of Spenser's works. It was hindered by my taking pupils in this college.—WARTON.

[3] Young students of the lowest rank at Oxford are so called.—WARTON

"There is an old English and Latin book of poems by Barclay, called 'The Ship of Fools:' at the end of which are a number of *Eglogues*,—so he writes it, from *Egloga*,—which are probably the first in our language. If you cannot find the book, I will get Mr. Dodsley to send it you.

"I shall be extremely glad to hear from you again, to know if the affair proceeds.[1] I have mentioned it to none of my friends, for fear of being laughed at for my disappointment.

"You know poor Mr. Dodsley has lost his wife; I believe he is much affected. I hope he will not suffer so much as I yet suffer for the loss of mine.

$$\text{Οἴμοι· τι δ' οἴμοι; θνητὰ γὰρ πεπόνθαμεν.}^{2}$$

I have ever since seemed to myself broken off from mankind; a kind of solitary wanderer in the wild of life, without any direction, or fixed point of view: a gloomy gazer on the world to which I have little relation. Yet I would endeavour, by the help of you and your brother, to supply the want of closer union, by friendship: and hope to have long the pleasure of being,

"Dear Sir,

"Most affectionately yours,

SAM. JOHNSON."

In 1755 we behold him to great advantage; his degree of Master of Arts conferred upon him, his Dictionary published, his correspondence animated, his benevolence exercised.

TO THE REVEREND MR. THOMAS WARTON.

"DEAR SIR,   *Feb.* 4, 1755.

"I wrote to you some weeks ago, but believe did not direct accurately, and therefore know not whether you had my letter. I would, likewise, write to your brother, but know not where to find him. I now begin to see land, after having wandered, according to Mr. Warburton's phrase, in this vast sea of words. What reception I shall meet with I know not; whether the sound of bells, and acclamations of the people, which Ariosto talks of in his last Canto, or a general murmur of dislike, I know not: whether I shall find upon the coast a Calypso that will court, or a Polypheme that will resist. But if Polypheme comes, have at his eye. I hope, however, the critics will let me be at peace; for though I do not much fear their skill and strength, I am a little afraid of myself, and would not willingly feel so much ill-will in my bosom as literary quarrels are apt to excite.

"Mr. Baretti is about a work, for which he is in great want of Crescimbeni, which you may have again when you please.

"There is nothing considerable done or doing among us here. We are not,

---

[1] Of the degree at Oxford.—WARTON.

[2] This verse is taken from the long lost "Bellerophon," a tragedy by Euripides. It is preserved by Suidas in his Lexicon, voc. Οἴμοι II. p. 666; where the reading is θνητὰ τοι πεπόνθαμεν.—REV. C. BURNEY.

perhaps, as innocent as villagers, but most of us seem to be as idle. I hope however, you are busy, and should be glad to know what you are doing.

"I am, dearest Sir,

"Your humble servant,

"Sam. Johnson."

TO THE SAME.

"Dear Sir,   *Feb. 4, 1755.*

"I received your letter this day, with great sense of the favour that has been done me ; [1] for which I return my most sincere thanks, and entreat you to pay to Mr. Wise such returns as I ought to make for so much kindness so little deserved.

"I sent Mr. Wise the Lexicon, and afterwards wrote to him; but know not whether he had either the book or letter. Be so good as to to contrive to inquire.

"But why does my dear Mr. Warton tell me nothing of himself? Where hangs the new volume ?[2] Can I help? Let not the past labour be lost for want of a little more : but snatch what time you can from the Hall, and the pupils, and the coffee-house, and the parks, and complete your design.

"I am, dear Sir, &c.   Sam. Johnson."

TO THE SAME.

"Dear Sir,   *Feb. 13, 1755.*

"I had a letter last week from Mr. Wise, but have yet heard nothing from you, nor know in what state my affair [3] stands ; of which I beg you to inform me, if you can, by the return of the post.

"Mr. Wise sends me word that he has not had the Finnick Lexicon yet which I sent some time ago ; and if he has it not, you must inquire after it. However, do not let your letter stay for that.

"Your brother, who is a better correspondent than you, and not much better, sends me word that your pupils keep you in college : but do they keep you from writing too? Let them, at least, give you time to write to, dear Sir,

"Your most affectionate, &c.

"Sam. Johnson."

TO THE SAME.

"Dear Sir,   *Feb. 1755.*

"Dr. King[4] was with me a few minutes before your letter ; this, however, is the first instance in which your kind intentions to me have ever been frustrated.[5] I have now the full effect of your care and benevolence; and am fa.

---

[1] His degree had now past, according to the usual form, the suffrages of the heads of colleges ; but was not yet finally granted by the University. It was carried without a single dissentient voice.—Warton.

[2] On Spenser.—Warton.   [3] Of the degree.—Warton.

[4] Principal of Saint Mary Hall at Oxford. He brought with him the diploma from Oxford.—Warton.

[5] I suppose Johnson means that my *kind intention* of being the *first* to give him the good news of the degree being granted was *frustrated*, because Dr. King brought it before my intelligence arrived.—Warton

from thinking it a slight honour, or a small advantage; since it will put the enjoyment of your conversation more frequently in the power of, dear Sir,

"Your most obliged and affectionate,

"SAM. JOHNSON."

"P.S. I have enclosed a letter to the Vice-Chancellor,[1] which you will read; and, if you like it, seal and give him."

As the public will doubtless be pleased to see the whole progress of this well-earned academical honour, I shall insert the Chancellor of Oxford's letter to the University,[2] the diploma, and Johnson's letter of thanks to the Vice-Chancellor.

"TO THE REVEREND DR. HUDDESFORD,

Vice-Chancellor of the University of Oxford; to be communicated to the Heads of Houses, and proposed in Convocation.

Grosvenor-street, Feb. 4, 1755.

"MR. VICE-CHANCELLOR AND GENTLEMEN,

"Mr. Samuel Johnson, who was formerly of Pembroke College, having very eminently distinguished himself by the publication of a series of essays, excellently calculated to form the manners of the people, and in which the cause of religion and morality is every where maintained by the strongest powers of argument and language; and who shortly intends to publish a Dictionary of the English Tongue, formed on a new plan, and executed with the greatest labour and judgment; I persuade myself that I shall act agreeable to the sentiments of the whole University, in desiring that it may be proposed in convocation to confer on him the degree of Master of Arts by diploma, to which I readily give my consent, and am, Mr. Vice-Chancellor and Gentlemen,

"Your affectionate friend and servant,

"ARRAN."

Term. S^{cti.}
Hilarii,   "DIPLOMA MAGISTRI JOHNSON.
1755.

"*CANCELLARIUS, Magistri et Scholares Universitatis Oxoniensis omnibus ad quos hoc presens scriptum pervenerit, salutem in Domino sempiternam.*

"*Cùm eum in finem gradus academici à majoribus nostris instituti fuerint, ut viri ingenio et doctrinâ præstantes titulis quoque præter cæteros insignirentur; cùmque vir doctissimus* Samuel Johnson *è Collegio Pembrochiensi, scriptis suis popularium mores informantibus dudum literato orbi innotuerit; quin et linguæ patriæ tum ornandæ tum stabiliendæ* (Lexicon *scilicet Anglicanum summo studio, summoâ se judicio congestum propediem editurus*) *etiam nunc utilissimam impendat operam; Nos igitur Cancellarius, Magistri, et Scholares antedicti, nè virum de literis humanioribus optimè meritum diutius inhonoratum prætereamus. in solenni Convocatione Doctorum, Magistrorum, Regentium, et non Regentium, decimo die Mensis Februarii Anno Domini Millesimo Septingentesimo Quinquagesimo quinto habitâ, præfatum virum* Samuelem Johnson (*conspirantibus omnium suffragiis*

---

[1] Dr. Huddesford, President of Trinity College.—WARTON.
[2] Extracted from the Convocation Register, Oxford.—BOSWELL.

Magistrum in Artibus renunciavimus et constituimus; eumque, virtute præsentis diplomatis, singulis juribus privilegiis et honoribus ad istum gradum, quàquà pertinentibus frui et gaudere jussimus.

" *In cujus rei testimonium sigillum Universitatis Oxoniensis præsentibus apponi fecimus.*

" *Datum in Domo nostræ Convocationis die* 20°

Mensis Feb. Anno Dom. prædicto.

" *Diploma supra scriptum per Registrarium lectum erat, et ex decreto venerabilis Domús communi Universitatis sigillo munitum.*"[1]

" *Londini, 4to Cal. Mart.* 1755.

" VIRO REVERENDO — HUDDESFORD, S.T.P.

" Universitatis Oxoniensis Vice-Cancellario Dignissimo, S.P.D.

SAM. JOHNSON.[2]

" *INGRATUS planè et tibi et mihi videar, nisi quanto me gaudio affecerint, quos nuper mihi honores (te, credo, auctore,) decrevit Senatus Academicus, literarum, quo tamen nihil levius, officio, significem; ingratus etiam, nisi comitatem, quá ir eximius[3] mihi vestri testimonium amoris in manus tradidit, agnoscam et laudem. Si quid est, undè rei tam gratæ accedat gratia, hoc ipso magis mihi placet, quod eo tempore in ordines Academicos denuò cooptatus sim, quo tuam imminuere auctoritatem, fumamque Oxonii lædere, omnibus modis conantur homines vafri, nec tamen acuti: quibus ego, prout viro umbratico licuit, semper restiti, semper restiturus. Qui enim, inter has rerum procellas, vel tibi vel Academiæ defuerit, illum virtuti et literis, sibique et posteris, defuturum cœstimo. Vale.*"

" TO THE REVEREND MR. THOMAS WARTON.

" DEAR SIR,   *March* 20, 1755.

" After I received my diploma, I wrote you a letter of thanks, with a letter to the Vice-Chancellor, and sent another to Mr. Wise; but have heard from nobody since, and begin to think myself forgotten. It is true, I sent you a double letter, and you may fear an expensive correspondent; but I would have taken it kindly, if you had returned it treble: and what is a double letter to a *petty king*, that, having *fellowship and fines*, can sleep without a *modus in his head?*[3]

" Dear Mr. Warton, let me hear from you, and tell me something, I care not what, so I hear it but from you. Something I will tell you:—I hope to see my Dictionary bound and lettered, next week;—*vastâ mole superbus.* And I have a great mind to come to Oxford at Easter; but you will not invite me.

---

[1] The original is in my possession.—BOSWELL.

[2] The superscription of this letter was not quite correct in the early editions of this work. It is here given from Dr. Johnson's original letter, now before me.—MALONE.

[3] We may conceive what a high gratification it must have been to Johnson to receive his diploma from the hands of the great Dr. King, whose principles were so congenial with his own.—BOSWELL.

[4] The words in italics are allusions to passages into Mr. Warton's poem, called ' The Progress of Discontent," now lately published.—WARTON.

Shall I come uninvited, or stay here where nobody perhaps would miss me if
I went? A hard choice! But such is the world to, dear Sir,

"Yours, &c.

"SAM. JOHNSON."

TO THE SAME.

"DEAR SIR,   *March* 25, 1755.

"Though not to write, when a man can write so well, is an offence
sufficiently heinous, yet I shall pass it by. I am very glad that the Vice-
Chancellor was pleased with my note. I shall impatiently expect you at
London, that we may consider what to do next. I intend in the winter to
open a *Bibliothèque*, and remember, that you are to subscribe a sheet a year:
let us try, likewise, if we cannot persuade your brother to subscribe another.
My book is now coming *in luminis oras*. What will be its fate I know not,
nor think much, because thinking is to no purpose. It must stand the censure
of the *great vulgar and the small;* of those that understand it, and that
understand it not. But in all this, I suffer not alone; every writer has the same
difficulties, and, perhaps, every writer talks of them more than he thinks.

"You will be pleased to make my compliments to all my friends; and be so
kind, at every idle hour, as to remember, dear Sir,

"Yours, &c.

"SAM. JOHNSON."

Dr. Adams told me, that this scheme of a *Bibliothèque* was a serious
one: for upon his visiting him one day, he found his parlour floor
covered with parcels of foreign and English literary journals, and he
told Dr. Adams he meant to undertake a Review. "How, Sir," said
Dr. Adams, "can you think of doing it alone? All branches of knowledge must be considered in it. Do you know Mathematics? Do you
know Natural History?" Johnson answered, "Why, Sir, I must do as
well as I can. My chief purpose is to give my countrymen a view of
what is doing in literature upon the continent; and I shall have, in a
good measure, the choice of my subject, for I shall select such books as
I best understand." Dr. Adams suggested, that as Dr. Maty had just
then finished his *Bibliothèque Britannique*, which was a well-executed
work, giving foreigners an account of British publications, he might,
with great advantage, assume him as an assistant. "*He*," said Johnson, "the little black dog! I'd throw him into the Thames." The
scheme, however, was dropped.

In one of his little memorandum-books I find the following hints for
his intended Review or Literary Journal; "*The Annals of Literature*,
foreign as well as domestic. Imitate Le Clerc—Bayle—Barberac. In-
felicity of Journals in England. 'Works of the learned.' We cannot
take in all. Sometimes copy from foreign Journalists. Always tell."

"TO DR. BIRCH.

"SIR,   *March* 29, 1755.

"I have sent some parts of my Dictionary, such as were at hand, for your inspection. The favour which I beg is, that if you do not like them, you will say nothing. I am, Sir,

"Your most affectionate humble servant,

"SAM. JOHNSON."

"TO MR. SAMUEL JOHNSON.

"SIR,   *Norfolk-street, April* 23, 1755.

"The part of your Dictionary which you have favoured me with the sight of has given me such an idea of the whole, that I most sincerely congratulate the public upon the acquisition of a work long wanted, and now executed with an industry, accuracy, and judgment, equal to the importance of the subject. You might, perhaps, have chosen one in which your genius would have appeared to more advantage, but you could not have fixed upon any other in which your labours would have done such substantial service to the present age and to posterity. I am glad that your health has supported the application necessary to the performance of so vast a task ; and can undertake to promise you as one (though perhaps the only) reward of it, the approbation and thanks of every well-wisher to the honour of the English language. I am, with the greatest regard, Sir,

"Your most faithful and

"Most affectionate humble servant,

"THO. BIRCH."

Mr. Charles Burney, who has since distinguished himself so much in the science of music, and obtained a doctor's degree from the University of Oxford, had been driven from the capital by bad health, and was now residing at Lynne Regis in Norfolk. He had been so much delighted with Johnson's "Rambler," and the plan of his Dictionary, that when the great work was announced in the newspapers as nearly finished, he wrote to Dr. Johnson, begging to be informed when and in what manner his Dictionary would be published ; entreating if it should be by subscription, or he should have any books at his own disposal, to to be favoured with six copies for himself and friends.

In answer to this application, Dr. Johnson wrote the following letter, of which (to use Mr. Burney's own words) "if it be remembered that it was written to an obscure young man, who at this time had not much distinguished himself even in his own profession, but whose name could never have reached the author of the 'Rambler,' the politeness and urbanity may be opposed to some of the stories which have been lately circulated of Dr. Johnson's natural rudeness and ferocity."

" TO MR. BURNEY, IN LYNNE REGIS, NORFOLK.

" SIR,   *Gough-square, Fleet-street, April* 8, 1755.

" If you imagine that by delaying my answer I intended to show any neglect of the notice with which you have favoured me, you will neither think justly of yourself nor of me. Your civilities were offered with too much elegance not to engage attention ; and I have too much pleasure in pleasing men like you, not to feel very sensibly the distinction which you have bestowed upon me.

" Few consequences of my endeavours to please or to benefit mankind have delighted me more than your friendship thus voluntarily offered, which now I have it I hope to keep, because I hope to continue to deserve it.

" I have no Dictionaries to dispose of for myself, but shall be glad to have you direct your friends to Mr. Dodsley, because it was by his recommendation that I was employed in the work.

" When you have leisure to think again upon me, let me be favoured with another letter ; and another yet, when you have looked into my Dictionary. If you find faults, I shall endeavour to mend them ; if you find none, I shall think you blinded by kind partiality : but to have made you partial in his favour, will very much gratify the ambition of, Sir, your most obliged

" And most humble servant,

" SAM. JOHNSON."

Mr. Andrew Millar, bookseller in the Strand, took the principal charge of conducting the publication of " Johnson's Dictionary ;" and as the patience of the proprietors was repeatedly tried and almost exhausted by their expecting that the work would be completed, within the time which Johnson had sanguinely supposed, the learned author was often goaded to despatch, more especially as he had received all the copy money, by different drafts, a considerable time before he had finished his task. When the messenger who carried the last sheet to Millar returned, Johnson asked him, " Well, what did he say ?"—" Sir," answered the messenger, " he said, ' Thank God I have done with him.' " " I am glad," replied Johnson, with a smile, " that he thanks God for anything." [1] It is remarkable, that those with whom Johnson chiefly contracted for his literary labours were Scotchmen, Mr. Millar and Mr. Strahan. Millar, though himself no great judge of literature, had good sense enough to have for his friends very able men, to give him their opinion and advice in the purchase of copyright ; the consequence of which was his acquiring a very large fortune, with great liberality. Johnson said of him, " I respect Millar, Sir ; he has raised the price of literature." The same praise may be justly given to

---

[1] Sir John Hawkins, p. 341, inserts two notes as having passed formally between Andrew Millar and Johnson, to the above effect. I am assured this was not the case. In the way of incidental remark it was a pleasant play of raillery. To have deliberately written notes in such terms would have been morose.—BOSWELL.

Panckoucke, the eminent bookseller of Paris.   Mr. Strahan's liberality
judgment, and success are well known.

" TO BENNET LANGTON, ESQ., AT LANGTON, NEAR SPILSBY,
LINCOLNSHIRE.

"SIR,   *May* 6, 1755.

" It has been long observed that men do not suspect faults which they do not
commit ; your own elegance of manners, and punctuality of complaisance, did
not suffer you to impute to me that negligence of which I was guilty, and [for]
which I have not since atoned.   I received both your letters, and received
them with pleasure proportioned to the esteem which so short an acquaintance
strongly impressed, and which I hope to confirm by nearer knowledge, though
I am afraid that gratification will be for a time withheld.

" I have, indeed, published my book [his Dictionary], of which I beg to know
your father's judgment, and yours ; and I have now staid long enough to watch
its progress in the world.   It has, you see, no patrons, and, I think, has yet had
no opponents, except the critics of the coffee-house, whose outcries are soon
dispersed into the air, and are thought on no more ; from this, therefore, I am
at liberty, and think of taking the opportunity of this interval to make an
excursion, and why not then into Lincolnshire ? or, to mention a stronger attraction, why not to dear Mr. Langton ?   I will give the true reason, which I know
you will approve :—I have a mother more than eighty years old, who has
counted the days to the publication of my book, in hopes of seeing me ; and to
her, if I can disengage myself here, I am resolved to go.

" As I know, dear Sir, that to delay my visit for a reason like this, will not
deprive me of your esteem, I beg it may not lessen your kindness.   I have very
seldom received an offer of friendship which I so earnestly desire to cultivate and
mature.   I shall rejoice to hear from you, till I can see you, and will see you as
soon as I can ; for when the duty that calls me to Lichfield is discharged, my
inclination will carry me to Langton.   I shall delight to hear the ocean roar, or
see the stars twinkle, in the company of men to whom Nature does not spread
her volumes or utter her voice in vain.

" Do not, dear Sir, make the slowness of this letter a precedent for delay, or
imagine that I approve the incivility that I have committed ; for I have known
you enough to love you, and sincerely to wish a further knowledge ; and I
assure you once more, that to live in a house that contains such a father, and
such a son, will be accounted a very uncommon degree of pleasure, by,
dear Sir,

" Your most obliged,
" And most humble servant,
" SAM. JOHNSON."

" TO THE REVEREND MR. THOMAS WARTON.

"DEAR SIR,   *May* 13, 1755.

" I am grieved that you should think me capable of neglecting your letters ;
and beg you will never admit any such suspicion again.   I purpose to come down

M 2

next week, if you shall be there ; or any other week that shall be more agreeable to you. Therefore let me know. I can stay this visit but a week, but intend to make preparations for a longer stay next time, being resolved not to lose sight of the University. How goes Apollonius ?[1] Don't let him be forgotten. Some things of this kind must be done, to keep us up. Pay my compliments to Mr. Wise, and all my other friends. I think to come to Kettel Hall.[2]

> "I am, Sir,
> "Your most affectionate, &c.
> "SAMUEL JOHNSON."

TO THE SAME.

"DEAR SIR,   *June* 10, 1755.

" It is strange how many things will happen to intercept every pleasure, though it [be] only that of two friends meeting together. I have promised myself every day to inform you when you might expect me at Oxford, and have not been able to fix a time. The time, however, is, I think, at last come, and I promise myself to repose in Kettel Hall, one of the first nights of the next week. I am afraid my stay with you cannot be long; but what is the inference? We must endeavour to make it cheerful. I wish your brother could meet us, that we might go and drink tea with Mr. Wise in a body. I hope he will be at Oxford, or at his nest of British and Saxon antiquities.[3] I shall expect to see Spenser finished, and many other things begun. Dodsley is gone to visit the Dutch. The Dictionary sells well. The rest of the world goes on as it did.

> " Dear Sir,
> " Your most affectionate, &c.
> " SAM. JOHNSON."

TO THE SAME.

"DEAR SIR,   *June* 24, 1755.

" To talk of coming to you, and not yet to come, has an air of trifling which I would not willingly have among you ; and which, I believe, you will not willingly impute to me, when I have told you, that since my promise, two of our partners[4] are dead, and that I was solicited to suspend my excursion till we could recover from our confusion.

"I have not laid aside my purpose; for every day makes me more impatient of staying from you. But death, you know, hears not supplications, nor pays

---

[1] A translation of Apollonius Rhodius is now intended by Mr. Warton.—WARTON.

[2] Kettel Hall is an ancient tenement, adjoining to Trinity College, built about the year 1615, by Dr. Ralph Kettel, then President, for the accommodation of commoners of that society. In this ancient *hostel*, then in a very ruinous state, about forty years after Johnson had lodged there, Mr. Windham and the present writer were accommodated with two chambers, of primitive simplicity, during the installation of the Duke of Portland, as Chancellor of the University of Oxford, in 1793. It has since been converted into a commodious private house.—MALONE.

[3] At Ellsfield, a village three miles from Oxford.—WARTON.

[4] Booksellers concerned in his Dictionary.—WARTON.

any regard to the convenience of mortals. I hope now to see you next week · but next week is but another name for to-morrow, which has been noted for promising and deceiving.

"I am, &c.

"SAM. JOHNSON."

TO THE SAME.

"DEAR SIR,   *Aug.* 7, 1755.

"I told you that among the manuscripts are some things of Sir Thomas More. I beg you to pass an hour in looking on them, and procure a transcript of the ten or twenty first lines of each, to be compared with what I have; that I may know whether they are yet published. The manuscripts are these :—

"Catalogue of Bodl. MS. pag. 122. F. 3. Sir Thomas More. 1. Fall of angels. 2. Creation and fall of mankind. 3. Determination of the Trinity for the rescue of mankind. 4. Five lectures of our Saviour's passion. 5. Of the institution of the Sacrament, three lectures. 6. How to receive the blessed body of our Lord sacramentally. 7. Neomenia, the new moon. 8. *De tristitia, tœdio, pavore, et oratione Christi ante captionem ejus.*

"Catalogue, page 154. Life of Sir Thomas More. *Qu.* Whether Roper's? Page 363. *De resignatione Magni Sigilli in manus Regis per D. Thomam Morum.* Page 364. *Mori Defensio Moriæ.*

"If you procure the young gentleman in the library to write out what you think fit to be written, I will send to Mr. Prince the bookseller to pay him what you shall think proper.

"Be pleased to make my compliments to Mr. Wise, and all my friends.

"I am, Sir,

"Your affectionate, &c.

"SAM. JOHNSON."

The Dictionary, with a Grammar and History of the English Language, being now at length published, in two volumes folio, the world contemplated with wonder so stupendous a work achieved by one man, while other countries had thought such undertakings fit only for whole academies. Vast as his powers were, I cannot but think that his imagination deceived him, when he supposed that by constant application he might have performed the task in three years. Let the Preface be attentively perused, in which is given, in a clear, strong, and glowing style, a comprehensive, yet particular view of what he had done; and it will be evident, that the time he employed upon it was comparatively short. I am unwilling to swell my book with long quotations from what is in everybody's hands, and I believe there are few prose compositions in the English language that are read with more delight, or are more impressed upon the memory, than that preliminary discourse. One of its excellencies has always struck me with peculiar admiration;

I mean the perspicuity with which he has expressed abstract scientific notions.   As an instance of this, I shall quote the following sentence :—

"When the radical idea branches out into parallel ramifications, how can a consecutive series be formed of senses in their own nature collateral ?"   We have here an example of what has been often said, and I believe with justice, that there is for every thought a certain nice adaptation of words which none other could equal, and which, when a man has been so fortunate as to hit, he has attained, in that particular case, the perfection of language."

The extensive reading which was absolutely necessary for the accumulation of authorities, and which alone may account for Johnson's retentive mind being enriched with a very large and various store of knowledge and imagery, must have occupied several years.   The Preface furnishes an eminent instance of a double talent, of which Johnson was fully conscious.   Sir Joshua Reynolds heard him say, "There are two things which I am confident I can do very well : one is an introduction to any literary work, stating what it is to contain, and how it should be executed in the most perfect manner : the other is a conclusion, showing from various causes, why the execution has not been equal to what the author promised to himself and to the public."

How should puny scribblers be abashed and disappointed, when they find him displaying a perfect theory of lexicographical excellence, yet at the same time candidly and modestly allowing that he "had not satisfied his own expectations."   Here was a fair occasion for the exercise of Johnson's modesty, when he was called upon to compare his own arduous performance, not with those of other individuals, (in which case his inflexible regard to truth would have been violated had he affected diffidence,) but with speculative perfection ; as he, who can outstrip all his competitors in the race, may yet be sensible of his deficiency when he runs against time.   Well might he say, that "the English Dictionary was written with little assistance of the learned ;" for he told me, that the only aid which he received was a paper containing twenty etymologies, sent to him by a person then unknown, who, he was afterwards informed, was Dr. Pearce, Bishop of Rochester.   The etymologies, though they exhibit learning and judgment, are not, I think, entitled to the first praise amongst the various parts of this immense work.   The definitions have always appeared to me such astonishing proofs of acuteness of intellect and precision of language, as indicate a genius of the highest rank.   This it is which marks the superior excellence of Johnson's Dictionary over others equally, or even more voluminous, and must have made it a work of much greater mental labour than mere Lexicons, or *Word-Books*, as the Dutch call them.   They, who will make the experiment of trying how they can define a few words of whatever nature, will soon be satisfied of the unquestionable justice of this observation, which I can assure my readers is founded upon much study, and upon communication with more minds than my own.

A few of his definitions must be admitted to be erroneous. Thus *Windward* and *Leeward*, though directly of opposite meaning, are defined identically the same way;[1] as to which inconsiderable specks it is enough to observe, that his Preface announces that he was aware there might be many such in so immense a work; nor was he at all disconcerted when an instance was pointed out to him. A lady once asked him how he came to define *Pastern* the *knee* of a horse; instead of making an elaborate defence, as she expected, he at once answered, "Ignorance, Madam,—pure ignorance." His definition of *Network* has been often quoted with sportive malignity, as obscuring a thing in itself very plain. But to these frivolous censures no other answer is necessary than that with which we are furnished by his own Preface:—

"To explain, requires the use of terms less abstruse than that which is to be explained, and such terms cannot always be found; for as nothing can be proved but by supposing something intuitively known, and evident without proof, so nothing can be defined but by the use of words too plain to admit of definition. Sometimes easier words are changed into harder; as, *burial*, into *sepulture* or *interment*; *dry*, into *desiccative*; *dryness*, into *siccity* or *aridity*; *fit*, into *paroxysm*: for, the *easiest* word, whatever it be, can never be translated into one more easy."

His introducing his own opinions, and even prejudices, under general definitions of words, while at the same time the original meaning of the words is not explained, as his *Tory*, *Whig*, *Pension*, *Oats*, *Excise*,[2] and a few more, cannot be fully defended, and must be placed to the account of capricious and humorous indulgence. Talking to me upon this subject when we were at Ashbourne in 1777, he mentioned a still stronger instance of the predominance of his private feelings in the

[1] He owns in his Preface the deficiency of the technical part of his work; and he said, he should be much obliged to me for definitions of musical terms for his next edition, which he did not live to superintend.—BURNEY.

[2] He thus defines Excise: "A hateful tax levied upon commodities, and adjudged not by the common judges of property, but wretches hired by those to whom Excise is paid." The Commissioners of Excise being offended by this severe reflection, consulted Mr. Murray, then Attorney-General, to know whether redress could be legally obtained. I wished to have procured for my readers a copy of the opinion which he gave, and which may now be justly considered as history; but the mysterious secrecy of office, it seems, would not permit it. I am, however, informed, by very good authority, that its import was, that the passage might be considered as actionable; but that it would be more prudent in the board not to prosecute. Johnson never made the smallest alteration in this passage. We find he still retained his early prejudice against Excise; for in "The Idler," No. 65, there is the following very extraordinary paragraph:—"The authenticity of *Clarendon's* history, though printed with the sanction of one of the first Universities of the world, had not an unexpected manuscript been happily discovered, would, with the help of factious credulity, have been brought into question by the two lowest of all human beings, a scribbler for a party, and a commissioner of Excise." The persons to whom he alludes were Mr. John Oldmixon, and George Ducket, Esq.—BOSWELL.

composition of this work, than any now to be found in it. " You know
Sir, Lord Gower forsook the old Jacobite interest. When I came to the
word *renegado,* after telling that it meant 'one who deserts to the
enemy, a revolter,' I added, *Sometimes we say a* GOWER. Thus it went
to the press ; but the printer had more wit than I, and struck it out."

Let it, however, be remembered, that this indulgence does not display
itself only in sarcasm towards others, but sometimes in playful allusion
to the notions commonly entertained of his own laborious task. Thus :
" *Grub-street,* the name of a street in London, much inhabited by writers
of small histories, *dictionaries,* and temporary poems ; whence any
mean production is called *Grub-street.*"—" *Lexicographer,* a writer of
dictionaries, a *harmless drudge.*"

At the time when he was concluding his very eloquent Preface,
Johnson's mind appears to have been in such a state of depression, that
we cannot contemplate without wonder the vigorous and splendid
thoughts which so highly distinguish that performance. "I," says he,
" may surely be contented without the praise of perfection, which if I
could obtain in this gloom of solitude, what would it avail me ? I have
protracted my work till most of those whom I wished to please have
sunk into the grave ; and success and miscarriage are empty sounds.
I therefore dismiss it with frigid tranquillity, having little to fear or
hope from censure or from praise." That this indifference was rather
a temporary than an habitual feeling, appears, I think, from his letters
to Mr. Warton ; and however he may have been affected for the
moment, certain it is that the honours which his great work procured
him, both at home and abroad, were very grateful to him. His friend,
the Earl of Cork and Orrery, being at Florence, presented it to the
Academia della Crusca. That Academy sent Johnson their *Vocabulario,*
and the French Academy sent him their *Dictionnaire,* which Mr.
Langton had the pleasure to convey to him.

It must undoubtedly seem strange, that the conclusion of his Preface
should be expressed in terms so desponding, when it is considered that
the author was then only in his forty-sixth year. But we must ascribe
its gloom to that miserable dejection of spirits to which he was constitutionally subject, and which was aggravated by the death of his wife
two years before. I have heard it ingeniously observed by a lady of
rank and elegance, that "his melancholy was then at its meridian." It
pleased God to grant him almost thirty years of life after this time ; and
once, when he was in a placid frame of mind, he was obliged to own to
me that he had enjoyed happier days, and had many more friends, since
that gloomy hour, than before.

It is a sad saying, that "most of those whom he wished to please
had sunk into the grave ;" and his case at forty-five was singularly unhappy, unless the circle of his friends was very narrow. I have often
thought, that as longevity is generally desired, and, I believe, generally

expected, it would be wise to be continually adding to the number of our friends, that the loss of some may be supplied by others. Friendship, "the wine of life," should, like a well-stocked cellar, be thus continually renewed; and it is consolatory to think, that although we can seldom add what will equal the generous *first growths* of our youth, yet friendship becomes insensibly old in much less time than is commonly imagined, and not many years are required to make it very mellow and pleasant. *Warmth* will, no doubt, make a considerable difference. Men of affectionate temper and bright fancy will coalesce a great deal sooner than those who are cold and dull.

The proposition which I have now endeavoured to illustrate was, at a subsequent period of his life, the opinion of Johnson himself. He said to Sir Joshua Reynolds, "If a man does not make new acquaintance as he advances through life, he will soon find himself left alone. A man, Sir, should keep his friendship *in constant repair*."

The celebrated Mr. Wilkes, whose notions and habits of life were very opposite to his, but who was ever eminent for literature and vivacity, sallied forth with a little *jeu d'esprit* upon the following passage in his Grammar of the English Tongue, prefixed to the Dictionary :— "*H* seldom, perhaps never, begins any but the first syllable." In an essay printed in the "Public Advertiser," this lively writer enumerated many instances in opposition to this remark : for example, "The author of this observation must be a man of quick *appre-hension*, and of a most, *compre-hensive* genius." The position is undoubtedly expressed with too much latitude.

This light sally, we may suppose, made no great impression on our lexicographer ; for we find that he did not alter the passage till many years afterwards.[1]

He had the pleasure of being treated in a very different manner by his old pupil Mr. Garrick, in the following complimentary epigram :—

"On Johnson's Dictionary.

"Talk of war with a Briton, he'll boldly advance,
    That one English soldier will beat ten of France ;
    Would we alter the boast from the sword to the pen,
    Our odds are still greater, still greater our men ;
    In the deep mines of science though Frenchmen may toil,
    Can their strength be compared to Locke, Newton, and Boyle?
    Let them rally their heroes, send forth all their pow'rs,
    Their verse-men and prose-men, then match them with ours !

---

[1] In the third edition, published in 1773, he left out the words *perhaps never*, and added the following paragraph :—

"It sometimes begins middle or final syllables in words compounded, as *block-head*, or derived from the Latin, as *compre-hended*."—Boswell

> First Shakspeare and Milton, like Gods in the fight,
> Have put their whole drama and epic to flight;
> In satires, epistles, and odes, would they cope,
> Their numbers retreat before Dryden and Pope;
> And Johnson, well-arm'd, like a hero of yore,
> Has beat forty French,[1] and will beat forty more!"

Johnson this year gave at once a proof of his benevolence, quickness of apprehension, and admirable art of composition, in the assistance which he gave to Mr. Zachariah Williams, father of the blind lady whom he had humanely received under his roof. Mr. Williams had followed the profession of physic in Wales; but having a very strong propensity to the study of natural philosophy, had made many ingenious advances towards a discovery of the longitude, and repaired to London in hopes of obtaining the great parliamentary reward. He failed of success; but Johnson having made himself master of his principles and experiments, wrote for him a pamphlet, published in quarto, with the following title: "An Account of an Attempt to ascertain the Longitude at Sea, by an exact Theory of the Variation of the Magnetical Needle; with a Table of the Variations at the most remarkable Cities in Europe, from the year 1660 to 1860."† To diffuse it more extensively, it was accompanied with an Italian translation on the opposite page, which it is supposed was the work of Signor Baretti,[2] an Italian of considerable literature, who having come to England a few years before, had been employed in the capacity both of a language master and an author, and formed an intimacy with Dr. Johnson. This pamphlet Johnson presented to the Bodleian library.[3] On a blank leaf of it is pasted a paragraph cut out of a newspaper, containing an account of the death and character of Williams, plainly written by Johnson.[4]

In July this year he had formed some scheme of mental improvement, the particular purpose of which does not appear. But we find in his "Prayers and Meditations," p. 25, a prayer entitled, "On the study of Philosophy, as an instrument of living;" and after it follows a note "This study was not pursued."

---

[1] The number of the French Academy employed in settling their language.—BOSWELL.

[2] This ingenious foreigner, who was a native of Piedmont, came to England about the year 1753, and died in London, May 5, 1789. A very candid and judicious account of him and his works, beginning with the words "So much asperity," and written, it is believed, by a distinguished dignitary in the Church, may be found in the "Gentleman's Magazine," for that year, p. 469.—MALONE.

[3] See note by Mr. Warton, pp. 185, 186, from which it appears that "12th" in the next note means the 12th of July, 1755.—MALONE.

[4] "On Saturday the 12th about 12 at night, died Mr. Zachariah Williams, in his eighty-third year, after an illness of eight months, in full possession of his mental faculties. He has been long known to philosophers and seamen for his skill in magnetism, and his proposal to ascertain the longitude by a peculiar system of the variation of the compass. He was a man of industry indefatigable, of conversation inoffensive, patient of adversity and disease, eminently sober, temperate, and pious; and worthy to have ended life with better fortune." —BOSWELL

On the 13th of the same month he wrote in his Journal the following scheme of life, for Sunday: "Having lived," as he with tenderness of conscience expresses himself, "not without an habitual reverence for the Sabbath, yet without that attention to its religious duties which Christianity requires;"

"1. To rise early, and in order to it, to go to sleep early on Saturday.

"2. To use some extraordinary devotion in the morning.

"3. To examine the tenor of my life, and particularly the last week; and to mark my advances in religion, or recession from it.

"4. To read the Scripture methodically with such helps as are at hand.

"5. To go to church twice.

"6. To read books of Divinity, either speculative or practical.

"7. To instruct my family.

"8. To wear off by meditation any worldly soil contracted in the week."

SAMUEL RICHARDSON.

CHAPTER IX.—1756—1758.

IN 1756 Johnson found that the great fame of his Dictionary had not set him above the necessity of "making provision for the day that was passing over him."[1] No royal or noble patron extended a munificent hand to give independence to the man who had conferred stability on the language of his country. We may feel indignant that there should have been such unworthy neglect; but we must, at the same time, congratulate ourselves, when we consider, that to this very neglect, operating to rouse the natural indolence of his constitution, we owe many valuable productions, which otherwise, perhaps, might never have appeared.

[1] He was so far from being "set above the necessity of·making provision for the day that was passing over him," that he appears to have been in this year in great pecuniary distress, having been arrested for debt; on which occasion his friend, Samuel Richardson, became his surety. See a letter from Johnson to him, on that subject, dated Feb. 19, 1756. Richardson's " Correspondence," vol. v. p. 283.—MALONE.

He had spent, during the progress of the work, the money for which he had contracted to write his Dictionary. We have seen that the reward of his labour was only fifteen hundred and seventy-five pounds ; and when the expense of amanuenses and paper, and other articles, are deducted, his clear profit was very inconsiderable. I once said to him, "I am sorry, Sir, you did not get more for your Dictionary." His answer was, "I am sorry too. But it was very well. The booksellers are generous liberal-minded men." He, upon all occasions, did ample justice to their character in this respect. He considered them as the patrons of literature ; and, indeed, although they have eventually been considerable gainers by his Dictionary, it is to them that we owe its having been undertaken and carried through at the risk of great expense, for they were not absolutely sure of being indemnified.

On the first day of this year[1] we find from his private devotions, that he had then recovered from sickness [Pr. and Med.], and in February, that his eye was restored to its use [Pr. and Med. p. 27]. The pious gratitude with which he acknowledges mercies upon every occasion is very edifying ; as is the humble submission which he breathes, when it is the will of his heavenly Father to try him with afflictions. As such dispositions become the state of man here, and are the true effects of religious discipline, we cannot but venerate in Johnson one of the most exercised minds that our holy religion hath ever formed. If there be any thoughtless enough to suppose such exercise the weakness of a great understanding, let them look up to Johnson, and be convinced that what he so earnestly practised must have a rational foundation.

His works this year were, an abstract or epitome, in octavo, of his folio Dictionary, and a few essays in a monthly publication, entitled "The Universal Visiter." Christopher Smart, with whose unhappy vacillation of mind he sincerely sympathised, was one of the stated undertakers of this miscellany ; and it was to assist him that Johnson sometimes employed his pen. All the essays marked with two *asterisks* have been ascribed to him ; but I am confident, from internal evidence, that of these, neither " The Life of Chaucer," " Reflections on the State of Portugal," nor an " Essay on Architecture," were written by him. I am equally confident, upon the same evidence, that he wrote " Further Thoughts on Agriculture ;"† being the sequel of a very inferior essay on the same subject, and which. though carried on as if by the same hand,

---

[1] In April in this year, Johnson wrote a letter to Dr. Joseph Warton, in consequence of having read a few pages of that gentleman's newly published "Essay on the Genius and Writings of Pope." The only paragraph in it that respects Johnson's personal history is this : "For my part, I have not lately done much. I have been ill in the winter, and my eye has been inflamed; but I please myself with the hopes of doing many things, with which I have long pleased and deceived myself!" Memoirs of Dr. J. Warton, &c. 4to. 1806.— Malone.

is both in thinking and expression so far above it, and so strikingly peculiar, as to leave no doubt of its true parent; and that he also wrote, " A Dissertation on the State of Literature and Authors,"† and " A Dissertation on the Epitaphs written by Pope."* The last of these, indeed, he afterwards added to his " Idler." Why the essays truly written by him are marked in the same manner with some which he did not write, I cannot explain: but with deference to those who have ascribed to him the three essays which I have ejected, they want all the characteristical marks of Johnsonian composition.

He engaged also to superintend and contribute largely to another monthly publication, entitled " The Literary Magazine, or Universal Review ; " * the first number of which came out in May this year. What were his emoluments from this undertaking, and what other writers were employed in it, I have not discovered. He continued to write in it, with intermissions, till the fifteenth number ; and I think that he never gave better proofs of the force, acuteness, and vivacity of his mind, than in this miscellany, whether we consider his original essays, or his reviews of the works of others. The "Preliminary Address " † to the public, is a proof how this great man could embellish, with the graces of superior composition, even so trite a thing as the plan of a magazine.

His original essays are, " An Introduction to the Political State of Great Britain ; " † " Remarks on the Militia Bill ; " † " Observations on his Britannic Majesty's Treaties with the Empress of Russia and the Landgrave of Hesse Cassel ; " † " Observations on the Present State of Affairs ; " † " and, " Memoirs of Frederick III., King of Prussia." † In all these he displays extensive political knowledge and sagacity, expressed with uncommon energy and perspicuity ; without any of those words which he sometimes took a pleasure in adopting, in imitation of Sir Thomas Brown ; of whose " Christian Morals " he this year gave an edition, with his " Life " * prefixed to it, which is one of Johnson's best biographical performances. In one instance only in these essays has he indulged his *Brownism*. Dr. Robertson, the historian, mentioned it to me, as having at once convinced him that Johnson was the author of the " Memoirs of the King of Prussia." Speaking of the pride which the old king, the father of his hero, took in being master of the tallest regiment in Europe, he says, " To review this *towering* regiment was his daily pleasure ; and to perpetuate it was so much his care, that when he met a tall woman he immediately commanded one of his *Titanian* retinue to marry her, that they might *propagate procerity*." For this Anglo-Latin word *procerity*, Johnson had, however, the authority of Addison.

His reviews are of the following books : " Birch's History of the Royal Society ; " † " Murphy's Gray's-Inn Journal ; " † " Warton's

Essay on the Writings and Genius of Pope," vol. i. ; † "Hampton's Translation of Polybius ;" † "Blackwell's Memoirs of the Court of Augustus ;" † "Russell's Natural History of Aleppo ;" † "Sir Isaac Newton's Arguments in Proof of a Deity ;" † "Borlase's History of the Isles of Scilly ;" † "Holme's Experiments on Bleaching ;" † "Browne's Christian Morals ;" † "Hales on Distilling Sea-Water, Ventilators in Ships, and Curing an ill Taste in Milk ;" † "Lucas's Essay on Waters ;" † "Keith's Catalogue of the Scottish Bishops ;" † "Browne's History of Jamaica ;" † "Philosophical Transactions," vol. xlix. "Mrs. Lennox's Translation of Sully's Memoirs ;" * "Miscellanies, by Elizabeth Harrison ;" † "Evans's Map and Account of the Middle Colonies in America ;" † "Letter on the Case of Admiral Byng ;" * "Appeal to the People concerning Admiral Byng ;" * "Hanway's Eight Days' Journey, and Essay on Tea ;" * "The Cadet, a Military Treatise ;" † "Some further Particulars in Relation to the Case of Admiral Byng, by a Gentleman of Oxford ;" * "The Conduct of the Ministry relating to the Present War impartially examined ;" † "A Free Inquiry into the Nature and Origin of Evil." * All these, from internal evidence, were written by Johnson : some of them I know he avowed, and have marked them with an *asterisk* accordingly. Mr. Thomas Davies, indeed, ascribed to him the Review of Mr. Burke's "Inquiry into the Origin of our Ideas of the Sublime and Beautiful;" and Sir John Hawkins, with equal discernment, has inserted it in his collection of Johnson's works ; whereas it has no resemblance to Johnson's composition, and is well known to have been written by Mr. Murphy, who has acknowledged it to me and many others.

It is worthy of remark, in justice to Johnson's political character, which has been misrepresented as abjectly submissive to power, that his "Observations on the present State of Affairs" glow with as animated a spirit of constitutional liberty as can be found anywhere. Thus he begins : "The time is now come, in which every Englishman expects to be informed of the national affairs ; and in which he has a right to have that expectation gratified. For, whatever may be urged by Ministers, or those whom vanity or interest make the followers of Ministers, concerning the necessity of confidence in our governors, and the presumption of prying with profane eyes into the recesses of policy, it is evident that this reverence can be claimed only by counsels yet unexecuted, and projects suspended in deliberation. But when a design has ended in miscarriage or success, when every eye and every ear is witness to general discontent, or general satisfaction, it is then a proper time to disentangle confusion and illustrate obscurity ; to show by what causes every event was produced, and in what effects it is likely to terminate ; to lay down with distinct particularity what rumour always huddles in general exclamation, or perplexes by indigested narratives ; to show whence happiness or calamity is derived, and whence it may be

expected; and honestly to lay before the people what inquiry can gather
of the past, and conjecture can estimate of the future."

Here we have it assumed as an incontrovertible principle, that in this
country the people are the superintendents of the conduct and measures
of those by whom Government is administered; of the beneficial effect of
which the present reign afforded an illustrious example, when addresses
from all parts of the kingdom controlled an audacious attempt to introduce a new power subversive of the Crown.

A still stronger proof of his patriotic spirit appears in his review of
an "Essay on Waters, by Dr. Lucas," of whom, after describing him
as a man well known to the world for his daring defiance of power, when
he thought it exerted on the side of wrong, he thus speaks :—

"The Irish ministers drove him from his native country by a proclamation,
in which they charge him with crimes of which they never intended to be
called to the proof, and oppressed him by methods equally irresistible by
guilt and innocence. Let the man thus driven into exile for having been the
friend of his country, be received in every other place as a confessor of
liberty; and let the tools of power be taught in time, that they may rob but
cannot impoverish."

Some of his reviews in this Magazine are very short accounts of the
pieces noticed; and I mention them only that Dr. Johnson's opinion of
the works may be known; but many of them are examples of elaborate
criticism in the most masterly style. In his review of the "Memoirs
of the Court of Augustus," he has the resolution to think and speak
from his own mind, regardless of the cant transmitted from age to age
in praise of the ancient Romans. Thus : "I know not why any one but
a schoolboy in his declamation should whine over the Commonwealth
of Rome, which grew great only by the misery of the rest of mankind.
The Romans, like others, as soon as they grew rich, grew corrupt; and
in their corruption sold the lives and freedoms of themselves, and of one
another." Again—"A people who, while they were poor, robbed mankind; and as soon as they became rich, robbed one another." In his
review of the Miscellanies in prose and verse, published by Elizabeth
Harrison, but written by many hands, he gives an eminent proof at once
of his orthodoxy and candour :—

"The authors of the essays in prose seem generally to have imitated, or
tried to imitate, the copiousness and luxuriance of Mrs. Rowe. This, however,
is not all their praise; they have laboured to add to her brightness of imagery,
her purity of sentiments. The poets have had Dr. Watts before their eyes, a
writer who, if he stood not in the first class of genius, compensated that defect
by a ready application of his powers to the promotion of piety. The attempt
to employ the ornaments of romance in the decoration of religion, was, I think,
first made by Mr. Boyle's 'Martyrdom of Theodora;' but Boyle's philosophical

studies did not allow him time for the cultivation of style ; and the completion of the great design was reserved for Mrs. Rowe. Dr. Watts was one of the first who taught the Dissenters to write and speak like other men, by showing them that elegance might consist with piety. They would have both done honour to a better society, for they had that charity which might well make their failings be forgotten, and with which the whole Christian world wish for communion. They were pure from all the heresies of an age, to which every opinion is become a favourite, that the universal church has hitherto detested! This praise the general interest of mankind requires to be given to writers who please and do not corrupt, who instruct and do not weary. But to them all human eulogies are vain, whom I believe applauded by angels, and numbered with the just."

His defence of tea against Mr. Jonas Hanway's violent attack upon that elegant and popular beverage, shows how very well a man of genius can write upon the slightest subject, when he writes, as the Italians say, *con amore;* I suppose no person ever enjoyed with more relish the infusion of that fragrant leaf than Johnson. The quantities which he drank of it at all hours were so great that his nerves must have been uncommonly strong not to have been extremely relaxed by such an intemperate use of it. He assured me that he never felt the least inconvenience from it, which is a proof that the fault of his constitution was rather a too great tension of fibres, than the contrary. Mr. Hanway wrote an angry answer to Johnson's review of his " Essay on Tea," and Johnson, after a full and deliberate pause, made a reply to it ; the only instance, I believe, in the whole course of his life, when he condescended to oppose any thing that was written against him. I suppose when he thought of any of his little antagonists, he was ever justly aware of the high sentiment of Ajax in Ovid :—

> " *Iste tulit pretium jam nunc certaminis hujus,*
> *Qui, cùm victus erit, mecum certasse feretur.*" [1]

But, indeed, the good Mr. Hanway laid himself so open to ridicule, that Johnson's animadversions upon his attack were chiefly to make sport.

The generosity with which he pleads the cause of Admiral Byng, is highly to the honour of his heart and spirit. Though Voltaire affects to be witty upon the fate of that unfortunate officer, observing that he was shot " *pour encourager les autres,*" the nation has long been satisfied that his life was sacrificed to the political fervour of the times. In the vault belonging to the Torrington family, in the church of Southill, in

Losing, he wins, because his name will be
Ennobled by defeat, who durst contend with me.—DRYDEN.

Bedfordshire, there is the following epitaph upon his monument, which I have transcribed :—

> "TO THE PERPETUAL DISGRACE
> OF PUBLIC JUSTICE,
> THE HONOURABLE JOHN BYNG, ESQ.
> ADMIRAL OF THE BLUE,
> FELL A MARTYR TO POLITICAL
> PERSECUTION,
> MARCH 14, IN THE YEAR 1757 ;
> WHEN BRAVERY AND LOYALTY
> WERE INSUFFICIENT SECURITIES
> FOR THE LIFE AND HONOUR OF
> A NAVAL OFFICER."

Johnson's most exquisite critical essay in the "Literary Magazine," and indeed anywhere, is his review of Soame Jenyns's "Inquiry into the Origin of Evil." Jenyns was possessed of lively talents, and a style eminently pure and easy, and could very happily play with a light subject, either in prose or verse ; but when he speculated on that most difficult and excruciating question, the Origin of Evil, he "ventured far beyond his depth," and, accordingly, was exposed by Johnson, both with acute argument and brilliant wit. I remember when the late Mr. Bicknell's humorous performance entitled "The Musical Travels of Joel Collyer" in which a slight attempt is made to ridicule Johnson, was ascribed to Soame Jenyns, "Ha !" said Johnson, "I thought I had given *him* enough of it."

His triumph over Jenyns is thus described by my friend Mr. Courtenay in his "Poetical Review of the literary and moral Character of Dr. Johnson ;" a performance of such merit, that had I not been honoured with a very kind and partial notice in it, I should echo the sentiments of men of the first taste loudly in its praise :—

> " When specious sophists with presumption scan
> The source of evil hidden still from man ;
> Revive Arabian tales, and vainly hope
> To rival St. John, and his scholar Pope :
> Though metaphysics spread the gloom of night,
> By reason's star he guides our aching sight ;
> The bounds of knowledge marks, and points the way
> To athless wastes, where wilder'd sages stray ;—
> Where, like a farthing link-boy, Jenyns stands,
> And the dim torch drops from his feeble hands."[1]

---

[1] Some time after Dr. Johnson's death, there appeared in the newspapers and magazines an illiberal and petulant attack upon him, in the form of an Epitaph, under the name of Mr. Soame Jenyns, very unworthy of that gentleman, who had quietly submitted to the critical lash while Johnson lived. It assumed, as characteristics of him, all the vulgar circumstances

This year Mr. William Payne, brother of the respectable bookseller of that name, published " An Introduction to the Game of Draughts," to which Johnson contributed a Dedication to the Earl of Rochford,* and a Preface,* both of which are admirably adapted to the treatise to which they are prefixed. Johnson, I believe, did not play at draughts after leaving College, by which he suffered ; for it would have afforded him an innocent, soothing relief from the melancholy which distressed him so often. I have heard him regret that he had not learned to play at cards ; and the game of draughts we know is peculiarly calculated to fix the attention without straining it. There is a composure and gravity in draughts which insensibly tranquillises the mind ; and accordingly, the Dutch are fond of it, as they are of smoking, of the sedative influence of which, though he himself never smoked, he had a high opinion.[1] Besides, there is in draughts some exercise of the faculties : and, accordingly Johnson, wishing to dignify the subject in his Dedication with what is most estimable in it, observes, " Triflers may find or make anything a trifle ; but since it is the great characteristic of a wise man to see events in their causes, to obviate consequences, and ascertain contingencies, your lordship will think nothing a trifle by which the mind is inured to caution, foresight, and circumspection."

As one of the little occasional advantages which he did not disdain to take by his pen, as a man whose profession was literature, he this year accepted of a guinea from Mr. Robert Dodsley, for writing the introduction to "The London Chronicle," an evening newspaper ; and even in so slight a performance exhibited peculiar talents. This Chronicle still subsists, and from what I observed, when I was abroad, has a more

of abuse which had circulated amongst the ignorant. It was an unbecoming indulgence of puny resentment, at a time when he himself was at a very advanced age, and had a near prospect of descending to the grave. I was truly sorry for it, for he was then become an avowed, and (as my Lord Bishop of London, who had a serious conversation with him on the subject, assures me) a sincere Christian. He could not expect that Johnson's numerous friends would patiently bear to have the memory of their master stigmatised by no mean pen, but that, at least, one would be found to retort. Accordingly, this unjust and sarcastic Epitaph was met in the same public field by an answer, in terms by no means soft, and such as wanton provocation only could justify :—

"EPITAPH.

" Prepared for a creature not quite dead *yet.*

" Here lies a little, ugly, nauseous elf,
  Who, judging only from its wretched self,
  Feebly attempted, petulant and vain,
  The ' Origin of Evil ' to explain.
  A mighty Genius at this elf displeas'd,
  With a strong critic grasp the urchin squeez'd.
  For thirty years its coward spleen it kept,
  Till in the dust the mighty Genius slept ;
  Then stunk and fretted in expiring snuff,
  And blink'd at JOHNSON with its last poor puff."—BOSWELL.

Journal of a Tour to the Hebrides, 3rd edit. 48.

extensive circulation upon the continent than any of the English newspapers. It was constantly read by Johnson himself; and it is but just to observe, that it has all along been distinguished for good sense, accuracy, moderation, and delicacy.

Another instance of the same nature has been communicated to me by the Rev. Dr. Thomas Campbell, who has done himself considerable credit by his own writings. "Sitting with Dr. Johnson one morning alone, he asked me if I had known Dr. Madden, who was author of the premium-scheme[1] in Ireland. On my answering in the affirmative, and also that I had for some years lived in his neighbourhood, &c., he begged of me that when I returned to Ireland, I would endeavour to procure for him a poem of Dr. Madden's, called ' Boulter's Monument.'[2] ' The reason,' said he, ' why I wish for it, is this : when Dr. Madden came to London, he submitted that work to my castigation : and I remember I blotted a great many lines, and might have blotted many more without making the poem worse.[3] However, the Doctor was very thankful, and very generous, for he gave me ten guineas, *which was to me at that time a great sum.*' "

He this year resumed his scheme of giving an edition of Shakspeare with notes. He issued Proposals of considerable length,[4] in which he showed that he perfectly well knew what a variety of research such an undertaking required ; but his indolence prevented him from pursuing it with that diligence which alone can collect those scattered facts, that genius, however acute, penetrating, and luminous, cannot discover by its own force. It is remarkable, that at this time his fancied activity was for the moment so vigorous, that he promised his work should be published before Christmas, 1757. Yet nine years elapsed before it saw the light. His throes in bringing it forth had been severe and remittent ; and at last we may almost conclude that thê Cæsarean operation was

[1] In the College of Dublin, four quarterly examinations of the students are held in each year, in various prescribed branches of literature and science; and premiums, consisting of books impressed with the College Arms, are adjudged by examiners (composed generally of the Junior Fellows), to those who have most distinguished themselves in the several classes, after a very rigid trial, which lasts two days. This regulation, which has subsisted about seventy years, has been attended with the most beneficial effects.

Dr. Samuel Madden was the first proposer of premiums in that University. They were instituted about the year 1734. He was also one of the founders of the Dublin Society for the encouragement of arts and agriculture. In addition to the premiums which were and are still annually given by that society for this purpose, Dr. Madden gave others from his own fund. Hence he was usually called " Premium Madden."—MALONE.

[2] Dr. Hugh Boulter, Archbishop of Armagh, and Primate of Ireland. He died Sept. 27 1742, at which time he was, for the thirteenth time, one of the Lords Justices of that kingdom. Johnson speaks of him in high terms of commendation, in his "Life of Ambrose Philips."—BOSWELL.

[3] Dr. Madden wrote very bad verses. See those prefixed to Leland's "Life of Philip of Macedon," 4to. 1758.—KEARNEY.

[4] They have been reprinted by Mr. Malone, in the Preface to his edition of Shakspeare.-BOSWELL.

performed by the knife of Churchill, whose upbraiding satire, I dare say, made Johnson's friends urge him to despatch.

> " He for subscribers baits his hook
> And takes your cash : but where's the book ?
> No matter where ? wise fear, you know,
> Forbids the robbing of a foe ;
> But what, to serve our private ends,
> Forbids the cheating of our friends ? "

About this period he was offered a living of considerable value in Lincolnshire, if he were inclined to enter into holy orders. It was a rectory in the gift of Mr. Langton, the father of his much valued friend. But he did not accept it ; partly I believe from a conscientious motive, being persuaded that his temper and habits rendered him unfit for that assiduous and familiar instruction of the vulgar and ignorant, which he held to be an essential duty in a clergyman; and partly because his love of a London life was so strong, that he would have thought himself an exile in any other place, particularly if residing in the country. Whoever would wish to see his thoughts upon that subject displayed in their full force, may peruse the " Adventurer," No. 126.

In 1757 it does not appear that he published anything, except some of those articles in the " Literary Magazine," which have been mentioned. That magazine, after Johnson ceased to write in it, gradually declined, though the popular epithet of *Antigallican* was added to it ; and in July, 1758, it expired. He probably prepared a part of his Shakspeare this year, and he dictated a speech on the subject of an address to the Throne, after the expedition to Rochfort, which was delivered by one of his friends, I know not in what public meeting. It is printed in the " Gentleman's Magazine" for October, 1785, as his, and bears sufficient marks of authenticity.

By the favour of Mr. Joseph Cooper Walker, of the Treasury, Dublin, I have obtained a copy of the following letter, from Johnson to the venerable author of " Dissertations on the History of Ireland :"—

" TO CHARLES O'CONNOR, ESQ.[1]

"SIR,   *London, April 9,* 1757.
" I have lately by the favour of Mr. Faulkner, seen your account of Ireland, and cannot forbear to solicit a prosecution of your design. Sir William Temple complains that Ireland is less known than any other country, as to its ancient

---

[1] Of this gentleman, who died at his seat at Ballinegare, in the county of Roscommon, in Ireland, July 1, 1791, in his 82nd year, some account may be found in the "Gentleman's Magazine" of that date. Of the work here alluded to by Dr. Johnson—" Dissertations on the History of Ireland "—a second and much improved edition was published by the author in 1766.—MALONE.

state. The natives have had little leisure and little encouragement for inquiry; and strangers, not knowing the language, have had no ability.

"I have long wished that the Irish literature were cultivated.[1] Ireland is known by tradition to have been once the seat of piety and learning; and surely it would be very acceptable to all those who are curious either in the original of nations, or the affinities of languages, to be further informed of the revolution of a people so ancient, and once so illustrious.

"What relation there is between the Welsh and Irish language, or between the language of Ireland and that of Biscay, deserves inquiry. Of these provincial and unextended tongues, it seldom happens that more than one are understood by any one man; and therefore it seldom happens that a fair comparison can be made. I hope you will continue to cultivate this kind of learning, which has too long lain neglected, and which, if it be suffered to remain in oblivion for another century, may, perhaps, never be retrieved. As I wish well to all useful undertakings, I would not forbear to let you know how much you deserve in my opinion, from all lovers of study, and how much pleasure your work has given to, Sir,

"Your most obliged, and most humble servant,

"SAM. JOHNSON."

"TO THE REVEREND MR. THOMAS WARTON.

"DEAR SIR,   *London, June* 21, 1757

"Dr. Marsili, of Padua, a learned gentleman and good Latin poet, has a mind to see Oxford. I have given him a letter to Dr. Huddesford,[2] and shall be glad if you will introduce him, and show him any thing in Oxford.

"I am printing my new edition of Shakspeare.

"I long to see you all, but cannot conveniently come yet. You might write to me now and then, if you were good for any thing. But *honores mutant mores.*[3] Professors forget their friends. I shall certainly complain to Miss Jones.[4]   I am, yours, &c.,   SAM. JOHNSON.

"Please to make my compliments to Mr. Wise."

---

[1] The celebrated orator, Mr. Flood, has shown himself to be of Dr. Johnson's opinion, having by his will bequeathed his estate, after the death of his wife, Lady Frances, to the University of Dublin: "desiring that immediately after the said estate shall come into their possession, they shall appoint two professors, one for the study of the native Erse or Irish language, and the other for the study of Irish antiquities and Irish history, and for the study of any other European language illustrative of, or auxiliary to, the study of Irish antiquities or Irish history; and that they shall give yearly two liberal premiums for two compositions, one in verse, and the other in prose, in the Irish language."—BOSWELL.

Since the above was written, Mr. Flood's will has been set aside, after a trial at bar, in the Court of Exchequer in Ireland.—MALONE.

[2] Now, or late, Vice-Chancellor.—WARTON.

[3] Mr. Warton was elected Professor of Poetry at Oxford in the preceding year.—WARTON.

[4] Miss Jones lived at Oxford, and was often of our parties. She was a very ingenious poetess, and published a volume of poems; and, on the whole, was a most sensible, agreeable, and amiable woman. She was sister to the Rev. River Jones, Chanter of Christchurch Cathedral, Oxford, and Johnson used to call her the *Chantress.* I have heard him often address her in this passage from "Il Penseroso:"

"Thee, Chantress, oft the woods among
I woo," &c.

She died unmarried.—WARTON

Mr. Burney having enclosed to him an extract from the review of his Dictionary in the *Bibliothèque des Savans,*[1] and a list of subscribers to his Shakspeare, which Mr. Burney had procured in Norfolk, he wrote the following answer :—

" TO MR. BURNEY, IN LYNNE, NORFOLK.

"Sir,   *Gough-square, Dec.* 24, 1757.

" That I may show myself sensible of your favours, and not commit the same fault a second time, I make haste to answer the letter which I received this morning.   The truth is, the other likewise was received, and I wrote an answer; but being desirous to transmit you some proposals and receipts, I waited till I could find a convenient conveyance, and day was passed after day, till other things drove it from my thoughts; yet not so, but that I remember with great pleasure your commendation of my Dictionary.   Your praise was welcome, not only because I believe it was sincere, but because praise has been very scarce. A man of your candour will be surprised when I tell you, that among all my acquaintance there were only two, who upon the publication of my book did not endeavour to depress me with threats of censure from the public, or with objections learned from those who had learned them from my own preface. Yours is the only letter of good-will that I have received ; though, indeed, I am promised something of that sort from Sweden.

" How my new edition [of Shakspeare] will be received I know not; the subscription has not been very successful.   I shall publish about March.

" If you can direct me how to send proposals, I should wish that they were in such hands.

" I remember, Sir, in some of the first letters with which you favoured me, you mentioned your lady.   May I inquire after her ?   In return for the favours which you have shown me, it is not much to tell you, that I wish you and her all that can conduce to your happiness.   I am, Sir,

" Your most obliged and most humble servant,

"Sam. Johnson."

In 1758 we find him, it should seem, in as easy and pleasant a state of existence as constitutional unhappiness ever permitted him to enjoy.

" TO BENNET LANGTON, ESQ., AT LANGTON, LINCOLNSHIRE.

" Dearest Sir,   *Jan.* 9, 1758.

" I must have indeed slept very fast not to have been awakened by your letter. None of your suspicions are true ; I am not much richer than when you left me ; and, what is worse, my omission of an answer to your first letter, will prove that I am not much wiser.   But I go on as I formerly did, designing to be some time or other both rich and wise ; and yet cultivate neither mind nor fortune. Do you take notice of my example, and learn the danger of delay.   When I was as you are now, towering in confidence of twenty-one, little did I suspect that I should be at forty-nine, what I now am.

· Tom. iii. p. 482.—Boswell.

"But you do not seem to need my admonition. You are busy in acquiring and in communicating knowledge, and while you are studying, enjoy the end of study, by making others wiser and happier. I was much pleased with the tale that you told me of being tutor to your sisters. I, who have no sisters nor brothers, look with some degree of innocent envy on those who may be said to be born to friends; and cannot see, without wonder, how rarely that native union is afterwards regarded. It sometimes, indeed, happens, that some supervenient cause of discord may overpower this original amity; but it seems to me more frequently thrown away with levity, or lost by neligence, than destroyed by injury or violence. We tell the ladies that good wives make good husbands; I believe it is a more certain position that good brothers make good sisters.

"I am satisfied with your stay at home, as Juvenal with his friend's retirement to Cumæ: I know that your absence is best, though it be not best for me.

> 'Quamvis digressu veteris confusus amici,
> Laudo tamen vacuis quod sedem figere Cumis
> Destinet, atque unum civem donare Sibyllæ.'

"Langton is a good Cumæ, but who must be Sibylla? Mrs. Langton is as wise as Sibyl, and as good; and will live, if my wishes can prolong life, till she shall in time be as old. But she differs in this, that she has not scattered her precepts in the wind, at least not those which she bestowed upon you.

"The two Wartons just looked into the town, and were taken to see 'Cleone,' where David [Garrick] says, they were starved for want of company to keep them warm. David and Doddy[1] have had a new quarrel, and, I think, cannot conveniently quarrel any more. 'Cleone' was well acted by all the characters, but Bellamy left nothing to be desired. I went the first night, and supported it as well as I might; for Doddy, you know, is my patron, and I would not desert him. The play was very well received. Doddy, after the danger was over, went every night to the stage-side, and cried at the distress of poor *Cleone*.

"I have left off housekeeping, and therefore made presents of the game which you were pleased to send me. The pheasant I gave to Mr. Richardson,[2] the bustard to Dr. Lawrence, and the pot I placed with Miss Williams, to be eaten by myself. She desires that her compliments and good wishes may be accepted by the family; and I make the same request for myself.

"Mr. Reynolds has within these few days raised his price to twenty guineas a head, and Miss is much employed in miniatures. I know not any body [else] whose prosperity has increased since you left them.

"Murphy is to have his 'Orphan of China' acted next month; and is, therefore, I suppose, happy. I wish I could tell you of any great good to which I was approaching, but at present my prospects do not much delight me; however, I am always pleased when I find that you, dear Sir, remember

"Your affectionate, humble servant,

"Sam. Johnson."

---

1 Mr. Dodsley, the author of "Cleone."—Boswell.
2 Mr. Samuel Richardson, author of "Clarissa."—Boswell.

"TO MR. BURNEY, AT LYNNE, NORFOLK.

"SIR,   *London, March* 8, 1758.

"Your kindness is so great, and my claim to any particular regard from you so little, that I am at a loss how to express my sense of your favours;[1] but I am, indeed, much pleased to be thus distinguished by you.

"I am ashamed to tell you that my Shakspeare will not be out so soon as I promised my subscribers; but I did not promise them more than I promised myself. It will, however, be published before summer.

"I have sent you a bundle of proposals, which, I think, do not profess more than I have hitherto performed. I have printed many of the plays, and have hitherto left very few passages unexplained; where I am quite at loss, I confess my ignorance, which is seldom done by commentators.

"I have, likewise, enclosed receipts; not that I mean to impose upon you the trouble of pushing them with more importunity than may seem proper, but that you may rather have more than fewer than you shall want. The proposals you will disseminate as there shall be an opportunity. I once printed them at length in the 'Chronicle,' and some of my friends (I believe Mr. Murphy, who formerly wrote the 'Gray's-Inn Journal,') introduced them with a splendid encomium.

"Since the 'Life of Browne,' I have been a little engaged, from time to time, in the 'Literary Magazine,' but not very lately. I have not the collection by me, and therefore cannot draw out a catalogue of my own parts, but will do it, and send it. Do not buy them, for I will gather all those that have any thing of mine in them, and send them to Mrs. Burney, as a small token of gratitude for the regard which she is pleased to bestow upon me.

"I am, Sir, your most obliged and most humble servant,

                               "SAM. JOHNSON."

Dr. Burney has kindly favoured me with the following memorandum, which I take the liberty to insert in his own genuine easy style. I love to exhibit sketches of my illustrious friend by various eminent hands.

DR. BURNEY.

"Soon after this, Mr. Burney, during a visit to the capital, had an interview with him in Gough-square, where he dined and drank tea with him, and was introduced to the acquaintance of Mrs. Williams. After dinner, Mr. Johnson proposed to Mr. Burney to go up with him into his garret, which being accepted, he there found about five or six Greek folios, a deal writing-desk, and a chair and a half. Johnson giving to his guest the entire seat, tottered himself on one with only three legs and one arm. Here he gave Mr. Burney Mrs. Williams's history, and showed him some volumes of Shakspeare already printed, to prove that he was in earnest. Upon Mr. Burney's opening the first volume, at the 'Merchant of Venice' he observed to him, that he seemed to be more severe on Warburton than Theobald. 'O poor Tib!' said Johnson, 'he was ready knocked down to my hands; Warburton stands between me and him.' 'But, Sir,' said Mr. Burney, 'you'll have Warburton upon your bones, wont you?' 'No, Sir; he'll not come out: he'll only growl in his den.' 'But you think, Sir, that Warburton is a superior critic to Theobald?'—'O, Sir, he'd make two-and-fifty Theobalds, cut into slices! The worst of Warburton is, that he has a rage for saying something, when there's nothing to be said.'—Mr. Burney then asked him whether he had seen the letter which Warburton had written in answer to a pamphlet, addressed, 'To the most impudent Man alive.' He answered in the negative. Mr. Burney told him it was supposed to be written by Mallet. The controversy now raged between the friends of Pope and Bolingbroke: and Warburton and Mallet were the leaders of the several parties. Mr. Burney asked him then if he had seen Warburton's book against Bolingbroke's Philosophy? 'No, Sir · I have never read Bolingbroke's impiety, and therefore am not interested about its confutation.'"

DR. JOHNSON AND FRANCIS BARBER.

CHAPTER X.—1758—1759.

ON the 15th of April, 1758, he began a new periodical paper, entitled "The Idler,"* which came out every Saturday in a weekly newspaper, called "The Universal Chronicle, or Weekly Gazette," published by Newbury.[1] These essays were continued till April 5, 1760. Of one hundred and three, their total number, twelve were contributed by his friends; of which, Nos. 33, 93, and 96, were written by Mr. Thomas Warton; No. 67 by Mr. Langton; and Nos. 69, 76, and 82, by Sir Joshua Reynolds; the concluding words of No. 82, "and pollute his canvas with deformity," being added by Johnson; as Sir Joshua informed me.

The "Idler" is evidently the work of the same mind which produced the "Rambler," but has less body and more spirit. It has more variety of real life, and greater facility of language. He describes the miseries

[1] This is a slight mistake. The first number of the "Idler" appeared on the 15th of April, 1758, in No. 2 of the "Universal Chronicle," &c., which was published by J. Payne, for whom, also, the "Rambler" had been printed. On the 29th of April this newspaper assumed the title of "Payne's Universal Chronicle," &c.—MALONE.

of idleness with the lively sensations of one who has felt them ; and in his private memorandums while engaged in it, we find, " This year I hope to learn diligence." [1]   Many of these excellent essays were written as hastily as an ordinary letter.   Mr. Langton remembers Johnson when on a visit at Oxford, asking him one evening how long it was til' the post went out ; and on being told about half-an-hour, he exclaimed, " Then we shall do very well."   He, upon this, instantly sat down and finished an "Idler," which it was necessary should be in London the next day.   Mr. Langton having signified a wish to read it, " Sir," said he, " you shall do no more than I have done myself."   He then folded it up, and sent it off.

Yet there are in the " Idler " several papers which show as much profundity of thought and labour of language as any of this great man's writings.   No. 14, " Robbery of time ;" No. 24, " Thinking ;" No. 41, " Death of a friend ;" No. 43, " Flight of time ;" No. 51, " Domestic greatness unattainable ;" No. 52, " Self-denial ;" No. 58, " Actual, how short of fancied, excellence ;" No. 89, " Physical evil moral good ;" and his concluding paper on " The horror of the last," will prove this assertion.   I know not why a motto, the usual trapping of periodical papers, is prefixed to very few of the " Idlers," as I have heard Johnson commend the custom : and he never could be at a loss for one, his memory being stored with innumerable passages of the classics.   In this series of essays he exhibits admirable instances of grave humour, of which he had an uncommon share.   Nor on some occasions has he repressed that power of sophistry which he possessed in so eminent a degree.   In No. 11, he treats with the utmost contempt the opinion that our mental faculties depend, in some degree, upon the weather ; an opinion, which they who have never experienced its truths are not to be envied, and of which he himself could not but be sensible, as the effects of weather upon him were very visible.   Yet thus he declaims :

" Surely nothing is more reproachful to a being endowed with reason than to resign its powers to the influence of the air, and live in dependence on the weather and the wind for the only blessings which nature has put into our power, tranquillity and benevolence.   This distinction of seasons is produced only by imagination operating on luxury.   To temperance, every day is bright ; and every hour is propitious to diligence.   He that shall resolutely excite his faculties or exert his virtues will soon make himself superior to the seasons, and may set at defiance the morning mist and the evening damp, the blasts of the east, and the clouds of the south."

Alas ! it is too certain that where the frame has delicate fibres, and there is a fine sensibility, such influences of the air are irresistible.

He might as well have bid defiance to the ague, the palsy, and other bodily disorders. Such boasting of the mind is false elevation.

> "I think the Romans call it Stoicism."

But in this number of his "Idler" his spirits seem to run riot; for in the wantonness of his disquisition he forgets, for a moment, even the reverence for that which he held in high respect, and describes, "the attendant on a *Court*," as one "whose business is to watch the looks of a being, weak and foolish as himself."

His unqualified ridicule of rhetorical gesture or action is not, surely, a test of truth; yet we cannot help admiring how well it is adapted to produce the effect which he wished:—

> "Neither the judges of our laws, nor the representatives of our people, would be much affected by laboured gesticulations, or believe any man the more because he rolled his eyes, or puffed his cheeks, or spread abroad his arms, or stamped the ground, or thumped his breast; or turned his eyes sometimes to the ceiling, and sometimes to the floor."

A casual coincidence with other writers, or an adoption of a sentiment or image which has been found in the writings of another, and afterwards appears in the mind as one's own, is not unfrequent. The richness of Johnson's fancy, which could supply his page abundantly on all occasions, and the strength of his memory, which at once detected the real owner of any thought, made him less liable to the imputation of plagiarism than, perhaps, any of our writers. In "The Idler," however, there is a paper in which conversation is assimilated to a bowl of punch, where there is the same train of comparison as in a poem of Blacklock, in his collection published in 1756, in which a parallel is ingeniously drawn between human life and that liquor. It ends,

> "Say then, physicians of each kind,
>   Who cure the body or the mind,
>   What harm in drinking can there be,
>   Since punch and life so well agree?"

To "The Idler," when collected in volumes, he added, beside the Essay on Epitaphs, and the Dissertation on those of Pope, an Essay on the Bravery of the English Common Soldiers. He, however, omitted one of the original papers, which in the folio copy is No. 22.[1]

"TO THE REV. MR. THOMAS WARTON.

"DEAR SIR,   *London, April* 14, 1758.

"Your notes upon my poet were very acceptable. I beg that you will be so kind as to continue your searches. It will be reputable to my work, and

---

[1] This paper may be found in Stockdale's supplemental volume of Johnson's Miscellaneous Pieces.—BOSWELL

suitable to your professorship, to have something of yours in the notes. As you have given no directions about your name, I shall therefore put it. I wish your brother would take the same trouble. A commentary must arise from the fortuitous discoveries of many men in devious walks of literature. Some of your remarks are on plays already printed : but I purpose to add an Appendix of Notes, so that nothing comes too late.

"You give yourself too much uneasiness, dear Sir, about the loss of the papers.[1] The loss is nothing, if nobody has found them; nor even then, perhaps, if the numbers be known. You are not the only friend that has had the same mischance. You may repair your want out of a stock, which is deposited with Mr. Allen, of Magdalen Hall, or out of a parcel which I have just sent to Mr. Chambers,[2] for the use of any body that will be so kind as to want them. Mr. Langtons are well; and Miss Roberts, whom I have at last brought to speak, upon the information which you gave me, that she had something to say.

"I am, &c.

"SAM. JOHNSON."

TO THE SAME.

"DEAR SIR,   <i>London, June</i> 1, 1758.

"You will receive this by Mr. Baretti, a gentleman particularly entitled to the notice and kindness of the Professor of poesy. He has time but for a short stay, and will be glad to have it filled up with as much as he can hear and see.

"In recommending another to your favour, I ought not to omit thanks for the kindness which you have shown to myself. Have you any more notes on Shakspeare? I shall be glad of them.

"I see your pupil sometimes;[3] his mind is as exalted as his stature. I am half afraid of him; but he is no less amiable than formidable. He will, if the forwardness of his spring be not blasted, be a credit to you and to the University. He brings some of my plays[4] with him, which he has my permission to show you, on condition you will hide them from every body else.

"I am, dear Sir, &c.

"SAM. JOHNSON."

"TO BENNET LANGTON, ESQ., TRINITY COLLEGE.

"DEAR SIR,   <i>June</i> 28, 1758.

"Though I might have expected to hear from you, upon your entrance into a new state of life at a new place, yet recollecting (not without some degree of shame) that I owe you a letter upon an old account, I think it my part to write first. This, indeed, I do not only from complaisance, but from interest ; for

---

[1] Receipts for Shakspeare.—WARTON.
[2] Then of Lincoln College. Now Sir Robert Chambers, one of the Judges in India.—WARTON.   [3] Mr. Langton.—WARTON.
[4] Part of the impression of the Shakspeare, which Dr. Johnson conducted alone, and published by subscription. This edition came out in 1765.—WARTON.

living on in the old way, I am very glad of a correspondent so capable as your-self, to diversify the hours. You have, at present, too many novelties about you to need any help from me to drive along your time.

"I know not any thing more pleasant, or more instructive, than to compare experience with expectation, or to register from time to time the difference between idea and reality. It is by this kind of observation that we grow daily less liable to be disappointed. You, who are very capable of anticipating futurity, and raising phantoms before your own eyes, must often have imagined to yourself an academical life, and have conceived what would be the manners, the views, and the conversation, of men devoted to letters; how they would choose their companions, how they would direct their studies, and how they would regulate their lives. Let me know what you expected, and what you have found. At least record it to yourself before custom has reconciled you to the scenes before you, and the disparity of your discoveries to your hopes has vanished from your mind. It is a rule never to be forgotten, that what-ever strikes strongly, should be described while the first impression remains fresh upon the mind.

"I love, dear Sir, to think on you, and therefore, should willingly write more to you, but that the post will not now give me leave to do more than send my compliments to Mr. Warton, and tell you that I am, dear Sir, most affectionately,

"Your very humble servant,

"SAM. JOHNSON."

"TO BENNET LANGTON, ESQ., AT LANGTON, NEAR SPILSBY, LINCOLNSHIRE.

"DEAR SIR,   *Sept.* 21, 1758.

"I should be sorry to think that what engrosses the attention of my friend should have no part of mine. Your mind is now full of the fate of Dury;[1] but his fate is past, and nothing remains but to try what reflection will suggest to mitigate the terrors of a violent death, which is more formidable at the first glance, than on a nearer and more steady view. A violent death is never very painful; the only danger is, lest it should be unprovided. But if a man can be supposed to make no provision for death in war, what can be the state that would have awakened him to the care of futurity? When would that man have prepared himself to die, who went to seek death without preparation? What then can be the reason why we lament more, him that dies of a wound, than him that dies of a fever? A man that languishes with disease, ends his life with more pain, but with less virtue: he leaves no example to his friends, nor bequeaths any honour to his descendants. The only reason why we lament a soldier's death, is, that we think he might have lived longer; yet this cause of grief is common to many other kinds of death, which are not so passionately bewailed. The truth is, that every death is violent which is the

---

[1] Major-General Alexander Dury, of the first regiment of foot-guards, who fell in the gallant discharge of his duty, near St. Cas, in the well-known unfortunate expedition against France, in 1758. His lady and Mr. Langton's mother were sisters. He left an only son, Lieutenant-Colonel Dury, who has a company in the same regiment.—BOSWELL.

effect of accident; every death, which is not gradually brought on by the miseries of age; or when life is extinguished for any other reason than that it is burnt out. He that dies before sixty, of a cold or consumption, dies, in reality, by a violent death; yet his death is borne with patience, only because the cause of his untimely end is silent and invisible. Let us endeavour to see things as they are, and then inquire whether we ought to complain. Whether to see life as it is, will give us much consolation, I know not; but the consolation which is drawn from truth, if any there be, is solid and durable : that which may be derived from error, must be, like its original, fallacious and fugitive.   "I am, dear Sir,

"Your most humble servant,

" SAM. JOHNSON."

In 1759, in the month of January, his mother died at the great age of ninety, an event which deeply affected him ; not that " his mind had acquired no firmness by the contemplation of mortality,"[1] but that his reverential affection for her was not abated by years, as indeed he retained all his tender feelings even to the latest period of his life. I have been told that he regretted much his not having gone to visit his mother for several years previous to her death. But he was constantly engaged in literary labours, which confined him to London ; and though he had not the comfort of seeing his aged parent, he contributed liberally to her support.

" TO MRS. JOHNSON, IN LICHFIELD.[2]

" HONOURED MADAM,   *Jan.* 13, 1758.[3]

" The account which Miss [Porter] gives me of your health, pierces my heart. God comfort, and preserve you, and save you, for the sake of Jesus Christ.

" I would have Miss read to you from time to time the Passion of our Saviour, and sometimes the sentences in the Communion Service—*Come unto me all ye that travail and are heavy laden, and I will give you rest.*

" I have just now read a physical book, which inclines me to think that a strong infusion of the bark would do you good. Do, dear mother, try it.

" Pray, send me your blessing, and forgive all that I have done amiss to you. And whatever you would have done, and what debts you would have paid first, or any thing else that you would direct, let Miss put it down ; I shall endeavour to obey you.

---

[1] Hawkins's " Life of Johnson," p. 395.—BOSWELL.

[2] Since the publication of the third edition of this work, the following letters of Dr. Johnson, occasioned by the last illness of his mother, were obligingly communicated to Mr. Malone by the Rev. Dr. Vyse. They are placed here agreeably to the chronological order almost uniformly observed by the author; and so strongly evince Dr. Johnson's piety and tenderness of heart, that every reader must be gratified by their insertion.—MALONE.

[3] Written by mistake for 1759, as the subsequent letters show. In the next letter, he had inadvertently fallen into the same error, but corrected it. On the *outside* of the letter of the 13th was written by another hand, " Pray acknowledge the receipt of this by return of the post, without fail."—MALONE.

"I have got twelve guineas [1] to send you, but unhappily am at a loss how to send it to-night. If I cannot send it to night, it will come by the next post.

"Pray, do not omit any thing mentioned in this letter. God bless you for ever and ever. I am,

"Your dutiful son,

"SAM. JOHNSON."

"TO MISS PORTER, AT MRS. JOHNSON'S, IN LICHFIELD

"MY DEAR MISS,   *Jan.* 16, 1759.

"I think myself obliged to you beyond all expression of gratitude for your care of my dear mother. God grant it may not be without success. Tell Kitty,[2] that I shall never forget her tenderness for her mistress. Whatever you can do, continue to do. My heart is very full.

"I hope you received twelve guineas on Monday. I found a way of sending them by means of the Postmaster, after I had written my letter, and hope they came safe. I will send you more in a few days. God bless you all.

"I am, my dear,

"Your most obliged and most humble servant,

"SAM. JOHNSON."

"Over the leaf is a letter to my mother."

"DEAR HONOURED MOTHER,   *Jan.* 16, 1759.

"Your weakness afflicts me beyond what I am willing to communicate to you. I do not think you unfit to face death, but I know not how to bear the thought of losing you. Endeavour to do all you ⌈can⌉ for yourself. Eat as much as you can.

"I pray often for you; do you pray for me.—I have nothing to add to my last letter. I am, dear, dear Mother,

"Your dutiful son,

"SAM. JOHNSON."

"TO MRS. JOHNSON IN LICHFIELD.

"DEAR HONOURED MOTHER,   *Jan.* 18, 1759.

"I fear you are too ill for long letters; therefore I will only tell you, you have from me all the regard that can possibly subsist in the heart. I pray God to bless you for evermore, for Jesus Christ's sake, Amen.

"Let Miss write to me every post, however short. I am, dear Mother,

"Your dutiful son,

"SAM. JOHNSON

[1] Six of these twelve guineas Johnson appears to have borrowed from Mr. Allen, the printer. See Hawkins's "Life of Johnson," p. 366 n.—MALONE.

[2] Catherine Chambers, Mrs. Johnson's maid-servant. She died in October, 1767. See Dr. Johnson's "Prayers and Meditations," p. 71: "Sunday, Oct. 18, 1767. Yesterday, Oct. 17, I took my leave for ever of my dear old friend, Catherine Chambers, who came to live with my mother about 1724, and has been but little parted from us since. She buried my father, my brother, and my mother. She is now fifty-eight years old."—MALONE.

"TO MISS PORTER, AT MRS. JOHNSON'S, IN LICHFIELD.

"DEAR MISS,   *Jan* 20, 1759.

"I will, if it be possible, come down to you. God grant that I may yet [find] my dear mother breathing and sensible. Do not tell her, lest I disappoint her. If I miss to write next post, I am on the road. I am, my dearest MISS,

"Your most humble servant,

"SAM. JOHNSON."

"*On the other side.*

"DEAR HONOURED MOTHER,[1]   *Jan.* 20, 1759.

"Neither your condition nor your character make it fit for me to say much. You have been the best mother, and I believe the best woman in the world. I thank you for your indulgence to me, and beg forgiveness of all that I have done ill, and all that I have omitted to do well.[2] God grant you his Holy Spirit, and receive you to everlasting happiness, for Jesus Christ's sake. Amen. Lord Jesus receive your spirit. Amen.

"I am, dear, dear, Mother,

"Your dutiful son,

"SAM. JOHNSON

"TO MISS PORTER, IN LICHFIELD.

"*Jan.* 23, 1759.[3]

"You will conceive my sorrow for the loss of my mother, of the best mother. If she were to live again, surely I should behave better to her. But she is happy, and what is past is nothing to her; and for me, since I cannot repair my faults to her, I hope repentance will efface them. I return you and all those that have been good to her, my sincerest thanks, and pray God to repay you all with infinite advantage. Write to me, and comfort me, dear child. I shall be glad likewise, if Kitty will write to me. I shall send a bill of twenty pounds in a few days which I thought to have brought to my mother; but God suffered it not. I have not power or composure to say much more. God bless you, and bless us all.

"I am, dear Miss,

"Your affectionate humble servant,

"SAM. JOHNSON."

Soon after this event, he wrote his "Rasselas, Prince of Abyssinia;"* concerning the publication of which Sir John Hawkins guesses vaguely and idly, instead of having taken the trouble to inform himself with

---

[1] This letter was written on the second leaf of the preceding, addressed to Miss Porter.—MALONE.

[2] So, in the Prayer which he composed on this occasion: "Almighty God, merciful Father, in whose hands are life and death, sanctify unto me the sorrow which I now feel. *Forgive me whatever I have done unkindly to my Mother, and whatever I have omitted to do kindly.* Make me to remember her good precepts and good example, and to reform my life according to thy holy word," &c.—"Prayers and Meditations," p. 31.—MALONE.

[3] Mrs. Johnson probably died on the 20th or 21st of January, and was buried on the day this letter was written.—MALONE.

authentic precision. Not to trouble my readers with a repetition of the Knight's reveries, I have to mention that the late Mr. Strahan, the printer, told me, that Johnson wrote it, that with the profits he might defray the expense of his mother's funeral, and pay some little debts which she had left. He told Sir Joshua Reynolds that he composed it in the evenings of one week,[1] sent it to the press in portions as it was written, and had never since read it over.[2] Mr. Strahan, Mr. Johnston, and Mr. Dodsley, purchased it for a hundred pounds, but afterwards paid him twenty-five pounds more when it came to a second edition.

Considering the large sums which have been received for compilations, and works requiring not much more genius than compilations, we cannot but wonder at the very low price which he was content to receive for this admirable performance; which, though he had written nothing else, would have rendered his name immortal in the world of literature. None of his writings have been so extensively diffused over Europe; for it has been translated into most, if not all, of the modern languages. This tale, with all the charms of oriental imagery, and all the force and beauty of which the English language is capable, leads us through the most important scenes of human life, and shows us that this stage of our being is full of " vanity and vexation of spirit." To those who look no further than the present life, or who maintain that human nature has not fallen from the state in which it was created, the instruction of this sublime story will be of no avail. But they who think justly, and feel with strong sensibility, will listen with eagerness and admiration to its truth and wisdom. Voltaire's " Candide," written to refute the system of Optimism, which it has accomplished with brilliant success, is wonderfully similar in its plan and conduct to Johnson's " Rasselas; " insomuch, that I have heard Johnson say, that if they had not been published so closely one after the other that there was not time for imitation, it would have been in vain to deny that the scheme of that which came latest was taken from the other. Though the proposition illustrated by both these works was the same, namely, that in our present state there is more evil than good, the intention of the writers was very different. Voltaire, I am afraid, meant only by wanton profaneness to obtain a sportive victory over religion, and to discredit the belief of a superintending Providence: Johnson meant, by showing the un satisfactory nature of things temporal, to direct the hopes of man to things eternal. Rasselas, as was observed to me by a very accomplished lady, may be considered as a more enlarged and more deeply philosophical discourse in prose, upon the interesting truth, which in his " Vanity of Human Wishes " he had so successfully enforced in verse.

---

[1] "Rasselas" was published in March or April, 1759.—BOSWELL.
[2] See vol. iv under June 2, 1781. Finding it then accidentally in a chaise with Mr Boswell, he read it eagerly. This was doubtless long after his declaration to Sir Joshua Reynolds.—MALONE.

The fund of thinking which this work contains is such, that almost every sentence of it may furnish a subject of long meditation. I am not satisfied if a year passes without my having read it through ; and at every perusal, my admiration of the mind which produced it is so highly raised that I can scarcely believe that I had the honour of enjoying the intimacy of such a man.

I restrain myself from quoting passages from this excellent work, or even referring to them, because I should not know what to select, or rather, what to omit. I shall, however, transcribe one, as it shows how well he could state the arguments of those who believe in the appearance of departed spirits ; a doctrine which it is a mistake to suppose that he himself ever positively held :—

"If all your fear be of apparitions," said the Prince, "I will promise you safety : there is no danger from the dead ; he that is once buried will be seen no more."

"That the dead are seen no more," said Imlac, "I will not undertake to maintain, against the concurrent and unvaried testimony of all ages, and of all nations. There is no people, rude or learned, among whom apparitions of the dead are not related and believed. This opinion, which prevails as far as human nature is diffused, could become universal only by its truth ; those that never heard of one another, would not have agreed in a tale which nothing but experience can make credible. That it is doubted by single cavillers, can very little weaken the general evidence ; and some who deny it with their tongues, confess it by their fears."

Notwithstanding my high admiration of "Rasselas," I will not maintain that the "morbid melancholy" in Johnson's constitution may not, perhaps, have made life appear to him more insipid and unhappy than it generally is ; for I am sure that he had less enjoyment from it than I have. Yet, whatever additional shade his own particular sensations may have thrown on his representation of life, attentive observation and close inquiry have convinced me that there is too much reality in the gloomy picture. The truth, however, is, that we judge of the happiness and misery of life differently at different times, according to the state of our changeable frame. I always remember a remark made to be by a Turkish lady, educated in France : "Ma foi, Monsieur, notre bonheur dépend de la façon que notre sang circule." This have I learnt from a pretty hard course of experience, and would, from sincere benevolence, impress upon all who honour this book with a perusal, that until a steady conviction is obtained, that the present life is an imperfect state, and only a passage to a better, if we comply with the divine scheme of progressive improvement ; and also that it is a part of the mysterious plan of Providence, that intellectual beings must "be made perfect through suffering ;" there will be a continual recurrence of disappointment and uneasiness. But if we walk with hope in "the mid-day sun" of revelation, our temper and disposition will be such, that the comforts and enjoyments in our way will be relished, while we patiently support the inconveniences and pains. After much speculation and various reasonings, I acknowledge myself convinced of the truth of Voltaire's conclusion, " *Après tout, c'est un monde passable.*" But we must not think too deeply :

> " ———— where ignorance is bliss,
> 'Tis folly to be wise,"

is, in many respects, more than poetically just. Let us cultivate, under the command of good principles, " *la théorie des sensations agréables :*" and, as Mr. Burke once admirably counselled a grave and anxious gentleman, " live pleasant."

The effect of " Rasselas," and of Johnson's other moral tales, is thus beautifully illustrated by Mr. Courtenay :—

> " Impressive truth, in splendid fiction drest,
> Checks the vain wish, and calms the troubled breast ;
> O'er the dark mind a light celestial throws,
> And soothes the angry passions to repose ;
> As oil effused illumes and smooths the deep,
> When round the bark the foaming surges sweep." [1]

It will be recollected that, during all this year, he carried on his " Idler," [2] and, no doubt, was proceeding, though slowly, in his edition

---

[1] Literary and Moral Character of Johnson.—BOSWELL.

[2] This paper was in such high estimation before it was collected into volumes, that it was seized on with avidity by various publishers of newspapers and magazines, to enrich their publications. Johnson, to put a stop to this unfair proceeding, wrote for the " Universal Chronicle" the following advertisement ; in which there is, perhaps, more pomp of words than the occasion demanded :

"London, Jan. 5, 1759. ADVERTISEMENT. The proprietors of the paper entitled ' The Idler,' having found that those essays are inserted in the newspapers and magazines with so little regard to justice or decency, that the ' Universal Chronicle,' in which they first appear is not always mentioned, think it necessary to declare to the publishers of those collections, that however patiently they have hitherto endured these injuries, made yet more injurious by contempt, they have now determined to endure them no longer. They have already seen essays, for which a very large price is paid, transferred with the most shameless rapacity into the weekly or monthly compilations, and their right, at least for the present, alienated from them, before they could themselves be said to enjoy it. But they would not willingly be thought to want tenderness, even for men by whom no tenderness hath been shown. The past is without remedy, and shall be without resentment. But those who have been thus busy with their sickles in the fields of their neighbours, are henceforward to take notice, that the time of impunity is at an end. Whoever shall, without our leave, lay the hand of rapine upon our papers, is to expect that we shall vindicate our due, by the means which justice prescribes, and which are warranted by the immemorial prescriptions of honourable trade. We shall lay hold in our turn, on their copies, degrade them from the pomp of wide margin and diffuse typography, contract them into a narrow space, and sell them at an humble price ; yet not with a view of growing rich by confiscations, for we think not much better of money got by punishment than by crimes. We shall, therefore, when our losses are repaid, give what profit shall remain to the *Magdalens ;* for we know not who can be more properly taxed for the support of penitent prostitutes, than prostitutes in whom there yet appears neither penitence nor shame."—BOSWELL.

of Shakspeare. He, however, from that liberality which never failed, when called upon to assist other labourers in literature, found time to translate for Mrs. Lenox's English version of Brumoy, " A Dissertation on the Greek Comedy," † and " The General Conclusion of the Book." †

An inquiry into the state of foreign countries was an object that seems at all times to have interested Johnson. Hence Mr. Newbery found no great difficulty in persuading him to write the Introduction * to a collection of voyages and travels published by him under the title of " The World Displayed," the first volume of which appeared this year, and the remaining volumes in subsequent years.

I would ascribe to this year the following letter to a son of one of his early friends at Lichfield, Mr. Joseph Simpson, Barrister, and author of a tract entitled " Reflections on the Study of the Law."

" TO JOSEPH SIMPSON, ESQ.

" DEAR SIR,

" Your father's inexorability not only grieves but amazes me : he is your father ; he was always accounted a wise man ; nor do I remember any thing to the disadvantage of his good nature ; but in his refusal to assist you there is neither good nature, fatherhood, nor wisdom. It is the practice of good nature to overlook faults which have already, by the consequences, punished the delinquent. It is natural for a father to think more favourably than others of his children ; and it is always wise to give assistance, while a little help will prevent the necessity of greater.

" If you married imprudently, you miscarried at your own hazard, at an age when you had a right of choice. It would be hard if the man might not choose his own wife, who has a right to plead before the judges of his country.

" If your imprudence has ended in difficulties and inconveniences, you are yourself to support them ; and, with the help of a little better health, you would support them and conquer them. Surely, that want which accident and sickness produces, is to be supported in every region of humanity, though there were neither friends nor fathers in the world. You have certainly from your father the highest claim of charity, though none of right ; and therefore I would counsel you to omit no decent nor manly degree of importunity. Your debts in the whole are not large, and of the whole but a small part is troublesome. Small debts are like small shot ; they are rattling on every side, and can scarcely be escaped without a wound ; great debts are like cannon ; of loud noise, but little danger. You must, therefore, be enabled to discharge petty debts, that you may have leisure with security, to struggle with the rest. Neither the great nor little debts disgrace you. I am sure you have my esteem for the courage with which you contracted them, and the spirit with which you endure them. I wish my esteem could be of more use. I have been invited, or have invited myself, to several parts of the kingdom ; and will not incommode my dear Lucy by coming to Lichfield, while her present lodging is of any use to her. I hope, in a few days, to be at leisure and to make visits. Whither I shall fly is matter of no importance. A man unconnected is at home every where ; unless he may be said to be at home no where. I am sorry, dear Sir, that where you have parents, a man of your merits should not have a home. I wish I could give it you.   " I am, my dear Sir, affectionately yours,

"SAM. JOHNSON."

He now refreshed himself by an excursion to Oxford, of which the following short characteristical notice, in his own words, is preserved :—

" ——————— is now making tea for me. I have been in my gown ever since I came here. It was at my first coming quite new and handsome. I have swum thrice, which I had disused for many years. I have proposed to Van sittart[1] climbing over the wall, but he has refused me. And I have clapped my hands till they are sore, at Dr. King's speech."[2]

His negro servant, Francis Barber, having left him, and been some time at sea, not pressed, as has been supposed, with his own consent, it appears, from a letter to John Wilkes, Esq., from Dr. Smollett, that his master kindly interested himself in procuring his release from a state of life of which Johnson always expressed the utmost abhorrence. He said, " No man will be a sailor who has contrivance enough to get himself into a jail ; for being in a ship is being in a jail, with the chance of being drowned."[3] And at another time, " A man in a jail has more room, better food, and commonly better company."[4] The letter was as follows :—

" DEAR SIR,   Chelsea, March 16, 1759.

" I am again your petitioner, in behalf of that great CHAM[5] of literature, Samuel Johnson. His black servant, whose name is Francis Barber, has been pressed on board the Stag frigate, Captain Angel, and our lexicographer is in great distress. He says, the boy is a sickly lad, of a delicate frame, and particularly subject to a malady in his throat, which renders him very unfit for his Majesty's service. You know what matter of animosity the said Johnson has against you : and I dare say you desire no other opportunity of resenting it, than that of laying him under an obligation. He was humble enough to desire

[1] Dr. Robert Vansittart, of the ancient and respectable family of that name in Berkshire He was eminent for learning and worth, and much esteemed by Dr. Johnson.—BOSWELL.

[2] Gentleman's Magazine, April 1785.—BOSWELL.

[3] Journal of a Tour to the Hebrides, 3rd edit. p. 126.—BOSWELL.

[4] Ibid. p. 251.—BOSWELL.

[5] In my first edition this word was printed *Chum*, as it appears in one of Mr. Wilkes's Miscellanies, and I animadverted on Dr. Smollett's ignorance; for which let me propitiate the *manes* of that ingenious and benevolent gentleman. CHUM was certainly a mistaken reading for CHAM, the title of the Sovereign of Tartary, which is well applied to Johnson, the Monarch of Literature : and was an epithet familiar to Smollett. See " Roderick Random," chap. 56. For this correction I am indebted to Lord Palmerston, whose talents and literary acquirements accord well with his respectable pedigree of Temple.—BOSWELL.

After the publication of the second edition of this work, the author was furnished by Mr. Abercrombie of Philadelphia, with a copy of a letter written by Dr. John Armstrong, the poet, to Dr. Smollett, at Leghorn, containing the following paragraph :—

" As to the King's Bench patriot, it is hard to say from what motive he published a letter of yours asking some trifling favour of him in behalf of somebody for whom the great CHAM of literature, Mr. Johnson, had interested himself."—MALONE.

my assistance on this occasion, though he and I were never cater-cousins ; and I ʼave him to understand that I would make application to my friend Mr. Wilkes, ♠ho, perhaps, by his interest with Dr. Hay and Mr. Elliot, might be able to procure the discharge of his lacquey.   It would be superfluous to say more on this subject, which I leave to your own consideration ; but I cannot let slip this opportunity of declaring that I am, with the most inviolable esteem and attachment, dear Sir,   " Your affectionate, obliged, humble servant,

                                                    " T. SMOLLETT."

Mr. Wilkes, who, upon all occasions, has acted as a private gentleman, with most polite liberality, applied to his friend, Sir George Hay, then one of the Lords Commissioners of the Admiralty ; and Francis Barber was discharged, as he has told me, without any wish of his own. He found his old master in chambers in the Inner Temple, and returned to his service.

What particular new scheme of life Johnson had in view this year, I have not discovered ; but that he meditated one of some sort, is clear from his private devotions, in which we find [Pr. and Med., pp. 30 and 40], " the change of outward things which I am now to make ; " and " Grant me the grace of thy Holy Spirit, that the course which I am now beginning may proceed according to thy laws, and end in the enjoyment of thy favour."   But he did not, in fact, make any external or visible change.[1]

At this time, there being a competition among the architects of London to be employed in the building of Blackfriars-bridge, a question was very warmly agitated, whether semi-circular or elliptical arches were preferable.   In the design offered by Mr. Mylne, the elliptical form was adopted, and therefore it was the great object of his rivals to attack it.   Johnson's regard for his friend, Mr. Gwyn, induced him to engage in this controversy against Mr. Mylne ;[2] and after being at

---

[1] It seems, from a note of his to Miss Porter, that Johnson, on the 23rd of March, of this year (1759), left his house in Gough-square, and went to reside in Staple Inn ; Miss Williams took separate lodgings.   It will appear from the list of Johnson's residences, subsequently given, that he removed from Staple Inn to Gray's Inn.—ED.

[2] Sir John Hawkins has given a long detail of it, in that manner vulgarly, but significantly called *rigmarole ;* in which, amidst an ostentatious exhibition of arts and artists he talks of " proportions of a column being taken from that of the human figure, and *adjusted by nature*— masculine and feminine—in a man, *sesquioctave* of the head, and in a woman *sesquinonal ;* " nor has he failed to introduce a jargon of musical terms, which do not seem much to correspond with the subject, but serve to make up the heterogeneous mass.   To follow the knight through all this, would be an useless fatigue to myself, and not a little disgusting to my readers.   I shall, therefore, only make a few remarks upon his statement.—He seems to exult in having detected Johnson in procuring " from a person eminently skilled in mathematics and the principles of architecture, answers to a string of questions drawn up by himself, touching the comparative strength of semicircular and elliptical arches."   Now I cannot conceive how Johnson could have acted more wisely.   Sir John complains that the opinion of that excellent mathematician, Mr. Thomas Simpson, did not preponderate in favour of the semicircular arch. But he should have known, that however eminent Mr. Simpson was in the higher parts of abstract mathematical science, he was little versed in mixed and practical mechanics.   Mr. Muller of Woolwich Academy, the scholastic father of all the great engineers which this

considerable pains to study the subject, he wrote three several letters in the " Gazetteer," in opposition to his plan.

If it should be remarked that this was a controversy which lay quite out of Johnson's way, let it be remembered that, after all, his employing his powers of reasoning and eloquence upon a subject which he had studied on the moment, is not more strange than what we often observe in lawyers, who, as *Quicquid agunt homines* is the matter of lawsuits, are sometimes obliged to pick up a temporary knowledge of an art or science of which they understood nothing till their brief was delivered, and appear to be much masters of it. In like manner, members of the legislature frequently introduce and expatiate upon subjects of which they have informed themselves for the occasion.

country has employed for forty years, decided the question by declaring clearly in favour of the elliptical arch.

It is ungraciously suggested, that Johnson's motive for opposing Mr. Mylne's scheme may have been his prejudice against him as a native of North Britain; when, in truth, as has been stated, he gave the aid of his able pen to a friend, who was one of the candidates ; and so far was he from having any illiberal antipathy to Mr. Mylne, that he afterwards lived with that gentleman upon very agreeable terms of acquaintance, and dined with him at his house. Sir John Hawkins, indeed, gives full vent to his own prejudice in abusing Blackfriars-bridge, calling it " an edifice, in which beauty and symmetry are in vain sought for; by which the citizens of London have perpetuated their own disgrace, and subjected a whole nation to the reproach of foreigners." Whoever has contemplated, *placido lumine*, this stately, elegant, and airy structure, which has so fine an effect, especially on approaching the capital on that quarter, must wonder at such unjust and ill-tempered censure ; and I appeal to all foreigners of good taste, whether this bridge be not one of the most distinguished ornaments of London. As to the stability of the fabric, it is certain that the City of London took every precaution to have the best Portland stone for it; but as this is to be found in the quarries belonging to the public, under the direction of the Lords of the Treasury, it so happened that parliamentary interest, which is often the bane of fair pursuits, thwarted their endeavours. Notwithstanding this disadvantage, it is well known that not only has Blackfriars-bridge never sunk either in its foundation or in its arches, which were so much the subject of contest, but any injuries which it has suffered from the effects of severe frosts have been already, in some measure, repaired with sounder stone, and every necessary renewal can be completed at a moderate expense—BOSWELL.

BLACKFRIARS BRIDGE

JOSEPH BARETTI.

CHAPTER XI.—1760—1763.

IN 1760 he wrote "An Address of the Painters to George III. on his Accession to the Throne of these Kingdoms," † which no monarch ever ascended with more sincere congratulations from his people. Two generations of foreign princes had prepared their minds to rejoice in having again a king, who gloried in being "born a Briton." He also wrote, for Mr. Baretti, the Dedication † of his Italian and English Dictionary, to the Marquis of Abreu, then Envoy-Extraordinary from Spain at the Court of Great Britain.

Johnson was now either very idle, or very busy with his Shakspeare ; for I can find no other public composition by him except an Introduction to the Proceedings of the Committee for clothing the French Prisoners ; * one of the many proofs that he was ever awake to the calls of humanity ; and an account which he gave in the " Gentleman's Magazine " of Mr. Tytler's acute and able vindication of Mary Queen of Scots.* The generosity of Johnson's feelings shines forth in the following sentence :

‘ It has now been fashionable for near half a century to defame and vilify the house of Stuart, and to exalt and magnify the reign of Elizabeth. The Stuarts have found few apologists, for the dead cannot pay for praise ; and who will, without reward, oppose the tide of popularity? Yet there remains still among us, not wholly extinguished, a zeal for truth, a desire of establishing right in opposition to fashion."

In this year I have not discovered a single private letter written by him to any of his friends. It should seem, however, that he had at this period a floating intention of writing a history of the recent and wonderful successes of the British arms in all quarters of the globe; for among his resolutions or memorandums, September 18, there is, " Send for books for Hist. of War." [1] How much is it to be regretted that this intention was not fulfilled! His majestic expression would have carried down to the latest posterity the glorious achievements of his country, with the same fervent glow which they produced on the mind at the time. He would have been under no temptation to deviate in any degree from truth, which he held very sacred, or to take a licence, which a learned divine told me he once seemed, in a conversation, jocularly to allow to historians.

"There are," said he, "inexcusable lies and consecrated lies. For instance we are told that on the arrival of the news of the unfortunate battle of Fontenoy, every heart beat, and every eye was in tears. Now we know that no man ate his dinner the worse, but there *should* have been all this concern; and to say there *was* (smiling), may be reckoned a consecrated lie."

This year, Mr. Murphy, having thought himself ill-treated by the Rev. Dr. Francklin, who was one of the writers of the " Critical Review," published an indignant vindication in " A Poetical Epistle to Samuel Johnson, A.M.," in which he compliments Johnson in a just and elegant manner :—

> "Transcendent Genius ! whose prolific vein
> Ne'er knew the frigid poet's toil and pain ;
> To whom APOLLO opens all his store,
> And every muse presents her sacred lore ;
> Say, powerful JOHNSON, whence thy verse is fraught
> With so much grace, such energy of thought ;
> Whether thy JUVENAL instructs the age
> In chaster numbers, and new-points his rage ;
> Or fair IRENE sees, alas ! too late
> Her innocence exchanged for guilty state ;
> Whate'er you write, in every golden line
> Sublimity and elegance combine ;
> Thy nervous phrase impresses every soul,
> While harmony gives rapture to the whole."

[1] Prayers and Meditations, p. 42.—BOSWELL.

Again, towards the conclusion :—

> " Thou then, my friend, who see'st the dangerous strife
> In which some demon bids me plunge my life,
> To the Aonian fount direct my feet,
> Say, where the Nine thy lonely musings meet ?
> Where warbles to thy ear the sacred throng,
> Thy moral sense, thy dignity of song ?
> Tell, for you can, by what unerring art
> You wake to finer feelings every heart ;
> In each bright page some truth important give,
> And bid to future times thy RAMBLER live."

I take this opportunity to relate the manner in which an acquaint-ance first commenced between Dr. Johnson and Mr. Murphy. During the publication of the " Gray's-Inn Journal," a periodical paper, which was successfully carried on by Mr. Murphy alone, when a very young man, he happened to be in the country with Mr. Foote ; and having mentioned that he was obliged to go to London in order to get ready for the press one of the numbers of that Journal, Foote said to him, " You need not go on that account. Here is a French magazine, in which you will find a very pretty oriental tale ; translate that, and send it to your printer." Mr. Murphy having read the tale, was highly pleased with it, and followed Foote's advice. When he returned to town, this tale was pointed out to him in the " Rambler," from whence it had been translated into the French magazine. Mr. Murphy then waited upon Johnson to explain this curious incident. His talents, literature, and gentleman-like manners, were soon perceived by Johnson, and a friend-ship was formed which was never broken.[1]

---

[1] When Mr. Murphy first became acquainted with Dr. Johnson, he was about thirty-one years old. He died at Knightsbridge, June 18, 1805, it is believed in his eighty-second year. In an account of this gentleman, published recently after his death, he is reported to have said, that " he was but *twenty-one*," when he had the impudence to write a periodical paper, during the time that Johnson was publishing the " Rambler."—In a subsequent page, in which Mr. Boswell gives an account of his first introduction to Johnson, will be found a striking instance of the incorrectness of Mr. Murphy's memory ; and the assertion above mentioned, if indeed he made it, which is by no means improbable, furnishes an additional proof of his inaccuracy ; for both the facts asserted are unfounded. He appears to have been eight years older than twenty-one, when he began the " Gray's-Inn Journal ; " and that paper instead of running a race with Johnson's production, did not appear till after the closing of the " Rambler," which ended March 14, 1752. The first number of the " Gray's-Inn Journal" made its appearance about seven months afterwards, in a newspaper of the time, called " The Craftsman," October 21, 1752 ; and in that form the first forty-nine numbers were given to the public. On Saturday, Sept. 29, 1753, it assumed a new form, and was published as a distinct periodical paper ; and in that shape it continued to be published till the 21st of Sept. 1754, when it finally closed ; forming in the whole one hundred and one Essays, in the folio copy. The extraordinary paper mentioned in the text, is No. 38 of the second series, published on June 15, 1754 ; which is a retranslation from the French version of Johnson's " Rambler," No. 190. It was omitted in the republication of these Essays in two volumes 12mo. in which one hundred and four are found, and in which the papers are not always dated on the days when

" TO BENNET LANGTON, ESQ., AT LANGTON, NEAR SPILSBY, LINCOLNSHIRE.

"DEAR SIR,   *Oct.* 18, 1760.

" You that travel about the world, have more materials for letters, than I who stay at home; and should, therefore, write with frequency equal to your opportunities. I should be glad to have all England surveyed by you, if you would impart your observations in narratives as agreeable as your last. Knowledge is always to be wished to those who can communicate it well. While you have been riding and running, and seeing the tombs of the learned, and the camps of the valiant, I have only stayed at home, and intended to do great things, which I have not done. Beau[1] went away to Cheshire, and has not yet found his way back. Chambers passed the vacation at Oxford.

" I am very sincerely solicitous for the preservation or curing of Mr. Langton's sight, and am glad that the chirurgeon at Coventry gives him so much hope. Mr. Sharpe is of opinion that the tedious maturation of the cataract is a vulgar error, and that it may be removed as soon as it is formed. This notion deserves to be considered; I doubt whether it be universally true; but if it be true in some cases, and those cases can be distinguished, it may save a long and uncomfortable delay.

" Of dear Mrs. Langton you give me no account; which is the less friendly, as you know how highly I think of her, and how much I interest myself in her health. I suppose you told her of my opinion, and likewise suppose it was not followed; however, I still believe it to be right.

" Let me hear from you again, wherever you are, or whatever you are doing; whether you wander or sit still, plant trees or make *Rustics*,[2] play with your sisters or muse alone; and in return I will tell you the success of Sheridan, who at this instant is playing *Cato*, and has already played *Richard* twice. He had more company the second than the first night, and will make, I believe, a good figure on the whole, though his faults seem to be very many; some of natural deficience, and some of laborious affectation. He has, I think, no power of assuming either that dignity or elegance which some men, who have little of either in common life, can exhibit on the stage. His voice when strained is

they really appeared; so that the motto prefixed to this Anglo-Gallic Eastern tale, *obscuris vera involvens*, might very properly have been prefixed to this work when republished. Mr. Murphy did not, I believe, wait on Johnson recently after the publication of this adumbration of one of his "Ramblers," as seems to be stated in the text; for, in his concluding Essay Sept. 21, 1754, we find the following paragraph:—

"Besides, why may not a person rather choose an air of bold negligence, than the obscure diligence of pedants and writers of affected phraseology. For my part, I have always thought an easy style more eligible than a pompous diction, lifted up by metaphor, amplified by epithet, and dignified by too frequent insertions of the Latin idiom." It is probable that the " Rambler " was here intended to be censured, and that the author, when he wrote it, was not acquainted with Johnson, whom, from his first introduction, he endeavoured to conciliate. Their acquaintance, therefore, it may be presumed, did not commence till towards the end of this year, 1754. Murphy, however, had highly praised Johnson in the preceding year, No. 14, of the second series, Dec. 22, 1753.—MALONE.

The " Rambler," No. 190, which Murphy retranslated, is the " History of Abouzaid, the son of Morad."— ED.

[1] Topham Beauclerk, Esq.—BOSWELL.

[2] Essays with that title, written about this time by Mr. Langton, but not published.

unpleasing, and when low is not always heard. He seems to think to much on the audience, and turns his face too often to the galleries.

"However, I wish him well, and among other reasons, because I like his wife.[1]

"Make haste to write to, dear Sir,

"Your most affectionate servan.,

"SAM. JOHNSON."

In 1761 Johnson appears to have done little. He was still, no doubt, proceeding in his edition of Shakspeare; but what advances he made in it cannot be ascertained. He certainly was at this time not active; for, in his scrupulous examination of himself, on Easter Eve, he laments, in his too rigorous mode of censuring his own conduct, that his life, since the communion of the preceding Easter, had been "dissipated and useless."[2] He, however, contributed, this year, the Preface * to "Rolt's Dictionary of Trade and Commerce," in which he displays such a clear and comprehensive knowledge of the subject, as might lead the reader to think that its author had devoted all his life to it. I asked him, whether he knew much of Rolt, and of his work. "Sir," said he, "I never saw the man, and never read the book. The booksellers wanted a Preface to a Dictionary of Trade and Commerce. I knew very well what such a Dictionary should be, and I wrote a Preface accordingly." Rolt, who wrote a great deal for the booksellers, was, as Johnson told me, a singular character. Though not in the least acquainted with him, he used to say, "I am just come from Sam. Johnson." This was a sufficient specimen of his vanity and impudence. But he gave a more eminent proof of it in our sister kingdom, as Dr. Johnson informed me. When Akenside's "Pleasures of the Imagination" first came out, he did not put his name to the poem. Rolt went over to Dublin, published an edition of it, and put his own name to it. Upon the fame of this, he lived for several months, being entertained at the best tables as "the ingenious Mr. Rolt."[3] His conversation, indeed, did not discover much of the fire of a poet; but it was recollected that both Addison and Thomson were equally dull till excited by wine. Akenside having been informed of this imposition, vindicated his right by publishing the poem with its real author's name. Several instances of such literary fraud have been detected. The Reverend Dr. Campbell, of St. Andrew's, wrote "An Enquiry into the Original of Moral Virtue," the manuscript

[1] Mrs. Sheridan was author of "Memoirs of Miss Sydney Biddulph," a novel of great merit, and of some other pieces.—BOSWELL.

[2] Prayers and Meditations, p. 44.—BOSWELL.

[3] I have had inquiry made in Ireland as to this story, but do not find it recollected there. I give it on the authority of Dr. Johnson, to which may be added, that of the "Biographical Dictionary," and "Biographia Dramatica;" in both of which it has stood many years. Mr. Malone observes, that the truth probably is, not that an edition was published with Rolt's name in the title-page, but that the poem being then anonymous Rolt acquiesced in its being attributed to him in conversation.—BOSWELL.

of which he sent to Mr. Innes, a clergyman in England, who was his countryman and acquaintance. Innes published it with his own name to it; and, before the imposition was discovered, obtained considerable promotion, as a reward of his merit.[1] The celebrated Dr. Hugh Blair, and his cousin, Mr. George Bannatine, when students in divinity, wrote a poem, entitled "The Resurrection," copies of which were handed about in manuscript. They were, at length, very much surprised to see a pompous edition of it in folio, dedicated to the Princess Dowager of Wales, by a Dr. Douglas, as his own. Some years ago a little novel, entitled "The Man of Feeling," was assumed by Mr. Eccles, a young Irish clergyman, who was afterwards drowned near Bath. He had been at the pains to transcribe the whole book, with blottings, interlineations, and corrections, that it might be shown to several people as an original. It was, in truth, the production of Mr. Henry Mackenzie, an attorney in the Exchequer at Edinburgh, who is the author of several other ingenious pieces; but the belief with regard to Mr. Eccles became so general, that it was thought necessary for Messrs. Strahan and Cadell to publish an advertisement in the newspapers, contradicting the report, and mentioning that they purchased the copyright of Mr. Mackenzie. I can conceive this kind of fraud to be very easily practised with successful effrontery. The *filiation* of a literary performance is difficult of proof; seldom is there any witness present at its birth. A man, either in confidence or by improper means, obtains possession of a copy of it in manuscript, and boldly publishes it as his own. The true author, in many cases, may not be able to make his title clear. Johnson, indeed, from the peculiar features of his literary offspring, might bid defiance to any attempt to appropriate them to others:—

> "But Shakspeare's magic could not copied be;
> Within that circle none durst walk but he."

He this year lent his friendly assistance to correct and improve a pamphlet written by Mr. Gwyn, the architect, entitled "Thoughts on the Coronation of George III." *

Johnson had now for some years admitted Mr. Baretti to his intimacy; nor did their friendship cease upon their being separated by Baretti's revisiting his native country, as appears from Johnson's letters to him.

"TO MR. JOSEPH BARETTI, AT MILAN.[2]

"[*London*] *June* 10, 1761.

"You reproach me very often with parsimony of writing; but you may discover by the extent of my paper that I design to recompense rarity by

---

[1] I have both the books. Innes was the clergyman who brought Psalmanazar to England, and was an accomplice in his extraordinary fiction.—BOSWELL.

[2] The originals of Dr. Johnson's three letters to Mr. Baretti, which are among the very

length. A short letter to a distant friend is, in my opinion, an insult, like that of a slight bow or cursory salutation ;—a proof of unwillingness to do much, even where there is a necessity of doing something. Yet it must be remembered, that he who continues the same course of life in the same place, will have little to tell. One week and one year are very like one another. The silent changes made by time are not always perceived ; and if they are not perceived, cannot be recounted. I have risen and lain down, talked and mused, while you have roved over a considerable part of Europe ; yet I have not envied my Baretti any of his pleasures, though, perhaps, I have envied others his company : and I am glad to have other nations made acquainted with the character of the English by a traveller who has so nicely inspected our manners, and so successfully studied our literature. I received your kind letter from Falmouth, in which you gave me notice of your departure for Lisbon ; and another from Lisbon, in which you told me, that you were to leave Portugal in a few days. To either of these how could any answer be returned? I have had a third from Turin, complaining that I have not answered the former. Your English style still continues in its purity and vigour. With vigour your genius will supply it : but its purity must be continued by close attention. To use two languages familiarly, and without contaminating one by the other, is very difficult ; and to use more than two is hardly to be hoped. The praises which some have received for their multiplicity of languages, may be sufficient to excite industry, but can hardly generate confidence.

" I know not whether I can heartily rejoice at the kind reception which you have found, or at the popularity to which you are exalted. I am willing that your merit should be distinguished ; but cannot wish that your affections may be gained. I would have you happy wherever you are ; yet I would have you wish to return to England. If ever you visit us again, you will find the kindness of your friends undiminished. To tell you how many inquiries are made after you, would be tedious, or if not tedious, would be vain ; because you may be told in a very few words, that all who knew you wish you well ; and that all that you embraced at your departure, will caress you at your return : therefore do not let Italian academicians nor Italian ladies drive us from your thoughts. You may find among us what you will leave behind, soft smiles and easy sonnets. Yet I shall not wonder if all our invitations should be rejected : for there is a pleasure in being considerable at home, which is not easily resisted.

" By conducting Mr. Southwell to Venice, you fulfilled, I know, the original contract : yet I would wish you not wholly to lose him from your notice, but to recommend him to such acquaintance as may best secure him from suffering by his own follies, and to take such general care both of his safety and his interest as may come within your power. His relations will thank you for any such gratuitous attention : at least they will not blame you for any evil that may happen, whether they thank you or not for any good.

" You know that we have a new king and a new parliament. Of the new

best he ever wrote, were communicated to the proprietors of that instructive and elegant monthly miscellany, the " European Magazine," in which they first appeared.—BOSWELL.

parliament Fitzherbert is a member. We were so weary of our old king, that we are much pleased with his   ccessor; of whom we are so much inclined to hope great things, that most of us begin already to believe them. The young man is hitherto blameless; but it would be unreasonable to expect much from one immaturity of juvenile years, and the ignorance of princely education. He has been long in the hands of the Scots, and has already favoured them more than the English will contentedly endure. But, perhaps, he scarcely knows whom he has distinguished, or whom he has disgusted.

"The Artists have instituted a yearly Exhibition of pictures and statues, in imitation, as I am told, of foreign academies. This year was the second exhibition. They please themselves much with the multitude of spectators, and imagine that the English School will rise in reputation. Reynolds is without a rival, and continues to add thousands to thousands, which he deserves, among other excellencies, by retaining his kindness for Baretti. This Exhibition has filled the heads of the artists and lovers of art. Surely life, if it be not long, is tedious, since we are forced to call in the assistance of so many trifles to rid us of our time, of that time which never can return.

"I know my Baretti will not be satisfied with a letter in which I give him no account of myself: yet what account shall I give him? I have not, since the day of our separation, suffered or done anything considerable. The only change in my way of life is, that I have frequented the theatre more than in former seasons. But I have gone thither only to escape from myself. We have had many new farces, and the comedy called 'The Jealous Wife,' which, though not written with much genius, was yet so well adapted to the stage, and so well exhibited by the actors, that it was crowded for near twenty nights. I am digressing from myself to the play-house; but a barren plan must be filled with episodes. Of myself I have nothing to say, but that I have hitherto lived without the concurrence of my own judgment; yet I continue to flatter myself, that, when you return, you will find me mended. I do not wonder that, where the monastic life is permitted, every order finds votaries, and every monastery inhabitants. Men will submit to any rule, by which they may be exempted from the tyranny of caprice and of chance. They are glad to supply by external authority their own want of constancy and resolution, and court the government of others, when long experience has convinced them of their own inability to govern themselves. If I were to visit Italy, my curiosity would be more attracted by convents than by palaces; though I am afraid that I should find expectation in both places equally disappointed, and life in both places supported with impatience and quitted with reluctance. That it must be so soon quitted, is a powerful remedy against impatience; but what shall free us from reluctance? Those who have endeavoured to teach us to die well, have taught few to die willingly: yet I cannot but hope that a good life might end at last in a contented death.

"You see to what a train of thought I am drawn by the mention of myself. Let me now turn my attention upon you. I hope you take care to keep an exact journal, and to register all occurrences and observations; for your friends here expect such a book of travels as has not been often seen. You have given us good specimens in your letters from Lisbon. I wish you had stayed longer in Spain, for no country is less known to the rest of Europe;

but the quickness of your discernment must make amends for the celerity of your motions. He that knows which way to direct his view, sees much in a little time.

"Write to me very often, and I will not neglect to write to you; and I may perhaps, in time, get something to write; at least you will know by my letters, whatever else they may have or want, that I continue to be

"Your most affectionate friend,

"SAM. JOHNSON."

In 1762 he wrote for the Reverend Dr. Kennedy, Rector of Bradley in Derbyshire, in a strain of very courtly elegance, a Dedication to the King* of that gentleman's work entitled "A complete System of Astronomical Chronology, unfolding the Scriptures." He had certainly looked at this work before it was printed ; for the concluding paragraph .s undoubtedly of his composition, of which let my readers judge :—

"Thus have I endeavoured to free Religion and History from the darkness of a disputed and uncertain chronology, from difficulties which have hitherto appeared insuperable, and darkness which no luminary of learning has hitherto been able to dissipate. I have established the truth of the Mosaical account, by evidence which no transcription can corrupt, no negligence can lose, and no interest can pervert. I have shown that the universe bears witness to the inspiration of its historian, by the revolution of its orbs and the succession of its seasons ; *that the stars in their courses fight against* incredulity, that the works of God give hourly confirmation to the *law*, the *prophets*, and the *gospel*, of which *one day telleth another, and one night certifieth another ;* and that the validity of the sacred writings never can be denied, while the moon shall increase and wane, and the sun shall know his going down."

He this year wrote also the Dedication † to the Earl of Middlesex, of Mrs. Lenox's "Female Quixote," and the Preface to the "Catalogue of the Artists' Exhibition."†

The following letter, which, on account of its intrinsic merit, it would have been unjust both to Johnson and the public to have withheld, was obtained for me by the solicitation of my friend Mr. Seward :—

' TO DR. STAUNTON.[1]

"DEAR SIR,   *June* 1, 1762.

"I make haste to answer your kind letter, in hope of hearing again from you before you leave us. I cannot but regret that a man of your qualifications should find it necessary to seek an establishment in Guadaloupe, which if a peace should restore to the French, I shall think it some alleviation of the loss that it must restore likewise Dr. Staunton to the English.

"It is a melancholy consideration, that so much of our time is necessarily to be spent upon the care of living, and that we can seldom obtain ease in

[1] Afterwards Sir G. Staunton, Baronet. He was originally a physician, and went as Secretary to Lord Macartney's embassy to China, and wrote the well-known account of it.

one respect but by resigning it in another; yet I suppose we are by this dispensation not less happy in the whole, than if the spontaneous bounty of Nature poured all that we want into our hands. A few, if they were left thus to themselves, would, perhaps, spend their time in laudable pursuits; but the greater part would prey upon the quiet of each other, or, in the want of other objects, would prey upon themselves.

"This, however, is our condition, which we must improve and solace as we can; and though we cannot choose always our place of residence, we may in every place find rational amusements, and possess in every place the comforts of piety and a pure conscience.

"In America there is little to be observed except natural curiosities. The new world must have many vegetables and animals with which philosophers are but little acquainted. I hope you will furnish yourself with some books of natural history, and some glasses and other instruments of observation. Trust as little as you can to report; examine all you can by your own senses. I do not doubt but you will be able to add much to knowledge, and, perhaps, to medicine. Wild nations trust to simples; and, perhaps, the Peruvian bark is not the only specific which those extensive regions may afford us.

"Wherever you are, and whatever be your fortune, be certain, dear Sir, that you carry with you my kind wishes; and that whether you return hither, or stay in the other hemisphere, to hear that you are happy will give pleasure to, Sir,

"Your most affectionate humble servant,
"Sam. Johnson."

A lady having at this time solicited him to obtain the Archbishop of Canterbury's patronage to have her son sent to the University, one of those solicitations which are too frequent, where people, anxious for a particular object, do not consider propriety, or the opportunity which the persons whom they solicit have to assist them, he wrote to her the following answer, with a copy of which I am favoured by the Reverend Dr. Farmer, Master of Emanuel College, Cambridge :—

"Madam,   *June* 8, 1762.
"I hope you will believe that my delay in answering your letter could proceed only from my unwillingness to destroy any hope that you had formed. Hope is itself a species of happiness, and, perhaps, the chief happiness which this world affords : but, like all other pleasures immoderately enjoyed, the excesses of hope must be expiated by pain; and expectations improperly indulged, must end in disappointment. If it be asked, what is the improper expectation which it is dangerous to indulge, experience will quickly answer, that it is such expectation as is dictated not by reason, but by desire; expectation raised, not by the common occurrences of life, but by the wants of the expectant; an expectation that requires the common course of things to be changed, and the general rules of action to be broken.

"When you made your request to me, you should have considered, Madam, what you were asking. You asked me to solicit a great man, to whom I never   oke, for a young person whom I had never seen, upon a supposition which I

P 2

had no means of knowing to be true. There is no reason why, amongst all the great, I should choose to supplicate the archbishop; nor why, among all the possible objects of his bounty, the archbishop should choose your son. I know, Madam, how unwillingly conviction is admitted, when interest opposes it; but surely, Madam, you must allow, that there is no reason why that should be done by me, which every other man may do with equal reason, and which, indeed, no man can do properly, without some very particular relation both to the archbishop and to you. If I could help you in this exigence by any proper means, it would give me pleasure; but this proposal is so very remote from usual methods, that I cannot comply with it, but at the risk of such answer and suspicions as I believe you do not wish me to undergo.

"I have seen your son this morning; he seems a pretty youth, and will, perhaps, find some better friend than I can procure him; but though he should at last miss the University, he may still be wise, useful, and happy.

"I am, Madam, your most humble servant,

"SAM. JOHNSON."

"TO MR. JOSEPH BARETTI, AT MILAN.

"SIR, *London, July* 20, 1762.

"However justly you may accuse me for want of punctuality in correspondence, I am not so far lost in negligence as to omit the opportunity of writing to you, which Mr. Beauclerk's passage through Milan affords me.

"I suppose you received the 'Idlers,' and I intend that you shall soon receive Shakspeare, that you may explain his works to the ladies of Italy, and tell them the story of the editor, among the other strange narratives with which your long residence in this unknown region has supplied you.

"As you have now been long away, I suppose your curiosity may pant for some news of your old friends. Miss Williams and I live much as we did. Miss Cotterel still continues to cling to Mrs. Porter, and Charlotte is now big of the fourth child. Mr. Reynolds gets six thousands a year. Levett is lately married, not without much suspicion that he has been wretchedly cheated in his match. Mr. Chambers is gone this day, for the first time, the circuit with the judges. Mr. Richardson[1] is dead of an apoplexy, and his second daughter has married a merchant.

"My vanity, or my kindness, makes me flatter myself, that you would rather hear of me than of those whom I have mentioned; but of myself I have very little which I care to tell. Last winter I went down to my native town, where I found the streets much narrower and shorter than I thought I had left them, inhabited by a new race of people, to whom I was very little known. My playfellows were grown old, and forced me to suspect that I was no longer young. My only remaining friend has changed his principles, and was become the tool of the predominant faction. My daughter-in-law, from whom I expected most, and whom I met with sincere benevolence, has lost the beauty and gaiety of youth, without having gained much of the wisdom of age. I wandered about

---

[1] Samuel Richardson, the author of "Clarissa," "Sir Charles Grandison," &c. He died July 4, 1761, aged 72.—MALONE

for five days, and took the first convenient opportunity of returning to a place, where, if there is not much happiness, there is, at least, such a diversity of good and evil, that slight vexations do not fix upon the heart.

" I think in a few weeks to try another excursion; though to what end ? Let me know, my Baretti, what has been the result of your return to your own country : whether time has made any alteration for the better, and whether, when the first raptures of salutation were over, you did not find your thoughts confessed their disappointment.

" Moral sentences appear ostentatious and tumid, when they have no greater occasions than the journey of a wit to his own town : yet such pleasures and such pains make up the general mass of life ; and as nothing is little to him that feels it with great sensibility, a mind able to see common incidents in their real state, is disposed by very common incidents to very serious contemplations. Let us trust that a time will come, when the present moment shall be no longer irksome ; when we shall not borrow all our happiness from hope, which at last is to end in disappointment.

" I beg that you will show Mr. Beauclerk all the civilities which you have in your power; for he has always been kind to me.

" I have lately seen Mr. Stratico, Professor of Padua, who has told me of your quarrel with an Abbot of the Celestine order; but had not the particulars very ready in his memory. When you write to Mr. Marsili, let him know that I remember him with kindness.

" May you, my Baretti, be very happy at Milan, or some other place nearer to, Sir,   " Your most affectionate humble servant,

" SAM. JOHNSON."

The accession of George the Third to the throne of these kingdoms, opened a new and brighter prospect to men of literary merit, who had been honoured with no mark of royal favour in the preceding reign. His present Majesty's education in this country, as well as his taste and beneficence, prompted him to be the patron of science and the arts ; and early this year, Johnson having been represented to him as a very learned and good man, without any certain provision, his Majesty was pleased to grant him a pension of three hundred pounds a year. The Earl of Bute, who was then Prime Minister, had the honour to announce this instance of his Sovereign's bounty, concerning which, many and various stories, all equally erroneous, have been propa-

LORD BUTE.

gated ; maliciously representing it as a political bribe to Johnson, to desert his avowed principles, and become the tool of a Government which he held to be founded in usurpation. I have taken care to have it in my power to refute them from the most authentic information. Lord Bute told me that Mr. Wedderburne, now Lord Loughborough was the person who first mentioned this subject to him. Lord Loughborough told me that the pension was granted to Johnson solely as the reward of his literary merit, without any stipulation whatever, or even tacit understanding that he should write for the administration. His lordship added, that he was confident the political tracts which Johnson afterwards did write, as they were entirely consonant with his own opinions, would have been written by him though no pension had been granted to him.

Mr. Thomas Sheridan and Mr. Murphy, who then lived a good deal both with him and Mr. Wedderburne, told me that they previously talked with Johnson upon this matter, and that it was perfectly understood by all parties that the pension was merely honorary. Sir Joshua Reynolds told me, that Johnson called on him after his Majesty's intention had been notified to him, and said he wished to consult his friends as to the propriety of his accepting this mark of the royal favour, after the definitions which he had given in his Dictionary of *pension* and *pensioners*. He said he should not have Sir Joshua's answer till next day, when he would call again, and desired he might think of it. Sir Joshua answered that he was clear to give his opinion then, that there could be no objection to his receiving from the King a reward for literary merit; and that certainly the definitions in his Dictionary were not applicable to him. Johnson, it should seem, was satisfied, for he did not call again till he had accepted the pension, and had waited on Lord Bute to thank him. He then told Sir Joshua that Lord Bute said to him expressly, "It is not given you for anything you are to do, but for what you have done."[1] His lordship, he said, behaved in the handsomest manner. He repeated the words twice, that he might be sure Johnson heard them, and thus set his mind perfectly at ease. This nobleman, who has been so virulently abused, acted with great honour in this instance, and displayed a mind truly liberal. A minister of a more narrow and selfish disposition would have availed himself of such an opportunity to fix an implied obligation on a man of Johnson's powerful talents to give him his support.

Mr. Murphy and the late Mr. Sheridan severally contended for the distinction of having been the first who mentioned to Mr. Wedderburne that Johnson ought to have a pension. When I spoke of this to Lord Loughborough, wishing to know if he recollected the prime mover in the business, he said, "All his friends assisted:" and when I told him that Mr. Sheridan strenuously asserted his claim to it, his lordship said,

[1] This was said by Lord Bute, as Dr. Burney was informed by Johnson himself, in answer to a question which he put, previously to his acceptance of the intended bounty: "Pray, my Lord, what am I expected to do for this pension?"—MALONE.

"He rang the bell." And it is but just to add, that Mr. Sheridan told me, that when he communicated to Dr. Johnson that a pension was to be granted him, he replied, in a fervour of gratitude, "The English language does not afford me terms adequate to my feelings on this occasion. I must have recourse to the French. I am *pénétré* with his Majesty's goodness." When I repeated this to Dr. Johnson, he did not contradict it.

His definitions of *pension* and *pensioner*, partly founded on the satirical verses of Pope, which he quotes, may be generally true ; and yet every body must allow, that there may be, and have been, instances of pensions given and received upon liberal and honourable terms. Thus, then, it is clear, that there was nothing inconsistent or humiliating in Johnson's accepting of a pension so unconditionally and so honourably offered to him.

But I shall not detain my readers longer by any words of my own, on a subject on which I am happily enabled, by the favour of the Earl of Bute, to present them with what Johnson himself wrote ; his lordship having been pleased to communicate to me a copy of the following letter to his father, which does great honour both to the writer and to the noble person to whom it is addressed :—

"TO THE RIGHT HONOURABLE THE EARL OF BUTE.

"MY LORD,   *July* 20, 1762.

"When the bills were yesterday delivered to me by Mr. Wedderburne, I was informed by him of the future favours which his Majesty has, by your Lordship's recommendation, been induced to intend for me.

"Bounty always receives part of its value from the manner in which it is bestowed; your Lordship's kindness includes every circumstance that can gratify delicacy, or enforce obligation. You have conferred favours on a man who has neither alliance nor interest, who has not merited them by services, nor courted them by officiousness ; you have spared him the shame of solicitation, and the anxiety of suspense.

"What has been thus elegantly given, will, I hope, be not reproachfully enjoyed ; I shall endeavour to give your Lordship the only recompence which generosity desires,—the gratification of finding that your benefits are not improperly bestowed. I am, my Lord,

"Your Lordship's most obliged,

"Most obedient, and most humble servant,

"SAM. JOHNSON."

This year his friend, Sir Joshua Reynolds, paid a visit of some weeks to his native county, Devonshire, in which he was accompanied by Johnson, who was much pleased with this jaunt, and declared he had derived from it a great accession of new ideas. He was entertained at the seats of several noblemen and gentlemen in the west of England ;[1]

[1] At one of these seats Dr. Amyat, physician in London, told me he happened to meet him. In order to amuse him till dinner should be ready, he was taken out to walk in the garden.

but the greatest part of this time was passed at Plymouth, where the magnificence of the navy, the ship-building and all its circumstances, afforded him a grand subject of contemplation. The Commissioner of

PLYMOUTH GARRISON.

the Dockyard paid him the compliment of ordering the yacht to convey him and his friend to the Eddystone, to which they accordingly sailed. But the weather was so tempestuous that they could not land.

Reynolds and he were at this time the guests of Dr. Mudge, the celebrated surgeon, and now physician of that place, not more distinguished for quickness of parts and variety of knowledge, than loved and esteemed for his amiable manners ; and here Johnson formed an acquaintance with Dr. Mudge's father, that very eminent divine, the Reverend Zachariah Mudge, Prebendary of Exeter, who was idolised in the west, both for his excellence as a preacher and the uniform perfect propriety of his private conduct. He preached a sermon purposely that Johnson might hear him ; and we shall see afterwards that Johnson honoured his memory by drawing his character. While Johnson was at Plymouth, he saw a great many of its inhabitants, and was not sparing of his very entertaining conversation. It was here that he made that frank and truly original confession, that " ignorance, pure ignorance," was the cause of a wrong definition, in his Dictionary, of the word *pastern*,[1] to the no small surprise of the lady who put the question to him ; who, having the most profound reverence for his character, so as almost to

The master of the house thinking it proper to introduce something scientific into the conversation, addressed him thus : " Are you a botanist, Dr. Johnson ? " " No, Sir," answered Johnson, " I am not a botanist ; and (alluding no doubt to his near-sightedness), should I wish to become a botanist, I must first turn myself into a reptile "—BOSWELL

[1] See p. 167.—BOSWELL.

suppose him endowed with infallibility, expected to hear an explanation (of what, to be sure, seemed strange to a common reader) drawn from some deep-learned source with which she was unacquainted.

Sir Joshua Reynolds, to whom I was obliged for my information concerning this excursion, mentions a very characteristical anecdote of Johnson while at Plymouth. Having observed that, in consequence of the dock-yard, a new town had arisen about two miles off as a rival to the old; and knowing, from his sagacity and just observation of human nature, that it is certain, if a man hates at all, he will hate his next neighbour, he concluded that this new and rising town could not but excite the envy and jealousy of the old, in which conjecture he was very soon confirmed; he, therefore, set himself resolutely on the side of the old town, the *established* town, in which his lot was cast, considering it as a kind of duty to *stand by* it. He accordingly entered warmly into its interests, and upon every occasion talked of the *dockers*, as the inhabitants of the new town were called, as upstarts and aliens. Plymouth is very plentifully supplied with water by a river brought into it from a great distance, which is so abundant that it runs to waste in the town. The Dock, or New-town, being totally destitute of water, petitioned Plymouth that a small portion of the conduit might be permitted to go to them, and this was now under consideration. Johnson, affecting to entertain the passions of the place, was violent in opposition; and, half laughing at himself for his pretended zeal, where he had no concern, exclaimed, "No, no; I am against the *dockers;* I am a Plymouth man. Rogues! let them die of thirst. They shall not have a drop!"[1]

Lord Macartney obligingly favoured me with a copy of the following letter, in his own handwriting, from the original, which was found, by the present Earl of Bute, among his father's papers.

"TO THE RIGHT HONOURABLE THE EARL OF BUTE.

"MY LORD,   *Temple-lane, Nov.* 3, 1762.

"That generosity by which I was recommended to the favour of his Majesty will not be offended at a solicitation necessary to make that favour permanent and effectual.

"The pension appointed to be paid me at Michaelmas I have not received, and know not where or from whom I am to ask it. I beg, therefore, that your Lordship will be pleased to supply Mr. Wedderburne with such directions as may be necessary, which, I believe, his friendship will make him think it no trouble to convey to me.

"To interrupt your Lordship at a time like this, with such petty difficulties, is improper and unseasonable; but your knowledge of the world has long since taught you that every man's affairs, however little, are important to himself. Every man hopes that he shall escape neglect; and, with reason, may every

[1] A friend of mine once heard him during this visit, exclaim with the utmost vehemence I HATE a Docker."—BLAKEWAY.

man whose vices do not preclude his claim, expect favour from that benificence which has been extended to, my Lord,

"Your Lordship's most obliged,

"And most humble servant,

"SAM. JOHNSON."

"TO MR. JOSEPH BARETTI, AT MILAN.

"SIR,   *London, Dec.* 21, 1762.

"You are not to suppose, with all your conviction of my idleness, that I have passed all this time without writing to my Baretti. I gave a letter to Mr. Beauclerk, who, in my opinion, and in his own, was hastening to Naples for the recovery of his health; but he has stopped at Paris, and I know not when he will proceed. Langton is with him.

"I will not trouble you with speculations about peace and war. The good or ill success of battles and embassies extends itself to a very small part of domestic life: we all have good and evil, which we feel more sensibly than our petty part of public miscarriage or prosperity. I am sorry for your disappointment, with which you seem more touched than I should expect a man of your resolution and experience to have been, did I not know that general truths are seldom applied to particular occasions, and that the fallacy of our self-love extends itself as wide as our interest or affections. Every man believes that mistresses are unfaithful, and patrons capricious; but he excepts his own mistress and his own patron. We have all learned that greatness is negligent and contemptuous, and that in courts life is often lavished away in ungratified expectation; but he that approaches greatness, or glitters in a court, imagines that destiny has at last exempted him from the common lot.

"Do not let such evils overwhelm you as thousands have suffered, and thousands have surmounted; but turn your thoughts with vigour to some other plan of life, and keep always in your mind, that, with due submission to Providence, a man of genius has been seldom ruined but by himself. Your patron's weakness or insensibility will finally do you little hurt, if he is not assisted by your own passions. Of your love I know not the propriety, nor can estimate the power; but in love, as in every other passion of which hope is the essence, we ought always to remember the uncertainty of events. There is, indeed, nothing that so much seduces reason from vigilance as the thought of passing life with an amiable woman; and if all would happen that a lover fancies, I know not what other terrestrial happiness would deserve pursuit. But love and marriage are different states. Those who are to suffer the evils together,[1] and to suffer often for the sake of one another, soon lose that tenderness of look and that benevolence of mind which arose from the participation of unmingled pleasure and successive amusement. A woman, we are sure, will not be always fair—we are not sure she will always be virtuous; and a man cannot retain through life that respect and assiduity by which he pleases for a day or for a month. I do not, however, pretend to have discovered that life has any thing more to be desired than a prudent and virtuous marriage, therefore know not what counsel to give you.

[1] Johnson probably wrote "the evils *of life* together." The words in italics, however, are not found in Baretti's original edition of this letter, but they may have been omitted inadvertently either in his transcript or at the press.—MALONE.

"If you can quit your imagination of love and greatness, and leave your hopes of preferment and bridal raptures to try once more the fortune of literature and industry, the way through France is now open, We flatter ourselves that we shall cultivate, with great diligence, the arts of peace; and every man will be welcome among us who can teach us any thing we do not know. For your part, you will find all your old friends willing to receive you.

"Reynolds still continues to increase in reputation and in riches. Miss Williams, who very much loves you, goes on in the old way; Miss Cotterel is still with Mrs. Porter; Miss Charlotte is married to Dean Lewis, and has three children; Mr. Levett has married a street-walker. But the gazette of my narration must now arrive to tell you, that Bathurst went physician to the army, and died at the Havannah.

"I know not whether I have not sent you word that Huggins and Richardson are both dead. When we see our enemies and friends gliding away before us, let us not forget that we are subject to the general law of mortality, and shall soon be where our doom will be fixed for ever.

"I pray God to bless you, and am, Sir,

"Your most affectionate humble servant,

"SAM. JOHNSON."

"Write soon."

In 1763, he furnished to the "Poetical Calendar," published by Fawkes and Woty, a character of Collins,* which he afterwards ingrafted into his entire life of that admirable poet, in the collection of lives which he wrote for the body of English poetry, formed and published by the booksellers of London. His account of the melancholy depression with which Collins was severely afflicted, and which brought him to his grave, is, I think, one of the most tender and interesting passages in the whole series of his writings. He also favoured Mr. Hoole with the Dedication of his translations of Tasso to the Queen,* which is so happily conceived and elegantly expressed, that I cannot but point it out to the peculiar notice of my readers.[1]

[1] "MADAM,

"To approach the high and illustrious has been in all ages the privilege of poets; and though translators cannot justly claim the same honour, yet they naturally follow their authors as attendants; and I hope that in return for having enabled Tasso to diffuse his fame through the British dominions, I may be introduced by him to the presence of your Majesty.

"Tasso has a peculiar claim to your Majesty's favour, as follower and panegyrist of the house of Este, which has one common ancestor with the House of Hanover; and in reviewing his life it is not easy to forbear a wish that he had lived in a happier time, when he might among the descendants of that illustrious family have found a more liberal and potent patronage.

"I cannot but observe, Madam, how unequally reward is proportioned to merit, when I reflect that the happiness which was withheld from Tasso is reserved for me; and that the poem which once hardly procured to its author the countenance of the princes of Ferrara, has attracted to its translator the favourable notice of a British Queen.

"Had this been the fate of Tasso, he would have been able to have celebrated the condescension of your Majesty in nobler language, but could not have felt it with more ardent gratitude than,   Madam, your Majesty's

"Most faithful and devoted servant,

BOSWELL.   "JOHN HOOLE."

CHAPTER XII.—1763.

First Interview of Boswell with Johnson, at the House of Davies the Bookseller—Record of Conversation—Boswell's Visit to his Chambers in the Temple—Description of Johnson—Meeting at "The Mitre" Tavern—Record of his Opinions of Gray, Goldsmith, &c.—Advice to Boswell.

THIS [1763] is to me a memorable year; for in it I had the happiness to obtain the acquaintance of that extraordinary man whose memoirs I am now writing: an acquaintance which I shall ever esteem as one of the most fortunate circumstances in my life. Though then but two-and-twenty, I had for several years read his works with delight and instruction, and had the highest reverence for their author, which had grown up in my fancy into a kind of mysterious veneration, by figuring to myself a state of solemn, elevated abstraction in which I supposed him to live in the immense metropolis of London. Mr. Gentleman, a native of Ireland, who passed some years in Scotland as a player, and as an instructor in the English language, a man whose talents and worth were depressed by misfortunes, had given me a representation of the figure and manner of DICTIONARY JOHNSON! as he was then generally called; [1] and during my first visit to London,

As great men of antiquity such as Scipio *Africanus* had an epithet added to their names

which was for three months in 1760, Mr. Derrick, the poet, who was Gentleman's friend and countryman, flattered me with hopes that he would introduce me to Johnson, an honour of which I was very ambitious. But he never found an opportunity, which made me doubt that he had promised to do what was not in his power ; till Johnson, some years afterwards, told me, " Derrick, Sir, might very well have introduced you. I had a kindness for Derrick, and am sorry he is dead."

In the summer of 1761 Mr. Thomas Sheridan[1] was at Edinburgh, and delivered lectures upon the English language and public speaking to large and respectable audiences.

THOMAS SHERIDAN.

I was often in his company, and heard him frequently expatiate upon Johnson's extraordinary knowledge, talents, and virtues, repeat his pointed sayings, describe his particularities, and boast of his being his guest sometimes till two or three in the morning. At his house I hoped to have many opportunities of seeing the sage, as Mr. Sheridan obligingly assured me I should not be disappointed.

When I returned to London in the end of 1762, to my surprise and regret I found an irreconcileable difference had taken place between Johnson and Sheridan. A pension of two hundred pounds a year had been given to Sheridan. Johnson, who, as has been already mentioned, thought slightingly of Sheridan's art, upon hearing that he was also pensioned, exclaimed, " What ! have they given *him* a pension ? Then it is time for me to give up mine." Whether this proceeded from a momentary indignation, as if it were an affront to his exalted merit that a player should be rewarded in the same manner with him, or was the sudden effect of a fit of peevishness, it was unluckily said, and indeed cannot be justified. Mr. Sheridan's pension was granted to him not as a player, but as a sufferer in the cause of Government, when he was manager of the Theatre Royal in Ireland, when parties ran high in 1753. And it must also be allowed that he was a man of literature, and had considerably improved the arts of reading and speaking with distinctness and propriety.

in consequence of some celebrated action, so my illustrious friend was often called DICTIONARY JOHNSON, from that wonderful achievement of genius and labour, his " Dictionary of the English Language;" the merit of which I contemplate with more and more admiration.— POSWELL.

[1] Thomas Sheridan was the son of Swift's friend, Dr. Sheridan, and father of the celebrated Richard Brinsley Sheridan, the dramatist and statesman —ED

Besides, Johnson should have recollected that Mr. Sheridan taught pronunciation to Mr. Alexander Wedderburne, whose sister was married to Sir Harry Erskine, an intimate friend of Lord Bute, who was the favourite of the king ; and surely the most outrageous Whig will not maintain that whatever ought to be the principle in the disposal of *offices*, a *pension* ought never to be granted from any bias of Court connection. Mr. Macklin, indeed, shared with Mr. Sheridan the honour of instructing Mr. Wedderburne ; and though it was too late in life for a Caledonian to acquire the genuine English cadence, yet so successful were Mr. Wedderburne's instructors, and his own unabating endeavours, that he got rid of the coarse part of his Scotch accent, retaining only as much of the " native wood-note wild " as to mark his country ; which, if any Scotchman should affect to forget, I should heartily despise him. Notwithstanding the difficulties which are to be encountered by those who have not had the advantage of an English education, he, by degrees, formed a mode of speaking to which Englishmen do not deny the praise of elegance. Hence his distinguished oratory, which he exerted in his own country as an advocate in the Court of Session, and a ruling elder of the *Kirk*, has had its fame and ample reward in much higher spheres. When I look back on this noble person at Edinburgh, in situations so unworthy of his brilliant powers, and behold Lord Loughborough at London, the change seems almost like one of the metamorphoses in Ovid ; and as his two preceptors, by refining his utterance, gave currency to his talents, we may say, in the words of that poet, " *Nam vos mutastis.*"

I have dwelt the longer upon this remarkable instance of successful parts and assiduity, because it affords animating encouragement to other gentlemen of North Britain to try their fortunes in the southern part of the island, where they may hope to gratify their utmost ambition ; and now that we are one people by the Union, it would surely be illiberal to maintain that they have not an equal title with the natives of any other part of his Majesty's dominions.

Johnson complained that a man who disliked him repeated his sarcasm to Mr. Sheridan, without telling him what followed, which was, that after a pause he added, "However, I am glad that Mr. Sheridan has a pension, for he is a very good man." Sheridan could never forgive this hasty contemptuous expression. It rankled in his mind ; and though I informed him of all that Johnson said, and that he would be very glad to meet him amicably, he positively declined repeated offers which I made, and once went off abruptly from a house where he and I were engaged to dine, because he was told that Dr. Johnson was to be there. I have no sympathetic feeling with such persevering resentment. It is painful when there is a breach between those who have lived together socially and cordially ; and I wonder that there is not in all such cases a mutual wish that it should be healed. I could perceive that Mr. Sheridan was by no means satisfied with Johnson's acknowledging him to be a good man. That could not soothe his injured vanity. I could not but smile, at the same time that I was offended, to observe Sheridan, in "The Life of Swift," which he afterwards published, attempting, in the writhings of his resentment, to depreciate Johnson, by characterising him as "a writer of gigantic fame, in these days of little men ;" that very Johnson whom he once so highly admired and venerated.

This rupture with Sheridan deprived Johnson of one of his most agreeable resources for amusement in his lonely evenings; for Sheridan's well-informed, animated, and bustling mind never suffered conversation to stagnate ; and Mrs. Sheridan was a most agreeable companion to an intellectual man. She was sensible, ingenious, unassuming, yet communicative. I recollect, with satisfaction, many pleasing hours which I passed with her under the hospitable roof of her husband, who was to me a very kind friend. Her novel, entitled "Memoirs of Miss Sydney Biddulph," contains an excellent moral, while it inculcates a future state of retribution ; [1] and what it teaches is impressed upon the mind by a series of as deep distress as can affect humanity, in the amiable and pious heroine who goes to her grave unrelieved, but resigned, and full of hope of "heaven's mercy." Johnson paid her this high compliment upon it : "I know not, Madam, that you have a right, upon moral principles, to make your readers suffer so much."

Mr. Thomas Davies, the actor, who then kept a bookseller's shop in Russell-street, Covent-garden, [2] told me that Johnson was very much

---

[1] My position has been very well illustrated by Mr. Belsham of Bedford, in his "Essay on Dramatic Poetry." "The fashionable doctrine," says he, "both of moralists and critics in these times is, that virtue and happiness are constant concomitants ; and it is regarded as a kind of dramatic impiety to maintain that virtue should not be rewarded, nor vice punished, in the last scene of the last act of every tragedy. This conduct in our modern poets is, however, in my opinion, extremely injudicious; for it labours in vain to inculcate a doctrine in theory, which every one knows to be false in fact, viz. that virtue in real life is always productive of happiness; and vice of misery. Thus Congreve concludes the tragedy of 'The Mourning Bride' with the following foolish couplet :

> 'For blessings ever wait on virtuous deeds,
> And, though a late, a sure reward succeeds.'

"When a man eminently virtuous, a Brutus, a Cato, or a Socrates, finally sinks under the pressure of accumulated misfortune, we are not only led to entertain a more indignant hatred of vice, than if he rose from his distress, but we are inevitably induced to cherish the sublime idea that a day of future retribution will arrive when he shall receive not merely poetical, but real and substantial justice."—Essays Philosophical, Historical, and Literary, London, 1791, vol. ii. 8vo, p. 317.

This is well reasoned and well expressed. I wish, indeed, that the ingenious author, had not thought it necessary to introduce any *instance* of "a man eminently virtuous ;" as he would then have avoided mentioning such a ruffian as Brutus under that description. Mr. Belsham discovers in his Essays so much reading, and thinking, and good composition, that I regret his not having been fortunate enough to be educated a member of our excellent national establishment. Had he not been nursed in nonconformity, he probably would not have been tainted with those heresies (as I sincerely, and on no slight investigation, think them) both in religion and politics, which, while I read, I am sure with candour, I cannot read without offence.— BOSWELL.

[2] No. 8.—The very place where I was fortunate enough to be introduced to the illustrious

his friend, and came frequently to his house, where he more than once invited me to meet him ; but by some unlucky accident or other he was prevented from coming to us.

NO. 8, RUSSELL STREET, COVENT GARDEN.

Mr. Thomas Davies was a man of good understanding and talents with the advantage of a liberal education. Though somewhat pompous, he was an entertaining companion ; and his literary performances have no inconsiderable share of merit. He was a friendly and very hospitable man ; both he and his wife (who has been celebrated for her beauty), though upon the stage for many years, maintained an uniform decency of character, and Johnson esteemed them, and lived in as easy an intimacy with them as with any family which he used to visit. Mr. Davies recollected several of Johnson's remarkable sayings, and was one of the best of the many imitators of his voice and manner, while relating them. He increased my impatience more and more to see the extraordinary man whose works I highly valued, and whose conversation was reported to be so peculiarly excellent.

subject of this work, deserves to be particularly marked. I never pass by it without feeling reverence and regret.—BOSWELL.

At last, on Monday, the 16th of May, when I was sitting in Mr Davies's back-parlour, after having drunk tea with him and Mrs. Davies. Johnson unexpectedly came into the shop ;[1] and Mr. Davies having perceived him, through the glass-door in the room in which we were sitting, advancing towards us,—he announced his awful approach to me, somewhat in the manner of an actor in the part of *Horatio*, when he addresses *Hamlet* on the appearance of his father's ghost, " Look, my Lord, it comes ! " I found that I had a very perfect idea of Johnson's figure, from the portrait of him painted by Sir Joshua Reynolds soon after he had published his Dictionary, in the attitude of sitting in his easy chair in deep meditation ; which was the first picture his friend did for him, which Sir Joshua very kindly presented to me, and from which an engraving has been made for this work.[2] Mr. Davies mentioned my name, and respectfully introduced

THOMAS DAVIES.

me to him. I was much agitated ; and recollecting his prejudice against the Scotch, of which I had heard much, I said to Davies, " Don't tell where I come from."—" From Scotland," cried Davies, roguishly. " Mr. Johnson," said I, " I do indeed come from Scotland, but I cannot help it." I am willing to flatter myself that I meant this as light pleasantry to soothe and conciliate him, and not as an humiliating abasement at the expense of my country. But however that might be, this speech was somewhat unlucky ; for with that quickness of wit for which he was so remarkable, he seized the expression, " come from Scotland," which I used in the sense of being of that country ; and, as if I had said that I had come away from it, or left it, retorted, " That, Sir, I find, is what a very great many of your countrymen cannot help." This stroke

[1] Mr. Murphy, in his " Essay on the Life and Genius of Dr. Johnson," has given an account of this meeting considerably different from mine, I am persuaded without any consciousness of error. His memory, at the end of near thirty years, has undoubtedly deceived him, and he supposes himself to have been present at a scene, which he has probably heard inaccurately described by others. In my note *taken on the very day*, in which I am confident I marked everything material that passed, no mention is made of this gentleman ; and I am sure, that I should not have omitted one so well known in the literary world. It may easily be imagined that this my first interview with Dr. Johnson, with all its circumstances, made a strong impression on my mind, and would be registered with peculiar attention.—Boswell.

It is remarkable, that in the editions of Murphy's " Life of Johnson," published subsequently to the appearance of this note, in 1791, he never corrected the mis-statement here mentioned. —Malone.

[2] The portrait referred to above is given on the title-page of the present volume.—Ed.

stunned me a good deal ; and when we had sat down, I felt myself not a little embarrassed, and apprehensive of what might come next. He then addressed himself to Davies : "What do you think of Garrick ? He has refused me an order for the play for Miss Williams, because he knows the house will be full, and that an order would be worth three shillings." Eager to take any opening to get into conversation with him, I ventured to say, "O Sir, I cannot think Mr. Garrick would grudge such a trifle to you." "Sir," said he, with a stern look, "I have known David Garrick longer than you have done ; and I know no right you have to talk to me on the subject." Perhaps I deserved this check ; for it was rather presumptuous in me, an entire stranger, to express any doubt of the justice of his animadversion upon his old acquaintance and pupil.[1] I now felt myself much mortified, and began to think that the hope which I had long indulged of obtaining his acquaintance was blasted. And, in truth, had not my ardour been uncommonly strong, and my resolution uncommonly persevering, so rough a reception might have deterred me for ever from making any further attempts. Fortunately, however, I remained upon the field not wholly discomfited ; and was soon rewarded by hearing some of his conversation, of which I preserved the following short minute, without marking the questions and observations by which it was produced.

"People," he remarked, "may be taken in once, who imagine that an author is greater in private life than other men. Uncommon parts require uncommon opportunities for their exertion.

"In barbarous society, superiority of parts is of real consequence. Great strength or great wisdom is of much value to an individual. But in more polished times there are people to do everything for money ; and then there are a number of other superiorities, such as those of birth, and fortune, and rank, that dissipate men's attention, and leave no extraordinary share of respect for personal and intellectual superiority. This is wisely ordered by Providence, to preserve some equality among mankind."

"Sir, this book ('The Elements of Criticism,' which he had taken up) is a pretty essay, and deserves to be held in some estimation, though much of it is chimerical."

Speaking of one who, with more than ordinary boldness, attacked public measures and the royal family, he said, "I think he is safe from the law, but he is an abusive scoundrel ; and instead of applying to my Lord Chief Justice to punish him, I would send half a dozen footmen, and have him well ducked."

[1] That this was a momentary sally against Garrick there can be no doubt ; for at Johnson's desire he had, some years before, given a benefit night at this theatre to this very person, by which she had got two hundred pounds. Johnson, indeed, upon all other occasions, when I was in his company, praised the very liberal charity of Garrick. I once mentioned to him, "It is observed, Sir, that you attack Garrick yourself, but will suffer nobody else to do it." Johnson (smiling), "Why, Sir, that is true."—BOSWELL.

" The notion of liberty amuses the people of England, and helps to keep off the *tædium vitæ*. When a butcher tells you that *his heart bleeds for his country*, he has, in fact, no uneasy feeling."

" Sheridan will not succeed at Bath with his oratory. Ridicule has gone down before him, and, I doubt, Derrick is his enemy." [1]

" Derrick may do very well, as long as he can outrun his character ; but the moment his character gets up with him, it is all over."

It is, however, but just to record, that, some years afterwards, when I reminded him of this sarcasm, he said, " Well, but Derrick has now got a character that he need not run away from."

I was highly pleased with the extraordinary vigour of his conversation, and regretted that I was drawn away from it by an engagement at another place. I had, for a part of the evening, been left alone with him, and had ventured to make an observation now and then, which he received very civilly ; so that I was satisfied that, though there was a roughness in his manner, there was no ill-nature in his disposition. Davies followed me to the door, and when I complained to him a little of the hard blows which the great man had given me, he kindly took upon him to console me by saying, " Don't be uneasy. I can see he likes you very well."

A few days afterwards I called on Davies, and asked him if he thought I might take the liberty of waiting on Mr. Johnson at his chambers in the Temple. He said I certainly might, and that Mr. Johnson would take it as a compliment. So, on Tuesday, the 24th of May, after having been enlivened by the witty sallies of Messieurs Thornton, Wilkes, Churchill, and Lloyd, with whom I had passed the morning, I boldly repaired to Johnson. His chambers were on the first floor of No. 1, Inner Temple-lane, and I entered them with an impression given me by the Reverend Dr. Blair, of Edinburgh, who had been introduced to him not long before, and described his having " found the Giant in his den ; " an expression which, when I came to be pretty well acquainted with Johnson, I repeated to him, and he was diverted at this picturesque account of himself. Dr. Blair had been presented to him by Dr. James Fordyce. At this time the controversy concerning the pieces published by Mr. James Macpherson, as translations of Ossian, was at its height. Johnson had all along denied their authenticity ; and, what was still more provoking to their admirers, maintained that they had no merit. The subject having been introduced by Dr. Fordyce, Dr. Blair, relying on the internal evidence of their antiquity, asked Dr. Johnson whether he thought any man of a modern age could have written such poems ? Johnson replied, " Yes, Sir, many men, many women, and many children." Johnson, at this time, did not know that Dr. Blair had just

Mr. Sheridan was then reading lectures upon oratory at Bath, where Derrick was Master of the Ceremonies; or, as the phrase is, KING.—BOSWELL.

published a Dissertation, not only defending their authenticity, but seriously ranking them with the poems of Homer and Virgil; and when he was afterwards informed of this circumstance, he expressed some displeasure at Dr. Fordyce's having suggested the topic, and said, "I am not sorry that they got thus much for their pains. Sir, it was like leading one to talk of a book, when the author is concealed behind the door."

He received me very courteously; but it must be confessed that his apartment, and furniture, and morning dress, were sufficiently uncouth. His brown suit of clothes looked very rusty; he had on a little old shrivelled unpowdered wig, which was too small for his head; his shirt-neck and knees of his breeches were loose; his black worsted stockings ill drawn up; and he had a pair of unbuckled shoes by way of slippers. But all these slovenly particularities were forgotten the moment that he began to talk. Some gentlemen, whom I do not recollect, were sitting with him; and when they went away, I also rose; but he said to me, "Nay, don't go."—"Sir," said I, "I am afraid that I intrude upon you. It is benevolent to allow me to sit and hear you." He seemed pleased with this compliment, which I sincerely paid him, and answered, "Sir, I am obliged to any man who visits me."—I have preserved the following short minute of what passed this day:—

"Madness frequently discovers itself merely by unnecessary deviation from the usual modes of the world. My poor friend Smart showed the disturbance of his mind, by falling upon his knees, and saying his prayers in the street, or in any other unusual place. Now, although, rationally speaking, it is greater madness not to pray at all, than to pray as Smart did, I am afraid there are so many who do not pray, that their understanding is not called in question."

Concerning this unfortunate poet, Christopher Smart, who was confined in a madhouse, he had, at another time, the following conversation with Dr. Burney.—BURNEY: "How does poor Smart do, Sir; is he likely to recover?"—JOHNSON: "It seems as if his mind had ceased to struggle with the disease: for he grows fat upon it."—BURNEY: "Perhaps, Sir, that may be from want of exercise."—JOHNSON: "No, Sir; he has partly as much exercise as he used to have, for he digs in the garden. Indeed, before his confinement, he used for exercise to walk to the alehouse; but he was *carried* back again. I did not think he ought to be shut up. His infirmities were not noxious to society. He insisted on people praying with him; and I'd as lief pray with Kit Smart as any one else. Another charge was, that he did not love clean linen; and I have no passion for it."

Johnson continued: "Mankind have a great aversion to intellectual labour; but even supposing knowledge to be easily attainable, more people would be content to be ignorant than would take even a little trouble to acquire it.

"The morality of an action depends on the motive from which we act. If I fling half-a-crown to a beggar, with intention to break his head, and he picks it up and buys victuals with it, the physical effect is good ; but, with respect to me, the action is very wrong. So religious exercises, if not performed with an intention to please God, avail us nothing. As our Saviour says of those who perform them from other motives, ' Verily they have their reward.'

"The Christian religion has very strong evidences. It, indeed, appears, in some degree, strange to reason ; but in History we have undoubted facts, against which, in reasoning *à priori*, we have more arguments than we have for them ; but, then, testimony has great weight, and casts the balance. I would recommend to every man whose faith is yet unsettled, Grotius, Dr. Pearson, and Dr. Clarke."

Talking of Garrick, he said, "He is the first man in the world for sprightly conversation."

When I rose a second time, he again pressed me to stay, which I did.

He told me, that he generally went abroad at four in the afternoon, and seldom came home till two in the morning. I took the liberty to ask if he did not think it wrong to live thus, and not make more use of his great talents. He owned it was a bad habit. On reviewing, at the distance of many years, my journal of this period, I wonder how, at my first visit, I ventured to talk to him so freely, and that he bore it with so much indulgence.

Before we parted, he was so good as to promise to favour me with his company one evening at my lodgings ; and, as I took my leave, shook me cordially by the hand. It is almost needless to add, that I felt no little elation at having now so happily established an acquaintance of which I had been so long ambitious.

My readers will, I trust, excuse me for being thus minutely circumstantial, when it is considered that the acquaintance of Dr. Johnson was to me a most valuable acquisition, and laid the foundation of whatever instruction and entertainment they may receive from my collections concerning the great subject of the work which they are now perusing

I did not visit him again till Monday, June 13, at which time I recollect no part of his conversation, except, that when I told him I had been to see Johnson ride upon three horses, he said, "Such a man, Sir, should be encouraged; for his performances show the extent of the human powers in one instance, and thus tend to raise our opinion of the faculties of man. He shows what may be attained by persevering application ; so that every man may hope, that by giving as much application, although, perhaps, he may never ride three horses at a time, or dance upon a wire, yet he may be equally expert in whatever profession he has chosen to pursue."

He again shook me by the hand at parting, and asked me why I did not come oftener to him. Trusting that I was now in his good graces, I answered, that he had not given me much encouragement, and reminded him of the check I had received from him at our first interview. "Poh, poh!" said he, with a complacent smile, "never mind these things. Come to me as often as you can. I shall be glad to see you."

I had learnt that his place of frequent resort was the Mitre tavern in Fleet-street, where he loved to sit up late, and I begged I might be allowed to pass an evening with him there soon, which he promised I should. A few days afterwards, I met him near Temple-bar about one o'clock in the morning, and asked if he would then go to the Mitre. "Sir," said he, "it is too late, they won't let us in. But I'll go with you another night, with all my heart."

A revolution of some importance in my plan of life had just taken place: for instead of procuring a commission in the foot guards, which was my own inclination, I had, in compliance with my father's wishes, agreed to study the law, and was soon to set out for Utrecht, to hear the lectures of an excellent civilian in that University, and then to proceed on my travels. Though very desirous of obtaining Dr. Johnson's advice and instructions on the mode of pursuing my studies, I was at this time so occupied, shall I call it? or so dissipated by the amusements of London, that our next meeting was not till Saturday, June 25, when, happening to dine at Clifton's eating-house, in Butcher-row, I was surprised to perceive Johnson come in and take his seat at another table. The mode of dining, or rather being fed, at such houses in London, is well known to many to be particularly unsocial, as there is no ordinary, or united company, but each person has his own mess, and is under no obligation to hold any intercourse with any one. A liberal and full-minded man, however, who loves to talk, will break through this churlish and unsocial restraint. Johnson and an Irish gentleman got into a dispute concerning the cause of some part of mankind being black. "Why, Sir," said Johnson, "it has been accounted for in three ways: either by supposing that they are the posterity of Ham, who was cursed, or that God at first created two kinds of men, one black, and another white, or that, by the heat of the sun, the skin is scorched, and so acquires a sooty hue. This matter has been much canvassed among naturalists, but has never been brought to any certain issue." What the Irishman said is totally obliterated from my mind; but I remember that he became very warm and intemperate in his expressions; upon which Johnson rose, and quietly walked away. When he had retired, his antagonist took his revenge, as he thought, by saying, "He has a most ungainly figure, and an affectation of pomposity, unworthy of a man of genius."

Johnson had not observed that I was in the room. I followed him, however, and he agreed to meet me in the evening at the Mitre. I called on him, and we went thither at nine. We had a good supper, and port wine, of which he then sometimes drank a bottle. The orthodox high-church sound of the Mitre,—the figure and manner of the celebrated Samuel Johnson,—the extraordinary power and precision of his conversation, and the pride, arising from finding myself admitted as his companion, produced a variety of sensations, and a pleasing elevation of

JOHNSON AND BOSWELL AT THE MITRE.

mind beyond what I had ever before experienced. I find in my Journal the following minute of our conversation, which, though it will give but a very faint notion of what passed, is, in some degree, a valuable record ; and it will be curious in this view, as showing how habitual to his mind were some opinions which appear in his works.

" Colley Cibber, Sir, was by no means a blockhead, but by arrogating to himself too much, he was in danger of losing that degree of estimation to which he was entitled. His friends gave out that he *intended* his Birthday Odes should be bad ; but that was not the case, Sir ; for he kept them many months by him, and a few years before he died he showed me one of them, with great solicitude to render it as perfect as might be, and I made some corrections, to which he was not very willing to submit.   I remember the following couplet in allusion to the King and himself :—

> ' Perched on the eagle's soaring wing,
> The lowly linnet loves to sing.'

Sir, he had heard something of the fabulous tale of the wren sitting upon the eagle's wing, and he had applied it to a linnet.   Cibber's familiar

COLLEY CIBBER.

style, however, was better than that which Whitehead[1] has assumed.   *Grand* nonsense is insupportable.   Whitehead is but a little man to inscribe verses to players."

I did not presume to controvert this censure, which was tinctured with his prejudice against players ; but I could not help thinking that a dramatic poet might with propriety pay a compliment to an eminent performer, as Whitehead has very happily done in his verses to Mr. Garrick.

"Sir, I do not think Gray a first-rate poet.   He has not a bold imagination, nor much command of words.   The obscurity in which he has involved himself will not persuade us that he is sublime.   His "Elegy in a Churchyard" has a happy selection of images, but I don't like what are called his great things.   His Ode which begins

> ' Ruin seize thee, ruthless King,
> Confusion on thy banners wait !

has been celebrated for its abruptness, and plunging into the subject all at once.   But such arts as these have no merit, unless when they are original.   We admire them only once ; and this abruptness has nothing new in it.   We have had it often before.   Nay, we have it in the old song of Johnny Armstrong :—

> Is there ever a man in all Scotland,
> From the highest estate to the lowest degree,' &c.

And then, Sir,

> ' Yes, there is a man in Westmorland,
> And Johnny Armstrong they do him call.'

There, now, you plunge at once into the subject.   You have no previous

---

[1] William Whitehead, who succeeded Cibber as Poet Laureate.

narration to lead you to it.—The two next lines in that Ode are. I think, very good :—

> ' Though fann'd by Conquest's crimson wing,
> They mock the air with idle state.' " [1]

Here let it be observed, that although his opinion of Gray's poetry was widely different from mine, and I believe from that of most men of taste, by whom it is with justice highly admired, there is certainly much absurdity in the clamour which has been raised, as if he had been culpably injurious to the merit of that bard, and had been actuated by envy. Alas ! ye little short-sighted critics, could Johnson be envious of the talents of any of his contemporaries ? That his opinion on this subject was what in private and in public he uniformly expressed, regardless of what others might think, we may wonder, and perhaps regret ; but it is shallow and unjust to charge him with expressing what he did not think.

Finding him in a placid humour, and wishing to avail myself of the opportunity which I fortunately had of consulting a sage, to hear whose wisdom, I conceived, in the ardour of youthful imagination, that men filled with a noble enthusiasm for intellectual improvement would gladly have resorted from distant lands,—I opened my mind to him ingenuously, and gave him a little sketch of my life, to which he was pleased to listen with great attention.

I acknowledged, that though educated very strictly in the principles of religion, I had for some time been misled into a certain degree of infidelity ; but that I was come now tô a better way of thinking, and was fully satisfied of the truth of the Christian revelation, though I was not clear as to every point considered to be orthodox. Being at all times a curious examiner of the human mind, and pleased with an undisguised display of what had passed in it, he called to me with warmth, " Give me your hand, I have taken a liking to you." He then began to descant upon the force of testimony, and the little we could know of final causes ; so that the objections of, " Why was it so ?" or "Why was it not so ?" ought not to disturb us : adding, that he himself had at one period been guilty of a temporary neglect of religion, but that it was not the result of argument, but mere absence of thought.

After having given credit to reports of his bigotry, I was agreeably surprised when he expressed the following very liberal sentiment, which has the additional value of obviating an objection to our holy religion, founded upon the discordant tenets of Christians themselves : " For my part, Sir, I think all Christians, whether Papists or Protestants, agree in the essential articles, and that their differences are trivial, and rather political than religious."

· My friend Mr. Malone, in his valuable comments on Shakspeare, has traced in that great poet the *disjecta membra* of these lines.—BOSWELL.

We talked of belief in ghosts. He said, " Sir, I make a distinction between what a man may experience by the mere strength of his imagination, and what imagination cannot possibly produce. Thus, suppose I should think that I saw a form, and heard a voice cry, ' Johnson, you are a very wicked fellow, and unless you repent you will certainly be punished ;' my own unworthiness is so deeply impressed upon my mind, that I might *imagine* I thus saw and heard, and therefore I should not believe that an external communication had been made to me. But if a form should appear, and a voice should tell me that a particular man had died at a particular place, and a particular hour, a fact which I had no apprehension of, nor any means of knowing, and this fact, with all its circumstances, should afterwards be unquestionably proved, I should in that case be persuaded that I had supernatural intelligence imparted to me."

Here it is proper, once for all, to give a true and fair statement of Johnson's way of thinking upon the question, whether departed spirits are ever permitted to appear in this world, or in any way to operate upon human life. He has been ignorantly misrepresented as weakly credulous upon that subject ; and, therefore, though I feel an inclination to disdain and treat with silent contempt so foolish a notion concerning my illustrious friend, yet, as I find it has gained ground, it is necessary to refute it. The real fact then is, that Johnson had a very philosophical mind, and such a rational respect for testimony, as to make him submit his understanding to what was authentically proved, though he could not comprehend why it was so. Being thus disposed, he was willing to inquire into the truth of any relation of supernatural agency, a general belief of which has prevailed in all nations and ages. But so far was he from being the dupe of implicit faith, that he examined the matter with a jealous attention, and no man was more ready to refute its falsehood when he had discovered it. Churchill, in his poem entitled " The Ghost," availed himself of the absurd credulity imputed to Johnson, and drew a caricature of him under the name of " Pomposo," representing him as one of the believers of the story of a ghost in Cocklane, which, in the year 1762, had gained very general credit in London. Many of my readers, I am convinced, are to this hour under an impression that Johnson was thus foolishly deceived. It will therefore surprise them a good deal when they are informed upon undoubted authority, that Johnson was one of those by whom the imposture was detected. The story had become so popular, that he thought it should be investigated ; and in this research he was assisted by the Rev. Dr. Douglas, now Bishop of Salisbury, the great detector of impostures ; who informs me that after the gentlemen who went and examined into the evidence were satisfied of its falsity, Johnson wrote in their presence an account of it, which was published in the newspapers and " Gentleman's Magazine," and undeceived the world.[1]

[1] The account was as follows:—" On the night of the 1st of February, many gentlemen

Our conversation proceeded. "Sir," said he, "I am a friend to subordination as most conducive to the happiness of society. There is a reciprocal pleasure in governing and being governed."

SCENE OF THE COCK-LANE GHOST'S EXPLOITS.

eminent for their rank and character, were, by the invitation of the Rev. Mr. Aldrich, of Clerkenwell, assembled at his house, for the examination of the noises supposed to be made by a departed spirit, for the detection of some enormous crime.

"About ten at night the gentlemen met in the chamber in which the girl, supposed to be disturbed by a spirit, had, with proper caution, been put to bed by several ladies. They sat rather more than an hour, and hearing nothing, went down stairs, when they interrogated the father of the girl, who denied in the strongest terms, any knowledge or belief of fraud.

"The supposed spirit had before publicly promised, by an affirmative knock, that it would attend one of the gentlemen into the vault under the church of St. John, Clerkenwell, where the body is deposited, and give a token of her presence there, by a knock upon her coffin; it was therefore determined to make this trial of the existence or veracity of the supposed spirit.

"While they were inquiring and deliberating, they were summoned into the girl's chamber by some ladies who were near her bed, and who had heard knocks and scratches. When the gentlemen entered, the girl declared that she felt the spirit like a mouse upon her back, and was required to hold her hands out of bed. From that time though the spirit was very solemnly required to manifest its existence by appearance, by impression on the hand or body of any present, by scratches, knocks, or any other agency, no evidence of any preternatural power was exhibited.

"The spirit was then very seriously advertised that the person to whom the promise was made of striking the coffin, was then about to visit the vault, and that the performance of the

"Dr. Goldsmith is one of the first men we now have as an author, and he is a very worthy man too. He has been loose in his principles, but he is coming right."

I mentioned Mallet's tragedy of "Elvira," which had been acted the preceding winter at Drury-lane, and that the Honourable Andrew Erskine, Mr. Dempster, and myself, had joined in writing a pamphlet, entitled "Critical Strictures," [1] against it. That the mildness of Dempster's disposition had, however, relented; and he had candidly said, "We have hardly a right to abuse this tragedy, for, bad as it is, how vain should either of us be to write one not near so good!" JOHNSON "Why, no, Sir ; this is not just reasoning. You *may* abuse a tragedy, though you cannot write one. You may scold a carpenter who has made you a bad table, though you cannot make a table. It is not your trade to make tables."

When I talked to him of the paternal estate to which I was heir, he said, "Sir, let me tell you, that to be a Scotch landlord, where you have a number of families dependent upon you, and attached to you, is, perhaps, as high a situation as humanity can arrive at. A merchant upon the 'Change of London, with a hundred thousand pounds, is nothing; an English duke, with an immense fortune, is nothing ; he has no tenants who consider themselves as under his patriarchal care, and who will follow him to the field upon an emergency."

His notion of the dignity of a Scotch landlord had been formed upon what he had heard of the Highland chiefs ; for it is long since a Lowland landlord has been so curtailed in his feudal authority that he has little more influence over his tenants than an English landlord ; and of late years most of the Highland chiefs have destroyed, by means too well known, the princely power which they once enjoyed.

He proceeded : "Your going abroad, Sir, and breaking off idle habits, may be of great importance to you. I would go where there are courts and learned men. There is a good deal of Spain that has not been perambulated. I would have you go thither. A man of inferior talents to yours may furnish us with useful observations upon that country." His supposing me, at that period of life, capable of writing

---

promise was then claimed. The company at one o'clock went into the church, and the gentleman to whom the promise was made, went with another into the vault. The spirit was solemnly required to perform its promise, but nothing more than silence ensued ; the person supposed to be accused by the spirit, then went down with several others but no effect was perceived. Upon their return they examined the girl, but could draw no confession from her between two and three she desired and was permitted to go home with her father.

"It is, therefore, the opinion of the whole assembly, that the child has some art of making or counterfeiting a particular noise, and that there is no agency of any higher cause."—BOSWELL.

[1] The "Critical Review," in which Mallet himself sometimes wrote, characterised this pamphlet as "the crude efforts of envy, petulance, and self-conceit." There being thus three epithets, we the three authors had a humorous contention how each should be appropriated.—BOSWELL

an account of my travels that would deserve to be read, elated me not a little.

I appeal to every impartial reader whether this faithful detail of his frankness, complacency, and kindness to a young man, a stranger and a Scotchman, does not refute the unjust opinion of the harshness of his general demeanour. His occasional reproofs of folly, impudence, or impiety, and even the sudden sallies of his constitutional irritability of temper, which have been preserved for the poignancy of their wit, have produced that opinion among those who have not considered that such instances, though collected by Mrs. Piozzi into a small volume, and read over in a few hours, were, in fact, scattered through a long series of years ; years, in which his time was chiefly spent in instructing and delighting mankind by his writings and conversation, in acts of piety to God, and good-will to men.

I complained to him that I had not yet acquired much knowledge, and asked his advice as to my studies. He said, "Don't talk of study, now. I will give you a plan ; but it will require some time to consider of it." "It is very good in you," I replied, "to allow me to be with you thus. Had it been foretold to me some years ago that I should pass an evening with the author of the 'Rambler,' how should I have exulted !" What I then expressed was sincerely from the heart. He was satisfied that it was, and cordially answered, "Sir, I am glad we have met. I hope we shall pass many evenings, and mornings too, together." We finished a couple of bottles of port, and sat till between one and two in the morning.

He wrote this year, in the "Critical Review," the account of "Telemachus, a Mask," by the Rev. George Graham, of Eton College. The subject of this beautiful poem was particularly interesting to Johnson, who had much experience of "the conflict of opposite prin ciples," which he describes as "the contention between pleasure and virtue, a struggle which will always be continued while the present system of nature shall subsist ; nor can history or poetry exhibit more than pleasure triumphing over virtue, and virtue subjugating pleasure."

JOHNSON READING THE VICAR OF WAKEFIELD.

CHAPTER XIII.—1763.

ACCOUNT OF GOLDSMITH—JOHNSON'S RELATION OF THEIR INTERVIEW, WHEN GOLDSMITH WAS ARRESTED BY HIS LANDLADY—BOSWELL SUPS WITH THEM AT THE MITRE—RECORD OF CONVERSATION—NIGHTLY TEA WITH MISS WILLIAMS—BOSWELL NOT YET ADMITTED TO THIS PRIVILEGE—SUBSEQUENT INTERVIEWS WITH JOHNSON, AND RECORD OF CONVERSATIONS ON THESE OCCASIONS.

AS Dr. Oliver Goldsmith will frequently appear in this narrative, I shall endeavour to make my readers in some degree acquainted with his singular character. He was a native of Ireland, and a contemporary with Mr. Burke, at Trinity College, Dublin, but did not then give much promise of future celebrity.[1] He, however, observed to

---

[1] Goldsmith got a premium at a Christmas examination in Trinity College, Dublin, which I have seen.—KEARNEY.

A premium obtained at the Christmas examination is generally more honourable than any other, because it ascertains the person who receives it to be the first in literary merit. At the other examinations, the person thus distinguished may be only the second in merit; he who has previously obtained the same honorary reward, sometimes receiving a written certificate that *he* was the best answerer, it being a rule that not more than one premium should be adjudged to the same person in one year. See p. 180.—MALONE.

Mr. Malone, that "though he made no great figure in mathematics, which was a study in much repute there, he could turn an Ode of Horace into English bet'er than any of them." He afterwards studied physic at Edinburgh, and upon the Continent : and, I have been informed, was enabled to pursue his travels on foot, partly by demanding, at Universities, to enter the lists as a disputant, by which according to the custom of many of them, he was entitled to the pre mium of a crown, when, luckily for him, his challenge was not accepted; so that, as I once observed to Dr. Johnson, he *disputed* his passage through Europe. He then came to England, and was employed successively in the capacities of an usher to an academy, a corrector of the press, a reviewer, and a writer for a newspaper. He had sagacity enough to cultivate assiduously the acquaintance of Johnson, and his faculties were gradually enlarged by the contemplation of such a model. To me and many others it appeared that he studiously copied the manner of Johnson, though, indeed, upon a smaller scale.

At this time I think he had published nothing with his name, though it was pretty generally known that *one Dr. Goldsmith* was the author of " An Inquiry into the present State of Polite Learning in Europe," and of " The Citizen of the World," a series of letters supposed to be written from London by a Chinese.[1] No man had the art of displaying with more advantage, as a writer, whatever literary acquisitions he made. " *Nihil quod tetigit non ornavit.*"[2] His mind resembled a fertile but thin soil. There was a quick, but not a strong, vegetation, of whatever chanced to be thrown upon it. No deep root could be struck. The oak of the forest did not grow there ; but the elegant shrubbery and the fragrant parterre appeared in gay succession. It has been generally circulated and believed that he was a mere fool in conversation ;[3] but, in truth, this has been greatly exaggerated. He had, no doubt, a more than common share of that hurry of ideas which we often find in his countrymen, and which sometimes produces a laughable confusion in expressing them. He was very much what the French call *un étourdi,*

[1] He had also published in 1759, "The Bee; being Essays on the most interesting Subjects."—MALONE.

[2] See his Epitaph in Westminster Abbey, written by Dr. Johnson.—BOSWELL.

[3] In allusion to this, Mr. Horace Walpole, who admired his writings, said he was "an inspired idiot;" and Garrick described him as one

"————————— for shortness call'd Noll,
Who wrote like an angel, and talk'd like poor Poll."

Sir Joshua Reynolds mentioned to me that he frequently heard Goldsmith talk warmly of the pleasure of being liked, and observe how hard it would be if literary excellence should preclude a man from that satisfaction, which he perceived it often did, from the envy which attended it; and therefore Sir Joshua was convinced that he was intentionally more absurd, in order to lessen himself in social intercourse, trusting that his character would be sufficiently supported by his work. If it indeed was his intention to appear absurd in company, he was often very successful. But with due deference to Sir Joshua's ingenuity, I think the conjecture too refined.—BOSWELL.

and from vanity and an eager desire of being conspicuous wherever he was, he frequently talked carelessly without knowledge of the subject, or even without thought. His person was short, his countenance coarse and vulgar, his deportment that of a scholar awkwardly affecting the easy gentleman. Those who were in any way distinguished, excited envy in him to so ridiculous an excess, that the instances of it are hardly credible. When accompanying two beautiful young ladies,[1] with their mother, on a tour in France, he was seriously angry that more attention was paid to them than to him ; and once at the exhibition of the *Fantoccini* in London, when those who sat next him observed with what dexterity a puppet was made to toss a pike, he could not bear that it should have such praise, and exclaimed, with some warmth, " Pshaw ! I can do it better myself." [2]

He, I am afraid, had no settled system of any sort, so that his conduct must not be strictly scrutinised ; but his affections were social and generous, and when he had money he gave it away very liberally. His desire of imaginary consequence predominated over his attention to truth. When he began to rise into notice, he said he had a brother who was Dean of Durham,[3] a fiction so easily detected, that it is wonderful how he should have been so inconsiderate as to hazard it. He boasted to me at this time of the power of his pen in commanding money, which I believe was true in a certain degree, though in the instance he gave he was by no means correct. He told me that he had sold a novel for four hundred pounds. This was his " Vicar of Wakefield." But Johnson informed me that he had made the bargain for Goldsmith, and the price was sixty pounds. " And, Sir," said he, " a sufficient price too, when it was sold; for then the fame of Goldsmith had not been elevated, as it afterwards was, by his ' Traveller ;' and the bookseller had such faint hopes of profit by his bargain, that he kept the manuscript by him a long time, and did not publish it till after the ' Traveller ' had appeared. Then, to be sure. it was accidentally worth more money."

Mrs. Piozzi[4] and Sir John Hawkins[5] have strangely mis-stated the history of Goldsmith's situation and Johnson's friendly interference, when this novel was sold. I shall give it authentically from Johnson's own exact narration :—

" I received one morning a message from poor Goldsmith that he was

---

[1] Miss Hornecks, one of whom is now married to Henry Bunbury, Esq., and the other to Colonel Gwyn.—BOSWELL.

[2] He went home with Mr. Burke to supper ; and broke his shin by attempting to exhibit to the company how much better he could jump over a stick than the puppets.—BOSWELL.

[3] I am willing to hope that there may have been some mistake as to this anecdote, though I had it from a dignitary of the church. Dr. Isaac Goldsmith, his near relation, was Dean of Cloyne, in 1747.—BOSWELL.

[4] Anecdotes of Johnson, p. 119.—BOSWELL.

Life of Johnson, p. 420.—BOSWELL.

in great distress, and, as it was not in his power to come to me, begging that I would come to him as soon as possible. I sent him a guinea, and promised to come to him directly. I accordingly went as soon as I was dressed, and found that his landlady had arrested him for his rent, at which he was in a violent passion. I perceived that he had already changed my guinea, and had got a bottle of Madeira and a glass before him. I put the cork into the bottle, desired he would be calm, and began to talk to him of the means by which he might be extricated. He then told me that he had a novel ready for the press, which he produced to me. I looked into it, and saw its merit; told the landlady I should soon return; and, having gone to a bookseller, sold it for sixty pounds. I brought Goldsmith the money, and he discharged his rent, not without rating his landlady in a high tone for having used him so ill." [1]

My next meeting with Johnson was on Friday, the 1st of July, when he and I and Dr. Goldsmith supped at the Mitre. I was before this time pretty well acquainted with Goldsmith, who was one of the brightest ornaments of the Johnsonian school. Goldsmith's respectful attachment to Johnson was then at its height; for his own literary reputation had not yet distinguished him so much as to excite a vain desire of competition with his great Master. He had increased my admiration of the goodness of Johnson - heart, by incidental remarks in the course of conversation, such as, when I mentioned Mr. Levett, whom he entertained under his roof, "He is poor and honest, which is recommendation enough to Johnson;" and when I wondered that he was very kind to a man of whom I had heard a very bad character, "He is now become miserable, and that ensures the protection of Johnson."

Goldsmith attempting this evening to maintain, I suppose from an affectation of paradox, "that knowledge was not desirable on its own account, for it often was a source of unhappiness:" Johnson: "Why, Sir, that knowledge may, in some cases, produce unhappiness, I allow. But, upon the whole, knowledge, *per se*, is certainly an object which every man would wish to attain, although, perhaps, he may not take the trouble necessary for attaining it."

---

[1] It may not be improper to annex here Mrs. Piozzi's account of this transaction, in her own words, as a specimen of the extreme inaccuracy with which all her anecdotes of Dr. Johnson are related, or rather discoloured and distorted. " I have forgotten the year, but it could scarcely, I think, be later than 1765 or 1766, that he was *called abruptly from our house after dinner*, and returning *in about three hours*, said he had been with an enraged author whose landlady pressed him for payment within doors, while the bailiffs beset him without; that he was *drinking himself drunk* with Madeira, to drown care, and fretting over a novel, which, when *finished*, was to be his *whole fortune*, but *he could not get it done for distraction*, nor could he step out of doors to offer it for sale. Mr. Johnson, therefore, sent away the bottle, and went to the bookseller, recommending the performance, and *desiring some immediate relief;* which when he brought back to the writer, *he called the woman of the house directly to partak of punch, and pass their time in merriment*."—Anecdotes of Dr. Johnson p. 119.—Boswell.

Dr. John Campbell, the celebrated political and biographical writer, being mentioned, Johnson said, " Campbell is a man of much knowledge, and has a good share of imagination. His 'Hermippus Redivivus' is very entertaining, as an account of the Hermetic philosophy, and as furnishing a curious history of the extravagancies of the human mind. If it were merely imaginary, it would be nothing at all. Campbell is not always rigidly careful of truth in his conversation ; but I do not believe there is anything of this carelessness in his books. Campbell is a good man, a pious man. I am afraid he has not been in the inside of a church for many years ;[1] but he never passes a church without pulling off his hat. This shows that he has good principles. I used to go pretty often to Campbell's on a Sunday evening, till I began to consider that the shoals of Scotchmen who flocked about him might probably say, when anything of mine was well done, 'Ay, ay, he has learnt this of Cawmell !' "

He talked very contemptuously of Churchill's poetry, observing, that "it had a temporary currency, only from its audacity of abuse, and being filled with living names, and that it would sink into oblivion." I ventured to hint that he was not quite a fair judge, as Churchill had attacked him violently. JOHNSON : "Nay, Sir, I am a very fair judge. He did not attack me violently till he found I did not like his poetry ; and his attack on me shall not prevent me from continuing to say what I think of him, from an apprehension that it may be ascribed to resentment. No, Sir, I called the fellow a blockhead at first, and I will call him a blockhead still. However, I will acknowledge that I have a better opinion of him now than I once had ; for he has shown more fertility than I expected. To be sure, he is a tree that cannot produce good fruit : he only bears crabs. But, Sir, a tree that produces a great many crabs, is better than a tree which produces only a few."

In this depreciation of Churchill's poetry, I could not agree with him. It is very true that the greatest part of it is upon the topics of the day, on which account, as it brought him great fame and profit at the time, it must proportionably slide out of the public attention, as other occasional objects succeed. But Churchill had extraordinary vigour both of thought and expression. His portraits of the players will ever

---

[1] I am inclined to think that he was misinformed as to this circumstance. I own I am jealous for my worthy friend Dr. John Campbell. For though Milton could without remorse absent himself from public worship, I cannot. On the contrary, I have the same habitual impressions upon my mind, with those of a truly venerable judge, who said to Mr. Langton, "Friend Langton, if I have not been at church on Sunday, I do not feel myself easy." Dr. Campbell was a sincerely religious man. Lord Macartney, who is eminent for his variety of knowledge, and attention to men of talents, and knew him well, told me, that when he called on him in a morning, he found him reading a chapter in the Greek New Testament, which he informed his lordship was his constant practice. The quantity of Dr. Campbell's composition is almost incredible, and his labours brought him large profits. Dr. Joseph Warton told me that Johnson said of him, "He is the richest author that ever grazed the common of literature."—BOSWELL.

be valuable to the true lovers of the drama ; and his strong caricatures of several eminent men of his age, will not be forgotten by the curious. Let me add, that there are in his works many passages which are of a general nature ; and his " Prophecy of Famine " is a poem of no ordinary merit. It is, indeed, falsely injurious to Scotland; but therefore, may be allowed a greater share of invention.

Bonnell Thornton had just published a burlesque "Ode on St. Cecilia's day," adapted to the ancient British music, viz. the salt-box, the Jew's-harp, the marrow-bones and cleaver, the hum-strum, or hurdy-gurdy, &c. Johnson praised its humour, and seemed much diverted with it. He repeated the following passage.:—

> " In strains more exalted the salt-box shall join,
> And clattering and battering and clapping combine ;
> With a rap and a tap, while the hollow side sounds,
> Up and down leaps the flap, and with rattling rebounds."[1]

I mentioned the periodical paper called " The Connoisseur." He said it wanted matter.—No doubt it had not the deep thinking of Johnson's writings. But surely it has just views of the surface of life, and a very sprightly manner.—His opinion of " The World," was not much higher than of " The Connoisseur."

Let me here apologise for the imperfect manner in which I am obliged to exhibit Johnson's conversation at this period. In the earl part of my acquaintance with him, I was so wrapt in admiration of his extraordinary colloquial talents, and so little accustomed to his peculiar mode of expression, that I found it extremely difficult to recollect and record his conversation with its genuine vigour and vivacity. In pro gress of time, when my mind was, as it were, *strongly impregnated with the Johnsonian æther*, I could with much more facility and exactness, carry in my memory and commit to paper the exuberant variety of his wisdom and wit.

At this time *Miss* Williams,[2] as she was then called, though she did not reside with him in the Temple under his roof, but had lodgings in Bolt-court, Fleet-street, had so much of his attention, that he every night drank tea with her before he went home, however late it might be,

---

[1] In 1769 I set for Smart and Newberry, Thornton's burlesque "Ode on St. Cecilia's day." It was performed at Ranelagh in masks, to a very crowded audience, as I was told, for I then resided in Norfolk. Beard sung the salt-box song, which was admirably accompanied on that instrument by Brent, the fencing master, and father of Miss Brent, the celebrated singer ; Skeggs on the broomstick, as bassoon ; and a remarkable performer on the Jew's-harp,— "Buzzing twangs the iron lyre." Cleavers were cast in bell-metal for this entertainment. All the performers of the old woman's oratory, employed by Foote, were, I believe, employed at Ranelagh, on this occasion.—BURNEY.

[2] See p. 160. This lady resided in Dr. Johnson's house in Gough-square from about 1753 to 1758 ; and in that year, on his removing to Gray's Inn, she went into lodgings At a subsequent period, she again became an inmate with Johnson, in Johnson's-court —MALONE.

and she always sat up for him. This it may be fairly conjectured, was not alone a proof of his regard for *her*, but of his own unwillingness to go into solitude, before that unseasonable hour at which he had habituated himself to expect the oblivion of repose. Dr. Goldsmith, being a privileged man, went with him this night, strutting away, and calling to me with an air of superiority, like that of an esoteric over an exoteric disciple of a sage of antiquity, "I go to Miss Williams." I confess, I then envied him this mighty privilege, of which he seemed so proud; but it was not long before I obtained the same mark of distinction.

On Tuesday, the 5th of July, I again visited Johnson. He told me he had looked into the poems of a pretty voluminous writer, Mr. (now Dr.) John Ogilvie, one of the Presbyterian ministers of Scotland, which had lately come out, but could find no thinking in them. BOSWELL: "Is there not imagination in them, Sir?" JOHNSON: "Why, Sir, there is in them what *was* imagination, but it is no more imagination in *him*, than sound is sound in the echo. And his diction too is not his own. We have long ago seen *white-robed innocence* and *flower-bespangled meads*."

Talking of London, he observed, "Sir, if you wish to have a just notion of the magnitude of this city, you must not be satisfied with seeing its great streets and squares, but must survey the innumerable little lanes and courts. It is not in the showy evolutions of buildings, but in the multiplicity of human habitations which are crowded together, that the wonderful immensity of London consists."—I have often amused myself with thinking how different a place London is to different people. They, whose narrow minds are contracted to the consideration of some one particular pursuit, view it only through that medium. A politician thinks of it merely as the seat of government in its different departments; a grazier, as a vast market for cattle; a mercantile man, as a place where a prodigious deal of business is done upon 'Change; a dramatic enthusiast, as the grand scene of theatrical entertainments; a man of pleasure as an assemblage of taverns, and the great emporium for ladies of easy virtue. But the intellectual man is struck with it, as comprehending the whole of human life in all its variety, the contemplation of which is inexhaustible.

On Wednesday, July 6, he was engaged to sup with me at my lodgings in Downing-street, Westminster. But on the preceding night my landlord having behaved very rudely to me and some company who were with me, I had resolved not to remain another night in his house. I was exceedingly uneasy at the awkward appearance I supposed I should make to Johnson and the other gentlemen whom I had invited, not being able to receive them at home, and being obliged to order supper at the Mitre. I went to Johnson in the morning, and talked of it as of a serious distress. He laughed, and said, "Consider, Sir how insignificant this will appear a twelvemonth hence." Were this consideration to be applied to most of the little vexatious incidents of life, by which our quiet is too often disturbed, it would prevent many painful sensations. I have tried it frequently with good effect. "There is nothing," continued he, "in this mighty misfortune ; nay, we shall be better at the Mitre." I told him that I had been at Sir John Fielding's office, complaining of my landlord, and had been informed that though I had taken my lodgings for a year, I might, upon proof of his bad behaviour, quit them when I pleased, without being under an obligation to pay rent for any longer time than while I possessed them. The fertility of Johnson's mind could show itself even upon so small a matter as this. "Why, Sir," said he, "I suppose this must be the law, since you have been told so in Bow-street. But if your landlord could hold you to your bargain, and the lodgings should be yours for a year you may certainly use them as you think fit. So, Sir, you may quarter two life-guardsmen upon him ; or you may send the greatest scoundrel you can find into your apartments ; or you may say that you want to make some experiments in natural philosophy, and may burn a large quantity of assafœtida in his house."

I had as my guests this evening at the Mitre Tavern, Dr. Johnson, Dr. Goldsmith, Mr. Thomas Davies, Mr. Eccles, an Irish gentleman, for whose agreeable company I was obliged to Mr. Davies, and the Rev. Mr. John Ogilvie,[1] who was desirous of being in company with my illustrious friend, while I, in my turn, was proud to have the honour of showing one of my countrymen upon what easy terms Johnson permitted me to live with him.

Goldsmith, as usual, endeavoured with too much eagerness to *shine* and disputed very warmly with Johnson against the well-known maxim of the British constitution, "the king can do no wrong ; " affirming, that "what was morally false could not be politically true ; and as the king might, in the exercise of his regal power, command and cause the doing of what was wrong, it certainly might be said, in sense and in reason, that he could do wrong." Johnson : "Sir, you are to consider that in our constitution, according to its true principles, the king is the head, he is supreme ; he is above every thing, and there is no power by which he can be tried. Therefore, it is, Sir, that we hold the king can do no wrong ; that whatever may happen to be wrong in government may not be above our reach by being ascribed to majesty. Redress is always to be had against oppression by punishing the immediate agents.

[1] The northern bard mentioned p. 244. When I asked Dr. Johnson's permission to introduce him, he obligingly agreed; adding, however, with a sly pleasantry, "But he must give us none of his poetry." It is remarkable that Johnson and Churchill, however, much they differed in other points, agreed on this subject. See Churchill's "Journey." It is, however, but justice to Dr. Ogilvie to observe, that his "Day of Judgment" has no inconsiderable share of merit.—Boswell.

The king, though he should command, cannot force a judge to condemn a man unjustly; therefore it is the judge whom we prosecute and punish. Political institutions are formed upon the consideration of what will most frequently tend to the good of the whole, although now and then exceptions may occur. Thus it is better in general that a nation should have a supreme legislative power, although it may at times be abused. And then, Sir, there is this consideration, that *if the abuse be enormous nature will rise up, and claiming her original rights, overturn a corrupt political system.*" I mark this animated sentence with peculiar pleasure, as a noble instance of that truly dignified spirit of freedom which ever glowed in his heart, though he was charged with slavish tenets by superficial observers, because he was at all times indignant against that false patriotism, that pretended love of freedom, that unruly restlessness which is inconsistent with the stable authority of any good government.

This generous sentiment, which he uttered with great fervour, struck me exceedingly, and stirred my blood to that pitch of fancied resistance, the possibility of which I am glad to keep in mind, but to which I trust I never shall be forced.

"Great abilities," said he, "are not requisite for an historian; for n historical composition all the greatest powers of the human mind are quiescent. He has facts ready to his hand, so there is no exercise of invention. Imagination is not required in any high degree; only about as much as is used in the lower kinds of poetry. Some penetration, accuracy, and colouring, will fit a man for the task, if he can give the application which is necessary."

"'Bayle's Dictionary' is a very useful work for those to consult who love the biographical part of literature, which is what I love most."

Talking of the eminent writers in Queen Anne's reign, he observed, "I think Dr. Arbuthnot the first man among them. He was the most universal genius, being an excellent physician, a man of deep learning, and a man of much humour. Mr. Addison was, to be sure, a great man; his learning was not profound, but his morality, his humour, and his elegance of writing set him very high."

Mr. Ogilvie was unlucky enough to choose for the topic of his conversation the praises of his native country. He began with saying, that there was very rich land around Edinburgh. Goldsmith, who had studied physic there, contradicted this, very untruly, with a sneering laugh. Disconcerted a little by this, Mr. Ogilvie then took a new ground, where, I suppose, he thought himself perfectly safe; for he observed, that Scotland had a great many noble wild prospects. JOHNSON: "I believe, Sir, you have a great many. Norway, too, has noble wild prospects; and Lapland is remarkable for prodigious noble wild prospects. But, Sir, let me tell you, the noblest prospect which a Scotchman ever sees, is the high-road that leads him to England!" This unexpected and pointed sally produced a roar of applause. After all, however, those who admire the rude grandeur of nature cannot deny it to Caledonia.

On Saturday, July 9, I found Johnson surrounded with a numerous levee, but have not preserved any part of his conversation. On the 14th we had another evening by ourselves at the Mitre. It happened to be a very rainy night, I made some commonplace observations on the relaxation of nerves and depression of spirits which such weather occasioned;[1] adding, however, that it was good for the vegetable creation. Johnson, who, as we have already seen, denied that the temperature of the air had any influence on the human frame, answered, with a smile of ridicule, "Why, yes, Sir, it is good for vegetables, and for the animals who eat those vegetables, and for the animals who eat those animals." This observation of his, aptly enough introduced a good supper and I soon forgot, in Johnson's company, the influence of a moist atmosphere.

Feeling myself now quite at ease as his companion, though I had all possible reverence for him, I expressed a regret that I could not be so easy with my father, though he was not much older than Johnson, and certainly, however respectable, had not more learning and greater abilities to depress me. I asked him the reason of this. JOHNSON: "Why, Sir, I am a man of the world. I live in the world, and I take, in some degree, the colour of the world as it moves along. Your father is a judge in a remote part of the island, and all his notions are taken from the old world. Besides, Sir, there must always be a struggle between a father and son, while one aims at power and the other at independence." I said, I was afraid my father would force me to be a lawyer. JOHNSON: "Sir, you need not be afraid of his forcing you to be a laborious practising lawyer; that is not in his power. For, as the proverb says, 'One man may lead a horse to the water, but twenty cannot make him drink.' He may be displeased that you are not what he wishes you to be; but that displeasure will not go far. If he insists only on your having as much law as is necessary for a man of property, and then endeavours to get you into parliament, he is quite in the right."

He enlarged very convincingly upon the excellence of rhyme over blank verse in English poetry. I mentioned to him that Dr. Adam Smith, in his lectures upon composition, when I studied under him in the College of Glasgow, had maintained the same opinion strenuously, and I repeated some of his arguments. JOHNSON: "Sir, I was once in company with Smith, and we did not take to each other; but had I known that he loved rhyme as much as you tell me he does, I should have HUGGED him."

[1] Johnson would suffer none of his friends to fill up chasms in conversation with remarks on the weather: "Let us not talk of the weather."—BURNEY.

Talking of those who denied the truth of Christianity, he said, "It is always easy to be on the negative side. If a man were now to deny that there is salt upon the table, you could not reduce him to an absurdity. Come, let us try this a little further. I deny that Canada is taken, and I can support my denial by pretty good arguments. The French are a much more numerous people than we ; and it is not likely that they would allow us to take it. 'But the ministry have assured us, in all the formality of the Gazette, that it is taken.'—Very true. But the ministry have put us to an enormous expense by the war in America, and it is their interest to persuade us that we have got something for our money.—'But the fact is confirmed by thousands of men who were at the taking of it.'—Ay, but these men have still more interest in deceiving us. They don't want that you should think the French have beat them, but that they have beat the French. Now suppose you should go over and find that it really is taken, that would only satisfy yourself ; for when you come home we will not believe you. We will say, you have been bribed.—Yet, Sir, notwithstanding all these plausible objections, we have no doubt that Canada is really ours. Such is the weight of common testimony. How much stronger are the evidences of the Christian religion ?"

"Idleness is a disease which must be combated ; but I would not advise a rigid adherence to a particular plan of study. I myself have never persisted in any plan for two days together. A man ought to read just as inclination leads him ; for what he reads as a task will do him little good. A young man should read five hours in a day, and so may acquire a great deal of knowledge."

To a man of vigorous intellect and ardent curiosity like his own, reading without a regular plan may be beneficial ; though even such a man must submit to it, if he would attain a full understanding of any of the sciences.

To such a degree of unrestrained frankness had he now accustomed me that in the course of this evening I talked of the numerous reflections which had been thrown out against him, on account of his having accepted a pension from his present Majesty. "Why, Sir," said he, with a hearty laugh, "it is a mighty foolish noise that they make.[1] I have accepted of a pension as a reward which has been thought due to my literary merit ; and now that I have this pension, I am the same man in every respect that I have ever been ; I retain the same principles It is true, that I cannot now curse (smiling) the house of Hanover ; nor would it be decent for me to drink King James's health in the wine that King George gives me money to pay for. But, Sir, I think that the pleasure of cursing the house of Hanover, and drinking

[1] When I mentioned the same idle clamour to him several years afterwards, he said, with a smile, "I wish my pension were twice as large, that they might make twice as much noise."—BOSWELL.

King James's health, **are** amply overbalanced by three hundred pounds a year."

There was here, most certainly, an affectation of more Jacobitism than he really had ; and indeed an intention of admitting, for the moment, in a much greater extent than it really existed, the charge of disaffection imputed to him by the world, merely for the purpose of showing how dexterously he could repel an attack, even though he were placed in the most disadvantageous position ; for I have heard him declare, that if holding up his right hand would have secured victory at Culloden to Prince Charles's army, he was not sure he would have held it up ; so little confidence had he in the right claimed by the house of Stuart, and so fearful was he of the consequences of another revolution on the throne of Great Britain ; and Mr. Topham Beauclerk assured me, he had heard him say this before he had his pension.   At another time he said to Mr. Langton, "Nothing has ever offered, that has made it worth my while to consider the question fully." He, however, also said to the same gentleman, talking of King James the Second, "It was become impossible for him to reign any longer in this country." He no doubt had an early attachment to the house of Stuart ; but his zeal had cooled as his reason strengthened.   Indeed I heard him once say, "that after the death of a violent Whig, with whom he used to contend with great eagerness, he felt his Toryism much abated."[1]   I suppose he meant Mr. Walmesley.

Yet there is no doubt that at earlier periods he was wont often to exercise both his pleasantry and ingenuity in talking Jacobitism.   My much respected friend, Dr. Douglas, now Bishop of Salisbury, has favoured me with the following admirable instance from his lordship's own recollection :—One day when dining at old Mr. Langton's, where Miss Roberts, his niece, was one of the company, Johnson, with his usual complacent attention to the fair sex, took her by the hand and said, "My dear, I hope you are a Jacobite."   Old Mr. Langton, who, though a high and steady Tory, was attached to the present royal family, seemed offended, and asked Johnson, with great warmth, what he could mean by putting such a question to his niece ?   "Why, Sir," said Johnson, "I meant no offence to your niece, I meant her a great compliment.   A Jacobite, Sir, believes in the divine right of kings.   He that believes in the divine right of kings believes in a Divinity.   A Jacobite believes in the divine right of bishops.   He that believes in the divine right of bishops, believes in the divine authority of the Christian religion.   Therefore, Sir, a Jacobite is neither an Atheist nor a Deist.   That cannot be said of a Whig ; for *Whiggism is a negation of all principle*."[2]

---

[1] Journal of a Tour to the Hebrides, 3rd edit. p. 420.—BOSWELL.

[2] He used to tell, with great humour, from my relation to him, the following little story ot my early years, which was literally true :—" Boswell, in the year 1745, was a fine boy, wore

He advised me, when abroad, to be as much as I could with the professors in the Universities, and with the clergy ; for from their conversation I might expect the best accounts of every thing in whatever country I should be, with the additional advantage of keeping my learning alive.

It will be observed, that when giving me advice as to my travels, Dr. Johnson did not dwell upon cities, and palaces, and pictures, and shows, and Arcadian scenes. He was of Lord Essex's opinion, who advises his kinsman, Roger Earl of Rutland, " rather to go a hundred miles to speak with one wise man, than five miles to see a fair town." [1]

I described to him an impudent fellow from Scotland, who affected to be a savage, and railed at all established systems. JOHNSON : "There is nothing surprising in this, Sir. He wants to make himself conspicuous. He would tumble in a hog-stye, as long as you looked at him and called to him to come out. But let him alone, never mind him, and he 'll soon give it over."

I added that the same person maintained that there was no distinction between virtue and vice. JOHNSON : " Why, Sir, if the fellow does not think as he speaks, he is lying ; and I see not what honour he can propose to himself from having the character of a liar. But if he does really think that there is no distinction between virtue and vice, why, Sir, when he leaves our houses let us count our spoons."

Sir David Dalrymple, now one of the judges of Scotland by the title of Lord Hailes, had contributed much to increase my high opinion of Johnson, on account of his writings, long before I attained to a personal acquaintance with him ; I, in return, had informed Johnson of Sir David's eminent character for learning and religion ; and Johnson was so much pleased, that at one of our evening meetings he gave him for his toast. I at this time kept up a very frequent correspondence with Sir David ; and I read to Dr. Johnson to-night the following passage from the letter which I had last received from him :—

" It gives me pleasure to think that you have obtained the friendship of Mr. Samuel Johnson. He is one of the best moral writers which England has produced. At the same time, I envy you the free and undisguised converse with such a man. May I beg you to present my best respects to him, and to assure him of the veneration which I entertain for the author of the ' Rambler' and of ' Rasselas ?' Let me recommend this last work to you ; with the ' Rambler' you certainly are acquainted. In ' Rasselas' you will see a tender-hearted operator, who probes the wound only to heal it. Swift, on the contrary, mangles human nature. He cuts and slashes, as if he took pleasure in the operation, like the tyrant who said, *Ita feri ut se sentiat emori.*"

Johnson seemed to be much gratified by this just and well-turned compliment.

He recommended to me to keep a journal of my life, full and unreserved. He said it would be a very good exercise, and would yield me great satisfaction when the particulars were faded from my remembrance. I was uncommonly fortunate in having had a previous coincidence of opinion with him upon this subject, for I had kept such a journal for some time; and it was no small pleasure to me to have this to tell him, and to receive his approbation. He counselled me to keep it private, and said I might surely have a friend who would burn it in case of my death. From this habit I have been enabled to give the world so many anecdotes, which would otherwise have been lost to posterity. I mentioned that I was afraid I put into my journal too many little incidents. JOHNSON: "There is nothing, Sir, too little for so little a creature as man. It is. by studying little things that we attain the great art of having as little misery and as much happiness as possible."

Next morning Mr. Dempster happened to call on me, and was so much struck even with the imperfect account which I gave him of Dr. Johnson's conversation, that to his honour be it recorded, when I complained of drinking port and sitting up late with him, affected my nerves for some time after, he said, "One had better be palsied at eighteen than not keep company with such a man."

On Tuesday, July 18, I found tall Sir Thomas Robinson sitting with Johnson. Sir Thomas said, that the King of Prussia valued himself upon three things; upon being a hero, a musician, and an author. JOHNSON: "Pretty well, Sir, for one man. As to his being an author, I have not looked at his poetry; but his prose is poor stuff. He writes just as you may suppose Voltaire's footboy to do, who has been his amanuensis. He has such parts as the valet might have, and about as much of the colouring of the style as might be got by transcribing his works." When I was at Ferney, I repeated this to Voltaire, in order to reconcile him somewhat to Johnson, whom he, in affecting the English mode of expression, had previously characterised as " a superstitious dog;" but after hearing such a criticism on Frederick the Great, with whom he was then on bad terms, he exclaimed, "An honest fellow!"

But I think the criticism much too severe; for the " Memoirs of the House of Brandenburgh " are written as well as many works of that kind. His poetry, for the style of which he himself makes a frank apology, "*jargonnant un François barbare*," though fraught with pernicious ravings of infidelity, has, in many places, great animation, and in some a pathetic tenderness.

Upon this contemptuous animadversion on the King of Prussia, I observed to Johnson, " It would seem then, Sir, that much less parts are necessary to make a king, than to make an author: for the King of

Prussia is confessedly the greatest king now in Europe, yet you think he makes a very poor figure as an author."

Mr. Levett this day showed me Dr. Johnson's library, which was contained in two garrets over his chambers, where Lintot, son of the celebrated bookseller of that name, had formerly his warehouse. I found a number of good books, but very dusty and in great confusion. The floor was strewed with manuscript leaves, in Johnson's own hand-writing, which I beheld with a degree of veneration, supposing they perhaps might contain portions of the " Rambler," or of " Rasselas." I observed an apparatus for chemical experiments, of which Johnson was all his life very fond. The place seemed to be very favourable for retirement and meditation. Johnson told me, that he went up thither without mentioning it to his servant when he wanted to study, secure from interruption ; for he would not allow his servant to say he was

not at home when he really was. " A servant's strict regard for truth," said he, " must be weakened by such a practice. A philosopher may know that it is merely a form of denial ; but few servants are such nice distinguish-ers. If I accustom a servant to tell a lie for *me,* have I not reason to appre-hend that he will tell many lies for *himself.*" I am, however, satisfied that every servant, of any degree of intelli-gence, understands saying his master is not at home, not at all as the affirmation of a fact, but as customary words, inti-mating that his master wishes not to

DR. JOHNSON'S CHAIR.

be seen ; so that there can be no bad effect from it.

Mr. Temple, now vicar of St. Gluvias, Cornwall, who had been my intimate friend for many years, had at this time chambers in Farrar's-buildings, at the bottom of inner Temple-lane, which he kindly lent me upon my quitting my lodgings, he being to return to Trinity Hall, Cam-bridge. I found them particularly convenient for me, as they were so near Dr. Johnson's.

On Wednesday, July 20, Dr. Johnson, Mr. Dempster, and my uncle, Dr. Boswell, who happened to be now in London, supped with me at these chambers. JOHNSON : " Pity is not natural to man. Children are always cruel. Savages are always cruel. Pity is acquired and improved by the cultivation of reason. We may have uneasy sensations from seeing a creature in distress, without pity: for we have not pity unless we wish to relieve them. When I am on my way to dine with friend, and finding it late, have bid the coachman make haste, if happen to attend when he whips his horses, I may feel unpleasant that the animals are put to pain, but I do not wish him to desist No, Sir, I wish him to drive on."

Mr. Alexander Donaldson, bookseller of Edinburgh, had for some time opened a shop in London, and sold his cheap editions of the most popular English books, in defiance of the supposed common-law right of *Literary Property*. Johnson, though he concurred in the opinion which was afterwards sanctioned by a judgment of the House of Lords, that there was no such right, was at this time very angry that the booksellers of London, for whom he uniformly professed much regard, should suffer from an invasion of what they had ever considered to be secure ; and he was loud and violent against Mr. Donaldson. "He is a fellow who takes advantage of the law to injure his brethren ; for, notwithstanding that the statute secures only fourteen years of exclusive right, it has always been understood by the *trade*, that he who buys the copyright of a book from the author obtains a perpetual property; and upon that belief, numberless bargains are made to transfer that property after the expiration of the statutory term. Now, Donaldson, I say, takes advantage here, of people who have really an equitable title from usage; and if we consider how few of the books, of which they buy the property, succeed so well as to bring profit, we should be of opinion that the term of fourteen years is too short; it should be sixty years." DEMPSTER : "Donaldson, Sir, is anxious for the encouragement of literature. He reduces the price of books, so that poor students may buy them." JOHNSON (laughing) : "Well, Sir, allowing that to be his motive, he is no better than Robin Hood, who robbed the rich in order to give to the poor."

It is remarkable, that when the great question concerning Literary Property came to be ultimately tried before the supreme tribunal of this country, in consequence of the very spirited exertions of Mr. Donaldson, Dr. Johnson was zealous against a perpetuity ; but he thought that the term of the exclusive right of authors should be considerably enlarged. He was then for granting a hundred years.

The conversation now turned upon Mr. David Hume's style. JOHNSON : "Why, Sir, his style is not English ; the structure of his sentences is French. Now the French structure and the English structure may, in the nature of things, be equally good. But if you allow that the English language is established, he is wrong. My name might originally have been Nicholson, as well as Johnson ; but were you to call me Nicholson now, you would call me very absurdly."

Rousseau's treatise on the inequality of mankind was at this time a fashionable topic. It gave rise to an observation by Mr. Dempster, that the advantages of fortune and rank were nothing to a wise man, who ought to value only merit. JOHNSON : "If man were a savage, living in the woods by himself, this might be true ; but in civilised society we all depend upon each other and our happiness is very much owing to tne good opinion of mankind. Now, Sir, in civilised society, external advantages make us more respected. A man with a good coat upon his back meets with a better reception than he who has a bad one. Sir, you may analyse this and say what is there in it? But that will avail you nothing, for it is part of a general system. Pound St. Paul's church into atoms, and consider any single atom; it is, to be sure, good for nothing; but put all these atoms together and you have St Paul's church. So it is with human felicity, which is made up of many ingredients, each of which may be shown to be very insignificant. In civilised society personal merit will not serve you so much as money will. Sir, you may make the experiment. Go into the street and give one man a lecture on morality and another a shilling, and see which will respect you most. If you wish only to support nature, Sir William Petty fixes your allowance at three pounds a year; but as times are much altered, let us call it six pounds. This sum will fill your belly, shelter you from the weather, and even get you a strong lasting coat, supposing it to be made of good bull's hide. Now, Sir, all beyond this is artificial, and is desired in order to obtain a greater degree of respect from our fellow-creatures. And, Sir, if six hundred pounds a year procure a man more consequence, and, of course, more happiness than six pounds a year, the same proportion will hold as to six thousand, and so on, as far as opulence can be carried. Perhaps he who has a large fortune may not be so happy as he who has a small one; but that must proceed from other causes than from his having the large fortune: for, *cœteris paribus*, he who is rich in a civilised society must be happier than he who is poor; as riches, if properly used, (and it is a man's own fault if they are not,) must be productive of the highest advantages. Money, to be sure, of itself is of no use: for its only use is to part with it. Rousseau, and all those who deal in paradoxes, are led away by a childish desire of novelty.[1] When I was a boy I used always to choose the wrong side of a debate, because most ingenious things, that is to say, most new things, could be said upon it. Sir, there is nothing for which you may not muster up more plausible arguments than those which are urged against wealth and other external advantages. Why, now, there is stealing: why should it be thought a crime? When we consider by what unjust methods property has been often acquired, and that what was unjustly got it must be unjust to keep, where is the harm in one man's taking the property of another from him? Besides, Sir, when we consider the bad use that many people make of their property, and how much better use the thief may make of it, it may be defended as a very allowable practice. Yet, Sir, the experience of mankind has discovered stealing to be so very bad a thing that they make no scruple

---

Johnson told Dr. Burney that Goldsmith said, when he first began to write he determined to commit to paper nothing but what was *new;* but he afterwards found that what was *new* was generally false, and from that time was no longer solicitous about novelty.—BURNEY

to hang a man for it. When I was running about this town a very poor fellow, I was a great arguer for the advantages of poverty; but I was, at the same time, very sorry to be poor. Sir, all the arguments which are brought to represent poverty as no evil, show it to be evidently a great evil. You never find people labouring to convince you that you may live very happily upon a plentiful fortune.—So you hear people talking how miserable a king must be, and yet they all wish to be in his place."

It was suggested that kings must be unhappy, because they are deprived of the greatest of all satisfactions, easy and unreserved society. JOHNSON: "This is an ill-founded notion. Being a king does not exclude a man from such society. Great kings have always been social. The King of Prussia, the only great king at present, is very social. Charles the Second, the last king of England who was a man of parts, was social; and our Henrys and Edwards were all social."

Mr. Dempster having endeavoured to maintain that intrinsic merit *ought* to make the only distinction among mankind. JOHNSON: "Why, Sir, mankind have found that this cannot be. How shall we determine the proportion of intrinsic merit? Were that to be the only distinction amongst mankind, we should soon quarrel about the degrees of it. Were all distinctions abolished, the strongest would not long acquiesce, but would endeavour to obtain a superiority by their bodily strength. But, Sir, as subordination is very necessary for society, and contentions for superiority very dangerous, mankind, that is to say, all civilised nations, have settled it upon a plain invariable principle. A man is born to hereditary rank; or his being appointed to certain offices gives him a certain rank. Subordination tends greatly to human happiness. Were we all upon an equality, we should have no other enjoyment than mere animal pleasure."

I said, I considered distinction or rank to be of so much importance in civilised society, that if I were asked on the same day to dine with the first duke in England, and with the first man in Britain for genius, I should hesitate which to prefer. JOHNSON: "To be sure, Sir, if you were to dine only once, and it were never to be known where you dined, you would choose rather to dine with the first man for genius; but to gain most respect, you should dine with the first duke in England. For nine people in ten that you meet with, would have a higher opinion of you for having dined with a duke; and the great genius himself would receive you better, because you had been with the great duke."

He took care to guard himself against any possible suspicion that his settled principles of reverence for rank and respect for wealth were at all owing to mean or interested motives; for he asserted his own independence as a literary man. "No man," said he, "who ever lived by literature, has lived more independently than I have done." He said he had taken longer time than he needed to have done in composing his

Dictionary. He received our compliments upon that great work with complacency, and told us that the Academy *della Crusca* could scarcely believe that it was done by one man.

Next morning I found him alone, and have preserved the following fragments of his conversation. Of a gentleman who was mentioned, he said, " I have not met with any man for a long time who has given me such general displeasure. He is totally unfixed in his principles, and wants to puzzle other people." I said his principles had been poisoned by a noted infidel writer, but that he was, nevertheless, a benevolent, good man. JOHNSON : " We can have no dependence upon that instinctive, that constitutional goodness, which is not founded upon principle. I grant you that such a man may be a very amiable member of society. I can conceive him placed in such a situation that he is not much tempted to deviate from what is right ; and as every man prefers virtue, when there is not some strong incitement to transgress its precepts, I can conceive him doing nothing wrong. But if such a man stood in need of money, I should not like to trust him ; and I should certainly not trust him with young ladies, for *there*, there is always temptation. Hume, and other sceptical innovators, are vain men, and will gratify themselves at any expense. Truth will not afford sufficient food to their vanity : so they have betaken themselves to error. Truth, Sir, is a cow which will yield such people no more milk, and so they are gone to milk the bull. If I could have allowed myself to gratify my vanity at the expense of truth, what fame might I have acquired ! Every thing which Hume has advanced against Christianity had passed through my mind long before he wrote. Always remember this, that after a system is well settled upon positive evidence, a few partial objections ought not to shake it. The human mind is so limited, that it cannot take in all the parts of a subject, so that there may be objections raised against any thing. There are objections against a *plenum*, and objections against a *vacuum ;* yet one of them must certainly be true."

I mentioned Hume's argument against the belief of miracles, that it is more probable that the witnesses to the truth of them are mistaken, or speak falsely, than that the miracles should be true. JOHNSON : " Why, Sir, the great difficulty of proving miracles should make us very cautious in believing them. But let us consider ; although God has made Nature to operate by certain fixed laws, yet it is not unreasonable to think that he may suspend those laws, in order to establish a system highly advantageous to mankind. Now the Christian religion is a most beneficial system, as it gives us light and certainty where we were before in darkness and doubt. The miracles which prove it are attested by men who had no interest in deceiving us ; but who, on the contrary, were told that they should suffer persecution, and did actually lay down their lives in confirmation of the truth of the facts which they asserted. Indeed, for some centuries the heathens did not pretend to deny the miracles ; but said they were performed by the aid of evil spirits. This is a circumstance of great weight. Then, Sir, when we take the proofs derived from prophecies which have been so exactly fulfilled, we have most satisfactory evidence. Supposing a miracle possible, as to which, in my opinion, there can be no doubt, we have as strong evidence for the miracles in support of Christianity as the nature of the thing admits."

At night, Mr. Johnson and I supped in a private room at the Turk's Head coffee-house, in the Strand. " I encourage this house," said he, " for the mistress of it is a good civil woman, and has not much business."

" Sir, I love the acquaintance of young people ; because, in the first place, I don't like to think myself growing old. In the next place, young acquaintances must last longest, if they do last ; and then, Sir, young men have more virtue than old men ; they have more generous sentiments in every respect. I love the young dogs of this age ; they have more wit and humour and knowledge of life than we had ; but then the dogs are not so good scholars. Sir, in my early years I read very hard. It is a sad reflection, but a true one, that I knew almost as much at eighteen as I do now.[1] My judgment, to be sure, was not so good, but I had all the facts. I remember very well when I was at Oxford, an old gentleman said to me, " Young man, ply your book diligently now, and acquire a stock of knowledge ; for when years come upon you, you will find that poring upon books will be but an irksome task."

This account of his reading, given by himself in plain words, sufficiently confirms what I have already advanced upon the disputed question as to his application. It reconciles any seeming inconsistency in his way of talking upon it at different times ; and shows that idleness and read-ing hard were with him relative terms, the import of which, as used by him, must be gathered from a comparison with what scholars of different degrees of ardour and assiduity have been known to do. And let it be remembered that he was now talking spontaneously, and expressing his genuine sentiments ; whereas at other times he might be induced from his spirit of contradiction, or more properly from his love of argu-mentative contest, to speak lightly of his own application to study. It is pleasing to consider that the old gentleman's gloomy prophecy as to the irksomeness of books to men of an advanced age, which is too often fulfilled, was so far from being verified in Johnson, that his ardour for literature never failed, and his last writings had more ease and vivacity than any of his earlier productions.

He mentioned to me now, for the first time, that he had been distressed

[1] His great period of study was from the age of twelve to that of eighteen ; as he told Mr. Langton, who gave me this information.—MALONE.

by melancholy, and for that reason had been obliged to fly from study and meditation, to the dissipating variety of life. Against melancholy he recommended constant occupation of mind, a great deal of exercise, moderation in eating and drinking, and especially to shun drinking at night. He said melancholy people were apt to fly to intemperance for relief, but that it sunk them much deeper in misery. He observed, that labouring men who work hard, and live sparingly, are seldom or never troubled with low spirits.

He again insisted on the duty of maintaining subordination of rank. " Sir, I would no more deprive a nobleman of his respect than of his money. I consider myself as acting a part in the great system of society, and I do to others as I would have them do to me. I would behave to a nobleman as I should expect he would behave to me, were I a nobleman, and he Sam. Johnson. Sir, there is one Mrs. Macaulay,[1] in this town, a great republican. One day when I was at her house, I put on a very grave countenance, and said to her, 'Madam, I am now become a convert to your way of thinking. I am convinced that all mankind are upon an equal footing ; and to give you an unquestionable proof, Madam, that I am in earnest, here is a very sensible, civil, well-behaved fellow-citizen, your footman ; I desire that he may be allowed to sit down and dine with us.' I thus, Sir, showed her the absurdity of the levelling doctrine. She has never liked me since. Sir, your levellers wish to level *down* as far as themselves ; but they cannot bear levelling *up* to themselves. They would all have some people under them ; why not then have some people above them ? "

JOSEPH WARTON.

I mentioned a certain author who disgusted me by his forwardness, and by showing no deference to noblemen into whose company he was admitted. JOHNSON : " Suppose a shoemaker should claim an equality with him, as he does with a lord : how he would stare. 'Why, Sir, do you stare ?' says the shoemaker, 'I do great service to society. 'Tis true I am paid for doing it ; but so are you, Sir ; and I am sorry to say it, better paid than I am, for doing something not so necessary. For mankind could do better without your books than without my shoes.' Thus, Sir, there would be a perpetual struggle for precedence, were there no fixed invariable rules for the

[1] This *one* Mrs. Macaulay was the same personage who afterwards made herself so much known as " the celebrated female historian."—BOSWELL.

distinction of rank, which creates no jealousy, as it is allowed to be accidental."

He said Dr. Joseph Warton was a very agreeable man, and his "Essay on the Genius and Writings of Pope" a very pleasing book. I wondered that he delayed so long to give us the continuation of it.— JOHNSON: "Why, Sir, I suppose he finds himself a little disappointed in not having been able to persuade the world to be of his opinion as to Pope."

We have now been favoured with the concluding volume, in which, to use a parliamentary expression, he has *explained*, so as not to appear quite so adverse to the opinion of the world, concerning Pope, as was at first thought; and we must all agree that his work is a most valuable accession to English literature.

A writer of deserved eminence being mentioned, Johnson said, "Why, Sir, he is a man of good parts, but being originally poor, he has got a love of mean company and low jocularity; a very bad thing, Sir. To laugh is good, and to talk is good. But you ought no more to think it enough if you laugh, than you are to think it enough if you talk. You may laugh in as many ways as you talk; and surely *every* way of talking that is practised cannot be esteemed."

I spoke of Sir James Macdonald as a young man of most distinguished merit, who united the highest reputation at Eton and Oxford, with the patriarchal spirit of a great Highland chieftain. I mentioned that Sir James had said to me, that he had never seen Mr. Johnson, but he had a great respect for him, though at the same time it was mixed with some degree of terror. JOHNSON: "Sir, if he were to be acquainted with me, it might lessen both."

The mention of this gentleman led us to talk of the Western Islands of Scotland, to visit which he expressed a wish that then appeared to me a very romantic fancy, which I little thought would be afterwards realised. He told me that his father had put Martin's account of those islands into his hands when he was very young, and that he was highly pleased with it; that he was particularly struck with the St. Kilda man's notion that the high church of Glasgow had been hollowed out of a rock; a circumstance to which old Mr. Johnson had directed his attention. He said he would go to the Hebrides with me when I returned from my travels, unless some very good companion should offer when I was absent, which he did not think probable; adding, "There are few people whom I take so much to as you." And when I talked of my leaving England, he said with a very affectionate air, "My dear Boswell, I should be very unhappy at parting, did I think we were not to meet again." I cannot too often remind my readers, that although such instances of his kindness are doubtless very flattering to me, yet I hope my recording them will be ascribed to a better motive than to vanity; for they afford unquestionable evidence of his tenderness and com-

s 2

placeney, which some, while they are forced to acknowledge his great powers, have been so strenuous to deny.

He maintained that a boy at school was the happiest of human beings. I supported a different opinion, from which I have never yet varied, that a man is happier ; and I enlarged upon the anxiety and sufferings which are endured at school. JOHNSON : " Ah, Sir, a boy's being flogged is not so severe as a man's having the hiss of the world against him. Men have a solicitude about fame ; and the greater share they have of it, the more afraid they are of losing it." I silently asked myself, " Is it possible that the great SAMUEL JOHNSON really entertains any such apprehension, and is not confident that his exalted fame is established upon a foundation never to be shaken ? "

He this evening drank a bumper to Sir David Dalrymple, "as a man of worth, a scholar, and a wit." " I have," said he, " never heard of him, except from you ; but let him know my opinion of him : for as he does not show himself much in the world, he should have the praise of the few who hear of him."

On Tuesday, July 26, I found Mr. Johnson alone. It was a very wet day, and I again complained of the disagreeable effects of such weather. JOHNSON : " Sir, this is all imagination, which physicians encourage ; for man lives in air as a fish lives in water ; so that if the atmosphere press heavy from above, there is an equal resistance from below. To be sure, bad weather is hard upon people who are obliged to be abroad ; and men cannot labour so well in the open air in bad weather as in good ; but, Sir, a smith, or a tailor, whose work is within doors, will surely do as much in rainy weather as in fair. Some very delicate frames, indeed, may be affected by wet weather ; but not common constitutions."

We talked of the education of children ; and I asked him what he thought was best to teach them first. JOHNSON : " Sir, it is no matter what you teach them first, any more than what leg you shall put into your breeches first. Sir, you may stand disputing which is best to put in first, but in the meantime your breech is bare. Sir, while you are considering which of two things you should teach your child first, another boy has learnt them both."

On Thursday, July 28, we again supped in private at the Turk's Head coffee-house. JOHNSON : " Swift has a higher reputation than he deserves. His excellence is strong sense ; for his humour, though very well, is not remarkably good. I doubt whether the ' Tale of a Tub ' be his ; for he never owned it, and it is much above his usual manner." [1]

" Thomson, I think, had as much of the poet about him as most writers. Every thing appeared to him through the medium of his

---

[1] This opinion was given by him more at large at a subsequent period. See " Journal of a Tour to the Hebrides," 3rd edit. p. 32.—BOSWELL.

favourite pursuit.   He could not have viewed those two candles burning but with a poetical eye."

"Has not —— a great deal of wit, Sir ?"   Johnson : "I do not think so, Sir.   He is, indeed, continually attempting wit, but he fails. And I have no more pleasure in hearing a man attempting wit and failing, than in seeing a man trying to leap over a ditch and tumbling into it."

He laughed heartily when I mentioned to him a saying of his concerning Mr. Thomas Sheridan, which Foote took a wicked pleasure to circulate.   "Why, Sir, Sherry is dull, naturally dull ; but it must have taken him a great deal of pains to become what we now see him.   Such an excess of stupidity, Sir, is not in Nature."—"So," said he, "I allowed him all his own merit."

He now added, "Sheridan cannot bear me.   I bring his declamation to a point.   I ask him a plain question, ' What do you mean to teach ?' Besides, Sir, what influence can Mr. Sheridan have upon the language of this great country, by his narrow exertions ?   Sir, it is burning a farthing candle at Dover, to show light at Calais."

Talking of a young man who was uneasy from thinking that he was very deficient in learning and knowledge, he said, "A man has no reason to complain who holds a middle place, and has many below him ; and perhaps he has not six of his years above him ;—perhaps not one Though he may not know anything perfectly, the general mass of knowledge that he has acquired is considerable.   Time will do for him all that is wanting."

The conversation then took a philosophical turn.   Johnson : "Human experience, which is constantly contradicting theory, is the great test of truth.   A system built upon the discoveries of a great many minds, is always of more strength, than what is produced by the mere workings of any one mind, which, of itself, can do little.   There is not so poor a book in the world that would not be a prodigious effort were it wrought out entirely by a single mind, without the aid of prior investigators. The French writers are superficial, because they are not scholars, and so proceed upon the mere power of their own minds ; and we see how very little power they have."

"As to the Christian religion, Sir, besides the strong evidence which we have for it, there is a balance in its favour from the number of great men who have been convinced of its truth, after a serious consideration of the question.   Grotius was an acute man, a lawyer, a man accustomed to examine evidence, and he was convinced.   Grotius was not a recluse, but a man of the world, who certainly had no bias to the side of religion.   Sir Isaac Newton set out an infidel, and came to be a very firm believer."

He this evening again recommended to me to perambulate Spain[1],

[1] I fully intended to have followed advice of such weight; but having staid much longer

I said it would amuse him to get a letter from me dated at Salamanca. JOHNSON: "I love the University of Salamanca; for when the Spaniards were in doubt as to the lawfulness of their conquering America, the University of Salamanca gave it as their opinion that it was not lawful." He spoke this with great emotion, and with that generous warmth which dictated the lines in his "London," against Spanish encroachment.

I expressed my opinion of my friend Derrick as but a poor writer. JOHNSON: "To be sure, Sir, he is; but you are to consider that his being a literary man has got for him all that he has. It has made him king of Bath. Sir, he has nothing to say for himself but that he is a writer. Had he not been a writer, he must have been sweeping the crossings in the streets, and asking halfpence from everybody that passed."

In justice, however, to the memory of Mr. Derrick, who was my first tutor in the ways of London, and showed me the town in all its variety of departments, both literary and sportive, the particulars of which Dr. Johnson advised me to put in writing, it is proper to mention what Johnson, at a subsequent period, said of him both as a writer and an editor: "Sir, I have often said, that if Derrick's letters had been written by one of a more established name, they would have been thought very pretty letters."[1] And "I sent Derrick to Dryden's relations to gather materials for his life; and I believe he got all that I myself should have got."[2]

Poor Derrick! I remember him with kindness. Yet I cannot withhold from my readers a pleasant humorous sally which could not have hurt him had he been alive, and now is perfectly harmless. In his collection of poems there is one upon entering the harbour of Dublin, his native city, after a long absence. It begins thus:—

> "Eblana! much loved city, hail!
> Where first I saw the light of day."

And after a solemn reflection on his being "numbered with forgotten dead," there is the following stanza:—

> "Unless my lines protract my fame,
>   And those, who chance to read them, cry,
> I knew him! Derrick was his name,
>   In yonder tomb his ashes lie——."

both in Germany and Italy than I proposed to do, and having also visited Corsica, I found that I had exceeded the time allowed me by my father, and hastened to France in my way homewards.—BOSWELL.

[1] Journal of a Tour to the Hebrides, 2nd edit. p. 104.—BOSWELL.

[2] Ibid. p. 142.—BOSWELL.

which was thus happily parodied by Mr. John Home, to whom we owe the beautiful and pathetic tragedy of " Douglas " :—

> " Unless my *deeds* protract my fame,
> *And he who passes sadly sings,*
> I knew him ! Derrick was his name,
> *On yonder tree his carcase swings !"*

I doubt much whether the amiable and ingenious author of these *burlesque* lines will recollect them ; for they were produced extempore one evening while he and I were walking together in the dining-room at Eglintoune Castle, in 1760, and I have never mentioned them to him since.

Johnson said once to me, " Sir, I honour Derrick for his presence of mind. One night, when Floyd, another poor author, was wandering about the streets in the night, he found Derrick fast asleep upon a bulk ; upon being suddenly waked, Derrick started up, 'My dear Floyd, I am sorry to see you in this destitute state ; will you come home with me to *my lodgings.*'"

I again begged his advice as to my method of study at Utrecht. " Come," said he, " let us make a day of it. Let us go down to Greenwich and dine, and talk of it there." The following Saturday was fixed for this excursion.

As we walked along the Strand to-night, arm in arm, a woman of the town accosted us, in the usual enticing manner. " No, no, my girl," said Johnson, " it won't do." He, however, did not treat her with harshness ; and we talked of the wretched life of such women, and agreed that much more misery than happiness, upon the whole, is produced by illicit commerce between the sexes.

On Saturday, July 30, Dr. Johnson and I took a sculler at the Temple-stairs, and set out for Greenwich. I asked him if he really thought a knowledge of the Greek and Latin languages an essential requisite to a good education. JOHNSON : " Most certainly, Sir ; for those who know them have a very great advantage over those who do not. Nay, Sir, it is wonderful what a difference learning makes upon people even in the common intercourse of life, which does not appear to be much connected with it." " And yet," said I, " people go through the world very well and carry on the business of life, to good advantage without learning." JOHNSON : " Why, Sir, that may be true in cases where learning cannot possibly be of any use ; for instance, this boy rows us as well without learning, as if he could sing the song of Orpheus to the Argonauts, who were the first sailors." He then called to the boy, " What would you give, my lad, to know about the Argonauts ?" " Sir," said the boy, " I would give what I have." Johnson

---

¹ He published a biographical work, containing an account of eminent writers, in 3 vols, 8vo.—BOSWELL.

was much pleased with his answer, and we gave him a double fare. Dr. Johnson then turning to me, "Sir," said he, "a desire of knowledge

TEMPLE STAIRS.

is the natural feeling of mankind; and every human being whose mind is not debauched, will be willing to give all that he has to get knowledge."

We landed at the Old Swan, and walked to Billingsgate, where we took oars and moved smoothly along the silver Thames. It was a very fine day. We were entertained with the immense number and variety of ships that were lying at anchor, and with the beautiful country on each side of the river.

I talked of preaching, and of the great success which those called methodists[1] have. JOHNSON: "Sir, it is owing to their expressing

---

[1] All who are acquainted with the history of religion, (the most important, surely, that concerns the human mind,) know that the appellation of *Methodists* was first given to a society of students in the University of Oxford, who about the year 1730, were distinguished by an earnest and *methodical* attention to devout exercises. This disposition of mind is not a novelty, or peculiar to any sect, but has been, and still may be found, in many Christians of every denomination. Johnson himself was, in a dignified manner, a methodist. In his "Rambler," No. 110, he mentions with respect " the whole discipline of regulated piety;" and in his "Prayers and Meditations," many instances occur of his anxious examination into his spiritual state. That this religious earnestness, and in particular an observation of the influence of the Holy Spirit, has sometimes degenerated into folly, and sometimes been counterfeited for base purposes, cannot be denied. But it is not, therefore, fair to decry it when genuine. The principal argument in reason and good sense against methodism is, that it tends to debase human nature, and prevent the generous exertions of goodness, by an unworthy supposition that God will pay no regard to them; although it is positively said in the scriptures, that he " will reward every man according to his works." But I am happy to have it in my power to do justice to those whom it is the fashion to ridicule, without any knowledge of their tenets; and this I can do by quoting a passage from one of their best apologists, Mr. Milner, who thus expresses their doctrine upon this subject: "Justified by

themselves in a plain and familiar manner, which is the only way to do good to the common people, and which clergymen of genius and learning ought to do from a principle of duty, when it is suited to their congregations ; a practice, for which they will be praised by men of sense. To insist against drunkenness as a crime, because it debases reason : the noblest faculty of man, would be of no service to the common people, but to tell them that they may die in a fit of drunkenness and show them how dreadful that would be, cannot fail to make a deep impression. Sir, when your Scotch clergy give up their homely manner, religion will soon decay in that country." Let this observation, as Johnson meant it, be ever remembered.

I was much pleased to find myself with Johnson at Greenwich, which he celebrates in his "London" as a favourite scene. I had the poem in my pocket, and read the lines aloud with enthusiasm :—

> " On Thames's banks in silent thought we stood,
> Where Greenwich smiles upon the silver flood ;
> Pleased with the seat which gave ELIZA birth,
> We kneel, and kiss the consecrated earth."

He remarked that the structure of Greenwich hospital was too magnificent for a place of charity, and that its parts were too much detached, to make one great whole.

Buchanan, he said, was a very fine poet ; and observed, that he was the first who complimented a lady, by ascribing to her the different perfections of the heathen goddesses ;[1] but that Johnstone improved upon this, by making his lady, at the same time, free from their defects.

He dwelt upon Buchanan's elegant verses to Mary Queen of Scots, *Nympha Caledoniæ*, &c., and spoke with enthusiasm of the beauty of Latin verse. " All the modern languages," said he, " cannot furnish so melodious a line as

> ' *Formosam resonare doces Amarillida silvas.*' "

Afterwards he entered upon the business of the day, which was to give me his advice as to a course of study. And here I am to mention with much regret, that my record of what he said is miserably scanty.

---

faith, renewed in his faculties, and constrained by the love of Christ, the believer moves in the sphere of love and gratitude, and all his *duties* flow more or less from this principle. And though *they are accumulating for him in heaven a treasure of bliss proportioned to his faithfulness and activity, and it is by no means inconsistent with his principles to feel the force of this consideration*, yet love itself sweetens every duty to his mind ; and he thinks there is no absurdity in his feeling the love of God as the grand commanding principle of his life."—*Essays on several religious Subjects, &c., by Joseph Milner, A.M., Master of the Grammar School of Kingstonupon-Hull*, 1789, p, 11.—BOSWELL.

[1] Epigram, Lib. II. " In Elizabeth. Angliæ Reg."—I suspect that the author's memory here deceived him, and that Johnson said, " the first *modern* poet ; " for there is a well-known epigram in the " Anthologia " containing this kind of eulogy.—MALONE

I recollect with admiration an animating blaze of eloquence, which roused every intellectual power in me to the highest pitch, but must have dazzled me so much that my memory could not preserve the substance of his discourse; for the note which I find of it is no more than this :—"He ran over the grand scale of human knowledge; advised me to select some particular branch to excel in, but to acquire a little of every kind." The defect of my minutes will be fully supplied by a long letter upon the subject, which he favoured me with after I had been some time at Utrecht, and which my readers will have the pleasure to peruse in its proper place.

We walked, in the evening, in Greenwich Park. He asked me, I suppose, by way of trying my disposition, "Is not this very fine?"—Having no exquisite relish of the beauties of nature, and being more delighted with "the busy hum of men," I answered, "Yes, Sir, but not equal to Fleet-street." JOHNSON: "You are right, Sir."

GREENWICH PARK.

I am aware that many of my readers may censure my want of taste. Let me, however, shelter myself under the authority of a very fashionable baronet[1] in the brilliant world, who, on his attention being called

1 My friend Sir Michael Le Fleming. This gentleman with all his experience of sprightly and elegant life, inherits, with the beautiful family domain, no inconsiderable share of that love of literature, which distinguished his venerable grandfather, the Bishop of Carlisle. He one day observed to me, of Dr. Johnson, in a felicity of phrase, "There is a blunt dignity about him on every occasion."—BOSWELL.

Sir Michael Le Fleming died of an apoplectic fit, while conversing at the Admiralty with Lord Howick, now Earl Grey, May 19, 1806.—MALONE.

to the fragrance of a May evening in the country, observed, "This may be very well; but for my part, I prefer the smell of a flambeau at the play-house."

We staid so long at Greenwich, that our sail up the river, in our return to London, was by no means so pleasant as in the morning ; for the night air was so cold that it made me shiver. I was the more sensible of it from having sat up all the night before recollecting and writing in my journal what I thought worthy of preservation ; an exertion which during the first part of my acquaintance with Johnson, I frequently made. I remember having sat up four nights in one week, without being much incommoded in the day-time.

Johnson, whose robust frame was not in the least affected by the cold, scolded me, as if my shivering had been a paltry effeminacy, saying, " Why do you shiver ?" Sir William Scott, of the Commons, told me that when he complained of a headache in the post-chaise, as they were travelling together to Scotland, Johnson treated him in the same manner : " At your age, Sir, I had no headache." It is not easy to make allowance for sensations in others, which we ourselves have not at the time. We must all have experienced how very differently we are affected by the complaints of our neighbours, when we are well, and when we are ill. In full health, we can scarcely believe that they suffer much ; so faint is the image of pain upon our imagination : when softened by sickness, we readily sympathise with the sufferings of others.

We concluded the day at the Turk's Head coffee-house very socially. He was pleased to listen to a particular account which I gave him of my family, and of its hereditary estate, as to the extent and population of which he asked questions, and made calculations; recommending, at the same time, a liberal kindness to the tenantry, as people over whom the proprietor was placed by Providence. He took delight in hearing my description of the romantic seat of my ancestors. "I must be there, Sir," said he, "and we will live in the old castle ; and if there is not a room in it remaining, we will build one." I was highly flattered, but could scarcely indulge a hope that Auchinleck would indeed be honoured by his presence, and celebrated by a description, as it afterwards was, in his " Journey to the Western Islands."

After we had again talked of my setting out for Holland, he said, " I must see thee out of England ; I will accompany you to Harwich." I could not find words to express what I felt upon this unexpected and very great mark of his affectionate regard.

Next day, Sunday, July 3, I told him I had been that morning at a meeting of the people called Quakers, where I had heard a woman preach. Johnson : " Sir, a woman's preaching is like a dog's walking on his hind legs. It is not done well ; but you are surprised to find it done at all."

On Tuesday, August 2, (the day of my departure from London having been fixed for the 5th,) Dr. Johnson did me the honour to pass a part of the morning with me at my chambers. He said, "that he always felt an inclination to do nothing." I observed, that it was strange to think that the most indolent man in Britain had written the most laborious work, "The English Dictionary."

I mentioned an imprudent publication by a certain friend of his, at an early period of life, and asked him if he thought it would hurt him. JOHNSON: "No, Sir; not much. It may perhaps be mentioned at an election."

I had now made good my title to be a privileged man, and was carried by him in the evening to drink tea with Miss Williams,[1] whom, though under the misfortune of having lost her sight, I found to be agreeable

[1] In a paper already referred to a lady who appears to have been well acquainted with Mrs. Williams, thus speaks of her:—

"Mrs. Williams was a person extremely interesting. She had an uncommon firmness of mind, a boundless curiosity, retentive memory, and strong judgment. She had various powers of pleasing. Her personal afflictions and slender fortune she seemed to forget, when she had the power of doing an act of kindness: she was social, cheerful, and active, in a state of body that was truly deplorable. Her regard to Dr. Johnson was formed with such strength of judgment and firm esteem, that her voice never hesitated when she repeated his maxims, or recited his good deeds; though upon many other occasions her want of sight had led her to make so much use of her ear as to affect her speech.

MRS. ANN WILLIAMS.

"Mrs. Williams was blind before she was acquainted with Dr. Johnson.—She had many resources, though none very great. With the Miss Wilkinsons she generally passed a part of the year, and received from them presents, and from the first who died, a legacy of clothes and money. The last of them, Mrs. Jane, left her an annual rent; but from the blundering manner of the will, I fear she never reaped the benefit of it. The lady left money to erect an hospital for ancient maids: but the number she had allotted, being too great for the donation, the Doctor (Johnson) said, it would be better to expunge the word *maintain*, and put in to *starve* such a number of old maids. They asked him what name should be given it? he replied, 'Let it be called JENNY'S WHIM,' the name of a well-known tavern near Chelsea, in former days.

"Lady Phillips made her a small annual allowance, and some other Welsh ladies, to all of whom she was related. Mrs. Montague, on the death of Mr. Montague, settled upon her (by deed), ten pounds per annum.—As near as I can calculate, Mrs. Williams had about thirty-five or forty pounds a year. The furniture she used in her apartment in Dr. Johnson's house was her own; her expenses were small, tea and bread and butter being at least half of her nourishment. Sometimes she had a servant or charwoman to do the ruder offices of the house; but she was herself active and industrious. I have frequently seen her at work. Upon remarking one day her facility in moving about the house, searching into drawers, and finding books without the help of sight, 'Believe me,' said she, 'persons who cannot do those common offices without sight, did but little while they enjoyed that blessing.' Scanty circumstances, bad health, and blindness, are surely a sufficient apology for her being sometimes impatient: her natural disposition was good, friendly, and humane."—MALONE.

in conversation, for she had a variety of literature, and expressed herself well; but her peculiar value was the intimacy in which she had long lived with Johnson, by which she was well acquainted with his habits, and knew how to lead him on to talk.

After tea he carried me to what he called his walk, which was a long narrow paved court in the neighbourhood,[1] overshadowed by some trees. There we sauntered a considerable time, and I complained to him that my love of London and of his company was such, that I shrunk almost from the thought of going away even to travel, which is generally so much desired by young men. He roused me by manly and spirited conversation. He advised me, when settled in any place abroad, to study with an eagerness after knowledge, and to apply to Greek an hour every day; and when I was moving about, to read diligently the great book of mankind.

On Wednesday, August 3, we had our last social evening at the Turk's Head coffee-house, before my setting out for foreign parts. I had the misfortune, before we parted, to irritate him unintentionally. I mentioned to him how common it was in the world to tell absurd stories of him, and to ascribe to him very strange sayings. JOHNSON: "What do they make me say, Sir?" BOSWELL: "Why, Sir, as an instance very strange indeed," laughing heartily as I spoke, "David Hume told me, you said that you would stand before a battery of cannon to restore the Convocation to its full powers." Little did I apprehend that he had actually said this: but I was soon convinced of my error; for, with a determined look he thundered out, "And would I not, Sir? Shall the Presbyterian *Kirk* of Scotland have its General Assembly, and the Church of England be denied its Convocation?" He was walking up and down the room while I told him the anecdote; but, when he uttered this explosion of high-church zeal he had come close to my chair, and his eyes flashed with indignation. I bowed to the storm, and diverted the force of it, by leading him to expatiate on the influence which religion derived from maintaining the church with great external respectability.

I must not omit to mention that he this year wrote "The Life of Ascham,"† and the Dedication to the Earl of Shaftesbury,† prefixed to the edition of that writer's English works, published by Mr. Bennet.

1 This was probably the court running off from the eastern corner of Gough-square, towards Shoe-lane. There are still two trees to be seen in the line, and there were probably many more at the time Boswell speaks of.—ED.

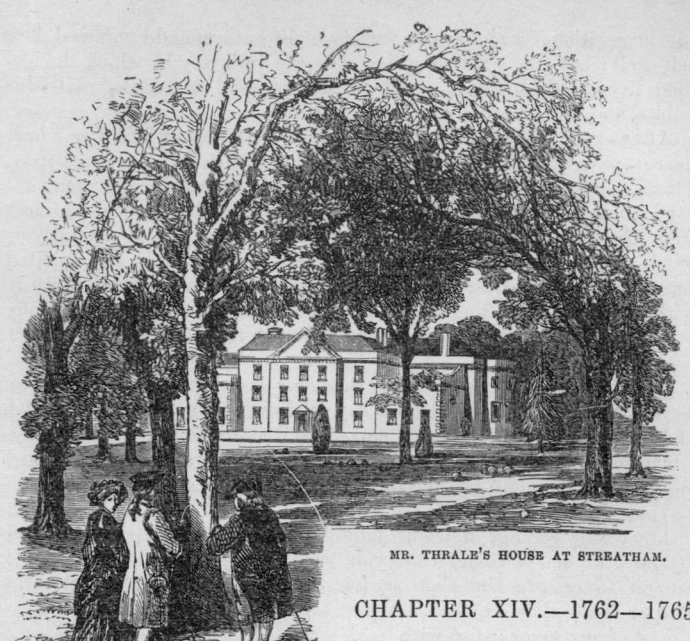

MR. THRALE'S HOUSE AT STREATHAM.

CHAPTER XIV.—1762—1765.

ON Friday, August 5, we set out early in the morning in the Harwich stage-coach. A fat elderly gentlewoman, and a young Dutchman, seemed the most inclined among us to conversation. At the inr. where we dined, the gentlewoman said that she had done her best to educate her children ; and, particularly, that she had never suffered them to be a moment idle. JOHNSON : "I wish, Madam, you would educate me too ; for I have been an idle fellow all my life." "I am sure, Sir," said she, "you have not been idle." JOHNSON : "Nay, madam, it is very true : and that gentleman there, (pointing to me,) has been idle. He was idle at Edinburgh. His father sent him to Glasgow, where he continued to be idle. He then came to London, where he has been very idle ; and now he is going to Utrecht, where he will be as idle as ever", I asked him privately how he could expose me so. JOHNSON : "Poh

poh ! " said he, " they knew nothing about you, and will think of it no more."

In the afternoon the gentlewoman talked violently against the Roman Catholics, and of the horrors of the Inquisition. To the utter astonishment of all the passengers but myself, who knew that he could talk upon any side of a question, he defended the Inquisition, and maintained that "false doctrine should be checked on its first appearance ; that the civil power should unite with the church in punishing those who dare to attack the established religion, and that such only were punished by the Inquisition."

He had in his pocket " *Pomponius Mela de Situ Orbis*," in which he read occasionally, and seemed very intent upon ancient geography.

Though by no means niggardly, his attention to what was generally right was so minute, that having observed at one of the stages that I ostentatiously gave a shilling to the coachman, when the custom was for each passenger to give only sixpence, he took me aside and scolded me, saying that what I had done would make the coachman dissatisfied with all the rest of the passengers, who gave him no more than his due This was a just reprimand ; for in whatever way a man may indulge his generosity or his vanity in spending his money, for the sake of others he ought not to raise the price of any article for which there is a constant demand.

He talked of Mr. Blacklock's poetry, so far as it was descriptive of visible objects ; and observed, that " as its author had the misfortune to be blind, we may be absolutely sure that such passages are combinations of what he has remembered of the works of other writers who could see. That foolish fellow Spence, has laboured to explain philosophically how Blacklock may have done, by means of his own faculties, what it is impossible he should do. The solution, as I have given it, is plain. Suppose, I know a man to be so lame that he is absolutely incapable to move himself, and I find him in a different room from that in which I left him ; shall I puzzle myself with idle conjectures that, perhaps, his nerves have by some unknown change all at once become effective ? No, Sir, it is clear how he got into a different room : he was *carried*."

Having stopped a night at Colchester, Johnson talked of that town with veneration, for having stood a siege for Charles the First. The Dutchman alone now remained with us. He spoke English tolerably well ; and thinking to recommend himself to us by expatiating on the superiority of the criminal jurisprudence of this country over that of Holland, he inveighed against the barbarity of putting an accused person to the torture, in order to force a confession. But Johnson was as ready for this as for the Inquisition. "Why, Sir, you do not, I find, understand the law of your own country. To torture in Holland is considered as a favour to an accused person ; for no man is put to the torture there, unless there is as much evidence against him as would amount to conviction in England. An accused person, among you, therefore, has one chance more to escape punishment than those who are tried among us."

At supper this night he taked of good eating with uncommon satisfaction. "Some people," said he, "have a foolish way of not minding, or pretending not to mind, what they eat. For my part, I mind my belly very studiously and very carefully; for I look upon it, that he who does not mind his belly will hardly mind anything else." He now appeared to me *Jean Bull philosophe*, and he was for the moment not only serious, but vehement. Yet I have heard him, upon other occasions, talk with great contempt of people who were anxious to gratify their palates; and the 206th number of his "Rambler" is a masterly essay against gulosity. His practice, indeed, I must acknowledge, may be considered as casting the balance of his different opinions upon this subject; for I never knew any man who relished good eating more than he did. When at table he was totally absorbed in the business of the moment: his looks seemed riveted to his plate; nor would he, unless when in very high company, say one word, or even pay the least attention to what was said by others, till he had satisfied his appetite, which was so fierce, and indulged with such intenseness, that while in the act of eating, the veins of his forehead swelled, and generally a strong perspiration was visible. To those whose sensations were delicate, this could not but be disgusting; and it was doubtless not very suitable to the character of a philosopher, who should be distinguished by self-command. But it must be owned that Johnson, though he could be rigidly *abstemious*, was not a *temperate* man either in eating or drinking. He could refrain, but he could not use moderately. He told me that he had fasted two days without inconvenience, and that he had never been hungry but once. They who beheld with wonder how much he ate upon all occasions, when his dinner was to his taste, could not easily conceive what he must have meant by hunger; and not only was he remarkable for the extraordinary quantity which he ate, but he was, or affected to be, a man of very nice discernment in the science of cookery. He used to descant critically on the dishes which had been at table where he had dined or supped, and to recollect very minutely what he had liked. I remember when he was in Scotland, his praising "*Gordon's palates*" (a dish of palates at the Honourable Alexander Gordon's) with a warmth of expression which might have done honour to more important subjects. "As for Maclaurin's imitation of a *made dish*, it was a wretched attempt." He about the same time was so much displeased with the performances of a nobleman's French cook, that he exclaimed with vehemence, "I'd throw such a rascal into the river;" and he then proceeded to alarm a lady at whose house he was to sup, by the following manifesto of his skill:—"I, Madam, who live at a variety of good tables, am a much better judge of cookery, than any person **who** has a very tolerable cook, but lives much at home ; for his palate is gradually adapted to the taste of his cook ; whereas, Madam, in trying by a wider range, I can more exquisitely judge." When invited to dine, even with an intimate friend, he was not pleased if something better than a plain dinner was not prepared for him. I have heard him say on such an occasion, " This was a good dinner enough to be sure ; but it was not a dinner to *ask* a man to." On the other hand, he was wont to express, with great glee, his satisfaction when he had been entertained quite to his mind. One day when he had dined with his neighbour and landlord, in Bolt-court, Mr. Allen, the printer, whose old housekeepeer had studied his taste in every thing, he pronounced this eulogy : " Sir, we could not have had a better dinner, had there been a *Synod of Cooks.*"

While we were left by ourselves, after the Dutchman had gone to bed, Dr. Johnson talked of that studied behaviour which many have recommended and practised. He disapproved of it ; and said, " I never considered whether I should be a grave man, or a merry man, but just let inclination, for the time, have its course."

He flattered me with some hopes that he would, in the course of the following summer, come over to Holland, and accompany me in a tour through the Netherlands.

I teased him with fanciful apprehensions of unhappiness. A moth having fluttered round the candle, and burnt itself, he laid hold of this little incident to admonish me ; saying, with a sly look, and in a solemn but a quiet tone, " That creature was its own tormentor, and I believe its name was Boswell."

Next day we got to Harwich, to dinner ; and my passage in the packet-boat to Helvoetsluys being secured, and my baggage put on board, we dined at our inn by ourselves. I happened to say it would be terrible if he should not find a speedy opportunity of returning to London, and be confined in so dull a place. Johnson : " Don't, Sir, accustom yourself to use big words for little matters. It would *not* be *terrible*, though I *were* to be detained some time here." The practice of using words of disproportionate magnitude, is, no doubt, too frequent everywhere ; but, I think, most remarkable among the French, of which all who have travelled in France must have been struck with innumerable instances.

We went and looked at the church, and having gone into it, and walked up to the altar, Johnson, whose piety was constant and fervent, sent me to my knees, saying, " Now that you are going to leave your native country, recommend yourself to the protection of your Creator and Redeemer."

After we came out of the church, we stood talking for some time together of Bishop Berkeley's ingenious sophistry to prove the non-existence of matter, and that everything in the universe is merely ideal

I observed that, though we are satisfied his doctrine is not true, it is impossible to refute it. I never shall forget the alacrity with which Johnson answered, striking his foot with mighty force against a large stone, till he rebounded from it,—" I refute it *thus*." [1] This was a stout exemplification of the *first truths* of *Père Bouffier*, or the *original principles* of Reid and of Beattie : without admitting which, we can no more argue in metaphysics, than we can argue in mathematics without axioms. To me it is not conceivable how Berkeley can be answered by pure reasoning ; but I know that the nice and difficult task was to have been undertaken by one of the most luminous minds of the present age, had not politics "turned him from calm philosophy aside." What an admirable display of subtilty, united with brilliance, might his contending with Berkeley have afforded us ! How must we, when we reflect on the loss of such an intellectual feast, regret that he should be characterised as the man,

> " Who, born for the universe, narrow'd his mind,
> And to party gave up what was meant for mankind !"

My revered friend walked down with me to the beach, where we embraced and parted with tenderness, and engaged to correspond by letters. I said, " I hope, Sir, you will not forget me in my absence." JOHNSON : " Nay, Sir, it is more likely you should forget me, than that I should forget you." As the vessel put out to sea, I kept my eyes upon him for a considerable time, while he remained rolling his majestic frame in his usual manner ; and at last I perceived him walk back into the town, and he disappeared.

Utrecht seeming at first very dull to me, after the animated scenes of London, my spirits were grievously affected ; and I wrote to Johnson a plaintive and desponding letter, to which he paid no regard. Afterwards, when I had acquired a firmer tone of mind, I wrote him a second letter, expressing much anxiety to hear from him. At length I received the following epistle, which was of important service to me, and, I trust, will be so to many others.

" A. M. M. BOSWELL, A LA COUR DE L'EMPEREUR, UTRECHT.

" DEAR SIR,   *London, Dec.* 8, 1763.
" You are not to think yourself forgotten, or criminally neglected, that you have had yet no letter from me. I love to see my friends, to hear from them,

---

[1] Dr. Johnson seems to have been imperfectly acquainted with Berkeley's doctrine : as his experiment only proves that we have the sensation of solidity, which Berkeley did not deny. —He admitted that we had sensations or ideas that are usually called sensible qualities, one of which is solidity : he only denied the existence of *matter*, i. e. an inert senseless substance, in which they are supposed to subsist.—Johnson's exemplification concurs with the vulgar notion, that solidity is matter.—KEARNEY.

to talk to them, and to talk of them; but it is not without a considerable effort of resolution that I prevail upon myself to write. I would not, however, gratify my own indolence, by the omission of any important duty, or any office of real kindness.

" To tell you that I am or am not well, that I have or have not been in the country, that I drank your health in the room in which we last sat together, and that your acquaintance continue to speak of you with their former kindness, topics with which those letters are commonly filled which are written only for the sake of writing, I seldom shall think worth communicating; but if I can have it in my power to calm any harassing disquiet, to excite any virtuous desire, to rectify any important opinion, or fortify any generous resolution, you need not doubt but I shall at least wish to prefer the pleasure of gratifying a friend much less esteemed than yourself, before the gloomy calm of idle vacancy. Whether I shall easily arrive at an exact punctuality of correspondence, I cannot tell. I shall, at present, expect that you will receive this in return for two which I have had from you. The first, indeed, gave me an account so hopeless of the state of your mind, that it hardly admitted or deserved an answer; by the second I was much better pleased; and the pleasure will still be increased by such a narrative of the progress of your studies, as may evince the continuance of an equal and rational application of your mind to some useful inquiry.

" You will, perhaps, wish to ask, what study I would recommend. I shall not speak of theology, because it ought not to be considered as a question whether you shall endeavour to know the will of God.

" I shall, therefore, consider only such studies as we are at liberty to pursue or to neglect; and of these I know not how you will make a better choice, than by studying the civil law as your father advises, and the ancient languages, as you had determined for yourself; at least resolve, while you remain in any settled residence, to spend a certain number of hours every day amongst your books. The dissipation of thought of which you complain, is nothing more than the vacillation of a mind suspended between different motives, and changing its direction as any motive gains or loses strength. If you can but kindle in your mind any strong desire, if you can but keep predominant any wish for some particular excellence or attainment, the gusts of imagination will break away, without any effect upon your conduct, and commonly without any traces left upon the memory.

" There lurks, perhaps, in every human heart a desire of distinction, which inclines every man first to hope, and then to believe, that nature has given him something peculiar to himself. This vanity makes one mind nurse aversion, and another actuate desires, till they rise by art much above their original state of power; and as affectation in time improves to habit, they at last tyrannise over him who at first encouraged them only for show. Every desire is a viper in the bosom, who, while he was chill, was harmless; but when warmth gave him strength, exerted it in poison. You know a gentleman, who, when he first set his foot in the gay world, as he prepared himself to whirl in the vortex of pleasure, imagined a total indifference and universal negligence to be the most agreeable concomitants of youth, and the strongest indication of an airy temper and a quick apprehension. Vacant to every object, and sensible of every impulse, he thought that all appearance of diligence would deduct something from the reputation of genius; and hoped that he should appear to attain, amidst all the ease of carelessness, and all the tumult of diversion, that knowledge and those accomplishments which mortals of the common fabric obtain only by mute abstraction and solitary drudgery. He tried this scheme of life awhile, was made weary of it by his sense and his virtue; he then wished to return to his studies; and finding long habits of idleness and pleasure harder to be cured than he expected, still willing to retain his claim to some extraordinary prerogatives, resolved the common consequences of irregularity into an unalterable decree of destiny, and concluded that Nature had originally formed him incapable of rational employment.

" Let all such fancies, illusive and destructive, be banished henceforward from your thoughts for ever. Resolve, and keep your resolution; choose, and pursue your choice. If you spend this day in study, you will find yourself still more able to study to-morrow; not that you are to expect that you shall at once obtain a complete victory. Depravity is not very easily overcome. Resolution will sometimes relax, and diligence will sometimes be interrupted; but let no accidental surprise or deviation, whether short or long, dispose you to despondency. Consider these failings as incident to all mankind. Begin again where you left off, and endeavour to avoid the seducements that prevailed over you before.

" This, my dear Boswell, is advice which, perhaps, has been often given you, and given you without effect. But this advice, if you will not take from others, you must take from your own reflections, if you propose to do the duties of the station to which the bounty of Providence has called you.

" Let me have a long letter from you as soon as you can. I hope you continue your journal, and enrich it with many observations upon the country in which you reside. It will be a favour if you can get me any books in the Frisick language, and can inquire how the poor are maintained in the Seven Provinces.

" I am, dear Sir, your most affectionate servant,

"SAM. JOHNSON."

I am sorry to observe that, neither in my own minutes, nor in my letters to Johnson, which have been preserved by him, can I find any information how the poor are maintained in the Seven Provinces. But I shall extract from one of my letters what I learnt concerning the other subject of his curiosity.

" I have made all possible inquiry with respect to the Frisick language,* and find that it has been less cultivated than any other of the northern dialects; a certain proof of which is their deficiency of books. Of the old Frisick, there are no remains, except some ancient laws preserved by Schotanus in his ' Beschryvinge van die Heerlykheid van Friesland;' and his ' Historia Frisica.' I have not yet been able to find these books. Professor Trotz, who formerly was of the University of Vranyken in Friesland, and is at present preparing an edition of all the Frisick laws, gave me this information. Of the modern Frisick, or what is spoken by the boors of this day, I have procured a specimen. It is Gisbert

Japix's '*Rymelerie*,' which is the only book that they have. It is amazing that they have no translation of the Bible, no treatises of devotion, nor even any of the ballads and story-books which are so agreeable to country people. You shall have Japix by the first convenient opportunity. I doubt not to pick up Schotanus. Mynheer Trotz has promised me his assistance."

Early in 1764 Johnson paid a visit to the Langton family, at their seat of Langton, in Lincolnshire, where he passed some time, much to his satisfaction. His friend, Bennet Langton, it will not be doubted, did everything in his power to make the place agreeable to so illustrious a guest; and the elder Mr. Langton and his lady, being fully capable of understanding his value, were not wanting in attention. He, however, told me that old Mr. Langton, though a man of considerable learning, had so little allowance to make for his occasional "laxity of talk," that because, in the course of discussion, he sometimes mentioned what might be said in favour of the peculiar tenets of the Romish church, he went to his grave believing him to be of that communion.

Johnson, during his stay at Langton, had the advantage of a good library, and saw several gentlemen of the neighbourhood. I have obtained from Mr. Langton, the following particulars of this period.

He was now fully convinced that he could not have been satisfied with a country living: for, talking of a respectable clergyman in Lincolnshire, he observed, "This man, Sir, fills up the duties of his life well. I approve of him, but could not imitate him."

To a lady who endeavoured to vindicate herself from blame for neglecting social attention to worthy neighbours, by saying, "I would go to them if it would do them any good;" he said, "What good, Madam, do you expect to have in your power to do them? It is showing them respect, and that is doing them good."

So socially accommodating was he, that once, when Mr. Langton and he were driving together in a coach, and Mr. Langton complained of being sick, he insisted that they should go out, and sit on the back of it in the open air, whi h they did; and being sensible how strange the appearance must be, observed that a countryman whom they saw in a field would probably be thinking, "If these two madmen should come down, what would become of me!"

Soon after his return to London, which was in February, was founded that club which existed long without a name, but at Mr. Garrick's funeral became distinguished by the title of THE LITERARY CLUB. Sir Joshua Reynolds had the merit of being the first proposer of it, to which Johnson acceded; and the original members were, Sir Joshua Reynolds, Dr. Johnson, Mr. Edmund Burke, Dr. Nugent, Mr. Beauclerk, Mr. Langton, Dr. Goldsmith, Mr. Chamier, and Sir John Hawkins. They met at the Turk's Head, in Gerrard-street, Soho, one evening in every week, at seven, and generally continued their conversation till a pretty late hour. This club has been gradually increased to its present number, thirty-five. After about ten years, instead of supping weekly, it was resolved to dine together once a fortnight during the meeting of Parliament. Their original tavern having been converted into a private house, they moved first to Prince's, in Sackville-street, then to Le Telier's, in Dover-street, and now meet at Parsloe's, St. James's-street. Between the time of its formation, and the time at which the work is passing through the press (June, 1792),[1] the following persons, now dead, were members of it : Mr. Dunning (afterwards Lord Ashburton), Mr. Samuel Dyer, Mr. Garrick, Dr. Shipley (Bishop of St. Asaph), Mr. Vesey, Mr. Thomas Warton, and Dr. Adam Smith. The present members are, Mr. Burke, Mr. Langton, Lord Charlemont, Sir Robert Chambers, Dr. Percy (Bishop of Dromore), Dr. Barnard (Bishop of Killaloe), Dr. Marlay (Bishop of Clonfert), Mr. Fox, Dr. George Fordyce, Sir William Scott, Sir Joseph Banks, Sir Charles Bunbury, Mr. Windham of Norfolk, Mr. Sheridan, Mr. Gibbon, Sir William Jones, Mr. Colman, Mr. Steevens, Dr. Burney, Dr. Joseph Warton, Mr. Malone, Lord Ossory, Lord Spencer, Lord Lucan, Lord Palmerston, Lord Eliot, Lord Macartney, Mr. Richard Burke, junior, Sir William Hamilton, Dr. Warren, Mr. Courtenay, Dr. Hinchliffe (Bishop of Peterborough), the Duke of Leeds, Dr. Douglas (Bishop of Salisbury), and the writer of this account.[2]

Sir John Hawkins[3] represents himself as a "*seceder*" from this society, and assigns as the reason of his "*withdrawing*" himself from it, that its late hours were inconsistent with his domestic arrangements

---

[1] The second edition is here spoken of.—MALONE.

[2] The Literary Club has since been deprived, by death, of Dr. Hinchliffe (Bishop of Peterborough), Mr. Gibbon, Sir William Jones, Mr. Richard Burke, Mr. Colman, Mr. Boswell (the author of this work), the Marquis of Bath, Dr. Warren, Mr. Burke, the Rev. Dr. Farmer, the Duke of Leeds, the Earl of Lucan, James Earl of Charlemont, Mr. Steevens, Dr. Warton, Mr. Langton, Lord Palmerston, Dr. Fordyce, Dr. Marlay (Bishop of Waterford), Sir William Hamilton, Sir Robert Chambers, Lord Eliot, Lord Macartney, Dr. Barnard (Bishop of Limerick), Mr. Fox, Dr. Horsley (Bishop of St. Asaph), Dr. Douglas (Bishop of Salisbury), and Dr. French Lawrence. Its latest, and its irreparable loss was that of the Right Hon. William Windham, the delight and admiration of this society, and of every other with whom he ever associated. Of the persons above-mentioned some were chosen members of it after the preceding account was written. It has since that time acquired Sir Charles Blagden, Major Rennell, the Hon. Frederick North, the Right Hon. George Canning, Mr. Marsden, the Right Hon. J. H. Frere, the Right Hon. Thomas Grenville, the Rev. Dr. Vincent, Dean of Westminster, Mr. William Lock, jun., Mr. George Ellis, Lord Minto, the Right Hon. Sir William Grant (Master of the Rolls), Sir George Staunton, Bart., Mr. Charles Wilkins, the Right Honourable Sir William Drummond, Sir Henry Halford, M.D., Sir Henry Englefield, Bart., Henry Lord Holland, John Earl of Aberdeen, Mr. Charles Hatchett, Mr. Charles Vaughan, Mr. Humphrey Davy, and the Rev. Dr. Burney. The club, some years after Mr. Boswell's death, removed (in 1799) from Parsloe's to the Thatched House, in St. James's-street, where they still continue to meet.

The total number of those who have been members of this club, from its foundation to the present time (October, 1810), is seventy-six, of whom fifty-five have been authors. Of the seventy-six members above-mentioned, forty-three are dead; thirty-three living.—MALONE.

[3] Life of Johnson, p. 425.—BOSWELL.

In this he is not accurate ; for the fact was that he one evening attacked Mr. Burke in so rude a manner that all the company testified their displeasure, and at their next meeting his reception was such that he never came again.[1]

He is equally inaccurate with respect to Mr. Garrick, of whom he says, "he trusted that the least intimation of a desire to come among us would procure him a ready admission ;" but in this he was mistaken. Johnson consulted me upon it, and when I could find no objection to receive him, exclaimed, "He will disturb us by his buffoonery ;" and afterwards so managed matters that he was never formally proposed, and, by consequence, never admitted.[2]

In justice both to Mr. Garrick and Dr. Johnson, I think it necessary to rectify this mis-statement. The truth is, that not very long after the institution of our club, Sir Joshua Reynolds was speaking of it to Garrick. "I like it much," said he, "I think I shall be of you." When Sir Joshua mentioned this to Dr. Johnson, he was much displeased with the actor's conceit. "*He'll be of us*," said Johnson, "how does he know we will *permit* him ? The first duke in England has no right to hold such language." However, when Garrick was regularly proposed some time afterwards, Johnson, though he had taken a momentary offence at his arrogance, warmly and kindly supported him, and he was accordingly elected,[3] was a most agreeable member, and continued to attend our meetings to the time of his death.

Mrs. Piozzi[4] has also given a similar misrepresentation of Johnson's treatment of Garrick in this particular, as if he had used these contemptuous expressions :—"If Garrick *does* apply, I'll black-ball him.— Surely, one ought to sit in a society like ours,

> ' Unelbow'd by a gamester, pimp, or player.' "

I am happy to be enabled by such unquestionable authority as that of Sir Joshua Reynolds, as well as from my own knowledge, to vindicate at once the heart of Johnson and the social merit of Garrick.

In this year, except what he may have done in revising Shakspeare, we do not find that he laboured much in literature. He wrote a review of Grainger's "Sugar Cane," a poem, in the "London Chronicle." He told me, that Dr. Percy wrote the greatest part of this review ; but, I imagine, he did not recollect it distinctly, for it appears to be mostly, if

---

[1] From Sir Joshua Reynolds.—BOSWELL. The knight having refused to pay his portion of the reckoning for supper, because he usually eat no supper at home, Johnson observed "Sir John, Sir, is a very *unclubable* man."—BURNEY.

[2] Life of Johnson, p. 425.—BOSWELL.

[3] Mr. Garrick was elected in March, 1773.—MALONE.

[4] Letters to and from Dr. Johnson, vol. ii. p. 278.—BOSWELL.

not altogether, his own. He also wrote in the "Critical Review," an account of Goldsmith's excellent poem, "The Traveller."

The ease and independence to which he had at last attained by royal munificence, increased his natural indolence. In his "Meditations," he thus accuses himself:—"Good Friday, April 20, 1764. I have made no reformation : I have lived totally useless, more sensual in thought, and more addicted to wine and meat."[1] And next morning he thus feelingly complains : "My indolence, since my last reception of the sacrament, has sunk into grosser sluggishness, and my dissipation spread into wilder negligence.   My thoughts have been clouded with sensuality ; and, except that from the beginning of this year I have, in some measure, forborne excess of strong drinks, my appetites have predominated over my reason. A kind of strange oblivion has overspread me, so that I know not what has become of the last year, and perceive that incidents and intelligence pass over me without leaving any impression." He then solemnly says, "This is not the life to which heaven is promised;"[2] and he earnestly resolves an amendment.

It was his custom to observe certain days with a pious abstraction : viz., New-year's day, the day of his wife's death, Good Friday, Easter-day, and his own birthday. He this year says, "I have now spent fifty-five years in resolving : having, from the earliest time almost that I can remember, been forming schemes of a better life. I have done nothing. The need of doing, therefore, is pressing, since the time of doing is short. O God, grant me to resolve aright, and to keep my resolutions, for Jesus Christ's sake. Amen."[3] Such a tenderness of conscience, such a fervent desire of improvement, will rarely be found. It is, surely, not decent in those who are hardened in indifference to spiritual improvement, to treat this pious anxiety of Johnson with contempt.

About this time he was afflicted with a very severe return of the hypochondriac disorder, which was ever lurking about him. He was so ill, as, notwithstanding his remarkable love of company, to be entirely averse to society, the most fatal symptom of that malady.   Dr. Adams told me, that, as an old friend he was admitted to visit him, and that he found him in a deplorable state, sighing, groaning, talking to himself, and restlessly walking from room to room. He then used this emphatical expression of the misery which he felt : "I would consent to have a limb amputated to recover my spirits."

Talking to himself was, indeed, one of his singularities ever since I knew him. I was certain that he was frequently uttering pious ejaculations; for fragments of the Lord's Prayer have been distinctly

Prayers and Meditations, p. 53.—BOSWELL.   [2] Ibid. p 1
[3] Ibid. p. 584.

overheard.[1] His friend, Mr. Thomas Davies, of whom Churchill says,

> " That Davies hath a very pretty wife,—"

when Dr. Johnson muttered—"lead us not into temptation," used, with waggish and gallant humour, to whisper Mrs. Davies, " You, my dear, are the cause of this."

He had another particularity, of which none of his friends ever ventured to ask an explanation. It appeared to me some superstitious habit, which he had contracted early, and from which he had never called upon his reason to disentangle him. This was his anxious care to go out or in at a door or passage, by a certain number of steps from a certain point, or at least so as that either his right or his left foot (I am not certain which), should constantly make the first actual movement when he came close to the door or passage. Thus I conjecture ; for I have, upon innumerable occasions, observed him suddenly stop, and then seem to count his steps with a deep earnestness ; and when he had neglected, or gone wrong in this sort of magical movement, I have seen him go back again, put himself in a proper posture to begin the ceremony, and, having gone through it, break from his abstraction, walk briskly on, and join his companion. A strange instance of something of this nature, even when on horseback, happened when he was in the Isle of Sky.[2] Sir Joshua Reynolds has observed him to go a good way about, rather than cross a particular alley in Leicester-fields ; but this Sir Joshua imputed to his having had some disagreeable recollection associated with it.

That the most minute singularities which belonged to him, and made very observable parts of his appearance and manner, may not be omitted, it is requisite to mention, that while talking, or even musing as he sat in his chair, he commonly held his head to one side towards his right shoulder, and shook it in a tremulous manner, moving his body backwards and forwards, and rubbing his left knee in the same direc-

---

[1] It used to be imagined at Mr. Thrale's, when Johnson retired to a window or corner of the room, by perceiving his lips in motion, and hearing a murmur without audible articulation that he was praying; but this was not always the case, for I was once, perhaps unperceived by him, writing at a table, so near the place of his retreat, that I heard him repeating some lines in an ode of Horace, over and over again, as if by iteration to exercise the organs of speech, and fix the ode in his memory :

> *Audiet cives acuisse ferrum,*
> *Quo graves* Persæ *melius perirent*
> *Audiet pugnas . . . .*

> "Our sons shall hear, shall hear to latest times,
> Of Roman arms with civil gore imbued,
> Which better had the Persian foe subdued."—Francis.

It was during the American war.—Burney.

[2] Journal of a Tour to the Hebrides 3rd edit. p. 316.—Boswell.

tion, with the palm of his hand. In the intervals of articulating, he made various sounds with his mouth ; sometimes as if ruminating, or what is called chewing the cud, sometimes giving a half whistle, sometimes making his tongue play backwards from the roof of his mouth, as if chuckling like a hen, and sometimes protruding it against his upper gums in front, as if pronouncing quickly under his breath, *too, too, too,* all this accompanied sometimes with a thoughtful look, but more frequently with a smile. Generally when he had concluded a period, in the course of a dispute, by which time he was a good deal exhausted by violence and vociferation, he used to blow out his breath like a whale. This, I suppose, was a relief to his lungs ; and seemed in him to be a contemptuous mode of expression, as if he had made the arguments of his opponent fly like chaff before the wind.

DR. PERCY.

I am fully aware how very obvious an occasion I here give for the sneering jocularity of such as have no relish of an exact likeness; which to render complete, he who draws it must not disdain the slightest strokes. But if witlings should be inclined to attack this account, let them have the candour to quote what I have offered in my defence.

He was for some time in the summer at Easton Maudit, Northamptonshire, on a visit to the Reverend Dr. Percy, now Bishop of Dromore. Whatever dissatisfaction he felt at what he considered a slow progress in intellectual improvement, we find that his heart was tender, and his affections warm, as appears from the following very kind letter :—

"TO JOSHUA REYNOLDS, ESQ., IN LEICESTER FIELDS, LONDON.

"*At the Rev. Mr. Percy's, at Easton Maudit, Northamptonshire,*
"DEAR SIR,   (*by Castle Ashby*), *Aug.* 19, 1764.

"I did not hear of your sickness till I heard likewise of your recovery, and therefore escaped that part of your pain, which every man must feel, to whom you are known as you are known to me.

"Having had no particular account of your disorder, I know not in what state it has left you. If the amusement of my company can exhilarate the languor of a slow recovery, I will not delay a day to come to you; for I know not how I can so effectually promote my own pleasure as by pleasing you, or my own interest as by preserving you, in whom, if I should lose you, I should lose almost the only man whom I call a friend.

"Pray let me hear of you from yourself, or from dear Miss Reynolds.[1] Make my compliments to Mr. Mudge. I am, dear Sir,

"Your most affectionate and most humble servant,

"SAM. JOHNSON."

Early in the year 1765 he paid a short visit to the University of Cambridge, with his friend Mr. Beauclerk. There is a lively picturesque account of his behaviour on this visit, in the "Gentleman's Magazine" for March, 1785, being an extract of a letter from the late Dr. John Sharp. The two following sentences are very characteristical : "He drank his large potations of tea with me, interrupted by many an indignant contradiction, and many a noble sentiment."—"Several persons got into his company the last evening at Trinity, where, about twelve, he began to be very great, stripped poor Mrs. Macaulay to the very skin, then gave her for his toast, and drank her in two bumpers."

The strictness of his self-examination, and scrupulous Christian humility, appear in his pious meditation on Easter-day this year :—

"I purpose again to partake of the blessed sacrament ; yet when I consider how vainly I have hitherto resolved at this annual commemoration of my Saviour's death, to regulate my life by his laws, I am almost afraid to renew my resolutions."

The concluding words are very remarkable, and show that he laboured under a severe depression of spirits :—

"Since the last Easter I have reformed no evil habit; my time has been unprofitably spent, and seems as a dream that has left nothing behind. *My memory grows confused, and I know not how the days pass over me.* Good Lord, deliver me !"[2]

No man was more gratefully sensible of any kindness done to him than Johnson. There is a little circumstance in his diary this year which shows him in a very amiable light :—

"July 2. I paid Mr. Simpson ten guineas, which he had formerly lent me in my necessity, and for which Tetty expressed her gratitude."

"July 8. I lent Mr. Simpson ten guineas more."

Here he had the pleasing opportunity of doing the same kindness to

[1] Sir Joshua's sister, for whom Johnson had a particular affection, and to whom he wrote many letters which I have seen, and which I am sorry her too nice delicacy will not permit to be published.—BOSWELL.

[2] Prayers and Meditations, p. 61.—BOSWELL.

an old friend, which he had formerly received from him. Indeed his liberality as to money was very remarkable. The next article in his diary is,—" July 16th, I received seventy-five pounds. Lent Mr. Davies twenty-five."

Trinity College, Dublin, at this time surprised Johnson with a spontaneous compliment of the highest academical honours, by creating him Doctor of Laws. The diploma, which is in my possession, is as follows:—

" *OMNIBUS ad quos præsentes literæ pervenerint, salutem. Nos Præpositus et Socii Seniores Collegii sacrosanctæ et individuæ Trinitatis Reginæ Elizabethæ juxta Dublin, testamur,* Samueli Johnson, *Armigero, ob egregiam scriptorum elegantiam et utilitatem, gratiam concessam fuisse pro gradu Doctoratûs in utroque Jure, octavo die Julii, Anno Domini millesimo septingentesimo sexagesimo-quinto. In cujus rei testimonium singulorum manus et sigillum quo in hisce utimur apposuimus ; vicesimo tertio die Julii, Anno Domini millesimo septingentesimo sexagesimo-quinto.*

GUL. CLEMENT.   FRAN. ANDREWS.   R. MURRAY.
THO. WILSON.   *Præp^s.*   ROB^{tus} LAW.
THO. LELAND.   MICH. KEARNEY."

This unsolicited mark of distinction, conferred on so great a literary character, did much honour to the judgment and liberal spirit of that learned body. Johnson acknowledged the favour in a letter to Dr. Leland, one of their number ; but I have not been able to obtain a copy of it.[1]

He appears this year to have been seized with a temporary fit of ambition, for he had thoughts both of studying law and of engaging in politics. His " Prayer before the Study of Law," is truly admirable :—

" *Sept.* 26, 1765.

" Almighty God, the giver of wisdom, without whose help resolutions are vain, without whose blessing study is ineffectual; enable me, if it be thy will, to attain such knowledge as may qualify me to direct the doubtful, and instruct the ignorant ; to prevent wrongs and terminate contentions; and grant that I

---

[1] Since the publication of the edition in 1804, a copy of this letter has been obligingly communicated to me by John Leland, Esq., son to the learned Historian, to whom it is addressed:

"TO THE REV. DR. LELAND.

" SIR,

" Among the names subscribed to the degree which I have had the honour of receiving from the University of Dublin, I find none of which I have any personal knowledge but those of Dr. Andrews and yourself.

" Men can be estimated by those who know them not, only as they are represented by those who know them : and therefore I flatter myself that I owe much of the pleasure which this distinction gives me, to your concurrence with Dr. Andrews in recommending me to the learned Society.

may use that knowledge which I shall attain, to thy glory and my own salvation, for Jesus Christ's sake.   Amen." [1]

His prayer in the view of becoming a politician is entitled, " Engaging in Politics with H——n," no doubt, his friend, the Right Honourable William Gerard Hamilton, for whom, during a long acquaintaince, he had a great esteem, and to whose conversations he once paid this high compliment : " I am very unwilling to be left alone, Sir, and therefore I go with my company down the first pair of stairs, in some hopes that they may, perhaps, return again : I go with you, Sir, as far as the street-door."   In what particular department he intended to engage,[2] does not appear, nor can Mr. Hamilton explain.   His prayer is in general terms :

" Enlighten my understanding with knowledge of right, and govern my will by thy laws, that no deceit may mislead me, nor temptation corrupt me ; that I may always endeavour to do good, and hinder evil." [3]

There is nothing upon the subject in his diary.

This year was distinguished by his being introduced into the family of Mr. Thrale, one of the most eminent brewers in England, and member of parliament for the borough of Southwark.   Foreigners are not a little amazed when they hear of brewers, distillers, and men in similar departments of trade, held forth as persons of considerable consequence. In this great commercial country it is natural that a situation which produces much wealth should be considered as very respectable ; and, no doubt, honest industry is entitled to esteem.   But, perhaps, the too rapid advances of men of low extraction tends to lessen the value of that distinction by birth and gentility which has ever been found beneficial to the grand scheme of subordination.   Johnson used to give this

---

" Having desired the Provost to return my general thanks to the University, I beg that you Sir, will accept my particular and immediate acknowledgments.

" I am, Sir,

" Your most obedient and most humble servant,

" Johnson's-court, Fleet-street,   " SAM. JOHNSON."

London, Oct. 17, 1765.

I have not been able to recover the letter which Johnson wrote to Dr. Andrews on this occasion.—MALONE.

[1] Prayers and Meditations, p. 66.—BOSWELL.

[2] In the Preface to a late Collection of Mr. Hamilton's Pieces, it has been observed, that our author was, by the generality of Johnson's words, " led to suppose that he was seized with a temporary fit of ambition, and that hence he was induced to apply his thoughts to law and politics.   But Mr. Boswell was certainly mistaken in this respect; and these words merely allude to Johnson's having at that time entered into some engagement with Mr. Hamilton occasionally to furnish him with his sentiments on the great political topics which should be considered in Parliament."   In consequence of this engagement, Johnson, in November, 1766, wrote a very valuable tract, entitled, " Considerations on Corn," which is printed as an Appendix to the works of Mr. Hamilton, published by T. Payne, in 1808.—MALONE.

[3] Prayers and Meditations, p. 67.—BOSWELL.

account of the rise of Mr. Thrale's father : " He worked at six shillings
a week for twenty years in the great brewery, which afterwards was his
own. The proprietor of it [1] had an only daughter, who was married to a
nobleman. It was not fit that a peer should continue the business. On
the old man's death, therefore, the brewery was to be sold. To find a
purchaser for so large a property was a difficult matter : and after some
time, it was suggested, that it would be advisable to treat with Thrale,
a sensible, active, honest man, who had been employed in the house, and
to transfer the whole to him for thirty thousand pounds, security being
taken upon the property. This was accordingly settled. In eleven
years Thrale paid the purchase-money. He acquired a large fortune,
and lived to be a member of parliament for Southwark.[2] But what was
most remarkable was the liberality with which he used his riches. He
gave his son and daughters the best education. The esteem which his
good conduct procured him from the nobleman who had married his
master's daughter made him be treated with much attention ; and his
son, both at school and at the University of Oxford, associated with
young men of the first rank. His allowance from his father after he
left college was splendid ; not less than a thousand a year. This, in a
man who had risen as old Thrale did, was a very extraordinary instance
of generosity. He used to say, ' If this young dog does not find so
much after I am gone as he expects, let him remember that he has had
a great deal in my own time.' "

The son, though in affluent circumstances, had good sense enough to
carry on his father's trade, which was of such extent, that I remember
he once told me he would not quit it for an annuity of ten thousand a
year : " Not," said he, " that I get ten thousand a year by it, but it is
an estate to a family." Having left daughters only, the property was
sold for the immense sum of one hundred and thirty-five thousand
pounds : a magnificent proof of what may be done by fair trade in a
long period of time.

There may be some who think that a new system of gentility[3] might

---

[1] The predecessor of old Thrale was Edmund Halsey, Esq.; the nobleman who married his
daughter, was Lord Cobham, great uncle of the Marquis of Buckingham. But I believe, Dr.
Johnson was mistaken in assigning so very low an origin to Mr. Thrale. The Clerk of
St. Alban's, a very aged man, told me, that he (the elder Thrale), married a sister of Mr.
Halsey. It is at least certain that the family of Thrale was of some consideration in that
town : in the abbey church is a handsome monument to the memory of Mr. John Thrale, late
of London, Merchant, who died in 1704, aged 54; Margaret, his wife, and three of their
children who died young, between the years 1676 and 1690. The arms upon this monument
are, paly of eight, gules and or, impaling, ermine, on a chief indented vert, three wolves (or
gryphons) heads, or, couped at the neck :—Crest on a ducal coronet, a tree, vert.—BLAKEWAY

[2] In 1733 he served the office of High Sheriff for Surrey ; and died April 9, 1758.—
A. CHALMERS.

[3] Mrs. Burney informs me that she heard Dr. Johnson say, " An English Merchant is a
new species of Gentleman." He, perhaps, had in his mind the following ingenious passage
in the " Conscious Lovers," Act. iv., Scene ii., where Mr. Sealand thus addresses Sir John

be established upon principles totally different from what have hitherto prevailed. Our present heraldry, it may be said, is suited to the barbarous times in which it had its origin. It is chiefly founded upon ferocious merit, upon military excellence. Why, in civilised times, we may be asked, should there not be rank and honours upon principles, which, independent of long custom, are certainly not less worthy, and which, when once allowed to be connected with elevation and precedency, would obtain the same dignity in our imagination? Why should not the knowledge, the skill, the expertness, the assiduity, and the spirited hazards of trade and commerce, when crowned with success, be entitled to give those flattering distinctions by which mankind are so universally captivated?

Such are the specious, but false, arguments for a proposition which always will find numerous advocates, in a nation where men are every day starting up from obscurity to wealth. To refute them is needless. The general sense of mankind cries out, with irresistible force, " *Un gentilhomme est toujours gentilhomme.*"

Mr. Thrale had married Miss Hesther Lynch Salisbury, of good Welch extraction, a lady of lively talents, improved by education. That Johnson's introduction into Mr. Thrale's family, which contributed so much to the happiness of his life was owing to her desire for his conversation, is a very probable and the general supposition; but it is not the truth. Mr. Murphy, who was intimate with Mr. Thrale, having spoken very highly of Dr. Johnson, he was requested to make them acquainted. This being mentioned to Johnson, he accepted of an invitation to dinner at Thrale's, and was so much pleased with his reception, both by Mr. and Mrs. Thrale, and they so much pleased with him, that his invitations to their house were more and more frequent, till at last he became one of the family, and an apartment was appropriated to him, both in their house at Southwark, and in their villa at Streatham.

Johnson had a very sincere esteem for Mr. Thrale, as a man of excellent principles, a good scholar, well skilled in trade, of a sound understanding, and of manners such as presented the character of a plain independent English 'Squire. As this family will frequently be mentioned in the course of the following pages, and as a false notion has prevailed that Mr. Thrale was inferior, and in some degree insignificant, compared with Mrs. Thrale, it may be proper to give a true

Bevil: "Give me leave to say, that we merchants are a species of gentry that have grown into the world this last century, and are as honourable, and almost as useful as you landed folks, that have always thought yourselves so much above us; for your trading forsooth is extended no farther than a load of hay, or a fat ox. You are pleasant people, indeed! because you are generally bred up to be lazy, therefore, I warrant you, industry is dishonourable" —BOSWELL.

state of the case, from the authority of Johnson himself in his own words.

"I know no man," said he, "who is more master of his wife and family than Thrale. If he but holds up a finger he is obeyed. It is

MR. AND MRS. THRALE.

a great mistake to suppose that she is above him in literary attainments. She is more flippant, but he has ten times her learning ; he is a regular scholar, but her learning is that of a school-boy in one of the lower forms." My readers may naturally wish for some representation of the figures of this couple. Mr. Thrale was tall, well-proportioned, and stately. As for *Madam*, or *my Mistress*, by which epithets Johnson used to mention Mrs. Thrale, she was short, plump, and brisk. She has herself given us a lively view of the idea which Johnson had of her person, on her appearing before him in a dark-coloured gown : "You little creatures should never wear those sort of clothes, however ; they are unsuitable in every way. What ! have not all insects gay colours ?"[1] Mr. Thrale gave his wife a liberal indulgence, both in the choice of their company, and in the mode of entertaining them. He understood and valued Johnson, without remission, from their first acquaintance to the day of his death. Mrs. Thrale was enchanted with Johnson's conversation for its own sake, and had also a very allowable vanity in appearing to be honoured with the attention of so celebrated a man.

Nothing could be more fortunate for Johnson than this connection. He had at Mr. Thrale's all the comforts and even luxuries of life : his melancholy was diverted, and his irregular habits lessened by association with an agreeable and well-ordered family. He was treated with the utmost respect and even affection. The vivacity of Mrs. Thrale's

[1] Mrs. Piozzi's Anecdotes, p. 279.—BOSWELL.

literary talk roused him to cheerfulness and exertion, even when they were alone. But this was not often the case ; for he found here a constant succession of what gave him the highest enjoyment—the society of the learned, the witty, and eminent in every way, who were assembled in numerous companies—called forth his wonderful powers, and gratified him with admiration, to which no man could be insensible.

In the October of this year[1] he at length gave to the world his edition of Shakspeare, which, if it had no other merit but that of producing his Preface, in which the excellences and defects of that immortal bard are displayed with a masterly hand, the nation would have had no reason to complain. A blind indiscriminate admiration of Shakspeare had exposed the British nation to the ridicule of foreigners. Johnson, by candidly admitting the faults of his poet, had the more credit in bestowing on him deserved and indisputable praise ; and doubtless none of all his panegyrists have done him half so much honour. Their praise was like that of a counsel upon his own side of the cause ; Johnson's was like the grave, well-considered, and impartial opinion of the judge, which falls from his lips with weight, and is received with reverence. What he did as a commentator has no small share of merit, though his researches were not so ample, and his investigations so acute as they might have been ; which we now certainly know from the labours of other able and ingenious critics who have followed him. He has enriched his edition with a concise account of each play, and of its characteristic excellence. Many of his notes have illustrated obscurities in the text, and placed passages eminent for beauty in a more conspicuous light ; and he has, in general, exhibited such a mode of annotation as may be beneficial to all subsequent editors.

His Shakspeare was virulently attacked by Mr. William Kenrick, who obtained the degree of LL.D. from a Scotch University, and wrote for the booksellers in a great variety of branches. Though he certainly was not without considerable merit, he wrote with so little regard to decency, and principles, and decorum, and in so hasty a manner, that his reputation was neither extensive nor lasting. I remember one evening, when some of his works were mentioned, Dr. Goldsmith said he had never heard of them ; upon which Dr. Johnson observed, " Sir, he is one of the many who have made themselves *public*, without making themselves *known*."

---

[1] From a letter written by Dr. Johnson to Dr. Joseph Warton, the day after the publication of his Shakspeare, Oct. 9, 1765 (see Wool's Memoirs of Dr. Warton, 4to. 1806) it appears that Johnson spent some time with that gentleman at Winchester in this year. In a letter written by Dr. Warton, to Mr. Thomas Warton, not long afterwards (January 28, 1766), is a paragraph which may throw some light on various passages in Dr. Warton's edition of Pope, relative to Johnson:—"I only dined with Johnson, who seemed cold and indifferent, and scarce said anything to me: perhaps he has heard what I said of his Shakspeare, or rather was offended at what I wrote to him :—as he pleases." The letter here alluded to, it is believed, has not been preserved : at least, it does not appear in the collection above referred to.—MALONE.

A young student of Oxford, of the name of Barclay, wrote an answer to Kenrick's review of Johnson's Shakspeare. Johnson was at first angry that Kenrick's attack should have the credit of an answer ; but, afterwards, considering the young man's good intention, he kindly noticed him, and probably would have done more, had not the young man died.

In his Preface to Shakspeare, Johnson treated Voltaire very con-temptuously, observing, upon some of his remarks, " These are the petty cavils of petty minds." Voltaire, in revenge, made an attack upon Johnson in one of his numerous literary sallies which I remember to have read ; but there being no general index to his voluminous works, have searched in vain, and therefore cannot quote it.[1]

Voltaire was an antagonist with whom I thought Johnson should not disdain to contend. I pressed him to answer. He said he perhaps might ; but he never did.

Mr. Burney having occasion to write to Johnson for some receipts for subscriptions to his Shakspeare, which Johnson had omitted to deliver when the money was paid, he availed himself of that opportunity of thanking Johnson for the great pleasure which he had received from the perusal of his Preface to Shakspeare ; which, although it excited much clamour against him at first, is now justly ranked among the most excellent of his writings. To this letter Johnson returned the following answer :—

" TO CHARLES BURNEY, ESQ., IN POLAND STREET

" SIR,

" I am sorry that your kindness to me has brought upon you so much trouble, though you have taken care to abate that sorrow, by the pleasure which I receive from your approbation. I defend my criticism in the same manner with you. We must confess the faults of our favourite to gain credit to our praise of his excellences. He that claims, either in himself or for another, the honours of perfection, will surely injure the reputation which he designs to assist.

" Be pleased to make my compliments to your family. I am, Sir,

" Your most obliged

" And most humble servant,

" *Oct.* 16, 1765.   " SAM. JOHNSON."

From one of his Journals I transcribed what follows :—

" At church, Oct.—65.

" To avoid all singularity. *Bonaventura.*[2]

---

[1] In the " Dictionnaire Philosophique," under the head " Art Dramatique."

[2] He was probably proposing to himself the model of this excellent person, who for his piety was named *the Seraphic Doctor*.—BOSWELL.

"To come in before service, and compose my mind by meditation, or by reading some portions of Scripture. *Tetty*.

"If I can hear the sermon, to attend it, unless attention be more troublesome than useful.

"To consider the act of prayer as a reposal of myself upon God, and a resignation of all into his holy hand."

END OF VOL I.

"Johnson started up and stood still. His Majesty approached him, and at once was courteously easy."

BOSWELL'S
LIFE OF JOHNSON

ILLUSTRATED

SAMUEL JOHNSON, LL.D.

VOL. II.

GEORGE ROUTLEDGE AND SONS

NEW YORK: 9 LAFAYETTE PLACE
LONDON, GLASGOW, AND MANCHESTER

CONTENTS OF VOLUME II.

CHAPTER I.—1766—1767.

Boswell returns to England—Voltaire's comparison of Pope and Dryden—Goldsmith's "Traveller," and "Deserted Village"—Renewal of the Suppers at the Mitre—Johnson's opinions of Rousseau—Specimens of his familiar Conversations—Letters to Bennet Langton—Johnson's Criticism on the Latin in Boswell's Thesis—Boswell's Reply—Publication of Mrs. Anna Williams's Miscellanies—Johnson advocates the Translation of the Bible in Gaelic—Cuthbert Shaw—The Hon. Thomas Hervey . **1**

CHAPTER II.—1767—1768.

Johnson introduced to George III. at Buckingham House—Visits Lichfield—Death of Catherine Chambers—Writes Prologue to Goldsmith's "Good-natured Man"—Boswell's account of Corsica published—Comparison of the Works of Fielding and Richardson—The Great Douglas Cause—St. Kilda—Johnson's Views of Conjugal Infidelity—Chastity and the Choice of a Wife—Baretti's Italy—Johnson visits Oxford—Returns to London—His contempt for Popular Liberty—Dr. Kenrick's Pamphlet—Johnson places Francis Barber at School—Conversational strictures on Thomson the Poet and Dr. Mounsey—Origin of the "Bear" epithet **23**

CHAPTER III.—1769.

Johnson appointed Professor of Ancient Literature—Boswell at the Stratford Jubilee—His account of Corsica—Scotch Gardening—Johnson and Boswell visit Mr. and Mrs. Thrale—Boswell introduces Johnson to General Paoli—Goldsmith's Tailor—Mrs. Montagu's Essay on Shakspeare—Foote—Baretti's Trial—Mrs. Williams's Tea Table—Johnson's Views of Romanism and Conversion to Popery—The Marriage Service **41**

CHAPTER IV.—1770—1771.

Johnson publishes "The False Alarm"—Letters to the Wartons, &c.—Dr. Maxwell's Collectanea—Johnson's Political Opinions—His general mode of Life—Love of Black-letter Books—Burton's "Anatomy of Melancholy"—Jacob Behmen—Dr. Priestley—French Novels—Père Boscovitch—Ossian—The Poetical Cobbler—Marriage—Foppery—The Poor of England—The Corn Laws—Mr. Burke—Fortune Hunters—Irish Clergy—Johnson publishes "Pamphlet on the Falkland Islands"—Mr. Strahan's effort to bring Johnson into Parliament—Boswell's Marriage—Johnson visits Lichfield and Ashbourne **67**

CHAPTER V.—1772.

Dr. Beattie—Boswell returns to London—Lord Monboddo—Scotch Church—Second Sight—Thirty-nine Articles—Royal Marriage Bill—Foote's Mimicry—Fourth Edition of the Dictionary prepared—Mr. Peyton—Origin of Languages—Flogging—Scottish Accent—Ghost Stories—Ranelagh—Hon. Thomas Erskine—General Oglethorpe—Goldsmith's Natural History—Johnson's advice to Authors—His Opinion on a point of Scotch Law **85**

CHAPTER VI.—1773.

CHAPTER VII.—1773.

CHAPTER VIII.—1773.

CHAPTER IX.—1775.

CHAPTER X.—1775.

CHAPTER XI.—1775.

CONTENTS.

LIST OF ILLUSTRATIONS.

VOL II.

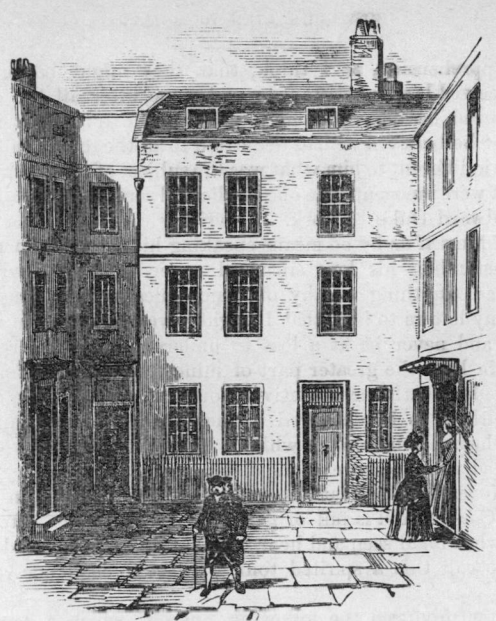

JOHNSON'S HOUSE IN JOHNSON'S-COURT.

CHAPTER I.—1766 1767.

IN 1764 and 1765 it should seem that Dr. Johnson was so busily employed with his edition of Shakspeare, as to have had little leisure for any other literary exertion, or, indeed, even for private correspondence. He did not favour me with a single letter for more than two years, for which it will appear that he afterwards apologised.

He was, however, at all times ready to give assistance to his friends, and others, in revising their works, and in writing for them, or greatly improving their dedications. In that courtly species of composition no man excelled Dr. Johnson. Though the loftiness of his mind prevented him from ever dedicating in his own person, he wrote a very great number of dedications for others. Some of these, the persons who were favoured with them, are unwilling should be mentioned, from a too anxious apprehension, as I think, that they might be suspected of having received larger assistance ; and some, after all the diligence I have bestowed, have escaped my inquiries. He told me, a great many years ago, " he believed he had dedicated to all the royal family round ; " and it was indifferent to him what was the subject of the work dedicated, provided it were innocent. He once dedicated some music for the German flute, to Edward Duke of York. In writing dedications for others, he considered himself as by no means speaking his own sentiments.

Notwithstanding his long silence, I never omitted to write to him, when I had anything worthy of communicating. I generally kept copies of my letters to him, that I might have a full view of our correspondence, and never be at a loss to understand any reference in his letters. He kept the greater part of mine very carefully ; and a short time before his death was attentive enough to seal them up in bundles, and order them to be delivered to me, which was accordingly done. Amongst them I found one, of which I had not made a copy, and which I own I read with pleasure at the distance of almost twenty years. It is dated November, 1765, at the palace of Pascal Paoli, in Corte, the capital of Corsica, and is full of generous enthusiasm. After giving a sketch of what I had seen and heard in that island, it proceeded thus :— " I dare to call this a spirited tour. I dare to challenge your approbation."

This letter produced the following answer, which I found on my arrival at Paris :—

À M. M. BOSWELL, CHEZ M. WATERS, BANQUIER, À PARIS.

" DEAR SIR,   *Johnson's-court, Fleet-street, January* 14, 1766.
" Apologies are seldom of any use. We will delay till your arrival the reasons, good or bad, which have made me such a sparing and ungrateful correspondent. Be assured, for the present, that nothing has lessened either the esteem or love with which I dismissed you at Harwich. Both have been increased by all that I have been told of you by yourself or others ; and when you return, you will return to an unaltered, and, I hope, unalterable friend.

" All that you have to fear from me is the vexation of disappointing me. No man loves to frustrate expectations which have been formed in his favour ; and the pleasure which I promise myself from your journals and remarks is so great, that perhaps no degree of attention or discernment will be sufficient to afford it.

" Come home, however, and take your chance. I long to see you, and to hear you ; and hope that we shall not be so long separated again. Come home, and expect such welcome as is due to him, whom a wise and noble curiosity has led, where perhaps no native of this country ever was before.

" I have no news to tell you that can deserve your notice ; nor would I willingly lessen the pleasure that any novelty may give you at your return. I am afraid we shall find it difficult to keep among us a mind which has been so long feasted with variety. But let us try what esteem and kindness can effect.

" As your father's liberality has indulged you with so long a ramble, I doubt not but you will think his sickness, or even his desire to see you, a sufficient reason for hastening your return. The longer we live, and the more we think, the higher value we learn to put on the friendship and tenderness of parents and of friends. Parents we can have but once; and he promises himself too much, who enters life with the expectation of finding many friends. Upon some motive, I hope, that you will be here soon; and am willing to think that it will be an inducement to your return, that it is sincerely desired by,

" Dear Sir, your affectionate and humble servant,

" SAM. JOHNSON."

I returned to London in February, and found Dr. Johnson in a good house in Johnson's-court, Fleet-street, in which he had accommodated Miss Williams with an apartment on the ground-floor, while Mr. Levett occupied his post in the garret; his faithful Francis was still attending upon him. He received me with much kindness. The fragments of our first conversation, which I have preserved, are these: I told him that Voltaire, in a conversation with me, had distinguished Pope and Dryden thus :—" Pope drives a handsome chariot, with a couple of neat trim nags; Dryden a coach, and six stately horses." JOHNSON : "Why Sir, the truth is, they both drive coaches and six; but Dryden's horses are either galloping or stumbling : Pope's go at a steady even trot." [1] He said of Goldsmith's " Traveller," which had been published in my absence, " There has not been so fine a poem since Pope's time."

And here it is proper to settle, with authentic precision, what has long floated in public report, as to Johnson's being himself the author of a considerable part of that poem. Much, no doubt, both of the sentiments and expression were derived from conversation with him : and it was certainly submitted to his friendly revision : but in the year 1783, he at my request marked with a pencil the lines which he had furnished, which are only line 420th,

" To stop too fearful, and too faint to go;"

and the concluding ten lines, except the last couplet but one, which I distinguish by the italic character :—

" How small of all that human hearts endure,
That part which kings or laws can cause or cure.
Still to ourselves in every place consign'd,
Our own felicity we make or find ;
With secret course, which no loud storms annoy,
Glides the smooth current of domestic joy:

[1] It is remarkable that Mr. Gray (" Ode on the Progress of Poesy ") has employed some what the same image to characterise Dryden. He, indeed, furnishes his car with but two horses; but they are of " ethereal race :"

" Behold where Dryden's less presumptuous car,
Wide o'er the fields of glory bear
Two coursers of ethereal race,
With necks in thunder cloth'd, and long-resounding pace."—BOSWELL.

> *The lifted axe, the agonizing wheel,*
> *Luke's iron crown, and Damien's bed of steel,*
> To men remote from power, but rarely known,
> Leave reason, faith, and conscience, all our own."

He added, " These are all of which I can be sure." They bear a small
proportion to the whole, which consists of four hundred and thirty-eight
verses. Goldsmith, in the couplet which he inserted, mentions *Luke* as
a person well known, and superficial readers have passed it over quite
smoothly ; while those of more attention have been as much perplexed
by *Luke* as by *Lydiat*, in " The Vanity of Human Wishes." The truth
is, that Goldsmith himself was in a mistake. In the " *Respublica
Hungarica*," there is an account of a desperate rebellion in the year
1514, headed by two brothers of the name of *Zeck*, George and Luke.
When it was quelled, *George*, not *Luke*, was punished by his head being
encircled with a red-hot iron crown : " *Coronâ candescente ferreâ coro-
natur*." The same severity of torture was exercised on the Earl of
Athol, one of the murderers of King James I. of Scotland.[1]

Dr. Johnson at the same time favoured me by marking the lines
which he furnished to Goldsmith's " Deserted Village," which are only
the last four :—

> ' That trade's proud empire hastes to swift decay,
> As ocean sweeps the labour'd mole away :
> While self-dependent power can time defy,
> As rocks resist the billows and the sky."

Talking of education, " People have now-a-days," said he, " got a
strange opinion that everything should be taught by lectures. Now, I
cannot see that lectures can do so much good as reading the books from
which the lectures are taken. I know nothing that can be best taught
by lectures, except where experiments are to be shown. You may teach
chemistry by lectures :—You might teach making of shoes by lectures ! "

At night I supped with him at the Mitre tavern, that we might renew
our social intimacy at the original place of meeting. But there was now
a considerable difference in his way of living. Having had an illness,
in which he was advised to leave off wine, he had, from that period,
continued to abstain from it, and drink only water, or lemonade.

I told him that a foreign friend of his, whom I had met with abroad,
was so wretchedly perverted to infidelity that he treated the hopes of
immortality with brutal levity : and said, " As man dies like a dog,
let him lie like a dog." JOHNSON : " *If* he dies like a dog, *let* him lie
like a dog." I added, that this man said to me, " I hate mankind, for
I think myself one of the best of them, and I know how bad I am."

---

[1] On the iron crown, see Mr. Steevens's note 7, on Act iv. sc. i. of "Richard III." It
seems to be alluded to in "Macbeth," Act iv. sc. i. "Thy crown does sear, &c." See also
Gough's "Camden." vol. iii. p. 396.—J. BLAKEWAY

Johnson : " Sir, he must be very singular in his opinion if he thinks himself one of the best of men, for none of his friends think him so."— He said, " No honest man could be a deist, for no man could be so after a fair examination of the proofs of Christianity." I named Hume. Johnson : "No, Sir ; Hume owned to a clergyman in the bishopric of Durham that he had never read the New Testament with attention."— I mentioned Hume's notion, that all who are happy are equally happy ; a little Miss with a new gown at a dancing-school ball, a general at the head of a victorious army, and an orator after having made an eloquent speech in a great assembly. Johnson : "Sir, that all who are happy are equally happy, is not true. A peasant and a philosopher may be equally *satisfied*, but not equally *happy*. Happiness consists in the multiplicity of agreeable consciousness. A peasant has not capacity for having equal happiness with a philosopher." I remember this very question very happily illustrated in opposition to Hume, by the Rev. Mr. Robert Brown, at Utrecht. " A small drinking-glass and a large one," said he, " may be equally full : but the large one holds more than the small." [1]

Dr. Johnson was very kind this evening, and said to me, "You have now lived five-and-twenty years, and you have employed them well." " Alas, Sir," said I, "I fear not. Do I know history ? Do I know mathematics ? Do I know law ? " Johnson : " Why, Sir, though you may know no science so well as to be able to teach it, and no profession so well as to be able to follow it, your general mass of knowledge of books and men renders you very capable to make yourself master of any science, or fit yourself for any profession." I mentioned that a gay friend had advised me against being a lawyer, because I should be excelled by plodding blockheads. Johnson : "Why, Sir, n the formulary and statutory part of law, a plodding blockhead may excel ; but in the ingenious and rational part of it a plodding blockhead can never excel."

I talked of the mode adopted by some to rise in the world, by courting great men, and asked him whether he had ever submitted to it. Johnson : "Why, Sir, I never was near enough to great men to

---

[1] Bishop Hall, in discussing this subject, has the same image : " Yet so conceive of these heavenly degrees that the least is glorious. *So do these vessels differ, that are all full.*" Epistles, Dec. iii. cp. 6. "Of the different degrees of heavenly glory." This most learned and ingenious writer, however, was not the first who suggested this image; for it is found also in an old book entitled "A Work worth the reading," by Charles Gibbon, 4to. 1591. In the fifth dialogue of this work, in which the question debated is, " whether there be degrees of glorie in heaven, or difference of paines in hell," one of the speakers observes, that "no doubt in the world to come, (where the least pleasure is unspeakable,) it cannot be but that he which hath bin most afflicted here, shall conceive and receive more exceeding joy than he which hath bin touched with lesse tribulation; and yet the joys of heaven are fitlie compared to *vessels filled with licour of all quantities ;* for everie man shall have his full measure there." By "*all* quantities" this writer, who seems to refer to a still more ancient author tha himself, I suppose, means *different* quantities.—Malone.

court them. You may be prudently attached to great men, and yet independent. You are not to do what you think wrong ; and, Sir, you are to calculate, and not to pay too dear for what you get. You must not give a shilling's worth of court for sixpence worth of good. But if you can get a shilling's worth of good for sixpence worth of court, you are a fool if you do not pay court."

He said, "If convents should be allowed at all, they should only be retreats for persons unable to serve the public, or who have served it. It is our first duty to serve society ; and, after we have done that, we may attend wholly to the salvation of our own souls. A youthful passion for abstracted devotion should not be encouraged."

I introduced the subject of second sight, and other mysterious manifestations ; the fulfilment of which, I suggested, might happen by chance. JOHNSON : "Yes, Sir, but they have happened so often, that mankind have agreed to think them not fortuitous."

I talked to him a great deal of what I had seen in Corsica, and of my intention to publish an account of it. He encouraged me by saying, "You cannot go to the bottom of the subject : but all that you tell us will be new to us. Give us as many anecdotes as you can."

Our next meeting at the Mitre was on Saturday the 15th of February, when I presented to him my old and most intimate friend, the Rev. Mr.

ROUSSEAU.

Temple, then of Cambridge. I having mentioned that I had passed some time with Rousseau, in his wild retreat, and having quoted some remark made by Mr. Wilkes, with whom I had spent many pleasant hours in Italy, Johnson said, sarcastically, "It seems, sir, you have kept very good company abroad, Rousseau and Wilkes ! " Thinking it enough to defend one at a time, I said nothing as to my gay friend, but answered with a smile, "My dear Sir, you don't call Rousseau bad company. Do you really think *him* a bad man ? " JOHNSON : "Sir, if you are talking jestingly of this, I don't talk with you. If you mean to be serious, I think him one of the worst of men ; a rascal, who ought to be hunted out of society, as he has been. Three or four nations have expelled him, and it is a shame that he is protected in this country." BOSWELL : "I don't deny, Sir, but that his novel may, perhaps, do harm ; but I cannot think his intention was bad." JOHNSON : "Sir, that will not do. We cannot prove any man's intention to be bad. You may shoot a man through the head, and say you intended to miss him ; but the judge will order you to be hanged. An alleged want of intention, when evil is committed, will not be allowed in a court of justice. Rousseau, Sir, is a very bad man. I would sooner sign a sentence for his transportation than that of any felon who has gone from the Old Bailey these many years. Yes, I should like to have him work in the plantations." BOSWELL : " Sir, do you think him as bad a man as Voltaire ? " JOHNSON : " Why, Sir, it is difficult to settle the proportion of iniquity between them."

This violence seemed very strange to me, who had read many of Rousseau's animated writings with great pleasure, and even edification ; had been much pleased with his society, and was just come from the continent where he was generally admired. Nor can I yet allow that he deserves the very severe censure which Johnson pronounced upon him. His absurd preference of savage to civilised life, and other singularities, are proofs rather of a defect in his understanding, than of any depravity in his heart. And notwithstanding the unfavourable opinion which many worthy men have expressed of his " *Profession de Foi du Vicaire Savoyard*," I cannot help admiring it as the performance of a man full of sincere reverential submission to Divine mystery, though beset with perplexing doubts : a state of mind to be viewed with pity rather than with anger.

On his favourite subject of subordination, Johnson said, " So far is it from being true that men are naturally equal, that no two people can be half an hour together, but one shall acquire an evident superiority over the other."

I mentioned the advice given us by philosophers, to console ourselves, when distressed or embarrassed, by thinking of those who are in a worse situation than ourselves. This, I observed, could not apply to all, for there must be some who have nobody worse than they are. JOHNSON : " Why, to be sure, Sir, there are ; but they don't know it. There is no being so poor and so contemptible, who does not think there is somebody still poorer, and still more contemptible."

As my stay in London at this time was very short, I had not many opportunities of being with Dr. Johnson ; but I felt my veneration for him in no degree lessened, by my having seen *multorum hominum more et urbes.* On the contrary, by having it in my power to compare him with many of the most celebrated persons of other countries, my admiration of his extraordinary mind was increased and confirmed.

The roughness, indeed, which sometimes appeared in his manners, was more striking to me now, from my having been accustomed to the studied, smooth, complying habits of the continent ; and I clearly recognised in him, not without respect for his honest conscientious zeal, the same indignant and sarcastical mode of treating every attempt to unhinge or weaken good principles.

One evening, when a young gentleman teased him with an account of the infidelity of his servant, who, he said, would not believe the scriptures, because he could not read them in the original tongues, and

be sure that they were not invented :—" Why, foolish fellow," said
Johnson, "has he any better authority for almost everything that he
believes ? " BOSWELL : " Then the vulgar, Sir, never can know they are
right, but must submit themselves to the learned." JOHNSON : " To be
sure, Sir. The vulgar are the children of the State, and must be taught
like children." BOSWELL : " Then, Sir, a poor Turk must be a Mahometan, just as a poor Englishman must be a Christian ? " JOHNSON :
" Why, yes, Sir ; and what then ? This, now, is such stuff as I used to
talk to my mother, when I first began to think myself a clever fellow ;
and she ought to have whipt me for it."

Another evening Dr. Goldsmith and I called on him, with the hope
of prevailing on him to sup with us at the Mitre. We found him indis-
posed, and resolved not to go abroad. " Come, then," said Goldsmith,
"we will not go to the Mitre to-night, since we cannot have the big
man with us." Johnson then called for a bottle of port, of which Gold
smith and I partook, while our friend, now a water-drinker, sat by us.
GOLDSMITH : " I think, Mr. Johnson, you don't go near the theatres
now. You give yourself no more concern about a new play, than if you
had never had anything to do with the stage." JOHNSON : " Why, Sir
our tastes greatly alter. The lad does not care for the child's rattle,
and the old man does not care for the young man's whore." GOLD-
SMITH : " Nay, Sir, but your Muse was not a whore." JOHNSON : "Sir,
I do not think she was. But as we advance in the journey of life, we
drop some of the things which have pleased us ; whether it be that we
are fatigued and don't choose to carry so many things any farther, or
that we find other things which we like better." BOSWELL : " But, Sir,
why don't you give us something in some other way ? " GOLDSMITH :
" Ay, Sir, we have a claim upon you." JOHNSON : " No, Sir, I am not
obliged to do any more. No man is obliged to do as much as he can
do. A man is to have part of his life to himself. If a soldier has
fought a good many campaigns, he is not to be blamed if he retires to
ease and tranquillity. A physician, who has practised long in a great
city, may be excused if he retires to a small town and takes less practice. Now, Sir, the good I can do by my conversation bears the same
proportion to the good I can do by my writings, that the practice of a
physician, retired to a small town, does to his practice in a great city."
BOSWELL : " But I wonder, Sir, you have not more pleasure in writing
than in not writing." JOHNSON : " Sir, you *may* wonder."

He talked of making verses, and observed, "The great difficulty is,
to know when you have made good ones. When composing, I have
generally had them in my mind, perhaps fifty at a time, walking up and
down in my room; and then I have written them down, and often, from
laziness, have written only half lines. I have written a hundred lines in
a day. I remember, I wrote a hundred lines of ' The Vanity of Human
Wishes ' in a day. Doctor (turning to Goldsmith), I am not quite idle ;

I made one line t'other day; but I made no more. GOLDSMITH: "Let us hear it; we'll put a bad one to it." JOHNSON: "No, Sir; I have forgot it."

Such specimens of the easy and playful conversation of the great Dr. Samuel Johnson, are, I think, to be prized, as exhibiting the little varieties of a mind so enlarged and so powerful when objects of consequence required its exertions, and as giving us a minute knowledge of his character and modes of thinking.

"TO BENNET LANGTON, ESQ., AT LANGTON, NEAR SPILSBY, LINCOLNSHIRE.

"DEAR SIR, *March 9, 1766; Johnson's-court, Fleet-street.*

"What your friends have done, that from your departure till now nothing has been heard of you, none of us are able to inform the rest; but as we are all neglected alike, no one thinks himself entitled to the privilege of complaint.

"I should have known nothing of you or of Langton, from the time that dear Miss Langton left us, had not I met Mr. Simpson, of Lincoln, one day in the street, by whom I was informed that Mr. Langton, your Mamma, and yourself, had been all ill, but that you were all recovered.

"That sickness should suspend your correspondence, I did not wonder; but hoped that it would be renewed at your recovery.

"Since you will not inform us where you are, or how you live, I know not whether you desire to know any thing of us. However, I will tell you that THE CLUB subsists; but we have the loss of Burke's company since he has been engaged in public business, in which he has gained more reputation than perhaps any man at his [first] appearance ever gained before. He made two speeches in the House for repealing the Stamp Act, which were publicly commended by Mr. Pitt, and have filled the town with wonder.

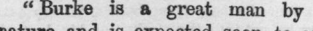

EDMUND BURKE.

"Burke is a great man by nature, and is expected soon to attain civil greatness. I am grown greater too, for I have maintained the newspapers these many weeks; and what is greater still, I have risen every morning since New-year's day, at about eight: when I was up, I have indeed done but little; yet it is no slight advancement to obtain for so many hours more the consciousness of being.

" I wish you were in my new study; I am now writing the first letter in it; I think it looks very pretty about me.

" Dyer [1] is constant at THE CLUB; Hawkins is remiss; I am not over diligent. Dr. Nugent, Dr. Goldsmith, and Mr. Reynolds, are very constant. Mr. Lye is printing his Saxon and Gothic Dictionary; all THE CLUB subscribes.

" You will pay my best respects to all my Lincolnshire friends.

" I am, dear Sir, most affectionately yours,

" SAM. JOHNSON."

" TO BENNET LANGTON, ESQ., AT LANGTON, NEAR SPILSBY, LINCOLNSHIRE.

" DEAR SIR,   *May* 10, 1766; *Johnson's-court, Fleet-street.*

" In supposing that I should be more than commonly affected by the death of Peregrine Langton,[2] you were not mistaken; he was one of those whom I loved at once by instinct and by reason. I have seldom indulged more hope of any thing than of being able to improve our acquaintance to friendship. Many a time have I placed myself again at Langton, and imagined the pleasure with which I should walk to Partney [3] in a summer morning; but this is no longer possible. We must now endeavour to preserve what is left us,—his example of piety and economy. I hope you make what inquiries you can, and write down what is told you. The little things which distinguish domestic characters are soon forgotten: if you delay to inquire, you will have no information; if you neglect to write, information will be vain.[4]

---

[1] Samuel Dyer, Esq., a most learned and ingenious member of the Literary Club, for whose understanding and attainments Dr. Johnson had great respect. He died Sept. 14, 1772. A more particular account of this gentleman may be found in a note on the " Life of Dryden," p. 186, prefixed to the edition of that great writer's Prose Works, in four volumes 8vo, 1800: in which his character is vindicated, and the very unfavourable and unjust representation of it, given by Sir John Hawkins in his " Life of Johnson," pp. 222—232, is minutely examined.—MALONE.

[2] Mr. Langton's uncle.—BOSWELL.

[3] The place of residence of Mr. Peregrine Langton.—BOSWELL.

[4] Mr. Langton did not disregard this counsel, but wrote the following account, which he has been pleased to communicate to me:—

"The circumstances of Mr. Peregrine Langton were these. He had an annuity for life of two hundred pounds per annum. He resided in a village in Lincolnshire; the rent of his house, with two or three small fields, was twenty-eight pounds; the county he lived in was not more than moderately cheap; his family consisted of a sister, who paid him eighteen pounds annually for her board, and a niece. The servants were two maids, and two men in livery. His common way of living, at his table, was three or four dishes; the appurtenances to his table were neat and handsome; he frequently entertained company at dinner, and then his table was well served with as many dishes as were usual at the tables of the other gentlemen in the neighbourhood. His own appearance, as to clothes, was genteelly neat and plain. He had always a postchaise, and kept three horses.

"Such, with the resources I have mentioned, was his way of living, which he did not suffer to employ his whole income; for he had always a sum of money lying by him for any extra ordinary expenses that might arise. Some money he put into the stocks: at his death the sum he had there amounted to one hundred and fifty pounds. He purchased out of his

" His art of life certainly deserves to be known and studied. He lived in plenty and elegance upon an income which to many would appear indigent. and to most, scanty. How he lived, therefore, every man has an interest in knowing. His death, I hope, was peaceful; it was surely happy.

income his household furniture and linen, of which latter he had a very ample store; and, as I am assured by those that had very good means of knowing, not less than the tenth part of his income was set apart for charity: at the time of his death, the sum of twenty-five pounds was found, with a direction to be employed in such uses.

" He had laid down a plan of living proportioned to his income, and did not practise any extraordinary degree of parsimony, but endeavoured that in his family there should be plenty without waste. As an instance that this was his endeavour, it may be worth while to mention a method he took in regulating a proper allowance of malt liquor to be drunk in his family, that there might not be a deficiency, or any intemperate profusion. On a complaint made that his allowance, of a hogshead in a month, was not enough for his own family, he ordered the quantity of a hogshead to be put into bottles, had it locked up from the servants, and distributed out, every day, eight quarts, which is the quantity each day at one hogshead in a month; and told his servants, that if that did not suffice, he would allow them more; but, by this method, it appeared at once that the allowance was much more than sufficient for his small family; and this proved a clear conviction, that could not be answered, and saved all future dispute. He was, in general, very diligently and punctually attended and obeyed by his servants; he was very considerate as to the injunctions he gave, and explained them distinctly; and, at their first coming to his service, steadily exacted a close compliance with them, without any remission: and the servants finding this to be the case, soon grew habitually accustomed to the practice of their business, and then very little further attention was necessary. On extraordinary instances of good behaviour, or diligent service, he was not wanting in particular encouragements and presents above their wages; it is remarkable that he would permit their relations to visit them, and stay at his house two or three days at a time.

" The wonder, with most that hear an account of his economy, will be, how he was able, with such an income, to do so much, especially when it is considered that he paid for every thing he had. He had no land, except the two or three small fields which I have said he rented; and, instead of gaining anything by their produce, I have reason to think he lost by them; however, they furnished him with no further assistance towards his housekeeping, than grass for his horses (not hay, for that I know he bought), and for two cows. Every Monday morning he settled his family accounts, and so kept up a constant attention to the confining his expenses within his income; and to do it more exactly, compared those expenses with a computation he had made, how much that income would afford him every week and day of the year. One of his economical practices was, as soon as any repair was wanting in or about his house, to have it immediately performed. When he had money to spare, he chose to lay in a provision of linen or clothes, or any other necessaries; as then, he said, he could afford it, which he might not be so well able to do when the actual want came in consequence of which method, he had a considerable supply of necessary articles lying by him, beside what was in use.

" But the main particular that seems to have enabled him to do so much with his income, was, that he paid for everything as soon as he had it, except, alone, what were current accounts, such as rent for his house, and servants' wages; and these he paid at the stated times with the utmost exactness. He gave notice to the tradesmen of the neighbouring market-towns that they should no longer have his custom, if they let any of his servants have anything without their paying for it. Thus he put it out of his power to commit those imprudences to which those are liable that defer their payments by using their money some other way than where it ought to go. And whatever money he had by him, he knew that it was not demanded elsewhere, but that he might safely employ it as he pleased.

" His example was confined, by the sequestered place of his abode, to the observation of few, though his prudence and virtue would have made it valuable to all who could have known it. These few particulars, which I knew myself, or have obtained from those who lived with him, may afford instruction, and be an incentive to that wise art of living, which he so successfully practised."—Boswell.

' I wish I had written sooner, lest, writing now, I should renew your grief; but I would not forbear saying what I have now said.

" This loss is, I hope, the only misfortune of a family to whom no misfortune at all should happen, if my wishes could avert it. Let me know how you all go on. Has Mr. Langton got him the little horse that I recommended? It would do him good to ride about his estate in fine weather.

" Be pleased to make my compliments to Mrs. Langton, and to dear Miss Langton, and Miss Di, and Miss Juliet, and to everybody else.

" THE CLUB holds very well together. Monday is my night.[1] I continue to rise tolerably well, and read more than I did. I hope something will ye' come on it. I am, Sir,

" Your most affectionate servant,
" SAM. JOHNSON."

After I had been some time in Scotland, I mentioned to him in a letter, that " on my first return to my native country, after some years of absence, I was told of a vast number of my acquaintance who were all gone to the land of forgetfulness, and I found myself like a man stalking over a field of battle, who every moment perceives some one 'ying dead." I complained of irresolution, and mentioned my having made a vow as a security for good conduct. I wrote to him again without being able to move his indolence : nor did I hear from him till he had received a copy of my inaugural Exercise, or Thesis in Civil Law, which I published at my admission as an Advocate, as is the custom in Scotland. He then wrote to me as follows :—

"TO JAMES BOSWELL, ESQ.

" DEAR SIR,   London, Aug. 21, 1766.

" The reception of your Thesis put me in mind of my debt to you. Why did you * * * * * * * * * * * * *.[2] I will punish you for it, by telling you that your Latin wants correction.[3] In the beginning, Spei alteræ, not to urge that it should be primæ, is not grammatical : alteræ should be alteri. In the next line you seem to use genus absolutely, for what we call family, that is, for illustrious extraction, I doubt without authority. Homines nullius originis for Nullis orti majoribus, or, Nullo loco nati, is, as I am afraid, barbarous.—Ruddiman is dead.

" I have now vexed you enough and will try to please you. Your resolution

---

[1] Of his being in the chair of THE LITERARY CLUB, which at this time met once a week in the evening.—BOSWELL.

[2] The passage omitted alluded to a private transaction.—BOSWELL.

[3] This censure of my Latin relates to the Dedication, which was as follows:—

"Viro nobilissimo, ornatissimo, Joanni, Vicecomiti Mountstuart, atavis edito regibus excelsæ familiæ de Bute spei alteræ; labente seculo, quum homines nullius originis genus æquare opibus aggrediuntur, sanguinis antiqui et illustris semper memori, natalium splendorem virtutibus augenti : ad publica populi comitia jam legato; in optimatium vero magnæ Britanniæ senatu, jure hæreditario, olim consessuro : vim insitam varia doctrina promovente, nec tamen se venditante, prædito: prisca fide animo liberrimo, et morum elegantia insigni : in Italiæ visitandæ itinere, socio suo honoratissimo, hasce jurisprudentiæ primitias devinctissimæ amicitiæ et observantiæ, monumentum, D.D.C.Q. JACOBUS BOSWELL."

to obey your father I sincerely approve; but do not accustom yourself to enchain your volatility by vows; they will sometimes leave a thorn in your mind, which you will, perhaps, never be able to extract or eject. Take this warning; it is of great importance.

" The study of the law is what you very justly term it, copious and generous; [1] and in adding your name to its professors, you have done exactly what I always wished, when I wished you best. I hope that you will continue to pursue it vigorously and constantly. You gain, at least, what is no small advantage, security from those troublesome and wearisome discontents, which are always obtruding themselves upon a mind vacant, unemployed, and undetermined.

" You ought to think it no small inducement to diligence and perseverance, that they will please your father. We all live upon the hope of pleasing somebody, and the pleasure of pleasing ought to be greatest, and at last always will be greatest, when our endeavours are exerted in consequence of our duty.

" Life is not long, and too much of it must not pass in idle deliberation how it shall be spent: deliberation, which those who begin it by prudence, and continue it with subtilty, must, after long expense of thought, conclude by chance. To prefer one future mode of life to another, upon just reasons, requires faculties which it has not pleased our Creator to give us.

" If therefore the profession you have chosen has some unexpected inconveniences, console yourself by reflecting that no profession is without them; and that all the importunities and perplexities of business are softness and luxury, compared with the incessant cravings of vacancy, and the unsatisfactory expedients of idleness.

> ' Hæc sunt quæ nostrâ potui te voce monere;
> Vade, age.'

" As to your History of Corsica, you have no materials which others have not, or may not have. You have, somehow or other, warmed your imagination. I wish there were some cure, like the lover's leap, for all heads of which some single idea has obtained an unreasonable and irregular possession. Mind your own affairs, and leave the Corsicans to theirs. I am, dear Sir,

" Your most humble servant,
" SAM. JOHNSON."

" TO DR. SAMUEL JOHNSON.

" MUCH ESTEEMED AND DEAR SIR,   *Auchinleck, Nov.* 6, 1766.
" I plead not guilty to [2]   *   *   *   *   *

" Having thus, I hope, cleared myself of the charge brought against me, I presume you will not be displeased if I escape the punishment which you have decreed for me unheard. If you have discharged the arrows of criticism against an innocent man, you must rejoice to find they have missed him, or have not been pointed so as to wound him.

---

[1] This alludes to the first sentence of the Proemium of my Thesis. "JURISPRUDENTIÆ, studio nullum uberius, nullum generosius: in legibus enim agitandis, populorum mores, variasque fortunæ vices ex quibus leges oriuntur, contemplari simul solemus."—BOSWELL.

[2] The passage omitted explained the transaction to which the preceding letter had alluded. BOSWELL.

" To talk no longer in allegory, I am, with all deference, going to offer a few observations in defence of my Latin, which you have found fault with.

" You think I should have used *spei primæ*, instead of *spei alteræ*. *Spes* is, indeed, often used to express something on which we have a future dependence, as in Virg. Eclog. i. l. 14.—

'———————— modo namque gemellos
Spem gregis, ah! silice in nudâ connixa reliquit:'

and in Georg. iii. l. 473,—

'*Spemque* gregemque simul,'

for the lambs and the sheep.   Yet it is also used to express anything on which we have a present dependence, and is well applied to a man of distinguished influence,—our support, our refuge, our *præsidium*, as Horace calls Mæcenas. So, Æneid xii. l. 57, Queen Amata addresses her son-in-law, Turnus:—' *Spes* tu nunc una:' and he was then no future hope, for she adds,—

'——— decus imperiumque Latini
Te penes;'

which might have been said of my Lord Bute some years ago.   Now I consider the present Earl of Bute to be ' Excelsæ familiæ de Bute *spes prima ;*' and my Lord Mountstuart, as his eldest son, to be ' *spes altera.*'   So in Æneid xii. l. 168, after having mentioned Pater Æneas, who was the *present* spes, the *reigning* spes, as my German friends would say, the *spes prima,* the poet adds,—

' Et juxta Ascanius, magnæ *spes altera* Romæ.'

" You think *alteræ* ungrammatical, and you tell me it should have been *alteri*.   You must recollect, that in old times *alter* was declined regularly; and when the ancient fragments preserved in the *Juris Civilis Fontes* were written, it was certainly declined in the way that I use it.   This, I should think, may protect a lawyer who writes *alteræ* in a dissertation upon part of his own science.   But as I could hardly venture to quote fragments of old law to so classical a man as Mr. Johnson, I have not made an accurate search into these remains, to find examples of what I am able to produce in poetical composition.   We find in Plaut. Rudens, act iii. scene 4,—

' Nam huic *alteræ* patria quæ sit profecto nescio.

Plautus is, to be sure, an old comic writer; but in the days of Scipio and Lelius, we find Terent. Heautontim. act ii. scene 3,—

'————————— hoc ipsa in itinere *alteræ*
Dum narrat, forte audivi.'

" You doubt my having authority for using *genus* absolutely, for what we call *family,* that is, for *illustrious extraction.*   Now I take *genus* in Latin, to have much the same signification with *birth* in English : both in their primary meaning expressing simply descent, but both made to stand κατ' ἐξοχην, for noble descent.   *Genus* is thus used in Hor. lib. ii. Sat. v. l. 8,—

' Et *genus* et virtus, nisi cum re, vilior alga est.'

And in lib. i. Epist vi. l. 37,—

    ' Et *genus* et formam Regina pecunia donat.'

And in the celebrated contest between Ajax and Ulysses, Ovid's Metamorph. lib. xiii. l. 140,—

    ' Nam *genus* et proavos, et quæ non fecimus ipsi,
      Vix ea nostra voco.'

" ' Homines nullius originis,' for ' nullis orti majoribus,' or ' nullo loco nati, is, ' you are afraid, barbarous.'

" *Origo* is used to signify extraction, as in Virg. Æneid i. 286,—

    ' Nascetur pulchrâ Trojanus *origine* Cæsar.'

And in Æneid x. l. 618,—

    ' Ille tamen nostrâ deducit *origine* nomen ; '

and as *nullus* is used for obscure, is it not in the genius of the Latin language to write *nullius originis*, for obscure extraction ?

" I have defended myself as well as I could.

" Might I venture to differ from you with regard to the utility of vows ? I am sensible that it would be very dangerous to make vows rashly, and without a due consideration. But I cannot help thinking that they may often be of great advantage to one of a variable judgment and irregular inclinations. I always remember a passage in one of your letters to our Italian friend, Baretti ; where, talking of the monastic life, you say you do not wonder that serious men should put themselves under the protection of a religious order, when they have found how unable they are to take care of themselves. For my own part, without affecting to be a Socrates, I am sure I have a more than ordinary struggle to maintain with *the Evil principle* ; and all the methods I can devise are little enough to keep me tolerably steady in the paths of rectitude.

    *   *   *   *   *   *

    " I am ever, with the highest veneration,
        " Your affectionate humble servant,
            " JAMES BOSWELL."

It appears from Johnson's diary, that he was this year at Mr. Thrale's, from before Midsummer till after Michaelmas, and that he afterwards passed a month at Oxford. He had then contracted a great intimacy with Mr. Chambers of that University, afterwards Sir Robert Chambers, one of the judges in India.

He published nothing this year in his own name ; but the noble dedication* to the King, of Gwyn's " London and Westminster Improved," was written by him ; and he furnished the preface,† and several of the pieces, which compose a volume of Miscellanies by Mrs. Anna Williams, the blind lady who had an asylum in his house.[1] Of these.

----

[1] In a paper already mentioned, (see vol. i., p. 41, and near the end of the year 1763) the following account of this publication is given by a lady (Lady Knight) well acquainted with Mrs. Williams :—

As to her poems, she many years attempted to publish them : the half-crowns she had

there are his "Epitaph on Phillips;" * "Translation of a Latin Epitaph
on Sir Thomas Hanmer;" † "Friendship, an Ode;" * and, "The Ant," *
a paraphrase from the Proverbs, of which I have a copy in his own
handwriting; and, from internal evidence, I ascribe to him, "To
Miss ——— on her giving the Author a gold and silk net-work Purse of
her own weaving;" † and "The Happy Life." † Most of the pieces in
this volume have evidently received additions from his superior pen,
particularly "Verses to Mr. Richardson, on his Sir Charles Grandison;"
"The Excursion;" "Reflections on a Grave digging in Westminster
Abbey." There is in this collection a poem, "On the Death of Stephen
Grey, the Electrician," * which, on reading it, appeared to me to be
undoubtedly Johnson's. I asked Mrs. Williams whether it was not
his. "Sir," said she, with some warmth, "I wrote that poem before I
had the honour of Dr. Johnson's acquaintance." I, however, was so
much impressed with my first notion, that I mentioned it to Johnson,
repeating, at the same time, what Mrs. Williams had said. His answer
was, "It is true, Sir, that she wrote it before she was acquainted with
me; but she has not told you that I wrote it all over again, except two
lines." "The Fountains," † a beautiful little fairy tale in prose,
written with exquisite simplicity, is one of Johnson's productions; and
I cannot withhold from Mrs. Thrale the praise of being the author of
that admirable poem, "The Three Warnings."

He wrote this year a letter, not intended for publication, which has,
perhaps, as strong marks of his sentiment and style, as any of his compositions. The original is in my possession. It is addressed to the late
Mr. William Drummond, bookseller, in Edinburgh, a gentleman of
good family, but small estate, who took arms for the house of Stuart in
1745; and during his concealment in London till the act of general
pardon came out, obtained the acquaintance of Dr. Johnson, who justly
esteemed him as a very worthy man. It seems, some of the members
of the Society in Scotland for propagating Christian knowledge had
opposed the scheme of translating the Holy Scriptures into the Erse or
Gaelic language, from political considerations of the disadvantage of
keeping up the distinction between the Highlanders and the other inhabitants of North Britain. Dr. Johnson being informed of this, I suppose
by Mr. Drummond, wrote, with a generous indignation, as follows :—

---

got towards the publication, she confessed to me, went for necessaries, and that the greatest
pain she ever felt was from the appearance of defrauding her subscribers: ' But what can
I do? the Doctor [Johnson] always puts me off with 'Well, we'll think about it,' and
Goldsmith says, ' Leave it to me.' However, two of her friends, under her directions, made
a new subscription at a crown, the whole price of the work, and in a very little time raised
sixty pounds. Mrs. Carter was applied to by Mrs. Williams's desire, and she with the utmost
activity and kindness, procured a long list of names. At length the work was published, in
which is a fine written, but gloomy tale of Dr. Johnson. The money Mrs. Williams had
various uses for, and a part of it was funded."—BOSWELL.

By this publication Mrs. Williams got £150.- -MALONE.

" TO MR. WILLIAM DRUMMOND.

" SIR,   *Johnson's-court, Fleet-street, Aug.* 13, 1766.

" I did not expect to hear that it could be, in an assembly convened for the propagation of Christian knowledge, a question whether any nation uninstructed in religion should receive instruction; or whether that instruction should be imparted to them by a translation of the holy books into their own language. If obedience to the will of GOD be necessary to happiness, and knowledge of his will be necessary to obedience, I know not how he that withholds this knowledge, or delays it, can be said to love his neighbour as himself. He that voluntarily continues ignorance, is guilty of all the crimes which ignorance produces; as to him that should extinguish the tapers of a lighthouse, might justly be imputed the calamities of shipwrecks. Christianity is the highest perfection of humanity; and as no man is good but as he wishes the good of others, no man can be good in the highest degree, who wishes not to others the largest measures of the greatest good. To omit for a year, or for a day, the most efficacious method of advancing Christianity, in compliance with any purposes that terminate on this side of the grave, is a crime of which I know not that the world has yet had an example, except in the practice of the planters of America, a race of mortals whom, I suppose, no other man wishes to resemble.

" The Papists have, indeed, denied to the laity the use of the Bible; but this prohibition, in few places now very rigorously enforced, is defended by arguments which have for their foundation the care of souls. To obscure, upon motives merely political, the light of revelation, is a practice reserved for the reformed; and, surely, the blackest midnight of Popery is meridian sunshine to such a reformation. I am not very willing that any language should be totally extinguished. The similitude and derivation of languages afford the most indubitable proof of the traduction of nations, and the genealogy of mankind. They add often physical certainty to historical evidence; and often supply the only evidence of ancient migrations, and of the revolutions of ages which left no written monuments behind them.

" Every man's opinions, at least his desires, are a little influenced by his favourite studies. My zeal for languages may seem, perhaps, rather overheated, even to those by whom I desire to be well esteemed. To those who have nothing in their thoughts but trade or policy, present power, or present money, I should not think it necessary to defend my opinions; but with men of letters I would not unwillingly compound, by wishing the continuance of every language, however narrow in its extent, or however incommodious for common purposes, till it is reposited in some version of a known book, that it may be always hereafter examined and compared with other languages, and then permitting its disuse. For this purpose the translation of the Bible is most to be desired. It is not certain that the same method will not preserve the Highland language, for the purposes of learning, and abolish it from daily use. When the Highlanders read the Bible, they will naturally wish to have its obscurities cleared and to know the history, collateral or appendant. Knowledge always desires increase; it is like fire, which must first be kindled by some external agent, but which will afterwards propagate itself. When they once desire to learn, they will naturally have recourse to the nearest language by which that desire can be gratified; and one will tell another that if he would attain knowledge, he must learn English.

" This speculation may, perhaps, be thought more subtle than the grossness of real life will easily admit. Let it, however, be remembered, that the efficacy of ignorance has long been tried, and has not produced the consequence expected. Let knowledge, therefore, take its turn; and let the patrons of privation stand awhile aside, and admit the operation of positive principles.

" You will be pleased, Sir, to assure the worthy man who is employed in the new translation,[1] that he has my wishes for his success; and if here or at Oxford I can be of any use, that I shall think it more than honour to promote his undertaking.

" I am sorry that I delayed so long to write.

" I am, Sir, your most humble servant,

" SAM. JOHNSON."

The opponents of this pious scheme being made ashamed of their conduct, the benevolent undertaking was allowed to go on.

The following letters, though not written till the year after, being chiefly upon the same subject, are here inserted :—

" TO MR. WILLIAM DRUMMOND.

" DEAR SIR,   *Johnson's-court, Fleet-street, April* 21, 1767

" That my letter should have had such effects as you mention, gives me great pleasure. I hope you do not flatter me by imputing to me more good than I have really done. Those whom my arguments have persuaded to change their opinion, show such modesty and candour as deserve great praise.

" I hope the worthy translator goes diligently forward. He has a higher reward in prospect than any honours which this world can bestow. I wish I could be useful to him.

" The publication of my letter, if it could be of use in a cause to which all other causes are nothing, I should not prohibit. But first, I would have you to consider whether the publication will really do any good; next, whether by printing and distributing a very small number, you may not attain all that you propose; and, what perhaps I should have said first, whether the letter, which I do not now perfectly remember, be fit to be printed.

" If you can consult Dr. Robertson, to whom I am a little known, I shall be satisfied about the propriety of whatever he shall direct. If he thinks that it should be printed, I entreat him to revise it; there may, perhaps, be some

---

[1] The Rev. Mr. John Campbell, Minister of the parish of Kippen, near Stirling, who has lately favoured me with a long, intelligent, and very obliging letter upon this work, makes the following remark: " Dr. Johnson has alluded to the worthy man employed in the trans- lation of the New Testament. Might not this have afforded you an opportunity of paying a proper tribute of respect to the memory of the Rev. Mr. James Stuart, late Minister of Killin, distinguished by his eminent piety, learning, and taste ? The amiable simplicity of his life, his warm benevolence, his indefatigable and successful exertions for civilising and improving the parish of which he was minister for upwards of fifty years, entitle him to the gratitude of his country, and the veneration of all good men. It certainly would be a pity if such a character should be permitted to sink into oblivion."—BOSWELL.

negligent lines written, and whatever is amiss, he knows very well how to rectify.[1]

"Be pleased to let me know, from time to time, how this excellent design goes forward.

"Make my compliments to young Mr. Drummond, whom I hope you will live to see such as you desire him.

"I have not lately seen Mr. Elphinston, but believe him to be prosperous. I shall be glad to hear the same of you, for I am, Sir,

"Your affectionate humble servant,

"Sam. Johnson."

TO THE SAME.

"Sir, *London, Johnson's-court, Fleet-street, Oct.* 24, 1767.

"I returned this week from the country, after an absence of near six months, and found your letter with many others, which I should have answered sooner, if I had sooner seen them.

"Dr. Robertson's opinion was surely right. Men should not be told of the faults which they have mended. I am glad the old language is taught, and honour the translator as a man whom God has distinguished by the high office of propagating his word.

"I must take the liberty of engaging you in an office of charity. Mrs. Heely, the wife of Mr. Heely, who had lately some office in your theatre, is my near relation, and now in great distress. They wrote me word of their situation some time ago, to which I returned them an answer which raised hopes of more than it is proper for me to give them. Their representation of their affairs I have discovered to be such as cannot be trusted ; and at this distance, though their case requires haste, I know not how to act. She, or her daughters, may be heard of at Canongate Head. I must beg, Sir, that you will inquire after them, and let me know what is to be done. I am willing to go to ten pounds, and will transmit you such a sum, if, upon examination, you find it likely to be of use. If they are in immediate want, advance them what you think proper. What I could do I would do for the woman, having no great reason to pay much regard to Heely himself.[2]

"I believe you may receive some intelligence from Mrs. Baker, of the theatre, whose letter I received at the same time with yours ; and to whom, if you see her, you will make my excuse for the seeming neglect of answering her.

"Whatever you advance within ten pounds shall be immediately returned to you, or paid as you shall order. I trust wholly to your judgment.

"I am, Sir, &c., Sam. Johnson.'

Mr. Cuthbert Shaw,[3] alike distinguished by his genius, misfortunes, and misconduct, published this year a poem, called " The Race, by

- This paragraph shows Johnson's real estimation of the character and abilities of the celebrated Scottish historian, however lightly, in a moment of caprice, he may have spoken of his works.—Boswell.

[2] This is the person concerning whom Sir John Hawkins has thrown out very unwarrantable reflections both against Dr. Johnson and Mr. Francis Barber.—Boswell.

[3] See an account of him in " The European Magazine," Jan. 1786.—Boswell.

Mercurius Spur, Esq.," in which he whimsically made the living poets of England contend for pre-eminence of fame by running :—

> " Prove by their heels the prowess of the head."

In this poem there was the following portrait of Johnson :—

> " Here Johnson comes,—unblest with outward grace,
> His rigid morals stamp'd upon his face,
> While strong conceptions struggle in his brain :
> (For even wit is brought to bed with pain :)
> To view him, porters with their loads would rest,
> And babes cling frighted to the nurse's breast.
> With looks convulsed, he roars in pompous strain,
> And, like an angry lion, shakes his mane.
> The nine, with terror struck, who ne'er had seen
> Aught human with so terrible a mien,
> Debating whether they should stay or run,
> Virtue steps forth, and claims him for her son.
> With gentle speech she warns him now to yield,
> Nor stain his glories in the doubtful field ;
> But wrapt in conscious worth, content sit down,
> Since Fame, resolved his various pleas to crown,
> Though forced his present claim to disavow,
> Had long reserved a chaplet for his brow.
> He bows, obeys ; for Time shall first expire,
> Ere Johnson stay, when Virtue bids retire."

The Honourable Thomas Hervey [1] and his lady, having unhappily disagreed, and being about to separate, Johnson interfered as their friend, and wrote him a letter of expostulation, which I have not been able to find ; but the substance of it is ascertained by a letter to Johnson in answer to it, which Mr. Hervey printed. The occasion of this correspondence between Dr. Johnson and Mr. Hervey, was thus related to me by Mr. Beauclerk.

"Tom Hervey had a great liking for Johnson, and in his will had left him a legacy of fifty pounds. One day he said to me, 'Johnson may want this money now, more than afterwards. I have a mind to give it him directly. Will you be so good as to carry a fifty pound note from me to him?' This I positively refused to do, as he might, perhaps, have knocked me down for insulting him, and have afterwards put the note in his pocket. But I said if Hervey would write him a letter, and enclose a fifty pound note, I should take care to deliver it. He accordingly did write him a letter, mentioning that he was only paying a legacy a little sooner. To his letter he added, ' *P.S. I am going to part with*

---

[1] The Honourable Thomas Hervey, whose letter to Sir Thomas Hanmer, in 1742, was much read at that time. He was the second son of John, the first Earl of Bristol, and one of the brothers of Johnson's early friend, Henry Hervey. He married in 1744, Anne, daughter of Francis Coughlan Esq. and died Jan. 20, 1775.—MALONE.

my wife.'   Johnson then wrote to him, saying nothing of the note, but remonstrating with him against parting with his wife."

When I mentioned to Johnson this story, in as delicate terms as I could, he told me that the fifty pound note was given to him by Mr. Hervey in consideration of his having written for him a pamphlet against Sir Charles Hanbury Williams, who, Mr. Hervey imagined, was the author of an attack upon him ; but that it was afterwards discovered to be the work of a garreteer, who wrote "The Fool ; " the pamphlet therefore against Sir Charles was not printed.

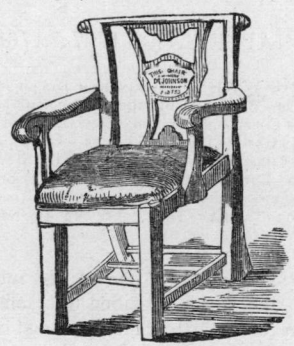

DR. JOHNSON'S CHAIR.

GEORGE III.

CHAPTER II.—1767—1768.

JOHNSON INTRODUCED TO GEORGE III. AT BUCKINGHAM HOUSE—VISITS LICHFIELD—DEATH OF CATHERINE CHAMBERS—WRITES PROLOGUE TO GOLDSMITH'S "GOOD-NATURED MAN"—BOSWELL'S ACCOUNT OF CORSICA PUBLISHED—COMPARISON OF THE WORKS OF FIELDING AND RICHARDSON—THE GREAT DOUGLAS CAUSE—ST. KILDA—JOHNSON'S VIEWS OF CONJUGAL INFIDELITY—CHASTITY AND THE CHOICE OF A WIFE—BARETTI'S ITALY—JOHNSON VISITS OXFORD—RETURNS TO LONDON—HIS CONTEMPT FOR POPULAR LIBERTY—DR. KENRICK'S PAMPHLET—JOHNSON PLACES FRANCIS BARBER AT SCHOOL—CONVERSATIONAL STRICTURES ON THOMSON THE POET AND DR. MOUNSEY—ORIGIN OF THE "BEAR" EPITHET.

IN February, 1767, there happened one of the most remarkable incidents of Johnson's life, which gratified his monarchical enthusiasm, and which he loved to relate with all its circumstances, when requested by his friends. This was his being honoured by a private conversation with his Majesty, in the library at the Queen's house. He had frequently visited those splendid rooms, and noble collection of books,[1] which he used to say was more numerous and curious than he supposed any person could have made in the time which the king had employed. Mr. Barnard, the librarian, took care that he should have every accom-

---

[1] Dr. Johnson had the honour of contributing his assistance towards the formation of this library; for I have read a long letter from him to Mr. Barnard, giving the most masterly instruction on the subject. I wished much to have gratified my readers with the perusal of this letter, and have reason to think that his Majesty would have been graciously pleased to permit its publication; but Mr. Barnard, to whom I applied, declined it "on his own account."—BOSWELL.

OLD BUCKINGHAM HOUSE.

modation that could contribute to his ease and convenience, while indulging his literary taste in that place—so that he had here a very agreeable resource at leisure hours.

His Majesty having been informed of his occasional visits, was pleased to signify a desire that he should be told when Dr. Johnson came next to the library. Accordingly, the next time that Johnson did come, as soon as he was fairly engaged with a book, on which, while he sat by the fire, he seemed quite intent, Mr. Barnard stole round to the apartment where the king was, and, in obedience to his Majesty's commands, mentioned that Dr. Johnson was then in the library. His Majesty said he was at leisure, and would go to him : upon which Mr. Barnard took one of the candles that stood on the king's table, and lighted his Majesty through a suite of rooms, till they came to a private door into the library, of which his Majesty had the key. Being entered, Mr. Barnard stepped forward hastily to Dr. Johnson, who was still in a profound study, and whispered him, " Sir, here is the king." Johnson started up, and stood still. His Majesty approached him, and at once was courteously easy.[1]

[1] The particulars of this conversation I have been at great pains to collect with the utmost authenticity, from Dr. Johnson's own detail to myself; from Mr. Langton, who was present when he gave an account of it to Dr. Joseph Warton, and several other friends, at Sir Joshua Reynolds's; from Mr. Barnard; from the copy of a letter written by the late Mr. Strahan, the printer, to Bishop Warburton; and from a minute, the original of which is among the papers of the late Sir James Caldwell, and a copy of which was most obligingly obtained for me from his son Sir John Caldwell, by Sir Francis Lumm. To all these gentlemen I beg leave to make my grateful acknowledgments, and particularly to Sir Francis Lumm, who was pleased to take a great deal of trouble, and even had the minute laid before the king by Lord Caermarthen now Duke of Leeds, then one of his Majesty's principal secretaries of state, who announced to Sir Francis the Royal pleasure concerning it by a letter, in these

His Majesty began by observing, that he understood he came sometimes to the library: and then mentioned his having heard that the Doctor
had been lately at Oxford, asked him if he was not fond of going thither.
To which Johnson answered, that he was indeed fond of going to Oxford
sometimes, but was likewise glad to come back again. The king then
asked him what they were doing at Oxford. Johnson answered, he
could not much commend their diligence, but that in some respects
they were mended, for they had put their press under better regula-
tions, and were at that time printing Polybius. He was then asked
whether there were better libraries at Oxford or Cambridge. He
answered, he believed the Bodleian was larger than any they had at
Cambridge ; at the same time adding, " I hope, whether we have more
books or not than they have at Cambridge, we shall make as good use
of them as they do." Being asked whether All-Souls or Christ-Church
library was the largest, he answered, "All-Souls library is the largest
we have, except the Bodleian." " Ay," said the king, "that is the
public library."

His Majesty inquired if he was then writing anything. He answered,
he was not, for he had pretty well told the world what he knew, and
must now read to acquire more knowledge. The king, as it should
seem with a view to urge him to rely on his own stores as an original
writer, and to continue his labours, then said, "I do not think you
borrow much from any body." Johnson said, he thought he had already
done his part as a writer. "I should have thought so too," said the
king, "if you had not written so well."—Johnson observed to me, upon
this, that "no man could have paid a handsomer compliment ; and it
was fit for a king to pay. It was decisive." When asked by another
friend, at Sir Joshua Reynolds's, whether he made any reply to this
high compliment, he answered, "No, Sir. When the king had said it,
it was to be so. It was not for me to bandy civilities with my
sovereign." Perhaps no man who had spent his whole life in courts
could have shown a more nice and dignified sense of true politeness
than Johnson did in this instance.

His Majesty having observed to him that he supposed he must have
read a great deal, Johnson answered, that he thought more than he
read ; that he had read a great deal in the early part of his life, but
having fallen into ill-health, he had not been able to read much,
compared with others ; for instance, he said he had not read much,
compared with Dr. Warburton. Upon which the king said, that he
heard Dr. Warburton was a man of such general knowledge, that you

words : "I have the king's commands to assure you, Sir, how sensible his Majesty is of your
attention in communicating the minute of the conversation previous to its publication. As
there appears no objection to your complying with Mr. Boswell's wishes on the subject, you
are at full liberty to deliver it to that gentleman, to make such use of in his 'Life of
Dr. Johnson,' as he may think proper."—BOSWELL.

could scarce talk with him on any subject on which he was not qualified to speak ; and that his learning resembled Garrick's acting, in its universality.[1] His Majesty then talked of the controversy between Warburton and Lowth, which he seems to have read, and asked Johnson what he thought of it. Johnson answered, " Warburton has most general, most scholastic learning : Lowth is the more correct scholar. I do not know which of them calls names best." The king was pleased to say he was of the same opinion : adding, " You do not think, then, Dr. Johnson, that there was much argument in the case." Johnson said, he did not think there was. " Why, truly," said the king, " when once it comes to calling names, argument is pretty well at an end."

His Majesty then asked him what he thought of Lord Lyttelton's history, which was then just published. Johnson said, he thought his style pretty good, but that he had blamed Henry the Second rather too much. " Why," said the king, " they seldom do these things by halves." " No, Sir," answered Johnson, " not to kings." But fearing to be misunderstood, he proceeded to explain himself ; and immediately subjoined, " That for those who spoke worse of kings than they deserved, he could find no excuse ; but that he could more easily conceive how some might speak better of them than they deserved, without any ill intention ; for, as kings had much in their power to give, those who were favoured by them would frequently, from grati-tude, exaggerate their praises ; and as this proceeded from a good motive, it was certainly excusable, as far as error could be excusable."

The king then asked him what he thought of Dr. Hill. Johnson answered, that he was an ingenious man, but had no veracity ; and immediately mentioned, as an instance of it, an assertion of that writer, that he had seen objects magnified to a much greater degree by using three or four microscopes at a time than by using one. " Now," added Johnson, " every one acquainted with microscopes knows, that the more of them he looks through, the less the object will appear." " Why," replied the king, " this is not telling an untruth, but telling it clumsily ; for, if that be the case, every one who can look through a microscope will be able to detect him."

" I now," said Johnson to his friends, when relating what had passed, " began to consider that I was depreciating this man in the estimation of his sovereign, and thought it was time for me to say something that might be more favourable." He added, therefore, that Dr. Hill was, notwithstanding, a very curious observer ; and if he would have been contented to tell the world no more than he knew, he might have been

---

[1] The Reverend Mr. Strahan clearly recollects having been told by Johnson, that the king observed that Pope made Warburton a bishop. " True, Sir," said Johnson, " but Warburton did more for Pope ; he made him a Christian : " alluding, no doubt, to his ingenious comments on " The Essay of Man."—Boswell.

a very considerable man, and needed not to have recourse to such mean expedients to raise his reputation.

The king then talked of literary journals, mentioned particularly the *Journal des savans,* and asked Johnson if it was well done. Johnson said, it was formerly very well done, and gave some account of the persons who began it, and carried it on for some years ; enlarging, at the same time, on the nature and use of such works. The king asked him if it was well done now. Johnson answered, he had no reason to think that it was. The king then asked him if there were any other literary journals published in this kingdom, except the Monthly and Critical Reviews ; and on being answered there was no other, his Majesty asked which of them was the best ; Johnson answered, that the Monthly Review was done with most care, the Critical upon the best principles ; adding, that the authors of the Monthly Review were enemies to the Church. This the king said he was sorry to hear.

The conversation next turned on the Philosophical Transactions, when Johnson observed that they had now a better method of arranging their materials than formerly. " Ay," said the king, " they are obliged to Dr. Johnson for that : " for his Majesty had heard and remembered the circumstance, which Johnson himself had forgot.

His Majesty expressed a desire to have the literary biography of this country ably executed, and proposed to Dr. Johnson to undertake it. Johnson signified his readiness to comply with his Majesty's wishes.

During the whole of this interview, Johnson talked to his Majesty with profound respect, but still in his firm manly manner, with a sonorous voice, and never in that subdued tone which is commonly used at the levee and in the drawing-room. After the king withdrew, Johnson showed himself highly pleased with his Majesty's conversation, and gracious behaviour. He said to Mr. Barnard, " Sir, they may talk of the king as they will ; but he is the finest gentleman I have ever seen." And he afterwards observed to Mr. Langton, " Sir, his manners are those of as fine a gentleman as we may suppose Louis the Fourteenth or Charles the Second."

At Sir Joshua Reynolds's, where a circle of Johnson's friends was collected round him to hear his account of this memorable conversation, Dr. Joseph Warton, in his frank and lively manner, was very active in pressing him to mention the particulars. " Come now, Sir, this is an interesting matter ; do favour us with it." Johnson, with great good humour, complied.

He told them, " I found his Majesty wished I should talk, and I made it my business to talk. I find it does a man good to be talked to by his sovereign. In the first place, a man cannot be in a passion—." Here some question interrupted him, which is to be regretted, as he certainly would have pointed out and illustrated many circumstances of advantage, from being in a situation where the powers of the mind are at once excited to vigorous exertion and tempered by reverential awe.

During all the time in which Dr. Johnson was employed in relating to the circle at Sir Joshua Reynolds's the particulars of what passed between the king and him, Dr. Goldsmith remained unmoved upon a sofa at some distance, affecting not to join in the least in the eager curiosity of the company. He assigned as a reason for his gloom and seeming inattention, that he apprehended Johnson had relinquished his purpose of furnishing him with a Prologue to his play, with the hopes of which he had been flattered; but it was strongly suspected that he was fretting with chagrin and envy at the singular honour Dr. Johnson had lately enjoyed. At length, the frankness and simplicity of his natural character prevailed. He sprung from the sofa, advanced to Johnson, and in a kind of flutter, from imagining himself in the situation which he had just been hearing described, exclaimed, " Well, you acquitted yourself in this conversation better than I should have done; for I should have bowed and stammered through the whole of it."

I received no letter from Johnson this year; nor have I discovered any of the correspondence[1] he had, except the two letters to Mr. Drummond, which have been inserted, for the sake of connection with that to the same gentlemen in 1766. His diary affords no light as to his employment at this time. He passed three months at Lichfield;[2] and I cannot omit an affecting and solemn scene there, as related by himself:—

"Sunday, Oct. 18, 1767. Yesterday, Oct. 17, at about ten in the morning, I took my leave for ever of my dear old friend, Catherine Chambers, who came to live with my mother about 1724, and has been but little parted from us since. She buried my father, my brother, and my mother. She is now fifty-eight years old.

"I desired all to withdraw, then told her that we were to part for ever; that, as Christians, we should part with prayer; and that I would, if she was willing, say a short prayer beside her. She expressed great desire to hear me; and held up her poor hands, as she lay in bed, with great fervour, while I prayed, kneeling by her, nearly in the following words:

" ' Almighty and most merciful Father, whose loving kindness is over all thy works, behold, visit, and relieve this thy servant, who is grieved with sickness. Grant that the sense of her weakness may add strength to her faith, and seriousness to her repentance. And grant that by the help of thy Holy Spirit, after the pains and labours of this short life, we may all obtain everlasting happiness, though JESUS CHRIST our Lord, for whose sake hear our prayers. Amen. Our Father, &c.'

---

[1] It is proper here to mention, that when I speak of his correspondence, I consider it independent of the voluminous collection of letters which, in the course of many years, he wrote to Mrs. Thrale, which forms a separate part of his works; and as a proof of the high estimation set on anything which came from his pen, was sold by that lady for the sum of five hundred pounds.—BOSWELL.

[2] In his letter to Mr. Drummond, dated Oct. 24, 1767, he mentions that he had arrived in London, after an absence of nearly *six months* in the country. Probably part of that time was spent at Oxford.—MALONE.

"I then kissed her. She told me that to part was the greatest pain that she had ever felt, and that she hoped we should meet again in a better place. I expressed, with swelled eyes, and great emotion of tenderness, the same hopes. We kissed, and parted. I humbly hope to meet again, and to part no more."[1]

By those who have been taught to look upon Johnson as a man of a harsh and stern character, let this tender and affectionate scene be candidly read ; and let them then judge whether more warmth of heart and grateful kindness, is often found in human nature.

We have the following notice in his devotional record :—

"August 2, 1767. I have been disturbed and unsettled for a long time, and have been without resolution to apply to study or to business, being hindered by sudden snatches."[2]

He, however, furnished Mr. Adams with a dedication * to the king of that ingenious gentleman's " Treatise on the Globes," conceived and expressed in such a manner as could not fail to be very grateful to a monarch, distinguished for his love of the sciences.

This year was published a ridicule of his style, under the title of " Lexiphanes." Sir John Hawkins ascribes it to Dr. Kenrick ; but its author was one Campbell, a Scotch purser in the navy. The ridicule consisted in applying Johnson's " words of large meaning," to insignificant matters, as if one should put the armour of Goliath upon a dwarf. The contrast might be laughable ; but the dignity of the armour must remain the same in all considerate minds. This malicious drollery, therefore, it may easily be supposed. could do no harm to its illustrious object.

"TO BENNET LANGTON, ESQ., AT MR. ROTHWELL'S, PERFUMER, IN NEW BOND-STREET, LONDON.

"DEAR SIR, *Lichfield, Oct.* 10, 1767.
" That you have been all summer in London is one more reason for which I regret my long stay in the country. I hope that you will not leave the town before my return. We have here only the chance of vacancies in the passing carriages, and I have bespoken one that may, if it happens, bring me to town on the 14th of this month ; but this is not certain.

"It will be a favour if you communicate this to Mrs. Williams : I long to see all my friends. I am, dear Sir,
" Your most humble servant,
" SAM. JOHNSON."

It appears from his notes of the state of his mind,[3] that he suffered great perturbation and distraction in 1768. Nothing of his writings was given to the public this year, except the Prologue* to his friend Goldsmith's comedy of " The Good-natured Man." The first lines of

[1] Prayers and Meditations. pp. 77, 78.—BOSWELL. [2] Ibid. p. 73. [3] Ibid. p. 81

this Prologue are strongly characteristical of the dismal gloom of his mind ; which, in his case, as in the case of all who are distressed with the same malady of imagination, transfers to others its own feelings. Who could suppose it was to introduce a comedy, when Mr. Bensley solemnly began :—

> " Press'd with the load of life, the weary mind,
> Surveys the general toil of human kind."

But this dark ground might make Goldsmith's humour shine the more.[1]

In the spring of this year, having published my " Account of Corsica, with the Journal of a Tour to that Island," I returned to London, very desirous to see Dr. Johnson, and hear him upon the subject. I found ne was at Oxford, with his friend Mr. Chambers, who was now Vinerian Professor, and lived in New Inn Hall. Having had no letter from him since that in which he criticised the Latinity of my Thesis, and having been told by somebody that he was offended at my having put into my book an extract of his letter to me at Paris, I was impatient to be with him, and therefore followed him to Oxford, where I was entertained by Mr. Chambers, with a civility which I shall ever gratefully remember. I found that Dr. Johnson had sent a letter to me to Scotland, and that I had nothing to complain of but his being more indifferent to my anxiety than I wished him to be. Instead of giving, with the circumstances of time and place, such fragments of his conversation as I preserved during this visit to Oxford, I shall throw them together in continuation.

I asked him whether, as a moralist, he did not think that the practice of the law, in some degree, hurt the nice feeling of honesty. Johnson : " Why no, Sir, if you act properly. You are not to deceive your clients with false representations of your opinion ; you are not to tell lies to a judge." Boswell : " But what do you think of supporting a cause which you know to be bad ? " Johnson : " Sir, you do not know it to be good or bad till the judge determines it. I have said that you are to state facts fairly ; so that your thinking, or what you call knowing, a cause to be bad, must be from reasoning, must be from your supposing your arguments to be weak and inconclusive. But, Sir,

---

[1] In this Prologue, as Mr. John Taylor informs me, after the fourth line—" And social sorrow loses half its pain," the following couplet was inserted :—

> " *Amidst the toils of this returning year,*
> *When senators and nobles learn to fear ;*
> Our *little* bard without complaint may share
> The bustling season's epidemic care : "

So the Prologue appeared in " The Public Advertiser," the theatrical gazette of that day, soon after the first representation of this comedy in 1768. Goldsmith probably thought that the lines printed in italic characters, which, however, seem necessary, or at least improve the sense, might give offence, and therefore prevailed on Johnson to omit them. The epithet *little*, which perhaps the author thought might diminish his dignity, was also changed to *anxious.*—Malone.

that is not enough. An argument which does not convince yourself may convince the judge to whom you urge it; and if it does convince him, why, then, sir, you are wrong, and he is right. It is his business to judge; and you are not to be confident in your own opinion that a cause is bad, but to say all you can for your client, and then hear the judge's opinion." BOSWELL : " But, Sir, does not affecting a warmth when you have no warmth, and appearing to be clearly of one opinion when you are in reality of another opinion, does not such dissimulation impair one's honesty? Is there not some danger that a lawyer may put on the same mask in common life in the intercourse with his friends?" JOHNSON : "Why no, Sir. Everybody knows you are paid for affecting warmth for your client; and it is, therefore, properly no dissimulation: the moment you come from the bar you resume your usual behaviour. Sir, a man will no more carry the artifice of the bar into the common intercourse of society, than a man who is paid for tumbling upon his hands will continue to tumble upon his hands when he should walk on his feet."[1]

Talking of some of the modern plays, he said, "False Delicacy" was totally void of character. He praised Goldsmith's "Good-natured Man;" said it was the best comedy that had appeared since "The Provoked Husband," and that there had not been of late any such character exhibited on the stage as that of Croaker. I observed it was the Suspirius of his "Rambler." He said, Goldsmith had owned he had borrowed it from thence. "Sir," continued he, "there is all the difference in the world between characters of nature and characters of manners; and *there* is the difference between the characters of Fielding and those

of Richardson. Characters of manners are very entertaining; but they are to be understood by a more superficial observer than characters of nature, where a man must dive into the recesses of the human heart."

It always appeared to me that he estimated the compositions of Richardson too highly, and that he had an unreasonable prejudice against Fielding. In comparing those two writers he used this expression : "that there was as great a difference between them as between a man who knew how a watch was made and a man who could tell the hour by looking on the

FIELDING.

dial-plate." This was a short and figurative state of his distinction

[1] See "The Journal of a Tour to the Hebrides," 4th edit. p. 14, where Johnson has supported the same argument.—J. BOSWELL, JUN.

between drawing characters of nature and characters only of manners. But I cannot help being of opinion, that the neat watches of Fielding are as well constructed as the large clocks of Richardson, and that his dial-plates are brighter. Fielding s characters, though they do not expand themselves so widely in dissertation, are as just pictures of human nature, and I will venture to say, have more striking features, and nicer touches of the pencil ; and though Johnson used to quote with approbation a saying of Richardson's, "that the virtues of Fielding's heroes were the vices of a truly good man," I will venture to add, that the moral tendency of Fielding's writings, though it does not encourage a strained and rarely possible virtue, is ever favourable to honour and honesty, and cherishes the benevolent and generous affections. He who is as good as Fielding would make him, is an amiable member of society, and may be led on by more regulated instructors, to a higher state of ethical perfection.

Johnson proceeded : "Even Sir Francis Wronghead[1] is a character of manners, though drawn with great humour." He then repeated, very happily, all Sir Francis's credulous account to Manly of his being with "the great man," and securing a place. I asked him, if "The Suspicious Husband" did not furnish a well-drawn character, that of Ranger. JOHNSON: "No, Sir ; Ranger is just a rake, a mere rake, and a lively young fellow, but no *character*."

The great Douglas cause was at this time a very general subject of discussion. I found he had not studied it with much attention, but had only heard parts of it occasionally. He, however, talked of it, and said, "I am of opinion that positive proof of fraud should not be required of the plaintiff, but that the judges should decide according as probability shall appear to preponderate, granting to the defendent the presumption of filiation to be strong in his favour. And I think, too, that a good deal of weight should be allowed to the dying declarations, because they were spontaneous. There is a great difference between what is said without our being urged to it, and what is said from a kind of compulsion. If I praise a man's book without being asked my opinion of it, that is honest praise, to which one may trust. But if an author asks me if I like his book, and I give him something like praise, it must not be taken as my real opinion."

"I have not been troubled for a long time with authors desiring my opinion of their works. I used once to be sadly plagued with a man who wrote verses, but who literally had no other notion of a verse, but that it consisted of ten syllables. *Lay your knife and your fork across your plate,* was to him a verse :

Lay yōur knife ānd your fōrk acrōss your plāte.

---

[1] In "The Provoked Husband," which was begun by Sir John Vanbrugh, and finished by Colley Cibber.—WRIGHT.

As he wrote a great number of verses, he sometimes by chance made good ones, though he did not know it."

He renewed his promise of coming to Scotland and going with me to the Hebrides, but said he would now content himself with seeing one or two of the most curious of them. He said, "Macaulay, who writes the account of St. Kilda, set out with a prejudice against prejudice, and wanted to be a smart modern thinker; and yet affirms for a truth, that when a ship arrives there all the inhabitants are seized with a cold."

Dr. John Campbell, the celebrated writer, took a great deal of pains to ascertain this fact, and attempted to account for it on physical principles, from the effect of effluvia from human bodies. Johnson, at another time, praised Macaulay, for his "*magnanimity*," in asserting this wonderful story, because it was well attested. A lady of Norfolk, by a letter to my friend Dr. Burney, has favoured me with the following solution:

"Now for the explication of this seeming mystery, which is so very obvious as, for that reason, to have escaped the penetration of Dr. Johnson and his friend, as well as that of the author. Reading the book with my ingenious friend, the late Reverend Mr. Christian, of Docking—after ruminating a little, 'The cause,' says he, 'is a natural one. The situation of St. Kilda renders a north-east wind indispensably necessary before a stranger can land. The wind, not the stranger, occasions an epidemic cold.' If I am not mistaken, Mr. Macaulay is dead; if living, this solution might please him, as I hope it will Mr. Boswell, in return for the many agreeable hours his works have afforded us."

Johnson expatiated on the advantages of Oxford for learning. "There is here, Sir," said he, "such a progressive emulation. The students are anxious to appear well to their tutors; the tutors are anxious to have their pupils appear well in the college; the colleges are anxious to have their students appear well in the university; and there are excellent rules of discipline in every college. That the rules are sometimes ill observed, may be true; but is nothing against the system. The members of an University may, for a season, be unmindful of their duty. I am arguing for the excellency of the institution."

Of Guthrie, he said, "Sir, he is a man of parts. He has no great regular fund of knowledge; but by reading so long, and writing so long, he no doubt has picked up a good deal."

He said he had lately been a long while at Lichfield, but had grown very weary before he left it. BOSWELL: "I wonder at that, Sir; it is your native place." JOHNSON: "Why so is Scotland *your* native place."

His prejudice against Scotland appeared remarkably strong at this time.[1] When I talked of our advancement in literature, "Sir," said

---

[1] Johnson's invectives against Scotland, in common conversation, were more in pleasantry and sport than real and malignant; for no man was more visited by natives of that country nor were there any for whom he had a greater esteem. It was to Dr. Grainger, a Scottish physician, that I owed my first acquaintance with Johnson in 1756.—PERCY.

he, "you have learnt a little from us, and you think yourselves very great men. Hume would never have written History, had not Voltaire written it before him. He is an echo of Voltaire." Boswell: "But, Sir, we have Lord Kames." Johnson: "You *have* Lord Kames. Keep him ; ha, ha, ha ! We don't envy you him. Do you ever see Dr. Robertson ? " Boswell: "Yes, Sir," Johnson: "Does the dog talk of me ? " Boswell: "Indeed, Sir, he does, and loves you." Thinking that I now had him in a corner, and being solicitous for the literary fame of my country, I pressed him for his opinion on the merit of Dr. Robertson's History of Scotland. But to my surprise, he escaped. " Sir, I love Robertson, and I won't talk of his book."

It is but justice both to him and Dr. Robertson to add, that though he indulged himself in this sally of wit, he had too good taste not to be fully sensible of the merits of that admirable work.

An essay, written by Mr. Deane, a Divine of the Church of England, maintaining the future life of brutes, by an explication of certain parts of the Scriptures, was mentioned, and the doctrine insisted on by a gentleman who seemed fond of curious speculation—Johnson, who did not like to hear anything concerning a future state which was not authorised by the regular canons of orthodoxy, discouraged this talk ; and being offended at its continuation, he watched an opportunity to give the gentleman a blow of reprehension. So, when the poor speculatist, with a serious, metaphysical, pensive face, addressed him, " But really, Sir, when we see a very sensible dog, we don't know what to think of him," Johnson, rolling with joy at the thought which beamed in his eye, turned quickly round, and replied, "True, Sir : and when we see a very foolish *fellow*, we don't know what to think of *him*." He then rose up, strided to the fire, and stood for some time laughing and exulting.

I told him that I had several times, when in Italy, seen the experiment of placing a scorpion within a circle of burning coals ; that it ran round and round in extreme pain, and finding no way to escape, retired to the centre, and like a true stoic philosopher, darted its sting into its head, and thus at once freed itself from its woes. *"This must end 'em."* I said this was a curious fact, as it showed deliberate suicide in a reptile. Johnson would not admit the fact. He said, Maupertuis [1] was of opinion that it does not kill itself, but dies of the heat ; that it gets to the centre of the circle, as the coolest place ; that its turning

* I should think it impossible not to wonder at the variety of Johnson's reading however desultory it might have been. Who could have imagined that the High Church of England-man would be so prompt in quoting *Maupertuis*, who, I am sorry to think, stands in the list of those unfortunate mistaken men, who call themselves *esprits forts*. I have, however, a high respect for that philosopher whom the great Frederick of Prussia loved and honoured, and addressed pathetically in one of his poems,—

" Maupertuis ! cher Maupertuis !
Que notre vie est peu de chose."

There was in Maupertuis a vigour and yet a tenderness of sentiment, united with strong

its tail in upon its head is merely a convulsion, and that it does not sting itself. He said he would be satisfied if the great anatomist Morgagni, after dissecting a scorpion on which the experiment had been tried, should certify that its sting had penetrated into its head.

He seemed pleased to talk of natural philosophy. "That woodcocks," said he, "fly over the northern countries, is proved, because they have been observed at sea. Swallows certainly sleep all the winter. A number of them conglobulate together, by flying round and round, and then all in a heap throw themselves under water, and lie in the bed of a river." He told us, one of his first essays was a Latin poem upon the glow-worm; I am sorry I did not ask where it was to be found.

Talking of the Russians and the Chinese, he advised me to read "Bell's Travels." I asked him whether I should read Du Halde's "Account of China." "Why, yes," said he, "as one reads such a book; that is to say, consult it."

He talked of the heinousness of the crime of adultery, by which the peace of families was destroyed. He said, "confusion of progeny constitutes the essence of the crime; and therefore a woman who breaks her marriage vows is much more criminal than a man who does it. A man, to be sure, is criminal in the sight of GOD; but he does not do his wife a very material injury, if he does not insult her; if, for instance, from mere wantonness of appetite, he steals privately to her chambermaid. Sir, a wife ought not greatly to resent this. I would not receive home a daughter who had run away from her husband on that account. A wife should study to reclaim her husband by more attention to please him. Sir, a man will not, once in a hundred instances, leave his wife and go to a harlot, if his wife has not been negligent of pleasing."

Here he discovered that acute discrimination, that solid judgment, and that knowledge of human nature, for which he was upon all occasions remarkable. Taking care to keep in view the moral and religious duty, as understood in our nation, he showed clearly from reason and good sense, the greater degree of culpability in the one sex deviating from it than the other; and, at the same time, inculcated a very useful lesson as to *the way to keep him.*

I asked him if it was not hard that one deviation from chastity should so absolutely ruin a young woman. JOHNSON: "Why no, Sir, it is the great principle which she is taught. When she has given up that principle, she has given up every notion of female honour and virtue, which are all included in chastity."

A gentleman talked to him of a lady whom he greatly admired and wished to marry, but was afraid of her superiority of talents. "Sir,"

intellectual powers, and uncommon ardour of soul. Would he had been a Christian! I cannot help earnestly venturing to hope that he is one now.—BOSWELL.

Maupertuis died in 1759 at the age of 62, in the arms of the Bernoullis, *tres Chretiennemens* —BURNEY

aid he, "you need not be afraid; marry her. Before a year goes about, you'll find that reason much weaker, and that wit not so bright." Yet the gentleman may be justified in his apprehension by one of Dr. Johnson's admirable sentences in his life of Waller: "He doubtless praised many whom he would have been afraid to marry; and, perhaps, married one whom he would have been ashamed to praise. Many qualities contribute to domestic happiness, upon which poetry has no colours to bestow: and many airs and sallies may delight imagination, which he who flatters them never can approve."

He praised Signor Baretti. "His account of Italy is a very entertaining book; and, Sir, I know no man who carries his head higher in conversation than Baretti. There are strong powers in his mind. He has not, indeed, many hooks; but with what hooks he has, he grapples very forcibly."

At this time I observed upon the dial-plate of his watch [1] a short Greek inscription, taken from the New Testament, Νυξ γαρ ερχεται, being the first words of our SAVIOUR's solemn admonition to the improvement of that time which is allowed us to prepare for eternity: "The night cometh when no man can work." He some time afterwards laid aside this dial-plate; and when I asked him the reason, he said, "It might do very well upon a clock which a man keeps in his closet; but to have it upon his watch which he carries about with him, and which is often looked at by others, might be censured as ostentatious." Mr. Steevens is now possessed of the dial-plate inscribed as above.

He remained at Oxford a considerable time; I was obliged to go to London, where I received his letter, which had been returned from Scotland.

"TO JAMES BOSWELL, ESQ.

"MY DEAR BOSWELL, Oxford, March 23, 1768.

"I have omitted a long time to write to you, without knowing very well why. I could now tell why I should not write; for who would write to men who publish the letters of their friends, without their leave? Yet I write to you in spite of my caution, to tell you that I shall be glad to see you, and that I wish you would empty your head of Corsica, which I think has filled it rather too long. But, at all events, I shall be glad, very glad, to see you.

"I am, Sir, yours affectionately,
"SAM. JOHNSON."

I answered thus:—

"TO MR. SAMUEL JOHNSON.

"MY DEAR SIR, London, 26th April, 1768.

"I have received your last letter, which, though very short, and by no means complimentary, yet gave me real pleasure, because it contains these words, 'I

[1] Sir John Hawkins says, that this watch was the first Johnson ever possessed. It was made for him by Mudge and Dutton in 1768. They were celebrated watchmakers of the last century, and their shop, situate at the left corner of Hind-court, was the last in Fleet-street to undergo the sweeping ordeal of modernisation, which it escaped up to the year 1850 —ED. D 2

shall be glad, very glad, to see you.'—Surely you have no reason to complain of my publishing a single paragraph of one of your letters; the temptation to it was so strong. An irrevocable grant of your friendship, and your dignifying my desire of visiting Corsica with the epithet of 'a wise and noble curiosity,' are to me more valuable than many of the grants of kings.

"But how can you bid me 'empty my head of Corsica?' My noble-minded friend, do you not feel for an oppressed nation bravely struggling to be free Consider fairly what is the case. The Corsicans never received any kindness from the Genoese. They never agreed to be subject to them. They owe them nothing; and when reduced to an abject state of slavery, by force, shall they not rise in the great cause of liberty, and break the galling yoke? And shall not every liberal soul be warm for them? Empty my head of Corsica! Empty it of honour, empty it of humanity, empty it of friendship, empty it of piety! No! while I live, Corsica and the cause of the brave islanders shall ever employ much of my attention, shall ever interest me in the sincerest manner.   *   *   *   *

"I am, &c.,

"JAMES BOSWELL."

"TO MRS. LUCY PORTER, IN LICHFIELD.

"MY DEAR DEAR LOVE,   *Oxford, April* 18, 1768.

You have had a very great loss. To lose an old friend, is to be cut off from a great part of the little pleasure that this life allows. But such is the condition of our nature, that as we live on we must see those whom we love drop successively, and find our circle of relation grow less and less, till we are almost unconnected with the world; and then it must soon be our turn to drop into the grave. There is always this consolation, that we have one Protector, who can never be lost but by our own fault; and every new experience of the uncertainty of all other comforts should determine us to fix our hearts where true joys are to be found. All union with the inhabitants of earth must in time be broken; and all the hopes that terminate here, must on [one] part or other end in disappointment.

"I am glad that Mrs. Adey and Mrs. Cobb do not leave you alone. Pay my respects to them, and the Sewards, and all my friends. When Mr. Porter comes, he will direct you. Let me know of his arrival, and I will write to him.

"When I go back to London, I will take care of your reading glass. Whenever I can do anything for you, remember, my dear darling, that one of my greatest pleasures is to please you.

"The punctuality of your correspondence I consider as a proof of great regard. When we shall see each other I know not, but let us often think on each other, and think with tenderness. Do not forget me in your prayers. I have for a long time back been very poorly; but of what use is it to complain?

"Write often, for your letters always give great pleasure to,

"My dear, your most affectionate and most humble servant,

"SAM. JOHNSON."

Upon his arrival in London in May, he surprised me one morning with a visit at my lodging in Half-moon-street, was quite satisfied with my explanation, and was in the kindest and most agreeable frame of mind. As he had objected to a part of one of his letters being published, I thought it right to take this opportunity of asking him explicitly whether it would be improper to publish his letters after his death. His answer was, " Nay, Sir, when I am dead, you may do as you will."

He talked in his usual style with a rough contempt of popular liberty. " They make a rout about *universal* liberty, without considering that all that is to be valued, or indeed can be enjoyed by individuals, is *private* liberty. Political liberty is good only so far as it produces private liberty. Now, Sir, there is the liberty of the press, which you know is a constant topic. Suppose you and I and two hundred more were restrained from printing our thoughts ; what then ? What proportion would that restraint upon us bear to the private happiness of the nation ? "

This mode of representing the inconveniences of restraint as light and insignificant, was a kind of sophistry in which he delighted to indulge himself, in opposition to the extreme laxity for which it has been fashionable for too many to argue, when it is evident, upon reflection, that the very essence of government is restraint ; and certain it is, that as government produces rational happiness, too much restraint is better than too little. But when restraint is unnecessary, and so close as to gall those who are subject to it, the people may and ought to remonstrate ; and, if relief is not granted, to resist. Of this manly and spirited principle, no man was more convinced than Johnson himself.

About this time Dr. Kenrick attacked him, through my sides, in a pamphlet, entitled " An Epistle to James Boswell, Esq., occasioned by his having transmitted the Moral Writings of Dr. Samuel Johnson to Pascal Paoli, General of the Corsicans." I was at first inclined to answer this pamphlet ; but Johnson, who knew that my doing so would only gratify Kenrick, by keeping alive what would soon die away of itself, would not suffer me to take any notice of it.

His sincere regard for Francis Barber, his faithful negro servant, made him so desirous of his further improvement, that he now placed him at a school at Bishop Stortford, in Hertfordshire. This humane attention does Johnson's heart much honour. Out of many letters which Mr. Barber received from his master, he has preserved three, which he kindly gave me, and which I shall insert according to their dates.

" TO MR. FRANCIS BARBER.

"Dear Francis,   *May* 28, 1768.

" I have been very much out of order. I am glad to hear that you are well, and design to come soon to you. I would have you stay at Mrs. Clapp's for the present, till I can determine what we shall do. Be a good boy.

" My compliments to Mrs. Clapp and to Mr. Fowler.

" I am, yours affectionately,

"Sam. Johnson."

Soon afterwards he supped at the Crown and Anchor tavern, in the Strand, with a company whom I collected to meet him. They were Dr. Percy, now Bishop of Dromore, Dr. Douglas, now Bishop of Salisbury, Mr. Langton, Dr. Robertson, the historian, Dr. Hugh Blair, and Mr. Thomas Davies, who wished much to be introduced to these eminent Scotch literati ; but on the present occasion he had very little

DR. ROBERTSON.

opportunity of hearing them talk, for with an excess of prudence, for which Johnson afterwards found fault with them, they hardly opened their lips, and that only to say something which they were certain would not expose them to the sword of Goliath ; such was their anxiety for their fame when in the presence of Johnson. He was this evening in remarkable vigour of mind, and eager to exert himself in conversation, which he did with great readiness and fluency ; but I am sorry to find that I have preserved but a small part of what passed.

He allowed high praise to Thomson as a poet ; but when one of the company said he was also a very good man,' our moralist contested this with great warmth, accusing him of gross sensuality and licentiousness of manners. I was very much afraid that in writing Thomson's life, Dr. Johnson would have treated his private character with a stern severity, but I was agreeably disappointed ; and I may claim a little merit in it, from my having been at pains to send him authentic accounts of the affectionate and generous conduct of that poet to his sisters, one of whom, the wife of Mr. Thomson, schoolmaster at Lanark I knew, and was presented by her with three of his letters, one of which Dr. Johnson has inserted in his life.

He was vehement against old Dr. Mounsey,[1] of Chelsea College, as "a fellow who swore and talked bawdy." "I have often been in his company," said Dr. Percy, "and never heard him swear or talk bawdy." Mr. Davies, who sat next to Dr. Percy, having after this had some conversation aside with him, made a discovery which, in his zeal to pay court to Dr. Johnson, he eagerly proclaimed aloud from the foot of the

[1] Messenger Mounsey, M.D., died at his apartments in Chelsea College, Dec. 26, 1788, at the great age of ninety-five. An extraordinary direction in his will may be found in the Gentleman's Magazine," vol. l., part ii., p 1183.—MALONE.

table : "Oh, Sir, I have found out a very good reason why Dr. Percy never heard Mounsey swear or talk bawdy, for he tells me he never saw him but at the Duke of Northumberland's table." "And so, Sir," said Dr. Johnson loudly to Dr. Percy, "you would shield this man from the charge of swearing and talking bawdy, because he did not do so at the Duke of Northumberland's table. Sir, you might as well tell us that you had seen him hold up his hand at the Old Bailey, and he neither swore nor talked bawdy ; or that you had seen him in the cart at Tyburn, and he neither swore nor talked bawdy. And is it thus, Sir, that you presume to controvert what I have related ?" Dr. Johnson's animadversion was uttered in such a manner, that Dr. Percy seemed to be displeased, and soon afterwards left the company, of which Johnson did not at that time take any notice.

Swift having been mentioned, Johnson, as usual, treated him with little respect as an author. Some of us endeavoured to support the Dean of St. Patrick's, by various arguments. One in par-

DR. MOUNSEY.

ticular praised his "Conduct of the Allies." JOHNSON : "Sir, his 'Conduct of the Allies' is a performance of very little ability." "Surely, Sir," said Dr. Douglas, "you must allow it has strong facts." [1] JOHNSON : "Why, yes, Sir ; but what is that to the merit of the composition ? In the Sessions-paper of the Old Bailey there are strong facts. House-breaking is a strong fact ; robbery is a strong fact ; and murder is a *mighty* strong fact : but is great praise due to the historian of those strong facts ? No, Sir, Swift has told what he had to tell distinctly enough, but that is all. He had to count ten, and he has counted it right."—Then recollecting that Mr. Davies, by acting as an *informer*, had been the occasion of his talking somewhat too harshly to his friend Dr. Percy, for which, probably, when the first ebullition was over he felt some compunction, he took an opportunity to give him a hit : so added, with a preparatory laugh, "Why, Sir, Tom Davies

[1] My respectable friend, upon reading this passage, observed that he probably must have said not simply " strong facts," but " strong facts well arranged." His lordship, however, knows too well the value of written documents to insist on setting his recollection against my notes taken at the time. He does not attempt to *traverse the record*. The fact, perhaps, may have been, either that the additional words escaped me in the noise of a numerous company, or that Dr. Johnson, from his impetuosity and eagerness to seize an opportunity to make a lively retort, did not allow Dr. Douglas to finish his sentence.—BOSWELL.

might have written the 'Conduct of the Allies.'" Poor Tom being thus suddenly dragged into ludicrous notice in presence of the Scottish Doctors, to whom he was ambitious of appearing to advantage, was grievously mortified. Nor did his punishment rest here ; for upon subsequent occasions, whenever he, "statesman all o'er,"[1] assumed a strutting importance, I used to hail him—" *The Author of the Conduct of the Allies.*"

When I called upon Dr. Johnson next morning, I found him highly satisfied with his colloquial prowess the preceding evening. " Well," said he, " we had good talk." BOSWELL : "Yes, Sir, you tossed and gored several persons."

The late Alexander Earl of Eglintoune, who loved wit more than wine, and men of genius more than sycophants, had a great admiration of Johnson ; but from the remarkable elegance of his own manners, was, perhaps, too delicately sensible of the roughness which sometimes appeared in Johnson's behaviour. One evening about this time, when his lordship did me the honour to sup at my lodgings with Dr. Robertson and several other men of literary distinction, he regretted that Johnson had not been educated with more refinement, and lived more in polished society. " No, no, my Lord," said Signor Baretti, "do with him what you would, he would always have been a bear." " True," answered the Earl, with a smile, " but he would have been a *dancing* bear."

To obviate all the reflections which have gone round the world to Johnson's prejudice, by applying to him the epithet of a *bear*, let me impress upon my readers a just and happy saying of my friend Goldsmith, who knew him well: " Johnson, to be sure, has a roughness in his manner ; but no man alive has a more tender heart. *He has nothing of the bear but his skin.*"

---

[1] See the hard drawing of him in Churchill's ROSCIAD.—BOSWELL.

STRATFORD JUBILEE.

CHAPTER III.—1769

JOHNSON APPOINTED PROFESSOR OF ANCIENT LITERATURE—BOSWELL AT THE STRATFORD JUBILEE HIS ACCOUNT OF CORSICA—SCOTCH GARDENING—JOHNSON AND BOSWELL VISIT MR. AND MRS. THRALE—BOSWELL INTRODUCES JOHNSON TO GENERAL PAOLI— GOLDSMITH'S TAILOR—MRS. MONTAGU'S ESSAY ON SHAKSPEARE—FOOTE—BARETTI'S TRIAL —MRS. WILLIAMS'S TEA-TABLE—JOHNSON'S VIEWS OF ROMANISM AND CONVERSION TO POPERY—THE MARRIAGE SERVICE.

IN 1769, so far as I can discover, the public was favoured with nothing of Johnson's composition, either for himself or any of his friends. His "Meditations" too strongly prove that he suffered much both in body and mind; yet was he perpetually striving against *evil*, and nobly endeavouring to advance his intellectual and devotional improvement. Every generous and grateful heart must feel for the distresses of so eminent a benefactor to mankind; and now that his unhappiness is certainly known, must respect that dignity of character which prevented him from complaining.

His Majesty having the preceding year instituted the Royal Academy of Arts in London, Johnson had now the honour of being appointed Professor in Ancient Literature.[1] In the course of the year he wrote some letters to Mrs. Thrale, passed some part of the summer at Oxford and at Lichfield, and when at Oxford he wrote the following letter :—

[1] In which place he has been succeeded by Bennet Langton, Esq. When that truly religious gentleman was elected to this honorary Professorship, at the same time that Edward Gibbon, Esq., noted for introducing a kind of sneering infidelity into his Historical Writings, was elected Professor in Ancient History, in the room of Dr. Goldsmith, I observed that it brought to my mind, "Wicked Will Whiston and good Mr. Ditton."—I am now also of that admirable institution as Secretary for Foreign Correspondence, by the favour of the Academicians and the approbation of the sovereign.—BOSWELL

"TO THE REVEREND MR. THOMAS WARTON.

"DEAR SIR,   *May* 31, 1769.

"Many years ago, when I used to read in the library of your college, I promised to recompense the college for that permission, by adding to their books a Baskerville's Virgil. I have now sent it, and desire you to deposit it on the shelves in my name.[1]

"If you will be pleased to let me know when you have an hour of leisure, I will drink tea with you. I am engaged for the afternoon, to-morrow, and on Friday : all my mornings are my own.[2]   I am, &c.,

"SAM. JOHNSON."

I came to London in the autumn, and having informed him that I was going to be married in a few months, I wished to have as much of

BOSWELL IN THE COSTUME OF A CORSICAN CHIEF.

his conversation as I could before engaging in a state of life which would probably keep me more in Scotland, and prevent me seeing him so often as when I was a single man ; but I found he was at Brighthelmstone with Mr. and Mrs. Thrale. I was very sorry that I had not his company with me at the Jubilee, in honour of Shakspeare, at Stratford-upon-Avon, the great poet's native town. Johnson's connection both with Shakspeare and Garrick founded a double claim to his presence ; and it would have been highly gratifying to Mr. Garrick. Upon this occasion I particularly lamented that he had not that warmth of friendship for his brilliant pupil, which we may suppose would have had a benignant effect on both. When almost every man of eminence in the literary world was happy to partake in this festival of genius, the absence of Johnson could not but be wondered at

1 "It has this inscription in a blank leaf: '*Hunc librum D. D. Samuel Johnson, eo quod hic loci studiis interdum vacaret.*' Of this library, which is an old Gothic room, he was very fond. On my observing to him that some of the *modern* libraries of the University were more commodious and pleasant for study, as being more spacious and airy, he replied 'Sir, if a man has a mind to *prance*, he must study at Christ Church and All-Souls.'"— WARTON

2 "During this visit he seldom or never dined out. He appeared to be deeply engaged in some literary work. Miss Williams was now with him at Oxford."—WARTON.

and regretted. The only trace of him there, was in the whimsical advertisement of a haberdasher, who sold *Shaksperian ribands* of various dyes ; and, by way of illustrating their appropriation to the bard, introduced a line from the celebrated Prologue at the opening of Drury-lane theatre :

"Each change of *many-colour'd* life he drew."

From Brighthelmstone Dr. Johnson wrote me the following letter, which they who may think I ought to have suppressed, must have less ardent feelings than I have always avowed.[1]

"TO JAMES BOSWELL, ESQ.

"DEAR SIR,   *Brighthelmstone, Sept. 9,* 1769.

"Why do you charge me with unkindness? I have omitted nothing that could do you good, or give you pleasure, unless it be that I have forborne to tell you my opinion of your 'Account of Corsica.' I believe my opinion, if you think well of my judgment, might have given you pleasure; but when it is considered how much vanity is excited by praise, I am not sure that it would have done you good. Your history is like other histories, but your Journal is, in a very high degree, curious and delightful. There is between the history and the journal that difference which there will always be found between notions borrowed from without, and notions generated within. Your history was copied from books; your journal rose out of your own experience and observation. You express images which operated strongly upon yourself, and you have impressed them with great force upon your readers. I know not whether I could name any narrative by which curiosity is better excited or better gratified.

"I am glad that you are going to be married; and as I wish you well in things of less importance, wish you well, with proportionate ardour, in this crisis of your life. What I can contribute to your happiness, I should be very unwilling to withhold : for I have always loved and valued you, and shall love you and value you still more, as you become more regular and useful : effects which a happy marriage will hardly fail to produce.

"I do not find that I am likely to come back very soon from this place. I

---

[1] In the Preface of my "Account of Corsica," published in 1768, I thus express myself:— "He who publishes a book affecting not to be an author, and professing an indifference for literary fame, may possibly impose upon many people such an idea of his consequence as he wishes may be received. For my part I should be proud to be known as an author, and I have an ardent ambition for literary fame; for, of all possessions I should imagine literary fame to be the most valuable. A man who has been able to furnish a book, which has been approved by the world, has established himself as a respectable character in distant society, without any danger of having that character lessened by the observation of his weaknesses. To preserve an uniform dignity among those who see us every day, is hardly possible; and to aim at it, must put us under the fetters of perpetual restraint. The author of an approved book may allow his natural disposition an easy play, and yet indulge the pride of superior genius, when he considers that by those who know him only as an author, he never ceases to be respected. Such an author, when in his hours of gloom and discontent, may have the consolation to think that his writings are at that very time giving pleasure to numbers; and such an author may cherish the hope of being remembered after death; which has been a great object to the noblest minds in all ages."—BOSWELL.

shall, perhaps, stay a fortnight longer : and a fortnight is a long time to a lover absent from his mistress. Would a fortnight ever have an end?

> "I am, dear Sir,
> " Your most affectionate humble servant,
> "SAM. JOHNSON."

After his return to town, we met frequently, and I continued the practice of making notes of his conversation, though not with so much assiduity as I wish I had done. At this time, indeed, I had a sufficient excuse for not being able to appropriate so much time to my journal ; for General Paoli, after Corsica had been overpowered by the monarchy of France, was now no longer at the head of his brave countrymen, but having with difficulty escaped from his native island, had sought an asylum in Great Britain ; and it was my duty, as well as my pleasure, to attend much upon him. Such particulars of Johnson's conversation at this period as I have committed to writing, I shall here introduce, without any strict attention to methodical arrangement. Sometimes short notes of different days shall be blended together, and sometimes a day may seem important enough to be separately distinguished.

He said, he would not have Sunday kept with rigid severity and gloom, but with a gravity and simplicity of behaviour.

I told him that David Hume had made a short collection of Scotticisms. " I wonder," said Johnson, "that *he* should find them." [1]

He would not admit the importance of the question concerning the legality of general warrants. " Such a power," he observed, " must be vested in every government, to answer particular cases of necessity ; and there can be no just complaint but when it is abused, for which those who administer government must be answerable. It is a matter of such indifference, a matter about which the people care so very little, that were a man to be sent over Britain to offer them an exemption from it at a halfpenny a piece, very few would purchase it." This was a specimen of that laxity of talking, which I had heard him fairly acknowledge ; for, surely, while the power of granting general warrants was supposed to be legal, and the apprehension of them hung over our heads, we did not possess that security of freedom, congenial to our happy constitution, and which, by the intrepid exertions of Mr. Wilkes, has been happily established.

He said, " The duration of Parliament, whether for seven years or the life of the King, appears to me so immaterial, that I would not give half-a-crown to turn the scale one way or the other. The *habeas corpus* is the single advantage which our government has over that of other countries."

On the 30th of September we dined together at the Mitre. I attempted to argue for the superior happiness of the savage life, upon the

---

The first edition of Hume's " History of England " was full of Scotticisms, many of which he corrected in subsequent editions.—MALONE.

usual fanciful topics. Johnson : "Sir, there can be nothing more false. The savages have no bodily advantages beyond those of civilized men. They have not better health ; and as to care or mental uneasiness, they are not above it, but below it, like bears. No, Sir ; you are not to talk such paradox: let me have no more on't. It cannot entertain, far less can it instruct. Lord Monboddo, one of your Scotch judges, talked a great deal of such nonsense. I suffered *him*, but I will not suffer *you*." Boswell : "But, Sir, does not Rousseau talk such nonsense ?" Johnson : "True, Sir ; but Rousseau *knows* he is talking nonsense, and laughs at the world for staring at him." Boswell : "How so, Sir ?" Johnson : "Why, Sir, a man who talks nonsense so well, must know that he is talking nonsense. But I am *afraid* (chuckling and laughing) Monboddo does *not* know that he is talking nonsense."[1] Boswell : "Is it wrong then, Sir, to affect singularity, in order to make people stare ?" Johnson : "Yes, if you do it by propagating error ; and, indeed, it is wrong in any way. There is in human nature a general inclination to make people stare ; and every wise man has himself to cure of it, and does cure himself. If you wish to make people stare by doing better than others, why make them stare till they stare their eyes out. But consider how easy it is to make people stare, by being absurd. I may do it by going into a drawing-room without my shoes. You remember the gentleman in 'The Spectator,' who had a commission **of** lunacy taken out against him for his extreme singularity, such as never wearing a wig, but a night-cap. Now, Sir, abstractedly, the night-cap was best : but, relatively, the advantage was overbalanced by his making the boys run after him."[2]

Talking of a London life, he said, "The happiness of London is no to be conceived but by those who have been in it. I will venture to say, there is more learning and science within the circumference of ten miles from where we now sit, than in all the rest of the kingdom." Boswell : "The only disadvantage is the great distance at which people live from one another." Johnson : "Yes, Sir ; but that is occasioned by the largeness of it, which is the cause of all the other advantages." Boswell : "Sometimes I have been in the humour of wishing to retire to a desert." Johnson : "Sir, you have desert enough in Scotland."

---

[1] His Lordship having frequently spoken in an abusive manner of Dr. Johnson in my company, I, on one occasion during the life-time of my illustrious friend, could not refrain from retaliation, and repeated to him this saying. He has since published I don't know how many pages in one of his curious books, attempting, in much anger, but with pitiful effect, to persuade mankind that my illustrious friend was not the great and good man which they esteemed and ever will esteem him to be.—Boswell.

[2] William Seward, Esq., F.R.S., editor of "Anecdotes of some Distinguished Persons," &c., in 4 vols. 8vo, well known to a numerous and valuable acquaintance for his literature, love of the fine arts, and social virtues. I am indebted to him for several communications concerning Johnson.—Boswell.

Mr. Seward was born in London in 1747, the son of a wealthy brewer, partner in the house of Calvert and Seward. He was educated at the Charter-house and at Oxford, and died April 24, 1799.—Malone.

Although I had promised myself a great deal of instructive conversation with him on the conduct of the married state, of which I had then a near prospect, he did not say much upon that topic. Mr. Seward heard him once say, that "a man has a very bad chance for happiness in that state, unless he marries a woman of very strong and fixed principles of religion." He maintained to me, contrary to the common notion, that a woman would not be the worse wife for being learned; in which, from all that I have observed of *Artemisias*, I humbly differed from him. That a woman should be sensible and well informed, I allow to be a great advantage ; and think that Sir Thomas Overbury, in his rude versification,[1] has very judiciously pointed out that degree of intelligence which is to be desired in a female companion :—

> " Give me, next *good*, an *understanding wife*,
>   By Nature *wise*, not *learned* by much art ;
> Some *knowledge* on her side with all my life
>   More scope of conversation impart ;
> Besides, her inborne virtue fortifie ;
> They are most firmly good, who best know why."

When I censured a gentleman of my acquaintance for marrying a second time, as it showed a disregard of his first wife, he said, "Not at all, Sir. On the contrary, were he not to marry again, it might be concluded that his first wife had given him a disgust to marriage ; but by taking a second wife he pays the highest compliment to the first, by showing that she made him so happy as a married man, that he wishes to be so a second time." So ingenious a turn did he give to this delicate question. And yet, on another occasion, he owned that he once had almost asked a promise of Mrs. Johnson that she would not marry again, but had checked himself. Indeed, I cannot help thinking, that in his case the request would have been unreasonable ; for if Mrs. Johnson forgot, or thought it no injury to the memory of her first love—the husband of her youth and the father of her children—to make a second marriage, why should she be precluded from a third, should she be so inclined ? In Johnson's persevering fond appropriation of his *Tetty*, even after her decease, he seems totally to have overlooked the prior claim of the honest Birmingham trader. I presume that her having been married before had, at times, given him some uneasiness ; for I remember his observing upon the marriage of one of our common friends, "He has done a very foolish thing ; he has married a widow, when he might have had a maid."

We drank tea with Mrs. Williams. I had last year the pleasure of seeing Mrs. Thrale at Dr. Johnson's one morning, and had conversation enough with her to admire her talents, and to show her that I was as Johnsonian as herself. Dr. Johnson had probably been kind enough to

[1] " A Wife," a poem, 1614.—BOSWELL.

speak well of me, for this evening he delivered me a very polite card from Mr. Thrale and her, inviting me to Streatham.

On the 6th of October I complied with this obliging invitation, and found, at an elegant villa, six miles from town, every circumstance that can make society pleasing. Johnson, though quite at home, was yet looked up to with an awe, tempered by affection, and seemed to be equally the care of his host and hostess. I rejoiced at seeing him so happy.

He played off his wit against Scotland with a good-humoured pleasantry, which gave me, though no bigot to national prejudices, an opportunity for a little contest with him. I having said that England was obliged to us for gardeners, almost all their good gardeners being Scotchmen—JOHNSON: "Why, Sir, that is because gardening is much more necessary amongst you than with us, which makes so many of your people learn it. It is *all* gardening with you. Things which grow wild here, must be cultivated with great care in Scotland. Pray now," throwing himself back in his chair, and laughing, " are you ever able to bring the *sloe* to perfection ? "

I boasted that we had the honour of being the first to abolish the unhospitable, troublesome, and ungracious custom of giving veils to servants. JOHNSON: " Sir, you abolished veils because you were too poor to be able to give them."

Mrs. Thrale disputed with him on the merit of Prior. He attacked him powerfully; said he wrote of love like a man who had never felt it : his love verses were college verses ; and he repeated the song " Alexis shunn'd his fellow swains," &c., in so ludicrous a manner, as to make us all wonder how any one could have been pleased with such fantastical stuff. Mrs. Thrale stood to her gun with great courage in defence of amorous ditties, which Johnson despised, till he at last silenced her by saying, " My dear lady, talk no more of this. Nonsense can be defended but by nonsense."

Mrs. Thrale then praised Garrick's talents for light gay poetry ; and, as a specimen, repeated his song in " Florizel and Perdita," and dwelt with peculiar pleasure on this line :

> "I'd smile with the simple, and feed with the poor."

JOHNSON: " Nay, my dear lady, this will never do. Poor David ! Smile with the simple. What folly is that ? And who would feed with the poor that can help it ? No, no ; let me smile with the wise, and feed with the rich." I repeated this sally to Garrick, and wondered to find his sensibility as a writer not a little irritated by it. To soothe him I observed that Johnson spared none of us ; and I quoted the passage in Horace, in which he compares one who attacks his friends for the sake of a laugh, to a pushing ox, that is marked by a bunch of hay put upon his horns : *fœnum habet in cornu.* " Ay," said Garrick, vehemently, " he has a whole *mow* of it."

Talking of history, Johnson said, "We may know historical facts to be true, as we may know facts in common life to be true. Motives are generally unknown. We cannot trust to the characters we find in history, unless when they are drawn by those who knew the persons; as those, for instance, by Sallust and by Lord Clarendon."

He would not allow much merit to Whitfield's oratory. "His popularity, Sir," said he, "is chiefly owing to the peculiarity of his manner. He would be followed by crowds were he to wear a night-cap in the pulpit, or were he to preach from a tree."

I know not from what spirit of contradiction he burst out into a violent declamation against the Corsicans, of whose heroism I talked in high terms. "Sir," said he, "what is all this rout about the Corsicans? They have been at war with the Genoese for upwards of twenty years, and have never yet taken their fortified towns. They might have battered down their walls and reduced them to powder in twenty years. They might have pulled the walls in pieces, and cracked the stones with their teeth in twenty years." It was in vain to argue with him upon the want of artillery; he was not to be resisted for the moment.

On the evening of October 10, I presented Dr. Johnson to General Paoli.[1] I had greatly wished that two men, for whom I had the highest esteem, should meet. They met with a manly ease, mutually conscious of their own abilities, and of the abilities of each other. The General spoke Italian, and Dr. Johnson English, and understood one another very well, with a little aid of interpretation from me, in which I compared myself to an isthmus which joins two great continents. Upon Johnson's

GENERAL PAOLI.

[1] Pascal Paoli was born at Stretta, in Corsica, followed his father into exile, and was educated at the Jesuit's College at Naples. His countrymen having elected him their generalissimo, he returned to Corsica and acted vigorously and successfully against the encroachments of the Genoese; but on their transferring the island to the French monarchy, he was eventually overpowered by its army, and sought refuge in England in 1769, where having obtained a pension of 1200l. a-year, he resided until 1789. The French Revolution having caused the island of Corsica to be recognised as a department of France, Paoli went to Paris in 1790, accompanied by deputies, and presented himself at the bar of the National Assembly, where he was received with enthusiasm, and took the oath of allegiance to the French government. The progress of the Revolution, however, disappointed the hopes he had conceived of ameliorating the condition of his country, and encouraged by assistance from Great Britain, he abandoned his allegiance to France. The result was a short-lived annexation to the British territory, and the eventual return of Paoli to England in embarrassed circumstances. The Government restored to him his pension and he resided in the metropolis until his death in 1807.—Ed.

approach, the General said, "From what I have read of your works, Sir, and from what Mr. Boswell has told me of you, I have long held you in great veneration." The General talked of languages being formed on the particular notions and manners of a people, without knowing which, we cannot know the language. We may know the direct signification of single words; but by these no beauty of expression, no sally of genius, no wit is conveyed to the mind. All this must be by allusion to other ideas. "Sir," said Johnson, "you talk of language, as if you had never done anything else but study it, instead of governing a nation." The General said, "*Questo è un troppo gran complimento :*" this is too great a compliment. Johnson answered, "I should have thought so, Sir, if I had not heard you talk." The General asked him what he thought of the spirit of infidelity which was so prevalent. JOHNSON: "Sir, this gloom of infidelity, I hope, is only a transient cloud passing through the hemisphere, which will soon be dissipated, and the sun break forth with his usual splendour." "You think then," said the General, "that they will change their principles like their clothes." JOHNSON: "Why, Sir, if they bestow no more thought on principles than on dress, it must be so." The General said, that "a great part of the fashionable infidelity was owing to a desire of showing courage. Men who have no opportunities of showing it as to things in this life, take death and futurity as objects on which to display it." JOHNSON: "That is mighty foolish affectation. Fear is one of the passions of human nature, of which it is impossible to divest it. You remember that the Emperor Charles V. when he read upon the tombstone of a Spanish nobleman, 'Here lies one who never knew fear,' wittily said, 'Then he never snuffed a candle with his fingers.'"

He talked a few words of French to the General; but finding he did not do it with facility, he asked for pen, ink, and paper, and wrote the following note :—

"*J'ai lu dans la géographie de Lucas de Linda un Pater-noster écrit dans une langue tout-à-fait différente de l'Italienne, et de toutes autres lesquelles se dérivent du Latin. L'auteur l'appelle linguam Corsicæ rusticam : elle a peut-être passé, peu à peu ; mais elle a certainement prévalu autrefois dans les montagnes et dans la campagne. Le même auteur dit la même chose en parlant de la Sardaigne ; qu'il y a deux langues dans l'Isle, une des villes, l'autre de la campagne.*"

The General immediately informed him that the *lingua rustica* was only in Sardinia.

Dr. Johnson went home with me, and drank tea till late in the night. He said, "General Paoli had the loftiest port of any man he had ever seen." He denied that military men were always the best bred men. "Perfect good breeding," he observed, "consists in having no particular mark of any profession, but a general elegance of manners ; whereas, in a military man, you can commonly distinguish the *brand* of a soldier, *l'homme d'épée.*"

Dr. Johnson shunned to-night any discussion of the perplexed question of fate and free will, which I attempted to agitate : "Sir," said he, "we *know* our will is free, and *there's* an end on't."

He honoured me with his company at dinner on the 16th of October, at my lodgings in Old Bond-street, with Sir Joshua Reynolds, Mr. Garrick, Dr. Goldsmith, Mr. Murphy, Mr. Bickerstaff, and Mr. Thomas Davies. Garrick played round him with a fond vivacity, taking hold of the breasts of his coat, and, looking up in his face with a lively archness, complimented him on the good health which he seemed then to enjoy ; while the sage, shaking his head, beheld him with a gentle complacency. One of the company not being come at the appointed hour, I proposed, as usual upon such occasions, to order dinner to be served ; adding, "Ought six people to be kept waiting for one ?" "Why, yes," answered Johnson, with a delicate humanity, "if the one will suffer more by your sitting down than the six will do by waiting." Goldsmith, to divert the

OLIVER GOLDSMITH.

tedious minutes, strutted about bragging of his dress, and I believe was seriously vain of it, for his mind was wonderfully prone to such impressions, "Come, come," said Garrick, "talk no more of that. You are perhaps the worst—eh, eh !" Goldsmith was eagerly attempting to interrupt him, when Garrick went on, laughing ironically, "Nay, you will always *look* like a gentleman ; but I am talking of being well or *ill drest.*" "Well, let me tell you," said Goldsmith, "when my tailor brought home my bloom-coloured coat, he said, 'Sir, I have a favour to beg of you. When anybody asks you who made

your clothes, be pleased to mention John Filby, at the Harrow, in Water-lane.'" JOHNSON : "Why, Sir, that was because he knew the strange colour would attract crowds to gaze at it, and thus they might hear of him, and see how well he could make a coat even of so absurd a colour."

After dinner our conversation first turned upon Pope. Johnson said, his characters of men were admirably drawn, those of women not so well. He repeated to us, in his forcible melodious manner, the concluding lines of the Dunciad.[1] While he was talking loudly in praise of those lines, one of the company ventured to say, "Too fine for such a

---

· Mr. Langton informed me that he once related to Johnson (on the authority of Spence) that Pope himself admired those lines so much, that when he repeated them, his voice faltered; "and well it might, Sir," said Johnson, "for they are noble lines."— J. BOSWELL, JUN.

poem :—a poem on what ?" JOHNSON (with a disdainful look) : "Why, on *dunces*. It was worth while being a dunce then. Ah, Sir, hadst *thou* lived in those days ! It is not worth while being a dunce now, when there are no wits." Bickerstaff observed, as a peculiar circumstance, that Pope's fame was higher when he was alive than it was then. Johnson said, his Pastorals were poor things, though the versification was fine. He told us, with high satisfaction, the anecdote of Pope's inquiring who was the author of his "London," and saying, he will be soon *déterré*. He observed, that in Dryden's poetry there were passages drawn from a profundity which Pope could never reach. He repeated some fine lines on love, by the former (which I have now forgotten), and gave great applause to the character of Zimri. Goldsmith said, that Pope's character of Addison showed a deep knowledge of the human heart. Johnson said, that the description of the temple, in "The Mourning Bride," [1] was the finest poetical passage he had ever read ; he recollected none in Shakspeare equal to it.—"But," said Garrick, all alarmed for "the God of his idolatry," "we know not the extent and variety of his powers. We are to suppose there are such passages in his works. Shakspeare must not suffer from the badness of our memories." Johnson, diverted by this enthusiastic jealousy, went on with great ardour : "No, Sir ; Congreve has *nature;*" (smiling on the tragic eagerness of Garrick) ; but composing himself, he added, "Sir, this is not comparing Congreve on the whole with Shakspeare on the whole ; but only maintaining that Congreve has one finer passage than any that can be found in Shakspeare. Sir, a man may have no more than ten guineas in the world, but he may have those ten guineas in one piece ; and so may have a finer piece than a man who has ten thousand pounds : but then he has only one ten-guinea piece.—What I mean is, that you can show me no passage, where there is simply a description of material objects, without any intermixture of moral notions,[2] which produces such an effect." Mr. Murphy mentioned Shakspeare's description of the night before the battle of Agincourt ; but it was observed it had *men* in it. Mr. Davies suggested the speech of Juliet, in which she figures herself awaking in the tomb of her ancestors. Some one mentioned the description of Dover Cliff. JOHNSON : "No, Sir ; it should be all precipice—all vacuum. The crows impede your fall. The

Act. ii., sc. 3.—MALONE.

> " How reverend is the face of this tall pile,
> Whose ancient pillars rear their marble heads,
> To bear aloft its arch'd and pond'rous roof,
> By its own weight made steadfast and unmoveable,
> Looking tranquillity ! It strikes an awe
> And terror on my aching sight."

[2] In Congreve's description there seems to be *an intermixture of moral notions ;* as the affecting power of the passage arises from the vivid impression of the described objects on the mind of the speaker : " And shoots a chillness," &c.—KEARNEY.

diminished appearance of the boats, and other circumstances, are all very good description ; but do not impress the mind at once with the horrible idea of immense height. The impression is divided ; you pass on by computation, from one stage of the tremendous space to another. Had the girl in 'The Mourning Bride' said, she could not cast her shoe to the top of one of the pillars in the temple, it would not have aided the idea, but weakened it."

Talking of a barrister who had a bad utterance, some one (to rouse Johnson) wickedly said, that he was unfortunate in not having been taught oratory by Sheridan. JOHNSON : "Nay, Sir, if he had been taught by Sheridan, he would have cleared the room." GARRICK : "Sheridan has too much vanity to be a good man."—We shall now see Johnson's mode of *defending* a man ; taking him into his own hands, and discriminating. JOHNSON : "No, Sir. There is, to be sure, in Sheridan, something to reprehend and everything to laugh at ; but, Sir, he is not a bad man. No, Sir ; were mankind to be divided into good and bad, he would stand considerably within the ranks of good. And, Sir, it must be allowed that Sheridan excels in plain declamation, though he can exhibit no character."

I should, perhaps, have suppressed this disquisition concerning a person of whose merit and worth I think with respect, had he not attacked Johnson so outrageously in his Life of Swift, and at the same time, treated us, his admirers, as a set of pigmies. He who has provoked the lash of wit, cannot complain that he smarts from it.

Mrs. Montague, a lady distinguished for having written an Essay on Shakspeare, being mentioned—REYNOLDS : "I think that essay does her honour." JOHNSON · " Yes, Sir ; it does *her* honour, but it would do nobody else honour. I have, indeed, not read it all. But when I take up the end of a web, and find it packthread, I do not expect, by looking further, to find embroidery. Sir, I will venture to say, there is not one sentence of true criticism in her book." GARRICK : " But, Sir, surely it shows how much Voltaire has mistaken Shakspeare, which nobody else has done." JOHNSON : "Sir, nobody else has thought it worth while. And what merit is there in that ? You may as well praise a schoolmaster for whipping a boy who has construed ill. No, Sir, there is no real criticism in it : none showing the beauty of thought, as formed on the workings of the human heart."

The admirers of this Essay [1] may be offended at the slighting manner

· Of whom I acknowledge myself to be one, considering it as a piece of the secondary or comparative species of criticism ; and not of that profound species which alone Dr. Johnson would allow to be " real criticism." It is, besides, clearly and elegantly expressed, and has done effectually what it professed to do ; namely, vindicated Shakspeare from the misrepre sentations of Voltaire; and considering how many young people were misled by his witty, though false observations, Mrs. Montague's Essay was of service to Shakspeare with a certain class of readers, and is, therefore, entitled to praise. Johnson, I am assured, allowed the merit which I have stated, saying (with reference to Voltaire), " it is conclusive *ad hominem*."—BOSWELL.

in which Johnson spoke of it ; but let it be remembered, that he gave his honest opinion unbiassed by any prejudice, or any proud jealousy of a woman intruding herself into the chair of criticism ; for Sir Joshua Reynolds has told me, that when the Essay first came out, and it was not known who had written it, Johnson wondered how Sir Joshua could like it. At this time Sir Joshua himself had received no information concerning the author, except being assured by one of our most eminent literati, that it was clear its author did not know the Greek tragedies in the original.   One day at Sir Joshua's table, when it was related that Mrs. Montague, in an excess of compliment to the author of a modern tragedy, had exclaimed, " I tremble for Shakspeare," Johnson said, " When Shakspeare has got ——— for his rival, and Mrs. Montague for his defender, he is in a poor state indeed."

Johnson proceeded : " The Scotchman has taken the right method in his ' Elements of Criticism.' I do not mean that he has taught us anything ; but he has told us old things in a new way." MURPHY : " He seems to have read a great deal of French criticism, and wants to make it his own : as if he had been for years anatomising the heart of man, and peeping into every cranny of it." GOLDSMITH : " It is easier to write that book than to read it." JOHNSON : " We have an example of true criticisim in Burke's ' Essay on the Sublime and Beautiful ; ' and, if I recollect, there is also Du Bos ; and Bouhours, who shows all beauty to depend on truth. There is no great merit in telling how many plays have ghosts in them, and how this ghost is better than that. You must show how terror is impressed on the human heart.—In the description of night in Macbeth, the beetle and the bat detract from the general idea of darkness,—inspissated gloom."

Politics being mentioned, he said, " This petitioning is a new mode of distressing government, and a mighty easy one. I will undertake to get petitions either against quarter guineas or half guineas, with the help of a little hot wine. There must be no yielding to encourage this. The object is not important enough.   We are not to blow up half a dozen palaces, because one cottage is burning."

The conversation then took another turn. JOHNSON : "It is amazing what ignorance of certain points one sometimes finds in men of eminence. A wit about town, who wrote Latin bawdy verses, asked me, how it happened that England and Scotland, which were once two kingdoms, were now one ; and Sir Fletcher Norton did not seem to know that there were such publications as the Reviews."

"The ballad of Hardyknute has no great merit, if it be really ancient.[1] People talk of nature. But mere obvious nature may be exhibited with very little power of mind."

---

[1] It is unquestionably a modern fiction. It was written by Sir John Bruce, of Kinross and first published at Edinburgh in folio, in 1719. See " Percy's Reliques of Ancient English Poetry," vol. ii., pp. 96, 111, 4th edit.—MALONE.

On Thursday, October 19, I passed the evening with him at his house. He advised me to complete a Dictionary of words peculiar to Scotland, of which I showed him a specimen. "Sir," said he, " Ray has made a collection of north country words. By collecting those of your country, you will do a useful thing towards the history of the language." He bade me also go on with collections which I was making upon the antiquities of Scotland. "Make a large book—a folio." BOSWELL : " But of what use will it be, Sir ? " JOHNSON : " Never mind the use ; do it."

I complained that he had not mentioned Garrick in his Preface to Shakspeare : and asked him if he did not admire him. JOHNSON : " Yes, as ' a poor player, who frets and struts his hour upon the stage ' —as a shadow." BOSWELL : " But has he not brought Shakspeare into notice ? " JOHNSON : " Sir, to allow that, would be to lampoon the age. Many of Shakspeare's plays are the worse for being acted : Macbeth, for instance." BOSWELL : " What, Sir ! is nothing gained by decoration and action ? Indeed, I do wish that you had mentioned Garrick." JOHNSON : " My dear Sir, had I mentioned him, I must have mentioned many more : Mrs. Pritchard, Mrs. Cibber,—nay, and Mr. Cibber too : he, too, altered Shakspeare." BOSWELL : " You have read his apology, Sir ? " JOHNSON : " Yes, it is very entertaining. But as for Cibber himself, taking from his conversation all that he ought not to have said, he was a poor creature. I remember when he brought me one of his Odes to have my opinion of it, I could not bear such nonsense, and would not let him read it to the end: so little respect had I for *that great man !* (laughing). Yet I remember Richardson wondering that I could treat him with familiarity."

I mentioned to him that I had seen the execution of several convicts at Tyburn, two days before, and that none of them seemed to be under any concern. JOHNSON : " Most of them, Sir, have never thought at all." BOSWELL : " But is not the fear of death natural to man ? " JOHNSON : " So much so, Sir, that the whole of life is but keeping away the thoughts of it." He then, in a low and earnest tone, talked of his meditating upon the awful hour of his own dissolution, and in what manner he should conduct himself upon that occasion : " I know not," said he, " whether I should wish to have a friend by me, or have it all between GOD and myself." Talking of our feeling for the distresses of others—JOHNSON : " Why, Sir, there is much noise made about it, but it is greatly exaggerated. No, Sir, we have a certain degree of feeling to prompt us to do good ; more than that, providence does not intend. It would be misery to no purpose." BOSWELL : " But suppose now, Sir, that one of your intimate friends were apprehended for an offence for which he might be hanged." JOHNSON : " I should do what I could to bail him, and give him any other assistance ; but if he were once fairly hanged, I should not suffer." BOSWELL : " Would you eat your dinner that day, Sir?" JOHNSON: "Yes, Sir, and eat it as if he were eating with me. Why, there's Baretti, who is to be tried for his life to-morrow; friends have risen up for him on every side; yet if he should be hanged, none of them will eat a slice of plum pudding the less. Sir, that sympathetic feeling goes a very little way in depressing the mind."

I told him that I had dined lately at Foote's, who showed me a letter which he had received from Tom Davies, telling him that he had not been able to sleep from the concern he felt on account of " *this sad affair of Baretti*," begging of him to try if he could suggest any thing that might be of service; and, at the same time, recommending to him an industrious young man who kept a pickle shop. JOHNSON: " Ay, Sir, here you have a specimen of human sympathy: a friend hanged, and a cucumber pickled. We know not whether Baretti or the pickleman has kept Davies from sleep: nor does he know himself. And as to his not sleeping, Sir, Tom Davies is a very great man; Tom has been upon the stage, and knows how to do those things: I have not been upon the stage, and cannot do those things." BOSWELL: "I have often blamed myself, Sir, for not feeling for others as sensibly as many say they do." JOHNSON: " Sir, don't be duped by them any more. You will find these very feeling people are not very ready to do you good. They *pay* you by *feeling*."

BOSWELL: " Foote has a great deal of humour." JOHNSON: "Yes, Sir." BOSWELL: " He has a singular talent of exhibiting character." JOHNSON: " Sir, it is not a talent—it is a vice; it is what others abstain from. It is not comedy, which exhibits the character of a species, as that of a miser gathered from many misers: it

FOOTE AS MAJOR STURGEON.

is farce, which exhibits individuals." BOSWELL: " Did not he think of exhibiting you, Sir?" JOHNSON: " Sir, fear restrained him; he knew I would have broken his bones. I would have saved him the trouble of cutting off a leg; I would not have left him a leg to cut off." BOSWELL: " Pray, Sir, is not Foote an infidel?" JOHNSON: " I do not know, Sir, that the fellow is an infidel; but if he be an infidel, he is an infidel as a dog is an infidel; that is to say, he has never thought upon the subject."[1] BOSWELL: "I suppose, Sir, he has thought superficially,

[1] When Mr. Foote was at Edinburgh, he thought fit to entertain a numerous Scotch company, with a great deal of coarse jocularity, at the expense of Dr. Johnson, imagining it would be acceptable. I felt this as not civil to me; but sat very patiently till he had exhausted his merriment on that subject; and then observed, that surely Johnson must be

and seized the first notions which occured to his mind." JOHNSON: " Why then, Sir, still he is like a dog, that snatches the piece next him. Did you never observe that dogs have not the power of comparing ? A dog will take a small bit of meat as readily as a large, when both are before him."

" Buchanan," he observed, " has fewer *centos* than any modern Latin Poet. He has not only had great knowledge of the Latin language, but was a great poetical genius. Both the Scaligers praise him."

He again talked of the passage in Congreve with high commendation, and said, " Shakspeare never has six lines together without a fault. Perhaps you may find seven ; but this does not refute my general assertion. If I come to an orchard and say there's no fruit here, and then comes a poring man, who finds two apples and three pears, and tells me, ' Sir, you are mistaken, I have found both apples and pears,' I should laugh at him : what would that be to the purpose ? "

BOSWELL : " What do you think of Dr. Young's ' Night Thoughts,' Sir ? " JOHNSON : " Why, Sir, there are very fine things in them." BOSWELL : " Is there not less religion in the nation now, Sir, than there was formerly ? " JOHNSON : " I don't know, Sir, that there is." BOSWELL : " For instance, there used to be a chaplain in every great family, which we do not find now." JOHNSON : " Neither do you find any of the state servants which great families used formerly to have. There is a change of modes in the whole department of life."

Next day, October 20, he appeared, for the only time I suppose in his life, as a witness in a court of justice, being called to give evidence to the character of Mr. Baretti, who having stabbed a man in the street, was arraigned at the Old Bailey for murder. Never did such a constellation of genius enlighten the awful Sessions-house, emphatically called Justice-hall : Mr. Burke, Mr. Garrick, Mr. Beauclerk, and Dr. Johnson ; and undoubtedly their favourable testimony had due weight with the court and Jury. Johnson gave his evidence in a slow, deliberate, and distinct manner, which was uncommonly impressive. It is well known that Mr. Baretti was acquitted.

On the 26th of October, we dined together at the Mitre Tavern. He found fault with Foote for indulging his talent of ridicule at the expense of his visitors, which I colloquially termed making fools of his company. JOHNSON : " Why, Sir, when you go to see Foote, you do not go to see a saint ; you go to see a man who will be entertained at your house, and

allowed to have some sterling wit, and that I had heard him say a very good thing of Mr. Foote himself. " Ah, my old Friend Sam," cried Foote, " no man says better things : do let us have it." Upon which I told the above story, which produced a very loud laugh from the company. But I never saw Foote so disconcerted. He looked grave and angry, and entered into a serious refutation of the justice of the remark. " What, Sir," said he, " talk thus of a man of liberal education—a man who for years was at the University of Oxford—a man who has added sixteen new characters to the English drama of his country ! "— BOSWELL.

then bring you on a public stage ; who will entertain you at his house for the very purpose of bringing you on a public stage. Sir, he does not make fools of his company ; they whom he exposes are fools already ; he only brings them into action."

Talking of trade, he observed, " It is a mistaken notion that a vast deal of money is brought into a nation by trade. It is not so. Commodities come from commodities ; but trade produces no capital accession of wealth. However, though there should be little profit in money, there is a considerable profit in pleasure, as it gives to one nation the productions of another ; as we have wines and fruits, and many other foreign articles brought to us." BOSWELL : " Yes, Sir, and there is a profit in pleasure, by its furnishing occupation to such numbers of mankind." JOHNSON : " Why, Sir, you cannot call that pleasure to which all are averse, and which none begin but with the hope of leaving off ; a thing which men dislike before they have tried it, and when they have tried it." BOSWELL : " But, Sir, the mind must be employed, and we grow weary when idle." JOHNSON : " That is, Sir, because others

being busy, we want company ; but if we were all idle, there would be no growing weary ; we should all entertain one another. There is, indeed, this in trade :—it gives men an opportunity of improving their situation. If there were no trade, many who are poor would always remain poor. But no man loves labour for itself." BOSWELL : " Yes, Sir, I know a person who does. He is a very laborious judge, and he loves the labour." JOHNSON : " Sir, that is because he loves respect and distinction. Could he have them without labour, he would like it less." BOSWELL : " He

MRS. WILLIAMS.

tells me he likes it for itself."—" Why, Sir, he fancies so, because he is not accustomed to abstract."

We went home to his house to tea. Mrs. Williams made it with sufficient dexterity, notwithstanding her blindness, though her manner of satisfying herself that the cups were full enough appeared to me a little awkward ; for I fancied she put her finger down a certain way, till she felt the tea touch it.[1] In my first elation at being allowed the privilege of attending Dr. Johnson at his late visits to this lady, which

[1] I have since had reason to think that I was mistaken; for I have been informed by a lady, who was long intimate with her, and likely to be a more accurate observer of such matters, that she had acquired such a niceness of touch as to know, by the feeling on the out side of the cup, how near it was to being full.—BOSWELL.

was like being *è secretioribus consiliis*, I willingly drank cup after cup, as if it had been the Heliconian spring. But as the charm of novelty went off, I grew more fastidious; and besides, I discovered that she was of a peevish temper.

There was a pretty large circle this evening. Dr. Johnson was in very good humour, lively, and ready to talk upon all subjects. Mr. Fergusson,[1] the self-taught philosopher, told him of a new invented machine which went without horses; a man who sat in it turned a handle, which worked a spring that drove it forward. "Then, Sir," said Johnson, "what is gained is, the man has his choice whether he will move himself alone, or himself and the machine too." Dominicetti being mentioned, he would not allow him any merit. "There is nothing in all this boasted system. No, Sir; medicated baths can be no better than warm water; their only effect can be that of tepid moisture." One of the company took the other side, maintaining that medicines of various sorts, and some too of most powerful effect, are introduced into the human frame by the medium of the pores; and, therefore, when warm water is impregnated with salutiferous substances, it may produce great effects as a bath. This appeared to me very satisfactory. Johnson did not answer it; but talking for victory, and determined to be master of the field, he had recourse to the device which Goldsmith imputed to him in the witty words of one of Cibber's comedies: "There is no arguing with Johnson; for when his pistol misses fire, he knocks you down with the butt-end of it." He turned to the gentleman, "Well, Sir, go to Dominicetti, and get thyself fumigated; but be sure that the steam be directed to thy *head*, for *that* is the *peccant part*." This produced a triumphant roar of laughter from the motley assembly of philosophers, printers, and dependents, male and female.

I know not how so whimsical a thought came into my mind, but I asked, "If, Sir, you were shut up in a castle, and a new-born child with you, what would you do?" JOHNSON: "Why, Sir, I should not much like my company." BOSWELL: "But would you take the trouble of rearing it?" He seemed, as may well be supposed, unwilling to pursue the subject; but upon my persevering in my question, replied, "Why yes, Sir, I would; but I must have all conveniences. If I had no garden, I would make a shed on the roof, and take it there for fresh air. I should feed it, and wash it much, and with warm water to

---

[1] James Fergusson was the son of a labourer, and born in 1710, at Keith, in Banffshire, Scotland. He learned to read in infancy by hearing his father teach one of his brothers; when only eight years of age he constructed a wooden clock. When old enough to work he was placed out as a servant to a farmer, and while tending his master's sheep he acquired a surprising knowledge of the stars, and constructed a celestial globe. Some neighbouring gentlemen, seeing his natural abilities, had him instructed. Eventually he went to Edinburgh, and chiefly supported himself by drawing miniature portraits with Indian ink, which profession he afterwards followed on his arrival in London. He wrote several volumes of mathematical and miscellaneous works, and died in 1776.—ED.

please it, not with cold water to give it pain." BOSWELL : "But, Sir, does not heat relax ?" JOHNSON : "Sir, you are not to imagine the water is to be very hot. I would not *coddle* the child. No, Sir, the hardy method of treating children does no good. I'll take you five children from London, who shall cuff five Highland children. Sir, a man bred in London will carry a burden, or run, or wrestle, as well as a man brought up in the hardest manner in the country." BOSWELL : " Good living, I suppose, makes the Londoners strong." JOHNSON " Why, Sir, I don't know that it does. Our chairmen from Ireland, who are as strong men as any, have been brought up upon potatoes. Quantity makes up for quality." BOSWELL : " Would you teach this child that I have furnished you with anything ?" JOHNSON : " No, I should not be apt to teach it." BOSWELL : " Would not you have a pleasure in teaching it ?" JOHNSON : " No, Sir, I should *not* have a pleasure in teaching it." BOSWELL : " Have you not a pleasure in teaching men ? *There* I have you. You have the same pleasure in teaching men that I should have in teaching children." JOHNSON : " Why, something about that."

BOSWELL : " Do you think, Sir, that what is called natural affection is born with us ? It seems to me to be the effect of habit, or of gratitude for kindness. No child has it for a parent whom it has not seen." JOHNSON : " Why, Sir, I think there is an instinctive natural affection in parents towards their children."

Russia being mentioned as likely to become a great empire, by the rapid increase of population :—JOHNSON : " Why, Sir, I see no prospect of their propagating more. They can have no more children than they can get. I know of no way to make them breed more than they do. It is not from reason and prudence that people marry, but from inclination. A man is poor ; he thinks, ' I cannot be worse, and so I'll e'en take Peggy.' " BOSWELL . " But have not nations been more populous at one period than another ?" JOHNSON : " Yes, Sir ; but that has been owing to the people being less thinned at one period than another, whether by emigrations, war, or pestilence, not by their being more or less prolific. Births at all times bear the same proportion to the same number of people." BOSWELL : " But to consider the state of our own country : does not throwing a number of farms into one hand hurt population ! " JOHNSON : " Why no, Sir ; the same quantity of food being produced, will be consumed by the same number of mouths, though the people may be disposed of in different ways. We see, if corn be dear and butchers' meat cheap, the farmers all apply themselves to the raising of corn, till it becomes plentiful and cheap, and then butchers' meat becomes dear ; so that an equality is always preserved. No, Sir, let fanciful men do as they will, depend upon it, it is difficult to disturb the system of life." BOSWELL : "But, Sir, is it not a very bad thing for landlords to oppress their tenants, by raising their rents ?"

JOHNSON : " Very bad. But, Sir, it can never have any general influence ; it may distress some individuals. For, consider this : landlords cannot do without tenants. Now, tenants will not give more for land than land is worth. If they can make more of their money by keeping a shop, or any other way, they'll do it, and so oblige landlords to let land come back to a reasonable rent, in order that they may get tenants Land in England is an article of commerce. A tenant who pays his landlord his rent, thinks himself no more obliged to him than you think yourself obliged to a man in whose shop you buy a piece of goods. He knows the landlord does not let him have his land for less than he can get from others, in the same manner as the shopkeeper sells his goods. No shopkeeper sells a yard of ribbon for sixpence when sevenpence is the current price." BOSWELL : " But, Sir, is it not better that tenants should be dependent on landlords ? " JOHNSON : " Why, Sir, as there are many more tenants than landlords, perhaps, strictly speaking, we should wish not. But if you please you may let your lands cheap, and so get the value, part in money and part in homage. I should agree with you in that." BOSWELL : " So, Sir, you laugh at schemes of political improvement." JOHNSON : " Why, Sir, most schemes of political improvement are very laughable things."

He observed, "Providence has wisely ordered that the more numerous men are, the more difficult it is for them to agree in anything, and so they are governed. There is no doubt, that if the poor should reason, ' We'll be the poor no longer, we'll make the rich take their turn,' they could easily do it, were it not that they can't agree. So the common soldiers, though so much more numerous than their officers, are governed by them for the same reason."

He said, " Mankind have a strong attachment to the habitations to which they have been accustomed. You see the inhabitants of Norway do not with one consent quit it, and go to some part of America, where there is a mild climate, and where they may have the same produce from land, with the tenth part of the labour. No, Sir ; their affection for their old dwellings, and the terror of a general change, keep them at home. Thus, we see many of the finest spots in the world thinly inhabited, and many rugged spots well inhabited."

"The London Chronicle," which was the only newspaper he constantly took in, being brought, the office of reading it aloud was assigned to me. I was diverted by his impatience. He made me pass over so many parts of it that my task was very easy. He would not suffer one of the petitions to the king about the Middlesex election to be read.

I had hired a Bohemian as my servant while I remained in London, and being much pleased with him, I asked Dr. Johnson whether his being a Roman Catholic should prevent my taking him with me to Scotland. JOHNSON : " Why no, Sir. If he has no objection, you can have none." BOSWELL : " So, Sir, you are no great enemy to the

Roman Catholic religion." JOHNSON : "No more, Sir, than to the Presbyterian religion." BOSWELL : "You are joking." JOHNSON : "No, Sir, I really think so. Nay, Sir, of the two, I prefer the Popish." BOSWELL : "How so, Sir ?" JOHNSON : "Why, Sir, the Presbyterians have no church, no apostolical ordination." BOSWELL : "And do you think that absolutely essential, Sir ?" JOHNSON : "Why, Sir, as it was an apostolical institution, I think it is dangerous to be without it. And, Sir, the Presbyterians have no public worship : they have no form of prayer in which they know they are to join. They go to hear a man pray, and are to judge whether they will join with him." BOSWELL : "But, Sir, their doctrine is the same with that of the Church of England. Their confession of faith, and the thirty-nine articles, contain the same points, even the doctrine of predestination." JOHNSON : "Why yes, Sir ; predestination was a part of the clamour of the times, so it is mentioned in our articles, but with as little positiveness as could be." BOSWELL : "Is it necessary, Sir, to believe all the thirty-nine articles ?" JOHNSON : "Why, Sir, that is a question which has been much agitated. Some have thought it necessary that they should all be believed ; others have considered them to be only articles of peace ; [1] that is to say, you are not to preach against them." BOSWELL : "It appears to me, Sir, that predestination, or what is equivalent to it, cannot be avoided, if we hold an universal prescience in the Deity." JOHNSON : "Why, Sir, does not GOD every day see things going on without preventing them." BOSWELL : "True, Sir ; but if a thing be *certainly* foreseen, it must be fixed and cannot happen otherwise ; and if we apply this consideration to the human mind, there is no free will, nor do I see how prayer can be of any avail." He mentioned Dr. Clarke and Bishop Bramhall on Liberty and Necessity, and bid me read "South's Sermons on Prayer ;" but avoided the question which has excruciated philosophers and divines beyond any other. I did not press it further when I perceived that he was displeased, and shrunk from any abridgment of an attribute usually ascribed to the Divinity, however irreconcilable in its full extent with the grand system of moral government. His supposed orthodoxy here cramped the vigorous powers of his understanding. He was confined by a chain which early imagination and long habit made him think massy and strong, but which, had he ventured to try, he could at once have snapt asunder.

[1] Dr. Simon Patrick (afterwards Bishop of Ely) thus expresses himself on this subject, in a letter to the learned Dr. John Mapletoft, dated Feb. 8, 1682-3 :—

"I always took the ARTICLES to be only articles of communion; and so Bishop Bramhall expressly maintains against the Bishop of Chalcedon; and I remember well, that Bishop Sanderson, when the king was first restored, received the subscription of an acquaintance of mine, which he declared was not to them as articles of *faith*, but *peace*. I think you need make no scruple of the matter, because all that I know so understand the meaning of the subscription, and upon other terms would not subscribe."—The above was printed some years ago in the "The European Magazine," from the original, now in the hands of Mr. Mapletoft surgeon at Chertsey, grandson to Dr. John Mapletoft.—MALONE.

I proceeded : " What do you think, Sir, of purgatory, as believed by the Roman Catholics ?" JOHNSON : " Why, Sir, it is a very harmless doctrine. They are of opinion that the generality of mankind are neither so obstinately wicked as to deserve everlasting punishment, nor so good as to merit being admitted into the society of blessed spirits ; and therefore that GOD is graciously pleased to allow of a middle state, where they may be purified by certain degrees of suffering. You see, Sir, there is nothing unreasonable in this." BOSWELL : " But then, Sir, their masses for the dead ?" JOHNSON : " Why, Sir, if it be once established that there are souls in purgatory, it is as proper to pray for *them*, as for our brethren of mankind who are yet in this life." BOSWELL : " The idolatry of the Mass ?" JOHNSON : " Sir, there is no idolatry in the Mass. They believe GOD to be there, and they adore him." BOSWELL : " The worship of Saints ?" JOHNSON : " Sir, they do not worship Saints ; they invoke them : they only ask their prayers. I am talking all this time of the *doctrines* of the Church of Rome. I grant you that, in *practice*, purgatory is made a lucrative imposition, and that the people do become idolatrous as they recommend themselves to the tutelary protection of particular saints. I think their giving the sacrament only in one kind is criminal, because it is contrary to the express institution of CHRIST, and I wonder how the Council of Trent admitted it." BOSWELL : " Confession ?" JOHNSON : " Why, I don't know but that is a good thing. The Scripture says, ' Confess your faults one to another,' and the priests confess as well as the laity. Then it must be considered that their absolution is only upon repentance, and often upon penance also. You think your sins may be forgiven without penance, upon repentance alone."

I thus ventured to mention all the common objections against the Roman Catholic Church, that I might hear so great a man upon them. What he said is here accurately recorded. But it is not improbable that if one had taken the other side, he might have reasoned differently.

I must, however, mention, that he had a respect for "*the old religior,*" as the mild Melancthon called that of the Roman Catholic Church, even while he was exerting himself for its reformation in some particulars. Sir William Scott informs me that he heard Johnson say, " A man who is converted from Protestantism to Popery may be sincere ; he parts with nothing : he is only superadding to what he already had. But a convert from Popery to Protestantism gives up so much of what he has held as sacred as anything that he retains ; there is so much *laceration of mind* in such a conversion, that it can hardly be sincere and lasting." The truth of this reflection may be confirmed by many and eminent instances, some of which will occur to most of my readers.

When we were alone, I introduced the subject of death, and endeavoured to maintain that the fear of it might be got over. I told him that David Hume said to me, he was no more uneasy to think he should *not be* after his life, than that he *had not been* before he began to exist. JOHNSON : " Sir, if he really thinks so, his perceptions are disturbed ; he is mad. If he does not think so, he lies. He may tell you he holds his finger in the flame of a candle, without feeling pain ; would you believe him ? When he dies, he at least gives up all he has." BOSWELL : " Foote, Sir, told me, that when he was very ill he was not afraid to die." JOHNSON : " It is not true, Sir. Hold a pistol to Foote's breast, or to Hume's breast, and threaten to kill them, and you'll see how they behave." BOSWELL : " But may we not fortify our minds for the approach of death ? "—Here I am sensible I was in the wrong, to bring before his view what he ever looked upon with horror ; for although when in a celestial frame of mind in his " Vanity of Human Wishes," he has supposed death to be " kind Nature's signal for retreat," from this state of being to "a happier seat," his thoughts upon this awful change were in general full of dismal apprehensions. His mind resembled the vast amphitheatre, the Coliseum at Rome. In the centre stood his judgment, which, like a mighty gladiator, combated those apprehensions that, like the wild beasts of the *Arena*, were all around in cells, ready to be let out upon him. After a conflict, he drives them back into their dens ; but not killing them, they were still assailing him. To my question, whether we might not fortify our minds for the approach of death, he answered, in a passion, " No, Sir, let it alone. It matters not how a man dies, but how he lives. The act of dying is not of importance, it lasts so short a time." He added, (with an earnest look), " A man knows it must be so, and submits. It will do him no good to whine."

I attempted to continue the conversation. He was so provoked that he said : " Give us no more of this : " and was thrown into such a state of agitation that he expressed himself in a way that alarmed and distressed me ; showed an impatience that I should leave him, and when I was going away, called to me sternly, " Don't let us meet to-morrow."

I went home exceedingly uneasy. All the harsh observations which I had ever heard made upon his character crowded into my mind : and I seemed to myself like the man who had put his head into the lion's mouth a great many times with perfect safety, but at last had it bit off.

Next morning I sent him a note, stating that I might have been in the wrong, but it was not intentionally ; he was therefore, I could not help thinking, too severe upon me. That, notwithstanding our agreement not to meet that day, I would call on him in my way to the city, and stay five minutes by my watch. " You are," said I, " in my mind, since last night, surrounded with cloud and storm. Let me have a glimpse of sunshine, and go about my affairs in serenity and cheerfulness."

Upon entering his study, I was glad that he was not alone, which would have made our meeting more awkward. There were with him Mr. Steevens and Mr. Tyers, both of whom I now saw for the first time. My note had, on his own reflection, softened him, for he received me very complacently ; so that I unexpectedly found myself at ease, and joined in the conversation.

He said, the critics had done too much honour to Sir Richard Blackmore, by writing so much against him. That in his " Creation " he had been helped by various wits,—a line by Phillips, and a line by Tickell ; so that by their aid, and that of others, the poem had been made out.[1]

I defended Blackmore's supposed lines, which have been ridiculed as absolute nonsense :

> "A painted vest Prince Vortiger had on,
> Which from a naked Pict his grandsire won."[2]

I maintained it to be a poetical conceit. A Pict being painted, if he is slain in battle, and a vest is made of his skin, it is a painted vest won from him, though he was naked.

Johnson spoke unfavourably of a certain pretty voluminous author, saying, " He used to write anonymous books, and then other books commending those books, in which there was something of rascality."

I whispered him, " Well, Sir, you are now in good humour." JOHNSON : " Yes, Sir." I was going to leave him, and had got as far as the staircase. He stopped me, and smiling, said, " Get you gone *in :* " a curious mode of inviting me to stay, which I accordingly did for some time longer.

This little incidental quarrel and reconciliation, which, perhaps, I may be thought to have detailed too minutely, must be esteemed as one of many proofs which his friends had, that though he might be charged with *bad humour* at times, he was always a *good-natured* man ; and I have heard Sir Joshua Reynolds, a nice and delicate observer of manners, particularly remark, that when upon any occasion Johnson

---

[1] Johnson himself has vindicated Blackmore upon this very point. See " The Lives of the Poets." vol. iii., p. 75, 8vo, 1791.—J. BOSWELL, JUN.

[2] An acute correspondent of " The European Magazine," April, 1792, has completely exposed a mistake which has been unaccountably frequent in ascribing these lines to Blackmore, notwithstanding that Sir Richard Steele, in that very popular work, " The Spectator," mentions them as written by the author of " The British Princes," the Hon. Edward Howard. The correspondent above mentioned, shows this mistake to be so inveterate, that not only *I* defended the lines as Blackmore's in the presence of Dr Johnson, without any contradiction or doubt of their authenticity, but that the Reverend Mr. Whitaker has asserted in print, that he understands they were *suppressed* in the late edition or editions of Blackmore. " After all," says this intelligent writer, " it is not unworthy of particular observation, that these lines so often quoted do not exist either in Blackmore or Howard." In " The British Princes." 8vo, 1669. now before me, p. 96, they stand thus:

> " A vest as admired Vortiger had on,
> Which from this Island's foes his grandsire won,
> Whose artful colour pass'd the Tyrian dye,
> Obliged to triumph in this legacy "

It is probable, I think, that some wag, in order to make Howard still more ridiculous than he really was. formed the couplet as it now circulates.—BOSWELL.

had been rough to any person in company, he took the first opportunity of reconciliation, by drinking to him, or addressing his discourse to him; but if he found his dignified indirect overtures sullenly neglected, he was quite indifferent, and considered himself as having done all that he ought to do, and the other as now in the wrong.

Being to set out for Scotland on the 10th of November, I wrote to him at Streatham, begging that he would meet me in town on the 9th: but if this should be very inconvenient to him, I would go thither. His answer was as follows :—

" TO JAMES BOSWELL, ESQ.

"Dear Sir, *Nov.* 9, 1769.

"Upon balancing the inconveniences of both parties, I find it will less incommode you to spend your night here, than me to come to town. I wish to see you, and am ordered by the lady of this house to invite you hither. Whether you can come or not, I shall not have any occasion of writing to you again before your marriage, and therefore tell you now, that with great sincerity I wish you happiness.

"I am, dear Sir, your most affectionate humble servant,

"Sam. Johnson."

I was detained in town till it was too late on the 9th, so went to him early in the morning of the 10th of November. "Now," said he, "that you are going to marry, do not expect more from life than life will afford. You may often find yourself out of humour, and you may often think your wife not studious enough to please you; and yet you may have reason to consider yourself as upon the whole very happily married."

Talking of marriage in general, he observed, "Our marriage service is too refined. It is calculated only for the best kind of marriages; whereas, we should have a form for matches of convenience, of which there are many." He agreed with me that there was no absolute necessity for having the marriage ceremony performed by a regular clergyman, for this was not commanded in scripture.

I was volatile enough to repeat to him a little epigrammatic song of mine, on matrimony, which Mr. Garrick had a few days before procured to be set to music by the very ingenious Mr. Dibdin.

"A MATRIMONIAL THOUGHT.

" In the blythe days of honeymoon,
With Kate's allurements smitten,
I loved her late, I loved her soon,
And call'd her dearest kitten.

" But now my kitten's grown a cat,
And cross like other wives,
Oh ! by my soul, my honest Mat,
I fear she has nine lives."

My illustrious friend said, " It is very well, Sir ; but you should not swear." Upon which I altered " Oh! by my soul," to " Alas, alas!"

He was so good as to accompany me to London, and see me into the post-chaise which was to carry me on my road to Scotland. And sure I am, that however inconsiderable many of the particulars recorded at this time may appear to some, they will be esteemed by the best part of my readers as genuine traits of his character, contributing together to give a full, fair, and distinct view of it.

MR. WILLIAM STRAHAN, THE KING'S PRINTER.

CHAPTER IV.—1770—1771.

IN 1770, he published a political pamphlet, entitled "The False Alarm," intended to justify the conduct of the ministry and their majority in the House of Commons, for having virtually assumed it as an axiom, that the expulsion of a member of parliament was equivalent to exclusion, and thus having declared Colonel Luttrell to be duly elected for the county of Middlesex, notwithstanding Mr. Wilkes had a great majority of votes. This being justly considered as a gross violation of the right of election, an alarm for the constitution extended itself all over the kingdom. To prove this alarm to be false was the purpose of Johnson's pamphlet; but even his vast powers are inadequate to cope with constitutional truth and reason, and his argument failed of effect; and the House of Commons have since expunged the offensive resolution from their Journals. That the House of Commons might have expelled Mr. Wilkes repeatedly, and as often as he should be re-chosen, was not denied but incapacitation cannot be but by an act of the whole legislature. It was wonderful to see how a prejudice in favour of government in general, and an aversion to popular clamour, could blind and contract such an understanding as Johnson's, in this particular case ; yet the wit, the sarcasm, the eloquent vivacity which this pamphlet displayed, made it be read with great avidity at the time, and it will ever be read with pleasure, for the sake of its composition. That it endeavoured to infuse a narcotic indifference, as to public concerns, into the minds of the people, and that it broke out sometimes into an extreme coarseness of contemptuous abuse, is but too evident.

It must not, however, be omitted, that when the storm of his violence subsides, he takes a fair opportunity to pay a grateful compliment to the king, who had rewarded his merit :

" These low-born railers have endeavoured, surely without effect, to alienate the affections of the people from the only king who, for almost a century, has much appeared to desire, or much endeavoured to deserve them." And, "Every honest man must lament, that the faction has been regarded with frigid neutrality by the Tories, who, being long accustomed to signalise their principles by opposition to the court, do not yet consider, that they have at last a king who knows not the name of party, and who wishes to be the common father of all his people."

To this pamphlet, which was at once discovered to be Johnson's, several answers came out, in which care was taken to remind the public of his former attacks upon government, and of his now being a pensioner, without allowing for the honourable terms upon which Johnson's pension was granted and accepted, or the change of system which the British court had undergone upon the accession of his present Majesty. He was, however, soothed in the highest strain of panegyric, in a poem called " The Remonstrance," by the Reverend Mr. Stockdale, to whom he was, upon many occasions, a kind protector.

The following admirable minute made by him, describe so well his own state and that of numbers to whom self-examination is habitual, that I cannot omit it :—

"June 1, 1770. Every man naturally persuades himself that he can keep his resolutions, nor is he convinced of his imbecility but by length of time and frequency of experiment. This opinion of our own constancy is so prevalent, that we always despise him who suffers his general and settled purpose to be overpowered by an occasional desire. They, therefore, whom frequent failures have made desperate, cease to form resolutions; and they who are become cunning, do not tell them. Those who do not make them are very few, but of their effect little is perceived ; for scarcely any man persists in a course of life planned by choice, but as he is restrained from deviation by some external power. He who may live as he will, seldom lives long in the observation of his own rules." [1]

Of this year I have obtained the following letters :—

"TO THE REVEREND DR. FARMER, CAMBRIDGE.

"SIR,   *Johnson's-court, Fleet-street, March* 21, 1770.

"As no man ought to keep wholly to himself any possession that may be useful to the public, I hope you will not think me unreasonably intrusive, if I have recourse to you for such information as you are more able to give me than any other man.

"In support of an opinion which you have already placed above the need of any more support, Mr. Steevens, a very ingenious gentleman, lately of King's College, has collected an account of all the translations which Shakspeare might have seen and used. He wishes his catalogue to be perfect; and, therefore, entreats that you will favour him by the insertion of such additions as the accuracy of your inquiries has enabled you to make. To this request I take the liberty of adding my own solicitation.

"We have no immediate use for this catalogue; and, therefore, do not desire that it should interrupt or hinder your more important employments. But it will be kind to let us know that you receive it. I am, Sir, &c.,

"SAM. JOHNSON."

"TO THE REVEREND MR. THOMAS WARTON.

"DEAR SIR,   *London, June* 23, 1770.

"The readiness with which you were pleased to promise me some notes on Shakspeare, was a new instance of your friendship. I shall not hurry you; but am desired by Mr. Steevens, who helps me in this edition, to let you know that we shall print the tragedies first, and shall, therefore, want first the notes which belong to them. We think not to incommode the readers with a supplement; and, therefore, what we cannot put into its proper place will do us no good. We shall not begin to print before the end of six weeks, perhaps not so soon.   I am, &c.,

"SAM. JOHNSON."

"TO THE REV. DR. JOSEPH WARTON.

"DEAR SIR,   *Sept.* 27, 1770.

"I am revising my edition of Shakspeare, and remember that I formerly misrepresented your opinion of Lear. Be pleased to write the paragraph as you would have it, and send it. If you have any remarks of your own upon that or any other play, I shall gladly receive them.

"Make my compliments to Mrs. Warton. I sometimes think of wandering for a few days to Winchester, but am apt to delay. I am, Sir,

"Your most humble servant,

"SAM. JOHNSON."

"TO MR. FRANCIS BARBER, AT MRS. CLAPP'S, BISHOP-STORTFORD, HERTFORDSHIRE.

"DEAR FRANCIS,   *London, Sept.* 25, 1770.

"I am at last sat down to write to you, and should very much blame myself for having neglected you so long, if I did not impute that and many other failings to want of health. I hope not to be so long silent again. I am very well satisfied with your progress, if you can really perform the exercises which you are set; and I hope Mr. Ellis does not suffer you to impose on him or on yourself.

"Make my compliments to Mr. Ellis, and to Mrs. Clapp, and Mr. Smith.

"Let me know what English books you read for your entertainment. You can never be wise unless you love reading.

"Do not imagine that I shall forget or forsake you; for if, when I examine you, I find that you have not lost your time, you shall want no encouragement from   Yours affectionately,

"SAM. JOHNSON."

TO THE SAME.

"DEAR FRANCIS,   December 7, 1770.

"I hope you mind your business. I design you shall stay with Mrs. Clapp these holidays. If you are invited out you may go, if Mr. Ellis gives leave. I have ordered you some clothes, which you will receive, I believe, next week. My compliments to Mrs. Clapp, and to Mr. Ellis, and Mr. Smith, &c. I am, your affectionate,   SAM. JOHNSON."

During this year there was a total cessation of all correspondence between Dr. Johnson and me, without any coldness on either side, but merely from procrastination, continued from day to day; and as I was not in London, I had no opportunity of enjoying his company and recording his conversation. To supply this blank, I shall present my readers with some *Collectanea*, obligingly furnished to me by the Rev. Dr. Maxwell, of Falkland, in Ireland, some time assistant-preacher at the Temple, and for many years the social friend of Johnson, who spoke of him with a very kind regard.

"COLLECTANEA.

"My acquaintance with that great and venerable character commenced in the year 1754. I was introduced to him by Mr. Grierson,[1] his Majesty's printer, at Dublin,—a gentleman of uncommon learning, and great wit and vivacity. Mr. Grierson died in Germany, at the age of twenty-seven. Dr. Johnson highly respected his abilities, and often observed, that he possessed more extensive knowledge than any man of his years he had ever known. His industry was equal to his talents; and he particularly excelled in every species of philological learning, and was, perhaps, the best critic of the age he lived in.

"I must always remember with gratitude my obligation to Mr. Grierson, for the honour and happiness of Dr. Johnson's acquaintance and friendship, which continued uninterrupted and undiminished to his death: a connection, that was at once the pride and happiness of my life.

"What pity it is, that so much wit and good sense as he continually exhibited in conversation, should perish unrecorded! Few persons quitted

[1] Son of the learned Mrs. Grierson, who was patronised by the late Lord Granville. and was the editor of several of the classics.—BOSWELL.

Her edition of Tacitus, with the notes of Rychius, in three volumes 8vo, 1730, was dedicated, in every elegant Latin, to John, Lord Carteret (afterwards Earl Granville), by whom she was patronised during his residence in Ireland as Lord Lieutenant between 1724 and 1730.—MALONE.

his company without perceiving themselves wiser and better than they were before. On serious subjects he flashed the most interesting conviction upon his auditors : and upon lighter topics, you might have supposed—*Albano musas de monte locutas.*

" Though I can hope to add but little to the celebrity of so exalted a character, by any communications I can furnish, yet out of pure respect to his memory, I will venture to transmit to you some anecdotes concerning him, which fell under my own observation. The very *minutiæ* of such a character must be interesting, and may be compared to the filings of diamonds.

" In politics he was deemed a Tory, but certainly was not so in the obnoxious or party sense of the term ; for while he asserted the legal and salutary prerogatives of the crown, he no less respected the constitutional liberties of the people. Whiggism, at the time of the Revolution, he said, was accompanied with certain principles ; but latterly, as a mere party distinction under Walpole and the Pelhams, was no better than the politics of stock-jobbers, and the religion of infidels.

" He detested the idea of governing by parliamentary corruption, and asserted most strenuously, that a prince steadily and conspicuously pursuing the interests of his people, could not fail of parliamentary concurrence. A prince of ability, he contended, might and should be the directing soul and spirit of his own administration ; in short, his own minister, and not the mere head of a party ; and then, and not till then, would the royal dignity be sincerely respected.

" Johnson seemed to think that a certain degree of crown influence over the Houses of Parliament (not meaning a corrupt and shameful dependence), was very salutary, nay, even necessary, in our mixed government. ' For,' said he, 'if the members were under no crown influence, and disqualified from receiving any gratification from court, and resembled, as they possibly might, Pym and Haslerig, and other stubborn and sturdy members of the Long Parliament, the wheels of government would be totally obstructed. Such men would oppose, merely to show their power, from envy, jealousy, and perversity of disposition ; and not gaining themselves, would hate and oppose all who did ; not loving the person of the prince, and conceiving they owed him little gratitude, from the mere spirit of insolence and contradiction, they would oppose and thwart him upon all occasions.'

" The inseparable imperfection annexed to all human governments, consisted, he said, in not being able to create a sufficient fund of virtue and principle to carry the laws into due and effectual execution. Wisdom might plan, but virtue alone could execute. And where could sufficient virtue be found ? A variety of delegated, and often discretionary, powers must be entrusted somewhere : which, if not governed by integrity and conscience, would necessarily be abused, till at last the constable would sell his for a shilling.

" This excellent person was sometimes charged with abetting slavish and arbitrary principles of government. Nothing in my opinion could be a grosser calumny and misrepresentation ; for how can it be rationally supposed that he should adopt such pernicious and absurd opinions, who supported his philosophical character with so much dignity, was extremely jealous of his personal liberty and independence,[1] and could not brook the smallest appearance of neglect or insult, even from the highest personages?

"But let us view him in some instances of more familiar life.

"His general mode of life, during my acquaintance, seemed to be pretty uniform. About twelve o'clock I commonly visited him, and frequently found him in bed, or declaiming over his tea, which he drank very plentifully. He generally had a levee of morning visitors, chiefly men of letters; Hawkesworth, Goldsmith, Murphy, Langton, Steevens, Beauclerk, &c. &c., and sometimes learned ladies; particularly I remember a French lady of wit and fashion doing him the honour of a visit. He seemed to me to be considered as a kind of public oracle, whom everybody thought they had a right to visit and consult; and, doubtless, they were well rewarded. I never could discover how

RANELAGH.

he found time for his compositions. He declaimed all the morning, then went to dinner at a tavern, where he commonly stayed late, and then drank his tea at some friend's house, over which he loitered a great while, but seldom took supper. I fancy he must have read and wrote chiefly in the night, for I can scarcely recollect that he ever refused going with me to a tavern, and he often went to Ranelagh,[2] which he deemed a place of innocent recreation.

[1] On the necessity of crown influence; see Boucher's "Sermons on the American Revolution," p. 218; and Paley's "Moral Philosophy," b. vi., c. vii., p. 491, 4to., there quoted.—BLAKEWAY.

[2] *Ranelagh*, a celebrated place of fashionable resort, somewhat similar to Vauxhall-gardens, was situate between Pimlico and Chelsea. It was so named from its occupying the site of Viscount Ranelagh's villa. At the present day not a vestige remains of it, although its memory is preserved by naming after it the streets, roads, and places which have been built upon its grounds.—ED.

"He frequently gave all the silver in his pocket to the poor, who watched him, between his house and the tavern where he dined. He walked the streets at all hours, and said he was never robbed, for the rogues knew he had little money, nor had the appearance of having much.

"Though the most accessible and communicative man alive, yet when he suspected he was invited to be exhibited, he constantly spurned the invitation.

"Two young women from Staffordshire visited him when I was present, to consult him on the subject of Methodism, to which they were inclined. 'Come,' said he, 'you pretty fools, dine with Maxwell and me at the Mitre, and we will talk over that subject;' which they did, and after dinner he took one of them upon his knee, and fondled her for half an hour together.

"Upon a visit to me at a country lodging near Twickenham, he asked what sort of society I had there. I told him but indifferent; as they chiefly consisted of opulent traders, retired from business. He said he never much liked that class of people; 'For, Sir,' said he, 'they have lost the civility of tradesmen, without acquiring the manners of gentlemen.'

"Johnson was much attached to London;[1] he observed, that a man stored his mind better there than anywhere else; and that in remote situations a man's body might be feasted, but his mind was starved, and his faculties apt to degenerate, from want of exercise and competition. No place, he said, cured a man's vanity or arrogance so well as London; for as no man was either great or good per se, but as compared with others not so good or great, he was sure to find in the metropolis many his equals, and some his superiors. He observed that a man in London was in less danger of falling in love indiscreetly than anywhere else; for there the difficulty of deciding between the conflicting pretensions of a vast variety of objects, kept him safe. He told me that he had frequently been offered country preferment, if he would consent to take orders; but he could not leave the improved society of the capital, or consent to exchange the exhilarating joys and splendid decorations of public life, for the obscurity, insipidity, and uniformity of remote situations.

"Speaking of Mr. Harte, Canon of Windsor, and writer of 'The History of Gustavus Adolphus,' he much commended him as a scholar, and a man of the most companionable talents he had ever known. He said the defects in his history proceeded not from imbecility, but from foppery.

"He loved, he said, the old black-letter books; they were rich in matter, though their style was inelegant; wonderfully so, considering how conversant the writers were with the best models of antiquity.

"Burton's 'Anatomy of Melancholy,' he said, was the only book that ever took him out of bed two hours sooner than he wished to rise.

"He frequently exhorted me to set about writing a History of Ireland, and archly remarked, there had been some good Irish writers, and that one Irishman might at least aspire to be equal to another. He had great compassion for the miseries and distresses of the Irish nation, particularly the

[1] Montaigne had the same affection for Paris which Johnson had for London. "Je l'aime tendrement," says he in his Essay on Vanity, "jusqu' à ses verrues et à ses taches. Je ne suis François que par cette grande cité, grande en peuples, grande en félicité de son assiette, mais sur tout grande et incomparable en variété et diversité des commoditez: la gloire de la France, et l'un des plus nobles ornemens du monde." Vol. iii., p. 321 edit Amsterdam, 1781.—Blakeway.

Papists; and severely reprobated the barbarous debilitating policy of the British government, which, he said, was the most detestable mode of persecution. To a gentleman, who hinted such policy might be necessary to support the authority of the English government, he replied by saying, ' Let the authority of the English government perish, rather than be maintained by iniquity. Better would it be to restrain the turbulence of the natives by the authority of the sword, and to make them amenable to law and justice by an effectual and vigorous police, than to grind them to powder by all manner of disabilities and incapacities. Better,' said he, ' to hang or drown people at once, than, by an unrelenting persecution, to beggar and starve them.' The moderation and humanity of the present times have, in some measure, justified the wisdom of his observations.

" Dr. Johnson was often accused of prejudices, nay, antipathy, with regard to the natives of Scotland. Surely, so illiberal a prejudice never entered his mind : and, it is well known, many natives of that respectable country possessed a large share in his esteem ; nor were any of them ever excluded from his good offices as far as opportunity permitted. True it is, he considered the Scotch, nationally, as a crafty, designing people, eagerly attentive to their own interest, and too apt to overlook the claims and pretensions of other people. ' While they confine their benevolence, in a manner, exclusively to those of their own country, they expect to share in the good offices of other people. Now,' said Johnson, ' this principle is either right or wrong; if right, we should do well to imitate such conduct; if wrong, we cannot too much detest it.'

" Being solicited to compose a funeral sermon for the daughter of a tradesman, he naturally inquired into the character of the deceased; and being told she was remarkable for her humility and condescension to inferiors, he observed that those were very laudable qualities, but it might not be so easy to discover who the lady's inferiors were.

" Of a certain player he remarked, that his conversation usually threatened and announced more than it performed; that he fed you with a continual renovation of hope, to end in a constant succession of disappointment.

" When exasperated by contradiction, he was apt to treat his opponents with too much acrimony: as, ' Sir, you don't see your way through that question. Sir, you talk the language of ignorance.' On my observing to him that a certain gentleman had remained silent the whole evening, in the midst of a very brilliant and learned society, ' Sir,' said he, ' the conversation over-flowed and drowned him.'

" His philosophy, though austere and solemn, was by no means morose and cynical, and never blunted the laudable sensibilities of his character, or exempted him from the influence of the tender passions. Want of tenderness, he always alleged, was want of parts, and was no less a proof of stupidity than depravity.

" Speaking of Mr. Hanway,[1] who published ' An Eight Days' Journey from

---

[1] Jonas Hanway, a wealthy Russian merchant and eminent philanthropist, born at Portsmouth, 1712, was the chief founder of the Marine Society and the Magdalen Hospital He wrote several religious works, the principal of which is entitled " Domestic Happiness Promoted." He died in 1786, and a monument was erected to his memory in Westminster Abbey.—ED.

London to Portsmouth,' 'Jonas,' said he, 'acquired some reputation by travelling abroad, but lost it all by travelling at home.'

" Of the passion of love he remarked, that its violence and ill effects were much exaggerated ; for who knows any real sufferings on that head, more than from the exorbitancy of any other passion?

" He much commended 'Law's Serious Call,' which he said was the finest piece of hortatory theology in any language. ' Law,' said he, ' fell latterly into the reveries of Jacob Behmen,[1] whom Law alleged to have been somewhat in the same state with St. Paul, and to have seen *unutterable things*. Were it even so,' said Johnson, ' Jacob would have resembled St. Paul still more, by not attempting to utter them.'

" He observed, that the established clergy in general did not preach plain enough ; and that polished periods and glittering sentences flew over the heads of the common people, without any impression upon their hearts. Something might be necessary, he observed, to excite the affections of the common people, who were sunk in languor and lethargy, and therefore he supposed that the new concomitants of methodism might probably produce so desirable an effect. The mind, like the body, he observed, delighted in change and novelty, and even in religion itself, courted new appearances and modifications. Whatever might be thought of some methodist teachers, he said, he could scarcely doubt the sincerity of that man, who travelled nine hundred miles in a month, and preached twelve times a week ; for no adequate reward, merely temporal, could be given for such indefatigable labour.

" Of Dr. Priestley's theological works, he remarked, that they tended to unsettle everything, and yet settled nothing.

" He was much affected by the death of his mother, and wrote to me to come and assist him to compose his mind, which indeed I found extremely agitated. He lamented that all serious and religious conversation was banished from the society of men, and yet great advantages might be derived from it. All acknowledged, he said, what hardly any body practised, the obligations we were under of making the concerns of eternity the governing principles of our lives. Every man, he observed, at last wishes for retreat : he sees his expectations frustrated in the world, and begins to wean himself from it, and to prepare for everlasting separation.

" He observed, that the influence of London now extended everywhere, and that from all manner of communication being opened, there shortly would be no remains of the ancient simplicity, or places of cheap retreat to be found.

" He was no admirer of blank verse, and said it always failed, unless sustained by the dignity of the subject. In blank verse, he said, the language suffered more distortion, to keep it out of prose, than any inconvenience or limitation to be apprehended from the shackles and circumspection of rhyme.

" He reproved me once for saying grace without mentioning the name of our LORD JESUS CHRIST, and hoped in future I would be more mindful of the apostolical injunction.

" He refused to go out of a room before me at Mr. Langton's house, saying, he hoped he knew his rank better than to presume to take place of a Doctor

: Jacob Behmen, or Böhmen, a German shoemaker and theological writer. He was the founder of a sect, sometimes called Behmenites, and sometimes Aureacrucians.—ED.

in Divinity I mention such little anecdotes, merely to show the peculiar turn and habit of his mind.

"He used frequently to observe, that there was more to be endured than enjoyed, in the general condition of human life; and frequently quoted those lines of Dryden:

> "Strange cozenage! none would live past years again,
> Yet all hope pleasure from what still remain."

For his part, he said, he never passed that week in his life which he would wish to repeat, were an angel to make the proposal to him.

"He was of opinion, that the English nation cultivated both their soil and their reason better than any other people; but admitted that the French, though not the highest, perhaps, in any department of literature, yet in every department were very high. Intellectual pre-eminence, he observed, was the highest superiority; and that every nation derived their highest reputation from the splendour and dignity of their writers. Voltaire, he said, was a good narrator, and that his principal merit consisted in a happy selection and arrangement of circumstances.

"Speaking of the French novels, compared with Richardson's, he said, they might be pretty baubles, but a wren was not an eagle.

"In a Latin conversation with the Père Boscovitch,[1] at the house of Mrs. Cholmondeley, I heard him maintain the superiority of Sir Isaac Newton over all foreign philosophers,[2] with a dignity and eloquence that surprised that learned foreigner. It being observed to him, that a rage for everything English prevailed much in France after Lord Chatham's glorious war, he said, he did not wonder at it, for that we had drubbed those fellows into a proper reverence for us, and that their national petulance required periodical chastisement.

"Lord Lyttelton's Dialogues, he deemed a nugatory performance. 'That man,' said he, 'sat down to write a book, to tell the world what the world had all his life been telling him.'

"Somebody observing that the Scotch Highlanders, in the year 1745, had made surprising efforts, considering their numerous wants and disadvantages: 'Yes, Sir,' said he, 'their wants were numerous; but you have not mentioned the greatest of them all—the want of law.'

"Speaking of the *inward light*, to which some methodists pretended, he said, it was a principle utterly incompatible with social or civil security. 'If a man,' said he, 'pretends to a principle of action of which I can know nothing, nay, not so much as that he has it, but only that he pretends to it; how can I tell what that person may be prompted to do? When a person professes to be governed by a written ascertained law, I can then know where to find him.'

"The poem of Fingal, he said, was a mere unconnected rhapsody, a tiresome

---

[1] Roger Joseph Boscovitch, a professor of mathematics in the Jesuits' College at Rome, was author of a Latin poem on Eclipses, &c. He died in 1787.—ED.

In a Discourse by Sir William Jones, addressed to the Asiatic Society, Feb. 24, 1785, is the following passage:—

One of the most sagacious men of this age who continues, I hope, to improve and adorn Samuel Johnson, remarked in my hearing, that if Newton had flourished in ancient Greece he would have been worshipped as a Divinity."—MALONE.

repetition of the same images. 'In vain shall we look for the *lucidus ordo,* where there is neither end nor object, design or moral, *nec certa recurrit imago.*'

" Being asked by a young nobleman, what was become of the gallantry and military spirit of the old English nobility, he replied, ' Why, my lord, I'll tell you what is become of it : it is gone into the city to look for a fortune.'

" Speaking of a dull, tiresome fellow, whom he chanced to meet, he said, ' That fellow seems to me to possess but one idea, and that is a wrong one.'

" Much inquiry having been made concerning a gentleman, who had quitted a company where Johnson was, and no information being obtained, at last Johnson observed, that ' he did not care to speak ill of any man behind his back, but he believed the gentleman was an *attorney.* '

" He spoke with much contempt of the notice taken of Woodhouse, the poetical shoemaker. He said, it was all vanity and childishness : and that such objects were, to those who patronised them, mere mirrors of their own superiority. ' They had better,' said he, ' furnish the man with good implements for his trade, than raise subscriptions for his poems. He may make an excellent shoemaker, but can never make a good poet. A schoolboy's exercise may be a pretty thing for a schoolboy ; but it is no treat for a man.'

" Speaking of Boetius, who was the favourite writer of the middle ages, he said, it was very surprising that, upon such a subject, and in such a situation, he should be *magis philosophus quam Christianus.*

" Speaking of Arthur Murphy, whom he very much loved, 'I don't know,' said he, ' that Arthur can be classed with the very first dramatic writers ; yet at present I doubt much whether we have anything superior to Arthur.'

" Speaking of the national debt, he said, 'It was an idle dream to suppose that the country could sink under it. Let the public creditors be ever so clamorous, the interest of millions must ever prevail over that of thousands.'

" Of Dr. Kennicott's Collations, he observed, that ' though the text should not be much mended thereby, yet it was no small advantage to know that we had as good a text as the most consummate industry and diligence could procure.'

" Johnson observed, ' that so many objections might be made to everything. that nothing could overcome them but the necessity of doing something. No man would be of any profession, as simply opposed to not being of it ; but every one must do something.'

" He remarked, that a London parish was a very comfortless thing ; for the clergyman seldom knew the face of one out of ten of his parishioners.

" Of the late Mr. Mallet he spoke with no great respect : said, he was ready for any dirty job ; that he had wrote against Byng at the instigation of the ministry, and was equally ready to write for him, provided he found his account in it.

" A gentleman who had been very unhappy in marriage, married immediately after his wife died : Johnson said, it was the triumph of hope over experience.

" He observed, that a man of sense and education should meet a suitable companion in a wife. It was a miserable thing when the conversation could only be such as, whether the mutton should be boiled or roasted, and probably a dispute about that.

" He did not approve of late marriages, observing, that more was lost in point of time, than compensated for by any possible advantages. Even ill assorted marriages were preferable to cheerless celibacy.

" Of Old Sheridan he remarked, that he neither wanted parts nor litera-ture ; but that his vanity and Quixotism obscured his merits.

" He said, foppery was never cured ; it was the bad stamina of the mind, which, like those of the body, were never rectified : once a coxcomb, and always a coxcomb.

" Being told that Gilbert Cooper called him the Caliban of literature, ' Well,' said he, ' I must dub him the Punchinello.'

" Speaking of the old Earl of Cork and Orrery, he said, ' That man spent his life in catching at an object, (literary eminence,) which he had not power to grasp.'

" To find a substitution for violated morality, he said, was the leading feature in all perversions of religion.

" He often used to quote, with great pathos, those fine lines of Virgil :—

> ' Optima quæque dies miseris mortalibus ævi
> Prima fugit ; subeunt morbi, tristisque senectus,
> Et labor, et duræ rapit inclementia mortis.'

" Speaking of Homer, whom he venerated as the prince of poets, Johnson remarked, that the advice given to Diomed [1] by his father, when he sent him to the Trojan war, was the noblest exhortation that could be instanced in any heathen writer, and comprised in a single line :—

> Αἰὲν ἀριστεύειν, καὶ ὑπείροχον ἔμμεναι ἄλλων :

which, if I recollect well, is translated by Dr. Clarke thus : *Semper appetere præstantissima, et omnibus aliis antecellere.*

" He observed, ' it was a most mortifying reflection for any man to consider *what he had done*, compared with what *he might have done*.'

" He said few people had intellectual resources sufficient to forego the pleasures of wine. They could not otherwise contrive how to fill the interval between dinner and supper.

" He went with me, one Sunday, to hear my old master, Gregory Sharpe, preach at the Temple.—In the prefatory prayer, Sharpe ranted about *liberty*, as a blessing most fervently to be implored, and its continuance prayed for. Johnson observed, that our *liberty* was in no sort of danger :—he would have done much better to pray against our *licentiousness*.

" One evening at Mrs. Montagu's, where a splendid company was assembled, consisting of the most eminent literary characters, I thought he seemed highly pleased with the respect and attention that were shown him, and asked him, on our return home, if he was not highly *gratified* by his visit : ' No, Sir,' said he, ' not highly *gratified ;* yet I do not recollect to have passed many evenings *with fewer objections.*'

" Though of no high extraction himself, he had much respect for birth and family, especially among ladies. He said, ' adventitious accomplishments may be possessed by all ranks ; but one may easily distinguish the *born gentlewoman.*'

---

[1] Dr. Maxwell's memory has deceived him. Glaucus is the person who received this counsel ; and Clarke's translation of the passage (II., lib. x., l. 208) is as follows :—

" Ut semper fortissime rem gererem, et superior virtute essem aliis."—J. BOSWELL, JUN

" He said, ' the poor in England were better provided for than in any other country of the same extent : he did not mean little cantons or petty republics ; where a great proportion of the people,' said he, ' are suffered to languish in helpless misery tha country must be ill policed, and wretchedly governed : a decent provision for the poor is the true test of civilisation. Gentlemen ot education,' he observed, ' were pretty much the same in all countries : the condition of the lower orders, the poor especially, was the true mark of national discrimination.'

" When the corn-laws were in agitation in Ireland, by which that country has been enabled not only to feed itself, but to export corn to a large amount, Sir Thomas Robinson observed, that those laws might be prejudicial to the corn-trade of England. ' Sir Thomas,' said he, ' you talk the language of a savage : what, Sir, would you prevent any people from feeding themselves, if by any honest means they can do it ?'

" It being mentioned that Garrick assisted Dr. Browne, the author of ' The Estimate,' in some dramatic composition, ' No, Sir,' said Johnson, ' he would no more suffer Garrick to write a line in his play, than he would suffer him to mount his pulpit.'

" Speaking of Burke, he said, ' It was commonly observed he spoke too often in parliament ; but nobody could say he did not speak well, though too frequently and too familiarly.'

" Speaking of economy, he remarked, it was hardly worth while to save anxiously twenty pounds a year. If a man could save to that degree, so as to enable him to assume a different rank in society, then, indeed, it might answer some purpose.

" He observed, a principal source of erroneous judgment was, viewing things partially and only on *one side :* as, for instance, *fortune hunters,* when they contemplated the fortunes *singly* and *separately,* it was a dazzling and tempting object ; but when they came to possess the wives and their fortunes *together,* they began to suspect they had not made quite so good a bargain.

" Speaking of the late Duke of Northumberland living very magnificently when Lord Lieutenant of Ireland, somebody remarked, it would be difficult to find a suitable successor to him : ' Then,' exclaimed Johnson, ' *he is only fit to succeed himself.*'

" He advised me, if possible, to have a good orchard. He knew, he said, a clergyman of small income, who brought up a family very reputably, which he chiefly fed with apple dumplings.

" He said, he had known several good scholars among the Irish gentlemen ; but scarcely any of them correct in *quality.* He extended the same observation to Scotland.

" Speaking of a certain prelate, who exerted himself very laudably in building churches and parsonage-houses ; ' however,' said he, ' I do not find that he is esteemed a man of much professional learning, or a liberal patron of it ; yet, it is well, where a man possesses any strong positive excellence. Few have all kinds of merit belonging to their character. We must not examine matters too deeply. No, Sir, *a fallible being will fail somewhere.*'

" Talking of the Irish clergy, he said, ' Swift was a man of great parts, and the instrument of much good to his country. Berkeley was a profound scholar, as well as a man of fine imagination ; but Usher,' he said, 'was the great luminary of the Irish church: and a greater,' he added, 'no church could boast of, at least in modern times.'

" We dined *tête-à-tête* at the Mitre, as I was preparing to return to Ireland, after an absence of many years. I regretted much leaving London, where I had formed many agreeable connections : 'Sir,' said he, 'I don't wonder at it ; no man, fond of letters, leaves London without regret. But remember, Sir, you have seen and enjoyed a great deal ; you have seen life in its highest decorations, and the world has nothing new to exhibit. No man is so well qualified to leave public life as he who has long tried it and known it well. We are always hankering after untried situations, and imagining greater felicity from them than they can afford. No, Sir, knowledge and virtue may be acquired in all countries, and your local consequence will make you some amends for the intellectual gratifications you relinquish.' Then he quoted the following lines with great pathos :—

> " 'He who has early known the pomps of state,
>   (For things unknown 'tis ignorance to condemn ;)
> And, after having view'd the gaudy bait,
>   Can boldly say, the trifle I contemn ;
> With such a one contented could I live,
>   Contented could I die.' [1]

" He then took a most affectionate leave of me ; said, he knew it was a point of *duty* that called me away. 'We shall all be sorry to lose you,' said he : '*laudo tamen.*' "

In 1771 he published another political pamphlet, entitled " Thoughts on the late Transactions respecting Falkland's Islands," in which, upon materials furnished to him by ministry, and upon general topics, expanded in his rich style, he successfully endeavoured to persuade the nation that it was wise and laudable to suffer the question of right to remain undecided, rather than involve our country in another war. It has been suggested by some, with what truth I shall not take upon me to decide, that he rated the consequence of those islands to Great Britain too low. But however this may be, every humane mind must

[1] Being desirous to trace these verses to the fountain-head, after having in vain turned over several of our elder poets with the hope of lighting on them, I applied to Dr. Maxwell, now resident at Bath, for the purpose of ascertaining their author: but that gentleman could furnish no aid on this occasion. At length the lines have been discovered by the author's second son, Mr. James Boswell, in " The London Magazine " for July, 1732, where they form part of a poem on " Retirement," there published anonymously, but in fact (as he afterwards found) copied, with some slight variations, from one of Walsh's smaller poems, entitled " The Retirement ; " and they exhibit another proof of what has been elsewhere observed by the author of the work before us, that Johnson retained in his memory fragments of obscure or neglected poetry. In quoting verses of that description, he appears by a slight deviation to have sometimes given them a moral turn, and to have dexterously adapted them to his own sentiments, where the original had a very different tendency. Thus, in the present instance (as Mr. J. Boswell observes to me), " the author of the poem above-mentioned exhibits himself as having retired to the country, to avoid the vain follies of a town life,—ambition avarice, and the pursuit of pleasure, contrasted with the enjoyments of the country, and the delightful conversation that the brooks, &c., furnish ; which he holds to be infinitely more pleasing and instructive than any which towns afford. He is then led to consider the weakness

surely applaud the earnestness with which he averted the calamity of war : a calamity so dreadful, that it is astonishing how civilised, nay, Christian nations can deliberately continue to renew it. His description of its miseries in this pamphlet, is one of the finest pieces of eloquence in the English language. Upon this occasion, too, we find Johnson lashing the party in opposition with unbounded severity, and

of the human mind, and, after lamenting that he (the writer), who is neither enslaved by avarice, ambition, or pleasure, has yet made himself a slave to *love*, he thus proceeds :

' If this dire passion never will be gone,
  If beauty always must my heart enthral,
O, rather let me be confined by *one*,
  Than madly thus become a slave to all :

' One *who has early known the pomp of state,*
  (*For things unknown 'tis ignorance to condemn ;*)
And, after having view'd the gaudy bait,
  Can coldly *say, the trifle I contemn* ;

In her blest arms *contented could I live,*
  Contented could I die. But O, my mind,
Imaginary scenes of bliss deceive
  With hopes of joys impossible to find.' "

Another instance of Johnson's retaining in his memory verses by obscure authors, is given in Mr. Boswell's " Journal of a Tour in the Hebrides;" where, in consequence of hearing a girl spinning in a chamber over that in which he was sitting, he repeated these lines, which he said were written by one Gifford, a clergyman ; but the poem in which they are introduced, has hitherto been undiscovered :—

" Verse sweetens toil, however rude the sound :
  All at her work the village maiden sings :
Nor while she turns the giddy wheel around,
  Revolves the sad vicissitude of things."

In the autumn of 1782, when he was at Brighthelmstone, he frequently accompanied Mr. Philip Metcalfe in his chaise, to take the air ; and the conversation in one of their excursions happening to turn on a celebrated historian, since deceased, he repeated, with great precision, some verses, as very characteristic of that gentleman. These furnish another proof of what has been above observed; for they are found in a very obscure quarter, among some anonymous poems appended to the second volume of a collection frequently printed by Lintot, under the title of " Pope's Miscellanies.

" See how the wand'ring Danube flows,
  Realms and religions parting ;
A friend to all true Christian foes,
  To Peter, Jack, and Martin.

" Now Protestant, and Papist now,
  Not constant long to either,
At length an infidel does grow,
  And ends his journey neither.

" Thus many a youth I've known set out,
  Half Protestant, half Papist,
And rambling long the world about,
  Turn infidel or atheist."

In reciting these verses I have no doubt that Johnson substituted some word for *infide* in the second stanza, to avoid the disagreeable repetition of the same expression.— MALONE.

making the fullest use of what he ever reckoned a most effectual argumentative instrument—contempt. His character of their very able mysterious champion, Junius, is executed with all the force of his genius, and finished with the highest care. He seems to have exulted in sallying forth to single combat against the boasted and formidable hero, who bade defiance to " principalities and powers, and the rulers of this world."

This pamphlet, it is observable, was softened in one particular, after the first edition ; for the conclusion of Mr. George Grenville's character stood thus : " Let him not, however, be depreciated in his grave. He had powers not universally possessed : could he have enforced payment of the Manilla ransom, *he could have counted it.*" Which instead of retaining its sly sharp point, was reduced to a mere flat unmeaning expression, or, if I may use the word—*truism :* " He had powers not universally possessed : and if he sometimes erred, he was likewise sometimes right."

" TO BENNET LANGTON, ESQ.

" DEAR SIR,   *March* 20, 1771.

" After much lingering of my own, and much of the ministry, I have at length got out my paper.[1] But delay is not yet at an end : not many had been dispersed before Lord North ordered the sale to stop. His reasons I do not distinctly know. You may try to find them in the perusal.[2] Before his order, a sufficient number were dispersed to do all the mischief, though, perhaps, not to make all the sport that might be expected from it.

" Soon after your departure, I had the pleasure of finding all the danger past with which your navigation was threatened. I hope nothing happens at home to abate your satisfaction ; but that Lady Rothes and Mrs. Langton, and the young ladies, are all well.

" I was last night at THE CLUB. Dr. Percy has written a long ballad in many *fits ;* it is pretty enough. He has printed, and will soon publish it. Goldsmith is at Bath with Lord Clare. At Mr. Thrale's, where I am now writing, all are well. I am, dear Sir, your most humble servant,

" SAM. JOHNSON."

Mr. Strahan, the printer, who had been long in intimacy with Johnson, in the course of his literary labours, who was at once his friendly agent in receiving his pension for him, and his banker in supplying him with money when he wanted it ; who was himself now a member of Parliament, and who loved much to be employed in political negociation : thought he should do eminent service, both to government and

---

[1] " Thoughts on the late Transactions respecting Falkland's Islands."

[2] By comparing the first with the subsequent editions, this curious circumstance of ministerial authorship may be discovered.

It can only be discovered (as Mr. Bindley observes to me) by him who possesses a copy of the first edition issued out before the sale was stopped.—MALONE.

Johnson, if he could be the means of his getting a seat in the House of Commons. With this view, he wrote a letter to one of the Secretaries of the Treasury, of which he gave me a copy in his own handwriting, which is as follows :—

"SIR, *New-street, March* 30, 1771.

" You will easily recollect, when I had the honour of waiting upon you some time ago, I took the liberty to observe to you, that Dr. Johnson would make an excellent figure in the House of Commons, and heartily wished he had a seat there. My reasons are briefly these :

" I know his perfect good affection to his Majesty and his government, which ɪ am certain he wishes to support by every means in his power.

" He possesses a great share of manly, nervous, and ready eloquence ; is quick in discerning the strength and weakness of an argument ; can express himself with clearness and precision, and fears the face of no man alive.

" His known character, as a man of extraordinary sense and unimpeached virtue, would secure him the attention of the House, and could not fail to givɪ him a proper weight there.

" He is capable of the greatest application, and can undergo any degree ᴏ labour, where he sees it necessary, and where his heart and affections are strongly engaged. His Majesty's ministers might therefore securely depend on his doing, upon every proper occasion, the utmost that could be expected from him. They would find him ready to vindicate such measures as tended to promote the stability of government, and resolute and steady in carrying them into execution. Nor is anything to be apprehended from the supposed impetuosity of his temper. To the friends of the king you will find him a lamb, to his enemies a lion.

" For these reasons I humbly apprehend that he would be a very able and useful member. And I will venture to say, the employment would not be disagreeable to him ; and knowing, as I do, his strong affection to the king, his ability to serve him in that capacity, and the extreme ardour with which I am convinced he would engage in that service, I must repeat that I wish most heartily to see him in the House.

" If you think this worthy of attention, you will be pleased to take a convenient opportunity of mentioning it to Lord North. If his lordship should happily approve of it, I shall have the satisfaction of having been, in some degree, the humble instrument of doing my country, in my opinion, a very essential service. I know your good nature, and your zeal for the public welfare, will plead my excuse for giving you this trouble. I am, with the greatest respect, Sir,

" Your most obedient and humble servant,
" WILLIAM STRAHAN."

This recommendation, we know, was not effectual ; but how, or for what reason, can only be conjectured. It is not to be believed that Mr. Strahan would have applied unless Johnson had approved of it. I never heard him mention the subject ; but at a later period of his life, when Sir Joshua Reynolds told him that Mr. Edmund Burke had said that, if he had come early into Parliament, he certainly would have been the greatest speaker that ever was there, Johnson exclaimed, " I should like to try my hand now."

It has been much agitated among his friends and others, whether he would have been a powerful speaker in Parliament, had he been brought in when advanced in life. I am inclined to think that his extensive knowledge, his quickness and force of mind, his vivacity and richness of expression, his wit and humour, and above all his poignancy of sarcasm, would have had great effect in a popular assembly ; and that the magnitude of his figure, and striking peculiarity of his manner, would have aided the effect. But I remember it was observed by Mr. Flood, that Johnson, having been long used to sententious brevity and the short flights o' conversation, might have failed in that continued and expanded kind of argument which is requisite in stating complicated matters in public speaking ; and, as a proof of this, he mentioned the supposed speeches in Parliament written by him for the magazine, none of which, in his opinion, were at all like real debates. The opinion of one who was himself so eminent an orator, must be allowed to have great weight. It was confirmed by Sir William Scott, who mentioned that Johnson had told him that he had several times tried to speak in the Society of Arts and Manufactures, but " had found he could not get on." [1] From Mr. William Gerard Hamilton I have heard that Johnson, when observing to him that it was prudent for a man who had not been accustomed to speak in public to begin his speech in as simple a manner as possible, acknowledged that he rose in that society to deliver a speech which he had prepared ; " but," said he, " all my flowers of oratory forsook me." I, however, cannot help wishing that he *had* " tried his hand in Parliament ; " and I wonder that the ministry did not make the experiment.

I at length renewed a correspondence which had been too long discontinued :—

" TO DR. JOHNSON.

" MY DEAR SIR, *Edinburgh, April* 18, 1771.
" I can now fully understand those intervals of silence in your correspondence with me, which have often given me anxiety and uneasiness ; for although I am conscious that my veneration and love for Mr. Johnson have never in the least abated, yet I have deferred for almost a year and a half to write to him."

In the subsequent part of this letter, I gave him an account of my comfortable life as a married man and a lawyer in practice at the Scotch bar ; invited him to Scotland, and promised to attend him to the Highlands and Hebrides.

[1] Dr. Kippis, however (" Biograph. Britan." article " J. Gilbert Cooper," p. 266, n. new edit.), says, that he " once heard Dr. Johnson speak in the Society of Arts and Manufactures, upon a subject relative to mechanics, with a propriety, perspicuity, and energy which excited general admiration."—MALONE.

" TO JAMES BOSWELL, ESQ.

" Dear Sir, *London, June* 20, 1771.

" If you are now able to comprehend that I might neglect to write without diminution of affection, you have taught me, likewise, how that neglect may be uneasily felt without resentment. I wished for your letter a long time, and when it came, it amply recompensed the delay. I never was so much pleased as now with your account of yourself; and sincerely hope, that between public business, improving studies, and domestic pleasures, neither melancholy nor caprice will find any place for entrance. Whatever philosophy may determine of material nature, it is certainly true of intellectual nature, that it *abhors a vacuum:* our minds cannot be empty; and evil will break in upon them, if they are not pre-occupied by good. My dear Sir, mind your studies, mind your business, make your lady happy, and be a good Christian. After this,

> ' *tristitiam et metus*
> *Trades protervis in mare Creticum*
> *Portare ventis.*'

"If we perform our duty, we shall be safe and steady, ' *Sive per,*' &c., whether we climb the Highlands, or are tossed among the Hebrides; and I hope the time will come when we may try our powers both with cliffs and water. I see but little of Lord Elibank, I know not why; perhaps by my own fault. I am this day going into Staffordshire and Derbyshire for six weeks.

" I am, dear Sir,

" Your most affectionate and most humble servant,

" Sam. Johnson."

" TO SIR JOSHUA REYNOLDS, IN LEICESTER FIELDS.

" Dear Sir, *Ashbourne, in Derbyshire, July* 17, 1771.

" When I came to Lichfield, I found that my portrait[1] had been much visited, and much admired. Every man has a lurking wish to appear considerable in his native place; and I was pleased with the dignity conferred by such a testimony of your regard.

"Be pleased, therefore, to accept the thanks of, Sir,

" Your most obliged and most humble servant,

" Sam. Johnson."

" Compliments to Miss Reynolds."

" TO DR. JOHNSON.

" My dear Sir, *Edinburgh, July* 27, 1771.

" The bearer of this, Mr. Beattie, professor of moral philosophy at Aberdeen, is desirous of being introduced to your acquaintance. His genius and learning, and labours in the service of virtue and religion, render him very worthy of it : and as he has a high esteem of your character, I hope you will give him a favourable reception. I ever am, &c., James Boswell."

The second portrait of Johnson, painted by Sir Joshua Reynolds; with his arms raised, and his hands bent. It was at this time, it is believed, in the possession of Miss Lucy Porter and is still probably at Lichfield.—Malone.

"TO BENNET LANGTON, ESQ., AT LANGTON, NEAR SPILSBY, LINCOLNSHIRE.

"DEAR SIR, *August* 29, 1771.

"I am lately returned from Staffordshire and Derbyshire. The last letter mentions two others which you have written to me since you received my pamphlet. Of these two I never had but one, in which you mentioned a design of visiting Scotland, and by consequence, put my journey to Langton

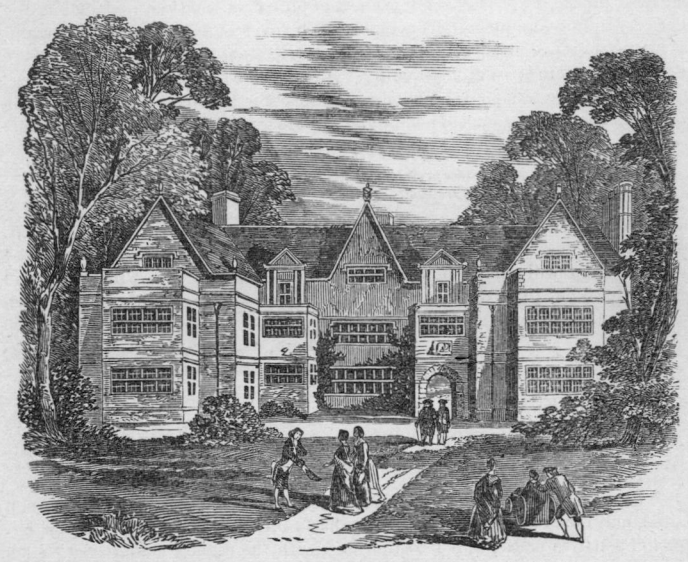

LANGTON HALL.

out of my thoughts. My summer wanderings are now over, and I am engaging in a very great work, the revision of my Dictionary; from which I know not, at present, how to get loose.

"If you have observed, or been told, any errors or omissions, you will do me a great favour by letting me know them.

'Lady Rothes, I find, has disappointed you and herself. Ladies will have these tricks. The Queen and Mrs. Thrale, both ladies of experience, yet both missed their reckoning this summer. I hope a few months will recompense your uneasiness.

"Please to tell Lady Rothes how highly I value the honour of her invitation, which it is my purpose to obey as soon as I have disengaged myself. In the meantime I shall hope to hear often of her ladyship, and every day better news and better, till I hear that you have both the happiness, which to both is very sincerely wished, by, Sir,

"Your most affectionate and most humble servant,

"SAM. JOHNSON."

In October I again wrote to him, thanking him for his last letter, and his obliging reception of Mr. Beattie ; informing him that I had been at Alnwick lately, and had good accounts of him from Dr. Percy.

In his religious record of this year we observe that he was better than usual, both in body and mind, and better satisfied with the regularity of his conduct. But he is still " trying his ways " too rigorously. He charges himself with not rising early enough ; yet he mentions what was surely a sufficient excuse for this, supposing it to be a duty seriously required, as he all his life appears to have thought it. " One great hindrance is want of rest ; my nocturnal complaints grow less troublesome towards morning : and I am tempted to repair the deficiencies of the night." [1] Alas ! how hard would it be, if this indulgence were to be imputed to a sick man as a crime. In his retrospect on the following Easter-eve, he says, " When I review the last year, I am able to recollect so little done, that shame and sorrow, though perhaps too weakly, come upon me." Had he been judging of any one else in the same circumstances, how clear would he have been on the favourable side. How very difficult, and, in my opinion, almost constitutionally impossible it was for him to be raised early, even by the strongest resolutions, appears from a note in one of his little paper-books (containing words arranged for his Dictionary), written I suppose about 1753 : " I do not remember that, since I left Oxford, I ever rose early by mere choice, but once or twice at Edial, and two or three times for ' The Rambler.' " I think he had fair ground enough to have quieted his mind on the subject, by concluding that he was physically incapable of what is at best but a commodious regulation.

" Prayers and Meditations," p. 101—BOSWELL.

DR. BEATTIE.

CHAPTER V.—1772.

Dr. Beattie—Boswell returns to London—Lord Monboddo—Scotch Church—Second Sight—Thirty-nine Articles Royal Marriage Bill—Foote's Mimicry—Fourth Edition of the Dictionary prepared—Mr. Peyton—Origin of Languages—Flogging—Scottish Accent—Ghost Stories—Ranelagh—Hon. Thomas Erskine—General Oglethorpe—Goldsmith's Natural History—Johnson's Advice to Authors—His Opinion on a point of Scotch Law.

IN 1772 he was altogether quiescent as an author; but it will be found, from the various evidences which I shall bring together, that his mind was acute, lively, and vigorous.

" TO SIR JOSHUA REYNOLDS.

"Dear Sir, *Feb.* 27, 1772.

"Be pleased to send to Mr. Banks, whose place of residence I do not know, this note, which I have sent open, that, if you please, you may read it.

"When you send it, do not use your own seal. I am, Sir, your most humble servant, "Sam. Johnson."

" TO JOSEPH BANKS, ESQ.

"Perpetua ambitâ bis terrâ præmia lactis
Hæc habet altrici Capra secunda Jovis." [1]

"Sir, *Johnson's-court, Fleet-street, February* 27, 1772.

"I return thanks to you and to Dr. Solander for the pleasure which I received in yesterday's conversation. I could not recollect a motto for your 'Goat,' but had given her one. You, Sir, may perhaps have an epic poem from some happier pen than, Sir, your most humble servant,

"Sam. Johnson."

[1] Thus translated by a friend:—
" In fame scarce second to the nurse of Jove,
This goat, who twice the world had traversed round,
Deserving both her master's care and love,
Ease and perpetual pasture now has found."—Boswell.

" TO DR. JOHNSON.

My dear Sir,

" It is hard that I cannot prevail on you to write to me oftener. But I am convinced that it is in vain to expect from you a private correspondence with any regularity. I must, therefore, look upon you as a fountain of wisdom, from whence few rills are communicated to a distance, and which must be approached at its source, to partake fully of its virtues.

* * * * * *

" I am coming to London soon, and am to appear in an appeal from the Court of Session in the House of Lords. A schoolmaster in Scotland was, by a court of inferior jurisdiction, deprived of his office, for being somewhat severe in the chastisement of his scholars. The Court of Session considering it to be dangerous to the interest of learning and education, to lessen the dignity of teachers, and make them afraid of too indulgent parents, instigated by the complaints of their children, restored him. His enemies have appealed to the House of Lords, though the salary is only twenty pounds a year. I was counsel for him here. I hope there will be little fear of a reversal; but I must beg to have your aid in my plan of supporting the decree. It is a general question and not a point of particular law.

* * * * * *

" I am, &c.,   JAMES BOSWELL."

" TO JAMES BOSWELL, ESQ.

" Dear Sir,   *March* 15, 1772.

" That you are coming so soon to town I am very glad; and still more glad that you are coming as an advocate. I think nothing more likely to make your life pass happily away, than that consciousness of your own value, which eminence in your profession will certainly confer. If I can give you any collateral help, I hope you do not suspect that it will be wanting. My kindness for you has neither the merit of singular virtue, nor the reproach of singular prejudice. Whether to love you be right or wrong, I have many on my side. Mrs. Thrale loves you, and Mrs. Williams loves you, and what would have inclined me to love you, if I had been neutral before, you are a great favourite of Dr. Beattie.

" Of Dr. Beattie I should have thought much, but that his lady puts him out of my head; she is a very lovely woman.

" The ejection which you come hither to oppose, appears very cruel, unreasonable, and oppressive. I should think there could not be much doubt of your success.

" My health grows better, yet I am not fully recovered. I believe it is held that men do not recover very fast after three score. I hope yet to see Beattie's College; and have not given up the western voyage. But however all this may be or not, let us try to make each other happy when we meet, and not refer our pleasure to distant times or distant places.

" How comes it that you tell me nothing of your lady? I hope to see her some time, and till then shall be glad to hear of her.

" I am, dear Sir, &c.,
" Sam. Johnson."

" Dear Sir,   *March* 14, 1772.

" I congratulate you and Lady Rothes [1] on your little man, and hope you will all be many years happy together.

" Poor Miss Langton can have little part in the joy of her family. She this day called her aunt Langton to receive the sacrament with her ; and made me talk yesterday on such subjects as suit her condition. It will probably be her *viaticum.* I surely need not mention again that she wishes to see her mother.   I am, Sir, your most humble servant,

" Sam. Johnson."

On the 21st of March, I was happy to find myself again in my friend's study, and was glad to see my old acquaintance, Mr. Francis Barber, who was now returned home. Dr. Johnson received me with a hearty welcome ; saying, " I am glad you are come, and glad you are come upon such an errand" (alluding to the cause of the schoolmaster). Boswell : "I hope, Sir, he will be in no danger. It is a very delicate matter to interfere between a master and his scholars : nor do I see how you can fix the degree of severity that a master may use." Johnson : " Why, Sir, till you can fix the degree of obstinacy and negligence of the scholars, you cannot fix the degree of severity of the master. Severity must be continued until obstinacy be subdued, and negligence be cured." He mentioned the severity of Hunter, his own master. " Sir," said I, " Hunter is a Scotch name : so it should seem this schoolmaster who beat you so severely was a Scotchman. I can now account for your prejudice against the Scotch." Johnson : " Sir, he was not Scotch ; and, abating his brutality, he was a very good master."

We talked of his two political pamphlets, " The False Alarm," and " Thoughts concerning Falkland's Islands." Johnson : " Well, Sir, which of them did you think the best ? " Boswell : " I liked the second best." Johnson : " Why, Sir, I liked the first best ; and Beattie liked the first best. Sir, there is a subtlety of disquisition in the first, that is worth all the fire of the second." Boswell : " Pray, Sir, is it true that Lord North paid you a visit, and that you got two hundred a year in addition to your pension ? " Johnson : " No, Sir. Except what I had from the bookseller, I did not get a farthing by them. And, between you and me, I believe Lord North is no friend to me." Boswell : " How so, Sir ? " Johnson : " Why, Sir, you cannot account for the fancies of men. Well, how does Lord Elibank ? and how does Lord Monboddo ? " Boswell : " Very well, Sir. Lord Monboddo still

[1] Mr. Langton married May 24, 1770, Jane, the daughter of —— Lloyd, Esq., and widow of John Earl of Rothes, many years Commander-in-Chief of the Forces in Ireland, who died in 1767.—Malone.

maintains the superiority of the savage life." [1] Johnson : " What strange narrowness of mind now is that, to think the things we have not known are better than the things which we have known." Boswell : " Why, Sir, that is a common prejudice." Johnson : " Yes, Sir, but a common prejudice should not be found in one whose trade it is to rectify error."

A gentleman having come in who was to go as a mate in the ship along with Mr. Banks and Dr. Solander, Dr. Johnson asked what were the names of the ships destined for the expedition. The gentleman answered, they were once to be called "The Drake " and "The Raleigh," but now they were to be called " The Resolution " and " The Adventure." Johnson : " Much better ; for had 'The Raleigh' returned without going round the world, it would have been ridiculous. To give them the names of ' The Drake' and 'The Raleigh ' was laying a trap for satire." Boswell : " Had not you some desire to go upon this expedition, Sir ? " Johnson : " Why, yes, but I soon laid it aside. Sir, there is very little of intellectual, in the course. Besides, I see but at a small distance. So it was not worth my while to go to see birds fly, which I should not have seen fly ; and fishes swim, which I should not have seen swim."

The gentleman being gone, and Dr. Johnson having left the room for some time, a debate arose between the Reverend Mr. Stockdale and Mrs. Desmoulins, whether Mr. Banks and Dr. Solander were entitled to any share of glory from their expedition. When Dr. Johnson returned to us, I told him the subject of their dispute. Johnson : "Why, Sir, it was properly for botany that they went out ; I believe they thought only of culling of simples."

I thanked him for showing civilities to Beattie. "Sir," said he, " I should thank *you*. We all love Beattie. Mrs. Thrale says, if ever she has another husband, she'll have Beattie. He sunk upon us [2] that he

---

[1] James Burnett, **Lord Monboddo**, a distinguished Scotch judge. Though both learned and acute, he exposed himself to much deserved ridicule by asserting the existence of mermaids and satyrs, but more particularly by his whimsical speculations relative to a supposed affinity between the human race and the monkey tribe.—Ed.

[2] " TO JAMES BOSWELL, ESQ.

" My dear Sir, *Edinburgh, May* 8, 1792.
" As I suppose your great work will soon be reprinted, I beg leave to trouble you with a remark on a passage of it, in which I am a little misrepresented. Be not alarmed ; the misrepresentation is not imputable to you. Not having the book at hand, I cannot specify the page, but I suppose you will easily find it. Dr. Johnson says, speaking of Mrs. Thrale's family, ' Dr. Beattie *sunk upon us* that he was married, or words to that purpose.' I am not sure that I understand *sunk upon us,* which is a very uncommon phrase; but it seems to me to imply, (and others I find have understood it in the same sense,) *studiously concealed from us his being married.* Now, Sir, this was by no means the case. I could have no motive to conceal a circumstance, of which I never was nor can be ashamed ; and of which Dr. Johnson seemed to think, when he afterwards became acquainted with Mrs. Beattie, that I had, as was true, reason to be proud. So far was I from concealing her, that my wife had at that time almost as numerous an acquaintance in London as I had myself; and was, not very long after, kindly invited and elegantly entertained at Streatham by Mr. and Mrs. Thrale

was married ; else we should have shown his lady more civilities. She is a very fine woman. But how can you show civilities to a nonentity I did not think he had been married. Nay, I did not think about it one way or other ; but he did not tell us of his lady till late."

He then spoke of St. Kilda, the most remote of the Hebrides. I told him, I thought of buying it. Johnson: "Pray do, Sir. We will go and pass a winter amid the blasts there. We shall have fine fish, and we will take some dried tongues with us, and some books. We will have a strong-built vessel, and some Orkney men to navigate her. We must build a tolerable house ; but we may carry with us a wooden house ready made, and requiring nothing but to be put up. Consider, Sir, by buying St. Kilda, you may keep the people from falling into worse hands. We must give them a clergyman, and he shall be one of Beattie's choosing. He shall be educated at Marischal College. I'll be your Lord Chancellor, or what you please." Boswell : "Are you serious, Sir, in advising me to buy St. Kilda—for if you should advise me to go to Japan, I believe I should do it ? " Johnson : "Why yes, Sir, I am serious." Boswell : "Why then I'll see what can be done."

I gave him an account of the two parties in the church of Scotland, those for supporting the rights of patrons, independent of the people, and those against it. Johnson : " It should be settled one way or other. I cannot wish well to a popular election of the clergy, when I consider that it occasions such animosities, such unworthy courting of the people, such slanders between the contending parties, and other disadvantages. It is enough to allow the people to remonstrate against the nomination of a minister for solid reasons." I suppose he meant heresy or immorality.

He was engaged to dine abroad, and asked me to return to him in the evening, at nine, which I accordingly did.

We drank tea with Mrs. Williams, who told us a story of second sight, which happened in Wales, where she was born. He listened to it very attentively, and said he should be glad to have some instances of that faculty well authenticated. His elevated wish for more and more evidence for spirit, in opposition to the grovelling belief of materialism, led him to a love of such mysterious disquisitions. He again justly observed, that we could have no certainty of the truth of supernatural appearances, unless something was told us which we could not know

" My request, therefore, is, that you would rectify this matter in your new edition. You are at liberty to make what use you please of this letter.

" My best wishes ever attend you and your family. Believe me to be, with the utmost regard and esteem, dear Sir,

" Your obliged and affectionate humble servant,

" J. Beattie."

I have, from my respect for my friend Dr. Beattie, and regard to his extreme sensibility, inserted the foregoing letter, though I cannot but wonder at his considering as any imputation a phrase commonly used among the best friends.—Boswell.

by ordinary means, or something done which could not be done but by supernatural power ; that Pharaoh in reason and justice required such evidence from Moses ; nay, that our Saviour said, " If I had not done among them the works which none other man did, they had not had sin." He had said in the morning, that Macaulay's "History of St. Kilda" was very well written, except some foppery about liberty and slavery. I mentioned to him that Macaulay told me, he was advised to leave out of his book the wonderful story that upon the approach of a stranger, all the inhabitants catch cold ; but that it had been so well authenticated, he determined to retain it. JOHNSON : "Sir, to leave things out of a book, merely because people tell you they will not be believed, is meanness. Macaulay acted with more magnanimity."

We talked of the Roman Catholic religion, and how little difference there was in essential matters between ours and it. JOHNSON : "True, Sir ; all denominations of Christians have really little difference in point of doctrine, though they may differ widely in external forms. There is a prodigious difference between the external form of one of your Presbyterian Churches in Scotland, and a church in Italy ; yet the doctrine taught is essentially the same."

I mentioned the petition to Parliament for removing the subscription to the Thirty-nine Articles. JOHNSON : "It was soon thrown out. Sir, they talk of not making boys at the University subscribe to what they do not understand ; but they ought to consider, that our Universities were founded to bring up members for the Church of England, and we must not supply our enemies with arms from our arsenal. No, Sir, the meaning of subscribing is, not that they fully understand all the articles, but that they will adhere to the Church of England. Now take it in this way, and suppose that they should only subscribe their adherence to the Church of England, there would be still the same difficulty ; for still the young men would be subscribing to what they do not understand. For if you should ask them, What do you mean by the Church of England ? Do you know in what it differs from the Presbyterian Church—from the Romish Church—from the Greek Church—from the Coptic Church ? they could not tell you. So, Sir, it comes to the same thing." BOSWELL : "But would it not be sufficient to subscribe the Bible ?" JOHNSON : " Why no, Sir ; for all sects will subscribe the Bible ; nay, the Mahometans will subscribe the Bible ; for the Mahometans acknowledge JESUS CHRIST, as well as Moses, but maintain that GOD sent Mahomet as a still greater prophet than either."

I mentioned the motion which had been made in the House of Commons, to abolish the fast of the 30th of January. JOHNSON : "Why, Sir, I could have wished that it had been a temporary act, perhaps, to have expired with the century. I am against abolishing it, because that would be declaring it wrong to establish it ; but I should have no objection to make an act, continuing it for another century, and then letting it expire."

He disapproved of the Royal Marriage Bill; "Because," said he, "I would not have the people think that the validity of marriage depends on the will of man, or that the right of a king depends on the will of man. I should not have been against making the marriage of any of the royal family, without the approbation of king and parliament, highly criminal."

In the morning we had talked of old families, and the respect due to them. JOHNSON : "Sir, you have a right to that kind of respect, and are arguing for yourself. I am for supporting the principle, and am disinterested in doing it, as I have no such right." BOSWELL : "Why, Sir, it is one more incitement to a man to do well." JOHNSON : "Yes, Sir, and it is a matter of opinion very necessary to keep society together. What is it but opinion, by which we have a respect for authority, that prevents us, who are the rabble, from rising up and pulling down you who are gentlemen from your places, and saying, 'We will be gentlemen in our turn!' Now, Sir, that respect for authority is much more easily granted to a man whose father has had it, than to an upstart, and so society is more easily supported." BOSWELL : "Perhaps, Sir, it might be done by the respect belonging to office, as among the Romans, where the dress, the *toga*, inspired reverence." JOHNSON : "Why, we know very little about the Romans. But, surely, it is much easier to respect a man who has always had respect, than to respect a man whom we know was last year no better than ourselves, and will be no better next year. In republics there is no respect to authority, but a fear of power." BOSWELL : "At present, Sir, I think riches seem to gain most respect." JOHNSON : "No, Sir, riches do not gain hearty respect; they only procure external attention. A very rich man, from low beginnings, may buy his election in a borough ; but, *cæteris paribus*, a man of family will be preferred. People will prefer a man for whose father their fathers have voted, though they should get no more money, or even less That shows that the respect for family is not merely fanciful, but has an actual operation. If gentlemen of family would allow the rich upstarts to spend their money profusely, which they are ready enough to do, and not vie with them in expense, the upstarts would soon be at an end, and the gentlemen would remain ; but if the gentlemen will vie in expense with the upstarts, which is very foolish, they must be ruined."

I gave him an account of the excellent mimicry of a friend of mine in Scotland ; observing, at the same time, that some people thought it a very mean thing. JOHNSON : "Why, Sir, it is making a very mean use of man's powers. But to be a good mimic requires great powers ; great acuteness of observation, great retention of what is observed, and great pliancy of organs to represent what is observed. I remember a lady of quality in this town, Lady —— ——, who was a wonderful mimic, and used to make me laugh immoderately. I have heard she is now gone mad." BOSWELL: "It is amazing how a mimic can not only give you the gestures and voice of a person whom he represents ; but even what a person would say on any particular subject." JOHNSON : "Why, Sir, you are to consider that the manner and some particular phrases of a person do much to impress you with an idea of him, and you are not sure that he would say what the mimic says in his character." BOSWELL: "I don't think Foote a good mimic, Sir." JOHNSON : "No, Sir ; his imitations are not like. He gives you some thing different from himself, but not the character which he means to assume. He goes out of himself, without going into other people. He cannot take off any person unless he is strongly marked, such as George Faulkner. He is like a painter who can draw the portrait of a man who has a wen upon his face, and who therefore is easily known. If a man hops upon one leg, Foote can hop upon one leg. But he has not that nice discrimination which your friend seems to possess. Foote is, however, very entertaining with a kind of conversation between wit and buffoonery."

On Monday, March 23, I found him busy, preparing a fourth edition of his folio Dictionary. Mr. Peyton, one of his original amanuenses, was writing for him. I put him in mind of a meaning of the word *side*, which he had omitted, viz. relationship ; as father's side, mother's side. He inserted it. I asked him if *humiliating* was a good word. He said, he had seen it frequently used, but he did not know it to be legitimate English. He would not admit *civilization*, but only *civility*. With great deference to him I thought *civilization*, from to *civilize*, better in the sense opposed to *barbarity* than *civility ;* as it is better to have a distinct word for each sense, than one word with two senses, which *civility* is, in his way of using it.

He seemed also to be intent on some sort of chemical operation. I was entertained by observing how he contrived to send Mr. Peyton on an errand, without seeming to degrade him. "Mr. Peyton,—Mr. Peyton, will you be so good as to take a walk to Temple-bar ? You will there see a chemist's shop, at which you will be pleased to buy for me an ounce of oil of vitriol ; not spirit of vitriol, but oil of vitriol. It will cost three halfpence." Peyton immediately went, and returned with it, and told him it cost but a penny.

I then reminded him of the schoolmaster's cause, and proposed to read to him the printed papers concerning it. "No, Sir," said he, "I can read quicker than I can hear." So he read them to himself.

After he had read for some time, we were interrupted by the entrance of Mr. Kristrom, a Swede, who was tutor to some young gentlemen in the city. He told me that there was a very good History of Sweden, by Daline. Having at that time an intention of writing the history of that country, I asked Dr. Johnson whether one might write a history of

Sweden without going thither.   " Yes, Sir," said he, " one for common use."

We talked of languages.   Johnson observed that Leibnitz had made some progress in a work, tracing all languages up to the Hebrew. "Why Sir," said he, "you would not imagine that the French *jour*, day, is derived from the Latin *dies*, and yet nothing is more certain ; and the intermediate steps are very clear.   From *dies*, comes *diurnus*.   *Diu* is, by inaccurate ears, or inaccurate pronunciation, easily confounded with *giu ;* then the Italians form a substantive of the ablative of an adjective, and thence *giurno*, or, as they make it, *giorno :* which is readily contracted into *giour* or *jour*."   He observed that the Bohemian language was true Sclavonic.   The Swede said, it had some similarity with the German.   JOHNSON : "Why, Sir, to be sure, such parts of Sclavonia as confine with Germany, will borrow German words ; and such parts as confine with Tartary will borrow Tartar words."

He said, he never had it properly ascertained that the Scotch Highlanders and the Irish understood each other.   I told him that my cousin, Colonel Graham, of the Royal Highlanders, whom I met at Drogheda, told me they did.   JOHNSON : " Sir, if the Highlanders understood Irish, why translate the New Testament into Erse, as was lately done at Edinburgh, when there is an Irish translation ?"   BOSWELL : "Although the Erse and Irish are both dialects of the same language, there may be a good deal of diversity between them, as between the different dialects in Italy."—The Swede went away, and Mr. Johnson continued his reading of the papers.   I said, "I am afraid, Sir, it is troublesome."   "Why, Sir," said he, "I do not take much delight in it ; but I'll go through it."

We went to the Mitre, and dined in the room where he and I first supped together.   He gave me great hopes of my cause.   " Sir," said he, " the government of a schoolmaster is somewhat of the nature of military government ; that is to say, it must be arbitrary, it must be exercised by the will of one man, according to particular circumstances. You must show some learning upon this occasion.   You must show that a schoolmaster has a prescriptive right to beat ; and that an action of assault and battery cannot be admitted against him unless there is some great excess, some barbarity.   This man has maimed none of his boys.   They are all left with the full exercise of their corporeal faculties. In our schools in England, many boys have been maimed ; yet I never heard of an action against a schoolmaster on that account.   Puffendorf, I think, maintains the right of a schoolmaster to beat his scholars."

On Saturday, March 27, I introduced to him Sir Alexander Macdonald, with whom he had expressed a wish to be acquainted.   He received him very courteously.

Sir Alexander observed, that the Chancellors in England are chosen from views much inferior to the office, being chosen from temporary political views.   JOHNSON : " Why, Sir, in such a government as ours, no man is appointed to an office because he is the fittest for it, nor hardly in any other government: because there are so many connections and dependencies to be studied. A despotic prince may choose a man to an office, merely because he is the fittest for it. The King of Prussia may do it." SIR A.: "I think, Sir, almost all great lawyers, such at least as have written upon law, have known only law, and nothing else." JOHNSON: "Why no, Sir; Judge Hale was a great lawyer, and wrote upon law ; and yet he knew a great many other things, and has written upon other things. Selden too." SIR A.: "Very true, Sir; and Lord Bacon. But was not Lord Coke a mere lawyer?" JOHNSON: "Why, I am afraid he was ; but he would have taken it very ill if you had told him so. He would have prosecuted you for scandal." BOSWELL: "Lord Mansfield is not a mere lawyer." JOHNSON: "No, Sir, I never was in Lord Mansfield's company ; but Lord Mansfield was distinguished at the University. Lord Mansfield, when he first came to town, ' drank champagne with the wits,' as Prior says. He was the friend of Pope." SIR A.: "Barristers, I believe, are not so abusive now as they were formerly. I fancy they had less law long ago, and so were obliged to take to abuse, to fill up the time. Now they have such a number of precedents, they have no occasion for abuse." JOHNSON: "Nay, Sir, they had more law long ago than they have now. As to precedents, to be sure they will increase in course of time ; but the more precedents there are, the less occasion is there for law ; that is to say, the less occasion is there for investigating principles." SIR A.: "I have been correcting several Scotch accents in my friend Boswell. I doubt, Sir, if any Scotchman ever attains to a perfect English pronunciation." JOHNSON: "Why, Sir, few of them do, because they do not persevere after acquiring a certain degree of it. But, Sir, there can be no doubt that they may attain to a perfect English pronunciation, if they will. We find how near they come to it ; and certainly a man who conquers nineteen parts of the Scottish accent, may conquer the twentieth. But, Sir, when a man has got the better of nine-tenths he grows weary, he relaxes his diligence, he finds he has corrected his accent so far as not to be disagreeable, and he no longer desires his friends to tell him when he is wrong ; nor does he choose to be told. Sir, when people watch me narrowly, and I do not watch myself, they will find me out to be of a particular county. In the same manner, Dunning[1] may be found out to be a Devonshire man. So most Scotchmen may be found out. But, Sir, little aberrations are of no disadvantage. I never catched Mallet in a Scotch accent ; and yet Mallet, I suppose, was past five-and-twenty before he came to London.

[1] John Dunning, Lord Ashburton, was born at Ashburton in 1731. After serving his clerkship in his father's office, he studied for the bar, and rapidly attained an eminent position in his profession. As counsel for Wilkes, he conducted his cause in such a manner as to establish his fame as a sound lawyer and adroit pleader.—ED.

Upon another occasion I talked to him on this subject, having myself taken some pains to improve my pronunciation, by the aid of the late Mr. Love, of Drury-lane Theatre, when he was a player at Edinburgh, and also of old Mr. Sheridan. Johnson said to me, " Sir, your pronunciation is not offensive." With this concession I was pretty well satisfied ; and let me give my countrymen of North Britain an advice not to aim at absolute perfection in this respect ; not to speak *High English*, as we are apt to call what is far removed from the *Scotch*, but which is by no means *good English*, and makes " the fools who use it " truly ridiculous. Good English is plain, easy, and smooth in the mouth of an unaffected English gentleman. A studied and facetious pronunciation, which requires perpetual attention, and imposes perpetual constraint, is exceedingly disgusting. A small intermixture of provincial peculiarities may, perhaps, have an agreeable effect, as the notes of different birds concur in the harmony of the grove, and please more than if they were all exactly alike. I could name some gentlemen of Ireland, to whom a slight proportion of the accent and recitative of that country is an advantage. The same observation will apply to the gentlemen of Scotland. I do not mean that we should speak as broad as a certain prosperous member of Parliament from that country (Mr. Dundas) ; though it has been well observed, that "it has been of no small use to him ; as it rouses the attention of the house by its uncommonness ; and is equal to tropes and figures in a good English speaker." I would give as an instance of what I mean to recommend to my countrymen, the pronunciation of the late Sir Gilbert Elliot ; and may I presume to add that of the present Earl of Marchmont, who told me, with great good humour, that the master of a shop in London, where he was not known, said to him, " I suppose, Sir, you are an American ! " " Why so, Sir ?" said his lordship. " Because, Sir," replied the shopkeeper, "you speak neither English nor Scotch, but something different from both, which I conclude is the language of America."

Boswell : " It may be of use, Sir, to have a Dictionary to ascertain pronunciation." Johnson : " Why, Sir, my Dictionary shows you the accent of words, if you can but remember them." Boswell : " But Sir, we want marks to ascertain the pronunciation of the vowels. Sheridan, I believe, has finished such a work." Johnson : " Why, Sir, consider how much easier it is to learn a language by the ear, than by any marks. Sheridan's Dictionary may do very well ; but you cannot always carry it about with you : and, when you want the word, you have not the Dictionary. It is like a man who has a sword that will not draw. It is an admirable sword, to be sure : but while your enemy is cutting your throat, you are unable to use it. Besides, Sir, what entitles Sheridan to fix the pronunciation of English ? He has, in the first place, the disadvantage of being an Irishman ; and if he says he will fix it after the example of the best company, why they differ among themselves. I remember an instance : when I published the plan for my Dictionary, Lord Chesterfield told me that the word *great* should be pronounced so as to rhyme to *state ;* and Sir William Yonge sent me word that it should be pronounced so as to rhyme to *seat*, and that none but an Irishman would pronounce it *grait.* Now here were two men of the highest rank, the one the best speaker in the House of Lords, the other the best speaker in the House of Commons, differing entirely."

I again visited him at night. Finding him in a very good humour, I ventured to lead him to the subject of our situation in a future state, having much curiosity to know his notions on that point. JOHNSON : " Why, Sir, the happiness of an unembodied spirit will consist in a consciousness of the favour of GOD, in the contemplation of truth, and in the possession of felicitating ideas." BOSWELL : " But, Sir, is there any harm in our forming to ourselves conjectures as to the particulars of our happiness, though the scripture has said but very little on the subject ? ' We know not what we shall be.' " JOHNSON : " Sir, there is no harm. What philosophy suggests to us on this topic is probable : what scripture tells us is certain. Dr. Henry More has carried it as far as philosophy can. You may buy both his theological and philosophical works in two volumes folio, for about eight shillings." BOSWELL : " One of the most pleasing thoughts is that we shall see our friends again." [1] JOHNSON : " Yes, Sir ; but you must consider, that when we are become purely rational, many of our friendships will be cut off. Many friendships are formed by a community of sensual pleasures : all these will be cut off. We form many friendships with bad men, because they have agreeable qualities, and they can be useful to us : but, after death, they can no longer be of use to us. We form many friendships by mistake, imagining people to be different from what they really are. After death, we shall see every one in a true light. Then, Sir, they talk of our meeting our relations ; but then all relationship is dissolved ; and we shall have no regard for one person more than another, but for their real value. However, we shall either have the satisfaction of meeting our friends, or be satisfied without meeting them." BOSWELL : " Yet, Sir, we see in scripture, that Dives still retained an anxious concern about his brethren." JOHNSON : " Why, Sir, we must either suppose that passage to be metaphorical, or hold with many divines, and all the Purgatorians, that departed souls do not all at once arrive at the utmost perfection of which they are capable." BOSWELL : " I think, Sir, that is a very rational supposition." JOHNSON : " Why, yes, Sir ; but we do not know it is a true one. There is no harm in believing it ; but you must not compel others to make it an article of faith ; for it is not revealed." BOSWELL : " Do you think, Sir, it is wrong in a man

[1] Bishop Hall, in his Epistle, " discoursing of the different degrees of heavenly glory, and of our mutual knowledge of each other above," (Dec. iii. c. 6,) holds the affirmative on both these questions.—MALONE.

who holds the doctrine of Purgatory, to pray for the souls of his deceased friends?" JOHNSON: "Why no, Sir." BOSWELL: "I have been told that in the Liturgy of the Episcopal Church of Scotland, there was a form of prayer for the dead." JOHNSON: "Sir, it is not in the Liturgy which Laud framed for the Episcopal Church of Scotland; if there is a liturgy older than that, I should be glad to see it." BOSWELL: "As to our employment in a future state, the sacred writings say little. The Revelation, however, of St. John gives us many ideas, and particularly mentions music." JOHNSON: "Why, Sir, ideas must be given you by means of something which you know; and as to music there are some philosophers and divines who have maintained that we shall not be spiritualised to such a degree, but that something of matter, very much refined, will remain. In that case, music may make a part of our future felicity."

BOSWELL: "I do not know whether there are any well-attested stories of the appearance of ghosts. You know there is a famous story of the appearance of Mrs. Veal, prefixed to 'Drelincourt on Death.'" JOHNSON: "I believe, Sir, that is given up. I believe the woman declared upon her death-bed that it was a lie." [1] BOSWELL: "This objection is made against the truth of ghosts appearing: that if they are in a state of happiness, it would be a punishment to them to return to this world; and if they are in a state of misery, it would be giving them a respite." JOHNSON: "Why, Sir, as the happiness or misery of embodied spirits does not depend upon place, but is intellectual, we cannot say that they are less happy or less miserable by appearing upon earth."

We went down between twelve and one to Mrs. Williams's room, and drank tea. I mentioned that we were to have the remains of Mr. Gray, in prose and verse, published by Mr. Mason. JOHNSON: "I think we have had enough of Gray. I see they have published a splendid edition of Akenside's works. One bad Ode may be suffered; but a number of them together makes one sick." BOSWELL: "Akenside's distinguished poem is his 'Pleasures of Imagination;' but for my part, I never could admire it so much as most people do." JOHNSON: "Sir, I could not read it through." BOSWELL: "I have read it through; but I did not find any great power in it."

I mentioned Elwal, the heretic, whose trial Sir John Pringle had given me to read. JOHNSON: "Sir, Mr. Elwal was, I think, an iron-monger at Wolverhampton; and he had a mind to make himself famous, by being the founder of a new sect, which he wished much should be called *Elwallians*. He held, that everything in the Old Testament that was not typical, was to be of perpetual observance: and so he wore a riband in the plaits of his coat, and he also wore a beard. I remember

---

[1] This fiction is known to have been invented by Daniel Defoe, and was added to the second edition of the English translation of Drelincourt's work (which was originally written in French) to make it sell. The first edition had it not.—MALONE.

I had the honour of dining in company with Mr. Elwal. There was one Barter, a miller, who wrote against him; and you had the controversy between Mr. Elwal and Mr. Barter. To try to make himself distinguished, he wrote a letter to King George the Second, challenging him to dispute with him, in which he said, ' George, if you be afraid to come by yourself, to dispute with a poor old man, you may bring a thousand of your *black*-guards with you; and if you should still be afraid, you may bring a thousand of your *red*-guards.' The letter had something of the impudence of Junius to our present king. But the men of Wolverhampton were not so inflammable as the common-council of London; so Mr. Elwal failed in his scheme of making himself a man of great consequence."

On Tuesday, March 31, he and I dined at General Paoli's. A question was started whether the state of marriage was natural to man. Johnson: " Sir, it is so far from being natural for a man and woman to live in a state of marriage, that we find all the motives which they have for remaining in that connection, and the restraints which civilised society imposes to prevent separation, are hardly sufficient to keep them together." The General said, that in a state of nature a man and woman uniting together, would form a strong and constant affection, by the mutual pleasure each would receive; and that the same causes of dissension would not arise between them, as occur between husband and wife in a civilised state." Johnson: " Sir, they would have dissensions enough, though of another kind. One would choose to go a-hunting in this wood, the other in that; one would choose to go a-fishing in this lake, the other in that; or perhaps one would choose to go a-hunting, when the other would choose to go a-fishing; and so they would part. Besides, Sir, a savage man and a savage woman meet by chance; and when the man sees another woman that pleases him better, he will leave the first."

We then fell into a disquisition whether there is any beauty independent of utility. The General maintained there was not. Dr. Johnson maintained that there was; and he instanced a coffee-cup which he held in his hand, the painting of which was of no real use, as the cup could hold the coffee equally well if plain; yet the painting was beautiful.

We talked of the strange custom of swearing in conversation. The General said, that all barbarous nations swore from a certain violence of temper, that could not be confined to earth, but was always reaching at the powers above. He said, too, that there was greater variety of swearing, in proportion as there was a greater variety of religious ceremonies."

Dr. Johnson went home with me to my lodgings in Conduit-street and drank tea, previous to our going to the Pantheon, which neither of us had seen before.

He said, " Goldsmith's Life of Parnell is poor; not that it is poorly written, but that he had poor materials; for nobody can write the life of a man, but those who have eat and drunk and lived in social intercourse with him."

I said, that if it was not troublesome and presuming too much, I would request him to tell me all the little circumstances of his life; what schools he attended, when he came to Oxford, when he came to London, &c. &c. He did not disapprove of my curiosity as to these particulars; but said, " They'll come out by degrees, as we talk together."

He censured Ruffhead's Life of Pope; and said, " he knew nothing of Pope, and nothing of poetry." He praised Dr. Joseph Warton's Essay on Pope; but said, " he supposed we should have no more of it, as the author had not been able to persuade the world to think of Pope as he did." BOSWELL : " Why, Sir, should that prevent him from continuing his work ? He is an ingenious counsel, who has made the most of his cause: he is not obliged to gain it." JOHNSON : " But, Sir, there is a difference when the cause is of a man's own making."

We talked of the proper use of riches. JOHNSON : " If I were a man of a great estate, I would drive all the rascals whom I did not like out of the county at an election."

I asked him, how far he thought wealth should be employed in hospitality. JOHNSON : " You are to consider that ancient hospitality, of which we hear so much, was in an uncommercial country, when men being idle, were glad to be entertained at rich men's tables. But in a commercial country, a busy country, time becomes precious, and therefore hospitality is not so much valued. No doubt there is still room for a certain degree of it ; and a man has a satisfaction in seeing his friends eating and drinking around him. But promiscuous hospitality is not the way to gain real influence. You must help some people at table before others ; you must ask some people how they like their wine oftener than others. You therefore offend more people than you please. You are like the French statesman, who said, when he granted a favour, ' J'ai ait x mécontents et un ingrat.'[1] Besides, Sir, being entertained ever so well at a man's table, impresses no lasting regard or esteem. No, Sir, the way to make sure of power and influence is, by lending money confidentially to your neighbours at a small interest, or perhaps at no interest at all, and having their bonds in your possession." BOSWELL : " May not a man, Sir, employ his riches to advantage, in educating young men of merit ? " JOHNSON : " Yes, Sir, if they fall in your way ; but if it be understood that you patronise young men of merit, you will be harassed with solicitations. You will have numbers forced upon you, who have no merit ; some will force them upon you from mistaken partiality; and some from downright interested motives, without scruple ; and you will be disgraced."

[1] A well-known saying of Louis the Fourteenth. —ED.

" Were I a rich man, I would propagate all kinds of trees that will grow in the open air. A greenhouse is childish. I would introduce foreign animals into the country : for instance, the reindeer."[1]

The conversation now turned on critical subjects. JOHNSON : " Bayes, in ' The Rehearsal,' is a mighty silly character. If it was intended to be like a particular man, it could only be diverting while that man was remembered. But I question whether it was meant for Dryden, as has been reported ; for we know some of the passages said to be ridiculed, were written since ' The Rehearsal ;' at least a passage mentioned in the Preface[2] is of a later date." I maintained that it had merit as a general satire on the self-importance of dramatic authors. But even in this light he held it very cheap.

We then walked to the Pantheon.[3] The first view of it did not strike us so much as Ranelagh, of which he said, the *coup d'œil* was the finest thing he had ever seen. The truth is, Ranelagh is of a more beautiful form ; more of it, or rather indeed the whole *rotunda*, appear at once, and it is better lighted. However, as Johnson observed, we saw the Pantheon in time of mourning, when there was a dull uniformity ; whereas we had seen Ranelagh when the view was enlivened with a gay profusion of colours. Mrs. Bosville, of Gunthwait, in Yorkshire, joined us, and entered into conversation with us. Johnson said to me afterwards, " Sir, this is a mighty intelligent lady."

I said there was not half a guinea's worth of pleasure in seeing this place. JOHNSON : " But, Sir, there is half a guinea's worth of inferiority to other people in not having seen it." BOSWELL : " I doubt, Sir, whether there are many happy people here." JOHNSON : " Yes, Sir, there are many happy people here. There are many people here who are watching hundreds, and who think hundreds are watching them."

Happening to meet Sir Adam Ferguson, I presented him to Dr. Johnson. Sir Adam expressed some apprehension that the Pantheon would encourage luxury. " Sir," said Johnson, " I am a great friend to public amusements ; for they keep people from vice. You now (addressing himself to me), would have been with a wench, had you not been here. Oh ! I forgot you were married."

[1] This project has since been realised. Sir Henry Liddel, who made a spirited tour into Lapland, brought two rein-deer to his estate in Northumberland, where they bred : but the race has unfortunately perished.—BOSWELL.

[2] There is no preface to " The Rehearsal," as originally published. Dr. Johnson seems to have meant the address to the Reader, with a Key subjoined to it, which have been prefixed to the modern editions of that play. He did not know, it appears, that several *additions* were made to " The Rehearsal " after the first edition. The ridicule on the passages here alluded to is found among those *additions*. They therefore furnish no ground for the doubts here suggested. Unquestionably Bayes was meant to be the representative of Dryden, whose familiar phrases in his ordinary conversation are frequently introduced in this piece.— MALONE.

In Oxford-street ; converted into the present bazaar in 1834.—ED.

Sir Adam suggested, that luxury corrupts a people, and destroys the spirit of liberty. JOHNSON: "Sir, that is all visionary. I would not give half a guinea to live under one form of government rather than another. It is of no moment to the happiness of an individual. Sir, the danger of the abuse of power is nothing to a private man. What Frenchman is prevented from passing his life as he pleases?" SIR ADAM: "But, Sir, in the British constitution it is surely of importance to keep up a spirit in the people, so as to preserve a balance against the crown." JOHNSON: "Sir, I perceive you are a vile Whig.—Why all this childish jealousy of the power of the crown? The crown has not power enough. When I say that all governments are alike, I consider that in no government power can be abused long. Mankind will not bear it. If a sovereign oppresses his people to a great degree, they will rise and cut off his head. There is a remedy in human nature against tyranny, that will keep us safe under every form of government. Had not the people of France thought themselves honoured in sharing in the brilliant actions of Louis XIV., they would not have endured him; and we may say the same of the King of Prussia's people." Sir Adam introduced the ancient Greeks and Romans. JOHNSON: "Sir, the mass of both of them were barbarians. The mass of every people must be barbarous where there is no printing, and consequently knowledge is not generally diffused. Knowledge is diffused among our people by the newspapers." Sir Adam mentioned the orators, poets, and artists of Greece. JOHNSON: "Sir, I am talking of the mass of the people. We see even what the boasted Athenians were. The little effect which Demosthenes's orations had upon them, shows that they were barbarians."

Sir Adam was unlucky in his topics; for he suggested a doubt of the propriety of bishops having seats in the House of Lords. JOHNSON: "How so, Sir? Who is more proper for having the dignity of a peer than a bishop, provided a bishop be what he ought to be; and if improper bishops be made, that is not the fault of the bishops, but of those who make them."

On Sunday, April 5, after attending divine service at St. Paul's church, I found him alone. Of a schoolmaster of his acquaintance, a native of Scotland, he said, "He has a great deal of good about him; but he is also very defective in some respects. His inner part is good, but his outer part is mighty awkward. You in Scotland do not attain that nice critical skill in languages which we get in our schools in England. I would not put a boy to him whom I intended for a man of learning. But for the sons of citizens, who are to learn a little, get good morals, and then go to trade, he may do very well."

I mentioned a cause in which I had appeared as counsel at the bar of the General Assembly of the Church of Scotland, where a *Probationer* (as one licensed to preach, but not yet ordained, is called), was opposed in his application to be inducted, because it was alleged that he had been guilty of fornication five years before. Johnson : " Why, Sir, if he has repented, it is not a sufficient objection. A man who is good enough to go to heaven, is good enough to be a clergyman." This was a humane and liberal sentiment. But the character of a clergyman is more sacred than that of an ordinary Christian. As he is to instruct with authority, he should be regarded with reverence, as one upon whom divine truth has had the effect to set him above such transgressions, as men, less exalted by spiritual habits, and yet upon the whole not to be excluded from heaven, have been betrayed into the predominance of passion. That clergymen may be considered as sinners in general, as all men are, cannot be denied ; but this reflection will not counteract their good precepts so much as the absolute knowledge of their having been guilty of certain specific immoral acts. I told him, that by the rules of the Church of Scotland, in their " Book of Discipline," if a *scandal,* as it is called, is not prosecuted for five years, it cannot afterwards be proceeded upon, " unless it be *of a heinous nature,* or again become flagrant ; " and that hence a question arose whether fornication was a sin of a heinous nature ; and that I had maintained that it did not deserve that epithet, inasmuch as it was not one of those sins which argue very great depravity of heart : in short, in the general acceptation of mankind, a heinous sin. Johnson : " No, Sir, it is not a heinous sin. A heinous sin is that for which a man is punished with death or banishment." Boswell: " But, Sir, after I had argued that it was not a heinous sin, an old clergyman rose up, and repeated the text of scripture denouncing judgment against whoremongers, asked whether, considering this, there could be any doubt of fornication being a heinous sin." Johnson : " Why, Sir, observe the word *whoremonger.* Every sin, if persisted in, would become heinous. Whoremonger is a dealer in whores, as ironmonger is a dealer in iron. But as you don't call a man an ironmonger for buying and selling a penknife, so you don't call a man a whoremonger for getting one wench with child." [1]

I spoke of the inequality of the livings of the clergy in England, and the scanty provisions of some of the curates. Johnson : " Why yes, Sir ; but it cannot be helped. You must consider that the revenues of the clergy are not at the disposal of the state, like the pay of the army. Different men have founded different churches ; and some are better endowed, some worse. The state cannot interfere and make an equal division of what has been particularly appropriated. Now when a clergyman has but a small living, or even two small livings, he can afford very little to the curate."

He said, he went more frequently to church when there were prayers

---

[1] It must not be presumed that Dr. Johnson meant to give any countenance to licentiousness, though in the character of an advocate he made a just and subtle distinction between occasional and habitual transgression.—Boswell.

only than when there was also a sermon, as the people required more an example for the one than the other; it being much easier for them to hear a sermon than to fix their minds on prayer.

On Monday, April 6, I dined with him at Sir Alexander Macdonald's, where was a young officer in the regimentals of the Scots Royal, who talked with a vivacity, fluency, and precision so uncommon, that he attracted particular attention. He proved to be the Honourable Thomas Erskine,[1] youngest brother to the Earl of Buchan, who has since risen into such brilliant reputation at the bar in Westminster-hall.

HON. THOMAS ERSKINE.

Fielding being mentioned, Johnson exclaimed, "he was a blockhead;" and upon my expressing my astonishment at so strange an assertion, he said, "What I mean by his being a blockhead is, that he was a barren rascal." BOSWELL : "Will you not allow, Sir, that he draws very natural pictures of human life?" JOHNSON : "Why, Sir, it is of very low life. Richardson used to say that, had he not known who Fielding was, he should have believed he was an ostler. Sir, there is more knowledge of the heart in one letter of Richardson's, than in all 'Tom Jones.'[2] I, indeed, never read 'Joseph Andrews.'" ERSKINE : "Surely, Sir, Richardson is very tedious." JOHNSON : "Why, Sir, if you were to read Richardson for the story, your impatience would be so much fretted that you would hang yourself. But you must read him for the sentiment, and consider the story as only giving occasion to the sentiment."—I have already given my opinion of Fielding; but I cannot refrain from repeating here my wonder at Johnson's excessive and unaccountable depreciation of one of the best writers that England has produced : "Tom Jones" has stood the test of public opinion with such success as to have established its great merit, both for the story, the sentiments, and the manners, and also the varieties of diction, so as to leave no doubt of its having an animated truth of execution throughout.

The book of travels, lately published under the title of *Coriat Junior*,

---

[1] Afterwards Lord Chancellor of England.

[2] Johnson's severity against Fielding did not arise from any viciousness in his style, but from his loose life, and the profligacy of almost all his male characters. Who would venture to read one of his novels aloud to modest women? His novels are *male* amusements, and very amusing they certainly are. Fielding's conversation was coarse, and so tinctured with the rank weeds of *the garden* that it would be thought only fit for a brothel.—BURNEY.

and written by Mr. Paterson,[1] was mentioned. Johnson said this book . was in imitation of Sterne,[2] and not of Coriat, whose name Paterson had chosen as a whimsical one. "Tom Coriat," said he, "was a humourist about the court of James the First. He had a mixture of learning, of wit, and of buffoonery. He first travelled through Europe, and published his travels. He afterwards travelled on foot through Asia, and had made many remarks; but he died at Mandoa, and his remarks were lost."

We talked of gaming, and animadverted on it with severity. JOHNSON : "Nay, gentlemen, let us not aggravate the matter. It is not roguery to play with a man who is ignorant of the game, while you are master of it, and so win his money : for he thinks he can play better than you, as you think you can play better than he; and the superior skill carries it." ERSKINE : "He is a fool, but you are not a rogue." JOHNSON : "That's much about the truth, Sir. It must be considered that a man who only does what every one of the society to which he belongs would do, is not a dishonest man. In the republic of Sparta it was agreed that stealing was not dishonourable if not discovered. I do not commend a society where there is an agreement that what would not otherwise be fair shall be fair; but I maintain, that an individual of any society, who practises what is allowed, is not a dishonest man." BOSWELL : "So then, Sir, you do not think ill of a man who wins perhaps forty thousand pounds in a winter ? " JOHNSON : "Sir, I do not call a gamester a dishonest man; but I call him an unsocial man, an unprofitable man. Gaming is a mode of transferring property without producing any intermediate good. Trade gives employment to numbers, and so produces intermediate good."

Mr. Erskine told us, that when he was in the island of Minorca, he not only read prayers, but preached two sermons to the regiment. He seemed to object to the passage in scripture, where we are told that the angel of the Lord smote, in one night, forty thousand Assyrians.[3] "Sir," said Johnson, "you should recollect that there was a supernatural interposition; they were destroyed by pestilence. You are not to suppose that the angel of the Lord went about and stabbed each of them with a dagger, or knocked them on the head, man by man."

After Mr. Erskine was gone, a discussion took place, whether the present Earl of Buchan, when Lord Cardross, did right to refuse to go Secretary of the Embassy to Spain, when Sir James Gray, a man of inferior rank, went Ambassador. Dr. Johnson said, that perhaps in point of interest he did wrong; but in point of dignity he did well. Sir

---

[1] Mr. Samuel Paterson, eminent for his knowledge of books.—BOSWELL.

[2] Mr. Paterson, in a pamphlet, produced some evidence to show that his work was written before Sterne's "Sentimental Journey" appeared.—BOSWELL.

[3] One hundred and eighty-five thousand. See Isaiah xxxvii. 36, and 2 Kings xix. 35,—MALONE

Alexander insisted that he was wrong ; and said that Mr. Pitt intended it as an advantageous thing for him. "Why, Sir," said Johnson, "Mr. Pitt might think it an advantageous thing for him to make him a vintner, and get him all the Portugal trade ; but he would have demeaned himself strangely had he accepted of such a situation. Sir, had he gone Secretary while his inferior was Ambassador, he would have been a traitor to his rank and family."

I talked of the little attachment which subsisted between near relations in London. "Sir," said Johnson, "in a country so commercial as ours, where every man can do for himself, there is not so much occasion for that attachment. No man is thought the worse of here whose brother was hanged. In uncommercial countries many of the branches of a family must depend on the stock ; so, in order to make the head of the family take care of them, they are represented as connected with his reputation, that, self-love being interested, he may exert himself to promote their interest. You have first large circles, or clans ; as commerce increases, the connection is confined to families ; by degrees, that, too, goes off, as having become unnecessary, and there being few opportunities of intercourse. One brother is a merchant in the city, and another is an officer in the guards ; how little intercourse can these two have !"

I argued warmly for the old feudal system. Sir Alexander opposed it, and talked of the pleasure of seeing all men free and independent. JOHNSON : "I agree with Mr. Boswell that there must be a high satisfaction in being a feudal lord ; but we are to consider that we ought not wish to have a number of men unhappy for the satisfaction of one." I maintained that numbers, namely the vassals or followers, were not unhappy ; for that there was a reciprocal satisfaction between the lord and them ; he being kind in his authority over them ; they being respectful and faithful to him.

On Thursday, April 9, I called on him to beg he would go and dine with me at the Mitre tavern. He had resolved not to dine at all this day, I know not for what reason ; and I was so unwilling to be deprived of his company, that I was content to submit to suffer a want which was at first somewhat painful, but he soon made me forget it ; and a man is always pleased with himself, when he finds his intellectual inclinations predominate.

He observed, that to reason philosophically on the nature of prayer was very unprofitable.

Talking of ghosts, he said, he knew one friend, who was an honest man, and a sensible man, who told him he had seen a ghost : old Mr. Edward Cave, the printer at St. John's Gate. He said Mr. Cave did not like to talk of it, and seemed to be in great horror whenever it was mentioned. BOSWELL : "Pray, Sir, what did he say was the appearance?" JOHNSON : "Why, Sir, something of a shadowy being."

I mentioned witches, and asked him what they properly meant, JOHNSON: "Why, Sir, they properly mean those who make use of the aid of evil spirits." BOSWELL: "There is no doubt, Sir, a general report and belief of their having existed." JOHNSON: "You have not only the general report and belief, but you have many voluntary solemn confessions." He did not affirm anything positively upon a subject which it is the fashion of the times to laugh at as a matter of absurd credulity. He only seemed willing, as a candid inquirer after truth, however strange and inexplicable, to show that he understood what might be urged for it.[1]

GENERAL OGLETHORPE.

On Friday, April 10, I dined with him at General Oglethorpe's, where we found Dr. Goldsmith.

Armorial bearings having been mentioned, Johnson said they were as ancient as the siege of Thebes, which he proved by a passage in one of the tragedies of Euripides.[2]

I started the question, whether duelling was consistent with moral duty. The brave old General fired at this, and said, with a lofty air, "Undoubtedly a man has a right to defend his honour." GOLDSMITH (turning to me): "I ask you first, Sir, what would you do if you were affronted?" I answered I should think it necessary to fight. "Why, then," replied Goldsmith, "that solves the question." JOHNSON: "No, Sir, it does not solve the question. It does not follow that what a man would do, is, therefore, right." I said, I wished to have it settled whether duelling was contrary to the laws of Christianity. Johnson immediately entered on the subject, and treated it in a masterly manner; and, so far as I have been able to recollect, his thoughts were these:—"Sir, as

---

[1] See this curious question treated by him with most acute ability, "Journal of a Tour to the Hebrides," 3rd edit. p. 33.—BOSWELL.

[2] The passage to which Johnson alluded, is to be found (as I conjecture) in the PHŒNISSÆ. l. 1120.

Καὶ πρῶτα μὲν προσῆγε, κ. τ. λ.

Ὁ τῆς κυναγοῦ Παρθενοπαῖος εκγονος,

ΕΠΙΣΗΜ, ἔχᾱν ΟΙΚΕΙΟΝ εν μεσω σακει.—J. BOSWELL.

Translation—"In the centre of his shield Parthenopæus bore the domestic symbol of Atalanta slaying the Ætolian boar."

men become in a high degree refined, various causes of offence arise, which are considered to be of such importance, that life must be staked to atone for them, though in reality they are not so. A body that has received a very fine polish may be easily hurt. Before men arrive at this artificial refinement, if one tells his neighbour—he lies, his neighbour tells him—he lies ; if one gives his neighbour a blow, his neighbour gives him a blow ; but in a state of highly polished society, an affront is held to be a serious injury. It must, therefore, be resented, or rather a duel must be fought upon it ; as men have agreed to banish from their society one who puts up with an affront without fighting a duel. Now, Sir, it is never unlawful to fight in self-defence. He, then, who fights a duel, does not fight from passion against his antagonist, but out of self-defence ; to avert the stigma of the world, and to prevent himself from being driven out of society. I could wish there was not that superfluity of refinement ; but while such notions prevail, no doubt a man may lawfully fight a duel."

Let it be remembered, that this justification is applicable only to the person who *receives* an affront. All mankind must condemn the aggressor.

The General told us that, when he was a very young man, I think only fifteen, serving under Prince Eugene of Savoy, he was sitting in a company at table with a Prince of Wirtemberg. The Prince took up a glass of wine, and, by a fillip, made some of it fly in Oglethorpe's face. Here was a nice dilemma. To have challenged him instantly might have fixed a quarrelsome character upon the young soldier : to have taken no notice of it, might have been considered as cowardice. Oglethorpe, therefore, keeping his eye upon the Prince, and smiling all the time, as if he took what his Highness had done in jest, said, " *Mon Prince,*—" (I forget the French words he used, the purport, however, was,) " That's a good joke : but we do it much better in England ; " and threw a whole glass of wine in the Prince's face. An old General, who sat by, said " *Il a bien fait, mon Prince, vous l'avez commencé :*" and thus all ended in good humour.

Dr. Johnson said, " Pray, General, give us an account of the siege of Belgrade." Upon which the General, pouring a little wine upon the table, described everything with a wet finger :—" Here we were, here were the Turks," &c. &c. Johnson listened with the closest attention.

A question was started, how far people who disagree in a capital point can live in friendship together. Johnson said they might. Goldsmith said they could not, as they had not the *idem velle atque idem nolle*—the same likings and the same aversions. JOHNSON : " Why Sir, you must shun the subject as to which you disagree. For instance, I can live very well with Burke ; I love his knowledge, his genius, his diffusion, and affluence of conversation ; but I would not talk to him of the Rockingham party." GOLDSMITH : " But, Sir, when people live *together* who have something as to which they disagree, and which they want to shun, they will be in the situation mentioned in the story of Bluebeard : 'You may look into all the chambers but one.' But we should have the greatest inclination to look into that chamber, to talk of that subject." JOHNSON (with a loud voice) : "Sir, I am not saying that *you* could live in friendship with a man from whom you differ as to some point : I am only saying that *I* could do it. You put me in mind of Sappho in Ovid." [1]

Goldsmith told us that he was now busy in writing a Natural History ; and, that he might have full leisure for it, he had taken lodgings at a farmer's house, near to the six mile-stone, on the Edgeware-road, and had carried down his books in two returned post-chaises. He said he believed the farmer's family thought him an odd character, similar to that in which the *Spectator* appeared to his landlady and her children : he was *The Gentleman*. Mr. Mickle, the translator of " The Lusiad," and I went to visit him at this place a few days afterwards : he was not at home ; but, having a curiosity to see his apartment, we went in, and found curious scraps of descriptions of animals, scrawled upon the wall with a black-lead pencil.

The subject of ghosts being introduced, Johnson repeated what he had told me of a friend of his, an honest man, and a man of sense, having asserted to him that he had seen an apparition. Goldsmith told us he was assured by his brother, the Reverend Mr. Goldsmith, that he also had seen one. General Oglethorpe told us that Prendergast, an officer in the Duke of Marlborough's army, had mentioned to many of his friends that he should die on a particular day ; that upon that day

---

[1] Mr. Boswell's note here being rather short, as taken at the time, (with a view perhaps to future revision,) Johnson's remark is obscure, and requires to be a little opened. What he said, probably was, " You seem to think that two friends, to live well together, must be in perfect harmony with each other ; that each should be to the other what Sappho beasts she was to her lover, and uniformly agree in every particular : but this is by no means necessary," &c.—The words of Sappho alluded to, are :—" *omnique à parte placebam*." Ovid. Epist. Sapp. ad Phaonem. l. 51.—MALONE.

I should rather conjecture that the passage which Johnson had in view was the following, l. 45—

" Si, nisi quæ facie poterit te digna videri
 Nulla futura tua est; nulla futura tua est.

His reasoning and its illustration I take to be this. If you are determined to associate with no one whose sentiments do not universally coincide with your own, you will, by such a resolution, exclude yourself from all society, for no two men can be found who, on all points, invariably think alike. So Sappho in Ovid tells Phaon, that if he will not unite himself to any one who is not a complete resemblance of himself, it will be impossible for him to form any union at all.

The lines which I have quoted are thus expanded in Pope's Paraphrase, which, to say the truth, I suspect was at this moment more in Johnson's recollection than the original :

" If to no charms thou wilt thy heart resign
 But such as merit, such as equal thine,
 By none, alas, by none, thou canst be moved,
 Phaon alone by Phaon must be loved."—J. BOSWELL.

a battle took place with the French ; that after it was over, and
Prendergast was still alive, his brother officers, while they were yet in
the field, jestingly asked him where was his prophecy now. Prendergast
gravely answered, " I shall die, notwithstanding what you see." Soon
afterwards there came a shot from a French battery, to which the orders
for a cessation of arms had not reached, and he was killed upon the spot.
Colonel Cecil, who took possession of his effects, found in his pocket-
book the following solemn entry :

[Here the date.] " Dreamt—or——————[1] Sir John Friend meets
me :" (here the very day on which he was killed was mentioned.) Prendergast had been connected with Sir John Friend, who was executed
for high treason. General Oglethorpe said he was with Colonel Cecil,
when Pope came and inquired into the truth of this story, which made
a great noise at the time, and was then confirmed by the Colonel.

On Saturday, April 11th, he appointed me to come to him in the
evening, when he should be at leisure to give me some assistance for
the defence of Hastie, the schoolmaster of Campbelltown, for whom I
was to appear in the House of Lords. When I came, I found him
unwilling to exert himself. I pressed him to write down his thoughts
upon the subject. He said, " There's no occasion for my writing. I'll
talk to you." He was, however, at last prevailed on to dictate to me,
while I wrote as follows :

" The charge is, that he has used immoderate and cruel correction.
Correction, in itself, is not cruel; children, being not reasonable, can be
governed only by fear. To impress this fear is, therefore, one of the
first duties of those who have the care of children. It is the duty of a
parent ; and has never been thought inconsistent with parental tenderness. It is the duty of a master, who is in his highest exaltation when
he is *loco parentis*. Yet, as good things become evil by excess, correction,
by being immoderate, may become cruel. But when is correction immoderate ? When it is more frequent or more severe than is required
ad monendum et docendum, for reformation and instruction. No severity
is cruel which obstinacy makes necessary ; for the greatest cruelty would
be to desist, and leave the scholar too careless for instruction, and too
much hardened for reproof. Locke, in his treatise of Education, mentions a mother, with applause, who whipped an infant eight times before
she had subdued it ; for had she stopped at the seventh act of correction,
her daughter, says he, would have been ruined. The degrees of
obstinacy in young minds are very different : as different must be the
degrees of persevering severity. A stubborn scholar must be corrected till he is subdued. The discipline of a school is military. There

---

[1] Here was a blank, which may be filled up thus:—"*was told by an apparition;* "—the
writer being probably uncertain whether he was asleep or awake, when his mind was
impressed with the solemn presentiment with which the fact afterwards happened so
wonderfully to correspond.—BOSWELL.

must be either unbounded licence or absolute authority. The master who punishes, not only consults the future happiness of him who is the immediate subject of correction, but he propagates obedience through the whole school ; and establishes regularity by exemplary justice. The victorious obstinacy of a single boy would make his future endeavours of reformation or instruction totally ineffectual. Obstinacy, therefore, must never be victorious. Yet, it is well known, that there sometimes occurs a sullen and hardy resolution, that laughs at all common punishment, and bids defiance to all common degrees of pain. Correction must be proportionate to occasions. The flexible will be reformed by gentle discipline, and the refractory must be subdued by harsher methods. The degrees of scholastic, as of military punishment, no stated rules can ascertain. It must be enforced till it overpowers temptation : till stubbornness becomes flexible, and perverseness regular. Custom and reason have, indeed, set some bounds to scholastic penalties. The schoolmaster inflicts no capital punishments ; nor enforces his edicts by either death or mutilation. The civil law has wisely determined, that a master who strikes at a scholar's eye shall be considered as criminal. But punishments, however severe, that produce no lasting evil, may be just and reasonable, because they may be necessary. Such have been the punishments used by the respondent. No scholar has gone from him either blind or lame, or with any of his limbs or powers injured or impaired. They were irregular, and he punished them , they were obstinate, and he enforced his punishment. But however provoked, he never exceeded the limits of moderation, for he inflicted nothing beyond present pain : and how much of that was required, no man is so little able to determine as those who have determined against him—the parents of the offenders.—It has been said, that he used unprecedented and improper instruments of correction. Of this accusation the meaning is not very easy to be found. No instrument of correction is more proper than another, but as it is better adapted to produce present pain without lasting mischief. Whatever were his instruments, no lasting mischief has ensued ; and therefore, however unusual, in hands so cautious, they were proper.—It has been objected, that the respondent admits the charge of cruelty, by producing no evidence to confute it. Let it be considered, that his scholars are either dispersed at large in the world, or continue to inhabit the place in which they were bred. Those who are dispersed cannot be found ; those who remain are the sons of his prosecutors, and are not likely to support a man to whom their fathers are enemies. If it be supposed that the enmity of their fathers proves the justness of the charge, it must be considered how often experience shows us, that men who are angry on one ground will accuse on another ; with how little kindness, in a town of low trade, a man who lives by learning is regarded ; and how implicitly, where the inhabitants are not very rich, a rich man is harkened to and followed

In a place like Campbelltown, it is easy for one of the principal inhabitants to make a party. It is easy for that party to heat themselves with imaginary grievances. It is easy for them to oppress a man poorer than themselves ; and natural to assert the dignity of riches, by persisting in oppression. The argument which attempts to prove the impropriety of restoring him to the school, by alleging that he has lost the confidence of the people, is not the subject of juridical consideration ; for he is to suffer, if he must suffer, not for their judgment, but for his own actions. It may be convenient for them to have another master ; but it is a convenience of their own making. It would be likewise convenient for him to find another school ; but this convenience he cannot obtain.— The question is not what is now convenient, but what is generally right. If the people of Campbelltown be distressed by the restoration of the respondent, they are distressed only by their own fault ; by turbulent passions and unreasonable desires ; by tyranny, which law has defeated, and by malice, which virtue has surmounted."

" This, Sir," said he, " you are to turn in your mind, and make the best use of it you can in your speech."

Of our friend Goldsmith he said, " Sir, he is so much afraid of being unnoticed, that he often talks merely lest you should forget that he is in the company." BOSWELL : " Yes, he stands forward." JOHNSON : " True, Sir ; but if a man is to stand forward, he should wish to do it not in an awkward posture, not in rags, not so as that he shall only be exposed to ridicule." BOSWELL : " For my part, I like very well to hear honest Goldsmith talk away carelessly." JOHNSON : " Why, yes, Sir, but he should not like to hear himself."

On Tuesday, April 14, the decree of the Court of Session in the schoolmaster's cause was reversed in the House of Lords, after a very eloquent speech by Lord Mansfield, who showed himself an adept in school discipline, but I thought was too rigorous towards my client. On the evening of the next day, I supped with Dr. Johnson, at the Crown and Anchor tavern, in the Strand, in company with Mr. Langton and his brother-in-law, Lord Binning. I repeated a sentence of Lord Mansfield's speech, of which, by the aid of Mr. Longlands, the solicitor on the other side, who obligingly allowed me to compare his note with my own, I have a full copy : " My Lords, severity is not the way to govern either boys or men." " Nay," said Johnson, " it is the way to *govern* them. I know not whether it be the way to *mend* them."

I talked of the recent expulsion of six students from the University of Oxford, who were methodists, and would not desist from publicly praying and exhorting. JOHNSON : " Sir, that expulsion was extremely just and proper. What have they to do at an University, who are not willing to be taught, but will presume to teach ? Where is religion to be learnt, but at an University ? Sir, they were examined, and found to be mighty ignorant fellows." BOSWELL : " But, was it not hard, Sir, to expel them, for I am told they were good beings ? " Johnson : " I believe they might be good beings, but they were not fit to be in the University of Oxford. A cow is a very good animal in the field, but we turn her out of a garden." Lord Elibank used to repeat this as an illustration uncommonly happy.

Desirous of calling Johnson forth to talk and exercise his wit, though I should myself be the object of it, I resolutely ventured to undertake the defence of convivial indulgence in wine, though he was not to night in the most genial humour. After urging the common plausible topics, I at last had recourse to the maxim *in vino veritas,* a man who is well warmed with wine will speak truth. Johnson : " Why, Sir, that may be an argument for drinking, if you suppose men in general to be liars. But, Sir, I would not keep company with a fellow who lies as long as he is sober, and whom you must make drunk before you can get a word of truth out of him." [1]

Mr. Langton told us he was about to establish a school upon his estate, but it had been suggested to him, that it might have a tendency to make the people less industrious. Johnson : " No, Sir. While learning to read and write is a distinction, the few who have that distinction may be the less inclined to work ; but when everybody learns to read and write it is no longer a distinction. A man who has a laced waistcoat is too fine a man to work ; but if everybody had laced waistcoats, we should have people working in laced waistcoats. There are no people whatever more industrious, none who work more, than our manufacturers ; yet they have all learned to read and write. Sir, you must not neglect doing a thing immediately good, from fear of remote evil—from fear of its being abused. A man who has candles may sit up too late, which he would not do if he had not candles ; but nobody will deny that the art of making candles, by which light is continued to us beyond the time that the sun gives us light, is a valuable art, and ought to be preserved." Boswell : " But, Sir, would it not be better to follow nature, and go to bed and rise just as nature gives us light or withholds it ?" Johnson : " No, Sir ; for then we should have no kind of equality in the partition of our time between sleeping and waking. It would be very different in different seasons and in different places. In some of the northern parts of Scotland how little light is there in the depth of winter ! "

We talked of Tacitus, and I hazarded an opinion, that with all his merit for penetration, shrewdness of judgment, and terseness of expression, he was too compact. too much broken into hints, as it were, and therefore too difficult to be understood. To my great satisfaction

---

[1] Mrs. Piozzi, in her Anecdotes, p. 261, has given an erroneous account of this incident, as of many others. She pretends to relate it from recollection, as if she herself had been present; when the fact is, that it was communicated to her by me. She has represented it as a personality, and the true point has escaped her.—Boswell.

Dr. Johnson sanctioned this opinion. "Tacitus, Sir, seems to me rather to have made notes for an historical work, than to have written a history." [1]

At this time it appears from his "Prayers and Meditations," that he had been more than commonly diligent in religious duties, particularly in reading the Holy Scriptures. It was Passion Week, that solemn season which the Christian world has appropriated to the commemoration of the mysteries of our redemption, and during which, whatever embers of religion are in our breasts, will be kindled into vious warmth.

I paid him short visits both on Friday and Saturday, and seeing his large folio Greek Testament before him, beheld him with a reverential awe, and would not intrude upon his time. While he was thus employed to such good purpose, and while his friends in their intercourse with him constantly found a vigorous intellect and a lively imagination, it is melancholy to read in his private register, "My mind is unsettled and my memory confused. I have of late turned my thoughts with a very useless earnestness upon past incidents. I have yet got no command over my thoughts; an unpleasing incident is almost certain to hinder my rest." [2] What philosophic heroism was it in him to appear with such manly fortitude to the world, while he was inwardly so distressed! We may surely believe that the mysterious principle of being "made perfect through suffering," was to be strongly exemplified in him.

On Sunday, April 19, being Easter-day, General Paoli and I paid him a visit before dinner. We talked of the notion that blind persons can distinguish colours by the touch. Johnson said, that Professor Sanderson [3] mentions his having attempted to do it, but that he found he was aiming at an impossibility; that to be sure a difference in the surface makes the difference of colours; but that difference is so fine that it is not sensible to the touch. The General mentioned jugglers and fraudulent gamesters, who could know cards by the touch. Dr. Johnson said, "The cards used by such persons must be less polished than ours commonly are."

We talked of sounds. The General said there was no beauty in a simple sound, but only in an harmonious composition of sounds. I presumed to differ from this opinion, and mentioned the soft and sweet sound of a fine woman's voice. JOHNSON : "No, Sir, if a serpent or a toad uttered it, you would think it ugly." BOSWELL : "So you would

---

[1] It is remarkable that Lord Monboddo, whom, on account of his resembling Dr. Johnson in some particulars, Foote called an Elzevir edition of him, has, by coincidence, made the very same remark. "Origin and Progress of Language," vol. iii. 2nd edit. p. 219.—BOSWELL.

[2] "Prayers and Meditations," p. 111.—BOSWELL.

[3] Nicholas Sanderson, LL.D., Lucasian Professor of Mathematics in the University of Cambridge, lost his sight by the small-pox when little more than twelvemonths old. He died 1739.—ED

think, Sir, were a beautiful tune to be uttered by one of those animals." JOHNSON : "No, Sir, it would be admired. We have seen fine fiddlers whom we liked as little as toads," (laughing.)

Talking on the subject of taste in the arts, he said, that difference of taste was, in truth, difference of skill. BOSWELL : " But, Sir, is there not a quality called taste, which consists merely in perception or in liking ; for instance, we find people differ much as to what is the best style of English composition. Some think Swift's the best ; others prefer a fuller and grander way of writing." JOHNSON : "Sir, you must first define what you mean by style, before you can judge who has a good taste in style, and who has a bad. The two classes of persons whom you have mentioned, don't suffer as to good and bad. They both agree that Swift has a good neat style ; but one loves a neat style another loves a style of more splendour. In like manner, one loves a plain coat, another loves a laced coat ; but neither will deny that each is good in its kind."

While I remained in London this spring, I was with him at several other times, both by himself and in company. I dined with him one day at the Crown and Anchor tavern, in the Strand, with Lord Elibank, Mr. Langton, and Dr. Vansittart, of Oxford. Without specifying each particular day, I have preserved the following memorable things :

I regretted the reflection in his Preface to Shakspeare against Garrick, to whom we cannot but apply the following passage : " I collated such copies as I could procure, and wished for more, but have not found the collectors of these rarities very communicative." I told him, that Garrick had complained to me of it, and had vindicated himself by assuring me, that Johnson was made welcome to the full use of his collection, and that he left the key of it with a servant, with orders to have a fire and every convenience for him. I found Johnson's notion was, that Garrick wanted to be courted for them, and that, on the contrary, Garrick should have courted him, and sent him the plays of his own accord. But, indeed, considering the slovenly and careless manner in which books were treated by Johnson, it could not be expected that scarce and valuable editions should have been lent to him.

A gentleman having, to some of the usual arguments for drinking, added this : "You know, Sir, drinking drives away care, and makes us forget whatever is disagreeable. Would not you allow a man to drink for that reason ? " JOHNSON : " Yes, Sir, if he sat next you."

I expressed a liking for Mr. Francis Osborne's works, and asked him what he thought of that writer. He answered, " A conceited fellow. Were a man to write so now, the boys would throw stones at him." He, however, did not alter my opinion of a favourite author, to whom I was first directed by his being quoted in "The Spectator," and in whom I have found much shrewd and lively sense, expressed indeed in a style somewhat quaint, which, however, I do not dislike. His book has an air of originality. We figure to ourselves an ancient gentleman talking to us.

When one of his friends endeavoured to maintain that a country gentleman might contrive to pass his life very agreeably, "Sir," said he, "you cannot give me an instance of any man who is permitted to lay out his own time, contriving not to have tedious hours." This observation, however, is equally applicable to gentlemen who live in cities, and are of no profession.

He said, "There is no permanent national character; it varies according to circumstances. Alexander the Great swept India; now the Turks sweep Greece."

A learned gentleman, who, in the course of conversation, wished to inform us of this simple fact, that the counsel upon the circuit at Shrewsbury were much bitten by fleas, took, I suppose, seven or eight minutes in relating it circumstantially. He, in a plenitude of phrase, told us, that large bales of woollen cloth were lodged in the town-hall; —that by reason of this, fleas nestled there in prodigious numbers; that the lodgings of the counsel were near the town-hall; and that those little animals moved from place to place with wonderful agility. Johnson sat in great impatience till the gentleman had finished his tedious narrative, and then burst out (playfully, however), "It is a pity, Sir, that you have not seen a lion; for a flea has taken you such a time, that a lion must have served you a twelvemonth." [1]

He would not allow Scotland to derive any credit from Lord Mansfield; for he was educated in England. "Much," said he, "may be made of a Scotchman, if he be *caught* young."

Talking of a modern historian and a modern moralist, he said, "There is more thought in the m   st than in the historian. There is but a shallow stream of thought in history." BOSWELL: "But surely, Sir, an historian has reflection." JOHNSON: "Why yes, Sir; and so has a cat when she catches a mouse for her kitten. But she cannot write like *   *   *   *; neither can *   *   *   *   *   *." [2]

He said, "I am very unwilling to read the manuscripts of authors, and give them my opinion. If the authors who apply to me have money, I bid them boldly print without a name; if they have written in order to get money, I tell them to go to the booksellers and make the best bargain they can." BOSWELL: "But, Sir, if a bookseller should bring you a manuscript to look at." JOHNSON: "Why, Sir, I would desire the bookseller to take it away."

I mentioned a friend of mine who had resided long in Spain, and was unwilling to return to Britain. JOHNSON: "Sir, he is attached to some **woman**." BOSWELL: "I rather believe, Sir, it is the fine climate

---

[1] Mrs. Piozzi, to whom I told this anecdote, has related it, as if the gentleman had given ' the *natural history of the mouse*." Anecdotes, p. 191.—BOSWELL.

[2] Mr Croker suggests that Doctors Beattie and Robertson are here alluded to.—ED

which keeps him there." Johnson : " Nay, Sir, how can you talk so ? What is *climate* to happiness ? Place me in the heart of Asia, should I not be exiled ? What proportion does climate bear to the complex system of human life ? You may advise me to go to live at Bologna to eat sausages. The sausages there are the best in the world ; they lose much by being carried."

On Saturday, May 9, Mr. Dempster and I had agreed to dine by ourselves at the British Coffee-house. Johnson, on whom I happened to call in the morning, said he would join us, which he did, and we spent a very agreeable day : though I recollect but little of what passed.

He said, " Walpole was a minister given by the king to the people : Pitt was a minister given by the people to the king,—as an adjunct."

" The misfortune of Goldsmith in conversation is this : he goes on without knowing how he is to get off. His genius is great, but his knowledge is small. As they say of a generous man, it is a pity he is not rich, we may say of Goldsmith, it is a pity he is not knowing. He would not keep his knowledge to himself."

Before leaving London this year, I consulted him upon a question purely of Scotch law. It was held of old, and continued for a long period, to be an established principle in that law that, whoever intermeddled with the effects of a person deceased, without the interposition of legal authority to guard against embezzlement, should be subjected to pay all the debts of the deceased, as having been guilty of what was technically called *vicious intromission*. The Court of Session had gradually relaxed the strictness of this principle, where the interference proved had been inconsiderable. In a case[1] which came before that Court the preceding winter, I had laboured to persuade the judge to return to the ancient law. It was my own sincere opinion that they ought to adhere to it ; but I had exhausted all my powers of reasoning in vain. Johnson thought as I did ; and in order to assist me in my application to the Court for a revision and alteration of the judgment he dictated to me the following argument :—

" This, we are told, is a law which has its force only from the long practice of the Court, and may, therefore, be suspended or modified as the Court shall think proper.

" Concerning the power of the Court to make or to suspend a law, we have no intention to inquire. It is sufficient for our purpose that every just law is dictated by reason ; and that the practice of every legal court is regulated by equity. It is the quality of reason to be invariable and constant ; and of equity, to give to one man what, in the same case, is given to another. The advantage which humanity derives from law is this : that the law gives every man a rule of action, and prescribes a mode of conduct which shall entitle him to the support and protection of society. That the law may be a rule of action, it is necessary that it be known; it is necessary that it be permanent and stable. The law is the measure of civil right; but if the measure be changeable, the extent of the thing measured never can be settled.

" To permit a law to be modified at discretion, is to leave the community without law. It is to withdraw the direction of that public wisdom, by which the deficiencies of private understanding are to be supplied. It is to suffer the rash and ignorant to act at discretion, and then to depend for the legality of that action on the sentence of the judge. He that is thus governed, lives not by law, but by opinion : not by a certain rule to which he can apply his intention before he acts, but by an uncertain and variable opinion, which he can never know but after he has committed the act on which that opinion shall be passed. He lives by a law (if a law it be) which he can never know before he has offended it. To this case may be justly applied that important principle, *misera est servitus ubi jus est aut incognitum aut vagum.* If intromission be not criminal till it exceeds a certain point, and that point be unsettled, and consequently different in different minds, the right of intromission, and the right of the creditor arising from it, are all *jura vaga*, and, by consequence, are *jura incognita ;* and the result can be no other than a *misera servitus,* an uncertainty concerning the event of action, a servile dependence on private opinion.

" It may be urged, and with great plausibility, that there may be intromission without fraud ; which, however true, will by no means justify an occasional and arbitrary relaxation of the law. The end of law is protection as well as vengeance. Indeed, vengeance is never used but to strengthen protection. That society only is well governed, where life is freed from danger, and from suspicion ; where possession is so sheltered by salutary prohibitions, that violation is prevented more frequently than punished. Such a prohibition was this, while it operated with its original force. The creditor of the deceased was not only without loss, but without fear. He was not to seek a remedy for an injury suffered ; for injury was warded off.

" As the law has been sometimes administered, it lays us open to wounds, because it is imagined to have the power of healing. To punish fraud when it is detected is the proper art of vindictive justice ; but to prevent frauds, and make punishment unnecessary, is the great employment of legislative wisdom. To permit intromission, and to punish fraud, is to make law no better than a pitfall. To tread upon the brink is safe ; but to come a step further is destruction. But, surely, it is better to enclose the gulf, and hinder all access, than, by encouraging us to advance a little, to entice us afterwards a little further, and let us perceive our folly only by our destruction.

" As law supplies the weak with adventitious strength, it likewise enlightens the ignorant with extrinsic understanding. Law teaches us to know when we commit injury and when we suffer it. It fixes certain marks upon actions, by which we are admonished to do or to forbear them. *Qui sibi bene temperat in licitis* (says one of the Fathers), *nunquam cadet in illicita.* He who never intromits at all, will never intromit with fraudulent intentions.

" The relaxation of the law against vicious intromission has been very favourably represented by a great master of jurisprudence, [1] whose words have

[1] Lord Kames, in his " Historical Law Tracts."—BOSWELL.

been exhibited with unnecessary pomp, and seem to be considered as irresistibly decisive. The great moment of his authority makes it necessary to examine his position. ' Some ages ago,' says he, 'before the ferocity of the inhabitants of this part of the island was subdued, the utmost severity of the civil law was necessary, to restrain individuals from plundering each other. Thus the man who intermeddled regularly with the moveables of a person deceased, was subjected to all the debts of the deceased without limitation. This makes a branch of the law of Scotland, known by the name of *vicious intromission* ; and so rigidly was this regulation applied in our courts of law, that the most trifling moveable abstracted *malá fide*, subjected the intermeddler to the foregoing consequences, which proved in many instances a most rigorous punishment. But this severity was necessary, in order to subdue the undisciplined nature of our people. It is extremely remarkable that, in proportion to our improvement in manners, this regulation has been gradually softened and applied by our sovereign Court with a sparing hand.'

" I find myself under a necessity of observing, that this learned and judicious writer has not accurately distinguished the deficiencies and demands of the different conditions of human life, which, from a degree of savageness and independence, in which all laws are vain, passes or may pass, by innumerable gradations, to a state of reciprocal benignity, in which laws shall be no longer necessary. Men are first wild and unsocial, living each man to himself, taking from the weak and losing to the strong. In their first coalitions of society, much of this original savageness is retained. Of general happiness, the product of general confidence, there is yet no thought. Men continue to prosecute their own advantages by the nearest way ; and the utmost severity of the civil law is necessary to restrain individuals from plundering each other. The restraints then necessary, are restraints from plunder, from acts of public violence, and undisguised oppression. The ferocity of our ancestors, as of all other nations, produced not fraud but rapine. They had not yet learned to cheat, and attempted only to rob. As manners grow more polished, with the knowledge of good, men attain likewise dexterity in evil. Open rapine becomes less frequent, and violence gives way to cunning. Those who before invaded pastures and stormed houses, now begin to enrich themselves by unequal contracts and fraudulent intromissions. It is not against the violence of ferocity, but the circumventions of deceit, that this law was framed; and I am afraid the increase of commerce, and the incessant struggle for riches which commerce excites, give us no prospect of an end speedily to be expected of artifice and fraud. It therefore seems to be no very conclusive reasoning which connects those two propositions :—' the nation is become less ferocious, and therefore the laws against fraud and *covin* shall be relaxed.'

" Whatever reason may have influenced the judges to a relaxation of the law, it was not that the nation was grown less fierce ; and, I am afraid, it cannot be affirmed that it is grown less fraudulent.

" Since this law has been represented as rigorously and unreasonably penal, it seems not improper to consider what are the conditions and qualities that make the justice or propriety of a penal law.

" To make a penal law reasonable and just, two conditions are necessary, and two proper. It is necessary that the law should be adequate to its end ;

that if it be observed, it shall prevent the evil against which it is directed. It is, secondly, necessary that the end of the law be of such importance as to deserve the security of a penal sanction. The other conditions of a penal law, which, though not absolutely necessary, are to a very high degree fit, are, that to the moral violation of the law there are many temptations, and that of the physical observance there is great facility.

" All these conditions apparently concur to justify the law which we are now considering. Its end is the security of property; and property very often of great value. The method by which it effects the security is efficacious, because it admits in its original rigour no gradations of injury; but keeps guilt and innocence apart, by a distinct and definite limitation. He that intromits is criminal; he that intromits not, is innocent. Of the two secondary considerations it cannot be denied that both are in our favour. The temptation to intromit is frequent and strong—so strong and so frequent as to require the utmost activity of justice, and vigilance of caution, to withstand its prevalence; and the method by which a man may entitle himself to legal intromission is so open and so facile, that to neglect it is a proof of fraudulent intention; for why should a man omit to do (but for reasons which he will not confess) that which he can do so easily, and that which he knows to be required by the law? If temptation were rare, a penal law might be deemed unnecessary. If the duty enjoined by the law were of difficult performance, omission, though it could not be justified, might be pitied. But in the present case, neither equity nor compassion operate against it. A useful, a necessary law is broken, not only without a reasonable motive, but with all the inducements to obedience that can be derived from safety and facility.

" I therefore return to my original position that a law, to have its effects, must be permanent and stable. It may be said, in the language of the schools, *Lex non recipit majus et minus*—we may have a law, or we may have no law, but we cannot have half a law. We must either have a rule of action, or be permitted to act by discretion and by chance. Deviations from the law must be uniformly punished, or no man can be certain when he shall be safe.

" That from the rigour of the original institution this Court has sometimes departed cannot be denied. But as it is evident that such deviations, as they make law uncertain, make life unsafe, I hope that of departing from it there will now be an end; that the wisdom of our ancestors will be treated with due reverence; and that consistent and steady decisions will furnish the people with a rule of action, and leave fraud and fraudulent intromissions no future hope of impunity or escape."

With such comprehension of mind, and such clearness of penetration did he thus treat a subject altogether new to him, without any other preparation than my having stated to him the arguments which had been used on each side of the question. His intellectual powers appeared with peculiar lustre, when tried against those of a writer of such fame as Lord Kames, and that too in his lordship's own department.

This masterly argument, after being prefaced, and concluded with some sentences of my own, and garnished with the usual formularies, was actually printed and laid before the Lords of the Session, but without success. My respected friend Lord Hailes, however, one of that honourable body, had critical sagacity enough to discover a more than ordinary hand in the *petition*. I told him Dr. Johnson had favoured me with his pen. His lordship with wonderful *acumen*, pointed out exactly where his composition began and where it ended. But that I may do impartial justice, and conform to the great rule of courts, *Suum cuique tribuito*, I must add that their lordships in general, though they were pleased to call this a " well-drawn paper," preferred the former very inferior petition which I had written ; thus confirming the truth of an observation made to me by one of their number, in a merry mood : " My dear Sir, give yourself no trouble in the composition of the papers you present to us ; for, indeed, it is casting pearls before swine."

I renewed my solicitations that Dr. Johnson would this year accomplish his long-intended visit to Scotland.

" TO JAMES BOSWELL, ESQ.

"DEAR SIR, *August*, 31, 1772.

" The regret has not been little with which I have missed a journey so pregnant with pleasing expectations, as that in which I could promise myself not only the gratification of curiosity, both rational and fanciful, but the delight of seeing those whom I love and esteem. * * * But such has been the course of things, that I could not come ; and such has been I am afraid, the state of my body, that it would not well have seconded my inclination. My body, I think, grows better, and I refer my hopes to another year; for I am very sincere in my design to pay the visit, and take the ramble. In the meantime, do not omit any opportunity of keeping up a favourable opinion of me in the minds of any of my friends. Beattie's book is, I believe, every day more liked ; at least I like it more, as I look more upon it.

" I am glad if you got credit by your cause, and am yet of opinion, that our cause was good, and that the determination ought to have been in your favour. Poor Hastie, I think, had but his deserts.

" You promised to get me a little ' Pindar;' you may add to it a little 'Anacreon.'

" The leisure which I cannot enjoy, it will be a pleasure to hear that you employ upon the antiquities of the feudal establishment. The whole system of ancient tenures is gradually passing away ; and I wish to have the knowledge of it preserved adequate and complete. For such an institution makes a very important part of the history of mankind. Do not forget a design so worthy of a scholar who studies the law of his country, and of a gentleman who may naturally be curious to know the condition of his own ancestors.

" I am, dear Sir, yours with great affection,

"SAM. JOHNSON."

" TO DR. JOHNSON.

" MY DEAR SIR, *Edinburgh, Dec.* 25, 1772.

* * * *

" I was much disappointed that you did not come to Scotland last autumn. However, I must own that your letter prevents me from complaining; not only because I am sensible that the state of your health was but too good an excuse, but because you write in a strain which shows that you have agreeable views of the scheme which we have so long proposed,

*　　*　　*　　*　　*

"I communicated to Beattie what you said of his book in your last letter to me.　He writes to me thus: 'You judge very rightly in supposing that Dr. Johnson's favourable opinion of my book must give me great delight.　Indeed it is impossible for me to say how much I am gratified by it; for there is not a man upon earth whose good opinion I would be more ambitious to cultivate. His talents and his virtues I reverence more than any words can express.　The extraordinary civilities, (the paternal attentions I should rather say,) and the many instructions I have had the honour to receive from him, will to me be a perpetual source of pleasure in the recollection,

Dum memor ipse mei, dum spiritus hos reget artus.'

"I had still some thoughts, while the summer lasted, of being obliged to go to London on some little business; otherwise I should certainly have troubled him with a letter several months ago, and given some vent to my gratitude and admiration.　This I intend to do, as soon as I am left a little at leisure.　Meantime, if you have occasion to write to him, I beg you will offer him my most respectful compliments, and assure him of the sincerity of my attachment and the warmth of my gratitude.

*　　*　　*　　*　　*　　*

"I am, &c.,

"JAMES BOSWELL."

GEORGE STEEVENS

CHAPTER VI.—1773.

NEW EDITIONS OF "THE DICTIONARY" AND "SHAKSPEARE" PUBLISHED—GEORGE STEEVENS
—LETTER TO BOSWELL, WHO RE-VISITS LONDON—GOLDSMITH'S COMEDY, "SHE STOOPS
TO CONQUER"—"THE SPECTATOR"—GOOD FRIDAY AND EASTER SUNDAY—A DINNER
AT JOHNSON'S HOUSE—THE STUARTS—LAW REPORTS—SIGNOR MARTINELLI—ALLAN
RAMSAY'S "GENTLE SHEPHERD"—CHARLES TOWNSHEND—JOHNSON DOUBTS THE PRAC-
TICABILITY OF SHORT-HAND REPORTING—HIS DEFENCE OF DUELLING—VANITY OF
GARRICK—SAVAGE LIFE—SUICIDE—EUSTACE BUDGELL—THE DOUGLAS CAUSE.

IN 1773, his only publication was an edition of his folio Dictionary
with additions and corrections ; nor did he, so far as is known,
furnish any productions of his fertile pen to any of his numerous friends
or dependents, except the preface [1] to his old amanuensis Macbean's
"Dictionary of Ancient Geography." His Shakspeare, indeed, which
had been received with high approbation by the public, and gone
through several editions, was this year re-published by George Steevens,
Esq., a gentleman not only deeply skilled in ancient learning, and of
very extensive reading in English literature, especially the early writers,
but at the same time of acute discernment and elegant taste. It is
almost unnecessary to say that, by his great and valuable additions to
Dr. Johnson's work, he justly obtained considerable reputation :

" *Divisum imperium cum Jove Cæsar habet.*"

[1] He, however, wrote, or partly wrote, an Epitaph on Mrs. Bell, wife of his friend John
Bell, Esq., brother of the Rev. Dr. Bell, Prebendary of Westminster, which is printed in
his works. It is in English prose, and has so little of his manner, that I did not believe
he had any hand in it, till I was satisfied of the fact by the authority of Mr. Bell.—BOSWELL.

"TO JAMES BOSWELL, ESQ.

"DEAR SIR,   *London, Feb.* 22, 1773.

"I have read your kind letter much more than the elegant Pindar which it accompanied. I am always glad to find myself not forgotten; and to be forgotten by you would give me great uneasiness. My northern friends have never been unkind to me; I have from you, dear Sir, testimonies of affection, which I have not often been able to excite; and Dr. Beattie rates the testimony which I was desirous of paying to his merit, much higher than I should have thought it reasonable to expect.

"I have heard of your masquerade.[1] What says your synod to such innovations? I am not studiously scrupulous, nor do I think a masquerade either evil in itself, or very likely to be the occasion of evil; yet, as the world thinks it a very licentious relaxation of manners, I would not have been one of the *first* masquers in a country where no masquerade had ever been before.[2]

"A new edition of my great Dictionary is printed, from a copy which I was persuaded to revise; but having made no preparation, I was able to do very little. Some superfluities I have expunged, and some faults I have corrected, and here and there have scattered a remark; but the main fabric of the work remains as it was. I have looked very little into it since I wrote it, and, I think, I found it full as often better, as worse, than I expected.

"Baretti and Davies have had a furious quarrel; a quarrel, I think, irreconcilable. Dr. Goldsmith has a new comedy, which is expected in the spring. No name is yet given it. The chief diversion arises from a stratagem by which a lover is made to mistake his future father-in-law's house for an inn. This, you see, borders upon farce. The dialogue is quick and gay, and the incidents are so prepared as not to seem improbable.

"I am sorry that you lost your cause of intromission, because I yet think the arguments on your side unanswerable. But you seem, I think, to say, that you gained reputation even by your defeat; and reputation you will daily gain, if you keep Lord Auchinleck's precept in your mind, and endeavour to consolidate in your mind a firm and regular system of law, instead of picking up occasional fragments.

"My health seems in general to improve; but I have been troubled for many weeks with a vexatious catarrh, which is sometimes sufficiently distressful. I have not found any great effects from bleeding and physic; and am afraid, that I must expect help from brighter days and softer air.

"Write to me now and then; and whenever any good befals you, make haste to let me know it, for no one will rejoice at it more than, dear Sir,

"Your most humble servant,

"SAM. JOHNSON."

"You continue to stand very high in the favour of Mrs. Thrale."

While a former edition of my work was passing through the press, I was unexpectedly favoured with a packet from Philadelphia, from Mr. James Abercrombie, a gentleman of that country, who is pleased to

---

[1] Given by a lady at Edinburgh.—BOSWELL.

[2] There had been masquerades in Scotland; but not for a very long time.—BOSWELL.

honour me with very high praise of my " Life of Dr. Johnson." To
have the fame of my illustrious friend, and his faithful biographer
echoed from the New World, is extremely flattering ; and my grateful
acknowledgments shall be wafted across the Atlantic.   Mr. Abercrombie has politely conferred on me a considerable additional obliga
tion, by transmitting to me copies of two letters from Dr. Johnson to
American gentlemen.   " Gladly, Sir," says he, " would I have sent
you the originals ; but being the only relics of the kind in America,
they are considered by the possessors of such inestimable value, that
no possible consideration would induce them to part with them.   In
some future publication of yours relative to that great and good man,
they may perhaps be thought worthy of insertion."

" TO MR. B————D.[1]

" SIR,   <i>London, Johnson's-court, Fleet-street, March</i> 4, 1773.
" That in the hurry of a sudden departure you should yet find leisure to
consult my convenience, is a degree of kindness, and an instance of regard, not
only beyond my claims, but above my expectation.   You are not mistaken in
supposing that I set a high value on my American friends, and that you should
confer a very valuable favour upon me by giving me an opportunity of keeping
myself in their memory.
" I have taken the liberty of troubling you with a packet, to which I wish a
safe and speedy conveyance, because I wish a safe and speedy voyage to him
that conveys it.   I am, Sir, your most humble servant,

" SAM. JOHNSON."

" TO THE REV. MR. WHITE.

" DEAR SIR,   <i>Johnson's-court, Fleet-street, London, March</i> 4, 1773.
" Your kindness for your friends accompanies you across the Atlantic.   It
was long since observed by Horace, that no ship could leave care behind : you
have been attended in your voyage by other powers,— by benevolence and
constancy : and I hope care did not often show her face in their company.
" I received the copy of Rasselas.   The impression is not magnificent, but
it flatters an author, because the printer seems to have expected that it would
be scattered among the people.   The little book has been well received, and is
translated into Italian, French, German and Dutch.   It has now one honour
more by an American edition.
" I know not that much has happened since your departure that can engage
your curiosity.   Of all public transactions the whole world is now informed by
the newspapers.   Opposition seems to despond ; and the dissenters, though

- This gentleman, who now resides in America in a public character of considerable
dignity, desired that his name might not be transcribed at full length.—BOSWELL.

2 Now Doctor White, and Bishop of the Episcopal Church in Pennsylvania.   During his
first visit to England in 1771, as a candidate for holy orders, he was several times in company
with Dr. Johnson, who expressed a wish to see the edition of Rasselas, which Dr. White told
him had been printed in America.   Dr. White, on his return, immediately sent him a copy.—
BOSWELL.

they have taken advantage of unsettled times, and a government much
enfeebled, seem not likely to gain any immunities.

"Dr. Goldsmith has a new comedy in rehearsal at Covent-garden, to which
the manager predicts ill success. I hope he will be mistaken. I think it
deserves a very kind reception.

"I shall soon publish a new edition of my large Dictionary: I have been
persuaded to revise it, and have mended some faults, but added little to its
usefulness.

"No book has been published since your departure, of which much notice
is taken. Faction only fills the town with pamphlets, and greater subjects are
forgotten in the noise of discord.

"Thus have I written, only to tell you how little I have to tell. Of myself
I can only add, that having been afflicted many weeks with a very troublsome
cough, I am now recovered.

"I take the liberty which you give me of troubling you with a letter, of
which you will be pleased to fill up the direction,   I am, Sir,

"Your most humble servant,

"SAM. JOHNSON."

On Saturday, April 3, the day after my arrival in London this year,
I went to his house late in the evening, and sat with Mrs. Williams till
he came home. I found in "The London Chronicle," Dr. Goldsmith's
apology to the public for beating Evans, a bookseller, on account of a
paragraph [1] in a newspaper published by him, which Goldsmith thought
impertinent to him and to a lady of his acquaintance. The apology was
written so much in Dr. Johnson's manner, that both Mrs. Williams and
I supposed it to be his; but when he came home he soon undeceived us.
When he said to Mrs. Williams, "Well, Dr. Goldsmith's *manifesto* has
got into your paper;" I asked him if Dr. Goldsmith had written it, with
an air that made him see I suspected it was his, though subscribed by
Goldsmith. JOHNSON: "Sir, Dr. Goldsmith would no more have asked
me to write such a thing as that for him than he would have asked me
to feed him with a spoon, or to do anything else that denoted his
imbecility. I as much believe that he wrote it as if I had seen him do
it. Sir, had he shown it to any one friend, he would not have been
allowed to publish it. He has, indeed, done it very well; but it is a
foolish thing well done. I suppose he has been so much elated with the
success of his new comedy that he has thought everything that concerned him must be of importance to the public." BOSWELL: "I fancy,
Sir, this is the first time that he has been engaged in such an adventure." JOHNSON: "Why, Sir, I believe it is the first time he has *beat;*
he may have *been beaten* before. This, Sir, is a new plume to him."

I mentioned Sir John Dalrymple's "Memoirs of Great Britain and

[1] The offence given, was a long abusive letter in "The London Packet." A particular
account of this transaction, and Goldsmith's Vindication (for such it was, rather than an
apology), may be found in the new Life of that Poet, prefixed to his Miscellaneous Works in
4 vols. 8vo. pp. 105—108.—MALONE.

Ireland," and his discoveries to the prejudice of Lord Russell and Algernon Sydney. JOHNSON : "Why, Sir, every body who had just notions of government thought them rascals before. It is well that all mankind now see them to be rascals." BOSWELL : "But, Sir, may not those discoveries be true without their being rascals." JOHNSON : "Consider, Sir, would any of them have been willing to have had it known that they intrigued with France ? (Depend upon it, Sir, he who does what he is afraid should be known, has something rotten about him.) This Dalrymple seems to be an honest fellow ; for he tells equally what makes against both sides. But nothing can be poorer than his mode of writing ; it is the mere bouncing of a schoolboy ! great he ![1] but greater she ! and such stuff."

I could not agree with him in this criticism : for though Sir John Dalrymple's style is not regularly formed in any respect, and one cannot help smiling sometimes at his affected *grandiloquence*, there is in his writing a pointed vivacity, and much of a gentlemanly spirit.

At Mr. Thrale's, in the evening, he repeated his usual paradoxical declamation against action in public speaking. "Action can have no effect upon reasonable minds. It may augment noise, but it never can enforce argument. If you speak to a dog, you use action : you hold up your hand thus, because he is a brute ; and in proportion as men are removed from brutes, action will have the less influence upon them." MRS. THRALE : "What then, Sir, becomes of Demosthenes' saying ? 'Action, action, action !'" JOHNSON : "Demosthenes, Madam, spoke to an assembly of brutes ; to a barbarous people."

I thought it extraordinary, that he should deny the power of rhetorical action upon human nature, when it is proved by innumerable facts in all stages of society. Reasonable beings are not solely reasonable. They have fancies which may be pleased, passions which may be roused.

Lord Chesterfield being mentioned, Johnson remarked, that almost all of that celebrated nobleman's witty sayings were puns. He, however, allowed the merit of good wit to his Lordship's saying of Lord Tyrawley and himself, when both very old and infirm : "Tyrawley and I have been dead these two years ; but we don't choose to have it known."

He talked with approbation of an intended edition of "The Spectator," with notes; two volumes of which had been prepared by a gentleman eminent in the literary world, and the materials which he had collected for the remainder had been transferred to another hand. He observed, that all works which describe manners, require notes in sixty or seventy years, or less ; and told us, he had communicated all he knew that could throw light upon "The Spectator." He said, "Addison had made his Sir Andrew Freeport a true Whig, arguing against giving charity to beggars, and throwing out other such ungracious sentiments ;

---

[1] A bombastic ode of Oldham's on Ben Jonson begins thus : "Great thou !" which perhaps his namesake remembered.—MALONE.

but that he had thought better, and made amends by making him found an hospital for decayed farmers." He called for the volume of "The Spectator," in which that account is contained, and read it aloud to us. He read so well, that everything acquired additional weight and grace from his utterance.

The conversation having turned on modern imitations of ancient ballads, and some one having praised their simplicity, he treated them with that ridicule which he always displayed when that subject was mentioned.

He disapproved of introducing scripture phrases into secular discourse. This seemed to me a question of some difficulty. A scripture expression may be used like a highly classical phrase, to produce an instantaneous strong expression ; and it may be done without being at all improper. Yet I own there is danger, that applying the language of our sacred book to ordinary subjects may tend to lessen our reverence for it. If therefore it be introduced at all, it should be with very great caution.

On Thursday, April 8, I sat a good part of the evening with him, but he was very silent. He said " Burnet's 'History of his own Times,' is very entertaining. The style, indeed, is mere chit-chat. I do not believe that Burnet intentionally lied ; but he was so much prejudiced that he took no pains to find out the truth. He was like a man who resolves to regulate his time by a certain watc but will not inquire whether the watch is right or not."

Though he was not disposed to talk, he was unwilling that I should leave him : and when I looked at my watch, and told him it was twelve o'clock, he cried, " What's that to you and me ?" and ordered Frank to tell Mrs. Williams that we were coming to drink tea with her, which we did. It was settled that we should go to church together next day.

On the 9th of April, being Good Friday, I breakfasted with him on tea and cross buns ; *Doctor* Levet, as Frank called him, making the tea. He carried me with him to the church of St. Clement Danes, where he had his seat ;[1] and his behaviour was, as I had imagined to myself, solemnly devout. I never shall forget the tremulous earnestness with which he pronounced the awful petition in the Litany : "In the hour of death, and at the day of judgment, good LORD deliver us."

[1] The Churchwardens of St. Clement Danes, having satisfactorily ascertained that a seat in the pew numbered 18, in the north gallery of that church, was regularly occupied for many years, by the great moralist, have, during the progress of this Edition, caused a neat brass tablet recording the fact to be affixed in a conspicuous position to the pillar against which the Doctor must often have reclined. The inscription on the tablet is understood to be from the pen of Dr. Croly, rector of St. Stephen's, Walbrook, and is as follows :—" In this pew and beside this pillar, for many years attended divine service the celebrated Dr. Samuel Johnson, the philosopher, the poet, the great lexicographer, the profound moralist, and chief writer of his time. Born 1709 ; died 1784. In the remembrance and honour of noble faculties, nobly employed, some inhabitants of the parish of St. Clement Danes have placed this slight memorial, A.D. 1851."—ED.

We went to church both in the morning and evening. In the interval between the two services we did not dine ; but he read in the Greek New Testament, and I turned over several of his books.

JOHNSON AT ST. CLEMENT DANES CHURCH.

In Archbishop Laud's Diary, I found the following passage, which I read to Dr. Johnson :

"1623, February 1, Sunday. I stood by the most Illustrious Prince Charles,[1] at dinner. He was then very merry, and talked occasionally of many things with his attendants. Among other things, he said, that if he were necessitated to take any particular profession of life, he could not be a lawyer, adding his reason : 'I cannot,' said he, 'defend a bad, nor yield in a good cause.' JOHNSON : 'Sir, this is false reasoning ; because every cause has a bad side : and a lawyer is not overcome, though the cause which he has endeavoured to support be determined against him."

I told him that Goldsmith had said to me a few days before, " As I take my shoes from the shoemaker, and my coat from the tailor, so I take my religion from the priest." I regretted this loose way of talking JOHNSON : "Sir, he knows nothing ; he has made up his mind about nothing."

To my great surprise he asked me to dine with him on Easter-day I never supposed that he had a dinner at his house ; for I had not then heard of any one of his friends having been entertained at his table. He

[1] Afterwards Charles I.—BOSWELL.

told me, "I have generally a meat-pie on Sunday ; it is baked at a public oven, which is very properly allowed, because one man can attend it ; and thus the advantage is obtained of not keeping servants from church to dress dinners."

April 11, being Easter Sunday, after having attended Divine Service at St. Paul's, I repaired to Dr. Johnson's. I had gratified my curiosity much in dining with Jean Jaques Rousseau, while he lived in the wilds of Neufchâtel : I had as great a curiosity to dine with Dr. Samuel Johnson, in the dusky recess of a court in Fleet-street. I supposed we should scarcely have knives and forks, and only some strange, uncouth, ill-dressed dish ; but I found everything in very good order. We had no other company but Mrs. Williams and a young woman whom I did not know. As a dinner here was considered as a singular phenomenon, and as I was frequently interrogated on the subject, my readers may perhaps be desirous to know our bill of fare. Foote, I remember, in allusion to Francis, the *negro*, was willing to suppose that our repast was *black broth*. But the fact was that we had a very good soup, a boiled leg of lamb and spinach, a veal pie, and a rice pudding.

Of Dr. John Campbell, the author, he said, "He is a very inquisitive and a very able man, and a man of good religious principles, though I am afraid he has been deficient in practice. Campbell is radically right ; and we may hope that in time there will be good practice."

He owned that he thought Hawkesworth was one of his imitators, but he did not think Goldsmith was. Goldsmith, he said, had great merit. BOSWELL : "But, Sir, he is much indebted to you for his getting so high in public estimation." JOHNSON : "Why, Sir, he has, perhaps, got *sooner* to it by his intimacy with me."

Goldsmith, though his vanity often excited him to occasional competition, had a very high regard for Johnson, which he had at this time expressed in the strongest manner in the Dedication of his comedy, entitled, "She Stoops to Conquer."[1]

Johnson observed, that there were very few books printed in Scotland before the Union. He had seen a complete collection of them in the possession of the Hon. Archibald Campbell, a nonjuring bishop.[2] I wish this collection had been kept entire. Many of them are in the library of the Faculty of Advocates at Edinburgh. I told Dr. Johnson that I had some intention to write the life of the learned and worthy Thomas Ruddiman. He said, "I should take pleasure in helping you to do honour to him. But his farewell letter to the faculty of Advocates,

---

[1] By inscribing this slight performance to you, I do not mean so much to compliment you as myself. It may do me some honour to inform the public, that I have lived many years in intimacy with you. It may serve the interests of mankind also to inform them, that the greatest wit may be found in a character, without impairing the most unaffected piety.— BOSWELL.

[2] See an account of this learned and respectable gentleman, and of his curious work on the *Middle State*, "Journal of a Tour to the Hebrides" 3rd edit. p. 371.— BOSWELL.

when he resigned the office of their librarian, should have been in Latin."

I put a question to him upon a fact in common life, which he could not answer, nor have I found any one else who could. "What is the reason that women servants, though obliged to be at the expense of purchasing their own clothes, have much lower wages than men servants, to whom a great proportion of that article is furnished, and when in fact our female house servants work much harder than the male ? "

He told me that he had twelve or fourteen times attempted to keep a journal of his life, but never could persevere. He advised me to do it. "The great thing to be recorded," said he, "is the state of your own mind ; and you should write down everything that you remember, for you cannot judge at first what is good or bad ; and write immediately, while the impression is fresh, for it will not be the same a week afterwards."

I again solicited him to communicate to me the particulars of his early life. He said, "You shall have them all for twopence. I hope you shall know a great deal more of me before you write my life." He mentioned to me this day many circumstances, which I wrote down when I went home, and have interwoven in the former part of this narrative.

On Tuesday, April 13, he and Dr. Goldsmith and I dined at General Oglethorpe's. Goldsmith expatiated on the common topic, that the race of our people was degenerated, and this was owing to luxury. Johnson : "Sir, in the first place I doubt the fact. I believe there are as many tall men in England now, as ever there were. But, secondly, supposing the stature of our people to be diminished, that is not owing to luxury ; for, Sir, consider to how very small a proportion of our people luxury can reach. Our soldiery, surely, are not luxurious, who live on sixpence a day ; and the same remark will apply to almost all the other classes. Luxury, so far as it reaches the poor, will do good to the race of people ; it will strengthen and multiply them. Sir, no nation was ever hurt by luxury ; for, as I said before, it can reach but to a very few. I admit that the great increase of commerce and manufactures hurts the military spirit of a people ; because it produces a competition for something else than martial honours—a competition for riches. It also hurts the bodies of the people : for you will observe, there is no man who works at any particular trade, but you may know him from his appearance to do so. One part or the other of his body being more used than the rest, he is in some degree deformed : but, Sir, that is not luxury. A tailor sits crossed-legged : but that is not luxury." Goldsmith : " Come, you're just going to the same place by another road." Johnson : " Nay, Sir, I say that is not *luxury*. Let us take a walk from Charing-cross to Whitechapel, through, I suppose, the greatest series of shops in the world, what is there in any of these shops (if you except gin-shops), that can do any human being any harm ? " GOLDSMITH : " Well, Sir, I'll accept your challenge. The very next shop to Northumberland-house is a pickle-shop." JOHNSON : " Well, Sir ; do we not know that a maid can in one afternoon make pickles sufficient to serve a whole family for a year ? nay, that five pickle-shops can serve all the kingdom ? Besides, Sir, there is no harm done to any body by the making of pickles or the eating of pickles."

We drank tea with the ladies ; and Goldsmith sung Tony Lumpkin's song in his comedy, "She Stoops to Conquer," and a very pretty one, to an Irish tune,[1] which he had designed for Miss Hardcastle ; but as Mrs. Bulkeley, who played the part, could not sing, it was left out. He afterwards wrote it down for me, by which means it w s preserved, and now appears amongst his poems. Dr. Johnson, in his way home, stopped at my lodgings in Piccadilly, and sat with me, drinking tea a second time, till a late hour.

I told him that Mrs. Macaulay said, she wondered how he could reconcile his political principles with his moral : his notions of inequality and subordination with wishing well to the happiness of all mankind who might live so agreeably, had they all their portions of land, and none to domineer over another. JOHNSON : " Why, Sir, I reconcile my principles very well, because mankind are happier in a state of inequality and subordination. Were they to be in this pretty state of equality, they would soon degenerate into brutes ;—they would become Monboddo's nation :—their tails would grow. Sir, all would be losers, were all to work for all : they would have no intellectual improvement. All intellectual improvement arises from leisure ; all leisure arises from one working for another."

Talking of the family of Stuart, he said, " It should seem that the family at present on the throne has now established as good a right as the former family, by the long consent of the people ; and that to disturb this right might be considered as culpable. At the same time I own, that it is a very difficult question, when considered with respect to the house of Stuart. To oblige people to take oaths as to the disputed right, is wrong. I know not whether I could take them : but I do not blame those who do." So conscientious and so delicate was he upon this subject, which has occasioned so much clamour against him.

Talking of law cases, he said, " The English reports, in general, are very poor : only the half of what has been said is taken down ; and of that half, much is mistaken. Whereas, in Scotland, the arguments on each side are deliberately put in writing, to be considered by the court. I think a collection of your cases upon subjects of importance, with the opinions of the judges upon them, would be valuable."

1 The " Humours of Ballamagairy."—BOSWELL.

On Thursday, April 15, I dined with him and Dr. Goldsmith at General Paoli's. We found here Signor Martinelli, of Florence, author of a History of England in Italian, printed at London.

I spoke of Allan Ramsay's "Gentle Shepherd," in the Scottish dialect, as the best pastoral that had ever been written; not only abounding with beautiful rural imagery, and just and pleasing sentiments, but being a real picture of manners; and I offered to teach Dr. Johnson to understand it. "No, Sir," said he, "I won't learn it. You shall retain your superiority by my not knowing it."

This brought on a question whether one man is lessened by another's acquiring an equal degree of knowledge with him. Johnson asserted the affirmative. I maintained that the position might be true in those kinds of knowledge which produce wisdom, power, and force, so as to enable one man to have the government of others; but

SIGNOR MARTINELLI.

that a man is not in any degree lessened by others knowing as well as he what ends in mere pleasure:—eating fine fruit, drinking delicious wines, reading exquisite poetry.

The General observed, that Martinelli was a Whig. JOHNSON: "I am sorry for it. It shows the spirit of the times: he is obliged to temporise." BOSWELL: "I rather think, Sir, that Toryism prevails in this reign." JOHNSON: "I know not why you should think so, Sir. You see your friend Lord Lyttelton, a nobleman, is obliged in his History to write the most vulgar Whiggism."

An animated debate took place whether Martinelli should continue his History of England to the present day. GOLDSMITH: "To be sure he should." JOHNSON: "No, Sir; he would give great offence. He would have to tell of almost all the living great what they do not wish told. ' GOLDSMITH: "It may, perhaps, be necessary for a native to be more cautious; but a foreigner who comes among us without prejudice, may be considered as holding the place of a judge, and may speak his mind freely." JOHNSON: "Sir, a foreigner, when he sends a work from the press, ought to be on his guard against catching the error and mistaken enthusiasm of the people among whom he happens to be." GOLDSMITH: "Sir, he wants only to sell his history, and to tell truth; one an honest, the other a laudable motive." JOHNSON: "Sir, they are both laudable motives. It is laudable in a man to wish to live by his labours; but he should write so as he may *live* by them, not so as he may be knocked on the head. I would advise him to be at Calais before he publishes his history of the present age. A foreigner who attaches himself to a political party in this country, is in the worst state that can be imagined : he is looked upon as a mere intermeddler. A native may do it from interest." BOSWELL : "Or principle." GOLDSMITH : "There are people who tell a hundred political lies every day, and are not hurt by it. Surely, then, one may tell truth with safety." JOHNSON : "Why, Sir, in the first place, he who tells a hundred lies has disarmed the force of his lies. But besides, a man had rather have a hundred lies told of him, than one truth which he does not wish should be told." GOLDSMITH : "For my part, I'd tell truth, and shame the devil." JOHNSON : "Yes, Sir ; but the devil will be angry. I wish to shame the devil as much as you do, but I should choose to be out of the reach of his claws." GOLDSMITH : "His claws can do you no harm, when you have the shield of truth."

It having been observed that there was little hospitality in London ; JOHNSON : "Nay, Sir, any man who has a name, or who has the power of pleasing, will be very generally invited in London. The man, Sterne, I have been told, has had engagements for three months." GOLDSMITH : "And a very dull fellow." JOHNSON : "Why, no, Sir."

Martinelli told us, that for several years he lived much with Charles Townshend, and that he ventured to tell him he was a bad joker. JOHNSON : "Why, Sir, thus much I can say upon the subject. One day he and a few more agreed to go and dine in the country, and each of them was to bring a friend in his carriage with him. Charles Townshend asked Fitzherbert to go with him, but told him, ' You must find somebody to bring you back : I can only carry you there.' Fitzherbert did not much like this arrangement. He, however, consented, observing sarcastically, ' It will do very well ; for then the same jokes will serve you in returning as in going.'"

An eminent public character being mentioned :—JOHNSON : "I remember being present when he showed himself to be so corrupted, or at least something so different from what I think right, as to maintain, that a member of parliament should go along with his party right or wrong. Now, Sir, this is so remote from native virtue, from scholastic virtue, that a good man must have undergone a great change before he can reconcile himself to such a doctrine. It is maintaining that you may lie to the public ; for you lie when you call that right which you think wrong, or the reverse. A friend of ours who is too much an echo of that gentleman, observed, ' that a man who does not stick uniformly to a party is only waiting to be bought.' Why, then, said I, he is only waiting to be what that gentleman is already."

We talked of the King's coming to see Goldsmith's new play.—"I wish he would," said Goldsmith ; adding, however, with an affected indifference, "Not that it would do me the least good." JOHNSON : "Well then, Sir let us say it would do *him* good (laughing). No, Sir this affectation will not pass : it is mighty idle. In such a state as ours who would not wish to please the chief magistrate ? " GOLDSMITH : " I *do* wish to please him. I remember a line in Dryden,

> ' And every poet is the monarch's friend.'

It ought to be reversed." JOHNSON : " Nay, there are finer lines in Dryden on the subject :—

> ' For colleges on bounteous kings depend,
> And never rebel was to arts a friend.' "

General Paoli observed, that successful rebels might. MARTINELLI : " Happy rebellions." GOLDSMITH : " We have no such phrase." GENERAL PAOLI : " But have you not the *thing* ? " GOLDSMITH : " Yes, all our *happy* revolutions. They have hurt our constitution, and will hurt it, till we mend it by another HAPPY REVOLUTION." I never before discovered that my friend Goldsmith had so much of the old prejudice in him.

General Paoli, talking of Goldsmith's new play, said, " *Il a fait un compliment très gracieux à une certaine grande dame;* " meaning a duchess of the first rank.

I expressed a doubt whether Goldsmith intended it, in order that I might hear the truth of it from himself. It perhaps was not quite fair to endeavour to bring him to a confession, as he might not wish to avow positively his taking part against the Court. He smiled and hesitated. The General at once relieved him by this beautiful image : *Monsieur Goldsmith est comme la mer, qui jette des perles et beaucoup d'autres belles choses, sans s'en appercevoir.*" GOLDSMITH : " *Très bien dit, et très élégamment.*"

A person was mentioned who, it was said, could take down in short-hand the speeches in parliament with perfect exactness. JOHNSON : " Sir, it is impossible. I remember one Angel who came to me to write for him a preface or dedication to a book upon short-hand, and he professed to write as fast as a man could speak. In order to try him, I took down a book, and read while he wrote ; and I favoured him, for I read more deliberately than usual. I had proceeded but a very little way, when he begged I would desist, for he could not follow me." Hearing now for the first time of this preface or dedication, I said, " What an expense, Sir, do you put us to in buying books, to which you have written prefaces or dedications." JOHNSON : " Why, I have dedicated to the royal family all round ; that is to say, to the last generation of the royal family." GOLDSMITH : " And, perhaps, Sir, not one sentence of wit in a whole dedication." JOHNSON : " Perhaps not, Sir." BOSWELL : " What then is the reason for applying to a particular person to do that which any one may do as well ? " JOHNSON : " Why, Sir, one man has a greater readiness at doing it than another."

I spoke of Mr. Harris,[1] of Salisbury, as being a very learned man, and in particular an eminent Grecian. JOHNSON : " I am not sure of that. His friends gave him out as such, but I know not who of his friends are able to judge of it." GOLDSMITH : " He is what is much better : he is a worthy humane man." JOHNSON : " Nay, Sir, that is not to the purpose of our argument : that will as much prove that he can play the fiddle as well as Giardini, as that he is an eminent Grecian." GOLDSMITH : " The greatest musical performers have but small emoluments. Giardini, I am told, does not get above seven hundred a year." JOHNSON : " That is indeed but little for a man to get, who does best that which so many endeavour to do. There is nothing, I think, in which the power of art is shown so much as in playing on the fiddle. In all other things we can do something at first. Any man will forge a bar of iron if you give him a hammer ; not so well as a smith, but tolerably. A man will saw a piece of wood, and make a box, though a clumsy one ; but give him a fiddle and a fiddlestick, and he can do nothing."

On Monday, April 19, he called on me with Mrs. Williams, in Mr. Strahan's coach, and carried me out to dine with Mr. Elphinston, at his Academy at Kensington. A printer having acquired a fortune sufficient to keep his coach was a good topic for the credit of literature. Mrs. Williams said that another printer, Mr. Hamilton, had not waited so long as Mr. Strahan, but had kept his coach several years sooner. JOHNSON : " He was in the right. Life is short. The sooner that a man begins to enjoy his wealth the better."

Mr. Elphinston talked of a new book that was much admired, and asked Dr. Johnson if he had read it. JOHNSON : " I have looked into it." " What," said Elphinston, " have you not read it through ? " JOHNSON (offended at being thus pressed, and so obliged to own his cursory mode of reading, answered tartly) : " No, Sir ; do *you* read books *through ?* "

He this day again defended duelling, and put his argument upon what I have ever thought the most solid basis : that if public war be allowed to be consistent with morality, private war must be equally so. Indeed, we may observe what strained arguments are used to reconcile war with the Christian religion. But, in my opinion, it is exceedingly clear that duelling having better reasons for its barbarous violence, is more justifiable than war in which thousands go forth without any cause of personal quarrel, and massacre each other.

On Wednesday, April 21, I dined with him at Mr. Thrale's. A gentleman attacked Garrick for being vain. JOHNSON : " No wonder, Sir, that he is vain ; a man who is perpetually flattered in every mode that can be conceived. So many bellows have blown the fire, that one

---

[1] Author of " Hermes, or a Philosophical Enquiry concerning Universal Grammar," a work displaying much ingenuity and an extensive acquaintance with the writings of the Greek poets and philosophers.—ED.

wonders he has not by this time become a cinder." BOSWELL: " And such bellows, too. Lord Mansfield with his cheeks like to burst. Lord Chatham like an Æolus. I have read such notes from them to him as were enough to turn his head." JOHNSON: "True. When he whom everybody else flatters, flatters me, I then am truly happy." MRS THRALE: "The sentiment is in Congreve, I think." JOHNSON: "Yes, Madam, in 'The Way of the World':—

> ' If there's delight in love, 'tis when I see
> That heart which others bleed for, bleed for me.'

No, Sir, I should not be surprised though Garrick chained the ocean and lashed the winds." BOSWELL: "Should it not be, Sir, lashed the ocean and chained the winds?" JOHNSON: "No, Sir, recollect the original—

> 'In Corum atque Eurum solitus sœvire flagellis
> Barbarus, Æolio nunquam hoc in carcere passos,
> Ipsum compedibus qui vinxerat Ennosigæum.'" [1]

This does very well when both the winds and the sea are personified, and mentioned by their mythological names, as in Juvenal; but when they are mentioned in plain language, the application of the epithets suggested by me is the most obvious; and accordingly, my friend himself in his imitation of the passage which describes Xerxes, has

"The waves he lashes, and enchains the wind."[2]

The modes of living in different countries, and the various views with which men travel in quest of new scenes, having been talked of, a learned gentleman who holds a considerable office in the law, expatiated on the happiness of a savage life, and mentioned an instance of an officer who had actually lived for some time in the wilds of America, of whom, when in that state, he quoted this reflection, with an air of admiration, as if it had been deeply philosophical: "Here am I, free and unrestrained, amidst the rude magnificence of Nature, with this Indian woman by my side, and this gun, with which I can procure food when I want it: what more can be desired for human happiness?" It did not require much sagacity to foresee that such a sentiment would not be permitted to pass without due animadversion. JOHNSON: "Do not allow yourself, Sir to be imposed upon by such gross absurdity. It is sad stuff; it is brutish. If a bull could speak, he might as well exclaim,—Here am I with this cow and this grass; what being can enjoy greater felicity?"

---

[1]
> "The proud barbarian, whose impatient ire
> Chastised the winds that disobeyed his nod,
> With stripes ne'er suffered from the Æolian God,
> Fetter'd the Shaker of the sea and land."—JUV. x. 182.—GIFFORD

[2] So also Butler, Hudibras, p. ii. c. i. v. 845.

> "A Persian Emperor *whipt* his grannam,
> The *sea* his mother Venus came on."—MALONE.

We talked of the melancholy end of a gentleman who had destroyed himself. JOHNSON: "It was owing to imaginary difficulties in his affairs, which, had he talked of with any friend, would soon have vanished." BOSWELL: "Do you think, Sir, that all who commit suicide are mad?" JOHNSON: "Sir, they are often not universally disordered in their intellects, but one passion presses so upon them, that they yield to it, and commit suicide, as a passionate man will stab another." He added, "I have often thought, that after a man has taken the resolution to kill himself, it is not courage in him to do anything, however desperate, because he has nothing to fear." GOLDSMITH: "I don't see that." JOHNSON: "Nay, but my dear Sir, why should not you see what every one else sees?" GOLDSMITH: "It is for fear of something that he has resolved to kill himself: and will not that timid disposition restrain him?" JOHNSON: "It does not signify that the fear of something made him resolve; it is upon the state of his mind after the resolution is taken that I argue. Suppose a man, either from fear, or pride, or conscience, or whatever motive, has resolved to kill himself; when once the resolution is taken, he has nothing to fear. He may then go and take the King of Prussia by the nose, at the head of his army. He cannot fear the rack, who is resolved to kill himself. When Eustace Budgel was walking down to the Thames, determined to drown himself, he might, if he pleased, without any apprehension of danger, have turned aside, and first set fire to St. James's Palace."

On Tuesday, April 27, Mr. Beauclerk and I called on him in the morning. As we walked up Johnson's court, I said, "I have a veneration for this court;" and was glad to find that Beauclerk had the same reverential enthusiasm. We found him alone. We talked of Sir Andrew Stuart's elegant and plausible letters to Lord Mansfield; a copy of which had been sent by the author to Dr. Johnson. JOHNSON: "They have not answered the end. They have not been talked of; I have never heard of them. This is owing to their not being sold. People seldom read a book which is given to them; and few are given. The way to spread a work is to sell it at a low price. No man will send to buy a thing that costs even sixpence without an intention to read it." BOSWELL: "May it not be doubted, Sir, whether it be proper to publish letters, arraigning the ultimate decision of an important cause by the supreme judicature of the nation?" JOHNSON: "No, Sir, I do not think it was wrong to publish these letters. If they are thought to do harm, why not answer them? But they will do no harm, if Mr. Douglas be indeed the son of Lady Jane he cannot be hurt; if he be not her son, and yet has the great estate of the family of Douglas, he may well submit to have a pamphlet against him by Andrew Stuart. Sir, I think such a publication does good, as it does good to show us the possibilities of human life. And, Sir, you will not say that the Douglas cause was a cause of easy decision, when it divided your court as much as it could do, to be determined at all. When your judges are seven and seven, the casting vote of the president must be given on one side or other no matter, for my argument, on which; one or the other *must* be taken; as when I am to move, there is no matter which leg I move first. And then, Sir, it was otherwise determined here. No, Sir, a more dubious determination of any question cannot be imagined."[1]

He said, "Goldsmith should not be for ever attempting to shine in conversation: he has not temper for it, he is so much mortified when he fails. Sir, a game of jokes is composed partly of skill, partly of chance, a man may be beat at times by one who has not the tenth part of his wit. Now Goldsmith's putting himself against another, is like a man laying a hundred to one who cannot spare the hundred. It is not worth a man's while. A man should not lay a hundred to one, unless he can easily spare it, though he has a hundred chances for him: he can get but a guinea, and he may lose a hundred. Goldsmith is in this state. When he contends, if he gets the better, it is a very little addition to a man of his literary reputation: if he does not get the better, he is miserably vexed."

Johnson's own superlative powers of wit set him above any risk of such uneasiness. Garrick had remarked to me of him, a few days before, "Rabelais and all other wits are nothing compared with him. You may be diverted by them; but Johnson gives you a forcible hug, and shakes laughter out of you whether you will or no."

Goldsmith, however, was often very fortunate in his witty contests, even when he entered the lists with Johnson himself. Sir Joshua Reynolds was in company with them one day, when Goldsmith said, that he thought he could write a good fable, mentioned the simplicity which that kind of composition requires, and observed, that in most fables the animals introduced seldom talk in character. "For instance," said he, "the fable of the little fishes, who saw birds fly over their heads, and envying them, petitioned Jupiter to be changed into birds. The skill," continued he, "consists in making them talk like little fishes." While he indulged himself in this fanciful reverie, he observed Johnson shaking his sides, and laughing. Upon which he smartly proceeded, "Why, Dr. Johnson, this is not so easy as you seem to think; for if you were to make little fishes talk, they would talk like WHALES."

Johnson, though remarkable for his great variety of composition, never exercised his talents in fable, except we allow his beautiful tale published in Mrs. Williams's Miscellanies to be of that species. I have,

---

[1] I regretted that Dr. Johnson never took the trouble to study a question which interested nations. He would not even read a pamphlet which I wrote upon it, entitled "The Essence of the Douglas Cause;" which, I have reason to flatter myself, had considerable effect in favour of Mr. Douglas; of whose legitimate filiation I was then, and am still, firmly convinced. Let me add, that no fact can be more respectably ascertained than by the judgment of the most august tribunal in the world; a judgment in which Lord Mansfield and Lord Camden united in 1769, and from which only five of a numerous body entered a protest.—BOSWELL

however, found among his manuscript collections the following sketch of one :—

" Glow-worm [1] lying in the garden saw a candle in a neighbouring palace, and complained of the littleness of his own light. Another observed—Wait a little—soon dark,—have outlasted πολλ [*many*] of these glaring lights which are only brighter as they haste to nothing."

On Thursday, April 29, I dined with him at General Oglethorpe's, where were Sir Joshua Reynolds, Mr. Langton, Dr. Goldsmith, and Mr. Thrale. I was very desirous to get Dr. Johnson absolutely fixed in his resolution to go with me to the Hebrides this year ; and I told him that I had received a letter from Dr. Robertson, the historian, upon the subject, with which he was much pleased, and now talked in such a manner of his long intended tour, that I was satisfied he meant to fulfil his engagement.

The custom of eating dogs at Otaheite being mentioned, Goldsmith observed, that this was also a custom in China : that a dog-butcher is as common there as any other butcher ; and that when he walks abroad all the dogs fall on him. JOHNSON : " That is not owing to his killing dogs, Sir. I remember a butcher at Lichfield, whom a dog that was in the house where I lived, always attacked. It is the smell of carnage which provokes this, let the animals he has killed be what they may." GOLDSMITH : " Yes, there is a general abhorrence in animals at the signs of massacre. If you put a tub full of blood into a stable, the horses are like to go mad." JOHNSON : " I doubt that." GOLDSMITH : " Nay, Sir, it is a fact well authenticated." THRALE : " You had better prove it before you put it into your book on natural history. You may do it in my stable if you will." JOHNSON : " Nay, Sir, I would not have him prove it. If he is content to take his information from others, he may get through his book with little trouble, and without much endangering his reputation. But if he makes experiments for so comprehensive a book as his, there would be no end to them ; his erroneous assertions would then fall upon himself ; and he might be blamed for not having made experiments as to every particular."

The character of Mallet having been introduced, and spoken of slightingly by Goldsmith. JOHNSON : " Why, Sir, Mallet had talent enough to keep his literary reputation alive as long as he himself lived ; and that, let me tell you, is a good deal." GOLDSMITH : " But I cannot agree that it was so. His literary reputation was dead long before his natural death. I consider an author's literary reputation to be alive only while his name will ensure a good price for his copy from the book-sellers. I will get you (to Johnson), a hundred guineas for anything whatever that you shall write, if you put your name to it."

---

[1] It has already been observed, that one of his first essays was a Latin poem on a glow-worm ; but whether it be anywhere extant has not been ascertained.—MALONE.

Dr. Goldsmith's new play, " She Stoops to Conquer," being mentioned—Johnson : " I know of no comedy for many years that has so much exhilarated an audience, that has answered so much the great end of comedy—making an audience merry."

Goldsmith having said, that Garrick's compliment to the Queen, which he introduced into the play of " The Chances," which he had altered and revised this year, was mean and gross flattery. Johnson : " Why, Sir, I would not *write*, I would not give solemnly under my hand, a character beyond what I thought really true ; but a speech on the stage, let it flatter ever so extravagantly, is formular. It has always been formular to flatter kings and queens ; so much so, that even in our church-service we have ' our most religious king,' used indiscriminately, whoever is king. Nay, they even flatter themselves— ' we have been graciously pleased to grant.' No modern flattery, however, is so gross as that of the Augustan age, where the emperor was deified. ' *Præsens Divus habebitur Augustus.*' And as to meanness (rising into warmth), how is it mean in a player—a showman—a fellow who exhibits himself for a shilling, to flatter his queen ? The attempt, indeed, was dangerous ; for if it had missed, what became of Garrick, and what became of the queen ? As Sir William Temple says of a great general, it is necessary not only that his designs be formed in a masterly manner, but that they should be attended with success. Sir, it is right, at a time when the royal family is not generally liked, to let it be seen that the people like at least one of them." Sir Joshua Reynolds : " I do not perceive why the profession of a player should be despised ; for the great and ultimate end of all the employments of mankind is to produce amusement. Garrick produces more amusement than any body." Boswell : " You say, Dr. Johnson, that Garrick exhibits himself for a shilling. In this respect he is only on a footing with a lawyer who exhibits himself for his fee, and even will maintain any nonsense or absurdity, if the case require it. Garrick refuses a play or a part which he does not like : a lawyer never refuses." Johnson : " Why Sir, what does this prove ? only that a lawyer is worse. Boswell is now like Jack in the ' Tale of a Tub,' who, when he is puzzled by an argument, hangs himself. He thinks I shall cut him down, but I'll let him hang" (laughing vociferously). Sir Joshua Reynolds : " Mr. Boswell thinks that the profession of a lawyer being unquestionably honourable, if he can show the profession of a player to be more honourable, he proves his argument."

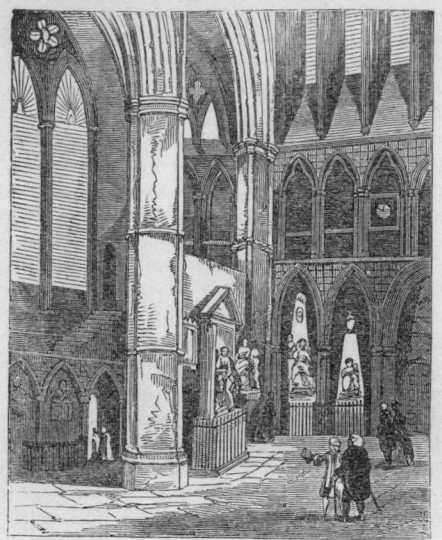

POETS' CORNER, WESTMINSTER ABBEY

CHAPTER VII.—1773.

DINNER AT BEAUCLERK'S—JOHNSON CRITICISES GOLDSMITH'S ABILITIES AS A WRITER—
BOSWELL ELECTED A MEMBER OF "THE CLUB"—MONUMENTS TO EMINENT PERSONS—
"THE WHOLE DUTY OF MAN"—JOHNSON'S OBSERVATIONS ON PUNNING—LAY PATRONAGE
—SOUTH SEA DISCOVERIES—REASONING OF BRUTES—TOLERATION AND MARTYRDOM—
JOHNSON EXCITES THE ANGER OF GOLDSMITH—DOCTRINE OF THE TRINITY—RECON-
CILIATION WITH "GOLDY"—LITERARY PROPERTY—LUDICROUS MERRIMENT OF JOHNSON.

ON Friday, April 30, I dined with him at Mr. Beauclerk's, where
were Lord Charlemont, Sir Joshua Reynolds, and some more
members of the LITERARY CLUB, whom he had obligingly invited to
meet me, as I was this evening to be balloted for as candidate for
admission into that distinguished society. Johnson had done me the
honour to propose me, and Beauclerk was very zealous for me.

Goldsmith being mentioned, JOHNSON: "It is amazing how little
Goldsmith knows. He seldom comes where he is not more ignorant
than any one else." SIR JOSHUA REYNOLDS: "Yet there is no man
whose company is more liked." JOHNSON: "To be sure, Sir. When
people find a man of the most distinguished abilities as a writer, their

inferior while he is with them, it must be highly gratifying to them. What Goldsmith comically says of himself is very true—he always gets the better when he argues alone ; meaning, that he is master of a subject in his study, and can write well upon it ; but when he comes into company, grows confused, and unable to talk. Take him as a poet, his 'Traveller' is a very fine performance ; aye, and so is his 'Deserted Village,' were it not sometimes too much the echo of his 'Traveller.' Whether, indeed, we take him as a poet, as a comic writer, or as an historian, he stands in the first class." BOSWELL : "An historian ? My dear Sir, you surely will not rank his compilation of the Roman History with the works of other historians of this age ? " JOHNSON : " Why, who are before him ? " BOSWELL : " Hume, Robertson, Lord Lyttleton." JOHNSON (his antipathy to the Scotch beginning to rise) : " I have not read Hume ; but, doubtless, Goldsmith's history is better than the *verbiage* of Robertson, or the foppery of Dalrymple." BOSWELL : " Will you not admit the superiority of Robertson, in whose history we find such penetration—such painting ? " JOHNSON : " Sir, you must consider how that penetration and that painting are employed. It is not history, it is imagination. He who describes what he never saw, draws from fancy. Robertson paints minds as Sir Joshua paints faces in a history piece : he imagines an heroic countenance. You must look upon Robertson's work as romance, and try it by that standard. History it is not. Besides, Sir, it is the great excellence of a writer to put into his book as much as his book will hold. Goldsmith has done this in his history. Now, Robertson might have put twice as much into his book. Robertson is like a man who has packed gold in wool ; the wool takes up more room than the gold. No, Sir ; I always thought Robertson would be crushed by his own weight—would be buried under his own ornaments. Goldsmith tells you shortly all you want to know : Robertson detains you a great deal too long. No man will read Robertson's cumbrous detail a second time ; but Goldsmith's plain narrative will please again and again. I would say to Robertson what an old tutor of a college said to one of his pupils : ' Read over your compositions, and wherever you meet with a passage which you think is particularly fine, strike it out.' Goldsmith's abridgment is better than that of Lucius Florus or Eutropius ; and I will venture to say, that if you compare him with Vertot, in the same places of the Roman History, you will find that he excels Vertot. Sir, he has the art of compiling, and of saying every thing he has to say in a pleasing manner. He is now writing a Natural History, and he will make it as entertaining as a Persian Tale."

I cannot dismiss the present topic without observing, that it is probable that Dr. Johnson, who owned that he often " talked for victory," rather urged plausible objections to Dr. Robertson's excellent historical works, in the ardour of contest, than expressed his real and decided opinion ; for it is not easy to suppose, that he should so widely differ from the rest of the literary world.

JOHNSON : " I remember once being with Goldsmith in Westminster Abbey. While we surveyed the Poets'Corner, I said to him,

' Forsitan et nostrum nomen miscebitur istis,[1]

When we got to Temple-bar, he stopped me, pointed to the heads upon it, and slily whispered me,

' Forsitan et nostrum nomen miscebitur ISTIS.' "[2]

Johnson praised John Bunyan highly : " His 'Pilgrim's Progress ' has great merit, both for invention, imagination, and the conduct of the story ; and it has had the best evidence of its merit, the general and continued approbation of mankind. Few books, I believe, have had a more extensive sale. It is remarkable, that it begins very much like the poem of Dante ; yet there was no translation of Dante when Bunyan wrote. There is reason to think that he had read Spenser."

A proposition which had been agitated, that monuments to eminent persons should, for the time to come, be erected in St. Paul's church as well as in Westminster Abbey, was mentioned ; and it was asked who should be honoured by having his monument first erected there. Somebody suggested Pope. JOHNSON : " Why, Sir, as Pope was a Roman Catholic, I would not have his to be first. I think Milton's rather should have the precedence.[3] I think more highly of him now than I did at twenty. There is more thinking in him and in Butler, than in any of our poets."

Some of the company expressed a wonder why the author of so excellent a book as " The Whole Duty of Man," should conceal himself.[4] JOHNSON : " There may be different reasons assigned for this, any one of which would be very sufficient. He may have been a clergyman, and may have thought that his religious counsels would have less weight when known to come from a man whose profession was theology. He may have been a man whose practice was not suitable to his principles, so that his character might injure the effect of his book, which he had written in a season of penitence. Or he may have been a man of rigid self-denial, so that he would have no reward for his pious labours while in this world, but refer it all to a future state."

The gentlemen went away to their club, and I was left at Beauclerk's

---

[1] Our name, perhaps, may be mixed with theirs. OVID. de Art. Amand. i. iii. v. 13.

[2] In allusion to Dr. Johnson's supposed political principles, and perhaps his own. BOSWELL.

[3] Here is another instance of his high admiration of Milton as a Poet, notwithstanding his just abhorrence of that sour Republican's political principles. His candour and discrimination are equally conspicuous. Let us hear no more of his "injustice to Milton."—BOSWELL.

[4] In a manuscript in the Bodleian Library several circumstances are stated which strongly incline me to believe that Dr. Accepted Frewen, Archbishop of York, was the author of this work.—MALONE

till the fate of my election should be announced to me. I sat in a state of anxiety which even the charming conversation of Lady Di Beauclerk could not entirely dissipate. In a short time I received the agreeable intelligence that I was chosen. I hastened to the place of meeting, and was introduced to such a society as can seldom be found. Mr. Edmund Burke, whom I then saw for the first time, and whose splendid talents had long made me ardently wish for his acquaintance ; Dr. Nugent, Mr. Garrick, Dr. Goldsmith, Mr. (afterwards Sir William) Jones, and the company with whom I had dined. Upon my entrance, Johnson placed himself behind a chair, on which he leaned as on a desk or pulpit, and with humourous formality gave me a *Charge*, pointing out the conduct expected from me as a good member of this club.

Goldsmith produced some very absurd verses which had been publicly recited to an audience for money. JOHNSON : " I can match this nonsense. There was a poem called ' Eugenio,' which came out some years ago, and concludes thus :—

> ' And now, ye trifling, self-assuming elves,
> Brimful of pride, of nothing, of yourselves,
> Survey Eugenio, view him o'er and o'er,
> Then sink into yourselves, and be no more.[1]

Nay, Dryden, in his poem on the Royal Society, has these lines :—

> ' Then we upon our globe's last verge shall go,
> And see the ocean leaning on the sky ;
> From thence our rolling neighbours we shall know,
> And on the lunar world securely pry.' "

Talking of puns, Johnson, who had a great contempt for that species of wit, deigned to allow that there was one good pun in " Menagiana " I think on the words *corps*.[2]

---

[1] Dr. Johnson's memory here was not perfectly accurate : "Eugenio" does not conclude thus. There are eight more lines after the last of those quoted by him; and the passage which he meant to recite is as follows :—

> "Say now, ye fluttering, poor assuming elves,
> Stark full of pride, of folly, of—yourselves ;
> Say, where's the wretch of all your impious crew
> Who dares confront his character to view ?
> Behold Eugenio, view him o'er and o'er,
> Then sink into yourselves, and be no more."

Mr. Reed informs me that the Author of Eugenio, Thomas Beech, a wine merchant at Wrexham, in Denbighshire, soon after its publication, viz. 17th May, 1737, cut his own throat; and that it appears by Swift's works, that the poem had been shown to him, and received some of his corrections. Johnson had read "Eugenio" on his first coming to town, for we see it mentioned in one of his letters to Mr. Cave, which has been inserted in this work.— BOSWELL.

[2] I formerly thought that I had perhaps mistaken the word, and imagined it to be *Corps*, from its similarity of sound to the real one. For an accurate and shrewd unknown gentleman, to whom I am indebted for some remarks on my work, observes on this passage—" Q. if not on the word, *Fort*? A vociferous French preacher said of Bourdaloue, ' Il prêche *fort bien*, et moi *bien fort*.'" Menagiana. See also " Anecdotes Littéraires " Article Bourdaloue. But my

Much pleasant conversation passed, which Johnson relished with great good humour. But his conversation alone, or what led to it, or was interwoven with it, is the business of this work.

On Saturday, May 1, we dined by ourselves at our old rendezvous, the Mitre tavern. He was placid, but not much disposed to talk. He observed, that " The Irish mix better with the English than the Scotch do ; their language is nearer to English ; as a proof of which, they succeed very well as players, which Scotchmen do not. Then, Sir, they have not that extreme nationality which we find in the Scotch. I will do you, Boswell, the justice to say, that you are the most *unscotchified* of your countrymen. You are almost the only instance of a Scotchman that I have known, who did not at every other sentence bring in some other Scotchman."

We drank tea with Mrs. Williams. I introduced a question which has been much agitated in the Church of Scotland, whether the claim of lay-patrons to present ministers to parishes be well founded ; and supposing it to be well founded, whether it ought to be exercised without the concurrence of the people ? That Church is composed of a series of judicatures ;—a Presbytery ; a Synod ; and finally, a General Assembly ; before all of which, this matter may be contended : and in some cases the Presbytery having refused to induct or *settle*, as they call it, the person presented by the patron, it has been found necessary to appeal to the General Assembly. He said, I might see the subject well treated in " The Defence of Pluralities ; " and although he thought that a patron should exercise his right with tenderness to the inclinations of the people of a parish, he was very clear as to his right. Then supposing the question to be pleaded before the General Assembly, he dictated to me what follows :—

" Against the right of patrons is commonly opposed, by the inferior judicatures, the plea of conscience. Their conscience tells them, that the people ought to choose their pastor ; their conscience tells them, that they ought not to impose upon a congregation a minister ungrateful and unacceptable to his auditors. Conscience is nothing more than a conviction felt by ourselves of something to be done, or something to be avoided ; and in questions of simple unperplexed morality, conscience is very often a guide that may be trusted. But before conscience can determine, the state of the question is supposed to be completely known. In questions of law, or of fact, conscience is very often confounded with opinion. No man's conscience can tell him the right of another

ingenious and obliging correspondent, Mr. Abercrombie, of Philadelphia, has pointed out to me the following passage in " Menagiana ; " which renders the preceding conjecture unnecessary, and confirms my original statement :

" Madame de Bourdonne, Chanoinesse de Remiremont, venoit d'entendre un discours plein de feu et d'esprit, mais fort peu solide, et tres irregulier. Une de ses amies, qui y prenoit intêret pour l'orateur, lui dit en sortant, ' Eh bien, Madame, que vous semble-t-il de ce que vous venez d'entendre ? Qu'il y a d'esprit ? '—' Il y a tant,' repondit Madame de Bourdonne, ' que, je n'y ai pas vû de *corps*.' " Menagiana, tome ii. p. 64. Amsterd. 1713.—BOSWELL.

man; they must be known by rational investigation, or historical inquiry. Opinion, which he that holds it may call his conscience, may teach some men that religion would be promoted, and quiet preserved by granting to the people universally the choice of their ministers. But it is a conscience very ill informed that violates the rights of one man, for the convenience of another. Religion cannot be promoted by injustice; and it was never yet found that a popular election was very quietly transacted.

" That justice would be violated by transferring to the people the right of patronage, is apparent to all who know whence that right had its original. The right of patronage was not at first a privilege torn by power from unresisting poverty. It is not an authority at first usurped in times of ignorance, and established only by succession and by precedents. It is not a grant capriciously made from a higher tyrant to a lower. It is a right dearly purchased by the first possessors, and justly inherited by those that succeeded them. When Christianity was established in this island, a regular mode of public worship was prescribed. Public worship requires a public place; and the proprietors of lands, as they were converted, built churches for their families and their vassals. For the maintenance of ministers, they settled a certain portion of their lands; and a district through which each minister was required to extend his care, was, by that circumscription, constituted a parish. This is a position so generally received in England, that the extent of a manor and of a parish are regularly received for each other. The churches which the proprietors of lands had thus built and thus endowed, they justly thought themselves entitled to provide with ministers; and where the episcopal government prevails the Bishop has no power to reject a man nominated by the patron, but for some crime that might exclude him from the priesthood. For the endowment of the church being the gift of the landlord, he was consequently at liberty to give it according to his choice, to any man capable of performing the holy offices. The people did not choose him because the people did not pay him.

" We hear it sometimes urged, that this original right is passed out of memory, and is obliterated and obscured by many translations of property and changes of government; that scarce any church is now in the hands of the heirs of the builders; and that the present persons have entered subsequently upon the pretended rights by a thousand accidental and unknown causes. Much of this, perhaps, is true. But how is the right of patronage extinguished? If the right followed the lands, it is possessed by the same equity by which the lands are possessed. It is, in effect, part of the manor, and protected by the same laws with every other privilege. Let us suppose an estate forfeited by treason, and granted by the Crown to a new family. With the lands were forfeited all the rights appendant to those lands; by the same power that grants the lands, the rights also are granted. The right lost by the patron falls not to the people, but is either retained by the Crown, or what to the people is the same thing, is by the Crown given away. Let it change hands ever so often, it is possessed by him that receives it with the same right as it was conveyed. It may, indeed, like all our possessions, be forcibly seized or fraudulently obtained ⋅ but no injury is still done to the people; for what they never had, they have never lost. Caius may usurp the right of Titius, but neither Caius nor Titius injures the people; and no man's conscience, however tender or however active, can prompt him to restore what may be proved to have never been taken away. Supposing, what I think cannot be proved, that a popular election of ministers were to be desired, our desires are not the measures of equity. It were to be desired that power should be only in the hands of the merciful, and riches in the possession of the generous; but the law must leave both riches and power where it finds them; and must often leave riches with the covetous, and power with the cruel. Convenience may be a rule in little things, where no other rule has been established. But as the great end of government is to give every man his own, no inconvenience is greater than that of making right uncertain. Nor is any man more an enemy to public peace, than he who fills weak heads with imaginary claims, and breaks the series of civil subordination, by inciting the lower classes of mankind to encroach upon the higher.

"Having thus shown that the right of patronage, being originally purchased, may be legally transferred, and that it is now in the hands of lawful possessors, at least as certainly as any other right;—we have left to the advocates of the people no other plea than that of convenience. Let us, therefore, now consider what the people would really gain by a general abolition of the right of patronage. What is most to be desired by such a change is, that the country should be supplied with better ministers. But why should we suppose that the parish will make a wiser choice than the patron? If we suppose mankind actuated by interest, the patron is more likely to choose with caution, because he will suffer more by choosing wrong. By the deficiencies of his minister, or by his vices, he is equally offended with the rest of the congregation; but he will have this reason more to lament them, that they will be imputed to his absurdity or corruption. The qualifications of a minister are well known to be learning and piety. Of his learning the patron is probably the only judge in the parish, and of his piety not less a judge than others; and is more likely to inquire minutely and dili-gently before he gives a presentation, than one of the parochial rabble, who can give nothing but a vote. It may be urged, that though the parish might not choose better ministers, they would at least choose ministers whom they like better, and who therefore officiate with greater efficacy. That ignorance and perverseness should always obtain what they like, was never considered as the end of government; of which it is the great and standing benefit, that the wise see for the simple, and the regular act for the capricious. But that this argu-ment supposes the people capable of judging, and resolute to act according to their best judgments, though this be sufficiently absurd, it is not all his absurdity. It supposes not only wisdom, but unanimity in those, who upon no other occa-sions are unanimous or wise. If by some strange concurrence all the voices of a parish should unite in the choice of any single man, though I could not charge the patron with injustice in presenting a minister, I should censure him as unkind and injudicious. But, it is evident, that as in all other popular elections, there will be contrariety of judgment and acrimony of passion, a parish upon every vacancy would break into factions, and the contest for the choice of a minister would set neighbours at variance, and bring discord into families. The minister would be taught all the arts of a candidate, would flatter some, and bribe others; and the electors, as in all other cases, would call for holidays and ale, and break the heads of each other during the jollity of the canvass. The time must, however, come at last, when one of the factions must prevail, and one of the ministers get possession of the church. On what terms does he enter upon his ministry but those of enmity with half his parish ? By what prudence or what diligence can he hope to conciliate the affections of that party by whose defeat he has obtained his living ? Every man who voted against him will enter the church with hanging head and downcast eyes, afraid to encounter that neighbour by whose vote and influence he has been overpowered. He will hate his neighbour for opposing him, and his minister for having prospered by the opposition ; and as he will never see him but with pain, he will never see him but with hatred. Of a minister presented by the patron, the parish has seldom any thing worse to say than that they do not know him. Of a minister chosen by a popular contest, all those who do not favour him, have nursed up in their bosoms principles of hatred and reasons of rejection. Anger is excited principally by pride. The pride of a common man is very little exasperated by the supposed usurpation of an acknowledged superior. He bears only his little share of a general evil, and suffers in common with the whole parish ; but when the contest is between equals, the defeat has many aggravations ; and he that is defeated by his next neighbour, is seldom satisfied without some revenge : and it is hard to say what bitterness of malignity would prevail in a parish where these elections should happen to be frequent, and the enmity of opposition should be re-kindled before it had cooled."

Though I present to my readers Dr. Johnson's masterly thoughts on the subject, I think it proper to declare that, notwithstanding I am myself a lay-patron, I do not entirely subscribe to his opinion.

On Friday, May 7, I breakfasted with him at Mr. Thrale's, in the Borough. While we were alone, I endeavoured as well as I could to apologise for a lady who had been divorced from her husband by act of Parliament. I said that he had used her very ill, had behaved brutally to her, and that she could not continue to live with him without having her delicacy contaminated ; that all affection for him was thus destroyed ; that the essence of conjugal union being gone, there remained only a cold form, a mere civil obligation ; that she was in the prime of life, with qualities to produce happiness ; that these ought not to be lost ; and, that the gentleman on whose account she was divorced had gained her heart while thus unhappily situated. Seduced, perhaps, by the charms of the lady in question, I thus attempted to palliate what I was sensible could not be justified ; for when I had finished my harangue, my venerable friend gave me a proper check : " My dear Sir, never accustom your mind to mingle virtue and vice. The woman's a whore, and there's an end on't."

He described the father of one of his friends thus : " Sir, he was so exuberant a talker at public meetings, that the gentlemen of his county were afraid of him. No business could be done for his declamation."

He did not give me full credit when I mentioned that I had carried on a short conversation by signs with some Esquimaux, who were then in London, particularly with one of them who was a priest. He thought I could not make them understand me. No man was more incredulous as to particular facts, which were at all extraordinary ; and therefore no man was more scrupulously inquisitive, in order to discover the truth.

I dined with him this day at the house of my friends, Messrs. Edward and Charles Dilly, booksellers in the Poultry : there were present, their elder brother, Mr. Dilly, of Bedfordshire, Dr. Goldsmith, Mr. Langton, Mr. Claxton, Reverend Dr. Mayo, a dissenting minister, the Reverend Mr. Toplady, and my friend the Reverend Mr. Temple.

Hawkesworth's compilation of the voyages to the South Sea being mentioned :—JOHNSON : " Sir, if you talk of it as a subject of commerce, it will be gainful ; if as a book that is to increase human knowledge, I believe there will not be much of that. Hawkesworth can tell only what the voyagers have told him ; and they have found very little, only one new animal, I think." BOSWELL : " But many insects, Sir." JOHNSON : " Why, Sir, as to insects, Ray reckons of British insects twenty thousand species. They might have stayed at home and discovered enough in that way."

Talking of birds, I mentioned Mr. Daines Barrington's ingenious essay against the received notion of their migration. JOHNSON : " I think we have as good evidence for the migration of woodcocks as can be desired. We find they disappear at a certain time of the year, and appear again at a certain time of the year ; and some of them, when weary in their flight, have been known to alight on the rigging of ships far out at sea." One of the company observed, that there had been instances of some of them found in summer in Essex. JOHNSON : " Sir, that strengthens our argument. *Exceptio probat regulam.* Some being found, shows that, if all remained, many would be found. A few sick or lame ones may be found." GOLDSMITH : " There is a partial migration of the swallows ; the stronger ones migrate, the others do not."

BOSWELL : " I am well assured that the people of Otaheite, who have the bread tree, the fruit of which serves them for bread, laughed heartily when they were informed of the tedious process necessary with us to have bread—ploughing, sowing, harrowing, reaping, threshing, grinding, baking." JOHNSON : " Why, Sir, all ignorant savages will laugh when they are told of the advantages of civilised life. Were you to tell men who live without houses, how we pile brick upon brick, and rafter upon rafter, and then after a house is raised to a certain height, a man tumbles off a scaffold, and breaks his neck ; he would laugh heartily at our folly in building ; but it does not follow that men are better without houses. No, Sir (holding up a slice of a good loaf), this is better than the bread tree."

He repeated an argument which is to be found in his " Rambler " against the notion that the brute creation is endowed with the faculty of reason : " Birds build by instinct ; they never improve ; they build their first nest as well as any one they ever build." GOLDSMITH : " Yet we see if you take away a bird's nest with the eggs in it, she will make a slighter nest and lay again." JOHNSON : "Sir, that is because at first she has full time and makes her nest deliberately. In the case you mention she is pressed to lay, and must therefore make her nest quickly and consequently it will be slight." GOLDSMITH : "The nidification of birds is what is least known in natural history, though one of the most curious things in it."

I introduced the subject of toleration. JOHNSON : "Every society has a right to preserve public peace and order, and therefore has a good right to prohibit the propagation of opinions which have a dangerous tendency. To say the *magistrate* has this right, is using an inadequate word ; it is the *society* for which the magistrate is agent. He may be morally or theologically wrong in restraining the propagation of opinions which he thinks dangerous, but he is politically right." MAYO: "I am of opinion, Sir, that every man is entitled to liberty of conscience in religion ; and that the magistrate cannot restrain that right." JOHNSON : "Sir, I agree with you. Every man has a right to liberty of conscience, and with that the magistrate cannot interfere. People confound liberty of thinking with liberty of talking ; nay, with liberty of preaching. Every man has a physical right to think as he pleases ; for it cannot be discovered how he thinks. He has not a moral right, for he ought to inform himself, and think justly. But, Sir, no member of a society has a right to *teach* any doctrine contrary to what the society holds to be true. The magistrate, I say, may be wrong in what he thinks ; but while he thinks himself right, he may and ought to enforce what he thinks." MAYO : "Then, Sir, we are to remain always in error, and truth never can prevail ; and the magistrate was right in persecuting the first Christians." JOHNSON : "Sir, the only method by which religious truth can be established is by martyrdom. The magistrate has a right to enforce what he thinks ; and he who is conscious of the truth has a right to suffer. I am afraid there is no other way of ascertaining the truth but by persecution on the one hand and enduring it on the other." GOLDSMITH : "But how is a man to act, Sir ? Though firmly convinced of the truth of his doctrine, may he not think it wrong to expose himself to persecution ? Has he a right to do so? Is it not, as it were, committing voluntary suicide ? " JOHNSON : "Sir, as to voluntary suicide, as you call it, there are twenty thousand men in an army, who will go without scruple to be shot at, and mount a breach for fivepence a day." GOLDSMITH : "But have they a moral right to do this ? " JOHNSON : "Nay, Sir, if you will not take the universal opinion of mankind, I have nothing to say. If mankind cannot defend their own way of thinking, I cannot defend it. Sir, if a man is in doubt whether it would be better for him to expose himself to martyrdom or not, he should not do it. He must be convinced that he has a delegation from Heaven." GOLDSMITH : "I would consider whether there is the greater chance of good or evil upon the whole. If I see a man who has fallen into a well, I would wish to help him out :

but if there is a greater probability that he shall pull me in, than that I shall pull him out, I would not attempt it. So were I to go to Turkey, I might wish to convert the Grand Signor to the Christian faith ; but when I considered that I should probably be put to death without effectuating my purpose in any degree, I should keep myself quiet." JOHNSON : " Sir, you must consider that we have perfect and imperfect obligations. Perfect obligations, which are generally not to do something, are clear and positive ; as, ' Thou shalt not kill.' But charity, for instance, is not definable by limits. It is a duty to give to the poor ; but no man can say how much another should give to the poor, or when a man has given too little to save his soul. In the same manner it is a duty to instruct the ignorant, and of consequence to convert infidels to Christianity ; but no man in the common course of things is obliged to carry this to such a degree as to incur the danger of martyrdom, as no man is obliged to strip himself to the shirt, in order to give charity. I have said that a man must be persuaded that he has a particular delegation from Heaven." GOLDSMITH : " How is this to be known ? Our first reformers, who were burnt for not believing bread and wine to be CHRIST—" JOHNSON (interrupting him) : " Sir, they were not burnt for not believing bread and wine to be CHRIST, but for insulting those who did believe it. And, Sir, when the first reformers began, they did not intend to be martyred ; as many of them ran away as could." BOSWELL : " But, Sir, there was your countryman Elwal, who, you told me, challenged King George with his black-guards and his red-guards." JOHNSON : " My countryman Elwal, Sir, should have been put in the stocks—a proper pulpit for him ; and he'd have had a numerous audience. A man who preaches in the stocks will always have hearers enough." BOSWELL : " But Elwal thought himself in the right." JOHNSON : " We are not providing for mad people ; there are places for them in the neighbourhood " (meaning Moorfields.) MAYO : " But, Sir, is it not very hard that I should not be allowed to teach my children what I really believe to be the truth ? " JOHNSON : " Why, Sir, you might contrive to teach your children *extrà scandalum ;* but, Sir, the magistrate, if he knows it, has a right to restrain you. Suppose you teach your children to be thieves ? " MAYO : " This is making a joke of the subject." JOHNSON : " Nay, Sir, take it thus,—that you teach them the community of goods ; for which there are as many plausible arguments as for most erroneous doctrines. You teach them that all things at first were in common, and that no man had a right to anything but as he laid his hands upon it ; and that this still is, or ought to be, the rule amongst mankind. Here, Sir, you sap a great principle in society —property. And don't you think the magistrate would have a right to prevent you ? Or, suppose you should teach your children the notion of the Adamites, and they should run naked into the streets, would not the magistrate have a right to flog 'em into their doublets ? " MAYO

"I think the magistrate has no right to interfere till there is some overt act." BOSWELL : " So, Sir, though he sees an enemy to the state charging a blunderbuss, he is not to interfere till it is fired off ! " MAYO : " He must be sure of its direction against the state." JOHNSON : "The magistrate is to judge of that. He has no right to restrain your thinking, because the evil centres in yourself. If a man were sitting at this table, and chopping off his fingers, the magistrate as guardian of the community, has no authority to restrain him, however he might do it from kindness as a parent. Though, indeed, upon more consideration, I think he may ; as it is probable, that he who is chopping off his own fingers, may soon proceed to chop off those of other people. If I think it right to steal Mr. Dilly's plate, I am a bad man ; but he can say nothing to me. If I make an open declaration that I think so, he will keep me out of his house. If I put forth my hand, I shall be sent to Newgate. This is the gradation of thinking, preaching, and acting ; if a man thinks erroneously, he may keep his thoughts to himself, and nobody will trouble him ; if he preaches erroneous doctrine, society may expel him ; if he acts in consequence of it, the law takes place, and he is hanged." MAYO : " But, Sir, ought not Christians to have liberty of conscience ? " JOHNSON : " I have already told you so, Sir. You are coming back to where you were." BOSWELL : " Dr. Mayo is always taking a return post-chaise, and going the stage over again. He has it at half-price." JOHNSON : " Dr. Mayo, like other champions for un-limited toleration, has got a set of words.[1] Sir, it is no matter, politically, whether the magistrate be right or wrong. Suppose a club were to be formed, to drink confusion to King George the Third, and a happy restoration to Charles the Third ; this would be very bad with respect to the state ; but every member of that club must either conform to its rules, or be turned out of it. Old Baxter, I remember, maintains that the magistrate should ' tolerate all things that are tolerable.' This is no good definition of toleration upon any principle ; but it shows that he thought some things were not tolerable." TOPLADY : " Sir, you have untwisted this difficult subject with great dexterity."

During this argument, Goldsmith sat in restless agitation, from a wish to get in and *shine.* Finding himself excluded, he had taken his hat to go away, but remained for some time with it in his hand, like a gamester, who, at the close of a long night lingers for a little while, to see if he can have a favourable opening to finish with success. Once when he was begin-ning to speak, he found himself overpowered by the loud voice of Johnson, who was at the opposite end of the table, and did not perceive Goldsmith's attempt. Thus disappointed of his wish to obtain the

[1] Dr. Mayo's calm temper and steady perseverance rendered him an admirable subject for the exercise of Dr. Johnson's powerful abilities. He never flinched : but, after reiterated blows, remained seemingly unmoved as at the first. The scintillations of Johnson's genius flashed every time he was struck, without his receiving any injury. Hence he obtained the epithet of THE LITERARY ANVIL.—BOSWELL

attention of the company, Goldsmith in a passion threw down his hat, looking angrily at Johnson, and exclaimed in a bitter tone, " *Take it.*" When Toplady was going to speak, Johnson uttered some sound, which led Goldsmith to think that he was beginning again, and taking the words from Toplady. Upon which, he seized this opportunity of venting his own envy and spleen, under the pretext of supporting another person: " Sir," said he, to Johnson, "the gentleman has heard you patiently for an hour; pray allow us now to hear him." JOHNSON (sternly): " Sir, I was not interrupting the gentleman. I was only giving him a signal of my attention. Sir, you are impertinent." Goldsmith made no reply, but continued in the company for some time.

A gentleman present ventured to ask Dr. Johnson if there was not a material difference as to toleration of opinions which lead to action, and opinions merely speculative; for instance, would it be wrong in the magistrate to tolerate those who preach against the doctrine of the TRINITY? Johnson was highly offended, and said, " I wonder, Sir, how a gentleman of your piety can introduce this subject in a mixed company." He told me afterwards, that the impropriety was, that perhaps some of the company might have talked on the subject in such terms as might have shocked him; or he might have been forced to appear in their eyes a narrow-minded man. The gentleman, with submissive deference, said he had only hinted at the question from a desire to hear Dr. Johnson's opinion upon it. JOHNSON: " Why, then, Sir, I think that permitting men to preach any opinion contrary to the doctrine of the Established Church, tends, in a certain degree, to lessen the authority of the Church, and consequently, to lessen the influence of religion." " It may be considered," said the gentleman, "whether it would not be politic to tolerate in such a case." JOHNSON: " Sir, we have been talking of *right :* this is another question. I think it *not* politic to tolerate in such a case."

Though he did not think it fit that so awful a subject should be introduced in a mixed company, and therefore at this time waved the theological question; yet his own orthodox belief in the sacred mystery of the TRINITY is evinced beyond doubt, by the following passage in his private devotions: " O Lord, hear my prayer, for Jesus Christ's sake; to whom with thee and the Holy Ghost, *three persons and one* God, be all honour and glory, world without end, Amen." [1]

BOSWELL: " Pray, Mr. Dilly, how does Dr. Leland's History of Ireland sell?" JOHNSON (bursting forth with a generous indignation): " The Irish are in a most unnatural state, for we see there the minority prevailing over the majority. There is no instance, even in the ten persecutions, of such severity as that which the Protestants of Ireland have exercised against the Catholics. Did we tell them we have conquered them, it would be above board: to punish them by confiscation

---

[1] Prayers and Meditations, p. 40.—BOSWELL.

and other penalties, as rebels, was monstrous injustice. King William was not their lawful sovereign : he had not been acknowledged by the Parliament of Ireland, when they apeared in arms against him."

I here suggested something favourable of the Roman Catholics. TOPLADY : " Does not their invocation of saints suppose omnipresence in the saints ? " JOHNSON : " No, Sir ; it supposes only pluri-presence ; and when spirits are divested of matter, it seems probable that they should see with more extent than in an embodied state. There is, therefore, no approach to an invasion of any of the divine attributes in the invocation of saints. But I think it is will-worship, and presumption. I see no command for it, and therefore think it is safer not to practise it."

He and Mr. Langton and I went together to the Club, where we found Mr. Burke, Mr. Garrick, and some other members, and amongst them our friend Goldsmith, who sat silently brooding over Johnson's reprimand to him after dinner. Johnson perceived this, and said aside to some of us, " I'll make Goldsmith forgive me ; " and then called to him in a loud voice, " Dr. Goldsmith, something passed to-day where you and I dined ; I ask your pardon." Goldsmith answered placidly, " It must be much from you, Sir, that I take ill." And so at once the difference was over, and they were on as easy terms as ever, and Goldsmith rattled away as usual.

In our way to the Club to-night, when I regretted that Goldsmith would, upon every occasion, endeavour to shine, by which he often exposed himself, Mr. Langton observed, that he was not like Addison, who was content with the fame of his writings, and did not aim also at excellency in conversation, for which he found himself unfit ; and that he said to a lady who complained of his having talked little in company " Madam, I have but ninepence in ready money, but I can draw for a thousand pounds." I observed that Goldsmith had a great deal of gold in his cabinet, but, not content with that, was always taking out his purse. JOHNSON : " Yes, Sir, and that so often an empty purse ! "

Goldsmith's incessant desire of being conspicuous in company, was the occasion of his sometimes appearing to such disadvantage as one should hardly have supposed possible in a man of his genius. When his literary reputation had risen deservedly high, and his society was much courted, he became very jealous of the extraordinary attention which was everywhere paid to Johnson. One evening, in a circle of wits, he found fault with me for talking of Johnson as entitled to the honour of unquestionable superiority. " Sir," said he, " you are for making a monarchy of what should be a republic."

He was still more mortified, when talking in a company with fluent vivacity, and, as he flattered himself, to the admiration of all who were present ; a German who sat next him, and perceived Johnson rolling himself, as if about to speak, suddenly stopped him, saying, " Stay,

stay—Toctor Shonson is going to say something." This was, no doubt, very provoking, especially to one so irritable as Goldsmith, who frequently mentioned it with strong expressions of indignation.

It may also be observed, that Goldsmith was sometimes content to be treated with an easy familiarity, but upon occasions would be consequential and important. An instance of this occurred in a small particular. Johnson had a way of contracting the names of his friends : as Beauclerk, Beau ; Boswell, Bozzy ; Langton, Lanky ; Murphy, Mur ; Sheridan, Sherry. I remember one day, when Tom Davies was telling that Dr. Johnson said, "We are all in labour for a name to *Goldy's* play," Goldsmith seemed displeased that such a liberty should be taken with his name, and said, "I have often desired him not to call me *Goldy*." Tom was remarkably attentive to the most minute circumstance about Johnson. I recollect his telling me once, on my arrival in London, "Sir, our great friend has made an improvement on his appellation of old Mr. Sheridan. He calls him now *Sherry derry*."

TO THE REVEREND MR. BAGSHAW, AT BROMLEY.[1]

"SIR,   May 8, 1773.

"I return you my sincere thanks for your additions to my Dictionary ; but the new edition has been published some time, and therefore I cannot now make use of them. Whether I shall ever revise it more, I know not. If many readers had been as judicious, as diligent, and as communicative as yourself, my work had been better. The world must at present take it as it is.

"I am, Sir,

"Your most obliged and most humble servant,

"SAM. JOHNSON."

On Sunday, May 8, I dined with Johnson at Mr. Langton's with Dr. Beattie and some other company. He descanted on the subject of Literary Property. "There seems," said he, "to be in authors a stronger right of property than that by occupancy ; a metaphysical right, a right, as it were, of creation, which should from its nature be perpetual ; but the consent of nations is against it ; and indeed reason and the interest of learning are against it ; for were it to be perpetual, no book, however useful, could be universally diffused amongst mankind, should the proprietor take it into his head to restrain its circulation.

[1] The Rev. Thomas Bagshaw, M.A., who died on November 20, 1787, in the seventy-seventh year of his age, Chaplain of Bromley College, in Kent, and Rector of Southfleet. He had resigned the cure of Bromley Parish some time before his death. For this and another letter from Dr. Johnson in 1784, to the same truly respectable man, I am indebted to Dr. John Loveday, of the Commons, a son of the late learned and pious John Loveday, Esq., of Caversham in Berkshire, who obligingly transcribed them for me from the originals in his possession. This worthy gentleman, having retired from business, now lives in Warwickshire. The world has been lately obliged to him as the Editor of the late Rev. Dr. Townson's excellent work, modestly entitled "A Discourse on the Evangelical History, from the Interment to the Ascension of our Lord and Saviour Jesus Christ;" to which is prefixed a truly interesting and pleasing account of the author by the Rev. Mr. Ralph Churton.—BOSWELL.

No book could have the advantage of being edited with notes, however necessary to its elucidation, should the proprietor perversely oppose it. For the general good of the world, therefore, whatever valuable book has once been created by an author, and issued out by him, should be understood as no longer in his power, but as belonging to the public; at the same time the author is entitled to an adequate reward. This he should have by an exclusive right to his work for a considerable number of years."

He attacked Lord Monboddo's strange speculation on the primitive state of human nature ; observing, " Sir, it is all conjecture about a thing useless, even were it known to be true. Knowledge of all kind is good. Conjecture, as to things useful, is good ; but conjecture as to what it would be useless to know, such as whether men went upon all four, is very idle."

On Monday, May 9, as I was to set out on my return to Scotland next morning, I was desirous to see as much of Dr. Johnson as I could. But I first called on Goldsmith to take leave of him. The jealousy and envy which, though possessed of many most amiable qualities, he frankly avowed, broke out violently at this interview. Upon another occasion, when Goldsmith confessed himself to be of an envious disposition, I contended with Johnson that we ought not to be angry with him, he was so candid in owning it. " Nay, Sir," said Johnson, " we must be angry that a man has such a superabundance of an odious quality that he cannot keep it within his own breast, but it boils over." In my opinion, however, Goldsmith had not more of it than other people have, but only talked of it freely.

He now seemed very angry that Johnson was going to be a traveller ; said, " he would be a dead weight for me to carry, and that I should never be able to lug him along through the Highlands and Hebrides." Nor would he patiently allow me to enlarge upon Johnson's wonderful abilities ; but exclaimed, " Is he like Burke, who winds into a subject like a serpent ? " " But," said I, " Johnson is the Hercules who strangled serpents in his cradle."

I dined with Dr. Johnson at General Paoli's. He was obliged, by indisposition, to leave the company early ; he appointed me, however, to meet him in the evening at Mr. (now Sir Robert) Chambers's in the Temple, where he accordingly came, though he continued to be very ill. Chambers, as is common on such occasions, prescribed various remedies to him. Johnson (fretted by pain) : " Prythee don't tease me. Stay till I am well, and then you shall tell me how to cure myself." He grew better, and talked with a noble enthusiasm of keeping up the representation of respectable families. His zeal on this subject was a circumstance in his character exceedingly remarkable, when it is considered that he himself had no pretensions to blood. I heard him once say, " I have great merit in being zealous for subordination and the honours of birth ; for I can hardly tell who was my grandfather." He maintained the dignity and propriety of male succession, in opposition to the opinion of one of our friends, who had that day employed Mr. Chambers to draw his will, devising his estate to his three sisters, in preference to a remote heir male. Johnson called them " three *dowdies*," and said, with as high a spirit as the boldest Baron in the most perfect days of the feudal system, " An ancient estate should always go to males. It is mighty foolish to let a stranger have it because he marries your daughter, and takes your name. As for an estate newly acquired by trade, you may give it, if you will, to the dog *Towser*, and let him keep his *own* name."

I have known him at times exceedingly diverted at what seemed to others a very small sport. He now laughed immoderately, without any reason that we could perceive, at our friend's making his will ; called him the *testator*, and added, "I dare say he thinks he has done a mighty thing. He won't stay till he gets home to his seat in the country, to produce this wonderful deed : he'll call up the landlord of the first inn on the road ; and, after a suitable preface upon the mortality and the uncertainty of life, will tell him that he should not delay making his will ; and ' here, Sir,' will he say, ' is my will, which I have just made, with the assistance of one of the ablest lawyers in the kingdom ; ' and he will read it to him (laughing all the time). He believes he has made this will ; but he did not make it : you, Chambers, made it for him. I trust you have had more conscience than to make him say, ' being of sound understanding ; ' ha, ha, ha ! I hope he has left me a legacy. I'd have his will turned into verse, like a ballad."

In this playful manner did he run on, exulting in his own pleasantry, which certainly was not such as might be expected from the author of " The Rambler," but which is here preserved, that my readers may be acquainted even with the slightest occasional characteristics of so eminent a man.

Mr. Chambers did not by any means relish this jocularity upon a matter of which *pars magna fuit*, and seemed impatient till he got rid of us. Johnson could not stop his merriment, but continued it all the way till he got without the Temple-gate. He then burst into such a fit of laughter, that he appeared to be almost in a convulsion ; and, in order to support himself, laid hold of one of the posts at the side of the foot pavement, and sent forth peals so loud, that in the silence of the night his voice seemed to resound from Temple-bar to Fleet-ditch.

This most ludicrous exhibition of the awful, melancholy, and venerable Johnson, happened well to counteract the feelings of sadness which I used to experience when parting with him for a considerable time. I accompanied him to his door, where he gave me his blessing.

He records of himself this year, " Between Easter and Whitsuntide, having always considered that time as propitious to study, I attempted to learn the Low Dutch Language." It is to be observed, that he here admits an opinion of the human mind being influenced by seasons, which he ridicules in his writings. His progress, he says, was interrupted by a fever " which, by the imprudent use of a small print, left an inflammation in his useful eye." We cannot but admire ' is spirit when we know

JOHNSON'S FIT OF LAUGHTER AT THE TEMPLE GATE.

that amidst a complication of bodily and mental distress, he was still animated with the desire of intellectual improvement.[1] Various notes of his studies appear on different days, in his manuscript diary of this year ; such as,

" *Inchoavi lectionem Pentateuchi—Finivi lectionem Conf. Fab. Burdonum.—Legi primum actum Troadum.—Legi Dissertationem Clerici postremam de Pent.—2 of Clark's Sermons.—L. Apollonii pugnam Betriciam.—L. centum versus Homeri.*"

Let this serve as a specimen of what accessions of literature he was perpetually infusing into his mind, while he charged himself with idleness.

This year died Mrs. Salusbury (mother of Mrs. Thrale), a lady whom he appears to have esteemed much, and whose memory he honoured with an Epitaph.[2]

---

[1] " Prayers and Meditations," p. 129.—Boswell.
[2] Mrs. Piozzi's " Anecdotes of Johnson," p. 131.—Boswell.

DR. JOHNSON IN HIS HEBRIDEAN COSTUME.

CHAPTER VIII.—1773.

IN a letter from Edinburgh, dated the 29th of May, I pressed him to persevere in his resolution to make this year the projected visit to the Hebrides, of which he and I had talked for many years, and which I was confident would afford us much entertainment.

"TO JAMES BOSWELL, ESQ.

"DEAR SIR, Johnson's-court, Fleet-street, July 5, 1773.

"When your letter came to me, I was so darkened by an inflammation in my eye that I could not for some time read it. I can now write without trouble, and can read large prints. My eye is gradually growing stronger; and I hope will be able to take some delight in the survey of a Caledonian loch.

"Chambers is going a Judge, with six thousand a-year, to Bengal. He and I shall come down together as far as Newcastle, and thence I shall easily get to Edinburgh. Let me know the exact time when your Courts intermit. I must conform a little to Chambers's occasions, and he must conform a little to mine. The time which you shall fix must be the common point to which we will come as near as we can. Except this eye, I am very well.

"Beattie is so caressed, and invited, and treated, and liked, and flattered by the great, that I can see nothing of him. I am in great hope that he will be well provided for, and then we will live upon him at the Marischal College, without pity or modesty.

"———— left the town without taking leave of me, and is gone in deep dudgeon to ————. Is not this very childish? Where is now my legacy?

"I hope your dear lady and her dear baby are both well. I shall see them too when I come; and I have that opinion of your choice, as to suspect that when I have seen Mrs. Boswell, I shall be less willing to go away.

"I am, dear Sir,
"Your affectionate humble servant,
"SAM. JOHNSON.

"Write to me as soon as you can. Chambers is now at Oxford."

I again wrote to him, informing him that the Court of Session rose on the 12th of August, hoping to see him before that time, and expressing, perhaps in too extravagant terms, my admiration of him, and my expectation of pleasure from our intended tour.

"TO JAMES BOSWELL, ESQ.

"DEAR SIR,　　　　　　　　　　　　　　　*August* 3, 1773.

"I shall set out from London on Friday the 6th of this month, and purpose not to loiter much by the way. Which day I shall be at Edinburgh I cannot exactly tell. I suppose I must drive to an inn, and send a porter to find you.

"I am afraid Beattie will not be at his College soon enough for us, and I shall be sorry to miss him; but there is no staying for the concurrence of all conveniences. We will do as well as we can.

"I am, Sir,
"Your most humble servant,
"SAM. JOHNSON."

TO THE SAME.

"DEAR SIR,　　　　　　　　　　　　　　　*August* 3, 1773.

"Not being at Mr. Thrale's when your letter came, I had written the inclosed paper and sealed it; bringing it hither for a frank, I found yours. If any thing could repress my ardour, it would be such a letter as yours. To disappoint a friend is unpleasing: and he that forms expectations like yours, must be disappointed. Think only when you see me, that you see a man who loves you, and is proud and glad that you love him.

"I am, Sir,
"Your most affectionate,
"SAM. JOHNSON."

M 2

TO THE SAME.

" DEAR SIR, *Newcastle, Aug.* 11, 1773.

" I came hither last night, and hope, but do not absolutely promise, to be in Edinburgh on Saturday. Beattie will not come so soon.

" I am, Sir,

" Your most humble servant,

" SAM. JOHNSON.

" My compliments to your lady."

TO THE SAME.

" *Saturday night.*

" Mr. Johnson sends his compliments to Mr. Boswell, being just arrived at Boyd's."

His stay in Scotland was from the 18th of August, on which day he arrived, till the 22nd of November, when he set out on his return to London ; and I believe ninety-four days were never passed by any man in a more vigorous exertion.

He came by the way of Berwick-upon-Tweed to Edinburgh, where he remained a few days, and then went by St. Andrews, Aberdeen, Inverness, and Fort Augustus, to the Hebrides, to visit which was the principal object he had in view. He visited the isles of Sky, Rasay Coll, Mull, Inchkenneth, and Icolmkill. He travelled through Argyleshire, by Inverary, and from thence by Lochlomond and Dumbarton to

CATHEDRAL OF ICOLMKILL, OR IONA.

Glasgow, then by Loudon to Auchinleck in Ayrshire, the seat of my family, and then by Hamilton, back to Edinburgh, where he again spent some time. He thus saw the four Universities of Scotland, its three principal cities, and as much of the Highland and insular life as was sufficient for his philosophical contemplation. I had the pleasure of accompanying him during the whole of his journey. He was respectfully entertained by the great, the learned, and the elegant wherever he went; nor was he less delighted with the hospitality which he experienced in humbler life.

His various adventures, and the force and vivacity of his mind, as exercised during this peregrination, upon innumerable topics, have been faithfully, and, to the best of my abilities, displayed in my " Journal of a Tour to the Hebrides," to which, as the public has been pleased to honour it by a very extensive circulation, I beg leave to refer, as to a separate and remarkable portion of his life,[1] which may be there seen in detail, and which exhibits as striking a view of his powers in conversation, as his works do of his excellence in writing. Nor can I deny to myself the very flattering gratification of inserting here the character which my friend Mr. Courtenay has been pleased to give of that work :

> " With Reynolds' pencil, vivid, bold, and true,
> So fervent Boswell gives him to our view :
> In every trait we see his mind expand ;
> The master rises by the pupil's hand ;
> We love the writer, praise his happy vein,
> Graced with the *naïveté* of the sage Montaigne.
> Hence not alone are brighter parts display'd,
> But e'en the specks of character portray'd :
> We *see* the Rambler with fastidious smile
> Mark the lone tree, and note the heath-clad isle ;
> But when the heroic tale of Flora[2] charms,
> Deck'd in a kilt, he wields a chieftain's arms :
> The tuneful piper sounds a martial strain,
> And Samuel sings ' The King shall have his *ain*.' "

During his stay at Edinburgh, after his return from the Hebrides, he was at great pains to obtain information concerning Scotland ; and it will appear, from his subsequent letters, that he was not less solicitous for intelligence on this subject after his return to London.

" TO JAMES BOSWELL, ESQ.

" Dear Sir, *Nov.* 27, 1773.

" I came home last night, without any incommodity, danger, or weariness, and am ready to begin a new journey. I shall go to Oxford on Monday.

---

[1] The author was not a small gainer by this extraordinary journey; for Dr. Johnson thus writes to Mrs. Thrale, Nov. 3, 1773 : "Boswell will praise my resolution and perseverance, and I shall in return celebrate his good humour and perpetual cheerfulness. He has better faculties than I had imagined; more justness of discernment, and more fecundity of images. It is very convenient to travel with him : for there is no house where he is not received with kindness and respect." Let. 90, to Mrs. Thrale.—Malone.

[2] " The celebrated Flora Macdonald." See Boswell's " Tour to the Hebrides."

I know Mrs. Boswell wished me well to go;[1] her wishes have not been disappointed. Mrs. Williams has received Sir A.'s[2] letter.

"Make my compliments to all those to whom my compliments may be welcome.

"Let the box[3] be sent as soon as it can, and let me know when to expect it.

"Inquire, if you can, the order of the Clans; Macdonald is first, Maclean second; further I cannot go. Quicken Dr. Webster.[4]

"I am, Sir,
"Yours affectionately,
"SAM. JOHNSON."

"MR. BOSWELL TO DR. JOHNSON.

"Edinburgh, Dec. 2, 1773.

*   *   *   *   *

"You shall have what information I can procure as to the order of the Clans. A gentleman of the name of Grant tells me that there is no settled order among them; and he says that the Macdonalds were not placed upon the right of the army at Culloden: the Stuarts were. I shall, however, examine witnesses of every name that I can find here. Dr. Webster shall be quickened too. I like your little memorandums; they are symptoms of your being in earnest with your book of northern travels.

"Your box shall be sent next week by sea. You will find in it some pieces of the broom bush, which you saw growing on the old castle of Auchinleck. The wood has a curious appearance when sawn across. You may either have a little writing-standish made of it, or get it formed into boards for a treatise on witchcraft, by way of a suitable binding."

*   *   *   *   *

"MR. BOSWELL TO DR. JOHNSON.

"Edinburgh, Dec. 18, 1773.

*   *   *   *   *

"You promised me an inscription for a print to be taken from an historical picture of Mary Queen of Scots, being forced to resign her crown, which Mr Hamilton at Rome has painted for me. The two following have been sent to me:—

---

[1] In this he showed a very acute penetration. My wife paid him the most assiduous and respectful attention, while he was our guest; so that I wonder how he discovered her wishing for his departure. The truth is, that his irregular hours and uncouth habits, such as turning the candles with their heads downwards when they did not burn bright enough, and letting the wax drop upon the carpet, could not but be disagreeable to a lady. Besides, she had not that high admiration of him which was felt by most of those who knew him; and what was very natural to a female mind, she thought he had too much influence over her husband. She once in a little warmth made, with more point than justice, this remark upon that subject: "I have seen many a bear led by a man; but I never before saw a man led by a bear."—BOSWELL.

[2] Sir Alexander Gordon, one of the Professors at Aberdeen.—BOSWELL.

[3] This was a box containing a number of curious things which he had picked up in Scotland, particularly some horn spoons.—BOSWELL.

[4] The Reverend Dr. Alexander Webster, one of the ministers of Edinburgh, a man of distinguished abilities, who had promised him information concerning the Highlands and Islands of Scotland.—BOSWELL.

' *Maria Scotorum Regina meliori seculo digna, jus regium civibus seditiosis invita resignat.*'

' *Cives seditiosi Mariam Scotorum Reginam sese muneri abdicare invitam cogunt.*'

" Be so good as to read the passage in Robertson, and see if you cannot give me a better inscription. I must have it both in Latin and English; so if you should not give me another Latin one, you will at least choose the best of these two, and send a translation of it."

*   *   *   *   *   *

His humane forgiving disposition was put to a pretty strong test on his return to London, by a liberty which Mr. Thomas Davies had taken with him in his absence, which was, to publish two volumes, entitled, " Miscellaneous and Fugitive Pieces," which he advertised in the newspapers, " By the Author of the Rambler." In this collection, several of Dr. Johnson's acknowledged writings, several of his anonymous performances, and some which he had written for others, were inserted ; but there were also some in which he had no concern whatever. He was at first very angry, as he had good reason to be. But, upon consideration of his poor friend's narrow circumstances, and that he had only a little profit in view, and meant no harm, he soon relented, and continued his kindness to him as formerly.

In the course of his self-examination with retrospect to this year, he seems to have been much dejected : for he says, January 1, 1774, " This year has passed with so little improvement, that I doubt whether I have not rather impaired than increased my learning," [1] and yet we have seen how he *read*, and we know how he *talked* during that period.

He was now seriously engaged in writing an account of our travels in the Hebrides, in consequence of which I had the pleasure of a more frequent correspondence with him.

" TO JAMES BOSWELL, ESQ.

" DEAR SIR,   *Jan.* 29, 1774.

" My operations have been hindered by a cough ; at least I flatter myself, that if my cough had not come, I should have been further advanced. But I have had no intelligence from Dr. W———, [Webster] nor from the Excise-office nor from you. No account of the little borough.[2] Nothing of the Erse language. I have yet heard nothing of my box.

" You must make haste and gather me all you can, and do it quickly, or I will and shall do without it.

" Make my compliments to Mrs. Boswell, and tell her that I do not love her the less for wishing me away. I gave her trouble enough, and shall be glad, in recompense, to give her any pleasure.

" I would send some porter into the Hebrides, if I knew which way it could be got to my kind friends there. Inquire, and let me know.

---

[1] " Prayers and Meditations," p. 129.—BOSWELL.

[2] The ancient Burgh of Prestick in Ayrshire.—BOSWELL.

"Make my compliments to all the Doctors of Edinburgh, and to all my friends, from one end of Scotland to the other.

"Write to me, and send me what intelligence you can : and if anything is too bulky for the post, let me have it by the carrier. I do not like trusting wind and waves.   I am, dear Sir, your most, &c.,

"SAM. JOHNSON."

TO THE SAME.

"DEAR SIR,   *London, Feb.* 7, 1774.

"In a day or two after I had written the last discontented letter, I received my box, which was very welcome. But still I must entreat you to hasten Dr. Webster, and continue to pick up what you can that may be useful.

"Mr. Oglethorpe was with me this morning, you know his errand. He was not unwelcome.

"Tell Mrs. Boswell that my good intentions towards her still continue. I should be glad to do anything that would either benefit or please her.

"Chambers is not yet gone, but so hurried or so negligent, or so proud, that I rarely see him. I have indeed, for some weeks past, been very ill of a cold and cough, and have been at Mrs. Thrale's, that I might be taken care of. I am much better ; *novæ redeunt in prælia vires ;* but I am yet tender, and easily disordered. How happy it was that neither of us were ill in the Hebrides.

"The question of Literary Property is this day before the Lords. Murphy drew up the Appellant's case, that is, the plea against the perpetual right. I have not seen it, nor heard the decision. I would not have the right perpetual.

"I will write to you as anything occurs, and do you send me something about my Scottish friends. I have very great kindness for them. Let me know likewise how fees come in, and when we are to see you.

"I am, Sir, yours affectionately,

"SAM. JOHNSON."

He at this time wrote the following letters to Mr. Steevens, his able associate in editing Shakspeare :—

"TO GEORGE STEEVENS, ESQ., HAMPSTEAD.

"SIR,   *Feb.* 7, 1774.

"If I am asked when I have seen Mr. Steevens, you know what answer I must give ; if I am asked when I shall see him, I wish you would tell me what to say.

"If you have ' Lesley's History of Scotland,' or any other book about Scotland, except Boetius and Buchanan, it will be a kindness if you send them to,

"Sir, your humble servant,

"SAM. JOHNSON."

TO THE SAME.

"SIR,   *Feb.* 21, 1774.

"We are thinking to augment our Club, and I am desirous of nominating you, if you care to stand the ballot, and can attend on Friday nights at least twice in five weeks; less than this is too little, and rather more will be expected. Be pleased to let me know before Friday.

" I am, Sir, your most, &c.,
" SAM. JOHNSON."

TO THE SAME.

" SIR,   *March* 5, 1774.

" Last night you became a member of the Club; if you call on me on Friday, I will introduce you. A gentleman proposed after you, was rejected. I thank you for Neander,[1] but wish he were not so fine. I will take care of him.

" I am, Sir,
" Your humble servant,
" SAM. JOHNSON."

" TO JAMES BOSWELL, ESQ.

" DEAR SIR.   *March* 5, 1774.

" Dr. Webster's informations were much less exact and much less determinate than I expected : they are, indeed, much less positive than, if he can trust his own book,[2] which he laid before me, he is able to give. But I believe it will always be found, that he who calls much for information will advance his work but slowly.

" I am, however, obliged to you, dear Sir, for your endeavours to help me, and hope, that between us something will some time be done, if not on this, on some occasion.

" Chambers is either married or almost married to Miss Wilton, a girl of sixteen, exquisitely beautiful, whom he has, with his lawyer's tongue, persuaded to take her chance with him in the East.

" We have added to the club, Charles Fox, Sir Charles Bunbury, Dr. Fordyce, and Mr. Steevens.

" Return my thanks to Dr. Webster. Tell Dr. Robertson I have not much to reply to his censure of my negligence : and tell Dr. Blair, that since he has written hither what I said to him, we must now consider ourselves as even, forgive one another, and begin again. I care not how soon, for he is a very pleasing man. Pay my compliments to all my friends, and remind Lord Elibank of his promise to give me all his works.

" I hope Mrs. Boswell and little Miss are well.—When shall I see them again? She is a sweet lady, only she was so glad to see me go, that I have almost a mind to come again, that she may again have the same pleasure.

" Inquire if it be practicable to send a small present of a cask of porter to Dunvegan, Rasay, and Col. I would not wish to be thought forgetful of civilities.   I am, Sir, your humble servant,
" SAM. JOHNSON."

---

[1] See the Catalogue of Mr. Steevens's Library, No. 265: " Neandri (Mich.) Opus aureum, Gr. et Lat. 2 tom. 4to. *corio turcico, foliis deauratis.* Lipsiæ, 1577."—This was doubtless the book which appears to have been lent by Mr. Steevens to Dr. Johnson.—MALONE.

[2] A manuscript account drawn by Dr. Webster of all the parishes in Scotland, ascertaining their length, breadth, number of inhabitants, and distinguishing Protestants and Roman Catholics. This book had been transmitted to government and Dr. Johnson saw a copy of it in Dr. Webster's possession.—BOSWELL.

On the 5th of March I wrote to him, requesting his counsel whether I should this spring come to London. I stated to him on the one hand some pecuniary embarrassments, which, together with my wife's situation at that time, made me hesitate : and, on the other, the pleasure and improvement which my annual visit to the metropolis always afforded me : and particularly mentioned a peculiar satisfaction which I experienced in celebrating the festival of Easter in St. Paul's Cathedral ; that to my fancy it appeared like going up to Jerusalem at the feast of the Passover ; and that the strong devotion which I felt on that occasion diffused its influence on my mind through the rest of the year.

" TO JAMES BOSWELL, ESQ.

" DEAR SIR,　　　　　　　[*Not dated, but written about the 15th of March.*]

" I am ashamed to think that since I received your letter I have passed so many days without answering it.

" I think there is no great difficulty in resolving your doubts. The reasons for which you are inclined to visit London, are, I think, not of sufficient strength to answer the objections. That you should delight to come once a year to the fountain of intelligence and pleasure, is very natural ; but both information and pleasure must be regulated by propriety. Pleasure, which cannot be obtained but by unseasonable or unsuitable expense, must always end in pain ; and pleasure which must be enjoyed at the expense of another's pain, can never be such as a worthy mind can fully delight in.

" What improvement you might gain by coming to London, you may easily supply or easily compensate, by enjoining yourself some particular study at home, or opening some new avenue to information. Edinburgh is not yet exhausted ; and I am sure you will find no pleasure here which can deserve either that you should anticipate any part of your future fortune, or that you should condemn yourself and your lady to penurious frugality for the rest of the year.

" I need not tell you what regard you owe to Mrs. Boswell's entreaties ; or how much you ought to study the happiness of her who studies yours with so much diligence, and of whose kindness you enjoy such good effects. Life cannot subsist in society but by reciprocal concessions. She permitted you to ramble last year, you must permit her now to keep you at home.

" Your last reason is so serious that I am unwilling to oppose it. Yet you must remember, that your image of worshipping once a year in a certain place, in imitation of the Jews, is but a comparison ; and *simile non est idem ;* if the annual resort to Jerusalem was a duty to the Jews, it was a duty because it was commanded ; and you have no such command, therefore no such duty. It may be dangerous to receive too readily, and indulge too fondly, opinions from which perhaps, no pious mind is wholly disengaged, of local sanctity and local devotion. You know what strange effects they have produced over a great part of the Christian world. I am now writing, and you, when you read this, are reading under the eye of Omnipresence.

" To what degree fancy is to be admitted into religious offices, it would require much deliberation to determine. I am far from intending totally to exclude it. Fancy is a faculty bestowed by our Creator, and it is reasonable that all his gifts should be used to his glory, that all our faculties should co-operate in his worship; but they are to co-operate according to the will of him that gave them, according to the order which his wisdom has established. As ceremonies prudential or convenient are less obligatory than positive ordinances, as bodily worship is only the token to others or ourselves of mental adoration, so Fancy is always to act in subordination to Reason. We may take Fancy for a companion, but must follow Reason as our guide. We may allow Fancy to suggest certain ideas in certain places; but Reason must always be heard, when she tells us that those ideas and those places have no natural or necessary relation. When we enter a church, we habitually recal to mind the duty of adoration, but we must not omit adoration for want of a temple; because we know, and ought to remember, that the Universal Lord is everywhere present; and that, therefore, to come to Jona, or to Jerusalem, though it may be useful, cannot be necessary.

" Thus I have answered your letter, and have not answered it negligently. I love you too well to be careless when you are serious.

" I think I shall be very diligent next week about our travels, which I have too long neglected.　　　　　I am, dear Sir, your most, &c.,

　　　　　　　　　　　　　　　　　　" SAM. JOHNSON.

" Compliments to Madam and Miss."

TO THE SAME.

　　　　　　　　　　　　　　　　　　" *May* 10, 1774.

" THE lady who delivers this has a lawsuit, in which she desires to make use of your skill and eloquence, and she seems to think that she shall have something more of both for a recommendation from me; which, though I know how little you want any external incitement to your duty, I could not refuse her, because I know that at least it will not hurt her, to tell you that I wish her well.　　　　　　　I am, Sir,

　　　　　　　　　　" Your most humble servant,

　　　　　　　　　　　　　" SAM. JOHNSON."

" MR. BOSWELL TO DR. JOHNSON.

　　　　　　　　　　　　" *Edinburgh, May* 12, 1774.

" LORD HAILES has begged of me to offer you his best respects, and to transmit to you specimens of ' Annals of Scotland, from the accession of Malcolm Kenmore, to the death of James V.,' in drawing up which his Lordship has been engaged for some time. His Lordship writes to me thus : ' If I could procure Dr. Johnson's criticisms, they would be of great use to me in the prosecution of my work, as they would be judicious and true. I have no right to ask that favour of him. If you could, it would highly oblige me.'

" Dr. Blair requests you may be assured that he did not write to London what you said to him, and that neither by word or letter has he made the least complaint of you; but on the contrary, has a high respect for you, and loves you much more since he saw you in Scotland. It would both divert and please you to see his eagerness about this matter,"

" TO JAMES BOSWELL, ESQ.

"DEAR SIR,   *Streatham, June* 12, 1774.

" Yesterday I put the first sheets of ' The Journey to the Hebrides' to the press. I have endeavoured to do you some justice in the first paragraph. It will be one volume in octavo, not thick.

" It will be proper to make some presents in Scotland. You shall tell me to whom I shall give; and I have stipulated twenty-five for you to give in your own name. Some will take the present better from me, others better from you. In this you who are to live in the place ought to direct. Consider it. Whatever you can get for my purpose send me; and make my compliments to your lady and both the young ones.

" I am, Sir, your, &c.

" SAM. JOHNSON."

" MR. BOSWELL TO DR. JOHNSON.

" *Edinburgh, June* 24, 1774.

" You do not acknowledge the receipt of the various packets which I have sent to you. Neither can I prevail with you to *answer* my letters, though you honour me with *returns*. You have said nothing to me about poor Goldsmith,[1] nothing about Langton.

" I have received for you, from the Society for Propagating Christian Knowledge in Scotland, the following Erse books:—' The New Testament;'— ' Baxter's Call;'—' The Confession of Faith of the Assembly of Divines at Westminster ·'—' The Mother's Catechism;'—' A Gaelic and English Vocabulary.' "

" TO JAMES BOSWELL, ESQ.

" DEAR SIR,   *July* 4, 1774.

"I wish you could have looked over my book before the printer, but it could not easily be. I suspect some mistakes; but as I deal, perhaps, more in notions than in facts, the matter is not great, and the second edition will be mended, if any such there be. The press will go on slowly for a time, because I am going into Wales to-morrow.

" I should be very sorry if I appeared to treat such a character as Lord Hailes otherwise than with high respect. I return the sheets,[3] to which I have done what mischief I could ; and finding it so little, thought not much of sending them. The narrative is clear, lively, and short.

" I have done worse to Lord Hailes than by neglecting his sheets; I have run him in debt. Dr. Horne, the President of Magdalen College, in Oxford, wrote to me about three months ago, that he purposed to reprint Walton's Lives, and desired me to contribute to the work ; my answer was, that Lord Hailes intended the same publication ; and Dr. Horne has resigned it to him. His Lordship must now think seriously about it.

<hr/>

[1] Dr. Goldsmith died April 4, this year.—BOSWELL.

[2] These books Dr. Johnson presented to the Bodleian Library.—BOSWELL.

[3] On the cover enclosing them, Dr. Johnson wrote—" If my delay has given any reason for supposing that I have not a very deep sense of the honour done me by asking my judgment I am very sorry."—BOSWELL.

" Of poor dear Dr. Goldsmith there is little to be told, more than the papers have made public. He died of a fever, made, I am afraid, more violent by uneasiness of mind. His debts began to be heavy, and all his resources were exhausted. Sir Joshua is of opinion that he owed not less than two thousand pounds. Was ever poet so trusted before?

" You may, if you please, put the inscription thus :—' *Maria Scotorum Regina nata* 15—, *a suis in exilium acta* 15—, *ab hospitâ neci data* 15—.' You must find the years.

" Of your second daughter, you certainly gave the account yourself, though you have forgotten it. While Mrs. Boswell is well, never doubt of a boy. Mrs Thrale brought, I think, five girls running, but while I was with you she had a boy.

" I am obliged to you for all your pamphlets, and of the last I hope to make some use. I made some of the former.

" I am, dear Sir, your most affectionate servant,
" Sam. Johnson.

" My compliments to all the three ladies."

" TO BENNET LANGTON, ESQ., AT LANGTON, NEAR SPILSBY
LINCOLNSHIRE.

" Dear Sir,   *July* 5, 1774.

" You have reason to reproach me that I have left your last letter so long unanswered, but I had nothing particular to say. Chambers, you find, is gone far, and poor Goldsmith is gone much further. He died of a fever, exasperated, as I believe, by the fear of distress. He had raised money and squandered it, by every artifice of acquisition and folly of expense. But let not his frailties be remembered ; he was a very great man.

" I have just begun to print my ' Journey to the Hebrides,' and am leaving the press to take another journey into Wales, whither Mr. Thrale is going, to take possession of, at least, five hundred a-year, fallen to his lady. All at Streatham, that are alive, are well.

" I have never recovered from the last dreadful illness, but flatter myself that I grow gradually better ; much, however, yet remains to mend. Κύριε ἐλέησον.

" If you have the Latin version of *Busy, curious, thirsty fly*, be so kind as to transcribe and send it ; but you need not be in haste, for I shall be I know not where for at least five weeks. I wrote the following tetrastich on poor Goldsmith :—

" Τὸν τάφον εἰσοράᾳς τὸν Ὀλιβάροιο, κονίην
Αφοοσι μὴ σέμνην, Ξεῖινε, πόδεσσι πάτει.
Οἶσι μέμηλε φύσις, μέτρων χάρις, ἔργα παλαιᾶ·
Κλαίετε ποιητὴν, ἱστόρικον, φυσικόν.

" Please to make my most respectful compliments to all the ladies, and remember me to young George and his sisters. I reckon George begins to show a pair of heels.

" Do not be sullen now, but let me find a letter when I come back.

" I am, dear Sir,
" Your affectionate humble servant,
" Sam. Johnson."

"TO MR. ROBERT LEVET.

"Dear Sir, _Llewenny, in Denbighshire, August_ 16, 1774.

Mr. Thrale's affairs have kept him here a great while, nor do I know exactly when we shall come hence. I have sent you a bill upon Mr. Strahan.

"I have made nothing of the ipecacuanha, but have taken abundance of pills, and hope that they have done me good.

"Wales, so far as I have yet seen of it, is a very beautiful and rich country, all enclosed and planted. Denbigh is not a mean town. Make my compliments to all my friends, and tell Frank I hope he remembers my advice. When his money is out, let him have more.

"I am, Sir, your humble servant.

"Sam. Johnson."

"MR. BOSWELL TO DR. JOHNSON.

"_Edinburgh, Aug._ 30, 1774.

"You have given me an inscription for a portrait of Mary Queen of Scots, in which you, in a short and striking manner, point out her hard fate. But you will be pleased to keep in mind that my picture is a representation of a particular scene in her history : her being forced to resign her crown, while she was imprisoned in the castle of Lochleven. I must, therefore, beg that you will be kind enough to give me an inscription suited to that particular scene, or determine which of the two formerly transmitted to you is the best; and, at any rate, favour me with an English translation. It will be doubly kind if you comply with my request speedily.

"Your critical notes on the specimen of Lord Hailes's ' Annals of Scotland,' are excellent. I agreed with you on every one of them. He himself objected only to the alteration of _free_ to _brave,_ in the passage where he says that Edward ' departed with the glory due to the conqueror of a free people.' He says, to call the Scots brave would only add to the glory of their conqueror. You will make allowance for the national zeal of our annalist. I now send a few more leaves of the ' Annals,' which I hope you will peruse, and return with observations, as you did upon the former occasion. Lord Hailes writes to me thus ' Mr. Boswell will be pleased to express the grateful sense which Sir David Dalrymple has of Dr. Johnson's attention to his little specimen. The further specimen will show, that

' Even in an _Edward_ he can see desert.'

"It gives me much pleasure to hear that a republication of Isaac Walton's 'Lives' is intended. You have been in a mistake in thinking that Lord Hailes had it in view. I remember one morning, while he sat with you in my house, he said that there should be a new edition of ' Walton's Lives;' and you said that ' they should be benoted a little.' This was all that passed on that subject. You must, therefore, inform Dr. Horne that he may resume his plan. I enclose a note concerning it ; and if Dr. Horne will write to me, all the attention that I can give, shall be cheerfully bestowed upon what I think a pious work,—the preservation and elucidation of Walton, by whose writings I have been most pleasingly edified.

* * * * * *

"MR. BOSWELL TO DR. JOHNSON.

" *Edinburgh, Sept.* 16, 1774.

" WALES has probably detained you longer than I supposed.   You will have become quite a mountaineer, by visiting Scotland one year and Wales another. You must next go to Switzerland. Cambria will complain, if you do not honour her also with some remarks. And I find *concessère columnæ*, the booksellers expect another book.   I am impatient to see your ' Tour to Scotland and the Hebrides.' Might you not send me a copy by the post as soon as it is printed off?"

*   *   *   *   *   *

"TO JAMES BOSWELL, ESQ.

" DEAR SIR,   *London, October* 1, 1774.

" Yesterday I returned from my Welsh journey.   I was sorry to leave my book suspended so long: but having an opportunity of seeing, with so much convenience, a new part of the island, I could not reject it.   I have been in five of the six counties of North Wales; and have seen St. Asaph and Bangor, the

SNOWDON.

two seats of their Bishops; have been upon Penmanmaur and Snowdon, and passed over into Anglesea.   But Wales is so little different from England, that it offers nothing to the speculation of the traveller.

" When I came home, I found several of your papers, with some pages of Lord Hailes's ' Annals,' which I will consider.   I am in haste to give you some account of myself, lest you should suspect me of negligence in the pressing business which I find recommended to my care, and which I knew nothing of till now, when all care is vain.[1]

" In the distribution of my books I propose to follow your advice, adding such as shall occur to me. I am not pleased with your notes of remembrance added to your names, for I hope I shall not easily forget them.

" I have received four Erse books, without any direction, and suspect that they are intended for the Oxford library. If that is the intention, I think it will be proper to add the metrical psalms, and whatever else is printed in Erse, that the present may be complete. The donor's name should be told.

" I wish you could have read the book before it was printed, but our distance does not easily permit it.

" I am sorry Lord Hailes does not intend to publish Walton ; I am afraid it will not be done so well, if it be done at all.

" I purpose now to drive the book forward. Make my compliments to Mrs. Boswell, and let me hear often from you.

" I am, dear Sir,

" Your affectionate humble servant,

" SAM. JOHNSON."

This tour to Wales, which was made in company with Mr. and Mrs. Thrale, though it no doubt contributed to his health and amusement, did not give an occasion to such a discursive exercise of his mind as our tour to the Hebrides. I do not find that he kept any journal or notes of what he saw there. All that I heard him say of it was, that " instead of bleak and barren mountains, there were green and fertile ones ; and that one of the castles in Wales would contain all the castles that he had seen in Scotland."

Parliament having been dissolved, and his friend Mr. Thrale, who was a steady supporter of government, having again to encounter the storm of a contested election, he wrote a short political pamphlet, entitled " The Patriot," addressed to the electors of Great Britain ; a title which, to factious men who consider a patriot only as an opposer of the measures of government, will appear strangely misapplied. It was, however, written with energetic vivacity ; and, except those passages in which it endeavours to vindicate the glaring outrage of the House of Commons in the case of the Middlesex election, and to justify the attempt to reduce our fellow-subjects in America to unconditional submission, it contained an admirable display of the properties of a real patriot, in the original and genuine sense ;—a sincere, steady, rational, and unbiassed friend to the interests and prosperity of his King and country. It must be acknowledged, however, that both in this and his two former pamphlets, there was, amidst many powerful arguments, not only a considerable portion of sophistry, but a contemptuous ridicule of his opponents, which was very provoking.

---

[1] I had written to him, to request his interposition in behalf of a convict, who I thought was very unjustly condemned.—BOSWELL.

"TO MR. PERKINS.[1]

" Sir,   *October* 25, 1774.

" You may do me a very great favour. Mrs. Williams, a gentlewoman whom you may have seen at Mr. Thrale's, is a petitioner for Mr. Hetherington's charity : petitions are this day issued at Christ's Hospital.

" I am a bad manager of business in a crowd ; and if I should send a mean man, he may be put away without his errand. I must therefore entreat that you will go, and ask for a petition for Anna Williams, whose paper of inquiries was delivered with answers at the counting-house of the hospital on Thursday the 20th. My servant will attend you thither, and bring the petition home when you have it.

" The petition which they are to give us, is a form which they deliver to every petitioner, and which the petitioner is afterwards to fill up, and return to them again. This we must have, or we cannot proceed according to their directions. You need, I believe, only ask for a petition ; if they inquire for whom you ask, you can tell them.

" I beg pardon for giving you this trouble ; but it is a matter of great importance.   I am, Sir,

" Your most humble servant.

" Sam. Johnson."

" TO JAMES BOSWELL, ESQ.

" Dear Sir,   *London, Oct.* 27, 1774.

" There has appeared lately in the papers an account of a boat overset between Mull and Ulva, in which many passengers were lost, and among them Maclean of Coll. We, you know, were once drowned ;[2] I hope, therefore, that the story is either wantonly or erroneously told. Pray satisfy me by the next post.

" I have printed two hundred and forty pages. I am able to do nothing much worth doing to dear Lord Hailes's book. I will, however, send back the sheets ; and hope, by degrees, to answer all your reasonable expectations.

" Mr. Thrale has happily surmounted a very violent and acrimonious opposition ; but all joys have their abatement—Mrs. Thrale has fallen from her horse and hurt herself very much. The rest of our friends, I believe, are well. My compliments to Mrs. Boswell.

" I am, Sir,

" Your most affectionate servant,

" Sam. Johnson."

· Mr. Perkins was for a number of years the worthy superintendent of Mr. Thrale's great brewery, and after his death became one of the proprietors of it ; and now resides (1791) in Mr. Thrale's house in Southwark, which was the scene of so many literary meetings, and in which he continues the liberal hospitality for which it was eminent. Dr. Johnson esteemed him much. He hung up in the counting-house a fine proof of the admirable mezzotinto of Dr. Johnson, by Doughty ; and when Mrs. Thrale asked him, somewhat flippantly, " Why do you put him up in the counting-house ? " He answered, " Because, Madam, I wish to have one wise man there." "Sir," said Johnson, " I thank you. It is a very handsome compliment, and I believe you speak sincerely."—Boswell.

[2] In the newspapers.—Boswell.

This letter, which shows his tender concern for an amiable young gentleman to whom he had been very much obliged in the Hebrides, I have inserted according to its date, though before receiving it I had informed him of the melancholy event that the young Laird of Coll was unfortunately drowned.

"TO JAMES BOSWELL, ESQ.

"DEAR SIR,   *Nov.* 26, 1774.

"Last night I corrected the last page of our 'Journey to the Hebrides.' The printer has detained it all this time, for I had, before I went into Wales, written all except two sheets. 'The Patriot' was called for by my political friends on Friday, was written on Saturday, and I have heard little of it. So vague are conjectures at a distance.[1] As soon as I can, I will take care that copies be sent to you, for I would wish that they might be given before they are bought : but I am afraid that Mr. Strahan will send to you and to the booksellers at the same time. Trade is as diligent as courtesy. I have mentioned all that you recommended. Pray make my compliments to Mrs. Boswell and the younglings. The club has, I think, not yet met.

"Tell me, and tell me honestly, what you think and what others say of our travels. Shall we touch the continent?[2]

"I am, dear Sir,
"Your most humble servant,
"SAM. JOHNSON."

In his manuscript diary of this year, there is the following entry :—

"Nov. 27. Advent Sunday. I considered that this day, being the beginning of the ecclesiastical year, was a proper time for a new course of life. I began to read the Greek Testament regularly, at one hundred and sixty verses every Sunday. This day I began the Acts.

"In this week I read Virgil's Pastorals. I learned to repeat the Pollio and Gallus. I read carelessly the first Georgic."

Such evidences of his unceasing ardour, both for "divine and human lore," when advanced into his sixty-fifth year, and notwithstanding his many disturbances from disease, must make us at once honour his spirit, and lament that it should be so grievously clogged by its material tegument. It is remarkable, that he was very fond of the precision which calculation produces. Thus we find in one of his manuscript diaries, "12 pages in 4to Gr. Test. and 30 pages in Beza's folio, comprise the whole in 40 days."

---

[1] Alluding to a passage in a letter of mine, where speaking of his "Journey to the Hebrides," I say, "But has not 'The Patriot' been an interruption, by the time taken to write it, and the time luxuriously spent in listening to its applauses?"—BOSWELL.

[2] We had projected a voyage together up the Baltic, and talked of visiting some of the more northern regions.—BOSWELL.

" DR. JOHNSON TO JOHN HOOLE, ESQ.

" DEAR SIR,   *December* 19, 1774.

" I have returned your play,[1] which you will find underscored with red, where there was a word which I did not like. The red will be washed off with a little water.

" The plot is so well framed, the intricacy so artful, and the disentanglement so easy, the suspense so affecting, and the passionate parts so properly interposed, that I have no doubt of its success.

" I am, Sir,

" Your most humble servant,

" SAM. JOHNSON

1 " Cleonice."—BOSWELL.

CHAPTER IX.—1775.

JOHNSON WRITES "PROPOSALS FOR PUBLISHING THE WORKS OF MRS. CHARLOTTE LENNOX," AND PREFACE TO BARETTI'S "EASY LESSONS"—CORRESPONDENCE WITH BOSWELL, AND WRITES LATIN INSCRIPTION FOR HIS PICTURE OF MARY QUEEN OF SCOTS—QUESTIONS THE AUTHENTICITY OF OSSIAN'S POEMS, AND REPLIES TO AN ANGRY LETTER FROM MACPHERSON—JOHNSON'S PERSONAL COURAGE—DEFEATS FOOTE'S INTENDED MIMICRY—"JOURNEY TO THE WESTERN ISLANDS" PUBLISHED, AND SCOTTISH JEALOUSY AROUSED—THE OSSIAN CONTROVERSY.

THE first effort of his pen in 1775 was, "Proposals for publishing the Works of Mrs. Charlotte Lennox," in three volumes quarto. In his diary, January 2, I find this entry—"Wrote Charlotte's Proposals." But, indeed, the internal evidence would have been quite sufficient. Her claim to the favour of the public was thus enforced :—

"Most of the pieces, as they appeared singly, have been read with approbation, perhaps above their merits, but of no great advantage to the writer. She hopes, therefore, that she shall not be considered as too indulgent to vanity, or too studious of interest, if from that labour which has hitherto been chiefly gainful to others, she endeavours to obtain at last some profit to herself and her children. She cannot decently enforce her claim by the praise of her own performances ; nor can she suppose, that, by the most artful and laboured address, an additional notice could be procured to a publication, of which HER MAJESTY has condescended to be the PATRONESS."

He this year also wrote the preface to Baretti's "Easy Lessons in Italian and English."

"TO JAMES BOSWELL, ESQ.

"DEAR SIR,   *January* 14, 1775.

"You never did ask for a book by the post till now, and I did not think on it. You see now it is done. I sent one to the King, and I hear he likes it.

"I shall send a parcel into Scotland for presents, and intend to give to many of my friends. In your catalogue you left out Lord Auchinleck.

"Let me know, as fast as you read it, how you like it; and let me know if any mistake is committed, or anything important left out. I wish you could have seen the sheets. My compliments to Mrs. Boswell, and to Veronica, and to all my friends.

"I am, Sir,

"Your most humble servant,

"SAM. JOHNSON."

"MR. BOSWELL TO DR. JOHNSON.

"*Edinburgh, Jan.* 19, 1775.

"BE pleased to accept of my best thanks for your 'Journey to the Hebrides,' which came to me by last night's post. I did really ask the favour twice; but you have been even with me by granting it so speedily. *Bis dat qui cito dat.* Though ill of a bad cold, you kept me up the greatest part of last night; for I did not stop till I had read every word of your book. I looked back to our first talking of a visit to the Hebrides, which was many years ago, when sitting by ourselves in the Mitre tavern in London, I think about *witching time o' night:* and then exulted in contemplating our scheme fulfilled, and a *monumentum perenne* of it erected by your superior abilities. I shall only say, that your book has afforded me a high gratification. I shall afterwards give you my thoughts on particular passages. In the mean time, I hasten to tell you of your having mistaken two names, which you will correct in London, as I shall do here, that the gentlemen who deserve the valuable compliments which you have paid them, may enjoy their honours. In page 106, for *Gordon* read *Murchison;* and in page 357, for *Maclean* read *Macleod.*

*   *   *   *   *   *

"But I am now to apply to you for immediate aid in my profession, which you have never refused to grant when I requested it. I inclose you a petition for Dr. Memis, a physician at Aberdeen, in which Sir John Dalrymple has exerted his talents, and which I am to answer as counsel for the managers of the Royal Infirmary in that city. Mr. Jopp, the Provost, who delivered to you your freedom, is one of my clients, and *as a citizen of Aberdeen,* you will support him.

"The fact is shortly this. In a translation of the charter of the Infirmary from Latin into English, made under the authority of the managers, the same phrase in the original is in one place rendered *Physician,* but when applied to Dr. Memis is rendered *Doctor of Medicine.* Dr. Memis complained of this before the translation was printed, but was not indulged in having it altered: and he has brought an action for damages, on account of a supposed injury, as if the designation given to him was an inferior one, tending to make it be supposed he is *not a Physician*, and consequently to hurt his practice. My father has dismissed the action as groundless, and now he has appealed to the whole court." [1]

" TO JAMES BOSWELL, ESQ.

" DEAR SIR,   *Jan.* 1, 1775.

" I long to hear how you like the book ; it is, I think, much liked here. But Macpherson is very furious; can you give me any more intelligence about him, or his Fingal? Do what you can, and do it quickly. Is Lord Hailes on our side ?

" Pray let me know what I owed you when I left you, that I may send it to you.

" I am going to write about the Americans. If you have picked up any hints among your lawyers, who are great masters of the law of nations, or if your own mind suggest anything, let me know. But mum, it is a secret.

" I will send your parcel of books as soon as I can; but I cannot do as I wish. However, you find everything mentioned in the book which you recommended.

" Langton is here; we are all that ever we were. He is a worthy fellow, without malice, though not without resentment.

" Poor Beauclerk is so ill, that his life is thought to be in danger. Lady D? nurses him with very great assiduity.

" Reynolds has taken too much to strong liquor,[2] and seems to delight in his new character.

" This is all the news that I have; but as you love verses, I will send you a few which I made upon Inchkenneth ;[3] but remember the condition, you shall not show them, except to Lord Hailes, whom I love better than any man whom I know so little. If he asks you to transcribe them for him, you may do it, but I think he must promise not to let them be copied again, nor to show them as mine.

" I have at last sent back Lord Hailes's sheets. I never think about returning them, because I alter nothing. You will see that I might as well have kept them. However I am ashamed of my delay; and if I have the honour of receiving any more, promise punctually to return them by the next post. Make my compliments to dear Mrs. Boswell, and to Miss Veronica.

" I am, dear Sir,

" Yours most faithfully,

"SAM. JOHNSON." [4]

In the Court of Session of Scotland an action is first tried by one of the judges, who is called the Lord Ordinary : and if either party is dissatisfied, he may appeal to the whole Court, consisting of fifteen, the Lord President and fourteen other judges, who have both in and out of court the title of Lords from the name of their estates; as, Lord Auchinleck, Lord Monboddo, &c.—BOSWELL.

[2] It should be recollected, that this fanciful description of his friend was given by Johnson after he himself had become a water-drinker.—BOSWELL.

[3] See them in "Journal of a Tour to the Hebrides," 3rd edit. p. 337.—BOSWELL.

[4] He now sent me a Latin inscription for my historical picture Mary Queen of Scots and

"MR. BOSWELL TO DR. JOHNSON.

"Edinburgh, Jan. 27, 1775.

*   *   *   *   *   *

"You rate our lawyers here too high, when you call them great masters of the law of nations.

*   *   *   *   *   *

"As for myself, I am ashamed to say I have read little and thought little on the subject of America. I will be much obliged to you, if you direct me where I shall find the best information of what is to be said on both sides. It is a subject vast in its present extent and future consequences. The imperfect hints which now float in my mind, tend rather to the formation of an opinion that our government has been precipitant and severe in the resolutions taken against the Bostonians. Well, do you know that I have no kindness for that race. But nations or bodies of men, should, as well as individuals, have a fair trial, and not be condemned on character alone. Have we not express contracts with our colonies, which afford a more certain foundation of judgment, than general political speculations on the mutual rights of States and their provinces or colonies? Pray let me know immediately what to read, and I shall diligently endeavour to gather for you anything that I can find. Is Burke's speech on American taxation published by himself? Is it authentic? I remember to have heard you say, that you had never considered East Indian affairs; though, surely, they are of much importance to Great Britain. Under the recollection of this, I shelter myself from the reproach of ignorance about the Americans. If you write upon the subject, I shall certainly understand it. But, since you seem to expect that I should know something of it, without your instruction, and that my own mind should suggest something, I trust you will put me in the way.

*   *   *   *   *   *

"What does Becket mean by the *Originals* of Fingal and other Poems of Ossian, which he advertises to have lain in his shop?

*   *   *   *   *   *

afterwards favoured me with an English translation. Mr. Alderman Boydell, that eminent Patron of the Arts, has subjoined them to the engraving from my picture.

> "*Maria Scotorum Regina,*
> *Hominum seditiosorum*
> *Contumeliis lassata,*
> *Minis territa, clamoribus victa,*
> *Libello, per quem*
> *Regno cedit,*
> *Lacrimans trepidansque*
> *Nomen apponit.*

> "Mary Queen of Scots,
> Harassed, terrified, and overpowered
> By the insults, menaces,
> And clamours
> Of her rebellious subjects,
> Sets her hand,
> With tears and confusion,
> To a resignation of the kingdom."—Bᴏsᴡᴇʟʟ.

" TO JAMES BOSWELL, ESQ.

" DEAR SIR,   *Jan.* 28, 1775.

" You sent me a case to consider, in which I have no facts but what are against us, nor any principles on which to reason. It is vain to write thus without materials. The fact seems to be against you ; at least, I cannot know nor say anything to the contrary. I am glad that you like the book so well. I hear no more of Macpherson. I shall long to know what Lord Hailes says of it. Lend it him privately. I shall send the parcel as soon as I can. Make my compliments to Mrs. Boswell.

> " I am, Sir, &c.,
> " SAM. JOHNSON."

" MR. BOSWELL TO DR. JOHNSON.

> "*Edinburgh, Feb.* 2, 1775.

*   *   *   *   *

" As to Macpherson, I am anxious to have from yourself a full and pointed account of what has passed between you and him. It is confidently told here, that before your book came out, he sent to you, to let you know that he understood you meant to deny the authenticity of Ossian's poems ; that the originals were in his possession ; that you might have inspection of them, and might take the evidence of people skilled in the Erse language ; and that he hoped, after this fair offer, you would not be so uncandid as to assert that he had refused reasonable proof. That you paid no regard to his message, but published your strong attack upon him ; and then he wrote a letter to you, in such terms as he thought suited to one who had not acted as a man of veracity. You may believe it gives me pain to hear your conduct represented as unfavourable, while I can only deny what is said, on the ground that your character refutes it, without having any information to oppose. Let me, I beg it of you, be furnished with a sufficient answer to any calumny upon this occasion.

" Lord Hailes writes to me (for we correspond more than we talk together), ' As to Fingal, I see a controversy arising, and purpose to keep out of its way. There is no doubt that I might mention some circumstances, but I do not choose to commit them to paper.' [1] What his opinion is, I do not know. He says, ' I am singularly obliged to Dr. Johnson for his accurate and useful criticisms. Had he given some strictures on the general plan of the work, it would have added much to its favours.' He is charmed with your verses on Inchkenneth, says they are very elegant, but bids me tell you he doubts whether

> ' *Legitimas faciunt pectora pura preces,*'

be according to the rubric. But that is your concern, for you know he is a Presbyterian."

*   *   *   *   *   *

[1] His Lordship, notwithstanding his resolution, did commit his sentiments to paper, and in one of his notes affixed to his Collection of Old Scottish Poetry, he says, that " to doubt the authenticity of those poems, is a refinement in scepticism indeed.'—J. BOSWELL, JUN.

" TO DR. LAWRENCE.[1]

"Sir,   *Feb.* 7, 1775.

" One of the Scotch physicians is now prosecuting a corporation that in some public instrument have styled him *Doctor of Medicine* instead of *Physician.* Boswell desires, being advocate for the corporation, to know whether *Doctor of Medicine* is not a legitimate title, and whether it may be considered as a disadvantageous distinction. I am to write to-night; be pleased to tell me.

" I am, Sir,

" Your most, &c.,

" SAM. JOHNSON."

" TO JAMES BOSWELL, ESQ.

"My dear Boswell,   *February* 7, 1775.

" I am surprised that, knowing, as you do, the disposition of your country-men to tell lies in favour of each other,[2] you can be at all affected by any reports that circulate among them. Macpherson never in his life offered me a sight of any original or of any evidence of any kind ;—but thought only of intimidating me by noise and threats, till my last answer,—that I would not be deterred from detecting what I thought a cheat, by the menaces of a ruffian,—put an end to our correspondence.

" The state of the question is this. He and Dr. Blair, whom I consider as deceived, say that he copied the poem from old manuscripts. His copies, if he had them, and I believe him to have none, are nothing. Where are the manuscripts? They can be shown if they exist, but they were never shown. '*De non existentibus et non apparentibus,*' says our law, '*eadem est ratio.*' No man has a claim to credit upon his own word, when better evidence, if he had it, may be easily produced. But so far as we can find, the Erse language was never written till very lately for the purposes of religion. A nation that cannot write, or a language that was never written, has no manuscripts.

" But whatever he has he never offered to show. If old manuscripts should now be mentioned, I should, unless there were more evidence than can be easily had, suppose them another proof of Scotch conspiracy in national falsehood.

" Do not censure the expression ; you know it to be true.

" Dr. Memis's question is so narrow as to allow no speculation ; and I have no facts before me but those which his advocate has produced against you.

" I consulted this morning the President of the London College of Physicians, who says, that with us, *Doctor of Physic* (we do not say *Doctor of Medicine*) is the highest title that a practiser of physic can have ; that *Doctor* implies not only *Physician,* but teacher of physic ; that every *Doctor* is legally a *Physician ;* but no man, not a *Doctor,* can *practise physic* but by *licence* particularly granted. The Doctorate is a licence of itself. It seems to us a very slender cause of prosecution.

*   *   *   *   *   *

---

[1] The learned and worthy Dr. Lawrence, whom Dr. Johnson respected and loved as his physician and friend.—BOSWELL.

[2] My friend has, in this letter, relied upon my testimony, with a confidence, of which the ground has escaped my recollection.—BOSWELL.

" I am now engaged, but in a little time I hope to do all you would have. My compliments to Madam and Veronica.

"I am, Sir, your most humble servant,
"SAM. JOHNSON."

What words were used by Mr. Macpherson in his letter to the venerable sage, I have never heard ; but they are generally said to have been of a nature very different from the language of literary contest. Dr Johnson's answer appeared in the newspapers of the day, and has since been frequently republished ; but not with perfect accuracy. I give it as dictated to me by himself, written down in his presence, and authenticated by a note in his own handwriting, " *This, I think, is a true copy.*" [1]

" MR. JAMES MACPHERSON,

" I received your foolish and impudent letter. Any violence offered me I shall do my best to repel ; and what I cannot do for myself, the law shall do for me. I hope I shall never be deterred from detecting what I think a cheat, by the menaces of a ruffian.

" What would you have me retract ? I thought your book an imposture ; I think it an imposture still. For this opinion I have given my reasons to the public, which I here dare you to refute. Your rage I defy. Your abilities, since your Homer, are not so formidable ; and what I hear of your morals inclines me to pay regard not to what you shall say, but to what you shall prove. You may print this if you will.

" SAM. JOHNSON."

Mr. Macpherson little knew the character of Dr. Johnson, if he supposed that he could be easily intimidated : for no man was ever more remarkable for personal courage. He had, indeed, an awful dread of death, or rather, " of something after death ; " and what rational man, who seriously thinks of quitting all that he has ever known, and going into a new and unknown state of being, can be without that dread ? But his fear was from reflection ; his courage natural. His fear, in that one instance, was the result of philosophical and religious consideration. He feared death, but he feared nothing else, not even what might occasion death. Many instances of his resolution may be mentioned. One day, at Mr. Beauclerk's house in the country, when two large dogs were fighting, he went up to them, and beat them till they separated ; and at another time, when told of the danger there was that a gun might burst if charged with many balls, he put in six or seven and fired it off against a wall. Mr. Langton told me, that when they were swimming together near Oxford, he cautioned Dr. Johnson against a pool, which was reckoned particularly dangerous ; upon which Johnson directly swam into it. He told me himself that one night he was attacked in the street by four men, to whom he would not yield, but kept them all at bay, till the watch came up, and carried both him and them to the round-house. In the playhouse at Lichfield, as Mr. Garrick informed me, Johnson having for a moment quitted a chair which was placed for him between the side scenes, a gentleman took possession of it, and when Johnson on his return civilly demanded his seat, rudely refused to give it up ; upon which Johnson laid hold of it, and tossed him and the chair into the pit. Foote, who so successfully revived the old comedy, by exhibiting living characters, had resolved to imitate Johnson on the stage ; expecting great profits from the ridicule of so celebrated a man. Johnson being informed of his intention, and being at dinner at Mr. Thomas Davies's, the bookseller, from whom I had the story, he asked Mr. Davies " what was the common price of an oak stick ; " and being answered sixpence, " Why then, Sir," said he, " give me leave to send your servant to purchase me a shilling one. I'll have a double quantity ; for I am told Foote means to *take me off*, as he calls it, and I am determined the fellow shall not do it with impunity." Davies took care to acquaint Foote of this, which effectually checked the wantonness of the mimic. Mr. Macpherson's menaces made Johnson provide himself with the same implement of defence ; and had he been attacked, I have no doubt that, old as he was, he would have made his corporal prowess be felt as much as his intellectual.

His " Journey to the Western Islands of Scotland " * is a most valuable performance. It abounds in extensive philosophical views of society, and in ingenious sentiment and lively description. A considerable part of it, indeed, consists of speculations, which many years before he saw the wild regions which we visited together, probably had employed his attention, though the actual sight of those scenes undoubtedly quickened and augmented them. Mr. Orme,[1] the very able historian, agreed with me in this opinion, which he thus strongly expressed :—" There are in that book, thoughts, which, by long revolution in the great mind of Johnson, have been formed and polished like pebbles rolled in the ocean ! "

That he was to some degree of excess a *true-born Englishman*, so as to have entertained an undue prejudice against both the country and the people of Scotland, must be allowed. But it was a prejudice of the head, and not of the heart. He had no ill-will to the Scotch ; for, if he had been conscious of that, he would never have thrown himself into the bosom of their country, and trusted to the protection of its remote inhabitants with a fearless confidence. His remark upon the nakedness of the country, from its being denuded of trees, was made after having travelled two hundred miles along the Eastern coast, where certainly trees are not to be found near the road ; and he said it was " a map of

[1] Robert Orme, author of " The History of the Military Transactions of the British Nation in Hindostan "

the road " which he gave. His disbelief of the authenticity of the poems ascribed to Ossian, a Highland bard, was confirmed in the course of his journey, by a very strict examination of the evidence offered for it ; and although their authenticity was made too much a national point by the Scotch, there were many respectable persons in that country, who did not concur in this ; so that his judgment upon the question ought not to be decided, even by those who differ from him. As to myself, I can only say, upon a subject now become very uninteresting, that when the fragments of Highland poetry first came out, I was much pleased with their wild peculiarity, and was one of those who subscribed to enable their editor, Mr. Macpherson, then a young man, to make a search in the Highlands and Hebrides for a long poem in the Erse language, which was reported to be preserved somewhere in those regions. But when there came forth an Epic Poem in six books, with all the common circumstances of former compositions of that nature; and when, upon an attentive examination of it, there was found a perpetual recurrence of the same images which appear in the fragments ; and when no ancient manuscript, to authenticate the work, was deposited in any public library, though that was insisted on as a reasonable proof, *who* could forbear to doubt ?

Johnson's grateful acknowledgments of kindness received in the course of this tour, completely refute the brutal reflections which have been thrown out against him, as if he had made an ungrateful return ; and his delicacy in sparing in his book those who we find from his letters to Mrs. Thrale were just objects of censure, is much to be admired. His candour and amiable disposition is conspicuous from his conduct, when informed by Mr. Macleod, of Rasay, that he had committed a mistake, which gave that gentleman some uneasiness. He wrote him a courteous and kind letter, and inserted in the newspapers an advertisement, correcting the mistake.[1]

The observations of my friend Mr. Dempster in a letter written to me, soon after he had read Dr. Johnson's book, are so just and liberal, that they cannot be too often repeated :

* * * * * *

"There is nothing in the book, from beginning to end, that a Scotchman need to take amiss. What he says of the country is true ; and his observations on the people are what must naturally occur to a sensible, observing, and reflecting inhabitant of a convenient metropolis, where a man on thirty pounds a-year may be better accommodated with all the little wants of life, than Coll or Sir Allan.

" I am charmed with his researches concerning the Erse language, and the antiquity of their manuscripts. I am quite convinced ; and I shall rank Ossian and his Fingals and Oscars, amongst the nursery tales, not the true history of our country, in all time to come.

[1] See "Journal of a Tour to the Hebrides," 3rd edit. p. 520.—BOSWELL.

"Upon the whole, the book cannot displease, for it has no pretensions. The author neither says he is a geographer, nor an antiquarian, nor very learned in the history of Scotland, nor a naturalist, nor a fossilist. The manners of the people, and the face of the country, are all he attempts to describe or seems to have thought of. Much were it to be wished that they who have travelled into more remote, and of course more curious regions, had all possessed his good sense. Of the state of learning, his observations on Glasgow University show he has formed a very sound judgment. He understands our climate too; and he has accurately observed the changes, however slow and imperceptible to us, which Scotland has undergone in consequence of the blessings of liberty and internal peace."

*   *   *   *   *

Mr. Knox, another native of Scotland, who has since made the same tour, and published an account of it, is equally liberal :—

"I have read," says he, "his book again and again, travelled with him from Berwick to Glenelg, through countries with which I am well acquainted; sailed with him from Glenelg to Rasay, Sky, Rum, Coll, Mull, and Icolmkill, but have not been able to correct him in any matter of consequence. I have often admired the accuracy, the precision, and the justness of what he advances respecting both the country and the people.

"The Doctor has everywhere delivered his sentiments with freedom, and in many instances with a seeming regard for the benefit of the inhabitants, and the ornament of the country. His remarks on the want of trees and hedges for shade, as well as for shelter to the cattle, are well founded, and merit the thanks, not the illiberal censure of the natives. He also felt for the distresses of the Highlanders, and explodes with great propriety the bad management of the grounds, and the neglect of timber in the Hebrides."

Having quoted Johnson's just compliments on the Rasay family, he says :—

"On the other hand, I found this family equally lavish in their encomiums upon the Doctor's conversation, and his subsequent civilities to a young gentleman of that country, who, upon waiting upon him at London, was well received, and experienced all the attention and regard that a warm friend could bestow. Mr. Macleod having also been in London, waited upon the Doctor, who provided a magnificent and expensive entertainment in honour of his old Hebridean acquaintance."

And talking of the military road by Fort Augustus, he says :—

"By this road, though one of the most rugged in Great Britain, the celebrated Dr. Johnson passed from Inverness to the Hebride Isles. His observations on the country and people are extremely correct, judicious, and instructive." [1]

Mr. Tytler, the acute and able vindicator of Mary Queen of Scots, in one of his letters to Mr. James Elphinstone, published in that gentleman's "Forty Years' Correspondence," says :—

[1] Page 103.—BOSWELL.

" I read Dr. Johnson's Tour with very great pleasure. Some few errors he has fallen into, but of no great importance, and those are lost in the numberless beauties of his work. If I had leisure, I could perhaps point out the most exceptionable places; but at present I am in the country, and have not his book at hand. It is plain he meant to speak well of Scotland ; and he has, in my apprehension, done us great honour in the most capital article, the character of the inhabitants."

His private letters to Mrs. Thrale, written during the course of his journey, which therefore may be supposed to convey his genuine feelings at the time, abound in such benignant sentiments towards the people who showed him civilities, that no man whose temper is not very harsh and sour, can retain a doubt of the goodness of his heart.

It is painful to recollect with what rancour he was assailed by numbers of shallow irritable North Britons, on account of his supposed injurious treatment of their country and countrymen, in his " Journey." Had there been any just ground for such a charge, would the virtuous and candid Dempster have given his opinion of the book, in the terms in which I have quoted ? Would the patriotic Knox[1] have spoken of it as he has done ? Would Mr. Tytler, surely

" —— a *Scot*, if ever *Scot* there were,"

have expressed himself thus ? And let me add, that, citizen of the world as I hold myself to be, I have that degree of predilection for my *natale solum*, nay, I have that just sense of the merit of an ancient nation which has been ever renowned for its valour, which in former times maintained its independence against a powerful neighbour, and in modern times has been equally distinguished for its ingenuity and industry in civilised life, that I should have felt a generous indignation at any injustice done to it. Johnson treated Scotland no worse than he did even his best friends, whose characters he used to give as they appeared to him, both in light and shade. Some people, who had not exercised their minds sufficiently, condemned him for censuring his friends. But Sir Joshua Reynolds, whose philosophical penetration and justness of thinking were not less known to those who lived with him, than his genius in his art is admired by the world, explained his conduct thus :—

" He was fond of discrimination, which he could not show without pointing out the bad as well as the good in every character; and as his friends were those whose characters he knew best, they afforded him the best opportunity for showing the acuteness of his judgment."

He expressed to his friend Mr. Windham, of Norfolk, his wonder at the extreme jealousy of the Scotch, and their resentment at having their

[1] I observed with much regret, while the first edition of this work was passing through the press (August, 1790), that this ingenious gentleman was dead.—BOSWELL.

country described by him as it really was ; when, to say that it was a
country as good as England, would have been a great falsehood.
" None of us," said he, " would be offended if a foreigner who
has travelled here should say, that vines and olives don't grow in
England." And as to his prejudice against the Scotch, which I always
ascribed to that nationality which he observed in *them*, he said to the
same gentleman, " When I find a Scotchman, to whom an Englishman
is as a Scotchman, that Scotchman shall be an Englishman to me."
His intimacy with many gentlemen of Scotland, and his employing so
many natives of that country as his amanuenses, prove that his prejudice was not virulent ; and I have deposited in the British Museum,
amongst other pieces of his writing, the following note in answer to one
from me, asking if he would meet me at dinner at the Mitre, though a
friend of mine, a Scotchman, was to be there :—

" Mr. Johnson does not see why Mr. Boswell should suppose a Scotchman
less acceptable than any other man. He will be at the Mitre."

My much-valued friend, Dr. Barnard, now Bishop of Killaloe, having
once expressed to him an apprehension, that if he should visit Ireland he
might treat the people of that country more unfavourably than he had
done the Scotch, he answered, with strong pointed double-edged wit,
" Sir, you have no reason to be afraid of me. The Irish are not in a
conspiracy to cheat the world by false representations of the merits of
their countrymen. No, Sir ; the Irish are a FAIR PEOPLE ;—they never
speak well of one another."

Johnson told me of an instance of Scottish nationality, which made a
very unfavourable impression upon his mind. A Scotchman of some
consideration in London, solicited him to recommend by the weight of
his learned authority, to be master of an English school, a person of
whom he who recommended him confessed he knew no more but that
he was his countryman. Johnson was shocked at this unconscientious
conduct.

All the miserable cavillings against his " Journey," in newspapers,
magazines, and other fugitive publications, I can speak from certain
knowledge, only furnished him with sport. At last there came out a
scurrilous volume, larger than Johnson's own, filled with malignant
abuse, under a name, real or fictitious, of some low man, in an obscure
corner of Scotland, though supposed to be the work of another Scotchman, who has found means to make himself well known both in
Scotland and England. The effect which it had upon Johnson was, to
produce this pleasant observation to Mr. Seward, to whom he lent the
book ; " This fellow must be a blockhead. They don't know how to go
about their abuse. Who will read a five shilling book against me ?
No, Sir, if they had wit, they should have kept pelting me with
pamphlets."

"MR. BOSWELL TO DR. JOHNSON.

"*Edinburgh, Feb.* 18, 1775.

"You would have been very well pleased if you had dined with me to-day. I had for my guests, Macquharrie, young Maclean of Coll, the successor of our friend, a very amiable man, though not marked with such active qualities as his brother; Mr. Maclean of Torloisk in Mull, a gentleman of Sir Allan's family: and two of the clan Grant; so that the Highland and Hebridean genius reigned. We had a great deal of conversation about you, and drank your health in a bumper. The toast was not proposed by me, which is a circumstance to be remarked, for I am now so connected with you, that anything that I say or do to your honour has not the value of an additional compliment. It is only giving you a guinea out of that treasure of admiration which already belongs to you, and which is no hidden treasure; for I suppose my admiration of you is co-existent with the knowledge of my character.

"I find that the Highlanders and Hebrideans in general are much fonder of your 'Journey,' than the low-country or *hither* Scots. One of the Grants said to day, that he was sure you were a man of a good heart, and a candid man, and seemed to hope that he should be able to convince you of the antiquity of a good proportion of the poems of Ossian. After all that has passed, I think the matter is capable of being proved to a certain degree. I am told that Macpherson got one old Erse MS. from Clanranald, for the restitution of which he executed a formal obligation; and it is affirmed, that the Gaelic (call it Erse or call it Irish) has been written in the Highlands and Hebrides for many centuries. It is reasonable to suppose, that such of the inhabitants as acquired any learning, possessed the art of writing as well as their Irish neighbours and Celtic cousins; and the question is, can sufficient evidence be shown of this?

"Those who are skilled in ancient writings can determine the age of MSS., or at least can ascertain the century in which they were written; and if men of veracity, who are so skilled, shall tell us that MSS. in the possession of families in the Highlands and the isles, are the works of a remote age, I think we should be convinced by their testimony.

"There is now come to this city Ranald Macdonald, from the Isle of Egg, who has several MSS. of Erse poetry, which he wishes to publish by subscription. I have engaged to take three copies of the book, the price of which is to be six shillings, as I would subscribe for all the Erse that can be printed, be it old or new, that the language may be preserved. This man says, that some of his manuscripts are ancient; and, to be sure, one of them which was shown to me does appear to have the duskiness of antiquity.

*   *   *   *   *

"The inquiry is not yet quite hopeless, and I should think that the exact truth may be discovered, if proper means be used.

"I am, &c.,

"JAMES BOSWELL."

" TO JAMES BOSWELL, ESQ.

"DEAR SIR,   *Feb.* 25, 1775.

" I am sorry that I could get no books for my friends in Scotland. Mr. Strahan has at last promised to send two dozen to you. If they come put the names of my friends into them : you may cut them out,[1] and paste them with a little starch in the book.

" You then are going wild about Ossian. Why do you think any part can be proved? The dusky manuscript of Egg is probably not fifty years old ; if it be an hundred, it proves nothing. The tale of Clanranald is no proof. Has Clanranald told it? Can he prove it? There are, I believe, no Erse manuscripts. None of the old families had a single letter in Erse that we heard of. You say it is likely that they could write. The learned, if any learned there were, could ; but knowing, by that learning, some written language, in that language they wrote, as letters had never been applied to their own. If there are manuscripts, let them be shown, with some proof that they are not forged for the occasion. You say many can remember parts of Ossian. I believe all those parts are versions of the English ; at least there is no proof of their antiquity.

" Macpherson is said to have made some translations himself; and having taught a boy to write it, ordered him to say that he had learned it of his grandmother. The boy, when he grew up, told the story. This Mrs. Williams heard at Mr. Strahan's table. Don't be credulous; you know how little a Highlander can be trusted. Macpherson is, so far as I know, very quiet. Is not that proof enough? Everything is against him. No visible manuscript: no inscription in the language: no correspondence among friends : no transaction of business, of which a single scrap remains in the ancient families. Macpherson's pretence is, that the character was Saxon. If he had not talked unskilfully of *manuscripts*, he might have fought with oral tradition much longer. As to Mr. Grant's information, I suppose he knows much less of the matter than ourselves.

" In the mean time, the bookseller says that the sale [2] is sufficiently quick. They printed four thousand. Correct your copy wherever it is wrong, and bring it up. Your friends will all be glad to see you. I think of going myself into the country about May,

" I am sorry that I have not managed to send the book sooner. I have left four for you, and do not restrict you absolutely to follow my directions in the distribution. You must use your own discretion.

" Make my compliments to Mrs. Boswell : I suppose she is now beginning to forgive me. I am, dear Sir, your humble servant,

"SAM. JOHNSON."

From a list in his handwriting.—BOSWELL.
[2] Of his " Journey to the Western Islands of Scotland."

EXTERIOR OF DRURY LANE THEATRE.—1775.

CHAPTER X.—1775.

BOSWELL RE-VISITS LONDON—JOHNSON PUBLISHES HIS PAMPHLET "TAXATION NO TYRANNY —DR. TOWERS'S REPLY—JOHNSON AND BOSWELL VISIT MR. STRAHAN.— GARRICK'S IMITATIONS—GRAY'S ODES—JOHNSON RECEIVES HIS DIPLOMA OF LL.D.—BRUCE, THE ABYSSINIAN TRAVELLER—JOHNSON'S OPINION OF PUBLIC SPEAKERS—HIS CONTEMPT FOR COLLEY CIBBER—CONVIVIAL DINNERS—"LILLIBURLERO"—PATRIOTISM—ADVISES GENERAL OGLETHORPE TO PUBLISH HIS LIFE.

ON Tuesday, March 21, I arrived in London ; and on repairing to Dr. Johnson's before dinner, found him in his study, sitting with Mr. Peter Garrick, the elder brother of David, strongly resembling him in countenance and voice, but of more sedate and placid manners. Johnson informed me, that though Mr. Beauclerk was in great pain it was hoped he was not in danger, and that he now wished to consult Dr. Heberden, to try the effect of a "new understanding." Both at this interview, and in the evening at Mr. Thrale's, where he and Mr. Peter Garrick and I met again, he was vehement on the subject of the Ossian controversy ; observing, "We do not know that there are any ancient Erse manuscripts : and we have no other reason to disbelieve that there are men with three heads, but that we do not know that there are any such men." He also was outrageous upon his supposition that my countrymen "loved Scotland better than truth," saying "All of them —nay, not all, but *droves* of them—would come up, and attest any thing for the honour of Scotland." He also persevered in his wild allegation, that he questioned if there was a tree between Edinburgh and the English border older than himself. I assured him he was mistaken, and suggested that the proper punishment would be, that he should receive a stripe at every tree above a hundred years old, that was found within that space. He laughed, and said, "I believe I might submit to it for a *baubee !*"

The doubts which, in my correspondence with him, I had ventured to state as to the justice and wisdom of the conduct of Great Britain towards the American colonies, while I at the same time requested that he would enable me to inform myself upon that momentous subject, he had altogether disregarded ; and had recently published a pamphlet, entitled, "Taxation no Tyranny: an answer to the Resolutions and Address of the American Congress." *

He had long before indulged most unfavourable sentiments of our fellow-subjects in America. For, as early as 1769, I was told by Dr. John Campbell, that he had said of them, "Sir, they are a race of convicts, and ought to be thankful for anything we allow them short of hanging."

Of this performance I avoided to talk with him ; for I had now formed a clear and settled opinion, that the people of America were well warranted to resist a claim that their fellow-subjects in the mother-country should have the entire command of their fortunes, by taxing them without their own consent ; and the extreme violence which it breathed, appeared to me so unsuitable to the mildness of a Christian philosopher, and so directly opposite to the principles of peace, which he had so beautifully recommended in his pamphlet respecting Falkland's Islands, that I was sorry to see him appear in so unfavourable a light. Besides, I could not perceive in it that ability of argument, or that felicity of expression, for which he was, upon other occasions, so eminent. Positive assertion, sarcastical severity, and extravagant ridicule, which he himself reprobated as a test of truth, were united in this rhapsody.

That this pamphlet was written at the desire of those who were then in power, I have no doubt ; and, indeed, he owned to me, that it had been revised and curtailed by some of them. He told me, that they had struck out one passage, which was to this effect :—

"That the colonists could with no solidity argue from their not having been taxed while in their infancy, that they should not now be taxed. We do not put a calf into the plough ; we wait till he is an ox."

He said, "They struck it out either critically as too ludicrous, or politically as too exasperating. I care not which. It was their business. If an architect says, I will build five stories, and the man who employs him says, I will have only three, the employer is to decide." " Yes, Sir," said I, "in ordinary cases. But should it be so when the architect gives his skill and labour *gratis ?* "

Unfavourable as I am constrained to say my opinion of this pamphlet was, yet, since it was congenial with the sentiments of numbers at that time, and as everything relating to the writings of Dr. Johnson is of importance in literary history, I shall therefore insert some passages which were struck out, it does not appear why, either by himself or those who revised it. They appear printed in a few proof leaves of it in my possession, marked with corrections in his own handwriting. I shall distinguish them by *italics.*

In the paragraph where he says, the Americans were incited to resistance by European intelligence from

"men whom they thought their friends, but who were friends only to themselves,"

there followed,—

" *and made by their selfishness, the enemies of their country.*"

And the next paragraph ran thus :—

" On the original contrivers of mischief, *rather than on those whom they have deluded,* let an insulted nation pour out its vengeance."

The paragraph which came next was in these words :—

" *Unhappy is that country in which men can hope for advancement by favouring its enemies. The tranquillity of stable government is not always easily preserved against the machinations of single innovators ; but what can be the hope of quiet, when factions hostile to the legislature can be openly formed and openly avowed ?*"

After the paragraph which now concludes the pamphlet, there followed this, in which he certainly means the great Earl of Chatham, and glances at a certain popular Lord Chancellor :—

" *If, by the fortune of war, they drive us utterly away, what they will do next ian only be conjectured. If a new monarchy is erected, they will want a* KING. *He who first takes into his hand the sceptre of America, should have a name of good omen.* WILLIAM *has been known both a conqueror and deliverer ; and perhaps England, however contemned, might yet supply them with* ANOTHER WILLIAM. *Whigs, indeed, are not willing to be governed ; and it is possible that* KING WILLIAM *may be strongly inclined to guide their measures : but Whigs have been cheated like other mortals, and suffered their leader to become their tyrant, under the name of their* PROTECTOR. *What more they will receive from England, no man can tell. In their rudiments of empire they may want a* CHANCELLOR.*"

Then came this paragraph :—

" *Their numbers are, at present, not quite sufficient for the greatness which, in some form of government or other, is to rival the ancient monarchies ; but by Dr. Franklin's rule of progression, they will, in a century and a quarter, be more than equal to the inhabitants of Europe. When the Whigs of America are thus multiplied, let the Princes of the earth tremble in their palaces. If they should continue to double and to double, their own hemisphere would not contain them. But let not our boldest oppugners of authority look forward with delight to this futurity of Whiggism."*

How it ended I know not, as it is cut off abruptly at the foot of the last of these proof pages.

His pamphlets in support of the measures of administration were published on his own account, and he afterwards collected them into a volume, with the title of "Political Tracts, by the Author of the Rambler," with this motto:—

> " *Fallitur egregio quisquis sub Principe credit*
> *Servitium ; nunquam libertas gratior extat*
> *Quam sub Rege pio.*"—CLAUDIANUS.

These pamphlets drew upon him numerous attacks. Against the common weapons of literary warfare he was hardened ; but there were two instances of animadversion which I communicated to him, and from what I could judge, both from his silence and his looks, appeared to me to impress him much.

One was, " A Letter to Dr. Samuel Johnson, occasioned by his late political Publications." It appeared previous to his " Taxation n- Tyranny," and was written by Dr. Joseph Towers. In that perform-ance, Dr. Johnson was treated with the respect due to so eminent a man, whilst his conduct as a political writer was boldly and pointedly arraigned, as inconsistent with the character of one, who, if he did employ his pen upon politics,

" it might reasonably be expected should distinguish himself, not by party violence and rancour, but by moderation and by wisdom."

It concluded thus :—

" I would, however, wish you to remember, should you again address the public under the character of a political writer, that luxuriance of imagination or energy of language, will ill compensate for the want of candour, of justice, and of truth. And I shall only add, that should I hereafter be disposed to read, as I heretofore have done, the most excellent of all your performances, ' The Rambler,' the pleasure which I have been accustomed to find in it will be much diminished by the reflection that the writer of so moral, so elegant, and so valuable a work, was capable of prostituting his talents in such produc-tions as ' The False Alarm,' the ' Thoughts on the Transactions respecting Falkland's Islands,' and ' The Patriot.' "

I am willing to do justice to the merit of Dr. Towers, of whom I will say, that although I abhor his Whiggish democratical notions and propensities (for I will not call them principles), I esteem him as an ingenious, knowing, and very convivial man.

The other instance was a paragraph of a letter to me, from my old and most intimate friend the Reverend Mr. Temple, who wrote the character of Gray, which has had the honour to be adopted both by

Mr. Mason and Dr. Johnson in their accounts of that poet. The words were—

"How can your great, I will not say your *pious*, but your *moral* friend, support the barbarous measures of administration, which they have not the face to ask even their infidel pensioner Hume to defend?"

However confident of the rectitude of his own mind, Johnson may have felt sincere uneasiness that his conduct should be erroneously imputed to unworthy motives, by good men ; and that the influence of his valuable writings should on that account be in any degree obstructed or lessened.

He complained to a right honourable friend of distinguished talents and very elegant manners, with whom he maintained a long intimacy, and whose generosity towards him will afterwards appear, that his pension having been given to him as a literary character, he had been applied to by the administration to write political pamphlets ; and he was even so much irritated, that he declared his resolution to resign his pension. His friend showed him the impropriety of such a measure, and he afterwards expressed his gratitude, and said he had received good advice. To that friend he once signified a wish to have his pension secured to him for life ; but he neither asked nor received from government any reward whatsoever for his political labours.

GEORGE COLMAN.

On Friday, March 24, I met him at the LITERARY CLUB, where were Mr. Beauclerk, Mr. Langton, Mr. Colman, Dr. Percy, Mr. Vesey, Sir Charles Bunbury, Dr. George Fordyce, Mr. Steevens, and Mr. Charles Fox. Before he came in, we talked of his "Journey to the Western Islands," and of his coming away, "willing to believe the second sight," which seemed to excite some ridicule. I was then so impressed with the truth of many of the stories of which I had been told, that I avowed my conviction, saying, "He is only *willing* to believe : I *do* believe. The evidence is enough for me, though not for his great mind. What will not fill a quart bottle, will fill a pint bottle. I am filled with belief." "Are you?" said Colman; "then cork it up."

I found his "Journey" the common topic of conversation in London at this time, wherever I happened to be. At one of Lord Mansfield's formal Sunday evening conversations, strangely called *Levées*, his

..ordship addressed me, " We have all been reading your travels, Mr. Boswell." I answered, "I was but the humble attendant of Dr. Johnson." The Chief-Justice replied, with that air and manner which none, who ever saw and heard him, can forget, " He speaks ill of nobody but Ossian."

Johnson was in high spirits this evening at the Club, and talked with great animation and success. He attacked Swift, as he used to do upon all occasions. " The ' Tale of a Tub ' is so much superior to his other writings, that one can hardly believe he was the author of it : [1] there is in it such a vigour of mind, such a swarm of thoughts, so much of nature, and art, and life." I wondered to hear him say of " Gulliver's Travels," " When once you have thought of big men and little men, it is very easy to do all the rest." I endeavoured to make a stand for Swift, and tried to rouse those who were much more able to defend him ; but in vain. Johnson at last, of his own accord, allowed very great merit to the inventory of articles found in the pocket of " The Man Mountain," particularly the description of his watch, which it was conjectured was his God, as he consulted it upon all occasions. He observed, that " Swift put his name to but two things (after he had a name to put), ' The Plan for the Improvement of the English Language,' and the last ' Drapier's Letter.' "

From Swift, there was an easy transition to Mr. Thomas Sheridan. Johnson : " Sheridan is a wonderful admirer of the tragedy of Douglas, and presented its author with a gold medal. Some years ago, at a coffee-house in Oxford, I called to him, ' Mr. Sheridan, Mr. Sheridan, how came you to give a gold medal to Home, for writing that foolish play ? ' This, you see, was wanton and insolent ; but I *meant* to be wanton and insolent. A medal has no value but as a stamp of merit. And was Sheridan to assume to himself the right of giving that stamp ? If Sheridan was magnificent enough to bestow a gold medal as an honorary reward of dramatic excellence, he should have requested one of the Universities to choose the person on whom it should be conferred. Sheridan had no right to give a stamp of merit : it was counterfeiting Apollo's coin."

[1] This doubt has been much agitated on both sides, I think without good reason. See Addison's " Freeholder," May 4, 1714; " An Apology for the Tale of a Tub;" Dr. Hawkesworth's " Preface to Swift's Works," and Swift's " Letter to Tooke the Printer," and Tooke's " Answer" in that collection; Sheridan's " Life of Swift;" Mr. Courtenay's note on p. 3 of his " Poetical Review of the Literary and Moral Character of Dr. Johnson;" and Mr. Cooksey's " Essay on the Life and Character of John Lord Somers, Baron of Evesham."

Dr. Johnson here speaks only to the *internal evidence.* I take leave to differ from him, having a very high estimation of the powers of Dr. Swift. His " Sentiments of a Church-of-England man;" his " Sermon on the Trinity," and other serious pieces, prove his learning as well as his acuteness in logic and metaphysics; and his various compositions of a different cast exhibit not only wit, humour, and ridicule; but a knowledge "of nature, and art, and life;" a combination therefore of those powers, when (as the " Apology " says) " the author was young, his invention at the height, and his reading fresh in his head," might surely produce " *The Tale of a Tub.*"—Boswell.

On Monday, March 27, I breakfasted with him at Mr. Strahan's. He told us, that he was engaged to go that evening to Mrs. Abington's benefit. "She was visiting some ladies whom I was visiting, and begged that I would come to her benefit. I told her I could not hear: but she insisted so much on my coming, that it would have been brutal to have refused her." This was a speech quite characteristical. He loved to bring forward his having been in the gay circles of life ; and he

MRS. ABINGTON.

was, perhaps, a little vain of the solicitations of this elegant and fashionable actress. He told us, the play was to be "The Hypocrite," altered from Cibber's "Nonjuror," so as to satirise the Methodists. "I do not think," said he, "the character of the Hypocrite justly applicable to the Methodists, but it was very applicable to the Nonjurors. I once said to Dr. Madan, a clergyman of Ireland, who was a great Whig, that perhaps a Nonjuror would have been less criminal in taking the oaths imposed by the ruling power, than refusing them ; because refusing them, necessarily laid him under almost an irresistible temptation to be more criminal ; for, a man *must* live, and if he precludes himself from the support furnished by the establishment, will probably be reduced to very wicked shifts to maintain himself." [1] BOSWELL : "I should think, Sir, that a man who took the oaths contrary to his principles, was a

· This was not merely a cursory remark ; for in his "Life of Fenton" he observes, "With many other wise and virtuous men, who at that time of discord and debate [about the beginning of this century], consulted conscience well or ill informed, more than interest, he doubted the legality of the government ; and refusing to qualify himself for public employment, by taking the oaths required, left the University without a degree." This conduct Johnson calls "perverseness of integrity."

The question concerning the morality of taking oaths, of whatever kind, imposed by the prevailing power at the time, rather than to be excluded from all consequence, or even any considerable usefulness in society, has been agitated with all the acuteness of casuistry. It is related, that he who devised the oath of abjuration, profligately boasted, that he had framed a test which should "damn one half of the nation, and starve the other." Upon minds not exalted to inflexible rectitude, or minds in which zeal for a party is predominant to excess, taking that oath against conviction, may have been palliated under the plea of necessity, or ventured upon in heat, as upon the whole producing more good than evil.

At a county election in Scotland, many years ago, when there was a warm contest between the friends of the Hanoverian succession, and those against it, the oath of abjuration having been demanded, the freeholders upon one side rose to go away. Upon which a very sanguine gentleman, one of their number, ran to the door to stop them, calling out with much earnestness, "Stay, stay, my friends, and let us swear the rogues out of it."—BOSWELL.

determined wicked man, because he was sure he was committing perjury, whereas a Nonjuror might be insensibly led to do what was wrong, without being so directly conscious of it." Johnson : " Why, Sir, a man who goes to bed to his patron's wife, is pretty sure that he is committing wickedness." Boswell : " Did the nonjuring clergymen do so, Sir ?" Johnson : " I am afraid many of them did."

I was startled at this argument, and could by no means think it convincing. Had not his own father complied with the requisition of government (as to which he once observed to me, when I pressed him upon it, " That, Sir, he was to settle with himself,") he would probably have thought more unfavourably of a Jacobite who took the oaths :—

> " ———had he not resembled
> My father as he *swore.*"

Mr. Strahan talked of launching into the great ocean of London, in order to have a chance for rising into eminence ; and, observing that many men were kept back from trying their fortunes there, because they were born to a competency, said, " Small certainties are the bane of men of talents ; " which Johnson confirmed. Mr. Strahan put Johnson in mind of a remark which he had made to him ; " There are few ways in which a man can be more innocently employed than in getting money." " The more one thinks of this," said Strahan, " the juster it will appear."

Mr. Strahan had taken a poor boy from the country as an apprentice, upon Johnson's recommendation. Johnson having inquired after him, said, " Mr. Strahan, let me have five guineas on account, and I'll give this boy one. Nay, if a man recommends a boy, and does nothing for him, it is sad work. Call him down."

I followed him into the court-yard, behind Mr. Strahan's house ; and there I had a proof of what I had heard him profess, that he talked alike to all. " Some people tell you that they let themselves down to the capacity of their hearers. I never do that. I speak uniformly, in as intelligible a manner as I can."

" Well, my boy, how do you go on ?" "Pretty well, Sir ; but they are afraid I an't strong enough for some parts of the business." Johnson : "Why, I shall be sorry for it ; for when you consider with how little mental power and corporeal labour a printer can get a guinea a week, it is a very desirable occupation for you. Do you hear—take all the pains you can ; and if this does not do, we must think of some other way of life for you. There's a guinea."

Here was one of the many, many instances of his active benevolence. At the same time, the slow and sonorous solemnity with which, while he bent himself down, he addressed a little thick short-legged boy, contrasted with the boy's awkwardness and awe could not but excite some ludicrous emotions.

I met him at Drury-lane playhouse in the evening. Sir Joshua Reynolds, at Mrs. Abington's request, had promised to bring a body of wits to her benefit; and having secured forty places in the front

COURT-YARD OF MR. STRAHAN'S HOUSE.

boxes, had done me the honour to put me in the group. Johnson sat on the seat directly behind me ; and as he could neither see nor hear at such a distance from the stage, he was wrapped up in grave abstraction, and seemed quite a cloud amidst all the sunshine of glitter and gaiety. I wondered at his patience in sitting out a play of five acts, and a farce of two. He said very little ; but after the prologue to "Bon Ton" had been spoken, which he could hear pretty well from the more slow and distinct utterance, he talked on prologue writing, and observed, "Dryden has written prologues superior to any that David Garrick has written ; but David Garrick has written more good prologues than Dryden has done. It is wonderful that he has been able to write such variety of them."

At Mr. Beauclerk's, where I supped, was Mr. Garrick, whom I
made happy with Johnson's praise of his prologues ; and I suppose, in
gratitude to him, he took up one of his favourite topics—the nationality
of the Scotch—which he maintained in a pleasant manner, with the

JOHNSON AT MRS. ABINGTON'S BENEFIT.

aid of a little poetical fiction. " Come, come, don't deny it : they are
really national. Why, now, the Adams [1] are as liberal-minded men as
any in the world : but, I don't know how it is, all their workmen are
Scotch. You are, to be sure, wonderfully free from that nationality ;
but so it happens, that you employ the only Scotch shoe-black in
London." He imitated the manner of his old master with ludicrous
exaggeration ; repeating, with pauses and half-whistlings interjected,

> " *Os homini sublime dedit,—cœlumque tueri*
> *Jussit,—et erectos ad sidera—tollere vultus :*"

Looking downwards all the time, and, while pronouncing the **four**
last words, absolutely touching the ground with a kind of contorted
gesticulation.

Garrick, however, when he pleased, could imitate Johnson **very**

---

[1] Architects of the *Adelphi buildings*.—**ED.**

exactly; for that great actor, with his distinguished powers of expression which were so universally admired, possessed also an admirable talent of mimicry. He was always jealous that Johnson spoke lightly of him. I recollect his exhibiting him to me one day, as if saying, "Davy has some convivial pleasantry about him, but 'tis a futile fellow;" which he uttered perfectly with the tone and air of Johnson.

I cannot too frequently request of my readers, while they peruse my account of Johnson's conversation, to endeavour to keep in mind his deliberate and strong utterance. His mode of speaking was indeed very impressive;[1] and I wish it could be preserved as music is written, according to the very ingenious method of Mr. Steele,[2] who has shown how the recitation of Mr. Garrick, and other eminent speakers, might be transmitted to posterity *in score.*[3]

Next day I dined with Johnson at Mr. Thrale's. He attacked Gray, calling him "a dull fellow." BOSWELL : " I understand he was reserved, and might appear dull in company ; but surely he was not dull in poetry." JOHNSON : " Sir, he was dull in company, dull in his closet, dull everywhere. He was dull in a new way, and that made many people think him GREAT. He was a mechanical poet." He then repeated some ludicrous lines, which have escaped my memory, and said, " Is not that GREAT, like his Odes ? " Mrs. Thrale maintained that his Odes were melodious ; upon which he exclaimed,

" Weave the warp, and weave the woof ;"—

I added, in a solemn tone,

" ' The winding-sheet of Edward's race.

There is a good line." " Ay," said he, " and the next line is a good one (pronouncing it contemptuously),

' Give ample verge and room enough.'

[1] My noble friend, Lord Pembroke, said once to me at Wilton, with a happy pleasantry and some truth, that " Dr. Johnson's sayings would not appear so extraordinary, were it not for his *bow-wow way.*" The sayings themselves are generally of sterling merit; but, doubtless, his *manner* was an addition to their effect; and therefore should be attended to as much as may be. It is necessary, however, to guard those who were not acquainted with him, against overcharged imitations or caricatures of his manner, which are frequenfly attempted, and many of which are second-hand copies from the late Mr. Henderson, the actor, who, though good mimic of some persons, did not represent Johnson correctly.—BOSWELL.

[2] See "Prosodia Rationalis; or, an Essay towards establishing the Melody and Measure of Speech, to be expressed and perpetuated by peculiar Symbols." London, 1779.—BOSWELL.

[3] I use the phrase *in score,* as Dr. Johnson has explained it in his Dictionary : " *A song in* SCORE, the words with the musical notes of a song annexed." But I understand that in scientific propriety it means all the parts of a musical composition noted down in the characters by which it is exhibited to the eye of the skilful.—BOSWELL.

It was *declamation* that Steele pretended to reduce to notation by new characters. This he called the *melody* of speech not the *harmony,* which the term in *score* implies.—BURNEY.

No, Sir, there are but two good stanzas in Gray's poetry, which are in his ' Elegy in a Country Churchyard.' " He then repeated the stanza,

" For who to dumb forgetfulness a prey," &c.

mistaking one word ; for instead of *precincts* he said *confines*. He added, " The other stanza I forget."

A young lady who had married a man much her inferior in rank being mentioned, a question arose how a woman's relations should behave to her in such a situation ; and, while I recapitulate the debate, and recollect what has since happened, I cannot but be struck in a manner that delicacy forbids me to express. While I contended that she ought to be treated with an inflexible steadiness of displeasure, Mrs. Thrale was all for mildness and forgiveness, and, according to the vulgar phrase, " making the best of a bad bargain." JOHNSON : " Madam, we must distinguish. Were I a man of rank, I would not let a daughter starve who had made a mean marriage ; but having voluntarily degraded herself from the station which she was originally entitled to hold, I would support her only in that which she herself had chosen ; and would not put her on a level with my other daughters. You are to consider, Madam, that it is our duty to maintain the subordination of civilized society ; and when there is a gross and shameful deviation from rank, it should be punished so as to deter others from the same perversion."

After frequently considering this subject, I am more and more confirmed in what I then meant to express, and which was sanctioned by the authority and illustrated by the wisdom of Johnson ; and I think it of the utmost consequence to the happiness of society, to which subordination is absolutely necessary. It is weak and contemptible, and unworthy in a parent to relax in such a case. It is sacrificing general advantage to private feelings. And let it be considered, that the claim of a daughter who has acted thus to be restored to her former situation, is either fantastical or unjust. If there be no value in the distinction of rank, what does she suffer by being kept in the situation to which she has descended ? If there be a value in that distinction, it ought to be steadily maintained. If indulgence be shown to such conduct, and the offenders know that in a longer or shorter time they shall be received as well as if they had not contaminated their blood by a base alliance, the great check upon that inordinate caprice which generally occasions low marriages, will be removed, and the fair and comfortable order of improved life will be miserably disturbed.

Lord Chesterfield's letters being mentioned, Johnson said, " It was not to be wondered at that they had so great a sale, considering that they were the letters of a statesman, a wit, one who had been so much in the mouths of mankind, one long accustomed *virûm volitare per ora.*"

On Friday, March 31, I supped with him and some friends at a tavern. One of the company attempted, with too much forwardness, to rally him on his late appearance at the theatre ; but had reason to repent of his temerity. "Why, Sir, did you go to Mrs. Abington's benefit ? Did you see ?" JOHNSON : "No, Sir." "Did you hear ?" JOHNSON : "No, Sir." "Why then, Sir, did you go ?" JOHNSON : "Because, Sir, she is a favourite of the public ; and when the public cares the thousandth part for you that it does for her, I will go to your benefit too."

Next morning I won a small bet from Lady Diana Beauclerk, by asking him as to one of his particularities, which her ladyship laid I durst not do. It seems he had been frequently observed at the Club to put into his pocket the Seville oranges, after he had squeezed the juice of them into the drink which he had made for himself. Beauclerk and Garrick talked of it to me, and seemed to think that he had a strange unwillingness to be discovered. We could not divine what he did with them ; and this was the bold question to be put. I saw on his table the spoils of the preceding night, some fresh peels nicely scraped and cut into pieces. "Oh, Sir," said I, "I now partly see what you do with the squeezed oranges you put into your pocket at the Club." JOHNSON : "I have a great love for them." BOSWELL : "And pray, Sir, what do you do with them ? You scrape them, it seems, very neatly, and what next ?" JOHNSON : "Let them dry, Sir." BOSWELL : "And what next ?" JOHNSON : "Nay, Sir, you shall know their fate no further." BOSWELL : "Then the world must be left in the dark. It must be said," assuming a mock solemnity, "he scraped them and let them dry ; but what he did with them next he never could be prevailed upon to tell." JOHNSON : "Nay, Sir, you should say it more emphatically :—he could not be prevailed upon, even by his dearest friends, to tell."

He had this morning received his diploma as Doctor of Laws from the University of Oxford. He did not vaunt of his new dignity, but I understood he was highly pleased with it. I shall here insert the progress and completion of that high academical honour, in the same manner as I have traced his obtaining that of Master of Arts.

"TO THE REVEREND DR. FOTHERGILL,

"Vice-Chancellor of the University of Oxford, to be communicated to the Heads of Houses, and proposed in Convocation.

"Downing-street, March 23, 1775.

"MR. VICE-CHANCELLOR AND GENTLEMEN,—
"The honour of the degree of M.A. by diploma, formerly conferred upon MR. SAMUEL JOHNSON, in consequence of his having eminently distinguished himself by the publication of a series of Essays, excellently calculated to form the manners of the people, and in which the cause of religion and morality

has been maintained and recommended by the strongest powers of argument and elegance of language, reflected an equal degree of lustre upon the University itself.

" The many learned labours which have since that time employed the attention and displayed the abilities of that great man, so much to the advancement of literature and the benefit of the community, render him worthy of more distinguished honours in the Republic of letters; and I persuade myself that I shall act agreeably to the sentiments of the whole University, in desiring that it may be proposed in Convocation to confer on him the degree of Doctor in Civil Law, by diploma, to which I readily give my consent; and am,   Mr. Vice-Chancellor and Gentlemen,

" Your affectionate friend and servant,

" NORTH." [1]

DIPLOMA.

" *CANCELLARIUS, Magistri, et Scholares Universitatis Oxoniensis omnibus ad quos presentes Literæ pervenerint, salutem in Domino Sempiternam.*

" SCIATIS, *virum illustrem* SAMUELEM JOHNSON, *in omni humaniorum literarum genere eruditum, omniumque scientiarum comprehensione felicissimum, scriptis suis, ad popularium mores formandos summâ verborum elegantiâ ac sententiarum gravitate compositis, ita olim inclaruisse, ut dignus videretur cui ab Academiâ suâ eximia quædam laudis præmia deferentur, quique venerabilem Magistrorum Ordinem summâ cum dignitate coöptaretur.*

" *Cùm verò eundem clarissimum virum tot posteâ tantique laboris, in patriâ præsertim linguâ ornandâ et stabiliendâ feliciter impensi, ita insigniverint, ut in Literarum Republicâ* PRINCEPS *jam et* PRIMARIUS *jure habeatur; Nos,* CANCELLARIUS, *Magistri, et Scholares Universitatis Oxoniensis, quò talis viri merita pari honoris remuneratione exæquentur, et perpetuum suæ simul laudis, nostræque ergà literas propensissimæ voluntatis extet monumentum, in solenni Convocatione Doctorum et Magistrorum Regentium, et non Regentium, prædictum* SAMUELEM JOHNSON, *Doctorem in Jure Civili renunciavimus et constituimus, eumque virtute præsentis Diplomatis singulis juribus, privilegiis et honoribus, ad istem gradum quàquà pertinentibus, frui et gaudere jussimus. In cujus rei testimonium commune Universitatis Oxoniensis sigillum præsentibus apponi fecimus.*

" *Datum in Domo nostræ Convocationis die tricesimo Mensis Martii, Anno Domini Millesimo septingentesimo, septuagesimo quinto.*" [2]

[1] Extracted from the Convocation Register, Oxford.—BOSWELL.

[2] The original is in my possession. He showed me the diploma, and allowed me to read it, but would not consent to my taking a copy of it, fearing perhaps that I should blaze it abroad in his life-time. His objection to this appears from his 99th letter to Mrs. Thrale, whom in that letter he thus scolds for the grossness of her flattery of him :—" The other Oxford news is, that they have sent me a degree of Doctor of Laws, with such praises in the diploma as perhaps ought to make me ashamed ; they are very like your praises. I wonder whether I shall ever show it to you."

It is remarkable that he never, so far as I know, assumed his title of *Doctor,* but called himself *Mr.* Johnson, as appears from many of his cards or notes to myself, and I have seen many from him to other persons, in which he uniformly takes that designation.—I once observed on his table a letter directed to him with the addition of *Esquire,* and objected to it as being a designation inferior to that of Doctor; but he checked me, and seemed pleased with it, because, as I conjectured, he liked to be sometimes taken out of the class of literary men, and to be merely *genteel—un gentilhomme comme un autre.*—BOSWELL.

"Viro Reverendo THOMÆ FOTHERGILL. *S.T.P. Universitatis Oxoniensis Vice-Cancellario. S. P.D.*

"SAM. JOHNSON.

"MULTIS non est opus, ut testimonium quo, te præside, Oxoniensis nomen meum posteris commendârunt, quali animo acceperim compertum faciam. Nemo sibi placens non lætatur ; nemo sibi non placet, qui vobis, literarum arbitris, placere potuit. Hoc tamen habet incommodi tantum beneficium, quod mihi nunquam posthâc sine vestræ famæ detrimento vel labi liceat vel cessare ; semperque sit timendum ne quod mihi tam eximiæ laudi est, vobis aliquando fiat opprobrio. Vale.[1]

"7. *Id. Apr.* 1775."

He revised some sheets of Lord Hailes's "Annals of Scotland," and wrote a few notes on the margin with red ink, which he bade me tell his Lordship did not sink into the paper, and might be wiped off with a wet sponge, so that it did not spoil his manuscript. I observed to him that there were very few of his friends so accurate as that I could venture to put down in writing what they told me as his sayings. JOHNSON : "Why should you write down *my* sayings ?" BOSWELL : "I write them when they are good ?" JOHNSON : "Nay, you may as well write down the sayings of any one else that are good." But *where*, I might with great propriety have added, can I find such ?

I visited him by appointment in the evening, and we drank tea with Mrs. Williams. He told me that he had been in the company of a gentleman[2] whose extraordinary travels had been much the subject of conversation. But I found he had not listened to him with that full confidence, without which there is little satisfaction in the society of travellers. I was curious to hear what opinion so able a judge as Johnson had formed of his abilities, and I asked if he was not a man of sense. JOHNSON : "Why, Sir, he is not a distinct relater ; and I should say, he is neither abounding nor deficient in sense. I did not perceive any superiority of understanding." BOSWELL : "But will you not allow him a nobleness of resolution, in penetrating into distant regions ?" JOHNSON : "That, Sir, is not to the present purpose. We are talking of sense. A fighting cock has a nobleness of resolution."

Next day, Sunday, April 2, I dined with him at Mr. Hoole's. We talked of Pope. JOHNSON : "He wrote his 'Dunciad' for fame. That was his primary motive. Had it not been for that, the dunces might have railed against him till they were weary, without his troubling himself about them. He delighted to vex them, no doubt ; but he had more delight in seeing how well he could vex them."

The "Odes to Obscurity and Oblivion," in ridicule of "cool Mason and warm Gray," being mentioned, Johnson said, "They are Colman's best things." Upon its being observed that it was believed these Odes

[1] The original is in the hands of Dr. Fothergill, then Vice Chancellor, who made this transcript.—T. WARTON

[2] James Bruce, the celebrated traveller, who had then recently returned from Abyssinia.— ED

were made by Colman and Lloyd jointly—JOHNSON : "Nay, Sir, how can two people make an Ode ? Perhaps one made one of them, and one the other." I observed that two people had made a play, and quoted the anecdote of Beaumont and Fletcher, who were brought under suspicion of treason, because while concerting the plan of a tragedy when sitting together at a tavern, one of them was overheard saying to the other, "I'll kill the King." JOHNSON : "The first of these odes is the best ; but they are both good. They exposed a very bad kind of writing." BOSWELL : "Surely, Sir, Mr. Mason's 'Elfrida' is a fine poem : at least you will allow there are some good passages in it." JOHNSON : "There are now and then some good imitations of Milton's bad manner."

I often wondered at his low estimation of the writings of Gray and Mason. Of Gray's poetry I have in a former part of this work expressed my high opinion ; and for that of Mr. Mason I have ever entertained a warm admiration. His "Elfrida" is exquisite, both in poetical description and moral sentiment ; and his "Caractacus" is a noble drama. Nor can I omit paying my tribute of praise to some of his smaller poems, which I have read with pleasure, and which no criticism shall persuade me not to like. If I wondered at Johnson's not tasting the works of Mason and Gray, still more have I wondered at their not tasting his works ; that they should be insensible to his energy of diction, to his splendour of images, and comprehension of thought. Tastes may differ as to the violin, the flute, the hautboy, in short, all the lesser instruments ; but who can be insensible to the powerful impressions of the majestic organ ?

His "Taxation no Tyranny" being mentioned, he said, "I think I have not been attacked enough for it. Attack is the reaction ; I never think I have hit hard, unless it rebounds." BOSWELL : "I don't know, Sir, what you would be at. Five or six shots of small arms in every newspaper, and repeated cannonading in pamphlets, might, I think, satisfy you. But, Sir, you'll never make out this match, of which we have talked, with a certain political lady, since you are so severe against her principles." JOHNSON : "Nay, Sir, I have the better chance for that. She is like the Amazons of old ; she must be courted by the sword. But I have not been severe upon her." BOSWELL : "Yes, Sir, you have made her ridiculous." JOHNSON : "That was already done, Sir. To endeavour to make her ridiculous, is like blacking the chimney."

I put him in mind that the landlord at Ellon in Scotland said, that he heard he was the greatest man in England,—next to Lord Mansfield. "Ay, Sir," said he, "the exception defined the idea. A Scotchman could go no farther

"The force of Nature could no farther go."

Lady Miller's collection of verses by fashionable people, which were put into her vase at Bath-Easton villa, near Bath, in competition for honorary prizes, being mentioned, he held them very cheap: *Bouterimès*," said he, "is a mere conceit, and an *old* conceit *now;* I wonder how people were persuaded to write in that manner for this lady." I named a gentleman of his acquaintance who wrote for the vase. JOHNSON: "He was a blockhead for his pains." BOSWELL: "The Duchess of Northumberland wrote." JOHNSON: "Sir, the Duchess of Northumberland may do what she pleases: nobody will say anything to a lady of her high rank. But I should be apt to throw ******'s verses in his face."

I talked of the cheerfulness of Fleet-street, owing to the constant quick succession of people which we perceive passing through it. JOHNSON: "Why, Sir, Fleet-street has a very animated appearance: but I think the tide of human existence is at Charing-cross."

FLEET STREET—1775.

He made the common remark on the unhappiness which men who have led a busy life experience, when they retire in expectation of enjoying themselves at ease, and that they generally languish for want of their habitual occupation, and wish to return to it. He mentioned as strong an instance of this as can well be imagined: "An eminent tallow-chandler in London, who had acquired a considerable fortune, gave up the trade in favour of his foreman, and went to live at a country-house near town. He soon grew weary, and paid frequent visits to his old shop, where he desired they might let him know their *melting-days*, and he would come and assist them; which he accordingly did. Here, Sir, was a man, to whom the most disgusting circumstances in the business to which he had been used was a relief from idleness."

On Wednesday, April 5, I dined with him at Messieurs Dilly's, with

Mr. John Scott of Amwell, the Quaker, Mr. Langton, Mr. Miller (now Sir John), and Dr. Thomas Campbell, an Irish clergyman, whom I took the liberty of inviting to Mr. Dilly's table, having seen him at Mr. Thrale's, and been told that he had come to England chiefly with a view to see Dr. Johnson, for whom he entertained the highest veneration. He has since published "A Philosophical Survey of the South of Ireland," a very entertaining book, which has, however, one 'ault :—that it assumes the fictitious character of an Englishman.

We talked of public speaking. JOHNSON : "We must not estimate a man's powers by his being able or not able to deliver his sentiments in public. Isaac Hawkins Browne, one of the first wits of this country, got into Parliament, and never opened his mouth. For my own part, I think it is more disgraceful never to try to speak, than to try it, and fail ; as it is more disgraceful not to fight, than to fight and be beaten." This argument appeared to me fallacious ; for if a man has not spoken, it may be said that he would have done very well if he had tried ; whereas, if he has tried and failed, there is nothing to be said for him. "Why then," I asked, "is it thought disgraceful for a man not to fight, and not disgraceful not to speak in public ?" JOHNSON : "Because there may be other reasons for a man's not speaking in public than want of resolution : he may have nothing to say (laughing). Whereas, Sir, you know courage is reckoned the greatest of all virtues; because, unless a man has that virtue, he has no security for preserving any other."

He observed, that "the statutes against bribery were intended to prevent upstarts with money from getting into Parliament :" adding, that "if he were a gentleman of landed property, he would turn out all his tenants who did not vote for the candidate whom he supported." LANGTON : "Would not that, Sir, be checking the freedom of election ?" JOHNSON : "Sir, the law does not mean that the privilege of voting should be independent of old family interest, of the permanent property of the country."

On Thursday, April 6, I dined with him at Mr. Thomas Davies's, with Mr. Hickey, the painter, and my old acquaintance Mr. Moody, the player.

Dr. Johnson, as usual, spoke contemptuously of Colley Cibber. "It is wonderful that a man, who for forty years had lived with the great and the witty, should have acquired so ill the talents of conversation ; and he had but half to furnish ; for one half of what he said was oaths." He, however, allowed considerable merit to some of his comedies, and said there was no reason to believe that "The Careless Husband" was not written by himself. Davies said, he was the first dramatic writer who introduced genteel ladies upon the stage. Johnson refuted his observation by instancing several such characters in comedies before his time. DAVIES (trying to defend himself from a charge of ignorance) : "I mean genteel moral characters." "I think," said Hickey, "gentility and morality are inseparable." BOSWELL : "By no means, Sir. The genteelest characters are often the most immoral. Does not Lord Chesterfield give precepts for uniting wickedness and the graces ? A man, indeed, is not genteel when he gets drunk ; but most vices may be committed very genteelly : a man may debauch his friend's wife genteelly : he may cheat at cards genteelly." HICKEY : "I do not think *that* is genteel." BOSWELL : "Sir, it may not be like a gentleman, but it may be genteel." JOHNSON : "You are meaning two different things. One means exterior grace ; the other honour. It is certain that a man may be very immoral with exterior grace. Lovelace, in ' Clarissa,' is a very genteel and a very wicked character. Tom Hervey, who died t'other day, though a vicious man, was one of the genteelest men that ever lived." Tom Davies instanced Charles the Second. JOHNSON (taking fire at any attack upon that Prince, for whom he had an extraordinary partiality) : "Charles the Second was licentious in his practice ; but he always had a reverence for what was good. Charles the Second knew his people, and rewarded merit. The Church was at no time better filled than in his reign. He was the best King we have had from his time till the reign of his present Majesty, except James the Second, who was a very good King, but unhappily believed that it was necessary for the salvation of his subjects that they should be Roman Catholics. *He* had the merit of endeavouring to do what he thought was for the salvation of the souls of his subjects, till he lost a great empire. *We*, who thought that we should *not* be saved if we were Roman Catholics, had the merit of maintaining our religion, at the expense of submitting ourselves to the government of King William (for it could not be done otherwise),—to the government of one of the most worthless scoundrels that ever existed. No ; Charles the Second was not such a man as ——— (naming another King). He did not destroy his father's will. He took money, indeed, from France : but he did not betray those over whom he ruled : he did not let the French fleet pass ours. George the First knew nothing, and desired to know nothing : did nothing, and desired to do nothing ; and the only good thing that is told of him is, that he wished to restore the crown to its hereditary successor." He roared with prodigious violence against George the Second. When he ceased, Moody interjected, in an Irish tone, and with a comic look, "Ah ! poor George the Second."

I mentioned that Dr. Thomas Campbell had come from Ireland to London, principally to see Dr. Johnson. He seemed angry at this observation. DAVIES : "Why, you know, Sir, there came a man from Spain to see Livy,[1] and Corelli came to England to see Purcell,[2] and, when he heard he was dead, went directly back again to Italy.'

---

[1] Plin. Epist Lib. ii. Ep. 3.—BOSWELL.
[2] Mr. Davies was here mistaken   Corelli never was in England.—BURNEY

JOHNSON : "I should not have wished to be dead to disappoint Campbell, had he been so foolish as you represent him ; but I should have wished to have been a hundred miles off:" This was apparently perverse ; and I do believe it was not his real way of thinking : he could not but like a man who came so far to see him. He laughed with some complacency, when I told him Campbell's odd expression to me concerning him : "That having seen such a man, was a thing to talk of a century hence," —as if he could live so long.

We got into an argument whether the Judges who went to India might with propriety engage in trade. Johnson warmly maintained that they might, "For why," he urged, "should not Judges get riches, as well as those who deserve them less ? " I said, they should have sufficient salaries, and have nothing to take off their attention from the affairs of the public. JOHNSON : "No Judge, Sir, can give his whole attention to his office ; and it is very proper that he should employ what time he has to himself, to his own advantage, in the most profitable manner." "Then, Sir," said Davies, who enlivened the dispute by making it somewhat dramatic, "he may become an insurer ; and when he is going to the bench he may be stopped,—' Your Lordship cannot go yet ; here is a bunch of invoices : several ships are about to sail.'" JOHNSON : "Sir, you may as well say a Judge should not have a house ; for they may come and tell him, ' Your Lordship's house is on fire ;' and so, instead of minding the business of his Court, he is to be occupied in getting the engine with the greatest speed. There is no end of this. Every Judge who has land, trades to a certain extent in corn or in cattle ; and in the land itself : undoubtedly his steward acts for him, and so do clerks for a great merchant. A Judge may be a farmer; but he is not to geld his own pigs. A Judge may play a little at cards for his amusement ; but he is not to play at marbles, or chuck farthings in the Piazza. No, Sir, there is no profession to which a man gives a very great proportion of his time. It is wonderful when a calculation is made, how little the mind is actually employed in the discharge of any profession. No man would be a Judge, upon the condition of being totally a Judge. The best employed lawyer has his mind at work but for a small proportion of his time : a great deal of his occupation is merely mechanical.—I once wrote for a magazine : I made a calculation that if I should write but a page a day, at the same rate, I should, in ten years, write nine volumes in folio, of an ordinary size and print." BOSWELL : "Such as Carte's History ? " JOHNSON : "Yes, Sir, when a man writes from his own mind, he writes very rapidly.[1] The greatest part of a writer's time is spent in reading, in order to write ; a man will turn over half a library to make one book."

[1] Johnson certainly did, who had a mind stored with knowledge, and teeming with imagery : but the observation is not applicable to writers in general.—BOSWELL.

I argued warmly against the Judges trading, and mentioned Hale as an instance of a perfect Judge, who devoted himself entirely to his office. JOHNSON : " Hale, Sir, attended to other things besides law : he left a great estate." BOSWELL : " That was because what he got accumulated without any exertion and anxiety on his part."

While the dispute went on, Moody once tried to say something on our side. Tom Davies clapped him on the back, to encourage him. Beauclerk, to whom I mentioned this circumstance, said, " that he could not conceive a more humiliating situation than to be clapped on the back by Tom Davies."

We spoke of Rolt, to whose Dictionary of Commerce Dr. Johnson wrote the Preface. JOHNSON : " Old Gardner, the bookseller, employed Rolt and Smart to write a monthly miscellany, called ' The Universal Visitor.' There was a formal written contract, which Allen the printer saw. Gardner thought as you do of the judge. They were bound to write nothing else ; they were to have, I think, a third of the profits of his sixpenny pamphlet ; and the contract was for ninety-nine years. I wish I had thought of giving this to Thurlow, in the cause about literary property. What an excellent instance would it have been of the oppression of booksellers towards poor authors ! " [1] (smiling). Davies, zealous for the honour of the trade, said, Gardner was not properly a bookseller. JOHNSON : " Nay, Sir ; he certainly was a bookseller. He had served his time regularly, was a member of the Stationers' Company, kept a shop in the face of mankind, purchased copyright, and was a *bibliopole*, Sir, in every sense. I wrote for some months in ' The Universal Visitor,' for poor Smart, while he was mad, not then knowing the terms on which he was engaged to write, and thinking I was doing him good. I hoped his wits would soon return to him. Mine returned to me, and I wrote in ' The Universal Visitor ' no longer."

Friday, April 7, I dined with him at a tavern, with a numerous company. JOHNSON : " I have been reading ' Twiss's Travels in Spain,' which are just come out. They are as good as the first book of travels that you will take up. They are as good as those of Keysler or Blainville : nay, as Addison's,[2] if you except the learning. They are not so good as Brydone's, but they are better than Pococke's. I have not, indeed, cut the leaves yet ; but I have read in them where the pages are

---

There has probably been some mistake as to the terms of this supposed extraordinary contract, the recital of which from hearsay afforded Johnson so much play for his sportive acuteness. Or if it was worded as he supposed, it is so strange that I should conclude it was a joke. Mr. Gardner, I am assured, was a worthy and liberal man.—BOSWELL.

[2] Speaking of Addison's *Remarks on Italy*, in " The Journal of a Tour to the Hebrides," (p. 320, 3rd edit.) he says, " It is a tedious book, and if it were not attached to Addison's previous reputation, one would not think much of it. Had he written nothing else, his name would not have lived. Addison does not seem to have gone deep into Italian literature. He shows nothing of it in his subsequent writings. He shows a great deal of French learning."—MALONE.

open, and I do not suppose that what is in the pages which are closed is worse than what is in the open pages.—It would seem," he added, "that Addison had not acquired much Italian learning, for we do not find it introduced into his writings. The only instance that I recollect, is his quoting ' *Stavo bene ; per star meglio, sto qui.*' " [1]

I mentioned Addison's having borrowed many of his classical remarks from Leandro Alberti. Mr. Beauclerk said, " It was alleged that he had borrowed also from another Italian author." JOHNSON. " Why, Sir, all who go to look for what the classics have said of Italy, must find the same passages : [2] and I should think it would be one of the first things the Italians would do on the revival of learning, to collect all that the Roman authors have said of their country."

Ossian being mentioned—JOHNSON : "Supposing the Irish and Erse languages to be the same, which I do not believe, yet as there is no reason to suppose that the inhabitants of the Highlands and Hebrides ever wrote their native language, it is not to be credited that a long poem was preserved among them. If we had no evidence of the art of writing being practised in one of the counties of England, we should not believe that a long poem was preserved *there*, though in the neighbouring counties, where the same language was spoken, the inhabitants could write." BEAUCLERK : " The ballad of Lillibuderlero was once in the mouths of all the people of this country, and is said to have had a great effect in bringing about the Revolution.

Yet I question whether any body can repeat it now ; which shows how improbable it is that much poetry should be preserved by tradition."

One of the company suggested an internal objection to the antiquity of the poetry said to be Ossian's, that we do not find the wolf in it, which must have been the case had it been of that age.

The mention of the wolf had led Johnson to think of other wild beasts ; and while Sir Joshua Reynolds and Mr. Langton were carrying on a dialogue about something which engaged them earnestly, he, in the midst

EDWARD GIBBON

of it, broke out, " Pennant tells of Bears." What he added, I have forgotten. They went on, which he, being dull of hearing, did not

---

[1] Addison, however, does not mention where this celebrated Epitaph, which has eluded a very diligent inquiry, is found.—MALONE.

[2] But if you find the same *applications* in another book, then Addison's learning falls to the ground. " Journal of a Tour to the Hebrides," *ut supra*.—MALONE.

perceive, or, if he did, was not willing to break off his talk ; so he continued to vociferate his remarks, and *Bear* (" like a word in a catch " as Beauclerk said,) was repeatedly heard at intervals, which coming from him who, by those who did not know him, had been so often assimilated to that ferocious animal, while we who were sitting around could hardly stifle laughter, produced a very ludicrous effect. Silence having ensued, he proceeded : " We are told, that the black bear is innocent ; but I should not like to trust myself with him." Mr. Gibbon muttered, in a low tone of voice, " I should not like to trust myself with *you*." This piece of sarcastic pleasantry was a prudent resolution, if applied to competition of abilities.

Patriotism having become one of our topics, Johnson suddenly uttered, in a strong determined tone, an apophthegm, at which many will start : " Patriotism is the last refuge of a scoundrel." But let it be considered, that he did not mean a real and generous love of our country, but that pretended patriotism which so many, in all ages and countries, have made a cloak for self-interest. I maintained, that certainly all patriots were not scoundrels. Being urged (not by Johnson), to name one exception, I mentioned an eminent person, whom we all greatly admired. JOHNSON : " Sir, I do not say that he is *not* honest ; but we have no reason to conclude from his political conduct that he *is* honest. Were he to accept a place from this ministry, he would lose that character of firmness which he has, and might be turned out of his place in a year. This ministry is neither stable, nor grateful to their friends, as Sir Robert Walpole was : so that he may think it more for his interest to take his chance of his party coming in."

Mrs Pritchard being mentioned, he said, " Her playing was quite mechanical. It is wonderful how little mind she had. Sir, she had never read the tragedy of Macbeth all through. She no more thought of the play out of which her part was taken, than a shoemaker thinks of the skin, out of which the piece of leather, of which he is making a pair of shoes, is cut."

On Saturday, May 8, I dined with him at Mr. Thrale's, where we met the Irish Dr. Campbell. Johnson had supped the night before at Mrs. Abington's with some fashionable people whom he named ; and he seemed much pleased with having made one in so elegant a circle. Nor did he omit to pique his *mistress* a little with jealousy of her house-wifery ; for he said, with a smile, " Mrs. Abington's jelly, my dear lady, was better than yours."

Mrs. Thrale, who frequently practised a coarse mode of flattery, by repeating his *bon-mots* in his hearing, told us that he had said, a certain celebrated actor was just fit to stand at the door of an auction-room with a long pole, and cry, " Pray, gentlemen, walk in ; " and that a certain author, upon hearing this, had said, that another still more celebrated actor was fit for nothing better than that, and would pick your pocket after you came out. JOHNSON : " Nay, my dear lady, there is no wit in what our friend added ; there is only abuse. You may as well say of any man that he will pick a pocket. Besides, the man who is stationed at the door does not pick people's pockets; that is done within, by the auctioneer."

Mrs. Thrale told us, that Tom Davies repeated, in a very bold manner, the story of Dr. Johnson's first repartee to me, which I have related exactly. He made me say, " I *was born* in Scotland," instead of " I *come from* Scotland ;" so that Johnson's saying, " That, Sir, is what a great many of your countrymen cannot help " had no point, or even meaning : and that upon this being mentioned to Mr. Fitzherbert, he observed, " it is not every man that can *carry a bon-mot.*"

On Monday, April 10, I dined with him at General Oglethorpe's, with Mr. Langton and the Irish Dr. Campbell, whom the General had obligingly given me leave to bring with me. This learned gentleman was thus gratified with a very high intellectual feast, by not only being in company with Dr. Johnson, but with General Oglethorpe, who had been so long a celebrated name both at home and abroad.[1]

I must, again and again, entreat of my readers not to suppose that my imperfect record of conversation contains the whole of what was said by Johnson, or other eminent persons who lived with him. What 1 have preserved, however, has the value of the most perfect authenticity

He this day enlarged upon Pope's melancholy remark,

> " Man never *is*, but always *to be* blest."

He asserted, that *the present* was never a happy state to any human being ; but that, as every part of life, of which we are conscious, was at some point of time a period yet to come, in which felicity was expected, there was some happiness produced by hope. Being pressed upon this subject, and asked if he really was of opinion, that though, in general, happiness was very rare in human life, a man was not sometimes happy in the moment that was present, he answered, " Never, but when he is drunk."

---

[1] Let me here be allowed to pay my tribute of most sincere gratitude to the memory of that excellent person, my intimacy with whom was the more valuable to me, because my first acquaintance with him was unexpected and unsolicited. Soon after the publication of my " Account of Corsica," he did me the honour to call on me, and approaching me with a frank and courteous air, said, " My name, Sir, is Oglethorpe, and I wish to be acquainted with you." I was not a little flattered to be thus addressed by an eminent man, of whom I had read in Pope, from my early years,

> " Or driven by strong benevolence of soul,
> Will fly, like Oglethorpe, from pole to pole."

I was fortunate enough to be found worthy of his good opinion, insomuch, that I not only was invited to make one in the many respectable companies whom he entertained at his table, but had a cover at his hospitable board every day when I happened to be disengaged ; and in his society I never failed to enjoy learned and animated conversation seasoned with genuine sentiments of virtue and religion. — BOSWELL.

He urged General Oglethorp to give the world his life.[1] He said, "I know no man whose life would be more interesting. If I were furnished with materials, I should be very glad to write it."

Mr. Scott of Amwell's Elegies were lying in the room. Dr. Johnson observed, "They are very well; but such as twenty people might write." Upon this I took occasion to controvert Horace's maxim

>"————————mediocribus esse poetis
>Non homines, non Dî, non concessere columnæ;"[2]

for here (I observed), was a very middle-rate poet, who pleased many readers, and therefore poetry of a middle sort was entitled to some esteem; nor could I see why poetry should not, like everything else, have different gradations of excellence, and consequently of value. Johnson repeated the common remark, that, "as there is no necessity for our having poetry at all, it being merely a luxury, an instrument of pleasure, it can have no value, unless when exquisite in its kind." I declared myself not satisfied. "Why, then, Sir," said he, "Horace and you must settle it." He was not much in the humour of talking.

No more of his conversation for some days appears in my journal, except that when a gentleman told him he had bought a suit of lace for his lady, he said, "Well, Sir, you have done a good thing and a wise thing." "I have done a good thing," said the gentleman, "but I do not know that I have done a wise thing." Johnson: "Yes, Sir; no money is better spent than what is laid out for domestic satisfaction. A man is pleased that his wife is dressed as well as other people; and a wife is pleased that she is dressed."

----

[1] The General seemed unwilling to enter upon it at this time; but upon a subsequent occasion he communicated to me a number of particulars, which I have committed to writing; but I was not sufficiently diligent in obtaining more from him, not apprehending that his friends were so soon to lose him; for notwithstanding his great age, he was very healthy and vigorous, and was at last carried off by a violent fever, which is often fatal at any period of life.—Boswell.

[2] De Art. Poet. v. 372.--Boswell.

JOHNSON AT MR. CAMBRIDGE'S.

CHAPTER XI.—1775.

ON Friday, April 14, being Good-Friday, I repaired to him in the morning, according to my usual custom on that day, and break-fasted with him. I observed that he fasted so very strictly, that he did not even taste bread, and took no milk with his tea; I suppose because it is a kind of animal food.

He entered upon the state of the nation, and thus discoursed: "Sir, the great misfortune now is, that government has too little power. All that it has to bestow must of necessity be given to support itself; so that it cannot reward merit. No man, for instance, can now be made a bishop for his learning and piety;[1] his only chance for promotion is his

---

[1] From this too just observation there are some eminent exceptions.—BOSWELL

being connected with somebody who has parliamentary interest. Our several ministers in this reign have outbid each other in concessions to the people. Lord Bute, though a very honourable man,—a man who meant well,—a man who had his blood full of prerogative,—was a theoretical statesman,—a book-minister,—and thought this country could be governed by the influence of the Crown alone. Then, Sir, he gave up a great deal. He advised the king to agree that the judges should hold their places for life, instead of losing them at the accession of a new king. Lord Bute, I suppose, thought to make the king popular by this con cession ; but the people never minded it ; and it was a most impolitic measure. There is no reason why a judge should hold his office for life, more than any other person in public trust. A judge may be partial otherwise than to the Crown: we have seen judges partial to the populace. A judge may become corrupt, and yet there may not be legal evidence against him. A judge may become froward from age. A judge may grow unfit for his office in many ways. It was desirable that there should be a possibility of being delivered from him by a new king. That is now gone by an act of Parliament *ex gratiâ* of the Crown. Lord Bute advised the king to give up a very large sum of money,[1] for which nobody thanked him. It was of consequence to the king, but nothing to the public, among whom it was divided. When I say Lord Bute advised, I mean, that such acts were done when he was minister, and we are to suppose that he advised them.—Lord Bute showed an undue partiality to Scotchmen. He turned out Dr. Nichols, a very eminent man, from being physician to the king, to make room for one of his countrymen, a man very low in his profession. He had * * * and * * * to go on errands for him. He had occasion for people to go on errands for him ; but he should not have had Scotchmen ; and, certainly, he should not have suffered them to have access to him before the first people in England."

I told him, that the admission of one of them before the first people in England, which had given the greatest offence, was no more than what happens at every minister's levee, where those who attend are admitted in the order that they have come, which is better than admitting them according to their rank ; for if that were to be the rule, a man who has waited all the morning might have the mortification to see a peer, newly

---

[1] The money arising from the property of the prizes taken before the declaration of war, which were given to his Majesty by the Peace of Paris, and amounted to upwards of 700,000*l.*, and from the lands in the ceded islands, which were estimated at 200,000*l.* more. Surely there was a noble munificence in this gift from a monarch to his people. And let it be remembered, that during the Earl of Bute's administration, the king was graciously pleased to give up the hereditary revenues of the Crown, and to accept, instead of them, of the limited sum of 800,000*l.* a year: upon which Blackstone observes, that " The hereditary revenues, being put under the same management as the other branches of the public patrimony, will produce more and be better collected than heretofore ; and the public is a gainer of upwards of 100,000*l.* per annum by this disinterested bounty of his Majesty."—Book i. chap. viii. p. 330. —BOSWELL.

come, go in before him, and keep him waiting still. Johnson : " True, Sir ; but * * * * should not have come to the levee, to be in the way of people of consequence. He saw Lord Bute at all times : and could have said what he had to say at any time, as well as at the levee. There is now no Prime Minister ; there is only an agent for government in the House of Commons. We are governed by the Cabinet ; but there is no one head there since Sir Robert Walpole's time." Boswell : " What then, Sir, is the use of Parliament ?" Johnson : "Why, Sir, Parliament is a large council to the king ; and the advantage of such a council is, having a great number of men of property concerned in the legislature, who, for their own interest, will not consent to bad laws. And you must have observed, Sir, the administration is feeble and timid, and cannot act with that authority and resolution which is necessary. Were I in power, I would turn out every man who dared to oppose me. Government has the distribution of offices, that it may be enabled to maintain its authority."

"Lord Bute," he added, "took down too fast, without building up something new." Boswell : " Because, Sir, he found a rotten building. The political coach was drawn by a set of bad horses ; it was necessary to change them." Johnson : "But he should have changed them one by one."

I told him that I had been informed by Mr. Orme, that many parts of the East Indies were better mapped than the Highlands of Scotland. Johnson : " That a country may be mapped, it must be travelled over." "Nay," said I, meaning to laugh with him at one of his prejudices, "can't you say, it is not *worth* mapping ?"

As we walked to St. Clement's Church, and saw several shops open upon this most solemn fast-day of the Christian world, I remarked, that one disadvantage arising from the immensity of London was, that nobody was heeded by his neighbour ; there was no fear of censure for not observing Good Friday, as it ought to be kept, and as it is kept in country towns. He said it was, upon the whole, very well observed even in London. He, however, owned that London was too large ; but added, " It is nonsense to say the head is too big for the body. It would be as much too big though the body were ever so large ; that is to say, though the country were ever so extensive. It has no similarity to a head connected with a body."

Dr. Wetherell, Master of University College, Oxford, accompanied us home from church ; and after he was gone, there came two other gentlemen, one of whom uttered the common-place complaints, that by the increase of taxes, labour would be dear, other nations would undersell us, and our commerce would be ruined. Johnson (smiling): " Never fear, Sir. Our commerce is in a very good state ; and suppose we had no commerce at all, we could live very well on the produce of our own country." I cannot omit to mention that I never knew any man who

was less disposed to be querulous than Johnson. Whether the subject
was his own situation, or the state of the public, or the state of human
nature in general, though he saw the evils, his mind was turned to
resolution, and never to whining or complaint.

We went again to St. Clement's in the afternoon. He had found
fault with the preacher in the morning for not choosing a text adapted
to the day. The preacher in the afternoon had chosen one extremely
proper : "It is finished."

After the evening service, he said, " Come, you shall go home with
me, and sit just an hour." But he was better than his word ; for, after
we had drunk tea with Mrs. Williams, he asked me to go up to his study
with him, where we sat a long while together in a serene, undisturbed
frame of mind, sometimes in silence, and sometimes conversing, as we
felt ourselves inclined, or more properly speaking, as *he* was inclined ;
for during all the course of my long intimacy with him, my respectful
attention never abated, and my wish to hear him was such, that I constantly watched every dawning of communication from that great and
illuminated mind.

He observed, " All knowledge is of itself of some value. There is
nothing so minute or inconsiderable, that I would not rather know it
than not. In the same manner, all power, of whatever sort, is of itself
desirable. A man would not submit to learn to hem a ruffle of his wife,
or of his wife's maid ; but if a mere wish could attain it, he would
rather wish to be able to hem a ruffle."

He again advised me to keep a journal fully and minutely, but
not to mention such trifles as that meat was too much or too little
done, or that the weather was fair or rainy. He had till very near
his death a contempt for the notion that the weather affects the human
frame.

I told him that our friend Goldsmith had said to me that he had come
too late into the world, for that Pope and other poets had taken up the
places in the Temple of Fame ; so that, as but a few at any period can
possess poetical reputation, a man of genius can now hardly acquire it.
JOHNSON : " That is one of the most sensible things I have ever heard of
Goldsmith. It is difficult to get literary fame, and it is every day growing
more difficult. Ah, Sir, that should make a man think of securing happiness in another world, which all who try sincerely for it may attain.
In comparison of that, how little are all other things ! The belief of
immortality is impressed upon all men, and all men act under an impression of it, however they may talk, and though, perhaps, they may be
scarcely sensible of it." I said, it appeared to me that some people had
not the least notion of immortality ; and I mentioned a distinguished
gentleman of our acquaintance. JOHNSON : " Sir, if it were not for the
notion of immortality, he would cut a throat to fill his pockets." When
I quoted this to Beauclerk, who knew much more of the gentleman than

we did, he said, in his acid manner, " He would cut a throat to fill his pockets, if it were not for fear of being hanged."

Dr. Johnson proceeded : " Sir, there is a great cry about infidelity ; but there are, in reality, very few infidels. I have heard a person, originally a Quaker, but now, I am afraid, a Deist, say that he did not believe there were, in all England, above two hundred infidels."

He was pleased to say, " If you come to settle here, we will have one day in the week on which we will meet by ourselves. That is the happiest conversation where there is no competition, no vanity, but a calm, quiet interchange of sentiment." In his private register this evening is thus marked :—

" Boswell sat with me till night ; we had some serious talk." [1]

It also appears from the same record, that after I left him he was occupied in religious duties, in

" giving Francis, his servant, some directions for preparation to communicate ; in reviewing his life, and resolving on better conduct."

The humility and piety which he discovers on such occasions, is truly edifying. No saint, however, in the course of his religious warfare, was more sensible of the unhappy failure of pious resolves, than Johnson. He said one day, talking to an acquaintance on this subject, " Sir, Hell is paved with good intentions." [2]

On Sunday, April 16, being Easter-day, after having attended the solemn service at St. Paul's, I dined with Dr. Johnson and Mrs. Williams. I maintained that Horace was wrong in placing happiness in *Nil admirari*, for that I thought admiration one of the most agreeable of all our feelings ; and I regretted that I had lost much of my disposition to admire, which people generally do as they advance in life. JOHNSON : " Sir, as a man advances in life, he gets what is better than admiration,—judgment, to estimate things at their true value." I still insisted that admiration was more pleasing than judgment, as love is more pleasing than friendship. The feeling of friendship is like that of being comfortably filled with roast beef ; love, like being enlivened with champagne. JOHNSON : " No, Sir : admiration and love are like being intoxicated with champagne ; judgment and friendship like being enlivened. Waller has hit upon the same thought with you ; [3] but I don't

---

[1] Prayers and Meditations, p. 138.

[2] This is a proverbial sentence. " Hell," says Herbert, "is full of good meanings and wishings." —JACULA PRUDENTUM, p. 11, edit. 1651.—MALONE.

[3] " Amoret's as sweet and good
As the most delicious food ;
Which but tasted does impart
Life and gladness to the heart.

" Sacharissa's beauty's wine,
Which to madness does incline
Such a liquor as no brain
That is mortal can sustain."—BOSWELL

believe you have borrowed from Waller. I wish you would enable yourself to borrow more."

He then took occasion to enlarge on the advantages of reading, and combated the idle, superficial notion, that knowledge enough may be acquired in conversation. " The foundation," said he, " must be laid by reading. General principles must be had from books, which, however, must be brought to the test of real life. In conversation you never get a system. What is said upon a subject is to be gathered from a hundred people. The parts of a truth, which a man gets thus, are at such a distance from each other that he never attains to a full view."

" TO BENNET LANGTON, ESQ.

"DEAR SIR,   *April* 17, 1775.

" I have enquired more minutely about the medicine for the rheumatism, which I am sorry to hear that you still want. The receipt is this :—

" Take equal quantities of flour of sulphur, and *flour* of mustard seed ; make them an electuary with honey or treacle, and take a bolus as big as a nutmeg several times a day, as you can bear it, drinking after it a quarter of a pint of the infusion of the root of Lovage.

" Lovage, in Ray's ' Nomenclature,' is Levisticum : perhaps the botanists may know the Latin name.

" Of this medicine I pretend not to judge. There is all the appearance of its efficacy, which a single instance can afford. The patient was very old, the pain very violent, and the relief, I think, speedy and lasting.

" My opinion of alterative medicine is not high, but *quid tentasse nocebit !* If it does harm, or does no good, it may be omitted ; but that it may do good, you have, I hope, reason to think is desired by, Sir,

" Your most affectionate humble servant,
"SAM. JOHNSON."

On Tuesday, April 11, he and I were engaged to go with Sir Joshua Reynolds to dine with Mr. Cambridge, at his beautiful villa on the banks of the Thames, near Twickenham. Dr. Johnson's tardiness was such, that Sir Joshua, who had an appointment at Richmond, early in the day, was obliged to go by himself on horseback, leaving his coach to Johnson and me. Johnson was in such good spirits, that everything seemed to please him as we drove along.

Our conversation turned on a variety of subjects. He thought portrait-painting an improper employment for a woman. " Public practice of any art," he observed, " and staring in men's faces, is very indelicate in a female." I happened to start a question, whether, when a man knows that some of his intimate friends are invited to the house of another friend with whom they are all equally intimate, he may join them without an invitation. JOHNSON : " No, Sir ; he is not to go when he is not invited. They may be invited on purpose to abuse him." (smiling).

As a curious instance how little a man knows, or wishes to know his own character in the world, or, rather as a convincing proof that Johnson's roughness was only external, and did not proceed from his heart, I insert the following dialogue. JOHNSON: "It is wonderful, Sir, how rare a quality good-humour is in life. We meet with very few good-humoured men." I mentioned four of our friends, none of whom he would allow to be good-humoured. One was *acid*, another was *muddy*, and to the others he had objections which have escaped me. Then, shaking his head and stretching himself at ease in the coach, and smiling with much complacency, he turned to me and said, "I look upon *myself* as a good-humoured fellow." The epithet *fellow*, applied to the great Lexicographer, the stately Moralist, the masterly Critic, as if he had been *Sam* Johnson, a mere pleasant companion, was highly diverting; and this light notion of himself struck me with wonder. I answered, also smiling, "No, no, Sir; that will *not* do. You are good-natured, but not good-humoured: you are irascible. You have not patience with folly and absurdity. I believe you would pardon them, if there were time to deprecate your vengeance; but punishment follows so quick after sentence, that they cannot escape."

I had brought with me a great bundle of Scotch magazines and newspapers, in which his "Journey to the Western Islands" was attacked in every mode; and I read a great part of them to him, knowing they would afford him entertainment. I wish the writers of them had been present: they would have been sufficiently vexed. One ludicrous imitation of his style, by Mr. Maclaurin, now one of the Scotch Judges, with the title of Lord Dreghorn, was distinguished by him from the rude mass. "This," said he, "is the best. But I could caricature my own style much better myself." He defended his remark upon the general insufficiency of education in Scotland; and confirmed to me the authenticity of his witty saying on the learning of the Scotch:—"Their learning is like bread in a besieged town: every man gets a little, but no man gets a full meal." "There is," said he, "in Scotland, a diffusion of learning, a certain portion of it widely and thinly spread. A merchant has as much learning as one of their clergy."

He talked of Isaac Walton's Lives, which was one of his most favourite books. Dr. Donne's Life, he said, was the most perfect of them. He observed, that "it was wonderful that Walton, who was in a very low situation in life, should have been familiarly received by so many great men, and that at a time when the ranks of society were kept more separate than they are now." He supposed that Walton had then given up his business as a linen-draper and sempster, and was only an author;[1]

Johnson's conjecture was erroneous. Walton did not retire from business till 1643. But in 1664, Dr. King, Bishop of Chichester, in a letter prefixed to his "Lives," mentions his having been familiarly acquainted with him for forty years; and in 1631 he was so intimate with Dr. Donne, that he was one of the friends who attended him on his death-bed.— J BOSWELL, JUN.

and added, "that he was a great panegyrist." BOSWELL : " No quality
will get a man more friends than a disposition to admire the qualities of
others. I do not mean flattery, but a sincere admiration." JOHNSON :
" Nay, Sir, flattery pleases very generally. In the first place, the
flatterer may think what he says to be true ; but in the second place,
whether he thinks so or not, he certainly thinks those whom he flatters
of consequence enough to be flattered."

No sooner had we made our bow to Mr. Cambridge, in his library,
than Johnson ran eagerly to one side of the room intent on poring over
the backs of the books.[1] Sir Joshua observed (aside), " He runs to the
books as I do to the pictures ; but I have the advantage. I can see
much more of the pictures than he can of the books." Mr. Cambridge,
upon this, politely said, " Dr. Johnson, I am going, with your pardon,
to accuse myself, for I have the same custom which I perceive you have.
But it seems odd that one should have such a desire to look at the backs
of books." Johnson, ever ready for contest, instantly started from his
reverie, wheeled about and answered, " Sir, the reason is very plain.
Knowledge is of two kinds. We know a subject ourselves, or we know
where we can find information upon it. When we inquire into any
subject, the first thing we have to do is to know what books have treated
of it. This leads us to look at catalogues, and the backs of books in
libraries." Sir Joshua observed to me the extraordinary promptitude
with which Johnson flew upon an argument. " Yes," said I, " he has
no formal preparation, no flourishing with his sword ; he is through
your body in an instant."

Johnson was here solaced with an elegant entertainment, a very
accomplished family, and much good company ; among whom was
Mr. Harris, of Salisbury, who paid him many compliments on his
" Journey to the Western Islands."

The common remark as to the utility of reading history being made ;
—JOHNSON : " We must consider how very little history there is ;
I mean real authentic history. That certain kings reigned, and certain
battles were fought, we can depend upon as true ; but all the colouring,
all the philosophy of history, is conjecture." BOSWELL : " Then, Sir,
you would reduce all history to no better than an almanac, a mere
chronological series of remarkable events." Mr. Gibbon, who must at
that time have been employed upon his history, of which he published
the first volume in the following year, was present ; but did not step
forth in defence of that species of writing. He probably did not like
to *trust* himself with Johnson.

---

1 The first time he dined with me, he was shown into my book-room, and instantly pored
over the lettering of each volume within his reach. My collection of books is very miscellaneous, and I feared there might be some among them that he would not like. But seeing
the number of volumes very considerable, he said, " You are an honest man to have formed
so great an accumulation of knowledge."—BURNEY.

Johnson observed, that the force of our early habits was so great that though reason approved, nay, though our senses relished a different course, almost every man returned to them. I do not believe there is any observation upon human nature better founded than this ; and, in many cases, it is a very painful truth ; for where early habits have been mean and wretched, the joy and elevation resulting from better modes of life must be damped by the gloomy consciousness of being under an almost inevitable doom to sink back into a situation which we recollect with disgust. It surely may be prevented, by constant attention and unremitting exertion to establish contrary habits of superior efficacy.

" The Beggars' Opera," and the common question, whether it was pernicious in its effects, having been introduced ;—JOHNSON : " As to this matter, which has been very much contested, I myself am of opinion, that more influence has been ascribed to ' The Beggars' Opera,' than it in reality ever had ; for I do not believe that any man was ever made a rogue by being present at its representation. At the same time I do not deny that it may have some influence, by making the character of a rogue familiar, and in some degree pleasing." [1] Then collecting himself, as it were, to give a heavy stroke : " There is in it such a *labefactation* of all principles as may be injurious to morality."

While he pronounced this response, we sat in a comical sort of restraint, smothering a laugh, which we were afraid might burst out. In his life of Gay, he has been still more decisive as to the inefficiency of " The Beggars' Opera " in corrupting society. But I have ever thought somewhat differently ; for, indeed, not only are the gaiety and heroism of a highwayman very captivating to a youthful imagination, but the arguments for adventurous depredation are so plausible, the allusions so lively, and the contrasts with the ordinary and more painful modes of acquiring property are so artfully displayed, that it requires a cool and strong judgment to resist so imposing an aggregate : yet, I own, I should be very sorry to have " The Beggars' Opera " suppressed ; for there is in it so much of real London life, so much brilliant wit, and such a variety of airs, which, from early association of ideas, engage, soothe, and enliven the mind, that no performance which the theatre exhibits delights me more.

The late "*worthy*" Duke of Queensbury, as Thomson, in his " Seasons," justly characterises him, told me, that when Gay showed

---

[1] A very eminent physician, whose discernment is as acute and penetrating in judging of the human character as it is in his own profession, remarked once at a club where I was, that a lively young man, fond of pleasure, and without money, would hardly resist a solicitation from his mistress to go upon the highway, immediately after being present at the representation of " The Beggars' Opera." I have been told of an ingenious observation by Mr. Gibbon that "The Beggars' Opera" may perhaps have sometimes increased the number of highwaymen ; but that it has had a beneficial effect in refining that class of men, making them less ferocious, more polite,—in short, more like gentlemen." Upon this, Mr. Courtenay said, that " Gay was the Orpheus of highwaymen."—BOSWELL.

him " The Beggars' Opera," his Grace's observation was, " This is a
very odd thing, Gay ; I am satisfied that it is either a very good thing,
or a very bad thing." It proved the former, beyond the warmest
expectations of the author or his friends. Mr. Cambridge, however,
showed us to-day, that there was good reason enough to doubt concerning its success. He was told by Quin, that during the first night
of its appearance it was long in a very dubious state ; that there was a
disposition to damn it, and that it was saved by the song,

> " Oh ponder well ! be not severe ! "

the audience being much affected by the innocent looks of Polly,
when she came to those two lines, which exhibit at once a painful and
ridiculous image,

> " For on the rope that hangs my dear,
> Depends poor Polly's life."

Quin himself had so bad an opinion of it, that he refused the part of
Captain Macheath, and gave it to Walker, who acquired great celebrity
by his grave yet animated performance of it.

We talked of a young gentleman's marriage with an eminent singer,
and his determination that she should no longer sing in public, though
his father was very earnest she should, because her talents would be
liberally rewarded, so as to make her a good fortune. It was questioned
whether the young gentleman, who had not a shilling in the world, but
was blest with very uncommon talents, was not foolishly delicate, or
foolishly proud, and his father truly rational, without being mean.
JOHNSON, with all the high spirit of a Roman senator, exclaimed, " He
resolved wisely and nobly to be sure. He is a brave man. Would not
a gentleman be disgraced by having his wife singing publicly for hire ?
No, Sir, there can be no doubt here. I know not if I should not
prepare myself for a public singer, as readily as let my wife be one."

Johnson arraigned the modern politics of this country, as entirely
devoid of all principle of whatever kind. " Politics," said he, " are now
nothing more than means of rising in the world. With this sole view do
men engage in politics, and their whole conduct proceeds upon it. How
different in that respect is the state of the nation now from what it was
in the time of Charles the First, during the Usurpation, and after the
Restoration, in the time of Charles the Second. Hudibras affords a
strong proof how much hold political principles had then upon the
minds of men. There is in Hudibras a great deal of bullion which will
always last. But, to be sure, the brightest strokes of his wit owed
their force to the impression of the characters, which was upon men's
minds at the time ; to their knowing them, at table and in the street ;
in short, being familiar with them ; and above all, to his satire being
directed against those whom a little while before they had hated and

feared. The nation in general has ever been loyal, has been at all times attached to the monarch, though a few daring rebels have been wonderfully powerful for a time. The murder of Charles the First was undoubtedly not committed with the approbation or consent of the people ; had that been the case, Parliament would not have ventured to consign the regicides to their deserved punishment ; and we know what exuberance of joy there was when Charles the Second was restored. If Charles the Second had bent all his mind to it, had made it his sole object, he might have been as absolute as Louis the Fourteenth." A gentleman observed, he would have done no harm if he had. JOHNSON : " Why, Sir, absolute princes seldom do any harm. But they who are governed by them are governed by chance. There is no security for good government." CAMBRIDGE: " There have been many sad victims to absolute government." JOHNSON : " So, Sir, have there been to popular factions." BOSWELL : " The question is, which is worst, one wild beast or many ? "

Johnson praised " The Spectator," particularly the character of Sir Roger de Coverley. He said, " Sir Roger did not die a violent death, as has been generally fancied. He was not killed ; he died only because others were to die, and because his death afforded an opportunity to Addison for some very fine writing. We have the example of Cervantes making Don Quixote die. I never could see why Sir Roger is represented as a little cracked. It appears to me that the story of the widow was intended to have something superinduced upon it ; but the superstructure did not come."

Somebody found fault with writing verses in a dead language, maintaining that they were merely arrangements of so many words, and laughed at the Universities of Oxford and Cambridge, for sending forth collections of them not only in Greek and Latin, but even in Syriac, Arabic, and other more unknown tongues. JOHNSON : " I would have as many of these as possible ; I would have verses in every language that there are the means of acquiring. Nobody imagines that an University is to have at once two hundred poets ; but it should be able to show two hundred scholars. Peiresc's death was lamented, I think, in forty languages. And I would have had at every coronation, and every death of a king, every *Gaudium*, and every *Luctus*, Universityverses, in as many languages as can be acquired. I would have the world to be thus told, ' Here is a school where everything may be learnt.' "

Having set out next day on a visit to the Earl of Pembroke, at Wilton, and to my friend, Mr. Temple, at Mamhead, in Devonshire, and not having returned to town till the second of May, I did not see Dr Johnson for a considerable time, and during the remaining part of my stay in London kept very imperfect notes of his conversation, which had I, according to my usual custom, written out at large soon after the time, much might have been preserved which is now irretrievably lost. I can now only record some particular scenes, and a few fragments of his *memorabilia*. But to make some amends for my relaxation of diligence in one respect, I have to present my readers with arguments upon two law cases, with which he favoured me.

On Saturday, the 6th of May, we dined by ourselves at the Mitre, and he dictated to me what follows, to obviate the complaint already mentioned, which had been made in the form of an action in the Court of Session, by Dr. Memis, of Aberdeen, that in the same translation of a charter in which *physicians* were mentioned, he was called *Doctor of Medicine*.

" There are but two reasons for which a physician can decline the title of *Doctor of Medicine*, because he supposes himself disgraced by the doctorship, or supposes the doctorship disgraced by himself. To be disgraced by a title which he shares in common with every illustrious name of his profession, with Boerhaave, with Arbuthnot, and with Cullen, can surely diminish no man's reputation. It is, I suppose, to the doctorate from which he shrinks, that he holds his rights of practising physic. A Doctor of Medicine is a physician under the protection of the laws, and by the stamp of authority. The physician who is not a doctor, usurps a profession, and is authorised only by himself to decide upon health and sickness, and life and death. That this gentleman is a Doctor his diploma makes evident; a diploma not obtruded upon him, but obtained by solicitation, and for which fees were paid. With what countenance any man can refuse the title which he has either begged or bought, is not easily discovered.

" All verbal injury must comprise in it either some false position or some unnecessary declaration of defamatory truth. That in calling him Doctor, a false appellation was given him, he himself will not pretend, who at the same time that he complains of the title would be offended if we supposed him to be not a doctor. If the title of Doctor be a defamatory truth, it is time to dissolve our colleges; for why should the public give salaries to men whose approbation is reproach? It may likewise deserve the notice of the public to consider what help can be given to the professors of physic, who all share with this unhappy gentleman the ignominious appellation, and of whom the very boys in the street are not afraid to say, ' *There goes the Doctor.*'

" What is implied by the term Doctor is well known. It distinguishes him to whom it is granted, as a man who has attained such knowledge of his profession as qualifies him to instruct others. A Doctor of Laws is a man who can form lawyers by his precepts. A Doctor of Medicine is a man who can teach the art of curing diseases. This is an old axiom which no man has yet thought fit to deny, *Nil dat quod non habet.* Upon this principle, to be Doctor implies skill, for *nemo docet quod non didicit.* In England, whoever practises physic, not being a Doctor, must practise by a license; but the doctorate conveys a license in itself.

" By what accident it happened that he and the other physicians were mentioned in different terms, where the terms themselves were equivalent, or where, in effect, that which was applied to him was the most honourable, perhaps they who wrote the paper cannot now remember. Had they expected a lawsuit to have been the consequence of such petty variation, I hope they would have avoided it. [1] But, probably, as they meant no ill, they suspected no danger, and therefore, consulted only what appeared to them propriety or convenience."

A few days afterwards, I consulted him upon a cause, *Paterson and others* against *Alexander and others*, which had been decided by a casting vote in the Court of Session, determining that the Corporation of Stirling was corrupt, and setting aside the election of some of their officers because it was proved that three of the leading men who influenced the majority, had entered into an unjustifiable compact, of which, however, the majority were ignorant. He dictated to me, after a little consideration, the following sentences upon the subject :

" There is a difference between majority and superiority ; majority is applied to number, and superiority to power; and power, like many other things, is to be estimated *non numero sed pondere.* Now though the greater *number* is not corrupt, the greater *weight* is corrupt, so that corruption predominates in the borough, taken *collectively,* though, perhaps, taken *numerically,* the greater part may be uncorrupt. That borough, which is so constituted as to act corruptly, is in the eye of reason corrupt, whether it be by the uncontrollable power of a few, or by an accidental pravity of the multitude. The objection in which is urged the injustice of making the innocent suffer with the guilty, is an objection not only against society, but against the possibility of society. All societies, great and small, subsist upon this condition ; that as the individuals derive advantages from union, they may likewise suffer inconveniences ; that as those who do nothing, and sometimes those who do ill, will have the honours and emoluments of general virtue and general prosperity, so those likewise who do nothing, or perhaps do well, must be involved in the consequences of predominant corruption."

This in my opinion was a very nice case ; but the decision was affirmed in the House of Lords.

On Monday, May 8, we went together and visited the mansions of Bedlam. I had been informed that he had once been there before with Mr. Wedderburn (now Lord Loughborough), Mr. Murphy, and Mr. Foote ; and I had heard Foote give a very entertaining account of Johnson's happening to have his attention arrested by a man who was very furious, and who, while beating his straw, supposed it was William Duke of Cumberland, whom he was punishing for his cruelties in Scotland, in 1746.[2] There was nothing peculiarly remarkable this day ;

---

[1] In justice to Dr. Memis, though I was against him as an Advocate, I must mention that he objected to the variation very earnestly, before the translation was printed off.—BOSWELL.

[2] My very honourable friend, General Sir George Howard, who served in the Duke of Cumberland's army, has assured me that the cruelties were not imputable to his Royal Highness.—BOSWELL.

but the general contemplation of insanity was very affecting. I accompanied him home, and dined and drank tea with him.

Talking of an acquaintance of ours, distinguished for knowing an uncommon variety of miscellaneous articles both in antiquities and polite literature, he observed, "You know, Sir, he runs about with little weight upon his mind." And talking of another very ingenious gentleman, who from the warmth of his temper was at variance with many of his acquaintance, and wished to avoid them, he said, " Sir, he leads the life of an outlaw."

On Friday, May 12, as he had been so good as to assign me a room in his house, where I might sleep occasionally, when I happened to sit with him to a late hour, I took possession of it this night, found every thing in excellent order, and was attended by honest Francis with a most civil assiduity. I asked Johnson whether I might go to a consultation with another lawyer upon Sunday, as that appeared to me to be doing work as much in my way, as if an artisan should work on the day appropriated for religious rest: JOHNSON : " Why, Sir, when you are of consequence enough to oppose the practice of consulting upon Sunday, you should do it : but you may go now. It is not criminal, though it is not what one should do who is anxious for the preservation and increase of piety, to which a peculiar observance of Sunday is a great help. The distinction is clear between what is of moral and what is of ritual obligation."

On Saturday, May 13, I breakfasted with him by invitation, accompanied by Mr. Andrew Crosbie, a Scotch Advocate, whom he had seen at Edinburgh, and the Hon. Colonel (now General) Edward Stopford, brother to Lord Courtown, who was desirous of being introduced to him. His tea, and rolls, and butter, and whole breakfast apparatus, were all in such decorum, and his behaviour was so courteous, that Colonel Stopford was quite surprised, and wondered at his having heard so much said of Johnson's slovenliness and roughness. I have preserved nothing of what passed, except that Crosbie pleased him much by talking learnedly of alchymy, as to which Johnson was not a positive unbeliever, but rather delighted in considering what progress had actually been made in the transmutation of metals, what near approaches there had been to the making of gold ; and told us that it was affirmed, that a person in the Russian dominions had discovered the secret, but died without revealing it, as imagining it would be prejudicial to society. He added, that it was not impossible but it might in time be generally known.

It being asked whether it was reasonable for a man to be angry at another whom a woman had preferred to him,—JOHNSON : " I do not see, Sir, that it is reasonable for a man to be angry at another, whom a woman has preferred to him : but angry he is, no doubt ; and he is loth to be angry at himself."

Before setting out for Scotland on the 23rd, I was frequently in his company at different places, but during this period have recorded only two remarks ; one concerning Garrick : "He has not Latin enough. He finds out the Latin by the meaning, rather than the meaning by the Latin : " and another concerning writers of travels, who, he observed, "were more defective than any other writers."

I passed many hours with him on the 17th, of which I find all my memorial is, "much laughing." It should seem he had that day been in a humour for jocularity and merriment, and upon such occasions I never knew a man laugh more heartily. We may suppose, that the high relish of a state so different from his habitual gloom, produced more than ordinary exertions of that distinguishing faculty of man, which has puzzled philosophers so much to explain. Johnson's laugh was as remarkable as any circumstance in his manner. It was a kind of good-humoured growl. Tom Davies described it drolly enough : " He laughs like a rhinoceros."

" TO BENNET LANGTON, ESQ.

"DEAR SIR, *May* 21, 1775.

"I have an old amanuensis in great distress. I have given what I think I can give, and begged till I cannot tell where to beg again. I put into his hands this morning four guineas. If you could collect three guineas more, it would clear him from his present difficulty.

"I am, Sir, your most humble servant,

"SAM. JOHNSON."

" TO JAMES BOSWELL, ESQ.

"DEAR SIR, *May* 27, 1775.

"I make no doubt but you are now safely lodged in your own habitation, and have told all your adventures to Mrs. Boswell and Miss Veronica. Pray teach Veronica to love me. Bid her not mind mamma.

"Mrs. Thrale has taken cold, and been very much disordered, but I hope is grown well. Mr. Langton went yesterday to Lincolnshire, and has invited Nicolaida[1] to follow him. Beauclerk talks of going to Bath. I am to set out on Monday ; so there is nothing but dispersion.

'I have returned Lord Hailes's entertaining sheets, but must stay till I come back for more, because it will be inconvenient to send them after me in my vagrant state.

"I promised Mrs. Macaulay[2] that I would try to serve her son at Oxford. I have not forgotten it, nor am unwilling to perform it. If they desire to give him an English education, it should be considered whether they cannot send him for a year or two to an English school. If he comes immediately from Scotland, he can make no figure in our Universities. The schools in the North, I believe, are cheap ; and, when I was a young man, were eminently good.

---

[1] A learned Greek.—BOSWELL.

[2] Wife of the Reverend Mr. Kenneth Macaulay, author of "The History of St. Kilda."—BOSWELL.

"There are two little books published by the Foulis, 'Telemachus,' and 'Collins's Poems,' each a shilling; I would be glad to have them.

"Make my compliments to Mrs. Boswell, though she does not love me. You see what perverse things ladies are, and how little fit to be trusted with feudal estates. When she mends and loves me, there may be more hope of her daughters.

"I will not send compliments to my friends by name, because I would be loth to leave any out in the enumeration. Tell them, as you see them, how well I speak of Scotch politeness, and Scotch hospitality, and Scotch beauty, and of everything Scotch, but Scotch oat-cakes, and Scotch prejudices.

"Let me know the answer of Rasay, and the decision relating to Sir Allan.[1]

"I am, my dearest Sir, with great affection,

"Your most obliged and most humble servant,

"SAM. JOHNSON.

After my return to Scotland, I wrote three letters to him, from which I extract the following passages :—

"I have seen Lord Hailes since I came down. He thinks it wonderful that you are pleased to take so much pains in revising his 'Annals.' I told him that you said you were well rewarded by the entertainment which you had in reading them.

"There has been a numerous flight of Hebrideans in Edinburgh this summer, whom I have been happy to entertain at my house. Mr. Donald Macqueen,[2] and Lord Monboddo supped with me one evening. They joined in controverting your proposition, that the Gaelic of the Highlands and Isles of Scotland was not written till of late.

"My mind has been somewhat dark this summer. I have need of your warming and vivifying rays; and I hope I shall have them frequently. I am going to pass some time with my father at Auchinleck."

"TO JAMES BOSWELL, ESQ.

"DEAR SIR,   *London, August 27, 1775.*

"I am returned from the annual ramble into the middle counties. Having seen nothing I had not seen before, I have nothing to relate. Time has left that part of the island few antiquities; and commerce has left the people no singularities. I was glad to go abroad, and, perhaps, glad to come home; which is, in other words, I was, I am afraid, weary of being at home, and weary of being abroad. Is not this the state of life? But, if we confess this weariness, let us not lament it; for all the wise and all the good say, that we may cure it.

"For the black fumes which rise in your mind, I can prescribe nothing but that you disperse them by honest business or innocent pleasure, and by reading, sometimes easy, and sometimes serious. Change of place is useful; and I hope that your residence at Auchinleck will have many good effects.

*   *   *   *   *   *

---

[1] A law-suit carried on by Sir Allan Maclean, chief of his clan, to recover certain parts of his family estates from the Duke of Argyle.—BOSWELL.

[2] A very learned minister in the Isle of Skye, whom both Dr. Johnson and I have mentioned with regard.—BOSWELL.

" That I should have given pain to Rasay, I am sincerely sorry; and am therefore very much pleased that he is no longer uneasy. He still thinks that I have represented him as personally giving up the Chieftainship. I meant only that it was no longer contested between the two houses, and supposed it settled, perhaps, by the cession of some remote generation, in the house of Dunvegan. I am sorry the advertisement was not continued for three or four times in the paper.

" That Lord Monboddo and Mr. Macqueen should controvert a position contrary to the imaginary interest of literary or national prejudice, might be easily imagined; but of a standing fact there ought to be no controversy; if there are men with tails, catch an *homo caudatus;* if there was writing of old in the Highlands or Hebrides, in the Erse language, produce the manuscripts. Where men write, they will write to one another; and some of their letters, in families studious of their ancestry, will be kept. In Wales there are many manuscripts.

" I have now three parcels of Lord Hailes's history, which I purpose to return all the next week : that his respect for my little observations should keep his work in suspense, makes one of the evils of my journey. It is in our language, I think, a new mode of history which tells all that is wanted, and, I suppose, all that is known, without laboured splendour of language, or affected subtlety of conjecture. The exactness of his dates raises my wonder. He seems to have the closeness of Henault without his constraint.

" Mrs. Thrale was so entertained with your ' Journal,'[1] that she almost read herself blind. She has a great regard for you.

" Of Mrs. Boswell, though she knows in her heart that she does not love me, I am always glad to hear any good, and hope that she and the little dear ladies will have neither sickness nor any other affliction. But she knows that she does not care what becomes of me, and for that she may be sure that I think her very much to blame.

" Never, my dear Sir, do you take it into your head to think that I do not love you; you may settle yourself in full confidence both of my love and my esteem; I love you as a kind man, I value you as a worthy man, and hope in time to reverence you as a man of exemplary piety. I hold you, as Hamlet has it, ' in my heart of hearts,' and, therefore, it is little to say, that I am, Sir,

" Your affectionate humble servant,

" SAM. JOHNSON."

TO THE SAME.

" SIR,   *August* 30, 1775.

" If in these papers [2] there is little alteration attempted, do not suppose me negligent. I have read them perhaps more closely than the rest; but I find nothing worthy of an objection.

" Write to me soon, and write often, and tell me all your honest heart.

" I am, Sir,

" Yours affectionately,

" SAM. JOHNSON."

---

[1] My " Journal of a Tour to the Hebrides," which that lady read in the original manuscript.—BOSWELL.

[2] Another parcel of Lord Hailes's " Annals of Scotland."—BOSWELL.

TO THE SAME.

"My Dear Sir,   *September* 14, 1775.

"I now write to you, lest in some of your freaks and humours you should fancy yourself neglected. Such fancies I must entreat you never to admit, at least never to indulge; for my regard for you is so radicated and fixed, that it is become part of my mind, and cannot be effaced but by some cause uncommonly violent; therefore whether I write or not, set your thoughts at rest. I now write to tell you that I shall not very soon write again, for I am to set out to-morrow on another journey.

*   *   *   *   *   *

"Your friends are all well at Streatham and in Leicester-fields.[1]   Make my compliments to Mrs. Boswell, if she is in good humour with me.

"I am, Sir, &c.,

"SAM. JOHNSON."

[1] Where Sir Joshua Reynolds lived.—BOSWELL.

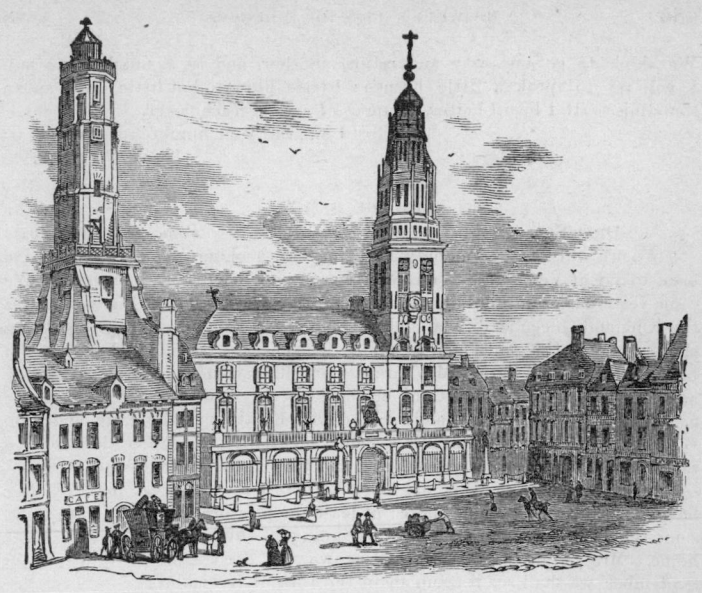

CALAIS.

CHAPTER XII.—1775.

JOHNSON ACCOMPANIES MR. AND MRS. THRALE ON A TOUR TO FRANCE—PARIS—ECOLE
MILITAIRE—THE GOBELINS—PALAIS ROYAL—MRS. FERMOR—PALAIS BOURBON—FON-
TAINEBLEAU—VERSAILLES AND TRIANON—SANTERRE THE BREWER—THE KING'S LIBRARY
—THE SORBONNE—ST. CLOUD—SEVRE—GRAND CHARTREUSE—LIBRARY OF ST. GERMAIN
—DEPARTURE FROM PARIS—CHANTILLY—COMPEIGNE—CAMBRAY.

WHAT he mentions in such light terms as, "I am to set out to-morrow on another journey," I soon afterwards discovered was no less than a tour to France with Mr. and Mrs. Thrale. This was the only time in his life that he went upon the Continent.

"TO MR. ROBERT LEVET.

" DEAR SIR, *Calais, Sept.* 13, 1775.

" We are here in France, after a very pleasing passage of no more than six hours. I know not when I shall write again, and therefore I write now, though you cannot suppose that I have much to say. You have seen France yourself. From this place we are going to Rouen, and from Rouen to Paris, where Mr. Thrale designs to stay about five or six weeks. We have a regular recommendation to the English resident, so we shall not be taken for vagabonds

We think to go one way and return another, and see as much as we can. I will try to speak a little French: I tried hitherto but little, but I spoke sometimes. If I heard better, I suppose I should learn faster.

> " I am, Sir, your humble servant,
>
> > " SAM. JOHNSON."

TO THE SAME.

" DEAR SIR,   *Paris, Oct.* 23, 1775.

" We are still here, commonly very busy in looking about us. We have been to-day at Versailles. You have seen it, and I shall not describe it. We came yesterday from Fontainebleau, where the Court is now. We went to see the King and Queen at dinner, and the Queen was so impressed by Miss,[1] that she sent one of the gentlemen to inquire who she was. I find all true that you have ever told me of Paris. Mr. Thrale is very liberal, and keeps us two coaches, and a very fine table; but I think our cookery very bad. Mrs. Thrale got into a convent of English nuns, and I talked with her through the grate, and I am very kindly used by the English Benedictine friars. But upon the whole I cannot make much acquaintance here; and though the churches, palaces, and some private houses are very magnificent, there is no very great pleasure after having seen many, in seeing more; at least the pleasure, whatever it be, must some time have an end, and we are beginning to think when we shall come home. Mr. Thrale calculates that as we left Streatham on the 15th of September, we shall see it again about the 15th of November.

" I think I had not been on this side of the sea five days before I found a sensible improvement in my health. I ran a race in the rain this day, and beat Baretti. Baretti is a fine fellow, and speaks French, I think, quite as well as English.

" Make my compliments to Mrs. Williams; and give my love to Francis, and tell my friends that I am not lost.   I am, dear Sir,

> " Your affectionate humble, &c.,
>
> > " SAM. JOHNSON."

" TO DR. SAMUEL JOHNSON.

" MY DEAR SIR,   *Edinburgh, Oct.* 24, 1775.

" If I had not been informed that you were at Paris, you should have had a letter from me by the earliest opportunity, announcing the birth of my son, on the 9th instant; I have named him Alexander, after my father. I now write, as I suppose your fellow-traveller, Mr. Thrale, will return to London this week, to attend his duty in Parliament, and that you will not stay behind him.

" I send another parcel of Lord Hailes's 'Annals.' I have undertaken to solicit you for a favour to him, which he thus requests in a letter to me: ' I intend soon to give you " The Life of Robert Bruce," which you will be pleased to transmit to Dr. Johnson. I wish that you could assist me in a fancy which I have taken, of getting Dr. Johnson to draw a character of Robert Bruce, from the account that I give of that prince. If he finds materials for it in my work,

---

[1] Miss Thrale.—BOSWELL

it will be a proof that I have been fortunate in selecting the most striking incidents.'

"I suppose by *The Life of Robert Bruce*, his lordship means that part of his 'Annals' which relates the history of that prince, and not a separate work.

"Shall we have *A Journey to Paris* from you in the winter? You will, I hope, at any rate, be kind enough to give me some account of your French travels very soon, for I am very impatient. What a different scene have you viewed this autumn, from that which you viewed in autumn 1773! I ever am, my dear Sir,   Your much obliged and

"Affectionate humble servant,

"JAMES BOSWELL."

"TO JAMES BOSWELL, ESQ.

"DEAR SIR,   *November* 16, 1775.

"I am glad that the young laird is born, and an end, as I hope, put to the only difference that you can ever have with Mrs. Boswell.[1] I know that she does not love me; but I intend to persist in wishing her well till I get the better of her.

"Paris is, indeed, a place very different from the Hebrides, but it is to a hasty traveller not so fertile of novelty, nor affords so many opportunities of remark. I cannot pretend to tell the public anything of a place better known to many of my readers than to myself. We can talk of it when we meet.

"I shall go next week to Streatham, from whence I purpose to send a parcel of the 'History' every post. Concerning the character of Bruce, I can only say, that I do not see any great reason for writing it; but I shall not easily deny what Lord Hailes and you concur in desiring.

"I have been remarkably healthy all the journey, and hope you and your family have known only that trouble and danger which has so happily terminated. Among all the congratulations that you may receive, I hope you believe none more warm or sincere, than those of, dear Sir,

"Your most affectionate,

"SAM. JOHNSON."

"TO MRS. LUCY PORTER, IN LICHFIELD.[2]

"DEAR MADAM,   *November* 16, 1775.

"This week I came home from Paris. I have brought you a little box, which I thought pretty; but I know not whether it is properly a snuff-box, or a box for some other use, I will send it, when I can find an opportunity. I have been through the whole journey remarkably well. My fellow-travellers were the same whom you saw at Lichfield, only we took Baretti with us. Paris is not so fine a place as you would expect. The palaces and churches, however,

---

[1] This alludes to my old feudal principle of preferring male to female succession.—BOSWELL.

[2] There can be no doubt that, many years previous to 1775, he corresponded with this lady, who was his step-daughter, but none of his earliest letters to her have been preserved.—BOSWELL.

Since the death of the author, several of Johnson's letters to Mrs. Lucy Porter, written before 1775, were obligingly communicated to me by the Rev. Dr. Vyse, and are printed in the present edition.—MALONE

are very splendid and magnificent; and what would please you, there are many very fine pictures; but I do not think their way of life commodious or pleasant.

"Let me know how your health has been all this while. I hope the fine summer has given you strength sufficient to encounter the winter.

"Make my compliments to all my friends; and if your fingers will let you, write to me, or let your maid write to me, if it be troublesome to you. I am, dear Madam,   "Your most affectionate humble servant,

"Sam. Johnson."

TO THE SAME.

"Dear Madam,   *December*, 1775.

"Some weeks ago I wrote to you to tell you that I was just come home from a ramble, and hoped that I should have heard from you. I am afraid winter has laid hold on your fingers, and hinders you from writing. However, let somebody write, if you cannot, and tell me how you do, and a little of what has happened at Lichfield among our friends. I hope you are all well.

"When I was in France, I thought myself growing young, but am afraid that cold weather will take part of my new vigour from me. Let us, however, take care of ourselves, and lose no part of our health by negligence.

"I never knew whether you received the Commentary on the New Testament, and the Travels, and the glasses.

"Do, my dear love, write to me; and do not let us forget each other. This is the season of good wishes, and I wish you all good. I have not lately seen Mr. Porter,[1] nor heard of him. Is he with you?

"Be pleased to make my compliments to Mrs. Adey, and Mrs. Cobb, and all my friends; and when I can do any good, let me know. I am, dear Madam,

"Yours most affectionately,
"Sam. Johnson."

It is to be regretted, that he did not write an account of his travels in France; for as he is reported to have once said, that "he could write the life of a broomstick,"[2] so, notwithstanding so many former travellers have exhausted almost every subject for remark in that great kingdom, his very accurate observation, and peculiar vigour of thought and illustration, would have produced a valuable work. During his visit to it, which lasted but about two months, he wrote notes or minutes of what he saw. He promised to show me them, but I neglected to put him in mind of it; and the greatest part of them has been lost, or, perhaps, destroyed in a precipitate burning of his papers a few days before his death, which must ever be lamented. One small paper-book, however, entitled "France II.," has been preserved, and is in my possession. It is a diurnal register of his life and observations, from

[1] Son of Mrs. Johnson, by her first husband.—Boswell.
[2] It is probable that the author's memory here deceived him, and that he was thinking of Stella's remark, that Swift could write finely upon a broomstick. See Johnson's Life of Swift.—J. Boswell, Jun

the 10th of October, to the 4th of November, inclusive, being twenty-six days, and shows an extraordinary attention to various minute particulars. Being the only memorial of this tour that remains, my readers, I am confident, will peruse it with pleasure, though his notes are very short, and evidently written only to assist his own recollection.

" *Tuesday*, Oct. 10.   We saw the *Ecole Militaire*, in which one hundred and fifty young boys are educated for the army.   They have arms of different sizes, according to the age;—flints of wood.   The building is very large, but nothing fine except the council-room.   The French have large squares in the windows;—they make good iron palisades.   Their meals are gross.

" We visited the observatory, a large building of a great height.   The upper stones of the parapet very large, but not cramped with iron.   The flat on the top is very extensive; but on the insulated part there is no parapet.   Though it was broad enough, I did not care to go upon it.   Maps were printing in one of the rooms.

" We walked to a small convent of the Fathers of the Oratory.   In the reading-desk of the refectory lay the Lives of the Saints.

" *Wednesday*, Oct. 11.   We went to the *Hôtel de Chatlois*, a house not very large, but very elegant.   One of the rooms was gilt to a degree that I never saw before.   The upper part for servants and their masters was pretty.

" Thence we went to Mr. Monville's, a house divided into small apartments, furnished with effeminate and minute elegance.—Porphyry.

" Thence we went to St. Roque's [*Roch*] Church, which is very large;—the lower part of the pillars incrusted with marble.—Three chapels behind the high altar; the last a mass of low arches.—Altars, I believe, all round.

" We passed through *Place de Vendôme*, a fine square, about as big as Hanover Square.—Inhabited by the high families.—Louis XIV. on horseback in the middle.

" Monville is the son of a farmer-general.   In the house of *Chatlois* is a room furnished with japan, fitted up in Europe.

" We dined with Bocage, the Marquis Blanchetti, and his lady.   The sweet-meats taken by the Marchioness Blanchetti, after observing that they were dear.   Mr. Le Roy, Count Manucci, the Abbé, the Prior, and Father Wilson, who stayed with me, till I took him home in the coach.

" Bathiani is gone.

" The French have no laws for the maintenance of their poor.—Monk not necessarily a priest.—Benedictines rise at four;—are at church an hour and half; at church again half an hour before, half an hour after, dinner; and again from half an hour after seven to eight.   They may sleep eight hours.   Bodily labour wanted in monasteries.

" The poor taken to hospitals, and miserably kept.—Monks in the convent, fifteen :—accounted poor.

" *Thursday*, Oct. 12.   We went to the Gobelins.—Tapestry makes a good picture : imitates flesh exactly.—One piece with a gold ground ; the birds not exactly coloured.—Thence we went to the King's cabinet ; very neat, not perhaps perfect.—Gold ore.—Candles of the candle-tree.—Seeds.—Woods.— Thence to Gagnier's house. where I saw rooms nine, furnished with a profusion of wealth and elegance which I had never seen before.—Vases.—Pictures.—The dragon china.—The lustre said to be of crystal, and to have cost 3500*l.*—The whole furniture said to have cost 125,000*l.*—Damask hangings covered with pictures.—Porphyry.—This house struck me.—Then we waited on the ladies to Monville's.—Captain Irwin with us.[1]—Spain.—Country towns all beggars.— At Dijon he could not find the way to Orleans.—Cross roads of France very bad. Five soldiers.—Woman.—Soldiers escaped.—The Colonel would not lose five men for the death of one woman.—The magistrates cannot seize a soldier but by the Colonel's permission.—Good inn at Nismes.—Moors of Barbary fond of Englishmen.—Gibraltar eminently healthy ; it has beef from Barbary.—There is a large garden.—Soldiers sometimes fall from the rock.

"*Friday,* Oct. 13. I stayed at home all day, only went to find the Prior, who was not at home. I read something in Canus.[2]—*Nec admiror, nec multum laudo.*

"*Saturday,* Oct. 14. We went to the house of Mr. [D'] Argenson, which was almost wainscotted with looking-glasses, and covered with gold.—The ladies' closet wainscotted with large squares of glass over painted paper. They always place mirrors to reflect their rooms.

" Then we went to Julien's, the Treasurer of the Clergy ; 30,000*l.* a year. —The house has no very large room, but is set with mirrors, and covered with gold.—Books of wood here, and in another library.

"At D' [Argenson's] I looked into the books in the lady's closet, and, in contempt, showed them to Mr. T[hrale].—*Prince Titi ; Bibl. des Fées,* and other books. She was offended, and shut up, as we heard afterwards, her apartment.

" Then we went to Julien Le Roy, the King's watchmaker, a man of character in his business, who showed a small clock made to find the longitude.— A decent man.

"Afterwards we saw the Palais Marchand, and the Courts of Justice, civil and criminal.—Queries on the Sellette.—This building has the old Gothic passages, and a great appearance of antiquity.—Three hundred prisoners sometimes in the gaol.

"Much disturbed ; hope no ill will be.[3]

" In the afternoon I visited Mr. Freron,[4] the journalist. He spoke Latin very scantily, but seemed to understand me.—His house not splendid, but of commodious size.—His family, wife, son, and daughter, not elevated, but decent.—I was pleased with my reception.—He is to translate my books, which I am to send him with notes.

"*Sunday,* Oct. 15. At Choisi, a royal palace on the banks of the Seine, about seven miles from Paris.—The terrace noble along the river.—The

1 The rest of this paragraph appears to be a minute of what was told by Capt. Irwin.— BOSWELL.

2 Melchior Canus, a celebrated Spanish Dominican, who died at Toledo, in 1560. He wrote a treatise, *De Locis Theologicis,* in Twelve books.—BOSWELL.

3 This passage, which so many think superstitious, reminds me of Archbishop Laud's Diary —BOSWELL.

4 Elie Catherine Freron, a celebrated French critic, and powerful opponent of Voltaire, was born at Quimper in 1719. He was originally a Jesuit, but quitted the society at the age of 20. He died in the year following Johnson's visit to Paris: and therefore the contemplated translation of the Doctor's works was put an end to,—ED.

rooms numerous and grand, but not discriminated from other palaces.—The chapel beautiful, but small.—China globes.—Inlaid tables.—Labyrinth.—Sinking table.—Toilet tables.

"*Monday*, Oct. 16. The Palais Royal very grand, large, and lofty.—A very great collection of pictures.—Three of Raphael.—Two Holy Family.—One small piece of M. Angelo.—One room of Rubens.—I thought the pictures of Raphael fine.

"The Tuileries.—Statues.—Venus.—Æn. and Anchises in his arms.—Nilus. —Many more.—The walks not open to mean persons.—Chairs at night hired for two sous a-piece.—Pont tournant.

"Austin Nuns.—Grate.—Mrs. Fermor, Abbess. She knew Pope, and thought him disagreeable.—Mrs. —— has many books; has seen life.—Their frontlet disagreeable.—Their hood.—Their life easy.—Rise about five; hour and half at chapel; dine at ten. Another hour and a half at chapel—half an hour about three, and half an hour more at seven; four hours in chapel.—A large garden.—Thirteen pensioners.—Teacher complained.

"At the Boulevards saw nothing, yet was glad to be there.—Rope-dancing and farce.—Egg-dance.

"N. [Note.] Near Paris, whether on week-days or Sundays, the roads empty.
"*Tuesday*, Oct. 17. At the Palais Marchand I bought

A snuff-box	.	.	.	.	.	24 livres.
————	.	.	.	.	.	6 „
Table book	.	.	.	.	.	15 „
Scissors 3 p (pair)	.	.	.	.	.	18 „
			(Livres)	.	.	63—£2 12s. 6d.

"We heard the lawyers plead.—N. As many killed at Paris as there are days in the year.—*Chambre de question.*—Tournelle at the Palais Marchand.—An old venerable building.

"The Palais Bourbon, belonging to the Prince of Condé. Only one small wing shown;—lofty;—splendid;—gold and glass.—The battles of the great Condé are painted in one of the rooms. The present Prince a grandsire at thirty-nine.

"The sight of palaces, and other great buildings, leaves no very distinct images, unless to those who talk of them. As I entered, my wife was in my mind :[1] she would have been pleased. Having now nobody to please, I am little pleased.

"N. In France there is no middle rank.

"So many shops open, that Sunday is little distinguished at Paris —The palaces of Louvre and Tuileries granted out in lodgings.

"In the *Palais de Bourbon*, gilt globes of metal at the fire-place.

"The French beds commended.—Much of the marble only paste.

"The colosseum a mere wooden building, at least much of it.

"*Wednesday*, Oct. 18. We went to Fontainebleau, which we found a large mean town, crowded with people.—The forest thick with woods, very extensive. —Manucci secured us lodgings.—The appearance of the country pleasant. No

---

[1] His tender affection for his departed wife, of which there are many evidences in his "Prayers and Meditations," appears very feelingly in this passage.—BOSWELL.

hills, few streams, only one hedge.—I remember no chapels nor crosses on the road.—Pavement still, and rows of trees.

"N. Nobody but mean people walk in Paris.

"*Thursday*, Oct. 19.   At court, we saw the apartments;—the King's bed-chamber and council-chamber extremely splendid.—Persons of all ranks in the external rooms through which the family passes; servants and masters.—Brunet with us the second time.

"The introductor came to us;—civil to me.—Presenting.—I had scruples—Not necessary.—We went and saw the king and queen at dinner.—We saw the other ladies at dinner—Madame Elizabeth, with the Princess of Guimené.—At night we went to a comedy.   I neither saw nor heard.—Drunken women.—Mrs. T [hrale] preferred one to the other.

"*Friday*, Oct. 20.   We saw the queen mount in the forest.—Brown habit: rode aside: one lady rode aside.—The queen's horse light grey;—martingale.—She galloped.—We then went to the apartments, and admired them.—Then wandered through the palace.—In the passages, stalls, and shops.—Painting in fresco by a great master, worn out.—We saw the king's horses and dogs.—The dogs almost all English.—Degenerate.

"The horses not much commended.—The stables cool; the kennel filthy.

"At night the ladies went to the Opera.   I refused, but should have been welcome.

"The king fed himself with his left hand, as we.

"*Saturday*, Oct. 21.   In the night I got round.—We came home to Paris.—I think we did not see the chapel.—Tree broken by the wind —The French chairs made all of boards painted.

"N. Soldiers at the court of justice.—Soldiers not amenable to the magistrates.—Dijon woman.

"Faggots in the palace.—Everything slovenly, except in the chief rooms.—Trees in the roads, some tall, none old, many very young and small.

"Women's saddles seem ill-made.   Queen's bridle woven with silver.—Tags to strike the horse.

"*Sunday*, Oct. 22.   To Versailles, a mean town.   Carriages of business passing.—Mean shops against the wall.—Our way lay through Sêve (Sêvres), where is the china manufacture.—Wooden bridge at Sêve, in the way to Versailles.—The palace of great extent.—The front long; I saw it not perfectly.—The Menagerie.   Cygnets dark; their black feet; on the ground; tame.—Halcyons, or gulls.—Stag and hind, young.—Aviary, very large: the net, wire.—Black stag of China, small.—Rhinoceros, the horn broken and pared away, which, I suppose, will grow; the basis, I think, four inches across; the skin folds like loose cloth doubled over his body, and cross his hips; a vast animal, though young: as big, perhaps, as four oxen.—The young elephant, with his tusks just appearing.—The brown bear put out his paws;—all very tame.—The lion.—The tigers I did not well view.—The camel or dromedary with two bunches called the Huguin,[1] taller than any horse.—Two camels with one bunch.—Among the birds was a pelican, who being let out, went to a fountain, and swam about to catch fish.   His feet well webbed: he dipped his head,

This epithet should be applied to this animal with one bunch.—BOSWELL.

and turned his long bill sidewise. He caught two or three fish, but did not eat them.

"Trianon is a kind of retreat appendant to Versailles. It has an open portico; the pavement, and I think, the pillars of marble.—There are many rooms which I do not distinctly remember.—A table of porphyry, about five feet long, and between two and three broad, given to Louis XIV. by the Venetian State.—In the council-room almost all that was not door or window, was, I think, looking-glass.—Little Trianon is a small palace like a gentleman's house.—The upper floor paved with brick.—Little Vienne.—The court is ill paved. The rooms at the top are small, fit to soothe the imagination with privacy. In the front of Versailles are small basons of water on the terrace, and

VERSAILLES.

other basons, I think, below them. There are little courts.—The great gallory is wainscotted with mirrors, not very large, but joined by frames. I suppose the large plates were not yet made.—The playhouse[1] was very large.—The chapel I do not remember if we saw.—We saw one chapel, but I am not certain whether there or at Trianon. The foreign office paved with bricks.—The dinner half a louis each, and, I think, a louis over.—Money given at menagerie, three livres; at palace, six livres.

"*Monday*, Oct. 23. Last night I wrote to Levet.—We went to see the looking-glasses wrought. They come from Normandy in cast plates, perhaps the third of an inch thick. At Paris they are ground upon a marble table, by rubbing one plate upon another with grit between them. The various sands, of which there are said to be five, I could not learn. The handle, by which

---

[1] " When at Versailles, the people showed us the theatre. As we stood on the stage looking at some machinery for playhouse purposes—' Now we are here, what shall we act, Dr. Johnson? The Englishman at Paris?'—' No, no,' replied he, ' we will try to act Harry the Fifth.'"—MRS. PIOZZI

the upper glass is moved, has the form of a wheel, which may be moved in all directions. The plates are sent up with their surfaces ground, but not polished, and so continue till they are bespoken, lest time should spoil the surface, as we are told. Those that are to be polished, are laid on a table covered with several thick cloths, hard strained, that the resistance may be equal: they are then rubbed with a hand rubber, held down hard by a contrivance which I did not well understand. The powder which is used last seemed to me to be iron dissolved in aquafortis: they called it, as Baretti said, *marc de l'eau forte*, which he thought was dregs. They mentioned vitriol and saltpetre. The cannon-ball swam in the quicksilver. To silver them, a leaf of beaten tin is laid, and rubbed with quicksilver, to which it unites. Then more quicksilver is poured upon it, which, by its mutual [attraction] rises very high. Then a paper is laid at the nearest end of the plate, over which the glass is slided till it lies upon the plate, having driven much of the quicksilver before it. It is then, I think, pressed upon cloth, and then set sloping to drop the superfluous mercury: the slope is daily heightened towards a perpendicular.

" In the way I saw the Grêve, the mayor's house, and the Bastile.

" We then went to Sans-terre, a brewer.[1] He brews with about as much malt as Mr. Thrale, and sells his beer at the same price, though he pays no duty for malt, and little more than half as much for beer. Beer is sold retail at 6d. a bottle. He brews 4000 barrels a-year. There are seventeen brewers in Paris, of whom none is supposed to brew more than he ; reckoning them at 3000 each, they make 51,000 a-year. They make their malt, for malting is here no trade.

" The moat of the Bastile is dry.

" *Tuesday*, Oct. 24. We visited the king's library—I saw the *Speculum humanæ Salvationis*, rudely printed, with ink, sometimes pale, sometimes black ; part supposed to be with wooden types, and part with pages cut in boards. The Bible, supposed to be older than that of Mentz, in '62 ; it has no date ; it is supposed to have been printed with wooden types.—I am in doubt ; the print is large and fair, in two folios. Another book was shown me, supposed to have been printed with wooden types ; I think *Durandi Sanctuarium* in '58. This is inferred from the difference of form sometimes seen in the same letter, which might be struck with different puncheons. The regular similitude of most letters proves better that they are metal. I saw nothing but the *Speculum*, which I had not seen, I think, before.

" Thence to the Sorbonne.—The library very large, not in lattices like the king's. *Marbone* and *Durandi*, q. collection, 14 vol. *Scriptores de rebus Gallicis*, many folios.—*Histoire Généalogique of France*, 9 vol.—*Gallia Christiana*, the first edition, 4to. the last, f. 12 vol.—The Prior and Librarian dined [with us] :—I waited on them home.—Their garden pretty, with covered walks, but small ; yet may hold many students. The Doctors of the Sorbonne are all equal ;—choose those who succeed to vacancies.--Profit little.

" *Wednesday*, Oct. 25. I went with the Prior to St. Cloud, to see Dr. Hooke. —We walked round the palace, and had some talk.—I dined with our whole company at the monastery.—In the library, *Beroald,—Cymon,—Titus*, from

---

[1] The detestable ruffian, who afterwards conducted Louis the Sixteenth to the scaffold, and commanded the troops that guarded it, during his murder.—MALONE.

Boccace.—*Oratio Proverbialis* to the Virgin, from Petrarch; Falkland to Sandys;—Dryden's Preface to the third vol. of Miscellanies.[1]

"*Thursday*, Oct. 26. We saw the china at Sève cut, glazed, painted.— Bellevue, a pleasing house, not great; fine prospect.—Meudon, an old palace. —Alexander, in porphyry: hollow between eyes and nose, thin cheeks.—Plato and Aristotle—Noble terrace overlooks the town—St. Cloud.—Gallery not very high, nor grand, but pleasing.—In the rooms, Michael Angelo, drawn by himself, Sir Thomas More, Des Cartes, Bochart, Naudæus, Mazarine.—Gilded wainscot, so common that it is not minded.—Gough and Keene.—Hooke came to us at the inn.—A message from Drumgold.

"*Friday*, Oct. 27. I stayed at home.—Gough and Keene, and Mrs. S——'s friend dined with us.—This day we began to have a fire.—The weather is grown very cold, and, I fear, has a bad effect upon my breath, which has grown much more free and easy in this country.

"*Saturday*, Oct. 28. I visited the Grand Chartreux built by St. Louis.—It is built for forty, but contains only twenty-four, and will not maintain more. The friar that spoke to us had a pretty apartment.—Mr. Baretti says four rooms; I remember but three.—His books seemed to be French.—His garden was neat; he gave me grapes. We saw the Place de Victoire, with the statues of the King, and the captive nations.

"We saw the palace and gardens of Luxembourg, but the gallery was shut. —We climbed to the top stairs.—I dined with Colbrooke, who had much company:—Foote, Sir George Rodney, Motteux, Udson, Taaf.—Called on the Prior, and found him in bed.

"Hotel—a guinea a day.—Coach, three guineas a week.—Valet de place, three l. a day.—*Avant coureur*, a guinea a week.—Ordinary dinner, six l. a head. —Our ordinary seems to be about five guineas a-day.—Our extraordinary expenses, as diversions, gratuities, clothes, I cannot reckon.—Our travelling is ten guineas a day.

"White stockings, 18 l.[2] Wig.—Hat.

"*Sunday*, Oct. 29. We saw the boarding-school.—the *Enfans trouvés*.—A room with about eighty-six children in cradles, as sweet as a parlour.—They lose a third; take in to perhaps more than seven [years old]; put them to trades; pin to them the papers sent with them.—Want nurses.—Saw their chapel.

"Went to St. Eustatia; saw an innumerable company of girls catechised, in many bodies, perhaps 100 to a catechist.—Boys taught at one time, girls at another.—The sermon; the preacher wears a cap, which he takes off at the name:—his action uniform, not very violent.

"*Monday*, Oct. 30. We saw the library of St. Germain.—A very noble collection.—*Codex Divinorum Officiorum*, 1459:—a letter, square like that of the *Offices*, perhaps the same.—The *Codex*, by Fust and Gernsheym.—*Meursius*, 12 v. fol.—*Amadis*, in French, 3 v. fol.—Catholicon *sine colophone*, but of 1460.—Two other editions,[3] one by *Augustin. de Civitate Dei* without name, date, or place, but of Fust's square letter as it seems.

He means, I suppose, that he read these different pieces, while he remained in the library.—Boswell.

[2] Eighteen *livres*. Two pair of white silk stockings were probably purchased.—Malone

[3] I have looked in vain into De Bure, Meerman, Mattaire, and other typographical books

"I dined with Col. Drumgold; had a pleasing afternoon.

"Some of the books of St. Germain's stand in presses from the wall, like those at Oxford.

"*Tuesday*, Oct. 31. I lived at the Benedictines; meagre day; soup meagre, herrings, eels, both with sauce; fried fish; lentils, tasteless in themselves. In the library; where I found *Maffeus's de Historiâ Indicâ : Promontorium flectere, to double the Cape.* I parted very tenderly from the Prior and Friar Wilkes.

"*Maitre des Arts,* 2 y.—*Bacc. Theol.* 3 y.—*Licentiate,* 2 y.—*Doctor Th.* 2 y. in all 9 years.—For the Doctorate three disputations, *Major, Minor, Sarbonica.* —Several colleges suppressed, and transferred to that which was the Jesuits' College.

"*Wednesday*, Nov. 1. We left Paris.—St. Denis, a large town; the church not very large, but the middle aisle is very lofty and awful.—On the left are chapels built beyond the line of the wall, which destroy the symmetry of the sides. The organ is higher above the pavement than any I have ever seen.— The gates are of brass.—On the middle gate is the history of our Lord.—The painted windows are historical, and said to be eminently beautiful.—We were at another church belonging to a convent, of which the portal is a dome; we could not enter further, and it was almost dark.

"*Thursday*, Nov. 2. We came this day to Chantilly, a seat belonging to the Prince of Condé.—This place is eminently beautified by all varieties of waters starting up in fountains, falling in cascades, running in streams, and spread in lakes.—The water seems to be too near the house.—All this water is brought from a source or river three leagues off, by an artificial canal, which for one league is carried under ground.—The house is magnificent.—The cabinet seems well stocked; what I remember was, the jaws of a hippopotamus, and a young hippopotamus preserved, which, however, is so small, that I doubt its reality. —It seems too hairy for an abortion, and too small for a mature birth.— Nothing was in spirits; all was dry.—The dog; the deer; the ant-bear with long snout.—The toucan, long broad beak.—The stables were of very great length.—The kennel had no scents.—There was a mockery of a village.—The menagerie had few animals.[1]—Two faussans,[2] or Brazilian weasels, spotted, very wild.—There is a forest, and I think, a park.—I walked till I was very weary, and next morning felt my feet battered, and with pains in the toes.

for the two editions of the "*Catholicon*," which Dr. Johnson mentions here, with *names* which I cannot make out, I read "one by *Latinius*, one by *Boedinus*." I have deposited the original MS. in the British Museum, where the curious may see it. My grateful acknowledgments are due to Mr. Planta for the trouble he was pleased to take in aiding my researches.— BOSWELL.

[1] The writing is so bad here, that the names of several of the animals could not be deciphered without much more acquaintance with natural history than I possess. Dr. Blagden, with his usual politeness, most obligingly examined the MS. To that gentleman, and to Dr. Gray, of the British Museum, who also very readily assisted me, I beg leave to express my best thanks.—BOSWELL.

[2] It is thus written by Johnson, from the French pronunciation of *fossane.* It should be observed, that the person who showed this menagerie was mistaken in supposing the *fossane* and the Brazilian weazel to be the same, the *fossane* being a different animal, and a native of Madagascar. I find them, however, upon one plate in Pennan's "Synopsis of Quadrupeds."— BOSWELL.

"*Friday*, Nov. 3. We came to Compeigne, a very large town, with a royal palace built round a pentagonal court.—The court is raised upon vaults, and has, I suppose, an entry on one side by a gentle rise.—Talk of painting.—The church is not very large, but very elegant and splendid.—I had at first great difficulty to walk, but motion grew continually easier.—At night we came to Noyon, an episcopal city.—The cathedral is very beautiful, the pillars alternately Gothic and Corinthian.—We entered a very noble parochial church.—Noyon is walled, and is said to be three miles round.

"*Saturday*, Nov. 4. We rose very early, and came through St. Quintin to Cambray, not long after three.—We went to an English nunnery, to give a letter to Father Welch, the confessor, who came to visit us in the evening.

"*Sunday*, Nov. 5. We saw the Cathedral.—It is very beautiful, with chapels on each side.—The choir splendid.—The balustrade in one part brass.—The Neff very high and grand. The altar, silver as far as it is seen.—The vestments very splendid.—At the Benedictines' Church ——"

Here his Journal [1] ends abruptly. Whether he wrote any more after this time, I know not; but probably not much, as he arrived in England about the 12th of November. These short notes of his tour, though they may seem minute taken singly, make together a considerable mass of information, and exhibit such an ardour of inquiry and acuteness of examination, as, I believe, are found in but few travellers, especially at an advanced age. They completely refute the idle notion which has been propagated, *that he could not see;* and, if he had taken the trouble to revise and digest them, he undoubtedly could have expanded them into a very entertaining narrative.

[1] My worthy and ingenious friend, Mr. Andrew Lumsden, by his accurate acquaintance with France, enabled me to make out many proper names which Dr. Johnson had written indistinctly, and sometimes spelt erroneously.—BOSWELL.

JOHNSON AND MADAME DE BOUFFLERS.

CHAPTER XIII—1775—1776.

WHEN I met him in London the following year, the account which he gave me of his French tour was, "Sir, I have seen all the visibilities of Paris, and around it; but to have formed an acquaintance with the people there, would have required more time than I could stay. I was just beginning to creep into acquaintance by means of Colonel Drumgold, a very high man, Sir, head of *L'Ecole Militaire*, a most complete character, for he had first been a professor of rhetoric, and then became a soldier. And, Sir, I was very kindly treated by the English Benedictines, and have a cell appropriated to me in their convent"

He observed, "The great in France live very magnificently, but the rest very miserably. There is no happy middle state as in England. The shops of Paris are mean ; the meat in the markets is such as would be sent to a gaol in England ; and Mr. Thrale justly observed, that the cookery of the French was forced upon them by necessity ; for they could not eat their meat, unless they added some taste to it. The French are an indelicate people ; they will spit upon any place. At Madame ——'s, a literary lady of rank, the footman took the sugar in his fingers, and threw it into my coffee. I was going to put it aside but hearing it was made on purpose for me, I e'en tasted Tom's fingers. The same lady would needs make tea *à l'Angloise.* The spout of the tea-pot did not pour freely ; she bade the footman blow into it. France is worse than Scotland in everything but climate. Nature has done more for the French ; but they have done less for themselves than the Scotch have done." [1]

It happened that Foote was at Paris at the same time with Dr. Johnson, and his description of my friend while there was abundantly ludicrous. He told me, that the French were quite astonished at his figure and manner, and at his dress, which he obstinately continued exactly as in London ; [2]—his brown clothes, black stockings, and plain shirt. He mentioned, that an Irish gentleman said to Johnson, "Sir, you have not seen the best French players." JOHNSON : "Players, Sir ! I look on them as no better than creatures set upon tables and joint-stools to make faces and produce laughter, like dancing dogs."—"But, Sir, you will allow that some players are better than others?" JOHNSON. "Yes, Sir, as some dogs dance better than others."

While Johnson was in France, he was generally very resolute in speaking Latin. It was a maxim with him that a man should not let himself down, by speaking a language which he speaks imperfectly. Indeed, we must have often observed how inferior, how much like a child a man appears, who speaks a broken tongue. When Sir Joshua Reynolds, at one of the dinners of the Royal Academy, presented him to a Frenchman of great distinction, he would not deign to speak French, but talked Latin, though his Excellency did not understand it,

[1] In a letter to a friend, written a few days after his return from France, he says, "The French have a clear air and a fruitful soil; but their mode of common life is gross and incommodious, and disgusting. I am come home convinced that no improvement of general use is to be found among them."—MALONE.

[2] Mr. Foote seems to have *embellished* a little in saying that Johnson did not alter his dress at Paris; as in his Journal is a memorandum about white stockings, wig, and hat. In another place we are told that "during his travels in France he was furnished with a French-made wig of handsome construction." That Johnson was not inattentive to his appearance is certain, from a circumstance related by Mr. Steevens, and inserted by Mr. Boswell, in vol iv., between June 15 and June 22, 1784.—J. BLAKEWAY.

Mr. Blakeway's observation is further confirmed by a note in Johnson's diary (quoted by Sir John Hawkins, *Life of Johnson,* p. 516), by which it appears, that he laid out thirty pounds in clothes for his French journey.—MALONE.

owing, perhaps, to Johnson's English pronunciation : yet upon another occasion he was observed to speak French to a Frenchman of high rank who spoke English ; and being asked the reason, with some expression of surprise, he answered, "because I think my French is as good as his English." Though Johnson understood French perfectly, he could not speak it readily, as I have observed at his first interview with General Paoli, in 1769 ; yet he wrote it, I imagine, pretty well, as appears in some of his letters in Mrs. Piozzi's collection, of which I shall transcribe one :—

"A MADAME LA COMTESSE DE ——

July 16, 1775.

"Oui, Madame, le moment est arrivé, et il faut que je parle. Mais pourquoi faut il partir? Est ce que je m'ennuye? Je m'ennuyerai ailleurs. Est ce que je cherche ou quelque plaisir, ou quelque soulagement? Je ne cherche rien, je n'espere rien. Aller voir ce que j'ai vû, être un peu rejoué, un peu degouté, me resouvenir que la vie se passe en vain, me plaindre de moi, m'endurcir aux dehors ; voici le tout de ce qu'on compte pour les delices de l'année. Que Dieu vous donne, Madame, tous les agrémens de la vie, avec un esprit qui peut en jouir sans s'y livrer trop."

Here let me not forget a curious anecdote, as related to me by Mr. Beauclerk, which I shall endeavour to exhibit as well as I can in that gentleman's lively manner : and in justice to him it is proper to add, that Dr. Johnson told me I might rely both on the correctness of his

SIR JOSHUA REYNOLDS.

memory, and the fidelity of his narrative. "When Madame de Boufflers was first in England," said Beauclerk, "she was desirous to see Johnson. I accordingly went with her to his chambers in the Temple, where she was entertained with his conversation for some time. When our visit was over, she and I left him, and were got into Inner Temple-lane, when all at once I heard a noise like thunder. This was occasioned by Johnson, who, it seems, upon a little recollection, had taken it into his head that he ought to have done the honours of his literary residence to a foreign lady of quality, and, eager to show himself a man of gallantry, was hurrying down the staircase in violent agitation. He overtook us before we reached the Temple-gate, and brushing in between me and Madame de Boufflers, seized her hand, and conducted her to her coach. His dress was a rusty-brown morning suit, a pair of old shoes by way of slippers, a little shrivelled wig sticking on the top of his head, and the sleeves of his shirt and the knees of his breeches hanging loose. A considerable crowd of people gathered round, and were not a little struck by this singular appearance."

He spoke Latin with wonderful fluency and elegance. When Père Boscovich was in England, Johnson dined in company with him at Sir Joshua Reynolds's and at Dr. Douglas's, now Bishop of Salisbury. Upon both occasions, that celebrated foreigner expressed his astonishment at Johnson's Latin conversation. When at Paris, Johnson thus characterised Voltaire to Freron the Journalist : " *Ver est acerrimi ingenii et paucarum literarum.*"

" TO DR. SAMUEL JOHNSON.

" My dear Sir,   *Edinburgh, Dec. 5,* 1775.
" Mr. Alexander Maclean, the young Laird of Coll, being to set out to-morrow for London, I give him this letter to introduce him to your acquaintance. The kindness which you and I experienced from his brother, whose unfortunate death we sincerely lament, will make us always desirous to show attention to any branch of the family. Indeed, you have so much of the true Highland cordiality, that I am sure you would have thought me to blame if I had neglected to recommend to you this Hebridean prince, in whose island we were hospitably entertained. I ever am with respectful attachment, my dear Sir,   Your most obliged,

" And most humble servant,

" James Boswell."

Mr. Maclean returned with the most agreeable accounts of the polite attention with which he was received by Dr. Johnson.

In the course of this year Dr. Burney informs me that " he very frequently met Dr. Johnson at Mr. Thrale's, at Streatham, where they had many long conversations, often sitting up as long as the fire and candles lasted, and much longer than the patience of the servants subsisted."

A few of Johnson's sayings, which that gentleman recollects, shall here be inserted :—

" I never take a nap after dinner but when I have had a bad night, and then the nap takes me."

" The writer of an epitaph should not be considered as saying nothing but what is strictly true. Allowance must be made for some degree of exaggerated praise. In lapidary inscriptions a man is not upon oath."

" There is now less flogging in our great schools than formerly, but then less is learned there ; so that what the boys get at one end they lose at the other."

" More is learned in public than in private schools from emulation ; there is the collision of mind with mind, or the radiation of many minds pointing to one centre. Though few boys make their own exercises, yet, if a good exercise is given up, out of a great number of boys, it is made by somebody."

" I hate by-roads in education. Education is as well known, and has long been as well known as ever it can be. Endeavouring to make children prematurely wise is useless labour. Suppose they have more knowledge at five or six years old than other children, what use can be made of it ? It will be lost before it is wanted, and the waste of so much time and labour of the teacher can never be repaid. Too much is expected from precocity, and too little performed. Miss [Aikin] [1] was an instance of early cultivation, but in what did it terminate ? In marrying a little Presbyterian parson, who keeps an infant boarding-school, so that all her employment now is,

> ' To suckle fools, and chronicle small beer.'

She tells the children, ' This is a cat, and that is a dog, with four legs and a tail ; see there ! you are much better than a cat or a dog, for you can speak.' If I had bestowed such an education on a daughter, and had discovered that she thought of marrying such a fellow, I would have sent her to the *Congress*."

" After having talked slightingly of music, he was observed to listen very attentively while Miss Thrale played on the harpsichord, and with eagerness he called to her, ' Why don't you dash away like Burney ?' Dr. Burney upon this said to him, ' I believe, Sir, we shall make a musician of you at last.' Johnson, with candid complacency, replied, ' Sir, I shall be glad to have a new sense given to me.' "

" He had come down one morning to the breakfast-room, and been a considerable time by himself before anybody appeared. When on a subsequent day he was twitted by Mrs. Thrale for being very late, which he generally was, he defended himself by alluding to the extraordinary morning when he had been too early. ' Madam, I do not like to come down to *vacuity*.' "

" Dr. Burney having remarked that Mr. Garrick was beginning to look old, he said, ' Why, Sir, you are not to wonder at that ; no man's face has had more wear and tear.' "

Not having heard from him for a longer time than I supposed he would be silent, I wrote to him December 18th, not in good spirits. " Sometimes I have been afraid that the cold which has gone over Europe this year like a sort of pestilence has seized you severely ; sometimes my imagination, which is upon occasions prolific of evil, hath figured that you may have somehow taken offence at some part of my conduct."

" TO JAMES BOSWELL, ESQ

"DEAR SIR,   *December* 23, 1775.

" Never dream of any offence. How should you offend me? I consider your friendship as a possession, which I intend to hold till you take it from me, and to lament if ever by my fault I should lose it. However, when such suspicions find their way into your mind, always give them vent ; I shall make haste to disperse them ; but hinder their first ingress if you can. Consider such thoughts as morbid.

"Such illness as may excuse my omission to Lord Hailes, I cannot honestly plead. I have been hindered, I know not how, by a succession of petty obstructions. I hope to mend immediately, and to send next post to his Lordship. Mr. Thrale would have written to you if I had omitted ; he sends his compliments, and wishes to see you.

"You and your lady will now have no more wrangling about feudal inheritance. How does the young Laird of Auchinleck? I suppose Miss Veronica is grown a reader and discourser.

" I have just now got a cough, but it has never yet hindered me from sleeping ; I have had quieter nights than are common with me.

"I cannot but rejoice that Joseph [1] has had the wit to find the way back. He is a fine fellow, and one of the best travellers in the world.

"Young Coll brought me your letter. He is a very pleasing youth. I took him two days ago to the Mitre, and we dined together. I was as civil as I had the means of being.

" I have had a letter from Rasay, acknowledging, with great appearance of satisfaction, the insertion in the Edinburgh paper. I am very glad that it was done.

"My compliments to Mrs. Boswell, who does not love me ; and of all the rest, I need only send them to those that do ; and I am afraid it will give you very little trouble to distribute them. I am, my dear, dear Sir,

" Your affectionate humble servant,

"SAM. JOHNSON."

In 1776, Johnson wrote, so far as I can discover, nothing for the public ; but that his mind was still ardent, and fraught with generous wishes to attain to still higher degrees of literary excellence, is proved by his private notes of this year, which I shall insert in their proper place.

---

[1] Joseph Ritter, a Bohemian, who was in my service many years, and attended Dr. Johnson and me in our Tour to the Hebrides. After having left me for some time, be had now returned to me.—BOSWELL.

" DEAR SIR,   *Jan.* 10, 1776.

" I have at last sent you all Lord Hailes's papers. While I was in France, I
looked very often into Henault ; but Lord Hailes, in my opinion, leaves him
far and far behind. Why I did not despatch so short a perusal sooner, when I
look back, I am utterly unable to discover ; but human moments are stolen
away by a thousand petty impediments which leave no trace behind them. I
have been afflicted, through the whole Christmas, with the general disorder, of
which the worst effect was a cough, which is now much mitigated, though the
country, on which I look from a window at Streatham, is now covered with a
deep snow. Mrs. Williams is very ill ; every body else is as usual.

" Among the papers, I found a letter to you which I think you had not
opened ; and a paper for 'The Chronicle,' which I suppose it not necessary now
to insert. I return them both.

" I have, within these few days, had the honour of receiving Lord Hailes's
first volume, for which I return my most respectful thanks.

" I wish you, my dearest friend, and your haughty lady, (for I know she
does not love me,) and the young ladies, and the young Laird, all happiness.
Teach the young gentleman, in spite of his mamma, to think and speak well
of, Sir,

              " Your affectionate humble servant,
                                          " SAM. JOHNSON."

At this time was in agitation a matter of great consequence to me
and my family, which I should not obtrude upon the world, were it not
that the part which Dr. Johnson's friendship for me made him take in
it, was the occasion of an exertion of his abilities, which it would be
injustice to conceal. That what he wrote upon the subject may be
understood, it is necessary to give a state of the question, which I shall
do as briefly as I can.

In the year 1504, the barony or manor of Auchinleck (pronounced
Affléck) in Ayrshire, which belonged to a family of the same name with
the lands, having fallen to the Crown by forfeiture, James the Fourth,
King of Scotland, granted it to Thomas Boswell, a branch of an ancient
family in the county of Fife, styling him in the character " *dilecto
familiari nostro ;* " and assigning, as the cause of the grant, " *pro
bono et fideli servitio nobis præstito.*" Thomas Boswell was slain in
battle fighting along with his sovereign, at the fatal field of Flodden,
in 1513.

From this very honourable founder of our family, the estate was
transmitted, in a direct series of heirs male, to David Boswell, my
father's great-grand-uncle, who had no sons, but four daughters, who
were all respectably married, the eldest to Lord Cathcart.

David Boswell, being resolute in the military feudal principle of continuing the male succession, passed by his daughters, and settled the
estate on his nephew by his next brother, who approved of the deed, and

renounced any pretensions which he might possibly have, in preference to his son. But the estate having been burthened with large portions to the daughters, and other debts, it was necessary for the nephew to sell a considerable part of it, and what remained was still much encumbered.

The frugality of the nephew preserved, and, in some degree, relieved the estate. His son, my grandfather, an eminent lawyer, not only repurchased a great part of what had been sold, but acquired other lands; and my father, who was one of the Judges of Scotland, and had added considerably to the estate, now signified his inclination to take the privilege allowed by our law, [1] to secure it to his family in perpetuity, by an entail, which on account of his marriage articles, could not be done without my consent.

In the plan of entailing the estate, I heartily concurred with him, though I was the first to be restrained by it ; but we unhappily differed as to the series of heirs which should be established, or in the language of our law, called to the succession. My father had declared a predilection for heirs general, that is, males and females indiscriminately. He was willing, however, that all males descending from his grandfather, should be preferred to females ; but would not extend that privilege to males deriving their descent from a higher source. I, on the other hand, had a zealous partiality for heirs male, however remote, which I maintained by arguments which appeared to me to have considerable weight.[2] And in the particular case of our family, I apprehended that we were under an implied obligation, in honour and good faith, to transmit the estate by the same tenure which we held it, which was as heirs male,

---

[1] Acts of Parliament of Scotland, 1685, Cap. 22.—BOSWELL.

[2] As first, the opinion of some distinguished naturalists, that our species is transmitted through males only, the female being all along no more than a *nidus*, or nurse as Mother Earth is to plants of every sort; which notion seems to be confirmed by that text of Scripture " He was yet *in the loins of his* FATHER when Melchisedeck met him; " (Heb. vii. 10), and consequently, that a man's grandson by a daughter, instead of being his *surest* descendant, as is vulgarly said, has, in reality, no connection whatever with his blood. And, secondly, independent of this theory, (which if true, should completely exclude heirs general), that if the preference of a male to a female, without regard to primogeniture (as a son, though much younger, nay, even a grandson by a son, to a daughter) be once admitted, as it universally is, it must be equally reasonable and proper in the most remote degree of descent from an original proprietor of an estate as in the nearest: because, however distant from the representative at the time, that remote heir male, upon the failure of those nearer to the *original proprietor* than he is, becomes in fact the nearest male to *him*, and is, therefore, preferable as *his* representative, to a female descendant. A little extension of mind will enable us easily to perceive that a son's son, in continuation to whatever length of time, is preferable to a son's daughter, in the succession to an ancient inheritance; in which regard should be had to the representation of the original proprietor, and not to that of one of his descendants.

I am aware of Blackstone's admirable demonstration of the reasonableness of the legal succession, upon the principle of there being the greatest probability that the nearest heir of the person who last dies proprietor of an estate, is of the blood of the first purchaser. But supposing a pedigree to be carefully authenticated through all its branches, instead of mere *probability* there will be a *certainty* that *the nearest heir male at whatever period,* has the same right of blood with the first heir male, namely, *the original purchaser's eldest son.*—BOSWELL.

excluding nearer females. I therefore, as I thought conscientiously, objected to my father's scheme.

My opposition was very displeasing to my father, who was entitled to great respect and deference; and I had reason to apprehend disagreeable consequences from my non-compliance with his wishes. After much perplexity and uneasiness, I wrote to Dr. Johnson, stating the case, with all its difficulties, at full length, and earnestly requesting that he would consider it at leisure, and favour me with his friendly opinion and advice.

" TO JAMES BOSWELL, ESQ.

"DEAR SIR,   *London, Jan.* 15, 1776.

" I was much impressed by your letter, and if I can form upon your case any resolution satisfactory to myself, will very gladly impart it; but whether I am equal to it, I do not know. It is a case compounded of law and justice, and requires a mind versed in juridical disquisitions. Could not you tell your whole mind to Lord Hailes? He is, you know, both a Christian and a lawyer. I suppose he is above partiality, and above loquacity; and, I believe, he will not think the time lost in which he may quiet a disturbed, or settle a wavering mind. Write to me as any thing occurs to you; and if I find myself stopped by want of facts necessary to be known, I will make inquiries of you as my doubts arise.

" If your former resolutions should be found only fanciful, you decide rightly in judging that your father's fancies may claim the preference; but whether they are fanciful or rational, is the question. I really think Lord Hailes could help us.

" Make my compliments to dear Mrs. Boswell, and tell her that I hope to be wanting in nothing that I can contribute to bring you all out of your troubles.

" I am, dear Sir, most affectionately,

" Your humble servant,

" SAM. JOHNSON."

TO THE SAME.

"DEAR SIR,   *Feb.* 3, 1776.

" I am going to write upon a question which requires more knowledge of local law, and more acquaintance with the general rules of inheritance, than I can claim; but I write because you request it.

" Land is, like any other possession, by natural right wholly in the power of its present owner: and may be sold, given, or bequeathed, absolutely or conditionally, as judgment shall direct, or passion incite.

" But natural right would avail little without the protection of law; and the primary notion of law is restraint in the exercise of natural right. A man is therefore, in society, not fully master of what he calls his own, but he still retains all the power which law does not take from him.

In the exercise of the right which law either leaves or gives, regard is to be paid to moral obligations.

" Of the estate which we are now considering, your father still retains such possession, with such power over it, that he can sell it, and do with the money what he will, without any legal impediment. But when he extends his power beyond his own life, by settling the order of succession, the law makes your consent necessary.

"Let us suppose that he sells the land to risk the money in some specious adventure, and in that adventure loses the whole; his posterity would be disappointed; but they could not think themselves injured or robbed. If he spent it upon vice or pleasure, his successors could only call him vicious and voluptuous; they could not say that he was injurious or unjust.

"He that may do more may do less. He that by selling or squandering, may disinherit a whole family, may certainly disinherit part, by a partial settlement.

"Laws are formed by the manners and exigencies of particular times, and it is but accidental that they last longer than their causes; the limitation of feudal succession to the male arose from the obligation of the tenant to attend his chief in war.

"As times and opinions are always changing, I know not whether it be not usurpation to prescribe rules to posterity, by presuming to judge of what we cannot know; and I know not whether I fully approve either your design or your father's, to limit that succession which descended to you unlimited. If we are to leave *sartum tectum* to posterity, what we have without any merit of our own received from our ancestors, should not choice and free-will be kept unviolated? Is land to be treated with more reverence than liberty?—If this consideration should restrain your father from disinheriting some of the males, does it leave you the power of disinheriting all the females?

"Can the possessor of a feudal estate make any will? Can he appoint, out of the inheritance, any portions to his daughter? There seems to be a very shadowy difference between the power of leaving land, and of leaving money to be raised from land; between leaving an estate to females, and leaving the male heir, in effect, only their steward.

"Suppose at one time a law that allowed only males to inherit, and during the continuance of this law many estates to have descended, passing by the females, to remoter heirs. Suppose afterwards the law repealed in correspondence with a change of manners, and women made capable of inheritance would not then the tenure of estates be changed? Could the women have no benefit from a law made in their favour? Must they be passed by upon moral principles for ever, because they were once excluded by a legal prohibition? Or may that which passed only to males by one law, pass likewise to females by another?

"You mention your resolution to maintain the right of your brothers:[1] I do not see how any of their rights are invaded.

"As your whole difficulty arises from the act of your ancestor, who diverted the succession from the females, you inquire, very properly, what were his motives, and what was his intention; for you certainly are not bound by his act more than he intended to bind you, nor hold your land on harder or stricter terms than those on which it was granted.

---

[1] Which term I applied to all the heirs male.—BOSWELL

"Intentions must be gathered from acts. When he left the estate to his nephew, by excluding his daughters, was it, or was it not, in his power to have perpetuated the succession to the males? If he could have done it, he seems to have shown, by omitting it, that he did not desire it to be done, and, upon your own principles, you will not easily prove your right to destroy that capacity of succession which your ancestors have left.

"If your ancestor had not the power of making a perpetual settlement, and if, therefore, we cannot judge distinctly of his intentions, yet his act can only be considered as an example; it makes not an obligation. And, as you observe, he set no example of rigorous adherence to the line of succession. He that overlooked a brother, would not wonder that little regard is shown to remote relations.

" As the rules of succession are, in a great part, purely legal, no man can be supposed to bequeath anything, but upon legal terms; he can grant no power which the law denies; and if he makes no special and definite limitation, he confers all the power which the law allows.

"Your ancestor, for some reason, disinherited his daughters; but it no more follows that he intended this act as a rule for posterity, than the disinheriting of his brother.

" If, therefore, you ask by what right your father admits daughters to inheritance, ask yourself, first, by what right you require them to be excluded?

" It appears, upon reflection, that your father excludes nobody; he only admits nearer females to inherit before males more remote; and the exclusion is purely consequential.

" These, dear Sir, are my thoughts, immethodical and deliberative; but, perhaps, you may find in them some glimmering of evidence.

" I cannot, however, but again recommend to you a conference with Lord Hailes, whom you know to be both a lawyer and a Christian.

" Make my compliments to Mrs. Boswell, though she does not love me.

" I am, Sir,
" Your affectionate servant,
" SAM. JOHNSON."

I had followed his recommendation and consulted Lord Hailes, who upon this subject had a firm opinion contrary to mine. His Lordship obligingly took the trouble to write me a letter, in which he discussed with legal and historical learning, the points in which I saw much difficulty, maintaining that " the succession of heirs general was the succession, by the law of Scotland, from the throne to the cottage, as far as we can learn it by record ; " observing that the estate of our family had not been limited to heirs male ; and that though an heir male had in one instance been chosen in preference to nearer females, that had been an arbitrary act, which had seemed to be best in the embarrassed state of affairs at that time ; and the fact was, that upon a fair computation of the value of land and money at the time, applied to the estate and the burthens upon it, there was nothing given the heir male but the skeleton of an estate.   " The plea of conscience," said his Lordship, " which you put, is a most respectable one, especially when *conscience* and *self* are on different sides. But I think that conscience is not well-informed, and that *self* and *she* ought on this occasion to be of a side."

This letter, which had considerable influence upon my mind, I sent to Dr. Johnson, begging to hear from him again, upon this interesting question.

" TO JAMES BOSWELL, ESQ.

"DEAR SIR,   *Feb.* 9, 1776.

" Having not any acquaintance with the laws or customs of Scotland, I endeavoured to consider your question upon general principles, and found nothing of much validity that I could oppose to this position : ' He who inherits a fief unlimited by his ancestors, inherits the power of limiting it according to his own judgment or opinion.' If this be true, you may join with your father.

"Further consideration produces another conclusion : ' He who receives a fief unlimited by his ancestors, gives his heirs some reason to complain, if he does not transmit it unlimited to posterity. For why should he make the state of others worse than his own, without a reason?' If this be true, though neither you nor your father are about to do what is quite right, but as your father violates (I think) the legal succession least, he seems to be nearer the right than yourself.

"It cannot but occur that 'Women have natural and equitable claims as well as men, and these claims are not to be capriciously or lightly superseded or infringed.' When fiefs implied military service, it is easily discerned why females could not inherit them ; but the reason is now at an end. As manners make laws, manners likewise repeal them.

"These are the general conclusions which I have attained. None of them are very favourable to your scheme of entail, nor perhaps to any scheme. My observation, that only he who acquires an estate may bequeath it capriciously,[1] if it contains any conviction, includes this position likewise, that only he who acquires an estate may entail it capriciously. But I think it may be safely presumed, that ' he who inherits an estate, inherits all the power legally concomitant ; ' and that ' He who gives or leaves unlimited an estate legally limitable, must be presumed to give that power of limitation which he omitted to take away, and to commit future contingencies to future prudence.' In these two positions I believe Lord Hailes will advise you to rest ; every other notion of possession seems to me full of difficulties, and embarrassed with scruples.

"If these axioms be allowed, you have arrived now at full liberty without the help of particular circumstances, which, however, have in your case great weight. You very rightly observe, that he who passing by his brother gave the inheritance to his nephew, could limit no more than he gave ; and by Lord Hailes's estimate of fourteen years' purchase, what he gave was no more than you may easily entail according to your own opinion, if that opinion should finally prevail.

"Lord Hailes's suspicion that entails are encroachments on the dominion of Providence, may be extended to all hereditary privileges and all permanent

---

[1] I had reminded him of his observation, mentioned *ante*.— BOSWELL.

institutions; I do not see why it may not be extended to any provision for the present hour, since all care about futurity proceeds upon a supposition, that we know at least in some degree what will be future. Of the future we certainly know nothing : but we may form conjectures from the past ; and the power of forming conjectures, includes, in my opinion, the duty of acting in conformity to that probability which we discover. Providence gives the power, of which reason teaches the use.

> " I am, dear Sir,
>> " Your most faithful servant,
>>> " SAM. JOHNSON."

" I hope I shall get some ground now with Mrs. Boswell ; make my com pliments to her, and to the little people.

" Don't burn papers : they may be safe enough in your own box,—you will wish to see them hereafter."

TO THE SAME.

"DEAR SIR,   *Feb.* 15, 1776.

" To the letters which I have written about your great question, I have nothing to add. If your conscience is satisfied, you have now only your prudence to consult. I long for a letter, that I may know how this troublesome and vexatious question is at last decided.[1] I hope that it will at last end well. Lord Hailes's letter was very friendly, and very seasonable, but I think his aversion from entails has something in it like superstition. Providence is not counteracted by any means which Providence puts into our power. The continuance and propagation of families makes a great part of the Jewish law, and is by no means prohibited in the Christian institution, though the necessity of it continues no longer. Hereditary tenures are established in all civilised countries, and are accompanied in most with hereditary authority. Sir William Temple considers our constitution as defective, that there is not an unalienable estate in land connected with a peerage : and Lord Bacon mentions as a proof that the Turks are Barbarians, their want of *Stirpes*, as he calls them, or hereditary rank. Do not let your mind, when it is freed from the supposed necessity of a rigorous entail, be entangled with contrary objections, and think all entails unlawful, till you have cogent arguments, which I believe you never will find. I am afraid of scruples.

" I have now sent all Lord Hailes's papers ; part I found hidden in a drawer in which I had laid them for security, and had forgotten them. Part of these are written twice ; I have returned both the copies. Part I had read before.

" Be so kind as to return Lord Hailes my most respectful thanks for his first volume : his accuracy strikes me with wonder ; his narrative is far superior to that of Henault, as I have formerly mentioned.

---

[1] The entail framed by my father with various judicious clauses, was settled by him and me, settling the estate upon the heirs male of his grandfather, which I found had been already done by my grandfather, imperfectly, but so as to be defeated only by selling the lands. I was freed by Dr. Johnson from scruples of conscientious obligation, and could, therefore, gratify my father. But my opinion and partiality for male succession in its full extent remained unshaken. Yet let me not be thought harsh or unkind to daughters ; for my notion is, that they should be treated with great affection and tenderness, and always participate of the prosperity of the family.—BOSWELL.

"I am afraid that the trouble which my irregularity and delay has cost him, is greater, far greater, than any good that I can do him will ever recompense but if I have any more copy, I will try to do better.

"Pray let me know if Mrs. Boswell is friends with me, and pay my respects to Veronica, and Euphemia, and Alexander.

"I am, Sir,

"Your most humble servant,

"SAM. JOHNSON."

"MR. BOSWELL TO DR. JOHNSON.

"*Edinburgh, Feb.* 20, 1776.

    *   *   *   *   *   *

"You have illuminated my mind, and relieved me from imaginary shackles of conscientious obligation. Were it necessary, I could immediately join in an entail upon the series of heirs approved by my father; but it is better not to act too suddenly,"

"DR. JOHNSON TO MR. BOSWELL.

"DEAR SIR,   *Feb.* 24, 1776.

"I am glad that what I could think or say has at all contributed to quiet your thoughts. Your resolution not to act, till your opinion is confirmed by more deliberation, is very just, If you have been scrupulous, do not be rash I hope that as you think more, and take opportunities of talking with men intelligent in questions of property, you will be able to free yourself from every difficulty.

"When I wrote last, I sent, I think, ten packets. Did you receive them all?

"You must tell Mrs. Boswell that I suspected her to have written without your knowledge,[1] and therefore did not return any answer, lest a clandestine correspondence should have been perniciously discovered. I will write to her soon. * * * * * *

"I am, dear Sir,

"Most affectionately yours,

"SAM. JOHNSON."

Having communicated to Lord Hailes what Dr. Johnson wrote concerning the question which perplexed me so much, his lordship wrote to me: "Your scruples have produced more fruit than I ever expected from them; an excellent dissertation on general principles of morals and law."

I wrote to Dr. Johnson on the 20th of February, complaining of melancholy, and expressing a strong desire to be with him; informing him that the ten packets came all safe; that Lord Hailes was much obliged to him, and said he had almost wholly removed his scruples against entails.

---

[1] A letter to him on the interesting subject of the family settlement, which I had read — BOSWELL.

"TO JAMES BOSWELL, ESQ.

"DEAR SIR,   *March* 5, 1776.

"I have not had your letter half-an-hour; as you lay so much weight upon my notions, I should think it not just to delay my answer.

"I am very sorry that your melancholy should return, and should be sorry likewise if it could have no relief but from my company. My counsel you may have when you are pleased to require it; but of my company you cannot in the next month have much, for Mr. Thrale will take me to Italy, he says, on the 1st of April.

"Let me warn you very earnestly against scruples. I am glad that you are reconciled to your settlement, and think it a great honour to have shaken Lord Hailes's opinion of entails. Do not, however, hope wholly to reason away your troubles; do not feed them with attention, and they will die imperceptibly away. Fix your thoughts upon your business, fill your intervals with company, and sunshine will again break in upon your mind. If you will come to me, you must come very quickly; and even then I know not but we may scour the country together, for I have a mind to see Oxford and Lichfield, before I set out on this long journey. To this I can only add that I am, dear Sir,

"Your most affectionate humble servant,

"SAM. JOHNSON."

TO THE SAME.

"DEAR SIR,   *March* 12, 1776.

"Very early in April we leave England, and in the beginning of the next week I shall leave London for a short time; of this I think it necessary to inform you, that you may not be disappointed in any of your enterprises. I had not fully resolved to go into the country before this day.

"Please to make my compliments to Lord Hailes; and mention very particularly to Mrs. Boswell my hope that she is reconciled to, Sir,

"Your faithful servant,

"SAM. JOHNSON."

Above thirty years ago, the heirs of Lord Chancellor Clarendon presented the University of Oxford with the continuation of his History, and such other of his Lordship's manuscripts as had not been published, on condition that the profits arising from their publication should be applied to the establishment of a *Manège* in the University. The gift was accepted in full convocation. A person being now recommended to Dr. Johnson, as fit to superintend this proposed riding school, he exerted himself with that zeal for which he was remarkable upon every similar occasion. But, on inquiry into the matter, he found that the scheme was not likely to be soon carried into execution: the profits arising from the Clarendon press being, from some mismanagement, very scanty This having been explained to him by a respectable dignitary of the church, who had good means of knowing it, he wrote a letter upon the subject, which at once exhibits his extraordinary precision and acuteness, and his warm attachment to his ALMA MATER.

" TO THE REVEREND DR. WETHERELL, MASTER OF UNIVERSITY-COLLEGE,
OXFORD.

" Dear Sir,   *March* 12, 1776.

" Few things are more unpleasant than the transaction of business with
men who are above knowing or caring what they have to do ; such as the
trustees for Lord Cornbury's institution will, perhaps, appear, when you have
read Dr. —— ——'s letter.

" The last part of the Doctor's letter is of great importance. The complaint [1] which he makes I have heard long ago, and did not know but it was
redressed. It is unhappy that a practice so erroneous has not been altered ;
for altered it must be, or our press will be useless with all its privileges.
The booksellers, who, like all other men, have strong prejudices in their own
favour, are enough inclined to think the practice of printing and selling books
by any but themselves, an encroachment on the rights of their fraternity ; and
have need of stronger inducements to circulate academical publications than
those of another ; for, of that mutual co-operation by which the general trade
is carried on, the University can bear no part. Of those whom he neither
loves nor fears, and from whom he expects no reciprocation of good offices,
why should any man promote the interest but for profit? I suppose, with all
our scholastic ignorance of mankind, we are still too knowing to expect that
the booksellers will erect themselves into patrons, and buy and sell under the
influence of a disinterested zeal for the promotion of learning.

" To the booksellers, if we look for either honour or profit from our press,
not only their common profit, but something more must be allowed ; and if books,
printed at Oxford, are expected to be rated at a high price, that price must be
levied on the public, and paid by the ultimate purchaser, not by the intermediate agents. What price shall be set upon the book, is, to the booksellers,
wholly indifferent, provided that they gain a proportionate profit by negocia-
ting the sale.

" Why books printed at Oxford should be particularly dear, I am, however,
unable to find. We pay no rent ; we inherit many of our instruments and
materials ; lodging and victuals are cheaper than at London ; and, therefore,
workmanship ought, at least, not to be dearer. Our expenses are naturally
less than those of booksellers ; and in most cases, communities are content
with less profit than individuals.

" It is, perhaps, not considered through how many hands a book often
passes, before it comes into those of the reader ; or what part of the profit each
hand must retain, as a motive for transmitting it to the next.

" We will call our primary agent in London, Mr. Cadell, who receives our
books from us, gives them room in his warehouse, and issues them on demand ;
by him they are sold to Mr. Dilly, a wholesale bookseller, who sends them into
the country ; and the last bookseller is the country bookseller. Here are three
profits to be paid between the printer and the reader, or in the style of commerce, between the manufacturer and the consumer ; and if any of these profits
is too penuriously distributed, the process of commerce is interrupted.

---

[1] I suppose the complaint was, that the trustees of the Oxford press did not allow the
London booksellers a sufficient profit upon vending their publications.—Boswell

"We are now come to the practical question, What is to be done? You will tell me, with reason, that I have said nothing, till I declare how much, according to my opinion, of the ultimate price ought to be distributed through the whole succession of sale.

"The deduction, I am afraid, will appear very great; but let it be considered before it is refused. We must allow, for profit, between thirty and thirty-five per cent., between six and seven shillings in the pound; that is for every book which costs the last buyer twenty shillings, we must charge Mr. Cadell with something less than fourteen. We must set the copies at fourteen shillings each, and superadd what is called the quarterly book, or for every hundred books so charged, we must deliver an hundred and four.

"The profits will then stand thus:

"Mr. Cadell, who runs no hazard, and gives no credit, will be paid for warehouse room and attendance by a shilling profit on each book, and his chance of the quarterly-book.

"Mr. Dilly, who buys the book for fifteen shillings, and who will expect the quarterly-book if he takes five-and-twenty, will send it to his country customer at sixteen and sixpence, by which, at the hazard of loss, and the certainty of long credit, he gains the regular profit of ten per cent. which is expected in the wholesale trade.

"The country bookseller, buying at sixteen and sixpence, and commonly trusting a considerable time, gains but three and sixpence; and if he trusts a year, not much more than two and sixpence; otherwise than as he may, perhaps, take as long credit as he gives.

"With less profit than this (and more you see he cannot have), the country bookseller cannot live; for his receipts are small, and his debts sometimes bad.

"Thus, dear Sir, I have been incited by Dr, ———'s letter to give you a detail of the circulation of books, which, perhaps, every man has not had opportunity of knowing; and which those who know it, do not, perhaps, always distinctly consider.

"I am, &c.,
"Sam. Johnson." [1]

[1] I am happy, in giving this full and clear statement to the public, to vindicate, by the authority of the greatest author of his age, that respectable body of men, the Booksellers of London, from vulgar reflections, as if their profits were exorbitant, when, in truth, Dr. Johnson has here allowed them more than they usually demand.—BOSWELL.

[This letter of Johnson's was extensively quoted and criticised during the disputes among the London Booksellers, in 1852, caused by some members of the retail trade selling books at less than the published price, and consequently underselling their neighbours. ED.]

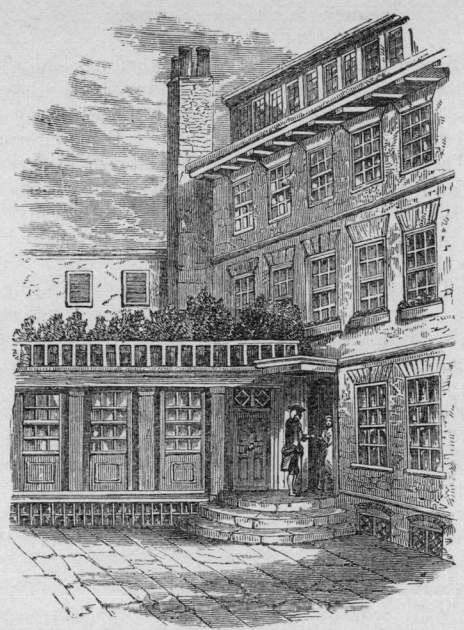

JOHNSON'S HOUSE, BOLT-COURT.

CHAPTER XIV.—1776.

HAVING arrived in London late on Friday, the 15th of March, I hastened next morning to wait on Dr. Johnson, at his house; but found he was removed from Johnson's-court, No. 7, to Bolt-court, No. 8, still keeping to his favourite Fleet-street. My reflection at the time upon this change, as marked in my Journal, is as follows: "I felt a foolish regret that he had left a court which bore his name;[1] but it was not foolish to be affected with some tenderness of regard for a place

---

[1] He said when in Scotland, that he was *Johnson of that Ilk.*—BOSWELL.

in which I had seen him a great deal, from whence I had often issued a
better and a happier man than I went in, and which had often appeared
to my imagination while I trod its pavement, in the solemn darkness of
the night, to be sacred to wisdom and piety." Being informed that he
was at Mr. Thrale's, in the Borough, I hastened thither, and found
Mrs. Thrale and him at breakfast. I was kindly welcomed. In a
moment he was in a full glow of conversation, and I felt myself elevated
as if brought into another state of being. Mrs. Thrale and I looked to
each other while he talked, and our looks expressed our congenial
admiration and affection for him. I shall ever recollect this scene with
great pleasure. I exclaimed to her, " I am now, intellectually, _Her-
mippus redivivus_, I am quite restored by him, by transfusion of _mind_."
"There are many," she replied, " who admire and respect Mr. Johnson ;
but you and I _love_ him."

He seemed very happy in the near prospect of going to Italy with
Mr. and Mrs. Thrale. " But," said he, " before leaving England I am
to take a jaunt to Oxford, Birmingham, my native city Lichfield, and
my old friend, Dr. Taylor's, at Ashbourne, in Derbyshire. I shall go
in a few days, and you, Boswell, shall go with me." I was ready to
accompany him, being willing even to leave London to have the pleasure
of his conversation.

I mentioned with much regret the extravagance of the representative
of a great family in Scotland, by which there was danger of its being
ruined ; and as Johnson respected it for its antiquity, he joined with me
in thinking it would be happy if this person should die. Mrs. Thrale
seemed shocked at this, as feudal barbarity ; and said, " I do not
understand this preference of the estate to its owner ; of the land to the
man who walks upon that land." JOHNSON : " Nay, Madam, it is not
a preference of the land to its owner ; it is the preference of a family
to an individual. Here is an establishment in a country, which is
of importance for ages, not only to the chief, but to his people ; an
establishment which extends upwards and downwards ; that this
should be destroyed by one idle fellow is a sad thing."

He said, " Entails are good, because it is good to preserve in a
country a series of men, to whom the people are accustomed to look up
as to their leaders. But I am for leaving a quantity of land in commerce, to excite industry, and keep money in the country ; for if no
land were to be bought in the country, there would be no encouragement
to acquire wealth, because a family could not be founded there ; or if
it were acquired, it must be carried away to another country where
land may be bought. And although the land in every country will
remain the same, and be as fertile where there is no money, as where
there is, yet all that portion of the happiness of civil life, which is produced by money circulating in a country, would be lost." BOSWELL :
" Then, Sir, would it be for the advantage of a country that all its

lands were sold at once?" Johnson: "So far, Sir, as money produces good, it would be an advantage; for, then that country would have as much money circulating in it as it is worth. But to be sure this would be counterbalanced by disadvantages attending a total change of proprietors."

I expressed my opinion that the power of entailing should be limited thus: "That there should be one-third, or perhaps one-half of the land of a country kept free for commerce; that the proportion allowed to be entailed, should be parcelled out so that no family could entail above a certain quantity. Let a family, according to the abilities of its representatives, be richer or poorer in different generations, or always rich if its representatives be always wise; but let its absolute permanency be moderate. In this way we should be certain of there being always a number of established roots; and as in the course of nature, there is in every age an extinction of some families, there would be continual openings for men ambitious of perpetuity, to plant a stock in the entailed ground." [1] Johnson: "Why, Sir, mankind will be better able to regulate the system of entails, when the evil of too much land being locked up by them is felt, than we can do at present when it is not felt."

I mentioned Dr. Adam Smith's book on "The Wealth of Nations," which was just published, and that Sir John Pringle had observed to me, that Dr. Smith, who had never been in trade, could not be expected to write well on that subject any more than a lawyer upon physic. Johnson: "He is mistaken, Sir; a man who has never been engaged in trade himself may undoubtedly write well upon trade, and there is nothing which requires more to be illustrated by philosophy than trade does. As to mere wealth, that is to say, money, it is clear that one nation or one individual cannot increase its store but by making another poorer; but trade procures what is more valuable, the reciprocation of the peculiar advantages of different countries. A merchant seldom thinks but of his own particular trade. To write a good book upon it, a man must have extensive views. It is not necessary to have practised, to write well upon a subject." I mentioned law as a subject on which no man could write well without practice. Johnson: "Why, Sir, in England, where so much money is to be got by the practice of the law, most of our writers upon it have been in practice; though Blackstone had not been much in practice when he published his

[1] The privilege of perpetuating in a family an estate and arms *indefeasibly* from generation to generation, is enjoyed by none of his Majesty's subjects except in Scotland, where the legal fiction of *fine* and *recovery* is unknown. It is a privilege so proud, that I should think it would be proper to have the exercise of it dependent on the royal prerogative. It seems absurd to permit the power of perpetuating their representation, to men, who having had no eminent merit, have truly no name. The king, as the impartial father of his people, would never refuse to grant the privilege to those who deserved it.—Boswell.

' Commentaries.' But upon the continent, the great writers on law have not all been in practice ; Grotius, indeed, was ; but Puffendorff was not, Burlamaqui was not."

When we had talked of the great consequence which a man acquired by being employed in his profession, I suggested a doubt of the justice of the general opinion, that it is improper in a lawyer to solicit employment ; for why, I urged, should it not be equally allowable to solicit that as a means of consequence, as it is to solicit votes to be elected a member of Parliament ?   Mr. Strahan had told me that a countryman of his and mine, who had risen to eminence in the law, had, when first making his way, solicited him to get him employed in city causes. JOHNSON : " Sir, it is wrong to stir up law-suits ; but when once it is certain that a law-suit is to go on, there is nothing wrong in a lawyer's endeavouring that he shall have the benefit rather than another." BOSWELL : " You would not solicit employment, Sir, if you were a lawyer." JOHNSON : " No, Sir ; but not because I should think it wrong, but because I should disdain it." This was a good distinction, which will be felt by men of just pride. He proceeded : " However, I would not have a lawyer to be wanting to himself in using fair means. I would have him to inject a little hint now and then, to prevent his being overlooked."

Lord Mountstuart's Bill for a Scotch Militia, in supporting which his lordship had made an able speech in the House of Commons, was now a pretty general topic of conversation.   JOHNSON : " As Scotland contributes so little land-tax towards the general support of the nation, it ought not to have a militia paid out of the general fund, unless it should be thought for the general interest that Scotland should be protected from an invasion, which no man can think will happen ; for what enemy would invade Scotland, where there is nothing to be got ? No, Sir ; now that the Scotch have not the pay of English soldiers spent among them, as so many troops are sent abroad, they are trying to get money another way, by having a militia paid. If they are afraid, and seriously desire to have an armed force to defend them, they should pay for it. Your scheme is to retain a part of your land-tax, by making us pay and clothe your militia."   BOSWELL : " You should not talk of *we* and *you*, Sir ; there is now an *Union*."   JOHNSON : " There must be a distinction of interest, while the proportions of land-tax are so unequal. If Yorkshire should say, ' Instead of paying our land-tax, we will keep a greater number of militia,' it would be unreasonable."   In this argument my friend was certainly in the wrong. The land-tax is as unequally proportioned between different parts of England, as between England and Scotland ; nay, it is considerably unequal in Scotland itself. But the land-tax is but a small part of the numerous branches of public revenue, all of which Scotland pays precisely as England does. A French invasion made in Scotland would soon penetrate into England.

He thus discoursed upon supposed obligation in settling estates :—
" Where a man gets the unlimited property of an estate, there is no
obligation upon him in *justice* to leave it to one person rather than
to another. There is a motive of preference from *kindness*, and this
kindness is generally entertained for the nearest relation. If I *owe* a
particular man a sum of money, I am obliged to let that man have the
next money I get, and cannot in justice let another have it ; but if I
owe money to no man, I may dispose of what I get as I please. There
is not a *debitum justitiæ* to a man's next heir ; there is only a *debitum
caritatis*. It is plain, then, that I have morally a choice according to
my liking. If I have a brother in want, he has a claim from affection
to my assistance ; but if I have also a brother in want, whom I like
better, he has a preferable claim. The right of an heir at law is only
this, that he is to have the succession to an estate, in case no other
person is appointed to it by the owner. His right is merely preferable
to that of the king."

We got into a boat to cross over to Blackfriars ; and as we moved
along the Thames, I talked to him of a little volume, which, altogether
unknown to him, was advertised to be published in a few days, under
the title of "*Johnsoniana, or Bon-Mots* of Dr. Johnson." JOHNSON :
" Sir, it is a mighty impudent thing." BOSWELL : " Pray, Sir, could
you have no redress if you were to prosecute a publisher for bringing
out, under your name, what you never said, and ascribing to you, dull,
stupid nonsense, or making you swear profanely as many ignorant
relaters of your *bon-mots* do ? " JOHNSON : " No, Sir ; there will
always be some truth mixed with the falsehood, and how can it be
ascertained how much is true and how much is false ? Besides, Sir,
what damages would a jury give me for having been represented as
swearing ? " BOSWELL : " I think, Sir, you should at least disavow
such a publication, because the world and posterity might with much
plausible foundation say, ' Here is a volume which was publicly advertised and came out in Dr. Johnson's own time, and by his silence, was
admitted by him to be genuine.' " JOHNSON : " I shall give myself no
trouble about the matter."

He was, perhaps, above suffering from such spurious publications ;
but I could not help thinking, that many men would be much injured
in their reputation, by having absurd and vicious sayings imputed to
them ; and that redress ought in such cases to be given.

He said, " The value of every story depends on its being true. A
story is a picture either of an individual or of human nature in general ;
if it be false, it is a picture of nothing. For instance : suppose a man
should tell that Johnson, before setting out for Italy, as he had to cross
the Alps, sat down to make himself wings. This many people would
believe ; but it would be a picture of nothing. * * * * (naming a
worthy friend of ours,) used to think a story, a story till I showed him

that truth was essential to it." I observed, tha Foote entertained us with stories which were not true ; but that, inaeed, it was properly not as narratives that Foote's stories pleased us, but as collections of ludicrous images. JOHNSON : "Foote is quite impartial, for he tells lies of every body."

The importance of strict and scrupulous veracity cannot be too often inculcated. Johnson was known to be so rigidly attentive to it, that even in his common conversation the slightest circumstance was mentioned with exact precision. The knowledge of his having such a principle and habit made his friends have a perfect reliance on the truth of everything that he told, however it might have been doubted if told by many others. As an instance of this, I may mention an odd incident which he related as having happened to him one night in Fleet-street : " A gentlewoman," said he, " begged I would give her my arm to assist her in crossing the street, which I accordingly did ; upon which she offered me a shilling, supposing me to be the watchman. I perceived that she was somewhat in liquor." This, if told by most people, would have been thought an invention ; when told by Johnson, it was believed by his friends as much as if they had seen what passed.

We landed at the Temple-stairs, where we parted.

I found him in the evening in Mrs. Williams's room. We talked of religious orders. He said, " It is as unreasonable for a man to go into a Carthusian convent for fear of being immoral, as for a man to cut off his hands for fear he should steal. There is, indeed, great resolution in the immediate act of dismembering himself ; but when that is once done, he has no longer any merit : for though it is out of his power to steal, yet he may all his life be a thief in his heart. So when a man has once become a Carthusian, he is obliged to continue so, whether he chooses it or not. Their silence, too, is absurd. We read in the Gospel of the apostles being sent to preach, but not to hold their tongues. All severity that does not tend to increase good or prevent evil, is idle. I said to the Lady Abbess of a convent, ' Madam, you are here, not for the love of virtue, but the fear of vice.' She said, ' she should remember this as long as she lived.' " I thought it hard to give her this view of her situation, when she could not help it ; and, indeed, I wondered at the whole of what he now said ; because, both in his " Rambler " and " Idler," he treats religious austerities with much solemnity of respect.

Finding him still persevering in his abstinence from wine, I ventured to speak to him of it. JOHNSON : " Sir, I have no objection to a man's drinking wine, if he can do it in moderation. I found myself apt to go to excess in it, and therefore, after having been for some time without it, on account of illness, I thought it better not to return to it. Every man is to judge for himself, according to the effects which he experiences. One of the Fathers tells us, he found fasting made him so peevish that he did not practise it."

Though he often enlarged upon the evil of intoxication, he was by no means harsh and unforgiving to those who indulged in occasional excess in wine. One of his friends, I well remember, came to sup at a tavern with him and some other gentlemen, and too plainly discovered that he had drunk too much at dinner. When one who loved mischief, thinking to produce a severe censure, asked Johnson, a few days afterwards, " Well, Sir, what did your friend say to you, as an apology for being in such a situation ? " Johnson answered : " Sir, he said all that a man *should* say : he said he was sorry for it."

I heard him once give a very judicious practical advice upon this subject : " A man who has been drinking wine at all freely, should never go into a new company. With those who have partaken of wine with him he may be pretty well in unison ; but he will probably be offensive or appear ridiculous to other people."

He allowed very great influence to education. " I do not deny, Sir, but there is some original difference in minds ; but it is nothing in comparison of what is formed by education. We may instance the science of *numbers*, which all minds are equally capable of attaining ; yet we find a prodigious difference in the powers of different men, in that respect, after they are grown up, because their minds have been more or less exercised in it ; and I think the same cause will explain the difference of excellence in other things, gradations admitting always some difference in the first principles."

This is a difficult subject ; but it is best to hope that diligence may do a great deal. We are *sure* of what it can do, in increasing our mechanical force and dexterity.

I again visited him on Monday. He took occasion to enlarge, as he often did, upon the wretchedness of a sea-life. " A ship is worse than a gaol. There is, in a gaol, better air, better company, better conveniency of every kind ; and a ship has the additional disadvantage of being in danger. When men come to like a sea-life, they are not fit to live on land. "—" Then," said I, " it would be cruel in a father to breed his son to the sea." JOHNSON : " It would be cruel in a father who thinks as I do. Men go to sea before they know the unhappiness of that way of life ; and when they have come to know it, they cannot escape from it, because it is then too late to choose another profession ; as, indeed, is generally the case with men, when they have once engaged in any particular way of life."

On Tuesday, March 19, which was fixed for our proposed jaunt, we met at the Somerset Coffee-house in the Strand, where we were taken up by the Oxford coach. He was accompanied by Mr. Gwyn, the architect ; and a gentleman of Merton College, whom he did not know, had the fourth seat. We soon got into conversation ; for it was very remarkable of Johnson, that the presence of a stranger had no restraint upon his talk. I observed that Garrick, who was about to quit the

stage, would soon have an easier life. JOHNSON : " I doubt that, Sir."
BOSWELL : " Why, Sir, he will be Atlas with the burden off his back."
JOHNSON : " But I know not if he will be so steady without his load.
However, he should never play any more, but be entirely the gentleman,
and not partly the player ; he should no longer subject himself to be
hissed by a mob, or to be insolently treated by performers, whom he
used to rule with a high hand, and who would gladly retaliate."
BOSWELL : " I think he should play once a year for the benefit of
decayed actors, as it has been said he means to do." JOHNSON : " Alas,
Sir, he will soon be a decayed actor himself."

Johnson expressed his disapprobation of ornamental architecture,
such as magnificent columns supporting a portico, or expensive pilasters
supporting merely their own capitals, " because it consumes labour disproportionate to its utility." For the same reason he satirized statuary.
" Painting," said he, " consumes labour not disproportionate to its effect :
but a fellow will hack half a year at a block of marble to make something in stone that hardly resembles a man. The value of statuary is
owing to its difficulty. You would not value the finest head cut upon a
carrot." Here he seemed to me to be strangely deficient in taste ; for
surely statuary is a noble art of imitation, and preserves a wonderful
expression of the varieties of the human frame ; and although it must
be allowed that the circumstances of difficulty enhance the value of a
marble head, we should consider that, if it requires a long time in the
performance, it has a proportionate value in durability.

Gwyn was a fine lively rattling fellow. Dr. Johnson kept him in
subjection, but with a kindly authority. The spirit of the artist, however, rose against what he thought a Gothic attack, and he made a brisk
defence. " What, Sir, you will allow no value to beauty in architecture
or in statuary ! Why should we allow it then in writing ? Why do
you take the trouble to give us so many fine allusions, and bright images,
and elegant phrases ? You might convey all your instruction without
these ornaments." Johnson smiled with complacency ; but said, "Why,
Sir, all these ornaments are useful, because they obtain an easier reception for truth ; but a building is not at all more convenient for being
decorated with superfluous carved work."

Gwyn at last was lucky enough to make one reply to Dr. Johnson
which he allowed to be excellent. Johnson censured him for taking
down a church which might have stood many years, and building a new
one at a different place, for no other reason, but that there might be a
direct road to a new bridge ; and his expression was, " You are taking
a church out of the way, that the people may go in a straight line to
the bridge." " No, Sir," said Gwyn, " I am putting the church *in* the
way, that the people may not *go out of the way*." JOHNSON (with a
hearty loud laugh of approbation) : " Speak no more. Rest your
colloquial fame upon this."

Upon our arrival at Oxford, Dr. Johnson and I went directly to University College, but were disappointed on finding that one of the fellows, his friend Mr. Scott, who accompanied him from Newcastle to Edinburgh, was gone to the country. We put up at the Angel Inn, and passed the evening by ourselves in easy and familiar conversation. Talking of constitutional melancholy, he observed, "A man so afflicted, Sir, must divert distressing thoughts, and not combat with them." Boswell: "May not he think them down, Sir?" Johnson: "No, Sir. To attempt to *think them down* is madness. He should have a lamp constantly burning in his bed-chamber during the night, and if wakefully disturbed, take a book and read, and compose himself to rest. To have the management of the mind is a great art, and it may be attained in a considerable degree by experience and habitual exercise." Boswell: "Should not he provide amusements for himself? Would it not, for instance, be right for him to take a course of chemistry?" Johnson: "Let him take a course of chemistry, or a course of rope-dancing, or a course of anything to which he is inclined at the time. Let him contrive to have as many retreats for his mind as he can, as many things to which it can fly from itself. Burton's 'Anatomy of Melancholy' is a valuable work. It is, perhaps, overloaded with quotation. But there is a great spirit and great power in what Burton says, when he writes from his own mind."

Next morning we visited Dr. Wetherell, Master of University College, with whom Dr. Johnson conferred on the most advantageous mode of disposing of the books printed at the Clarendon press, on which subject his letter has been inserted in a former page. I often had occasion to remark, Johnson loved business, loved to have his wisdom actually operate on real life. Dr. Wetherell and I talked of him without reserve in his own presence. Wetherell: "I would have given him a hundred guineas if he would have written a Preface to his 'Political Tracts,' by way of a Discourse on the British Constitution." Boswell: "Dr. Johnson, though in his writings, and upon all occasions, a great friend to the constitution, both in church and state, has never written expressly in support of either. There is really a claim upon him for both. I am sure he could give a volume of no great bulk upon each which would comprise all the substance, and with his spirit would effectually maintain them. He should erect a fort on the confines of each." I could perceive that he was displeased with this dialogue. He burst out, "Why should I be always writing?" I hoped he was conscious that the debt was just, and meant to discharge it, though he disliked being dunned.

We then went to Pembroke College, and waited on his old friend Dr. Adams, the master of it, whom I found to be a most polite, pleasing, communicative man. Before his advancement to the headship of his college, I had intended to go and visit him at Shrewsbury, where he was rector of St. Chad's, in order to get from him what particulars he could recollect of Johnson's academical life. He now obligingly gave me part of that authentic information, which, with what I afterwards owed to his kindness, will be found incorporated in its proper place in this work.

Dr. Adams had distinguished himself by an able answer to David Hume's "Essay on Miracles." He told me he had once dined in company with Hume, in London; that Hume shook hands with him, and said, "You have treated me much better than I deserve;" and that they exchanged visits. I took the liberty to object to treating an infidel writer with smooth civility. Where there is a controversy concerning a passage in a classic author, or concerning a question in antiquities, or any other subject in which human happiness is not deeply interested, a man may treat his antagonist with politeness and even respect. But where the controversy is concerning the truth of religion, it is of such vast importance to him who maintains it, to obtain the victory, that the person of an opponent ought not to be spared. If a man firmly believes that religion is an invaluable treasure, he will consider a writer who endeavours to deprive mankind of it as a *robber;* he will look upon him as *odious,* though the infidel might think himself in the right. A robber who reasons as the gang do in the "Beggars' Opera," who call themselves *practical* philosophers, and may have as much sincerity as pernicious *speculative* philosophers, is not the less an object of just indignation. An abandoned profligate may think that it is not wrong to debauch my wife; but shall I, therefore, not detest him? And if I catch him in making an attempt, shall I treat him with politeness? No, I will kick him down stairs, or run him through the body; that is, if I really love my wife, or have a true rational notion of honour. An infidel then shall not be treated handsomely by a Christian, merely because he endeavours to rob with ingenuity. I do declare, however, that I am exceedingly unwilling to be provoked to anger, and could I be persuaded that truth would not suffer from a cool moderation in its defenders, I should wish to preserve good humour, at least, in every controversy; nor, indeed, do I see why a man should lose his temper while he does all he can to refute an opponent. I think ridicule may be fairly used against an infidel; for instance, if he be an ugly fellow, and yet absurdly vain of his person, we may contrast his appearance with Cicero's beautiful image of Virtue, could she be seen. Johnson coincided with me, and said, "When a man voluntarily engages in an important controversy, he is to do all he can to lessen his antagonist, because authority from personal respect has much weight with most people, and often more than reasoning. If my antagonist writes bad language, though that may not be essential to the question, I will attack him for his bad language." ADAMS: "You would not jostle a chimney-sweeper." JOHNSON: "Yes, Sir, if it were necessary to jostle him *down.*"

Dr. Adams told us, that in some of the colleges at Oxford, the fellows had excluded the students from social intercourse with them in the common room. JOHNSON : "They are in the right, Sir ; there can be no real conversation, no fair exertion of mind amongst them, if the young men are by : for a man who has a character does not choose to stake it in their presence." BOSWELL : "But, Sir, may there not be very good conversation without a contest for superiority ?" JOHNSON "No animated conversation, Sir ; for it cannot be but one or other will come off superior. I do not mean that the victor must have the better of the argument, for he may take the weak side ; but his superiority of parts and knowledge will necessarily appear ; and he to whom he thus shows himself superior is lessened in the eyes of the young men. You know it was said, ' *Mallem cum Scaligero errare quam cum Clavio recte sapere.*' In the same manner take Bentley's and Jason de Nores' Comments upon Horace, you will admire Bentley more when wrong, than Jason when right.

We walked with Dr. Adams into the master's garden, and into the common room. JOHNSON (after a reverie of meditation) : "Ay ! Here I used to play at draughts with Phil. Jones and Fludyer. Jones loved beer, and did not get very forward in the Church. Fludyer turned out a scoundrel, a Whig, and said he was ashamed of having been bred at Oxford. He had a living at Putney, and got under the eye of some retainers to the court at that time, and so became a violent Whig: but he had been a scoundrel all along to be sure." BOSWELL : "Was he a scoundrel, Sir, in any other way than that of being a political scoundrel ? Did he cheat at draughts ?" JOHNSON : "Sir, we never played for *money*."

He then carried me to visit Dr. Bentham, Canon of Christ Church, and divinity professor, with whose learned and lively conversation we were much pleased. He gave us an invitation to dinner, which Dr. Johnson told me was a high honour. "Sir, it is a great thing to dine with the canons of Christ Church." We could not accept his invitation, as we were engaged to dine at University College. We had an excellent dinner there, with the masters and fellows, it being St.

DR. HORNE, BISHOP OF NORWICH.

Cuthbert's day, which is kept by them as a festival, as he was a saint of Durham, with which this college is much connected.

We drank tea with Dr. Horne, late President of Magdalen College and Bishop of Norwich, of whose abilities, in different respects, the public has had eminent proofs, and the esteem annexed to whose character was increased by knowing him personally. He had talked of publishing an edition of Walton's Lives, but had laid aside that design, upon Dr. Johnson's telling him, from mistake, that Lord Hailes intended to do it. I had wished to negotiate between Lord Hailes and him, that one or other should perform so good a work. JOHNSON: "In order to do it well, it would be necessary to collect all the editions of Walton's Lives. By way of adapting the book to the taste of the present age, they have, in a late edition, left out a vision which he relates Dr. Donne had, but it should be restored;[1] and there should be a critical catalogue given of the works of the different persons whose lives were written by Walton, and therefore their works must be carefully read by the editor."

We then went to Trinity College, where he introduced me to Mr. Thomas Warton, with whom we passed a part of the evening. We talked of biography. JOHNSON: "It is rarely well executed. They only, who live with a man, can write his life with any genuine exactness and discrimination; and few people who have lived with a man know what to remark about him. The chaplain of a late bishop, whom I was to assist in writing some memoirs of his lordship, could tell me scarcely anything."[2]

I said, Mr. Robert Dodsley's life should be written, as he had been so much connected with the wits of his time, and by his literary merit had raised himself from the station of a footman. Mr. Warton said, he had published a little volume under the title of "The Muse in Livery." JOHNSON: "I doubt whether Dodsley's brother would thank a man who should write his life; yet Dodsley himself was not unwilling that his original low condition should be recollected. When Lord Lyttelton's 'Dialogues of the Dead' came out, one of which is between Apicius, an ancient epicure, and Dartineuf, a modern epicure, Dodsley said to me, 'I knew Dartineuf well, for I was once his footman.'"

Biography led us to speak of Dr. John Campbell, who had written a considerable part of "The Biographia Britannica." Johnson, though he valued him highly, was of opinion that there was not so much in his great work, "A Political Survey of Great Britain," as the world had been taught to expect;[3] and had said to me, that he believed Campbell's disappointment on account of the bad success of that work, had killed

---

[1] The vision which Johnson speaks of, was not in the original publication of Walton's Life of Dr. Donne, in 1640. It is not found in the three earliest editions; but was first introduced into the fourth, in 1675. I have not been able to discover what modern republication is alluded to, in which it was omitted. It has very properly been restored by Dr. Zouch.—JAMES BOSWELL, JUN.

[2] It has been mentioned to me by an accurate English friend, that Dr. Johnson could never have used the phrase *almost nothing*, as not being English; and therefore I have put another in its place. At the same time, I am not quite convinced it is not good English. For the best writers use this phrase, "*little or nothing;*" *i. e.* almost so little as to be nothing. —BOSWELL.

[3] Yet surely it is a very useful work, and of wonderful research and labour for one man to have executed.—BOSWELL

him. He this evening observed of it, "That work was his death."
Mr. Warton, not adverting to his meaning, answered, "I believe so ;
from the great attention he bestowed on it." JOHNSON : "Nay, Sir,
he died of *want* of attention, if he died at all by that book."

We talked of a work much in vogue at that time, written in a very
mellifluous style, but which, under pretext of another subject, contained
much artful infidelity. I said it was not fair to attack us unexpectedly ;
he should have warned us of our danger before we entered his garden of
flowery eloquence, by advertising, "Spring-guns and men-traps set
here." The author [1] had been an Oxonian, and was remembered there
for having "turned Papist." I observed, that as he had changed
several times—from the Church of England to the Church of Rome,
from the Church of Rome to infidelity—I did not despair yet of seeing
him a Methodist preacher. JOHNSON (laughing) : "It is said that his
range has been more extensive, and that he has once been Mahometan.
However, now that he has published his infidelity, he will probably
persist in it." BOSWELL : "I am not quite sure of that, Sir."

I mentioned Sir Richard Steele having published his "Christian
Hero," with the avowed purpose of obliging himself to lead a religious
life ; yet that his conduct was by no means strictly suitable. JOHN-
SON : "Steele, I believe, practised the lighter vices."

Mr. Warton, being engaged, could not sup with us at our inn ; we
had therefore another evening by ourselves. I asked Johnson whether
a man's being forward to make himself known to eminent people, and
seeing as much of life, and getting as much information as he could in
every way, was not yet lessening himself by his forwardness ? JOHNSON :
"No, Sir ; a man always makes himself greater as he increases his
knowledge."

I censured some ludicrous fantastic dialogues between two coach-
horses, and other such stuff, which Baretti had lately published. He
joined with me, and said, "Nothing odd will do long. 'Tristram
Shandy' did not last." I expressed a desire to be acquainted with a
lady who had been much talked of, and universally celebrated for extraordinary address and insinuation. JOHNSON : "Never believe extraordinary characters which you hear of people. Depend upon it, Sir,
they are exaggerated. You do not see one man shoot a great deal
higher than another." I mentioned Mr. Burke. JOHNSON : "Yes,
Burke *is* an extraordinary man. His stream of mind is perpetual."
It is very pleasing to me to record, that Johnson's high estimation of
the talents of this gentleman was uniform, from their early acquaintance. Sir Joshua Reynolds informs me, that when Mr. Burke was first
elected a member of Parliament, and Sir J. Hawkins expressed a wonder
at his attaining a seat, Johnson said : "Now, we who know Mr. Burke,
know that he will be one of the first men in the country." And once

when Johnson was ill, and unable to exert himself as much as usual without fatigue, Mr. Burke having been mentioned, he said, " That fellow calls forth all my powers. Were I to see Burke now it would kill me." So much was he accustomed to consider conversation as a contest, and such was his notion of Burke as an opponent.

Next morning, Thursday, March 21, we set out in a post-chaise to pursue our ramble. It was a delightful day, and we rode through Blenheim-park. When I looked at the magnificent bridge built by John, Duke of Marlborough, over a small rivulet, and recollected the epigram made upon it—

> "The lofty arch his high ambition shows;
> The stream an emblem of his bounty flows :"

and saw that now, by the genius of Brown, a magnificent body of water was collected, I said, " They have *drowned* the epigram." I observed to him, while in the midst of the noble scene around us, " You and I, Sir, have, I think, seen together the extremes of what can be seen in Britain—the wild, rough island of Mull, and Blenheim-park."

We dined at an excellent inn at Chapel-house, where he expatiated on the felicity of England in its taverns and inns, and triumphed over the French for not having, in any perfection, the tavern life. " There is no private house," said he, " in which people can enjoy themselves so well as at a capital tavern. Let there be ever so great plenty of good things, ever so much grandeur, ever so much elegance, ever so much desire that everybody should be easy, in the nature of things it cannot be : there must always be some degree of care and anxiety. The master of the house is anxious to entertain his guests—the guests are anxious to be agreeable to him ; and no man, but a very impudent dog indeed, can as freely command what is in another man's house, as if it were his own. Whereas, at a tavern, there is a general freedom from anxiety. You are sure you are welcome ; and the more noise you make, the more trouble you give, the more good things you call for, the welcomer you are. No servants will attend you with the alacrity which waiters do, who are incited by the prospect of an immediate reward in proportion as they please. No, Sir, there is nothing which has yet been contrived by man, by which so much happiness is produced as by a good tavern or inn." [1] He then repeated, with great emotion, Shenstone's lines :

[1] Sir John Hawkins has preserved very few *Memorabilia* of Johnson. There is, however to be found in his bulky tome, a very excellent one upon this subject. " In contradiction to those, who, having a wife and childen, prefer domestic enjoyments to those which a tavern affords, I have heard him assert, *that a tavern chair was the throne of human felicity.*—' As soon, said he, 'as I enter the door of a tavern, I experience an oblivion of care, and a freedom from solicitude : when I am seated, I find the master courteous, and the servants obsequious to my call; anxious to know and ready to supply my wants; wine there exhilarates my spirits, and prompts me to free conversation and an interchange of discourse with those whom I most love ; I dogmatise and am contradicted, and in this conflict of opinion and sentiments I find delight.'"—BOSWELL.

> "Whoe'er has travell'd life's dull round,
> Where'er his stages may have been,
> May sigh to think he still has found
> The warmest welcome at an inn." [1]

My illustrious friend, I thought, did not sufficiently admire Shenstone. That ingenious and elegant gentleman's opinion of Johnson appears in one of his letters to Mr. Greaves, dated Feb. 9, 1760. " I have lately been reading one or two volumes of the Rambler ; who, excepting against some few hardnesses [2] in his manner, and the want of more examples to enliven, is one of the most nervous, most perspicuous, most concise, most harmonious prose writers I know. A learned diction improves by time."

In the afternoon, as we were driven rapidly along in the post-chaise, he said to me, " Life has not many things better than this."

We stopped at Stratford-upon-Avon, and drank tea and coffee ; and it pleased me to be with him upon the classic ground of Shakspeare's native place.

He spoke slightingly of Dyer's " Fleece."—"The subject, Sir, cannot be made poetical. How can a man write poetically of serges and druggets ? Yet you will hear many people talk to you gravely of that excellent poem, ' The Fleece.' " Having talked of Grainger's " Sugar Cane," I mentioned to him Mr. Langton's having told me, that this poem, when read in manuscript at Sir Joshua Reynolds's, had made all the assembled wits burst into a laugh, when, after much blank-verse pomp, the poet began a new paragraph thus :—

> "Now, Muse, let's sing of *rats*."

And what increased the ridicule was, that one of the company, who slily overlooked the reader, perceived that the word had been originally *mice*, and had been altered to *rats*, as more dignified. [3]

This passage does not appear in the printed work, Dr. Grainger, or some of his friends, it should seem, having become sensible that introducing even *rats*, in a grave poem, might be liable to banter. He, however, could not bring himself to relinquish the idea ; for they are

[1] We happened to lie this night at the inn at Henley, where Shenstone wrote these lines. I give them as they are found in the corrected edition of his works, published after his death. In Dodsley's collection the stanza ran thus :—

> " Whoe'er has travell'd life's dull round,
> Whate'er his *various tour has* been,
> May sigh to think *how oft* he found
> *His* warmest welcome at an inn.'—BOSWELL.

[2] He too often makes use of the *abstract* for the *concrete*.—BOSWELL.

[3] Such is this little laughable incident, which has been often related. Dr. Percy, the Bishop of Dromore, who was an intimate friend of Dr. Grainger, and has a particular regard for his memory, has communicated to me the following explanation :—

" The passage in question was originally not liable to such perversion ; for the author having occasion in that part of his work to mention the havoc made by rats and mice, had introduced the subject in a kind of mock heroic, and a parody of Homer's battle of the frogs thus, in a still more ludicrous manner, periphrastically exhibited in his poem as it now stands :—

> " Nor with less waste the whisker'd vermin race,
> A countless clan, despoil the lowland cane."

Johnson said that Dr. Grainger was an agreeable man ; a man who would do any good that was in his power. His translation of Tibullus, he thought, was very well done ; but " The Sugar-Cane, a Poem," [1] did not please him ; for he exclaimed, " What could be made of a sugar-cane ? One might as well write ' The Parsley-Bed, a Poem ;' or ' The Cabbage Garden, a Poem.'" BOSWELL : " You must then *pickle* your cabbage with the *sal atticum*." JOHNSON : " You know there is already ' The Hop-Garden, a Poem ;' and, I think, one could say a great deal about cabbage. The poem might begin with the advantages of civilised society over a rude state, exemplified by the Scotch, who had no cabbages till Oliver Cromwell's soldiers introduced them ; and one might thus show how arts are propagated by conquest, as they were by the Roman arms." He seemed to be much diverted with the fertility of his own fancy.

I told him, that I heard Dr. Percy was writing the history of the wolf in Great Britain. JOHNSON : " The wolf, Sir ! why the wolf ? Why does he not write of the bear, which we had formerly ? Nay, it is said we had the beaver. Or why does he not write of the grey rat, the Hanover rat, as it is called, because it is said to have come into this country about the time that the family of Hanover came ? I should like to see ' *The History of the Grey Rat, by Thomas Percy, D.D., Chaplain in Ordinary to His Majesty,*' " (laughing immoderately). BOSWELL : " I am afraid a court chaplain could not decently write of the grey rat." JOHNSON : " Sir, he need not give it the name of the Hanover rat." Thus could he indulge a luxuriant, sportive imagination, when talking of a friend whom he loved and esteemed.

He mentioned to me the singular history of an ingenious acquaintance · " He had practised physic in various situations with no great emolument. A West India gentleman, whom he delighted by his conversation, gave him a bond for a handsome annuity during his life, on the condition of

---

and mice, invoking the Muse of the old Grecian bard in an elegant and well-turned manner. In that state I had seen it ; but afterwards, unknown to me and other friends, he had been persuaded, contrary to his own better judgment, to alter it, so as to produce the unlucky effect above mentioned."

The above was written by the Bishop when he had not the poem itself to recur to ; and though the account given was true of it at one period, yet as Dr. Grainger afterwards altered the passage in question, the remarks in the text do not now apply to the printed poem.

The Bishop gives this character of Dr. Grainger :—" He was not only a man of genius and learning, but had many excellent virtues ; being one of the most generous, friendly, and benevolent men I ever knew."—BOSWELL.

[1] Dr. Johnson said to me, "Percy, Sir, was angry with me for laughing at the ' Sugar-cane ' for he had a mind to make a great thing of Grainger's rats.—BOSWELL.

his accompanying him into the West Indies, and living with him there for two years. He accordingly embarked with the gentleman ; but upon the voyage fell in love with a young woman who happened to be one of the passengers, and married the wench. From the imprudence of his disposition he quarrelled with the gentleman, and declared he would have no connection with him. So he forfeited the annuity. He settled as a physician in one of the Leeward Islands. A man was sent out to him merely to compound his medicines. This fellow set up as rival to him in his practice of physic, and got so much the better of him in the opinion of the people of the island, that he carried away all the business, upon which he returned to England, and soon after died."

On Friday, March 22, having set out early from Henley, where we had lain the preceding night, we arrived at Birmingham about nine o'clock, and, after breakfast, went to call on his old schoolfellow, Mr. Hector. A very stupid maid, who opened the door, told us that " her master was gone out ; he was gone to the country ; she could not tell when he would return." In short, she gave us a miserable reception ; and Johnson observed, " She would have behaved no better to people who wanted him in the way of his profession." He said to her, " My name is Johnson ; tell him I called. Will you remember the name ? " She answered with rustic simplicity, in the Warwickshire pronunciation, " I don't understand you, Sir." " Blockhead ! " said he, " I'll write." I never heard the word *blockhead* applied to a woman before, though I do not see why it should not, when there is evident occasion for it.[1] He however, made another attempt to make her understand him, and roared loud in her ear, " *Johnson*," and then she catched the sound.

We next called on Mr. Lloyd, one of the people called Quakers. He too was not at home, but Mrs. Lloyd was, and received us courteously, and asked us to dinner. Johnson said to me, " After the uncertainty of all human things at Hector's, this invitation came very well." We walked about the town, and he was pleased to see it increasing.

I talked of legitimation by subsequent marriage, which obtained in the Roman law, and still obtains in the law of Scotland. Johnson : " I think it a bad thing ; because the chastity of women being of the utmost importance, as all property depends upon it, they who forfeit it should not have any possibility of being restored to good character ; nor should the children by illicit connection attain the full right of lawful children, by the posterior consent of the offending parties." His opinion upon this subject deserves consideration. Upon his principle there may

---

[1] My worthy friend Mr. Langton, to whom I am under innumerable obligations in the course of my Johnsonian History, has furnished me with a droll illustration of this question. An honest carpenter, after giving some anecdote, in his presence, of the ill-treatment which he had received from a clergyman's wife, who was a noted termagant, and whom he accused of unjust dealing in some transaction with him, added, " I took care to let her know what I thought of her." And being asked, " What did you say ? " answered, " I told her she was a *scoundrel.*"—Boswell.

at times, be a hardship, and seemingly a strange one, upon individuals ; but the general good of society is better secured. And, after all, it is unreasonable in an individual to repine that he has not the advantage of a state which is made different from his own by the social institution under which he is born. A woman does not complain that her brother who is younger than her, gets their common father's estate. Why, then, should a natural son complain that a younger brother, by the same parents lawfully begotten, gets it ? The operation of law is similar in both cases. Besides, an illegitimate son, who has a younger legitimate brother by the same father and mother, has no stronger claim to the father's estate, than if that legitimate brother had only the same father, from whom alone the estate descends.

Mr. Lloyd joined us in the street, and in a little while we met *Friend Hector*, as Mr. Lloyd called him. It gave me pleasure to observe

MR. HECTOR.

the joy which Johnson and he expressed on seeing each other again. Mr. Lloyd and I left them together, while he obligingly showed me some of the manufactures of this very curious assemblage of artificers. We all met at dinner at Mr. Lloyd's, where we were entertained with great hospitality. Mr. and Mrs. Lloyd had been married the same year with their Majesties, and like them, had been blessed with a numerous family of fine children, their numbers being exactly the same. Johnson said, "Marriage is the best state for a man in general ; and every man is a worse man in proportion as he is unfit for the married state."

I have always loved the simplicity of manners, and the spiritual-mindedness of the Quakers and, talking with Mr. Lloyd, I observed that the essential part of religion was piety—a devout intercourse with the Divinity, and that many a man was a Quaker without knowing it.

As Dr. Johnson had said to me in the morning, while we walked together, that he liked individuals among the Quakers, but not the sect, when we were at Mr. Lloyd's I kept clear of introducing any questions concerning the peculiarities of their faith. But I having asked to look at Baskerville's edition of " Barclay's Apology," Johnson laid hold of it ; and the chapter on baptism happening to open, Johnson remarked, " He says there is neither precept nor practice for baptism in the scriptures. That is false." Here he was the aggressor, by no means in a gentle manner : and the good Quakers had the advantage of him, for he had read negligently, and had not observed that

Barclay speaks of *infant* baptism, which they calmly made him perceive. Mr. Lloyd, however, was in a great mistake ; for, when insisting that the rite of baptism by water was to cease when the *spiritual* administration of Christ began, he maintained that John the Baptist said, " *My baptism* shall decrease, but *his* shall increase." Whereas the words are, " *He* must increase, but I *must* decrease." [1]

One of them having objected to the " observance of days, and months, and years," Johnson answered, " The Church does not superstitiously observe days merely as days, but as memorials of important facts. Christmas might be kept as well upon one day of the year as another ; but there should be a stated day for commemorating the birth of our Saviour, because there is danger that what may be done on any day will be neglected."

He said to me at another time, " Sir, the holidays observed by our Church are of great use in our religion." There can be no doubt of this in a limited sense—I mean if the number of such consecrated portions of time be not too extensive. The excellent Mr. Nelson's " Festivals and Fasts," which has, I understand, the greatest sale of any book ever printed in England—except the Bible—is a most valuable help to devotion ; and in addition to it I would recommend two sermons on the same subject by Mr. Pott, Archdeacon of St. Alban's, equally distinguished for piety and elegance. I am sorry to have it to say that Scotland is the only Christian country, Catholic or Protestant, where the great events of our religion are not solemnly commemorated by its ecclesiastical establishment on days set apart for the purpose.

Mr. Hector was so good as to accompany me to see the great works of Mr. Boulton, at a place which he has called Soho, about two miles from Birmingham, which the very ingenious proprietor showed me himself to the best advantage. I wished Johnson had been with us ; for it was a scene which I should have been glad to contemplate by his light. The vastness and the contrivance of some of the machinery would have " matched his mighty mind." I shall never forget Mr. Boulton's expression to me, " I sell here, Sir, what all the world desires to have—Power." He had about seven hundred people at work. I contemplated him as an *iron chieftain*, and he seemed to be a father to his tribe. One of them came to him, complaining grievously of his landlord for having distrained his goods. " Your landlord is in the right, Smith," said Boulton. " But I'll tell you what—find you a friend who will lay down one half of your rent, and I'll lay down the other half, and you shall have your goods again."

From Mr. Hector I now learnt many particulars of Dr. Johnson's early life, which, with others that he gave me at different times since, have contributed to the formation of this work.

John, chap. iii. v. 30.—Boswell.

Dr. Johnson said to me in the morning, "You will see, Sir, at Mr. Hector's, his sister, Mrs. Careless, a clergyman's widow. She was the first woman with whom I was in love. It dropt out of my head imperceptibly ; but she and I shall always have a kindness for each other." He laughed at the notion that a man can never be really in love but once, and considered it as a mere romantic fancy.

On our return from Mr. Boulton's, Mr. Hector took me to his house, where we found Johnson sitting placidly at tea, with his *first love ;* who though now advanced in years, was a genteel woman, very agreeable and well bred.

Johnson lamented to Mr. Hector the state of one of their school-fellows, Mr. Charles Congreve, a clergyman, which he thus described : "He obtained, I believe, considerable preferment in Ireland, but now lives in London, quite as a valetudinarian, afraid to go into any house but his own. He takes a short airing in his post-chaise every day. He has an elderly woman, whom he calls cousin, who lives with him, and jogs his elbow when his glass has stood too long empty, and encourages him in drinking, in which he is very willing to be encouraged : not that he gets drunk, for he is a very pious man, but he is always muddy. He confesses to one bottle of port every day, and he probably drinks more. He is quite unsocial ; his conversation is quite monosyllabical ; and when, at my last visit, I asked him what o'clock it was, that signal of my departure had so pleasing an effect on him, that he sprung up to look at his watch, like a greyhound bounding at a hare." When Johnson took leave of Mr. Hector, he said, "Don't grow like Congreve ; nor let me grow like him, when you are near me."

When he again talked of Mrs. Careless to-night, he seemed to have had his affection revived ; for he said, " If I had married her, it might have been as happy for me." BOSWELL ; " Pray, Sir, do you not suppose that there are fifty women in the world, with any one of whom a man may be as happy as with any one woman in particular." JOHNSON : " Ay, Sir, fifty thousand." BOSWELL : " Then, Sir, you are not of opinion with some who imagine that certain men and certain women are made for each other ; and that they cannot be happy if they miss their counterparts." JOHNSON : " To be sure not, Sir. I believe marriages would in general be as happy, and often more so, if they were all made by the Lord Chancellor, upon a due consideration of the characters and circumstances, without the parties having any choice in the matter."

I wished to have stayed at Birmingham to-night, to have talked more with Mr. Hector ; but my friend was impatient to reach his native city ; so we drove on that stage in the dark, and were long pensive and silent. When we came within the focus of the Lichfield lamps, " Now," said he, " we are getting out of a state of death." We put up at the " Three Crowns," not one of the great inns, but a good old-fashioned one, which was kept by Mr. Wilkins, and was the very next house to that in which Johnson was born and brought up, and which was still his own property.[1] We had a comfortable supper, and got

THE THREE CROWNS INN.

into high spirits. I felt all my Toryism glow in this old capital of Staffordshire. I could have offered incense *genio loci;* and I indulged in libations of that ale, which Boniface, in "The Beaux Stratagem," recommends with such an eloquent jollity.

Next morning he introduced me to Mrs. Lucy Porter, his step-daughter. She was now an old maid, with much simplicity of manner. She had never been in London. Her brother, a captain in the navy, had left her a fortune of ten thousand pounds, about a third of which she had laid out in building a stately house, and making a handsome garden, in an elevated situation in Lichfield. Johnson, when here by himself, used to live at her house. She reverenced him, and he had a parental tenderness for her.

We then visited Mr. Peter Garrick, who had that morning received a letter from his brother David, announcing our coming to Lichfield. He was engaged to dinner, but asked us to tea, and to sleep at his house. Johnson, however, would not quit his old acquaintance Wilkins, of the "Three Crowns." The family likeness of the Garricks was very

---

[1] I went through the house where my illustrious friend was born, with a reverence with which it doubtless will long be visited.—BOSWELL.

triking; and Johnson thought that David's vivacity was not so peculiar to himself as was supposed. "Sir," said he, "I don't know but if Peter had cultivated all the arts of gaiety as much as David has done, he might have been as brisk and lively. Depend upon it, Sir, vivacity is much an art, and depends greatly on habit." I believe there is a good deal of truth in this, notwithstanding a ludicrous story told me by a lady abroad, of a heavy German baron, who had lived much with the young English at Geneva, and was ambitious to be as lively as they; with which view, he, with assiduous attention, was jumping over the chairs and tables in his lodgings; and when the people of the house ran in and asked with surprise, what was the matter, he answered, "*Sh' apprens t'etre fif.*"

PARLOUR OF THE THREE CROWNS INN.

We dined at our inn, and had with us a Mr. Jackson, one of Johnson's schoolfellows, whom he treated with much kindness, though he seemed to be a low man, dull and untaught. He had a coarse grey coat, black waistcoat, greasy leather breeches, and a yellow uncurled wig; and his countenance had the ruddiness which betokens one who is in no haste to "leave his can." He drank only ale. He had tried to be a cutler at Birmingham, but had not succeeded; and now he lived poorly at home, and had some scheme of dressing leather in a better manner than common; to his indistinct account of which, Dr. Johnson listened with patient attention, that he might assist him with his advice.

Here was an instance of genuine humanity and real kindness in this great man, who has been most unjustly represented as altogether harsh and destitute of tenderness. A thousand such instances might have been recorded in the course of his long life ; though that his temper was warm and hasty, and his manner often rough, cannot be denied.

I saw here, for the first time, *oat ale ;* and oat cakes, not hard as in Scotland, but soft like Yorkshire cakes, were served at breakfast. It was pleasant to me to find, that *" Oats,"* the *"food of horses,"* were so much used as the *food of the people* in Dr. Johnson's own town. He expatiated in praise of Lichfield and its inhabitants, who, he said, were " the most sober, decent people in England, the genteelest in proportion to their wealth, and spoke the purest English." I doubted as to the last article of this eulogy, for they had several provincial sounds ; as *there* pronounced like *fear*, instead of like *fair ; once* pronounced *woonse,* instead of *wunse,* or *wonse.* Johnson himself never got entirely free of those provincial accents. Garrick sometimes used to take him off, squeezing a lemon into a punch-bowl, with uncouth gesticulations, looking round the company, and calling out, " Who's for *poonsh ?*"[1]

Very little business appeared to be going forward in Lichfield. I found, however, two strange manufactures for so inland a place, sailcloth and streamers for ships ; and I observed them making some saddle-cloths, and dressing sheep-skins ; but, upon the whole, the busy hand of industry seemed to be quite slackened. " Surely, Sir," said I, " you are an idle set of people." " Sir " said Johnson, " we are a city of philosophers ; we work with our heads, and make the boobies of Birmingham work for us with their hands."

There was at this time a company of players performing at Lichfield. The manager, Mr. Stanton, sent his compliments, and begged leave to wait on Dr. Johnson. Johnson received him very courteously, and he drank a glass of wine with us. He was a plain, decent, well-behaved man, and expressed his gratitude to Dr. Johnson for having once got him permission from Dr. Taylor at Ashbourne to play there upon moderate terms. Garrick's name was soon introduced. JOHNSON . " Garrick's conversation is gay and grotesque. It is a dish of all sorts, but all good things. There is no solid meat in it ; there is a want of sentiment in it. Not but that he has sentiment sometimes, and sentiment, too, very powerful and very pleasing ; but it has not its full proportion in his conversation."

When we were by ourselves he told me, " Forty years ago, Sir, I was in love with an actress here, Mrs. Emmet, who acted Flora in 'Hob in the Well.'" What merit this lady had as an actress, or what was

[1] Garrick himself, like the Lichfieldians, always said, *shupreme, shuperior.*—BURNEY.
This is still the vulgar pronunciation of Ireland, where the pronunciation of the English nguage by those who have not expatriated, is doubtless that which generally prevailed in land in the time of Queen Elizabeth.—MALONE.

her figure or her manner, I have not been informed : but, if we may believe Mr. Garrick, his old master's taste in theatrical merit was by no means refined ; he was not an *elegans formarum spectator*. Garrick used to tell that Johnson said of an actor, who played Sir Harry Wildair, at Lichfield, "There is a courtly vivacity about the fellow ; " when, in fact, according to Garrick's account. " he was the most vulgar ruffian that ever went upon *boards*."

We had promised Mr. Stanton to be at his theatre on Monday. Dr. Johnson jocularly proposed to me to write a Prologue for the occasion : " A Prologue, by James Boswell, Esq., from the Hebrides." I was really inclined to take the hint. Methought, " Prologue, spoken before Dr. Samuel Johnson at Lichfield, 1776," would have sounded as well as " Prologue, spoken before the Duke of York at Oxford," in Charles the Second's time. Much might have been said of what Lichfield had done for Shakspeare, by producing Johnson and Garrick. But I found he was averse to it.

We went and viewed the museum of Mr. Richard Green, apothecary here, who told me he was proud of being a relation of Dr. Johnson's. It was, truly, a wonderful collection, both of antiquities and natural curiosities, and ingenious works of art. He had all the articles accurately arranged, with their names upon labels, printed at his own little press ; and on the staircase leading to it was a board, with the names of contributors marked in gold letters. A printed catalogue of the collection was to be had at a bookseller's. Johnson expressed his admiration of the activity and diligence and good fortune of Mr. Green, in getting together, in his situation, so great a variety of things ; and Mr. Green told me that Johnson once said to him, " Sir, I should as soon have thought of building a man-of-war as of collecting such a museum." Mr. Green's obliging alacrity in showing it was very pleasing. His engraved portrait, with which he has favoured me, has a motto truly characteristical of his disposition, " *Nemo sibi vivat*."

A physician being mentioned who had lost his practice, because his whimsically changing his religion had made people distrustful of him, I maintained that this was unreasonable, as religion is unconnected with medical skill. JOHNSON : " Sir, it is not unreasonable ; for when people see a man absurd in what they understand, they may conclude the same of him in what they do not understand. If a physician were to take to eating of horse-flesh, nobody would employ him ; though one may eat horse-flesh, and be a very skilful physician. If a man were educated in an absurd religion, his continuing to profess it would not hurt him, though his changing to it would." [1]

We drank tea and coffee at Mr. Peter Garrick's, where was Mrs. Aston, one of the maiden sisters of Mrs. Walmsley, wife of Johnson's first

---

[1] Fothergill, a Quaker, and Schomberg, a Jew, had the greatest practice of any two physicians of their time.—PUTNEY.

friend, and sister also of the lady of whom Johnson used to speak with the warmest admiration, by the name of Molly Aston, who was afterwards married to Captain Brodie, of the navy.

On Sunday, March 24, we breakfasted with Mrs. Cobb, a widow lady who lived in an agreeable, sequestered place close by the town, called the Friary, it having been formerly a religious house. She and her niece, Miss Adey, were great admirers of Dr. Johnson ; and he behaved to them with a kindness and easy pleasantry, such as we see between old and intimate acquaintance. He accompanied Mrs. Cobb to St. Mary's Church, and I went to the Cathedral, where I was very much delighted with the music, finding it to be peculiarly solemn, and accordant with the words of the service.

We dined at Mr. Peter Garrick's, who was in a very lively humour, and verified Johnson's saying, that if he had cultivated gaiety as much as his brother David, he might have equally excelled in it. He was to-day quite a London narrator, telling us a variety of anecdotes with that earnestness and attempt at mimicry, which we usually find in the wits of the metropolis. Dr. Johnson went with me to the Cathedral in the afternoon. It was grand and pleasing to contemplate this illustrious writer, now full of fame, worshipping in "the solemn temple" of his native city.

I returned to tea and coffee at Mr. Peter Garrick's, and then found Dr. Johnson at the Rev. Mr. Seward's, Canon Residentiary, who

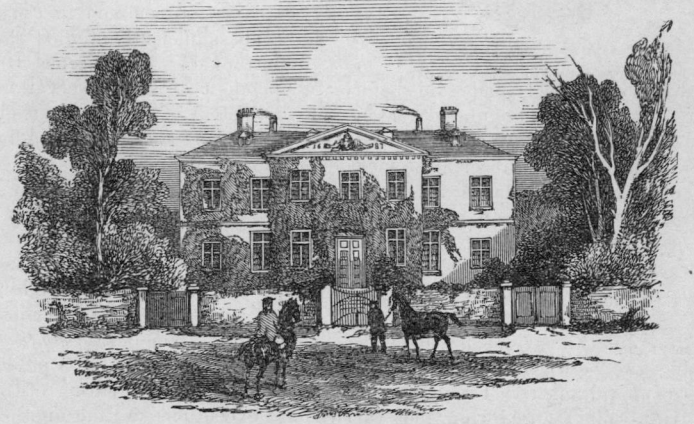

THE BISHOP S PALACE, LICHFIELD.

inhabited the Bishop's palace, in which Mr. Walmsley lived, and which had been the scene of many happy hours in Johnson's early life. Mr. Seward had, with ecclesiastical hospitality and politeness, asked me in the morning, merely as a stranger, to dine with him ; and in the afternoon, when I was introduced to him, he asked Dr. Johnson and me to spend the evening and sup with him. He was a genteel, well-bred, dignified clergyman, had travelled with Lord Charles Fitzroy, uncle of the present Duke of Grafton, who died when abroad, and he had lived much in the great world. He was an ingenious and literary man, had published an edition of Beaumont and Fletcher, and written verses in Dodsley's collection. His lady was the daughter of Mr. Hunter, Johnson's first schoolmaster. And now, for the first time, I had the pleasure of seeing his celebrated daughter, Miss Anna Seward, to whom

MISS ANNA SEWARD.

I have since been indebted for many civilities, as well as some obliging communications concerning Johnson.

Mr. Seward mentioned to us the observations which he had made upon the strata of earth in volcanos, from which it appeared, that they were so very different in depth at different periods, that no calculation whatever could be made as to the time required for their formation. This fully refuted an anti-mosaical remark introduced into Captain Brydone's entertaining tour, I hope heedlessly, from a kind of vanity which is too common in those who have not sufficiently studied the most important of all subjects. Dr. Johnson, indeed, had said before, independent of this observation, "Shall all the accumulated evidence of the history of the world—shall the authority of what is unquestionably the most ancient writing, be overturned by an uncertain remark such as this ?"

On Monday, March 25, we breakfasted at Mrs. Lucy Porter's. Johnson had sent an express to Dr. Taylor's, acquainting him of our being at Lichfield, and Taylor had returned an answer that his post-chaise should come for us this day. While we sat at breakfast, Dr. Johnson received a letter by the post, which seemed to agitate him very much. When he had read it, he exclaimed, "One of the most dreadful things that has happened in my time." The phrase *my time*, like the word *age*, is usually understood to refer to an event of a public or general nature. I imagined something like an assassination of the King—like a gunpowder plot carried into execution—or like another fire of London. When asked, "What is it, Sir ?" he answered, "Mr. Thrale has lost his only son !" This was, no doubt, a very great affliction to Mr. and Mrs. Thrale, which their friends would consider accordingly ; but from the manner in which the intelligence of it was communicated by Johnson, it appeared for the moment to be comparatively small. I, however, soon felt a sincere concern, and was curious to observe how Dr. Johnson would be affected. He said, "This

MRS. LUCY PORTER'S HOUSE.

is a total extinction to their family, as much as if they were sold into captivity." Upon my mentioning that Mr. Thrale had daughters, who might inherit his wealth, "Daughters," said Johnson, warmly, "he'll no more value his daughters than—" I was going to speak. "Sir," said he, "don't you know how you yourself think? Sir, he wishes to propagate his name." In short, I saw male succession strong in his mind, even where there was no name, no family of any long standing. I said, it was lucky he was not present when this misfortune happened. JOHNSON: "It is lucky for *me*. People in distress never think that you feel enough." BOSWELL: "And, Sir, they will have the hope of seeing you, which will be a relief in the meantime; and when you get to them, the pain will be so far abated, that they will be capable of being consoled by you, which, in the first violence of it, I believe would not be the case." JOHNSON: "No, Sir; violent pain of mind, like violent pain of body, *must* be severely felt." BOSWELL: "I own, Sir, I have not so much feeling for the distress of others as some people have, or pretend to have; but I know this, that I would do all in my power to relieve them." JOHNSON: "Sir, it is affectation to pretend to feel the distress of others as much as they do themselves. It is equally so, as if one should pretend to feel as much pain while a friend's leg is cutting off as he does. No, Sir; you have expressed the rational and just nature of sympathy. I would have gone to the extremity of the earth to have preserved this boy."

He was soon quite calm. The letter was from Mr. Thrale's clerk, and concluded, "I need not say how much they wish to see you in London." He said, "We shall hasten back from Taylor's."

Mrs. Lucy Porter, and some other ladies of the place, talked a great deal of him when he was out of the room, not only with veneration, but affection. It pleased me to find that he was so much *beloved* in his native city.

Mrs. Aston, whom I had seen the preceding night, and her sister, Mrs. Gastrel, a widow lady, had each a house and garden, and pleasure-ground, prettily situate upon Stowhill, a gentle eminence adjoining to

STOWHILL—RESIDENCES OF MRS. ASTON AND MRS. GASTREL.

Lichfield. Johnson walked away to dinner there, leaving me by myself, without any apology. I wonder at this want of that facility of manners, from which a man has no difficulty in carrying a friend to a house where he is intimate. I felt it very unpleasant to be thus left in solitude in a country town, where I was an entire stranger, and began to think myself unkindly deserted; but I was soon relieved, and convinced that my friend, instead of being deficient in delicacy, had conducted the matter with perfect propriety, for I received the following note in his handwriting:—

"Mrs. Gastrel, at the lower house on Stowhill, desires Mr. Boswell's company to dinner at two."

I accepted of the invitation, and had here another proof how amiable his character was in the opinion of those who knew him best. I was not informed till afterwards that Mrs. Gastrel's husband was the clergyman who, while he lived at Stratford upon-Avon, where he was proprietor of Shakspeare's garden, with Gothic barbarity cut down his mulberry-tree,[1] and, as Dr. Johnson told me, did it to vex his neighbours. His lady, I have reason to believe, on the same authority, participated in the guilt of what the enthusiasts of our immortal bard deem almost a species of sacrilege.

After dinner, Dr. Johnson wrote a letter to Mrs. Thrale, on the death of her son. I said it would be very distressing to Thrale, but she would soon forget it, as she had so many things to think of. Johnson : " No, Sir, Thrale will forget it first. *She* has many things that she *may* think of. *He* has many things that he *must* think of." This was a very just remark upon the different effects of those light pursuits which occupy a vacant and easy mind, and those serious engagements which arrest attention, and keep us from brooding over grief.

He observed of Lord Bute, " It was said of Augustus, that it would have been better for Rome that he had never been born, or had never died. So it would have been better for this nation, if Lord Bute had never been minister, or had never resigned."

In the evening we went to the Town-hall, which was converted into a temporary theatre, and saw " Theodosius," with " The Stratford Jubilee." I was happy to see Dr. Johnson sitting in a conspicuous part of the pit, and receiving affectionate homage from all his acquaintance. We were quite gay and merry. I afterwards mentioned to him that I condemned myself for being so when poor Mr. and Mrs. Thrale were in such distress. Johnson : " You are wrong, Sir ; twenty years hence Mr. and Mrs. Thrale will not suffer much pain from the death of their son. Now, Sir, you are to consider that distance of place, as well as distance of time, operates upon the human feelings. I would not have you be gay in the presence of the distressed, because it would shock them ; but you may be gay at a distance. Pain for the loss of a friend, or of a relation whom we love, is occasioned by the want which we feel. In time the vacuity is filled with something else ; or sometimes the vacuity closes up of itself."

Mr. Seward and Mr. Pearson, another clergyman here, supped with us at our inn. and after they left us we sat up late, as we used to do in London.

Here I shall record some fragments of my friend's conversation during this jaunt.

" Marriage, Sir, is much more necessary to a man than to a woman :

---

[1] See an accurate and animated statement of Mr. Gastrel's barbarity, by Mr. Malone, in a note on " Some account of the Life of William Shakspeare," prefixed to his admirable edition of that poet's works vol. i. p. 118.—BOSWELL.

for he is much less able to supply himself with domestic comforts. You will recollect my saying to some ladies the other day, that I had often wondered why young women should marry, as they have so much more freedom, and so much more attention paid to them while unmarried than when married. I indeed did not mention the *strong* reason for their marrying—the *mechanical* reason." BOSWELL: "Why that is a strong one. But does not imagination make it much more important than it is in reality? Is it not, to a certain degree, a delusion in us as well as in women?" JOHNSON: "Why yes, Sir; but it is a delusion that is always beginning again." BOSWELL: "I don't know but there is upon the whole more misery than happiness produced by that passion." JOHNSON: "I don't think so, Sir."

"Never speak of a man in his own presence. It is always indelicate, and may be offensive."

"Questioning is not the mode of conversation among gentlemen. It is assuming a superiority, and it is particularly wrong to question a man concerning himself. There may be parts of his former life which he may not wish to be made known to other persons, or even brought to his own recollection."

"A man should be careful never to tell tales of himself to his own disadvantage. People may be amused and laugh at the time, but they will be remembered and brought out against him upon some subsequent occasion."

"Much may be done if a man puts his whole mind to a particular object. By doing so, Norton[1] has made himself the great lawyer that he is allowed to be."

I mentioned an acquaintance of mine, a sectary, who was a very religious man, who not only attended regularly on public worship with those of his communion, but made a particular study of the Scriptures, and even wrote a commentary on some parts of them, yet was known to be very licentious in indulging himself with women; maintaining that men are to be saved by faith alone, and that the Christian religior had not prescribed any fixed rule for the intercourse between the sexes JOHNSON: "Sir, there is no trusting to that crazy piety."

I observed that it was strange how well Scotchmen were known to one another in their own country, though born in very distant counties; for we do not find that the gentlemen of neighbouring counties in England are mutually known to each other. JOHNSON, with his usual acuteness, at once saw and explained the reason of this: "Why, Sir, you have Edinburgh, where the gentlemen from all your counties meet, and which is not so large but they are all known. There is no such common place of collection in England, except London, where from its

[1] Sir Fletcher Norton, afterwards Speaker of the House of Commons, and, in 1782, created Baron Grantly.—MALONE

great size and diffusion, many of those who reside in contiguous counties of England, may long remain unknown to each other."

On Tuesday, March 26, there came for us an equipage properly suited to a wealthy, well-beneficed clergyman : Dr. Taylor's large, roomy post chaise, drawn by four stout, plump horses, and driven by two steady jolly postilions, which conveyed us to Ashbourne ; where I found my friend's schoolfellow living upon an establishment perfectly corresponding with his substantial, creditable equipage ; his house, garden, pleasure-grounds, table—in short, everything good, and no scantiness appearing. Every man should form such a plan of living as he can execute completely. Let him not draw an outline wider than he can fill up. I have seen many skeletons of show and magnificence which excite at once ridicule and pity. Dr. Taylor had a good estate of his own and good preferment in the church, being a prebendary of Westminster and rector of Bosworth. He was a diligent justice of the peace, and presided over the town of Ashbourne, to the inhabitants of which I was told he was very liberal ; and as a proof of this it was mentioned to me, he had the preceding winter distributed two hundred pounds among such of them as stood in need of his assistance. He had consequently a considerable political interest in the county of Derby which he employed to support the Devonshire family ; for though the schoolfellow and friend of Johnson, he was a Whig. I could not perceive in his character much congeniality of any sort with that of Johnson, who, however, said to me, " Sir, he has a very strong understanding." His size, and figure, and countenance, and manner, were that of a hearty English 'squire, with the parson superinduced ; and I took particular notice of his upper-servant, Mr. Peters, a decent, grave man, in purple clothes, and a large white wig, like the butler or *major domo* of a bishop.

Dr. Johnson and Dr. Taylor met with great cordiality ; and Johnson soon gave him the same sad account of their schoolfellow, Congreve, that he had given to Mr. Hector ; adding a remark of such moment to the rational conduct of a man in the decline of life, that deserves to be imprinted upon every mind : " There is nothing against which an old man should be so much upon his guard as putting himself to nurse." Innumerable have been the melancholy instances of men once distinguished for firmness, resolution, and spirit, who in their latter days have been governed like children, by interested female artifice.

Dr. Taylor commended a physician who was known to him and Dr. Johnson, and said, " I fight many battles for him, as many people in the country dislike him." Johnson : " But you should consider, Sir, that by every one of your victories he is a loser ; for every man of whom you get the better will be very angry, and resolve not to employ him ; whereas, if people get the better of you in argument about him, they'll think, ' We'll send for Dr. ——, nevertheless.' " This was an observation deep and sure in human nature.

Next day we talked of a book in which an eminent judge was arraigned before the bar of the public, as having pronounced an unjust decision in a great cause. Dr. Johnson maintained that this publication would not give any uneasiness to the judge. " For," said he, " either he acted honestly, or he meant to do injustice. If he acted honestly, his own consciousness will protect him ; if he meant to do injustice, he will be glad to see the man who attacks him so much vexed."

Next day, as Dr. Johnson had acquainted Dr. Taylor of the reason for his returning speedily to London, it was resolved that we should set out after dinner. A few of Dr. Taylor's neighbours were his guests that day.

Dr. Johnson talked with approbation of one who had attained to the state of the philosophical wise man, that is, to have no want of anything. "Then, Sir," said I, "the savage is a wise man." " Sir," said he, " I do not mean simply being without, but not having a want." I maintained, against this proposition, that it was better to have fine clothes, for instance, than not to feel the want of them. JOHNSON : "No, Sir ; fine clothes are good only as they supply the want of other means of procuring respect. Was Charles the Twelfth, think you, less respected for his coarse blue coat and black stock ? And you find the King of Prussia dresses plain, because the dignity of his character is sufficient." I here brought myself into a scrape, for I heedlessly said, "Would not *you*, Sir, be the better for velvet embroidery ?" JOHNSON : "Sir, you put an end to all argument, when you introduce your opponent himself. Have you no better manners ? There is *your want*." I apologised by saying, I had mentioned him as an instance of one who wanted as little as any man in the world, and yet, perhaps might receive some additional lustre from dress.

END OF VOL. II.